LILLIAN ROXON'S
ROCK
ENCYCLOPEDIA

LILLIAN ROXON'S ROCK ENCYCLOPEDIA

Compiled by Ed Naha

GROSSET & DUNLAP
A FILMWAYS COMPANY
Publishers • New York

For the Halibut

ACKNOWLEDGMENTS

I would like to thank the following people for the help, encouragement, sympathy, prayers, and hairshirts needed during the construction of this tome: Ken Sasano (the Smithsonian of West Coast rock), Janis Cercone, Joyce Frommer, Pat Hill, my family, Diane Del Grosso, Denise Gatto, Madeleine, Michael Klenfner, Jo Buckley, Jim Foley, Gary Kenton and the wunnerful Warners staff, Debbie Hawkins, Ron Oberman, Lynn Kellermann, Diane Marie Bobal, Jessica Falcon, Kathy Brisker, Danny Dorph, Toi Moritomo, Tracy Gold, Steven X. Rea, Faye Evans, Bob Kauss, Susan Blonde, Gabby, Hoto and Zeke (the music mavens), Karin Berg, Janis Azrak, Sacco, Sari Becker, Pat Fisher, Bob Abrams, Soozin K., Tom Vickers, the folks at London, Kathy Schenker, Annette Monaco, Sheryl Feuerstein, and Susan Scivoletti.

I would also like to thank the following record companies for their help and/or benign neglect: Atlantic Records, Mercury, Warners, Elektra, Asylum, Epic, ABC-Dunhill, London, Columbia, MCA, United Artists, Casablanca, RSO, A&M, and Capitol.

INTRODUCTION

"Trying to get the rock world to keep still long enough for me to take its picture was one of the most difficult tasks in putting this book together. Groups split even as I wrote of their inner harmony, and got themselves together just as I had acknowledged their tragic demise. Baritones turned sopranos overnight; bands expanded and contracted their personnel like concertinas; fine performers degenerated swiftly and inexplicably while supposed second-raters found their promise all too late to make our deadlines."

That's how rock journalist Lillian Roxon described the first edition of this book, published way back in 1969. The original *Rock Encyclopedia* was the only one of its kind. It was written and published during an era when the "big time" rock biz was still in its naively wondrous stage. Rock writing was still ebullient and kinetic. Music magazines were springing up left and right (most decidedly left), delighted to latch onto some of rock and roll's greased lightning *Zeitgeist*. The sounds were alive. The groups were zany. Flower power ran head on into Vietnam. It was the sixties. The age of Aquarius. The pop realm was young in mind and spirit. Cynicism had not yet floated to the surface of the long-playing grooves. The distorted sense of self-importance had not yet attached itself to the typewriter keys of the rock press. Rock was fun. Rock was angry. Rock was magic.

Well, a lot has changed on the rock scene over the past ten years or so. The record industry has become an *industry,* replete with three-pieced hipsters (pocket calculators optional) who deal with rock groups on a basis of dollars and cents. Most of the superstars of the sixties are gone, either physically or musically, leaving behind a lot of historic memories, forgotten dreams, and great adjectives. This past decade of rock and roll has been as erratic, eclectic, traumatic, and silly as the real world around it. While the nation turned its attention to Watergate a go go, rock and roll was busily backpedaling in its own way. Psychedelia fell under the blows of heavy metal, which in turn made way for disco, which at present coexists peacefully with country-rock, pop, pap, easy listening, rock, R&B, and jazz fusion. FM stations, which first came into their own as the anti-establishment "underground" sensations of the sixties, are more popular than ever, although these days they are for the most part solidly above-ground, playing all the hits that make you happy, (or crazy, as the case may be). Rock journalists emerged as superstars, some more deserving than others, with many of them discarding their happy-go-lucky spirit of yesteryear in favor of a zaniness comparable to that of the Pope during Easter week. Lillian Roxon herself became one of the nation's most prestigious and best-loved rock writers, holding court weekly within the pages of the *New York Daily News* until her untimely death in 1973. Until the very end, she was a rare example of delightful journalism. She dearly loved her music and her legion of music fans. She is still missed.

During this decade's long period of evolution (and regression), rock has somehow survived. Despite the ups, the downs, the trends, and the taboos, the essence of the music has remained unchanged. Rock was, and is, a restless animal. Powerful. Exultant. And just a little bit off the wall. The faces, the fads, the sounds may come and go, but the sheer urgency of the music forever resounds in the minds of its listeners. And those listeners now span several generations.

In essence, rock is eternal.

And pretty wacky.

In updating Lillian's original concept, I've tried to reflect rock and roll as it is today, spotlighting the contemporary artists as well as the prototypical ravers. From the sublime to the ridiculous to the neanderthal. The pompadours. The shags. The mascara. Secret origins. Biggest sellers. Rankest stiffs. The zeniths and the nadirs. They're all here, just waiting for the gaze of the ardent rockophile to bring them to life.

Read on.

Rock on.

And don't sit too close to the pages, you'll hurt your ears.

A&R MEN/A&R men are the fellows who actually venture forth into the concrete jungle and sign bands to labels. They are talent scouts, administrators (they ride shotgun on the budget problems of each individual recording in their sphere of influence), and producers (many heads of A&R are producers present or past tense). A&R itself stands for artists and repertoire and, in days of yore, that stood for clout. In record-dom's fledgling days it was possible for an A&R whiz like John Hammond, one of the greatest ever, to return to his label with the likes of Bob Dylan, Aretha Franklin, Bessie Smith, or Bruce Springsteen in tow. Today, however, the record business has become more of a *business*. In larger labels' dealings, A&R men are often discouraged from signing new acts and are instructed to see if they can woo established acts from other prestigious labels. This is done for a number of reasons. Many record companies would rather sink a great deal of money into an established act via advertising and promotion in order to ensure greater sales returns (Superstar Jack on label X sells 1,000,000 records with $200,000 going into advertising. Therefore, Superstar Jack on new label Y will probably sell 2,000,000 copies with $400,000 in advertising) than sink a few hundred thousand into a brand new rock and roll band which could either evolve into superstardom or stiff city. More often than not, the A in A&R today stands for Atrophy. The times they are a-changin'.

ABBA/*Frida Lyngstad-Fredriksson (vocals), Benny Anderson (vocals, keyboards), Anna Ulvaeus (vocals), Bjorn Ulvaeus (vocals, guitars).*
Abba is the uncontested champion of four-part harmony on the Continent. Their sound is crisp, clean, and catchy and their European singles have made them the top-selling AM group on the other side of the Atlantic. The group has finally started to happen big in the states and all indications point toward the well-scrubbed foursome's becoming top tenners first class in America before long.

The quartet started in 1972. Frida was a well-known television personality and Anna was a solo performer. The two ladies joined forces with Benny (who came to the troupe from The Hep-Stars) and Bjorn (who played with Anderson in The Hootenanny Singers). Their first success came in 1974 when they copped first prize in the Eurovision song contest. They immediately took all of Europe by storm with their slickly produced songs *Waterloo and SOS*.

In spite of advanced promotion in the United States, however, the band just didn't click until 1976, when they exploded with hits like *Dancing Queen, Mamma Mia,* and *Fernando.* All systems are go for this Swedish entourage and their top-ten-oriented sound.

Albums/WATERLOO (7/74): *Waterloo; Sitting in the Palmtree; King Kong Song; Hasta Mañana; My Mama Said; Dance (While the Music Still Goes On); Honey, Honey; Watch Out; What About Livingstone; Gonna Sing You My Lovesong; Suzy-Hang-Around; Ring Ring.* ABBA (9/75): *Mamma Mia; Hey, Hey Helen; Tropical Loveland; SOS; Man in the Middle; Bang-A-Boomerang; I Do, I Do, I Do; Rock Me; Intermezzo No. 1; I've Been Waiting for You; So Long.* GREATEST HITS (8/76); SOS: *He Is Your Brother; Ring Ring; Another Town, Another Train; Honey Honey; So Long; Mamma Mia; I Do, I Do, I Do, I Do; Waterloo; People Need Love; Nina Pretty Ballerina; Bang-A-Boomerang; Dance (While the Music Still Goes On); Fernando.* ARRIVAL (12/76): *When I Kissed the Teacher; Dancing Queen; My Love, My Life; Dum Dum Diddle; Knowing Me, Knowing You; Money, Money, Money; That's Me; Why Did I Have to Be Me; Tiger; Arrival.*

Singles/*Waterloo/Watch Out* (5/74); *Honey Honey/Dance* (8/74); *Ring Ring/Hasta Mañana* (12/74); *SOS/Man in the Middle* (6/75); *Waterloo/Honey Honey* (8/75); *I Do, I Do, I Do, I Do/Bang-A-Boomerang* (12/75); SOS/Ring Ring (2/76); *Mamma Mia/I Do, I Do, I Do, I Do* (4/76); *Mamma Mia/Tropical Loveland* (5/76); *Fernando/Rock Me* (8/76); *Dancing Queen* (11/76); *Knowing Me, Knowing You/Happy Hawaii* (4/77).

ACID ROCK/Originally, acid rock was music that tried to reproduce the distorted hearing of a person under the influence of lysergic acid diethylamide (LSD). The idea was to recreate for someone who was not drugged the illusion of an LSD experience through music (an illusion heightened by light shows designed to reproduce *visual* aspects of a trip).

LSD hit San Francisco in 1965 just a little before the big dance scene started to happen there, a scene touched off by the general exuberance of a community that had just discovered chemical ecstasy. All the music did was mirror that ecstasy. It was slower and more languid than hard rock, incorporating much of the Oriental music that was providing background sounds for the drug experiences of that period. Numbers tended to run on longer as though time as one knows it had lost its meaning. Notes and phrasings lurched and warped in a way that had not, until then, been considered acceptable in rock. Lyrics conjured up images previously confined to the verses of poets like Samuel Taylor Coleridge and William Blake.

The acid rock and light shows of the San Francisco ballrooms did provide for many a joyous journey to the center of the mind without any of the inconvenient side effects, let alone the expense, of hallucinatory drugs. However, there is not much doubt that a sizable percentage of those 1966–67 audiences did not need musical help so much as sympathetic musical companionship for a voyage that had already been triggered with chemicals. Thus, the term acid rock could be taken to mean *enhancing* as well as *inducing* psychedelic transports.

AEROSMITH/*Steve Tyler (vocals), Tom Hamilton (bass), Joe Perry (guitar), Joey Kramer (drums), Brad Whitford (guitar).*
With *Dream On* serving as their national anthem, Aerosmith has, in the span of four years, taken the rock world by storm, wiggling and wailing their way into the stereo speakers of millions. Starting out in Sunapee, New Hampshire, in 1970, the embryonic entourage of would-be rockers moved to Boston in an effort to launch their careers in a major city (Boston being the closest major city to Sunapee). The city, however, made no effort to help the lads achieve stardom; thus the entire year of 1971 found the group sharing a small apartment with their equipment and doing the things that most newly formed rock bands do best: starving and looking for work.

Jobs were painfully slow in coming, but by mid-1972, Aerosmith had played enough to garner them both a ragamuffin following and a local manager. In July of 1972, the fivesome found themselves in New York's famed Max's Kansas City, where their performance earned them a second set of managers. A few months later, at a similar gig attended by record executive Clive Davis, the band was rewarded with a recording contract.

Their first album, *AEROSMITH,* was dismissed by the rock press as being a mild ripoff of the Rolling Stones, and the band was placed in the unexpected position of having to prove their worth to a skeptical world. A few ill-chosen concert dates with such non-rock bands as the Mahavishnu Orchestra and the then-concept-oriented Kinks didn't help matters much. A single, *Dream On,* was released in an effort to save the group from instant obscurity, but it did little outside the Boston area. Still, Aerosmith refused to be discouraged.

Uniting with top producer Jack Douglas, they released a second long-player, *GET YOUR WINGS.* When it hit the stores in 1974, the rock critics had already seen fit to dismiss Steve Tyler as a second-rate Jagger and the rest of the band as a gang of loud louts. Then, something extraordinary occurred. In spite of the odds stacked against them, the teeth-gnashing, double-guitar sound of Aerosmith began to click. They toured. They toured in the spring. They toured in the summer. They toured in the fall. By the time their third LP, *TOYS IN THE ATTIC,* was released, the band was making it big with the critics who really counted . . . the rock fans themselves. The writers still ignored them, the record execs still couldn't figure out their brashness, but the fans flocked to their concerts by the thousands.

During the summer of '75, the ear-splitting *TOYS* went gold, then platinum, selling over one million copies. All three existing albums vaulted onto the best-seller charts, with the first two now turning gold. The boys then recorded a fourth platinum album, *ROCKS.* In early 1976, *Dream On* was re-released as a single, going top ten and earning itself a gold record nearly three years after its first appearance. The five bawdy boys from Boston had finally snared their niche on top-forty radio.

And their success shows no signs of slowing down. Currently recording a fifth hard-rock fest with producer Douglas, the no-holds-barred rock 'n' rollers have long since lived down the Rolling Stone stigma and have earned the respect of the critics for their own tough brand of music. As a matter of fact, Aerosmith is one of the press's very favorite bands at the moment. Those critics knew it all along.

Albums/AEROSMITH (1/73); *Make It: Somebody; Dream On; One Way Street; Mama Kin; Write Me; Movin' Out; Walkin' the Dog.* GET YOUR WINGS (3/74): *Train Kept a-Rollin'; Spaced; Woman of the World; Season of Wither; Same Old Song and Dance; Pandora's Box; SOS; Lord of the Thighs.* TOYS IN THE ATTIC (4/75): *Toys in the Attic; Uncle Salty; No More No More; Round and Round; You See Me Crying; Adam's Apple; Walk This Way; Big Ten-Inch Record; Sweet Emotion.* ROCKS (5/76): *Back in the Saddle; Last Child; Rats in the Cellar; Combination; Sick As*

*a Dog; Nobody's Fault; Get the Lead Out; Lick and a Promise;
Home Tonight.* DRAW THE LINE (12/77): *Draw the Line; I
Wanna Know Why; Critical Mass; Get It Up; Bright Light Fright;
Kings and Queens; The Hand That Feeds; Sight for Sore Eyes;
Milk Cow Blues.*

Singles/*Same Old Song and Dance/Pandora's Box* (3/73); *Dream
On/Somebody* (6/73); *Train Kept a-Rollin'/Spaced* (9/74);
SOS/Spaced (2/75); *Sweet Emotion/Uncle Salty* (5/75); *Walk
This Way/Round and Round* (8/75); *You See Me Crying/Toys in
the Attic* (11/75); *Dream On/Somebody* (12/75); *Last
Child/Combination* (5/76); *Home Tonight/Pandora's Box* (8/76);
Walk This Way/Uncle Salty (11/76); *Dream On/Sweet Emotion*
(11/76); *Back in the Saddle/Nobody's Fault* (3/77); *Draw the Line*
(10/77).

THE ALLMAN BROTHERS BAND/*Original members: Duane
Allman (lead, acoustic, and slide guitars), Dicky Betts (lead guitar),
Gregg Allman (keyboards and vocals), Berry Oakley (bass and vocals), Jai Johanny Johanson (drums, congas, timbales, and
percussion), Butch Trucks (drums and tympani), Thom Doucette
(harmonica and percussion). Other members: Chuck Leavell (piano), Lamar Williams (bass).*
Idols of the early seventies, the blues-oriented Allman Brothers
Band quickly gave a needed shot in the arm to the dying blues-
rock movement and established the nation's South as a stomping
ground for a horde of new and exciting rock bands. Formed in
1969, the band was the brainchild of brothers Gregg and Duane
Allman, two Nashville-born musicians who had tried unsuccessfully to launch their professional careers while still in their
teens, during the early sixties. Their first band, the Allman Joys,
never got past the local gigging stage but their second, Hourglass,
finally wangled a recording contract with Liberty Records in
1968. Hourglass cut two albums' worth of material, disbanding
shortly thereafter. Both Duane and Gregg were displeased with
the pop-oriented trend their band was pursuing and decided to
opt for the session-man's life.
    Gregg and Duane remained together for a time, drifting in and
out of future Allman Band–member Butch Trucks' band.
Duane's solo career, however, began to soar. His inspired guitar
lines on Wilson Pickett's album sessions and *Hey Jude* single soon
made him a much-sought-after R&B session musician. Subse-

quent stints with Clarence Carter, Aretha Franklin, Herbie Mann, King Curtis, Arthur Conley, and Boz Scaggs enhanced his near-legendary status. He was tasteful, versatile, and melodic in riffing technique. His wailing, snarling guitar licks became the rage of the session world of that time.

As his fame spread, Duane began seeking newer inroads into music. He sought a solo career. Beginning an aborted solo album, he joined with his brother, Butch Trucks' band, and a local group called the Second Coming, which accidentally created a new sound and a new band: the Allman Brothers Band. Signed by Capricorn Records, the group began to woodshed in 1969, cutting their debut album the same year. Duane and Gregg took the band on torturous coast-to-coast tours, which brought the group's slide-guitar–oriented sound to eager fans everywhere. As their popularity increased, the Allman Brothers Band's albums began to sell. As they sold more, the concert halls grew in size. Soon, the Brothers Band's career mushroomed.

Duane continued with his outside activities, lending his talents to a number of albums, including sessions by Delaney and Bonnie, Ronnie Hawkins, and Eric Clapton for his Derek and the Dominoes offering. Meanwhile, with albums such as *IDLEWILD SOUTH* and *AT THE FILLMORE EAST* attaining gold status, the Allman troupe won an assuredly superstar status on the music front. In 1971, however, tragedy nearly destroyed the band. On October 29, guitar genius Duane died in a freak motorcycle accident in Macon, Georgia—a town the band called home. A year later, Berry Oakley met a similar fate in almost exactly the same circumstances.

Reeling under the blows of the double loss, the band rallied triumphantly, becoming one of the nation's biggest bands the following year. By 1974, however, the entourage showed signs of fragmentation. Newfound leader Gregg Allman embarked on a solo career that initially proved fairly catatonic before moving on to a nearly nonexistent status. The Allman Brothers struggled valiantly onward without the benefit of an Allman before sputtering into the shadows with 1975's greatest hits package, *THE ROAD GOES ON FOREVER,* and the similar collection of '76, *WIPE THE WINDOWS . . . A DOLLAR GAS.* Gregg, meanwhile, continued on his fairly inactive solo career. In late 1977, he began a fairly strange chapter of his musical life by embarking on a career with his wife of two years, songstress Cher, premiering with an LP, *ALLMAN AND WOMAN*. A European tour got the duo off to a rocky start.

Albums/THE ALLMAN BROTHERS BAND (12/69): *Don't You Want No More; It's Not My Cross to Bear; Black-Hearted Woman; Trouble No More; Every Hungry Woman; Dreams; Whipping Post.* IDLEWILD SOUTH (9/70): *Revival; Don't Leave Me Wandering; Midnight Rider; Memories of Elizabeth Reed; Hoochie Coochie Man; Please Call Home; Leave My Blues at Home.* AT THE FILLMORE EAST (6/71): *Statesboro Blues; Done Somebody Wrong; Stormy Monday; Whipping Post; You Don't Love Me; Hot 'Lanta; In Memory of Elizabeth Reed.* EAT A PEACH (2/72): *Mountain Jam; One Way Out; Trouble No More; Stand Back; Little Martha; Blue Sky; Ain't Wastin' Time No More; Les Brers in a Minor; Melissa.* BEGINNINGS (A two-record repackage of THE ALLMAN BROTHERS BAND and IDLEWILD SOUTH; 2/73). BROTHERS AND SISTERS (8/73): *Wasted Words; Ramblin' Man; Southbound; Jessica; Come and Go Blues; Pony Boy.* WIN, LOSE OR DRAW (8/75): *Can't Lose What You Never Had; Just Another Love Song; Nevertheless; Win, Lose or Draw; Louisiana Lou and 3-Card Monty John; High Falls; Sweet Mama.* THE ROAD GOES ON FOREVER ... GREATEST HITS (11/75): *Black-Hearted Woman; Dreams; Whipping Post; Midnight Rider; Stormy Monday; Stand Back; Hoochie Coochie Man; Statesboro Blues.* WIPE THE WINDOWS ... A DOLLAR GAS (11/76): *Wasted Words; Southbound; Ramblin' Man; In Memory of Elizabeth Reed; Ain't Wastin' No More Time; Come and Go Blues; Can't Lose What You Never Had; Don't Want You No More; Jessica; It's Not My Cross to Bear.*

Singles/*Revival* (12/70); *Ain't Wastin' Time No More* (3/72); *Melissa* (7/72); *Ain't Wastin' Time No More/Blue Sky* (9/72); *Just One Way Out/Stand Back* (10/72); *Ramblin' Man/Pony Boy* (6/73); *Jessica/Come and Go Blues* (12/73); *Ramblin' Man/Melissa* (1/74).

AMERICA/*Dan Peek (guitar, vocals), Dewey Bunnell (guitar, vocals), Gerry Beckley (guitar, vocals).*
The sons of three British-based American servicemen, Peek, Bun-

nell and Beckley first joined forces in the late nineteen sixties in the United Kingdom, conjuring up a harmonious brand of music that was influenced greatly by the Crosby, Stills and Nash–itis that was gripping the music industry at that time. In 1972, after three years of recording and practicing, the band exploded onto the singles charts with a fairly innocuous tune. *A Horse with No Name*. Although Neil Young fans were fairly outraged by this blatant sound-alike group, the trio went on to garner quite a following for itself. Long after Crosby, Stills, Nash and Young ceased to be a commercially successful venture, the sweet-sounding style of America continued to impress with such top-tenning tunes as *Tin Man, Lonely People, Ventura Highway, I Need You,* and *The Sandman.* America's career eased off somewhat in the 1976–'77 period, and by the end of 1977 there were on-again, off-again rumors that the threesome was to be a twosome from that point onward. A live release in November of 1977 proved the rumor to be fact, with Beckley and Bunnell going it alone.

Albums/AMERICA (1/72): *Riverside; Sandman; Three Roses; Children; Hire; I Need You; Rainy Day; Never Found the Time; Pigeon Song; Donkey Jaw; Clarice; Horse with No Name.* HOME-COMING (11/72): *Ventura Highway; To Each His Own; Don't Cross the River; Moon Song; Only in Your Heart; Till the Sun Comes Up Again; Cornwall Blank; Head and Heart; California Revisited; Saturn Nights.* HAT TRICK (10/73): *Hat Trick; Muskrat Love; Wind Wave; Molten Love; Goodbye; Willow Tree Lullaby; Green Monkey; It's Life; Submarine Ladies; Rainbow Song.* HOLIDAY (11/74): *Mad Dog; Tin Man; In the Country; Old Man Took; Hollywood; It's Up to You; Lonely People; Another Try; Glad to See You; What Does It Matter.* HEARTS (3/75): *Daisy Jane; Half a Man; Midnight; Bell Tree; Old Virginia; People in the Valley; Company; Woman Tonight; The Story of a Teenager; Sister Golden Hair; Tomorrow; Seasons.* GREATEST HITS (11/75): *A Horse with No Name; I Need You; Sandman; Ventura Highway; Don't Cross the River; Only in Your Heart; Muskrat Love; Tin Man; Lonely People; Sister Golden Hair; Daisy Jane; Woman Tonight.* HIDEAWAY (3/76): *Lovely Night; Amber Cascades; Don't Let It Get You Down; Can't You See; Watership Down; She's Beside You; Hideway (I and II); She's a Liar; Letter; Today's the Day; Jet Boy Blue; Who Loves You.* LIVE (11/77): *Tin Man; Muskrat Love; I Need You; Old Man Took; Daisy Jane;*

Company; Hollywood; Another Try; Ventura Highway; Sister Golden Hair; Horse with No Name; Amber Cascades; To Each His Own; Sergeant Darkness.

Singles/*Horse with No Name/Everyone I Meet Is from California* (2/72); *I Need You/Riverside* (4/72); *Ventura Highway/Saturn Nights* (9/72); *Horse with No Name/I Need You* (9/72); *Don't Cross the River/To Each His Own* (12/72); *Muskrat Love/Cornwell Blank* (6/73); *Rainbow Song/Willow Tree Lullaby* (11/73); *Tin Man/In the Country* (7/74). *Lonely People/Mad Dog* (10/74); *Daisy Jane/Tomorrow* (6/75); *Woman Tonight/Bell Tree* (10/75); *Today's the Day/Hideaway* (4/76); *Who Loves You/Amber Cascades* (7/76); *She's a Liar/She's beside You* (10/76); *Don't Cry, Baby/Monster* (5/77).

AMERICAN TEARS/*Mark Mangold (vocals, keyboards), Craig Evan Brooks (guitar, vocals), Glenn Kithcart (drums), Kirk Powers (bass, vocals). Previous members: Gary Sonny (bass), Tommy Gunn (drums), Greg Baze (bass).*
The logical successor to Lee Michaels' demented keyboard-dominated riffing of the sixties, this seventies, New York band emerged in 1974 with an interesting, albeit poorly produced, debut album. From there, the only direction to go was up . . . and up they went. Led by keyboardist Mark Mangold, the group reformed and emerged victorious with a keyboard extravaganza, *TEAR GAS,* a heavy "ivory" album that harkened back to the plod-rocking days of '69. The public and radio programmers, however, were just not ready for a guitarless band. Mangold dropped and added new members, coming up with a guitar-keyboard quartet. *POWERHOUSE,* their finest LP to date, was the result. As a reward for their hard work and redesigning, the band was dropped by their label.

Albums/BRANDED BAD (8/74): *Sweet Changes; Doctor Abreaction; Low Down, Need You Badly; Crooked Is Quicker; Pauline; Lock and Chain; Take Me, Lord; Louie (I've Been Arrested); Pennywall; Slidin' Home.* TEAR GAS (10/75): *Back Like Me (2 parts); Charon; Serious Boy Blue; I Saw a Soldier; The War Lover; Franki and the Midget.* POWERHOUSE (3/77): *Slow Train; Promise to Be Free; Listen (Can You Feel It); Lookin' for Love; Can't Keep from Cryin'; Don't Give It Away; Say You'll Stay; Last Chance for Love.*

Singles/*He Don't Want Your Money (Dr. Abreaction)*/*Pennywall* (2/75); *Born to Love*/*Franki and the Midget* (6/76); *Listen (Can You Feel It)* (promotional single—disc jockies only; 5/77).

ANGEL/*Punky Meadows (guitar), Frank DiMino (vocals), Greg Guiffria (keyboards), Mickie Jones (bass), Barry Brandt (drums).* Dressed in white flowing robes and introduced on stage by a gigantic, talking head, Angel is one of the newest members of the Casablanca Records entourage—the people who gave the world Kiss. Hailing from Washington, D.C., the group started and was signed in 1975. In 1977 they were chosen the "Newcomer Group of the Year" by *Circus* Magazine and have become well known for their innovative stage show, which includes a large heaping of futuristic holography.
Albums/ANGEL (10/75): *Tower; Long Time; Rock and Rollers; Broken Dreams; Mariner; Sunday Morning; One and One; Angel Theme.* HELLUVA BAND (5/76): *Feelin' Right; The Fortune; Anyway You Want It; Dr. Ice; Mirrors; Feelings; Pressure Point; Chicken Soup; Angel Theme.* ON EARTH AS IT IS IN HEAVEN (1/77): *Can You Feel It; She's a Mover; Big Boy (Let's Do It Again); Telephone Exchange; White Lightning; On the Rocks; You're Not Fooling Me; That Magic Touch; Cast the First Stone; Just a Dream.*
Singles/*Rock and Rollers* (1/76); *That Magic Touch* (3/77).

JON ANDERSON/Lancashire-born Briton Jon Anderson is best known as the lead singer of the band Yes. Together with bassist Chris Squire, Anderson started Yes in 1968. Prior to that, he toured for over a decade as lead singer with various semi-successful bands in the United Kingdom. In 1976, he released his first solo album.
Album/OLIAS OF SUNHILLOW (6/76): *Ocean Song; Meeting; Sound Out the Galleon; Dance of Ranyart; Olias; Quoquag en Transic; Naon; Transic To; Flight of the Moonglade; Solid Space; Moon Ra; Chords; Song of Search; To the Runner.*
Single/*Flight of the Moonglade*/*To the Runner.*

THE ANIMALS/*Eric Burdon (vocals), Charles Chandler (bass), Alan Price (keyboards), John Steel (drums), Hilton Valentine (guitar). Additional members: Andy Somers (guitar), Barry Jenkins* *(drums), John Weider (guitar, violin, bass), Zoot Money (organ), Dave Roweberry (keyboards).*

It was the long hot summer of 1964 and Beatlemania was rampant when the hardy, raspy voice of Eric Burdon hit the airwaves with *The House of the Rising Sun.* That was when America knew the English meant business. With Eric up there on the charts, they knew that the British invasion was for real, that England had more than just the Beatles. The Animals were the antithesis of British pop. They were from Newcastle, a town as rough as Liverpool. Alan Price, the organist, had attained fame as leader of the Alan Price Combo, which Burdon joined in 1962. The locals thought they looked like animals, so the Animals they became. Eric was very much into blues, as were so many other English groups emerging at that time (a reaction against the polite, clean rock of the then-top groups, who wore suits on stage and sang songs to match). The Animals' sound was incredibly black, and black and bluesy, dominated by Eric's riveting vocals and Price's rumbling organ solos. Their early exercise in funk was an incredible success stateside with hit albums, singles, and tours. They were so much of that black community's music scene that *Ebony* magazine gave them a five-page spread.

Then in 1966 Price and Burdon had a major disagreement, which resulted in the fragmentation of the original troupe. A new group, a new sound, and a new billing emerged. Eric Burdon and the New Animals tossed aside the R&B flavor of old in pursuit of the soon-to-be popular psychedelia. The San Francisco scene made a big impression on the ever-mellow king of blue-eyed funk and tunes like *San Franciscan Nights* and *Monterey* tolled the death knell for the once-hard-as-nails grit army. The Animals barely made it into the seventies. Burdon staged a funky comeback, of sorts, with Eric Burdon and War. Eric's association with the band lasted for two albums. He re-emerged with a surprisingly guitar-oriented band: the Eric Burdon Band. This highly touted assembly bit the dust after some intense problems between Eric and his manager. The original Animals rallied 'round the sagging lead singer and recorded an album in early 1976 to bolster his spirits. The record finally appeared nearly two years later to little or no critical acclaim.

Albums/THE ANIMALS (10/64): *House of the Rising Sun; Blue*

Feeling; Girl Can't Help It; Baby, Let Me Take You Home; Right Time; Talkin' 'bout You; Around and Around; I'm in Love Again; Gonna Send You Back to Walker; Memphis, Tennessee; I'm Mad Again; I've Been Around. ANIMALS ON TOUR (3/65): *Boom Boom; My, How You've Changed; I Believe to My Soul; Mess Around; Bright Lights, Big City; Worried Life Blues; Let the Good Times Roll; Ain't Got You; Hallelujah, I Love Her So; I'm Crying; Dimples; She Said Yeah.* ANIMAL TRACKS (9/65): *We Gotta Get Outta This Place; Take It Easy, Baby; Bring It On Home to Me; Roberta; Story of Bo Diddley; I Can't Believe It; For Miss Caulker; Club a-Go-Go; Don't Let Me Be Misunderstood; Bury My Body.* BEST OF THE ANIMALS (2/66): *It's My Life; Gonna Send You Back to Walker; Bring It On Home to Me; I'm Mad; House of the Rising Sun; We Gotta Get Outta This Place; Boom Boom; I'm in Love Again; I'm Crying; Don't Let Me Be Misunderstood.* ANIMALIZATION (9/66): *Don't Bring Me Down; One Monkey Don't Stop the Show; You're on My Mind; She'll Return It; Cheating; Inside—Looking Out; See See Rider; Gin House Blues; Maudie; What Am I Living For; Sweet Little Sixteen; I Put a Spell on You.* ANIMALISM (12/66): *All Night Long; Shake; Other Side of This Life; Rock Me, Baby; Lucille; Smoke Stack Lightning; Hey, Gyp; Hit the Road, Jack; Outcast; Louisiana Blue; That's All I Am to You; Going Down Slow.* ERIC IS HERE (3/67): *Help Me, Girl; In the Night; Mama Told Me Not to Come; I Think It's Gonna Rain Today; This Side of Goodbye; That Ain't Where It's At; Wait till Next Year; Losin' Control; It's Not Easy; True Love (Comes Only Once in a Lifetime); Biggest Bundle of Them All; It's Been a Long Time Comin'.* BEST OF ERIC BURDON AND THE ANIMALS, VOLUME 2 (6/67): *When I Was Young; Girl Named Sandoz; Don't Bring Me Down; She'll Return It; See See Rider; Other Side of This Life; Hey, Gyp; Inside —Looking Out; Help Me, Girl; Cheating; You're on My Mind; That Ain't Where It's At.* WINDS OF CHANGE (10/67): *San Franciscan Nights; Good Times; Winds of Change; Poem by the Sea; Paint It Black; Black Plague; Yes, I Am Experienced; Man-Woman; Hotel Hell; Anything; It's All Meat.* TWAIN SHALL MEET (5/68): *Monterey; Just the Thought; Closer to the Truth; No Self Pity; Orange and Red Beams; Sky Pilot; We Love You, Lil; All Is One.* EVERY ONE OF US (7/68): *White Houses; Uppers and Downers; Serenade to a Sweet Lady; The Immigrant Lad;*

*Year of the Guru; St. James Infirmary; New York 1963–America
1968.* LOVE IS (12/68): *River Deep, Mountain High; I'm an
Angel; I'm Dying, or Am I; Ring of Fire; Coloured Rain; To Love
Somebody; As the Years Go Passing; Gemini—the Madman.*
GREATEST HITS (3/69). BEST OF THE ANIMALS (1973):
*House of the Rising Sun; I'm Crying; Baby, Let Me Take You
Home; Around and Around; Don't Let Me Be Misunderstood;
We've Gotta Get Out of This Place; It's My Life; Help Me, Girl;
When I Was Young; Story of Bo Diddley; Bring It On Home to Me;
Gonna Send You Back to Walker; Boom Boom; Bury My Body;
Cheating; A Girl Named Sandoz; Dimples; She'll Return It; Talk-
in' 'bout You; I'm in Love Again.* BEFORE WE WERE SO
RUDELY INTERRUPTED (9/77): *Riverside Country; Lonely
Avenue; Brother Bill; It's All Over Now, Baby Blue; other titles.*

Singles/*The House of the Rising Sun* (7/64); *Gonna Send You Back
to Walker* (8/64); *I'm Crying* (9/64); *Boom Boom/Blue Feeling*
(11/64); *Don't Let Me Be Misunderstood/Club a-Go-Go* (1/65);
Bring It On Home to Me/For Miss Caulker (4/65); *We Gotta Get
Outta Of This Place/I Can't Believe It* (7/65); *It's My Life*
(10/65); *Inside—Looking Out* (1/66); *Don't Bring Me Down*
(5/66); *See See Rider* (8/66); *Help Me, Girl* (10/66); *When I Was
Young/Don't Bring Me Down* (3/67); *San Franciscan Nights/Good
Times* (7/67); *Monterey/Ain't It So* (11/67); *Anything* (3/68); *Sky
Pilot (two parts)* (5/68); *White Houses/River Deep, Mountain
High* (10/68).

PAUL ANKA/In 1958, when he was fifteen, Paul Anka had a
number-one hit with a song he wrote called *Diana*. That was the
teen agony era of American pop music. If you were fifteen and
suffering over an older woman of seventeen or eighteen and could
write a song about it . . . success was yours. By early 1959, Anka
(at the ripe old age of sixteen) had three major hits. At seventeen
he was a millionaire. At eighteen he made his nightclub debut (he
was old enough to drink then). By twenty-one, he'd written over
two hundred songs and made millions, which was not all that
surprising when you consider he had a huge following in different
parts of the world and still does, especially in Europe.

Anka's success in Europe sustained him, financially, during his
cold spell as a performer stateside. His success as a songwriter,
however, never paled. Remaining behind the scenes, the Ottawa,

Canada–born Anka constantly came up with hits, including Frank Sinatra's epic *My Way.* In 1974 Anka staged a remarkable comeback as a singer-songwriter with the smash single *You're Having My Baby.* His second career in full swing, Anka still packs them in on the nightclub circuit.

Albums/PAUL ANKA SINGS HIS BIG 15 (7/60). SONGS I WISH I'D WRITTEN (1960): *Ramblin' Rose; I Can't Stop Loving You; End of the World; He'll Have to Go; All I Have to Do Is Dream; Can't Get Used to Losing You; Oh, Lonesome Me; Save the Last Dance for Me; Blue on Blue; Moon River; It's Not for Me To Say; Memories Are Made of This; You Always Hurt the One You Love; Cry; Who's Sorry Now.* ANKA AT THE COPA (11/60). PAUL ANKA SINGS HIS BIG 15, VOL. 2 (9/61). YOUNG, ALIVE AND IN LOVE (3/62). LET'S SIT THIS ONE OUT (8/62). PAUL ANKA'S 21 GOLDEN HITS (5/63): *Diana; Put Your Head on My Shoulder; Time to Cry; Lonely Boy; Puppy Love; I Love You in the Same Old Way; You Are My Destiny; I Love You; Baby; Crazy Love; Don't Ever Leave Me; Summer's Gone; Adam and Eve; Don't Gamble with Love; I'm Still Waiting Here for You; It Doesn't Matter Any More; Love Land; Tonight My Love; Tonight; My Home Town; Cinderella; Dance on Little Girl; Longest Day.* STRICTLY NASHVILLE (8/66): *Bonaparte's Retreat; I Wish; Oh, Such a Stranger; There Won't Be No Runnin' Back (to You); I Went to Your Wedding; Story of Yours; Legend in My Time; I Didn't Mean to Hurt You; Once a Day.* PAUL ANKA LIVE (10/67): *It Only Takes a Moment; Everybody Has the Right to Be Wrong; How Insensitive; Satin Doll; When I Take My Sugar to Tea; Goin' Out of My Head; Everybody Loves Somebody; What the World Needs Now Is Love; Memphis, Tennessee; Medley.* GOODNIGHT MY LOVE (2/69): Picking Up the Pieces; Daddy's Home; In the Still of the Night; Next Year; Forgive and Forget; Goodnight My Love; You Send Me; Think It Over; Baby; For Once in My Life; I Gotta Be Me; Silhouettes. SINCERELY (9/69): *Sincerely; Watch What Happens; The Nearness of You; Can't Take My Eyes Off of You; My Way; Crazy World; Satin Doll; By the Time I Get to Phoenix; Gentle on My Mind; He's Got the Whole World in His Hands; Goodnight My Love.* LIFE GOES ON (11/69): *Can't Get You Out of My Mind; Find My Way; Tell It Like It Is; Eleanor Rigby; Life Goes On;*

Happy; I Was There; Keeping One Foot in the Door. 70'S (4/70): *Before It's Too Late; This Land Is Your Land; Midnight Mistress; Daddy; Rainy Monday; Crazy World; She's a Lady; City Life; Amanda; Anna May; I'm in Love with You; Real People.* PAUL ANKA (1/72). JUBILATION (6/72). MY WAY (8/74): *My Way; You Send Me; Memphis; Daddy's Home; I've Gotta Be Me; For Once in My Life; Silhouettes; Goodnight My Love.* ANKA (11/74): PAUL ANKA GOLD (10/74): *Diana; I Love You, Baby; Let the Bells Keep Ringing; Don't Gamble with Love; Crazy Love; Just Young; Midnight; It's Time to Cry; You Are My Destiny; Don't Ever Leave Me; I Miss You So; Your Love; Waiting for You; Puppy Love; Lonely Boy; Summer's Gone; Something Happened; The Story of My Love; My Home Town; Adam and Eve; My Heart Sings; Dance On, Little Girl; Tonight My Love; Cinderella; Kissin' on the Phone; Hello, Young Lovers; I Love You in the Same Old Way; Put Your Head on My Shoulder.* ANKA (11/74): *Bring the Wine; One Man Woman—One Woman Man; Something About You; You're Having My Baby; Let Me Get To Know You; Love Is a Lonely Song; How Can Anything Be Beautiful (After You); I Gave a Little and Lost a Lot; Papa; It Doesn't Matter Anymore.* FEELINGS (3/75): *Anytime (I'll Be There); I Don't Like to Sleep Alone; Out of My Mind in Love; It's So Sad to See the Old Hometown Again; There's Nothing Stronger Than Our Love; Wake Up; Today I Became a Fool; Girl, You Turn Me On; Walk Away; Water Runs Deep.* TIMES OF YOUR LIFE (11/75): *Having My Baby; One Man Woman—One Woman Man; Wake Up; Bring the Wine; Times of Your Life; I Don't Like to Sleep Alone; Let Me Get to Know You; There's Nothing Stronger Than Our Love; Papa; Anytime (I'll Be There).* THE PAINTER (8/76): *You Bring Out the Best in Me; Wildflower; The Painter; Closing Doors; Happier; Living Isn't Living; Aldous; I'll Help You; Never Gonna Fall in Love Again; Do I Love You?; Prelude.* THE MUSIC MAN (4/77): *Dannon; Slowdown; Jealous Lady; Everybody Ought to Be in Love; A Mexican Night; Second Thoughts; My Best Friend's Wife; My Little Girl's Become a Big Girl Now; If I Had My Life to Live Over; Tonight; Music Man.*

Singles/*Diana* (6/57); *I Love You, Baby* (11/57); *You Are My Destiny* (1/58); *Crazy Love* (3/58); *Let the Bells Keep Ringing* (3/58); *Midnight*(6/58); *Just Young* (9/58); *My Heart Sings* (12/58); *I*

Miss You So (3/59); *Lonely Boy* (6/59); *Put Your Head on My Shoulder* (8/59); *It's Time to Cry* (11/59); *Puppy Love* (1/60); *Adam and Eve* (3/60); *My Home Town* (5/60); *Something Happened* (5/60); *Hello Young Lovers* (7/60); *I Love You in the Same Old Way* (7/60); *Summer's Gone* (9/60); *The Story of My Love* (1/61); *Tonight My Love/Tonight* (2/61); *Dance On Little Girl* (5/61); *Kissin' on the Phone* (8/61); *Cinderella* (9/61); *Love Me Warm and Tender* (1/62); *A Steel Guitar and a Glass of Wine* (5/62); *I'm Coming Home* (7/62); *Every Night* (7/62); *Eso Beso* (10/62); *Love Makes the World Go Round* (1/63); *Remember/Diana* (3/63); *Hello Jim* (5/69); *Did You Have a Happy Birthday?* (12/63); *This Crazy World* (10/68); *Goodnight My Love* (12/68); *In the Still of the Night* (2/69); *Sincerely/Next Year* (5/69); *Happy* (10/69); *Midnight Mistress* (4/70); *Do I Love You* (9/71); *Jubilation* (2/72); *Flashback/Let Me Get to Know You* (10/73); *Having My Baby/Papa* (6/74); *One Man Woman—One Woman Man/Let Me Get to Know You* (10/74); *I Don't Like to Sleep Alone/How Can Anything Be Beautiful (After You)* (2/75); *There's Nothing Stronger Than Our Love/Today I Became a Fool* (7/75); *The Times of Your Life/Water Runs Deep* (10/75); *Anytime/Something about You* (3/76); *Happier/Closing Doors* (11/76); *My Best Friend's Wife/Never Gonna Fall in Love Again* (3/77); *Everybody Ought to Be in Love/Tonight* (6/77).

ANTHONY AND THE IMPERIALS (formerly LITTLE ANTHONY AND THE IMPERIALS)/*Anthony Gourdine (vocals), Clarence Collins (vocals), Kenny Seymour (guitar), Ernest Wright (vocals), Sam Strain (vocals).*
Beginning to vocalize in Brooklyn in 1958, Anthony and the Imperials were signed by the small End label and their careers were launched with a smash single, *Tears on My Pillow.* Dubbed "little" Anthony and the Imperials by dj Alan Freed because of lead singer Gourdine's diminutive stature, the group went on to become one of the most successful groups of the fifties. The sixties saw their careers slowing down. By the seventies, they had just about forsaken the recording world altogether for live gigs in some of the nation's more exclusive nightclubs.

Albums/GOIN' OUT OF MY HEAD (1964): *Goin' Out of My Head; What a Difference a Day Makes; Reputation; Hurt; It's Just a Matter of Time; Never Again; Hurt So Bad; Who's Sorry Now;*

Where Are You; Take Me Back; I Miss You So; Get Out of My Life. I'M ON THE OUTSIDE (12/64): *I'm on the Outside; People; Our Song; Where Did Our Love Go; Make It Easy on Yourself; Girl from Ipanema; Walk On By; Letter a Day; Please Go; Exodus; Funny; Tears on My Pillow.* BEST OF LITTLE ANTHONY AND THE IMPERIALS (2/66): *Goin' Out of My Head; Hurt So Bad; Hurt; Take Me Back; Shimmy Shimmy Ko-Ko Bop; Tears on My Pillow; I Miss You So; I'm on the Outside; Reputation; Our Song; Never Again; Get Out of My Life.* GREATEST HITS: *Tears on My Pillow; Two People in the World; Shimmy Shimmy Ko-Ko Bop; The Diary; Prayer and a Jukebox; I'm All Right; So Much; So Near and Yet So Far; When You Wish upon a Star; I'm Still in Love with You; Over the Rainbow; River Path.* PAYIN' OUR DUES (4/66): *Better Use Your Head; Call Me the Joker; Good for a Lifetime; Cry My Eyes Out; You Better Take It Easy, Baby; Hungry Heart; It's Not the Same; Wonder of It All; Gonna Fix You Good; Lost without You; You're Not That Girl Anymore; Your Own Little World.* REFLECTIONS (5/67): *Don't Tie Me Down; My Love Is a Rainbow; If I Remember to Forget; Keep It Up; Hold On to Someone; Yesterday Has Gone; Trick or Treat; Lost in Love; The Mirrors of Your Mind; I Love You; Better Off without You; Thousand Miles Away.* MOVIE GRABBERS (9/67): *You Only Live Twice; Georgy Girl; Love theme from* The Sandpiper; *This Is My Song; I Will Wait for You; Somewhere, My Love; Man and a Woman; Who Can Say; Watch What Happens; Born Free; Gentle Rain; Restless One.* BEST OF LITTLE ANTHONY AND THE IMPERIALS, VOL. 2 (2/68): *I'm Hypnotized; Beautiful People; Georgy Girl; Thousand Miles Away; You Only Live Twice; Goin' Out of My Head; Two People in the World; Prayer and a Jukebox; When You Wish upon a Star; You Better Take It Easy, Baby; If I Remember to Forget.* OUT OF SIGHT, OUT OF MIND (9/69). THE VERY BEST OF LITTLE ANTHONY AND THE IMPERIALS (1974): *The Diary; Tears on My Pillow; Shimmy Shimmy Ko-Ko Bop; Two People in the World; Hurt So Bad; Goin' Out of My Head; Take Me Back; I Miss You So; Out of Sight, Out of Mind; I'm on the Outside (Looking In); Better Use Your Head; When You Wish upon a Star.*

Singles/*Tears on My Pillow* (7/58); *So Much* (12/58); *Wishful Thinking* (2/59); *A Prayer and a Juke Box* (5/59); *Shimmy Shim-*

my Ko-Ko Bop (11/59); *My Empty Room* (3/60); *I'm on the Outside (Looking In)* (7/64); *Goin' Out of My Head* (10/64); *Hurt So Bad* (1/65); *Take Me Back* (6/65); *I Miss You So* (9/65); *Hurt* (12/65); *Better Use Your Head* (4/66); *It's Not the Same* (10/66); *I'm Hypnotized* (1/68); *Out of Sight, Out of Mind* (7/69); *The Ten Commandments of Love* (10/69); *Help Me Find a Way (to Say I Love You)* (11/70).

ARGENT/*Rod Argent (keyboards, vocals), John Verity (guitar, vocals), Robert Henrit (drums), Jim Rodford (bass).*

Argent is a perfect example of a good idea never fully realized. After dissolving The Zombies in 1969, Rod Argent and Russ Ballard joined forces with Bob Henrit and Jim Rodford and formed Argent. The group's initial excursion into recordom was fairly Zombies-esque, but by the time *RING OF HANDS,* Argent's second album, was released, it looked like they were well on their way to developing a keyboard heavy sound of their own. This embryonic direction, however, was short-lived. Immediately thereafter, the group adopted a scattergun approach to music with lilting melodies and admirable riffing lost amidst an ocean of overindulgent soloing and overdrawn arrangements. The band did manage to keep their heads above water with two singles, *Hold Your Head Up* and *God Gave Rock and Roll to You,* but the first tune's main claim to fame rested solely on a repetitious phrase that was ground out to the point of extinction and the second was an uptempo dirge that reminded one of a happy funeral mass. In 1974, after the release of *NEXUS,* chief songwriter Russ Ballard decided to go it alone. Guitarist John Verity and rhythm guitarist John Grimaldi then joined the force. Grimaldi lasted until early 1976. After his departure, the band decided to pack it in as well, leaving a toe-tapping history of musical confusion behind. At this point, Rod is mulling a solo outing while Ballard continues on his critically acclaimed but publicly ignored path.

Albums/ARGENT (1/69): *Like Honey; Liar; Be Free; Schoolgirl; Dancer in the Smoke; Lonely Hard Road; The Feeling Is Inside; Freefall; Stepping Stone; Bring You Joy.* RING OF HANDS (2/71): *Celebration; Sweet Mary; Cast Your Spell Uranus; Lolklorien; Chained; Rejoice; Pleasure; Sleep Won't Help Me; Where Are We Going Wrong.* ALL TOGETHER NOW (5/72):

Hold Your Head Up; Keep on Rollin'; Tragedy; I Am the Dance of Ages; Be My Lover, Be My Friend; He's a Dynamo; Pure Love. IN DEEP (3/73): *God Gave Rock and Roll to You; It's Only Money (I and II); Losing Hold; Be Glad; Christmas for the Free; Candles on the River; Rosie.* NEXUS (4/74): *The Coming of Kohoutek; Once Around the Sun; Infinite Wanderer; Love; Music of the Spheres; Thunder and Lightning; Keeper of the Flame; Man for All Reasons; Gonna Meet My Maker.* ENCORE (11/74): *Coming of Kohoutek; It's Only Money (I and II); God Gave Rock and Roll to You; Thunder and Lightning; Music of the Spheres; I Don't Believe in Miracles; I Am the Dance of Ages; Keep On Rollin'; Hold Your Head Up; Time of the Season.* CIRCUS (2/75): *Circus; Highwire; Clown; Trapeze; Shine On Sunshine; The Ring; The Jester.* COUNTERPOINTS (4/76): *On My Feet Again; I Can't Remember, But Yes; Time; Waiting for the Yellow One; It's Fallin' Off; Be Strong; Rock 'n' Roll Show; Butterfly Road Back Home.*

Singles/*Liar*/*Schoolgirl* (10/69); *Sweet Mary*/*Rejoice* (3/71); *Celebration*/*Kingdom* (5/71); *Hold Your Head Up*/*Closer To Heaven* (5/72); *Tragedy*/*He's a Dynamo* (10/72); *God Gave Rock and Roll to You*/*Christmas for the Free* (3/73); *It's Only Money*/*Losing Hold* (6/73); *Hold Your Head Up*/*God Gave Rock and Roll to You* (3/74); *Man for All Reasons*/*Music from the Spheres* (5/74); *Thunder and Lightning*/*The Coming of Kohoutek* (8/74).

JOAN ARMATRADING/A remarkable young singer-songwriter hailing from the West Indies, Joan Armatrading first came to the public's attention in 1973 with the release of her first album, *WHATEVER IS FOR US*. A brief tour (with then-partner Pam Nestor) resulted in critical acclaim, but a reaffirmation of a low-profile stance with radio stations. By 1976, however, all that had changed and Joan's rambling, quivering vocals could be heard bursting forth from FM radio stations coast to coast.

Albums/WHATEVER IS FOR US (3/73): *My Family; City Girl; Spend a Little Time; Whatever Is for Us, For Us; Child Star; Visionary Mountains; It Could Have Been Better; Head of the Table; Mister Remember Me; Give It a Try; Alice; Conversation; Mean Old Man; All the King's Gardens.* BACK TO THE NIGHT (4/75): *No Love for Free; Travel So Far; Steppin' Out; Dry Land;*

Cool Blue Stole My Heart; Get in Touch with Jesus; Body to Dust; Back to the Night; So Good; Let's Go Dancing; Come When You Need Me. JOAN ARMATRADING (7/76): *Down to Zero; Help Yourself; Water with the Wine; Love and Affection; Save Me; Join the Boys; People; Somebody Who Loves You; Like Fire; Tall in the Saddle.* SHOW SOME EMOTION (10/77): *Woncha Come On Home; Show Some Emotion; Warm Love; Never Is Too Late; Peace in Mind; Opportunity; Mama Mercy; Get in the Sun; Willow; Kissin' and a-Huggin'.*

Singles/*Lonely Lady* (6/73); *Love and Affection* (9/76); *Down to Zero* (1/77); *Water with the Wine* (3/77).

THE ASSOCIATION/*Russ Giguere (vocals, guitar), Ted Bluechel, Jr. (drums), Brian Cole (bass vocals, bass guitar, clarinet), Terry Kirkman (vocals, twenty-three instruments including recorder, fluegel horn, drums), Larry Ramos (replacing Gary Alexander; lead guitar, vocals), Jim Yester (rhythm guitar, vocals, keyboards).*

In the mid-sixties, when flower power was about to happen and psychedelic confusion was something yet to look forward to, the incredibly melodic innocuousness of the Association took hold with a little tune entitled *Along Comes Mary.* Linked with the emergence of the wonderous world of marijuana (Mary, get it, huh?) the song immediately became a hit. Later songs such as *Cherish, Windy,* and *Never My Love* proved non-addictive but popular nonetheless. As the group limped through the sunshiny sixties into the sneering seventies, their personalities took on a desperate note and their albums promptly stopped selling like hotcakes, cold cakes, or any other digestible material. The group faded from view after a kiss-of-death album on Columbia Records.

Albums/AND THEN . . . ALONG COMES THE ASSOCIATION (4/66): *Along Comes Mary; Enter the Young; Your Own Love; Don't Blame It on Me; Blistered; I'll Be Your Man; Cherish; Standing Still; Message of Our Love; Round Again; Remember; Changes.* RENAISSANCE (5/67): *Pandora's Golden Heebie Jeebies; Memories of You; Songs in the Wind; You Hear Me Call Your Name; I'm the One; You May Think; All Is Mine; Looking Glass; Come to Me; No Fair At All; Another Time, Another Place;*

Angeline. INSIGHT OUT (8/67): *Windy; Wasn't It a Bit Like Now; On a Quiet Night; We Love Us; When Love Comes to Me; Reputation; Never My Love; Happiness; Sometime; Wantin' Ain't Gettin'; Requiem for the Masses.* BIRTHDAY (5/68): *Everything That Touches You; Come On In; Rose Petals, Incense and Kitten; Like Always; Toymaker; Barefoot Gentleman; Time for Livin'; Hear in Here; Time It Is Today; Bus Song; Birthday Morning.* ASSOCIATION'S GREATEST HITS (11/68): *Cherish; Windy; Never My Love; Along Comes Mary; Enter the Young; Everything That Touches You; No Fair At All; Six Man Band; Time for Livin'; We Love Us; The Time It Is Today; Like Always; Requiem for the Masses.* GOODBYE COLUMBUS (soundtrack; 3/69): *Goodbye Columbus; How Well I Know You; Dartmouth?!; A Moment to Share; Love Has a Way; So Kind to Me; It's Gotta Be Real; Reverie; A Time for Love; other titles.* ASSOCIATION (8/69): *Look at Me, Look at You; Yes I Will; Love Affair; The Nest; What Were the World; Are You Ready; Broccoli; Boy on the Mountain; Goodbye Forever; I Am Up for Europe; Under Branches; other titles.* LIVE (6/70). STOP YOUR MOTOR (7/71): *Bring Yourself Home; That's Racin'; P.F. Sloan; Silver Morning; Funny Kind of Song; It's Gotta Be Real; Traveler's Guide; Seven Virgins; Along the Way; The First Sound.* WATERBEDS IN TRINIDAD (5/72): *Silent Song thru the Lord; Darling Be Home Soon; Midnight Wind; Come the Fall; Kicking the Gong Around; Rainbows Bent; Snow Queen; Indian Wells; Woman; Please Don't Go; Little Road and a Stone to Roll.*

Singles/*Along Comes Mary* (5/66); *Cherish* (7/66); *Pandora's Golden Heebie Jeebies* (10/66); *No Fair At All* (1/67); *Windy/Sometime* (4/67); *Never My Love/Requiem for the Masses* (8/67); *Everything That Touches You/We Love Us* (1/68); *Time for Livin'/Birthday Morning* (4/68); *Six Man Band/Like Always* (8/68); *Time It Is Today/Enter the Young* (11/68); *Goodbye Columbus/The Time It Is Today* (2/69); *Under Branches/Hear in Here* (4/69); *Just About the Same/Look at Me, Look at You* (2/70); *Along The Way/Travelers Guide* (10/70); *Bring Yourself Home/It's Gotta Be Real* (7/71); *That's Racin'/Makes Me Cry* (9/71); *Darling Be Home Soon/Indian Wells Woman* (4/72); *Come the Fall/Kicking the Gong Around* (7/72); *Names, Tags, Numbers and Labels/Rainbows Bent* (1/73).

THE ATLANTA RHYTHM SECTION/*Ronnie Hammond (vocals), Dean Daughtry (keyboards), Robert Nix (drums), J.R. Cobb (guitar), Paul Goddard (guitar), Barry Baily (guitar). Former member: Rodney Justo (vocals).*

One of the foremost examples of Southern rock expertise, the Atlanta Rhythm Section is basically a story of a group of seasoned sessionmen who have fought long and hard to establish their credentials as legitimate artists. The band signed a recording deal in 1974, and by 1977 they were hitting both the album and single best-seller lists. Baily, Justo, Daughtry, Nix, and Goodard had recorded years previously as the Candymen on ABC, as well as playing throughout the country as Roy Orbison's backup group. The lack of success with the Candymen after two critically acclaimed albums led them back to the session-musician stage. But by 1974 they felt ready to take the plunge once again. This time, happily for all concerned, the band proved a success.

Albums/THIRD ANNUAL PIPE DREAM (6/74): *Doraville; Jesus-Hearted People; Close the Door; Blues in Maude's Flat; Join the Race; Angel; Get Your Head out of Your Heart; Who You Gonna Run To; Help Yourself; The Wars Is Over.* DOG DAYS (4/75): *Crazy; Boogie Smoogie; Cuban Crises; It Just Ain't Your Moon; Dog Days; Bless My Soul; Silent Treatment; All Night Rain.* RED TAPE (4/76): *Jukin'; Mixed Emotion; Shanghaied; Police! Police!; Beautiful Dreamers; Oh, What a Feeling; Free Spirit; Another Man's Woman.* ROCK AND ROLL ALTERNATIVE (12/76): *Sky High; Hitch-Hiker's Hero; Don't Miss the Message; Georgia Rhythm; So in to You; Outside Woman Blues; Everybody Gotta Go; Neon Lites.*

Singles/*Doraville/Angel* (6/74); *Doraville/Who You Gonna Run To* (8/74); *Angel/Help Yourself* (10/74); *Get Your Head out of Your Heart/Jesus-Hearted People* (4/75); *Dog Days/Cuban Crises* (7/75); *Crazy/Bless My Soul* (10/75); *So in to You/Everybody's Gotta Go* (12/76); *Neon Lites/Don't Miss the Message* (5/77).

AVERAGE WHITE BAND/*Alan Gorrie (bass, vocals), Roger Ball (keyboards, reeds), Malcolm Duncan (tenor sax), Hamish Stuart (guitar, vocals), Onnie McIntyre (vocals, rhythm guitar), Steve Ferrone (drums). Previous member: Robbie McIntosh (drums).*

The foremost exponent of blue-eyed soul from the United Kingdom, the Average White Band is a troupe steeped in black

R&B, hailing from Scotland. Beginning in 1972, they soon achieved notoriety on the pub circuit before blossoming as Eric Clapton's opening act at his famous comeback concert at the Rainbow in London in January, 1973. A premier album garnered critical acclaim stateside but remained an uncommercial venture. Soon the group found themselves on another label (Atlantic) and with a new producer (Atlantic's Arif Mardin).

The Mardin-produced AWB release proved an immense success. The six-man army was on their way to fame. A subsequent single, *Cut the Cake,* was an international hit. As their fame began to grow, tragedy struck. In September of 1974, drummer Robbie McIntosh died of an accidental overdose of heroin at a L.A. rock party. The poisoning made headlines and the rock stars in attendance at the fete were oft quoted on the fact that no one was aware that heroin was being distributed.

Robbie was replaced by former Bloodstone drummer Steve Ferrone. AWB's career has remained constant over the years but their *Cut The Cake* days remain their strongest commercially.

Albums/SHOW YOUR HAND (1973). AVERAGE WHITE BAND (8/74): *You Got It; Got the Love; Pick Up the Pieces; Person to Person; Work to Do; Nothing You Can Do; Just Wanna Love You Tonight; Keepin' It to Myself; I Just Can't Give You Up; There's Always Someone Waiting.* CUT THE CAKE (6/75): *Cut the Cake; School Boy Crush; It's a Mystery; Groovin' the Night Away; If I Ever Lose This Heaven; Why; High-Flyin' Woman; Cloudy; How Sweet Can You Get; When They Bring Down the Curtain.* SOUL SEARCHING (6/76): *Overture; Love Your Life; I'm the One; A Love of Your Own; Queen of My Soul; Soul Searching; Goin' Home; Everybody's Darling; Would You Stay; Sunny Days; Digging Deeper.* PERSON TO PERSON (12/76): *Person to Person; Cut the Cake; If I Ever Lose This Heaven; Cloudy; T.L.C.; I'm the One; Pick Up the Pieces; Love Your Life; School Boy Crush; I Heard It through the Grapevine.* BENNY AND US (with Ben E. King; 6/77): *Get It Up for Love; Keepin' It to Myself; Imagine; Fool for You Anyway; A Star in the Ghetto; The Message; What Is Soul; Someday We'll All Be Free.*

Singles/*Nothing You Can Do/I Just Can't Give You Up* (7/74); *Pick Up the Pieces/Work to Do* (10/74); *Cut the Cake/Person to Person* (3/75); *If I Ever Lose This Heaven/High-flyin' Woman*

(7/75); *Person to Person/Pick Up the Pieces* (8/75); *School Boy Crush/Groovin' the Night Away* (10/75); *If I Ever Lose This Heaven/Work to Do* (2/76); *Queen of My Soul/Would You Stay* (8/76); *A Love of Your Own/Soul Searching* (10/76); *School Boy Crush/Queen of My Soul* (11/76); *Cloudy/Love Your Life* (2/77).

BACHMAN-TURNER OVERDRIVE/*Randy Bachman (guitars, vocals), Robbie Bachman (drums), Fred Turner (bass, vocals), Blair Thorton (guitar).*

Bachman-Turner Overdrive (BTO) has all the subtlety of a steamroller and the finesse of a barroom brawl. The band is a direct result of Randy Bachman's exodus from the Guess Who. After a brief stab at soloing, Randy got a band together called Brave Belt (with brother Robbie, Fred Turner and original Guess Who singer Chad Allan)—a fairly bizarre concoction that hovered unsuccessfully between rock and country. After two LPs, Brave Belt went below the belt and emerged as the neolithic BTO with the lineup being Randy, Fred, Robbie, and Tim Bachman on guitar. Their first slbum, *BACHMAN-TURNER OVERDRIVE,* was released in '73 and confused a lot of people. Mercury Records brought the Godzilla troupe into New York for a gig at Max's Kansas City (a famous club with a stage the size of a washroom) and deafened several key critics as a result. No matter, at least the name BTO would be remembered.

By the Time BTO's second album was out, so was brother Tim, replaced by Blair Thorton. After the release of the second LP, things started happening in a big way for BTO and they haven't stopped happening since. The quartet has enjoyed an amazing success with their thunderthudding style. Songs like *You Ain't Seen Nothin' Yet* and *Takin' Care of Business* have made the name BTO synonymous with primo–head-knocking rock. True to form, however, Randy Bachman has done his best to prove himself unpredictable. In late 1977, he left the band, allowing BTO to make it or break it as a trio.

Albums/BACHMAN-TURNER OVERDRIVE (5/73): *Gimme Your Money Please; Hold Back the Water; Blue Collar; Little Gandy Dancer; Stayed Awake; Down and Out Man; Don't Get Yourself in Trouble; Thank You for the Feelin'.*
BACHMAN TURNER OVERDRIVE II (12/73): *Blown; Welcome Home; Stonegates; Let It Ride; Give It Time; Tramp; I Don't*

Have to Hide; Takin' Care of Business. NOT FRAGILE (8/74): *Not Fragile; Rock Is My Life; Roll On Down the Highway; You Ain't Seen Nothing Yet; Free Wheelin' Sledgehammer; Blue Moanin'; Second Hand; Givin' It All Away.* FOUR WHEEL DRIVE (5/75): *Four Wheel Drive; She's a Devil; Hey You; Flat Broke Love; She's Keepin' Time; Quick Change Artist; Lowland Fling; Don't Let the Blues Get You Down.* HEAD ON (12/75): *Find Out About Love; It's Over; Average Man; Woncha Take Me for a While; Take It Like a Man; Lookin' Out for #1; Away from Home; Stay Alive.* THE BEST OF BTO (SO FAR) (7/76): *Roll On Down the Highway; Hey You; Lookin' Out For #1; Gimme Your Money Please; Let It Ride; Take It Like a Man; You Ain't Seen Nothing Yet; Blue Collar; Takin' Care of Business.* FREE-WAYS (2/77): *Can We All Come Together; Life Still Goes On (I'm Lonely); Shotgun Rider; Just for You; My Wheels Won't Turn; Down, Down; Easy Groove; Freeways.*

Singles/*Stayed Awake All Night/Gimme Your Money Please* (5/73); *Hold Back the Water/Blue Collar* (8/73); *Tramp/Let It Ride* (1/74); *Stonegates/Takin' Care of Business* (4/74); *Let It Ride* (6/74); *You Ain't Seen Nothing Yet/Free Wheelin'* (8/74); *Roll On Down the Highway/Sledgehammer* (1/75); *Hey You/Flat Broke Love* (5/75); *She's a Devil/Down to the Line* (11/75); *Woncha Take Me for a While/Take It Like a Man* (1/76); *Find Out About Love/Lookin' Out for #1* (3/76); *Down, Down/Shotgun Rider* (5/77).

BACK STREET CRAWLER/CRAWLER/*Original members; Terry Wilson Slesser (vocals), Paul Kossoff (lead guitar), Terry Wilson (bass), Tony Braunagel (drums), Mike Montgomery (keyboards). Present members: Slesser, Braunagel, Wilson, Geoff Whitehorn (guitars), John "Rabbit" Bundrick (keyboards).*
Named after an early solo album by former Free guitarist Paul Kossoff, Back Street Crawler came into being in 1975 as an extension of Kossoff's dazzling, albeit sparse, guitar style. Kossoff, a former drug user, was plagued by ill health in his later years and died in 1976 of an apparent heart attack. A posthumous album, *2ND STREET,* was dedicated "To Koss." The band regrouped in 1977 as Crawler and, releasing an album of the same name, began a new career as sort of a grandson of Free . . . a hard-rocking band with an economical sound.

Albums/PAUL KOSSOFF: BACK STREET CRAWLER (British release 1973): *Tuesday Morning; I'm Ready; Time Away; Molten Gold; Back Street Crawler (Don't Need You No More).* THE BAND PLAYS ON (10/75): *Hoo Doo Woman; New York, New York; Stealing My Way; Survivor; It's a Long Way Down to the Top; All the Girls Are Crazy; Jason Blue; Train Song; Rock and Roll Junkie; The Band Plays On.* 2ND STREET (11/76): *Selfish Lover; Blue Soul; Stop Doing What You're Doing; Raging River; Some Kind of Happy; Sweet Beauty; Just for You; On Your Life; Leaves in the Wind.* CRAWLER (8/77): *Without You Babe; You Got Money; Sold On Down the Line; One Too Many Lovers; You Are My Saviour; Pastime Dreamer; Never Loved a Woman; You and Me; Stone Cold Sober.*

BAD COMPANY/*Paul Rodgers (vocals, guitar), Simon Kirke (drums), Mick Ralphs (guitar), Boz Burrell (bass).*
If Bad Company was not a group, they would probably be a nuclear warhead ... or, on a more personal level, a left hook below the belt. The Masters of stark, no-holds barred, sledgehammer rock, Bad Company is a relatively new band (in existence since 1973) whose roots can be traced back to the late sixties. Rodgers and Kirke first met as one-half of the primo British band Free. Free was one of the first bands of that period to promote the use of "space" in their music. Their sound was clean, crisp, and lethal, with anvil drums and bass laying down a pattern interrupted only occasionally by blinding flashes of guitar. It was only natural that when this much underrated band band broke up, the two friends should search for an outlook that, while similar in approach, would carry this train of thought to its next plane of existence.

Also on the look for a band was founder-member–guitarist of the original Mott the Hoople, Mick Ralphs. Mick had grown tired of the pressures his old group presented and grew a bit disgusted with the ornate stage antics that surrounded every guitar lick he came up with. He was looking for something simple and to the point—a no-frills approach to rock and roll. The seeds of Bad Company were born and the band was solidified with the addition of former King Crimson bassist Boz Burrell, a singer who had been taught bass by Crimson's lead genius, Robert Fripp.

The newly born foursome were signed to Led Zepplin's embryonic SwanSong label and the hits haven't stopped coming since. Their first single, *Can't Get Enough of Your Love,* went top-five in the United States and a six-week introduction tour of the country turned into a three-month stay. After crashing through the U.S. music scene like a wild-riffing bull, Bad Company went on to garner gold and platinum album awards for every long-player they've released since 1973. Onstage they perform without the aid of ornate costumes or flashy visual effects. They pick up their instruments and microphones, throttle them for a few hours and leave, exhausted. To millions of fans, Bad Company is sheer rock personified.

Albums/BAD CO. (6/74): *Can't Get Enough; Rock Steady; Ready for Love; Don't Let Me Down; Bad Company; The Way I Choose; Movin' On; Seagull.* STRAIGHT SHOOTER (4/75): *Good Lovin' Gone Bad; Feel Like Makin' Love; Weep No More; Shooting Star; Deal with the Preacher; Wild Fire Woman; Anna; Call on Me.* RUN WITH THE PACK (3/76): *Live for the Music; Simple Man; Honey Child; Love Me, Somebody; Run with the Pack; Silver, Blue & Gold; Young Blood; Do Right by Your Woman; Sweet Li'l Sister; Fade Away.* BURNING SKY (3/77): *Burnin' Sky; Morning Sun; Leaving You; Like Water; Everything I Need; Heartbeat; Peace of Mind; Passing Time; Too Bad; Man Needs Woman; Master of Ceremony.*

Singles/*Can't Get Enough* (7/74); *Movin' On* (12/74); *Good Lovin' Gone Bad* (4/75); *Feel Like Makin' Love* (6/75); *Young Blood/Do Right by Your Woman* (3/76); *Honey Child/Fade Away* (6/76); *Burnin' Sky/Everything I Need* (4/77).

BADFINGER/*Pete Ham (vocals, keyboards, guitar), Joey Molland (guitar, vocals), Tom Evans (bass, vocals), Mike Gibbins (drums).*
Badfinger is one of the few bands to be done in by having instant successes. Coming together in the late sixties as the Iveys, they had a worldwide hit with *Maybe Tomorrow.* Subsequently, the band found themselves caught up in the business end of the late sixties' Beatlemania, including the notorious financial antics of the Beatles' Apple Records company. The band submitted a demo tape to the embryonic label and were signed by the Beatles themselves; the fab four really enjoyed the band's fresh, veddy

British approach to rock, which was, in some respects, similar to the Beatles' own a few years before.

The Iveys became Badfinger and immediately plunged into work, scoring the soundtrack for the Ringo Starr starrer, *Magic Christian*. McCartney penned a tune, *Come and Get It,* Badfinger recorded it, and a gold record was born. Badfinger's career took off immediately and albums such as *NO DICE* and *STRAIGHT UP* quickly established them as a group of considerable performing and composing merit. Their Beatles-inspired success, however, had a tendency to overshadow their own songwriting skills. The Kafkaesque turn for the worse at Apple Records put a strain on the band's relationship with the Beatles, now four solo friends. Although working with several ex-Beatles on solo albums, Badfinger split from the label, joining Warner Brothers.

Their post-Apple releases proved schizoid affairs, offering both classic Badfinger tunes and utter banality. The lack of success in their later years began to irritate the members. A discouraged Pete Ham announced his plans to quit the band in 1975. Shortly thereafter, on May 1, he committed suicide. With the loss of one of their founder-members, the band fragmented and disappeared.

Albums/MAGIC CHRISTIAN MUSIC (2/70): *Come and Get It; Crimson Ship; Dear Angie; Fisherman; Midnight Sun; Beautiful and Blue; Rock of All Ages; Carry On 'til Tomorrow; I'm in Love; Walk Out in the Rain; Angelique; Knocking Down Our Homes; Give It a Try; Maybe Tomorrow.* NO DICE (9/70): *I Can't Take It; I Don't Mind; Love Me Do; Midnight Caller; No Matter What; Without You; Blodwyn; Better Days; It Had to Be; Waterford John; Believe Me; We're for the Dark.* STRAIGHT UP (12/71): *Take It All; Baby Blue; Money; Flying; I'd Die, Babe; Name of the Game; Suitcase; Sweet Tuesday Morning; Day after Day; Sometimes; Perfection; It's Over.* ASS (11/73): *Apple of My Eye; Get Away Icicles; The Winner; Blind Owl; Constitution; When I Say; Cowboy; Timeless; I Can Love You.* BADFINGER (2/74): *I Miss You; Shine On; Love Is Easy; Song for a Lost Friend; Why Don't We Talk; Island; Matted Spam; Where Do We Go from Here?; My Heart Goes Out; Lonely You; Give It Up; Andy Norris.* WISH YOU WERE HERE (11/74): *Just a Chance; You're So Fine; Got to Get Out of Here; Know One Knows; Dennis; In the Meantime; Love Time; Some Other Time; King of the Load; Meanwhile, Back at the Ranch; Should I Smoke.*

Singles/*Come and Get It*/*Rock of All Ages* (1/70); *No Matter What*/*Carry On 'til Tomorrow* (10/70); *Day after Day*/*Money* (11/71); *Baby Blue*/*Flying* (3/72); *Apple of My Eye*/*Blind Owl* (12/73); *I Miss You*/*Shine On* (3/74).

THE BAND/*Rick Danko (bass, vocals), Levon Helm (drums, vocals), Garth Hudson (organ, vocals), Richard Menuel (piano, vocals), Robbie Robertson (guitar, vocals).*
Together since the early sixties (when they backed rock and rolling Ronnie Hawkins under the name of The Hawks), The Band was a legend before the release of their first album in 1968. The main cause of their "instant fame" was a fellow by the name of Dylan. During 1966, The Band backed Dylan on his tour of the United Kingdom (the notorious "electric folk" concerts) and, in 1967, after Dylan's motorcycle mishap, they recorded the historic Dylan "Basement Tapes" at their sprawling Woodstock headquarters, Big Pink.

In '68, their debut disc, *MUSIC FROM BIG PINK,* was released and progressive rockers around the world praised the album as being the greatest thing to come along since sliced bread. The Band was, at this point, in rather a unique situation. Robbie Robertson's rural songwriting style was anything but slick and preordained, yet The Band was tossed into the same superstar sweepstakes as any Rolling-Zepplin-and-Englishmen band and faced all the pressures, demands, and lunacy that came with this position. Surprised at the sudden critical acclaim, the unit attempted to "tighten" the musical end of things with their second release, *THE BAND.* They had, once again, come up with a brilliant record. They were besieged by reporters, both underground and straight. Stardom was assuredly theirs. Photos were taken. Flashbulbs went off in their faces. Big Pink was viewed as a shrine, of sorts.

STAGE FRIGHT, their third album, was written in three weeks and saw a subtle change of attitude in The Band. They were becoming more, uh, aware of the hazardous duties of rockdom. In *CAHOOTS,* they purposely turned from the folksy approach to music for which they had been lionized and branched out into a more experimental realm. It was their first real *studio* album and the song *Where Do We Go from Here* accurately summed up their feeling at the time.

CAHOOTS shocked a lot of critics. It was intended to. But the real jolts were yet to come as The Band began cautiously to retreat from the whirlwind spotlight life. *ROCK OF AGES* was a crazy-quilt of their favorite songs, both original and otherwise, and *MOONDOG MATINEE* was an album of moldie oldies, featuring material made famous by The Platters, Fats Domino and others. The Band rallied somewhat in 1975 for the release of *NORTHERN LIGHTS/SOUTHERN CROSS*, their first studio album of original material in years. Although Band critics found it less inspiring than their earlier classics (Well, ya know, it ain't no *PINK*), loyal fans embraced it dutifully.

The pressure of living up to legend culminated with The Band's Last Waltz concert on Thanksgiving Day, 1976. After playing together for over a decade and a half, the group announced that they were never going to tour as The Band again. A studio album was released in 1977, *ISLANDS,* wherein the Band made it clear that they were still their own men. They would play what they wanted to play when they wanted to play it and would be known, from now on, as musicians' musicians and not fantasy-laden superstars.

Albums/MUSIC FROM BIG PINK (7/68): *Tears of Rage; To Kingdom Come; In a Station; Caledonia Mission; The Weight; We Can Talk; Long Black Veil; Chest Fever; Lonesome Suzie; This Wheel's on Fire; I Shall Be Released.* THE BAND (9/69): *Across the Great Divide; Rag Mama Rag; The Night They Drove Old Dixie Down; When You Awake; Up on Cripple Creek; Whispering Pines; Jemina Surrender; Rockin' Chair; Jawbone; Look Out Cleveland; The Unfaithful Servant; King Harvest (Has Surely Come).* STAGE FRIGHT (8/70): *Strawberry Wine; Sleeping; Time to Kill; Just Another Whistle Stop; All La Glory; The Shape I'm In; The W. S. Walcott Medicine Show; Daniel and the Sacred Harp; Stage Fright; The Rumor.* CAHOOTS (9/71): *Life Is a Carnival; When I Paint My Masterpiece; Last of the Blacksmiths; Where Do We Go From Here?; 4% Pantomime; The Moon Struck One; Thinkin' Out Loud; Smoke Signal; Volcano; Shoot Out in Chinatown; The River Hymn.* ROCK OF AGES (6/72): *Don't Do It; King Harvest (Has Surely Come); Caledonia Mission; Get Up Jake; Chest Fever; W. S. Walcott Medicine Show; The Genetic Method; (I Don't Want to) Hand Up My Rock and Roll Shoes;*

Stage Fright; The Night They Drove Old Dixie Down; Across the Great Divide; This Wheel's on Fire; The Weight; The Shape I'm In; Rag Mama Rag; The Unfaithful Servant; Life Is a Carnival. MOONDOG MATINEE (10/73): *Ain't Got No Home; Holy Cow; Share Your Love with Me; Mystery Train; Third Man Theme; The Promised Land; The Great Pretender; I'm Ready; Saved; A Change Is Gonna Come.* NORTHERN LIGHTS/SOUTHERN CROSS (11/75): *Forbidden Fruit; Hobo Jungle; Ophelia; Acadian Driftwood; Ring Your Bell; It Makes No Difference; Jupiter Hollow; Rags and Bones.* THE BEST OF THE BAND (7/76): *Up On Cripple Creek; The Shape I'm In; The Weight; It Makes No Difference; Life Is a Carnival; Ophelia; The Night They Drove Old Dixie Down; Stage Fright; Twilight; Don't Do It; Tears of Rage.* ISLANDS (3/77): *Right As Rain; Street Walker; Let the Night Fall; Ain't That a Lot of Love; Christmas Must Be Tonight; Islands; The Saga of Pepote Rouge; Georgia on My Mind; Knockin' Lost John; Living in a Dream.*

Singles/*The Weight/I Shall Be Released* (8/68); *Up On Cripple Creek/The Night They Drove Old Dixie Down* (10/69); *Rag Mama Rag/Unfaithful Servant* (2/20); *Time to Kill/The Shape I'm In* (9/70); *Carnival/The Moon Struck One* (10/71); *Don't Do It/Rag Mama Rag* (8/72); *(I Don't Want to Hand Up) My Rock and Roll Shoes/Caledonia Mission* (11/72); *Ain't Got No Home/Get Up Jake* (10/73); *The Third Man Theme/W. S. Walcott Medicine Show* (1/74); *Ophelia/Hobo Jungle* (2/76); *Twilight/Acadian Driftwood* (8/76); *Georgia on My Mind/The Night They Drove Old Dixie Down* (11/76).

BAROQUE ROCK/On Procol Harum's *A Whiter Shade of Pale* (1967), it was a Bach cantata. With The Left Banke (1967) it was a harpsichord. Vintage groups like Ars Nova, The New York Rock and Roll Ensemble, and Chrysalis attempted to mix rock rhythms with baroque instrumentation with varied success. It was a small movement, which blossomed in the late sixties and was dedicated but not very successful commercially.

THE BEACH BOYS/*Brian Wilson (vocals), Dennis Wilson (vocals, drums), Mike Love (vocals), Al Jardine (vocals, guitar), Carl Wilson (vocals, guitar). Additional members: Bruce Johnston (vocals).*

During the mind-numbing days of the early sixties, the sweet sounds of the Beach Boys were more than just a breath of fresh air —they were a revolutionary gust of harmony-laden word-paintings that conjured up visions of endless summers, long-haired beach bunnies, and that big wave. The Beach Boys *were* California. They re-introduced the art of vocalizing to a stagnant rock world. They were kinetic, sharp, and snappy. They were something totally, wondrously different. For that reason, and rightfully so, they were one of the biggest American groups of the sixties, earning a large following of would-be surfers across the globe. Since those days, however, their music has hovered between the spectacular and the silly.

The band formed in 1961 as Carl and the Passions, playing at California dances and school functions under both that name and Kenny and the Cadets. In 1961, Brian penned the epic *Surfin'*, the group cut a demo for the Candix label, and the Beach Boys began. Wilson, in one unexpected move, had invented the West Coast sound. Mixing his wet-suit imagery with Chuck Berry Rhythms, he came up with a succession of vocally crazed smashes: *Surfin Safari, Surfin' U.S.A., Fun, Fun, Fun, Little Honda,* and *I Get Around.*

The pressures of being in the number-one American group got the best of Brian, however, who suffered a nervous breakdown in 1965. He vowed to participate only on recording sessions and was replaced by Bruce Johnston. With Brian away from the band, a schism of sorts formed. The group, live, was still cranking out those groovy West Coast tales of sun and surf as evidenced in *Help Me Rhonda* and *California Girls.* Wilson, on the other hand, was planning introspective musical intricacies with the aid of critically acclaimed lyricist and commercial albatross Van Dyke Parks. The duo's masterpiece, *PET SOUNDS,* was a commercial stiff, totally enraging the working band, although a hit single, *Good Vibrations,* did calm them down a bit.

Brian, retreating deeper and deeper into an isolated fantasy world, concocted the epic LP *SMILE,* an album that was never released. Fearing the popularity of the Beatles via their *SGT. PEPPER* LP, Wilson truncated his work, releasing it as *SMILEY SMILE,* yet another commercial failure. The Beach Boys began reaching their nadir with *WILD HONEY, FRIENDS,* and *SUNFLOWER.* Repackages started to appear, reminding stalwart

fans of the golden years of the Beach Boys. *SURF'S UP,* a 1971
LP consisting of aborted *SMILE* material, saw the band on the
upswing. They suddenly became very popular as a live act, although their newer albums continued to disappoint and/or revolt
their fans. *CARL AND THE PASSIONS* and *HOLLAND* virtually drove their fans up the wall. Brian's surreal world of wired-
out land became legendary, with friends alternately reporting that
he was on the mend mentally or beyond the valley of the dolls.

During the seventies, the Beach Boys are still remembered for
the great achievements of a decade ago. Their reputations are
kept alive by moldie-oldie repackages and by superb, harmonious
concert dates. In 1976–77, Brian Wilson staged a "therapeutic"
come-back as a solo artist with an album and an appearance on
the nationwide TV-er, *Saturday Night Live.*

It was different.

Albums/SURFIN' SAFARI (10/62): *Surfin' Safari; Country
Fair; Ten Little Indians; Chug-A-Lug; Little Girl (You're My Miss
America); 409; Surfin'; Heads you Win—Tails I Lose; Sum-
mertime Blues; Cuckoo Clock; Moon Dawg; The Shift;* SURFIN'
USA (4/63): *Surfin' USA; Farmer's Daughter; Misirlou; Stoked;
Lonely Sea; Shut Down; Noble Surfer; Honky Tonk; Lana; Surf
Jam; Let's Go Trippin'; Finders Keepers.* SHUT DOWN (1963):
*Shut Down; Chicken; Wide Track; Brontosaurus Stomp; Four on
the Floor; Black Denim Trousers and Motorcycle Boots; 409;
Street Machine; The Ballad of Thunder Road; Hot Rod Race; Car
Trouble; Cheater Slicks.* SURFER GIRL (9/63): *Surfer Girl;
Catch a Wave; The Surfer Moon; South Bay Surfer; The Rocking
Surfer; Little Deuce Coupe; In My Room; Hawaii; Surfer's Rule;
Our Car Club; Your Summer Dream; Boogie Woogie.* LITTLE
DEUCE COUPE (10/63): *Little Deuce Coupe; Ballad of Ole'
Betsy; Be True to Your School; Car Crazy Cutie; Cherry, Cherry
Coupe; Shut Down; Spirit of America; 409; Our Car Club; No-Go
Showboat; A Young Man Is Gone; Custom Machine.* SHUT
DOWN, VOLUME 2 (3/64): *Fun, Fun, Fun; Don't Worry Baby;
In the Parkin' Lot; "Cassius" Love vs. "Sonny" Wilson; The
Warmth of the Sun; This Car of Mine; Why Do Fools Fall in Love;
Pom Pom Play Girl; Keep an Eye on Summer; Shut Down, Part II;
Louie, Louie; Denny's Drums.* ALL SUMMER LONG (7/64):
Get Around; All Summer Long; Hushabye; Little Honda; We'll

Run Away; Carl's Big Chance; Wendy; Do You Remember; Girls on the Beach; Drive-In; Our Favorite Recording Sessions; Don't Back Down. BEACH BOYS CHRISTMAS ALBUM (10/64): *Little Saint Ñick; The Man with All the Toys; Santa's Beard; Merry Christmas, Baby; Christmas Day; Frosty the Snowman; We Three Kings of Orient Are; Blue Christmas; Santa Claus Is Coming to Town; White Christmas; I'll Be Home for Christmas; Auld Lang Syne.* BEACH BOYS CONCERT (10/64): *Fun, Fun, Fun; The Little Old Lady from Pasadena; Little Deuce Coupe; Long, Tall Texan; In My Room; The Monster Mash; Let's Go Trippin'; Papa-Oom-Mow-Mow; The Wanderer; Hawaii; Graduation Day; I Get Around; Johnny B. Goode.* BEACH BOYS TODAY (3/65): *Do You Wanna Dance; Good to My Baby; Don't Hurt My Little Sister; When I Grow Up; Help Me, Rhonda; Dance, Dance, Dance; Please Let Me Wonder; I'm So Young; Kiss Me, Baby; She Knows Me Too Well; In the Back of My Mind; Bull Session with the "Big Daddy."* SUMMER DAYS (6/65): *The Girl from New York City; Amusement Parks USA; Then I Kissed Her; Salt Lake City; Girl Don't Tell Me; Help Me; Rhonda; California Girls; Let Him Run Wild; You're So Good to Me; Summer Means New Love; I'm Bugged at My Old Man; And Your Dreams Come True.* BEACH BOYS PARTY (11/65): *Hully Gully; I Should Have Known Better; Tell Me Why; Papa-Ooom-Mow-Mow; Mountain of Love; You've Got to Hide Your Love Away; Devoted to You; Alley Oop; There's No Other; Medley; I Get Around; Little Deuce Coupe; The Times They Are A-Changin'; Barbara Ann.* PET SOUNDS (4/66): *Wouldn't It Be Nice; You Still Believe in Me; That's Not Me; Don't Talk; I'm Waiting for the Day; Let's Go Away for Awhile; Sloop John B.; God Only Knows; I Know There's an Answer; Here Today; I Just Wasn't Made for These Times; Caroline, No; Pet Sounds.* BEST OF THE BEACH BOYS (6/66): *Surfin' USA; Catch a Wave; Surfer Girl; Little Deuce Coupe; In My Room; Little Honda; Fun, Fun, Fun; The Warmth of the Sun; Louie, Louie; Kiss Me, Baby; You're So Good to Me; Wendy.* BEST OF THE BEACH BOYS, VOLUME II (7/67): *Barbara Ann; When I Grow Up; Long, Tall Texan; Please Let Me Wonder; 409; Let Him Run Wild; Don't Worry Baby; Surfin' Safari; Little Saint Nick; California Girls; Help Me, Rhonda; I Get Around.* SMILEY SMILE (9/67): *Heroes and Villains; Vegetables; Fall*

*Breaks and Back to Winter; Little Pad; She's Goin' Bald; Good
Vibrations; With Me Tonight; Wind Chimes; Gettin' Hungry;
Wonderful; Whistle In.* WILD HONEY (11/67): *Wild Honey;
Aren't You Glad; I Was Made to Love Her; Country Air; Thing or
Two; Here Comes the Night; Darlin'; I'd Love Just Once to See
You; Let the Wind Blow; How She Boogalooed It; Mama Says.*
FRIENDS (6/68): *Mean for You; Friends; Wake the World; Be
Here in the Morning; When a Man Needs a Woman; Passing By;
Anna Lee; The Healer; Little Bird; Be Still; Busy Doin' Nothin';
Diamond Head; Transcendental Meditation.* 20/20 (2/69): *Do It
Again; I Can Hear Music; Bluebirds over the Mountain; Be with
Me; All I Want to Do; The Nearest Faraway Place; Cotton Fields;
I Went to Sleep; Time to Get Alone; Never Learn Not to Love; Our
Prayer; Cabinessence.* CLOSE UP (7/69). SUNFLOWER (7/70):
*Slip On Through; Tears in the Morning; All I Wanna Do; Forever;
Cool, Cool Water; At My Window; Our Sweet Love; It's About
Time; Deirdre; Got to Know the Woman; This Whole World; Add
Some Music to Your Day.* FUN, FUN, FUN/DANCE, DANCE,
DANCE (2/71): *Fun, Fun, Fun; Don't Worry Baby; The Warmth
of the Sun; This Car of Mine; Why Do Fools Fall in Love; Pom
Pom Play Girl; Keep an Eye on Summer; Louie, Louie; Shut Down,
Part 2; Denny's Drums; Do You Wanna Dance?; Good to My
Baby; Don't Hurt My Little Sister; Help Me, Rhonda; When I
Grow Up; Dance, Dance, Dance; I'm So Young; Kiss Me, Baby;
She Knows Me Too Well.* SURF'S UP (8/71): *Don't Go Near the
Water; Long Promised Road; Take a Load Off Your Feet; Disney
Girls; Student Demonstration Time; Feet Flows; Lookin' at Tomor-
row; Till I Die; Surf's Up; A Day in the Life of a Tree.* PET
SOUNDS/CARL & THE PASSIONS "SO TOUGH" (5/72):
*You Need a Mess of Help to Stand Alone; He Comes Down;
Mercella; Here She Comes; Hold On Dear Brother; Make It Good;
Cuddle Up; All this Is That; plus all titles from previously released
PET SOUNDS.* HOLLAND (12/72): *Sail on Sailor; Steamboat;
California Saga; Big Sur; The Beach of Eagles; California; The
Trader; Leaving This Town; Funky Pretty; Only with You.* 20/20
(re-released 7/73). IN CONCERT (11/73): *In Concert; Sail On
Sailor; Sloop John B.; The Trader; You Still Believe in Me;
Darlin'; Marcella; California Girls; Leaving This Town; Heroes
and Villains; Funky Pretty; Let the Wind Blow; Help Me, Rhonda;*

Surfer Girl; Wouldn't It Be Nice; We Got Love; Surfin' USA; Fun, Fun, Fun; Good Vibrations; Don't Worry Baby. PET SOUNDS (re-released 2/74). ENDLESS SUMMER (6/74): *Surfin' Safari; Surfer Girl; Help Me, Rhonda; Girl Don't Tell Me; You're So Good to Me; All Summer Long; Be True to Your School; Little Deuce Coupe; In My Room; Shut Down; Fun, Fun, Fun; I Get Around; The Girls on the Beach; Wendy Let Him Run Wild; Don't Worry Baby.* WILD HONEY (re-released 7/74). SMILEY SMILE (re-released 10/74). FRIENDS/SMILEY SMILE (re-released 10/74). SPIRIT OF AMERICA (4/75): *Dance, Dance, Dance; Break Away; A Young Man Is Gone; 409; The Little Girl I Once Knew; Don't Back Down; Barbara Ann; Spirit of America; When I Grow Up; Do You Wanna Dance; Graduation Day; Little Honda; Hushabye; Hawaii; Drive-In; Tell Me Why; Do You Remember?; This Car of Mine; Please Let Me Wonder; Why Do Fools Fall in Love; Custom Machine.* GOOD VIBRATIONS (6/75): *Sail on Sailor; Sloop John B.; God Only Knows; Darlin'; Add Some Music to Your Day; Wouldn't It Be Nice; Good Vibrations; Do It Again; Caroline, No; Friends; Surf's Up; Heroes and Villains.* 15 BIG ONES (7/76): *Rock and Roll Music; It's OK; Had to Phone Ya; Chapel of Love; Everyone's in Love with You; Talk to Me; That Same Song; TM Song; Palisades Park; Susie Cincinnatti; A Casual Look; Blueberry Hill; Back Home; In the Still of the Night; Just Once in My Life.* LIVE IN LONDON (11/76): *Darlin'; Wouldn't It Be Nice; Sloop John B.; California Girls; Do It Again; Wake the World; Aren't You Glad; Bluebirds over the Mountain; Good Vibrations; God Only Knows; Barbara Ann; Their Hearts Were Full of Spring.* THE BEACH BOYS LOVE YOU (3/77): *Roller Skating Child; I'll Bet He's Nice; Airplane; Love Is a Woman; Johnny Carson; Let Us Go On This Way; I Wanna Pick You Up; Let's Put Our Hearts Together; Solar System; The Night Was So Young; Ding Dang; Mona; Honkin' Down the Highway; Good Time.*

Singles/*Surfin'* (1/62); *Surfin' Safari/409* (7/62); *Ten Little Indians* (11/62); *Surfin' USA/Shutdown* (2/63); *Surfer Girl/Little Deuce Coupe* (7/63); *Be True to Your School/In My Room* (10/63); *Little Saint Nick/The Lord's Prayer* (12/63); *Fun, Fun, Fun;/Why Do Fools Fall in Love* (2/64); *I Get Around/Don't Worry Baby* (5/64); *When I Grow Up* (8/64); *Wendy/Little Honda* (9/64); *Dance, Dance, Dance/The Warmth of the Sun* (10/64); *Do*

You Wanna Dance?/Please Let Me Wonder (1/65); *Help Me, Rhonda* (3/65); *California Girls/Let Him Run Wild* (7/65); *The Little Girl I Once Knew* (10/65); *Barbara Ann/Girl Don't Tell Me* (12/65); *Sloop John B./You're So Good to Me* (3/66); *Wouldn't It Be Nice/God Only Knows* (7/66); *Good Vibrations/Let's Go Away for a While* (10/66); *Heroes and Villains/You're Welcome* (7/67); *Wild Honey/Wind Chimes* (10/67); *Darlin'/Here Today* (12/67); *Friends/Little Bird* (4/68); *Bluebirds over the Mountain/Never Learn Not to Love* (12/68); *I Can Hear Music/All I Want to Do* (3/69); *Break Away/Celebrate the News* (6/69); *Add Some Music to Your Day/Suzie Cincinatti* (2/70); *Cottonfields/Nearest Faraway Place* (4/40); *Slip On Through/This Whole World* (6/70); *Tears in the Morning/It's About Time* (9/70); *Cool, Cool Water/Forever* (2/71); *Long Promised Road/Deirdre* (3/71); *Long Promised Road/Till I Die* (10/71); *Surf's Up/Don't Go Near the Water* (11/71); *You Need a Mess of Help to Stand Alone/Cuddle Up* (5/72); *Marcella/Hold On Dear Brother* (6/72); *Sail On Sailor/Only with You* (1/73); *California Saga/Funky Pretty* (4/73); *Surfin' USA/The Warmth of the Sun* (7/74); *I Can Hear Music/Let the Wind Blow* (8/74); *Sail On Sailor/Only with You* (1/75); *Little Honda/Hawaii* (5/75); *Barbara Ann/Little Honda* (6/75); *Wouldn't It Be Nice/Caroline, No* (7/75); *Rock and Roll Music/The TM Song* (5/76); *It's OK/Had to Phone Ya* (7/76); *Be True to Your School/Graduation Day* (9/76); *Suzie Cincinnatti/Everyone's in Love with You* (11/76); *Honkin' Down the Highway/Solar System* (5/77).

THE BEATLES/*John Lennon (guitar, vocals), George Harrison (guitar, vocals), Paul McCartney (bass, vocals), Ringo Starr (drums, vocals). Previous members: Pete Best (drums), Stu Sutcliffe (bass).*
To a lot of young rock fans, deeply entrenched in the intricacies of Kiss and Blue Oyster Cult, the Beatles are nothing but a name. The band that Paul McCartney of Wings used to play in. But for a generation of music lovers during the sixties, indeed for most of the music world of that decade, the Beatles were more than just a band: they were innovators. Prime movers. They were the spark that ignited the music explosion later termed the British Invasion.
    All four of the Beatles (Lennon, Harrison, Starr, and Mc-Cartney) were born in Liverpool and all were musically acquainted

with the slightly syrupy songs of their time. It wasn't until the Beatles got into their teens, in the fifties, that something happened that was destined to change the face of popular music and to lay the groundwork for the revolution that the Beatles themselves were to bring about in the sixties. That something was Bill Haley's *Rock around the Clock,* a song that, while it was sung by an adult, was distinctly addressed to the younger generation. It had nothing to do with cocktails and moonlight, and a lot to do with being young and rebellious. The Beatles were exactly the right age to be hit hard by that song when it came out in 1955.

That was the year John, fifteen and still in school, started his own group, the Quarrymen. When the historic meeting between Quarryman Lennon and new friend Paul McCartney took place on June 15, 1956, Elvis Presley's *Heartbreak Hotel* had been number-one on the U.S. hit parade for over six weeks. One of the big attractions Paul, just fourteen, had for Lennon, sixteen, was that he looked a bit like Elvis. England was absolutely Elvis-happy at the time and, of course, rock-happy. Plastic Elvises sprang up everywhere, with Tommy Steele and Cliff Richard getting the same hysterical, screaming adulation in England that Elvis had in the States. Paul joined the Quarrymen. He and John started writing songs together and, in 1957, when Elvis was singing *All Shook Up,* they penned *Love Me Do.* Five years later, in 1962, it would be their first English release.

In 1958, George Harrison, who wore tight pants and had a group called the Rebels, disbanded it to join the Quarrymen. In 1959, the Quarrymen changed their name several times, ending up as the Silver Beatles. By now the lineup included Pete Best on drums and Stu Sutcliffe on bass. Musically, they were fairly hideous, but what they lacked in talent they made up for in enthusiasm. It wasn't really until a concert job in Hamburg earned them steady work in that city that they started to get themselves together as a band. Their image was very rough-trade rocker, all leather and menace, as opposed to the more established rocker look of another English group in Hamburg at the time, Rory Storme and the Hurricanes, who wore drape-shaped suits with curved lapels and string ties. Their drummer, Ringo Starr, would eventually join the Beatles, but not before he learned to brush his hair down instead of up in a greasy pompadour and shave his outrageous goatee.

Beginning to build a reputation in both England and Germany, the Beatles lost the aid of Pete Best, who opted for a career in art. He died in 1962 of a brain hemorrhage. That same year, record store owner Brian Epstein took the boys under his wing and negotiated a contract for them with EMI. He replaced Best with Starr and the Beatles were born. George Martin, the Obi-Wan Kenobi of the Beatles' star-crossed career, entered the picture as their producer, and by the end of the year had the boys on the bottom half of the pop charts with *Love Me Do.*

Each subsequent release reached a high mark on the charts. *Please Please Me, From Me to You, She Loves You.* But it was their fifth single, *I Want to Hold Your Hand,* that exploded across the world. That started it. While their success spread in England, in America their five singles occupied the top five positions on the trade charts. Beatlemania had begun. Although they launched a plethora of similarly inclined British pop-rock bands, the Beatles always managed to remain ahead of the pack. They were always the originators, always the innovators. With uncanny skill, they drifted from pop to rock to balladeering to psychedelic to Eastern to, well, Beatles.

Their initial success spawned the revolutionary film by Richard Lester, *A Hard Day's Night,* which took the Beatle hysteria to new heights. Each of the four were now "personalities." Paul was the romantic one. Lennon was the intellectual wise-guy. George was reliable. Ringo was cuddly. Lennon's novel, *In His Own Write,* proved to the world that there was more to this band than mere "Yeah, yeah, yeah"s, and fans and critics of all ages began to sit up and take notice.

As the Beatles withstood the fickleness of the pop world, they began to change, to evolve. Their lyrics took on new meanings, culling quite a bit of introspective influence from the budding genius of Dylan. Within a year or two they would launch yet another film vehicle, *Help,* and set the music industry on its ear with the phenomenal *RUBBER SOUL* LP. Gone were the rock and roll rip-offs of days gone by. (On *BEATLES VI* the fab four were still playing things like *Dizzy Miss Lizzie.*) Present and accounted for was a new, matured sound as evidenced by *Norwegian Wood, In My Life,* and *Michelle.*

The Beatles kept on progressing, with albums like *REVOLVER* and singles like *Paperback Writer.* Nineteen sixty-seven proved a banner year for the Beatles. The era of psychedelia was dawning and the foursome from Great Britain were there (first) to usher it in. The extraordinary single *Penny Lane/Strawberry Fields Forever* created a total furor in the music industry, to be surpassed only by the commotion caused by *SGT. PEPPER'S LONELY HEARTS CLUB BAND,* possibly the finest album ever conceived of in the rock realm, decidedly the Beatle's finest hour, and one of the first, if not *the* first, concept albums ever attempted in pop. The Beatles were now officially gods in the world of rock and roll.

Change was in the air, however, and the changes were not all for the better. The foursome allied themselves with the oncoming trend of Eastern mysticism. And that trend began to permeate their work, occasionally to the point of extinction. A self-made feature, *Magical Mystery Tour,* proved surreal to the umpteenth degree, occasionally losing both the audience and, apparently, the cast and crew. A soundtrack LP helped salvage the debacle. *THE BEATLES* double white album followed that within a year, once more elevating the group into the world of rock Titans with its enigmatic passages. (This is the ditty that featured *Number 9* trivia. Is Paul dead? Is he alive? Does anyone care?)

Lennon's coupling with Japanese artist Yoko Ono began to act as a bit of a turnoff to many of their fans, a fact that surfaced in the heart-wrenching single *The Ballad of John and Yoko.* ("Christ, you know it ain't easy," caroused the chorus. A lot of music critics agreed.) The film *Yellow Submarine* made the Beatles palatable even for kiddies, and a soundtrack album proved a popular item indeed. Still, friction within the band was building. The creators. The inventors. The frustrated artists. Overshadowed by their own success.

John and Paul were not seeing eye-to-eye- in a series of encounters, allegedly caused by Yoko's presence on every recording session. George felt that his songs were being overlooked by his illustrious songwriting peers. Ringo was, well, Ringo. Pleasant sot, he. *ABBEY ROAD* was next to be released, a delightful concoction of sound featuring more tunes by Harrison, vocals by Starr, and a host of McCartney-Lennon material. By this time, however, the pair was not really writing together, although co-credit was given on the songs penned individually.

Their final release, *LET IT BE,* marked the end of the Beatles.

A subsequent film of the same name gave a bird's-eye view of the final throes of chaos endured by the fab four. Everyone was hurt, angry, frustrated. None would come out and say exactly why. John had Yoko. Paul had his songs. George had his frustration. Ringo had his pleasant personality. The band severed ties, with some amount of bitterness, in 1970, with all four taking off on solo careers.

The McCartney-Lennon feud lasted some years, with each of them issuing parting shots at each other via songs. The rift has since been patched up. Harrison used his Eastern mysticism in a pop way, coming up with the smash ALL THINGS MUST PASS. Starr futzed about a bit before emerging as a pop crooner par excellence.

All in all, the brief but bright career of the Beatles did more than simply shape the music of the sixties. They shaped rock and roll. Period. They took the state of the art for a quantum leap past countless intermediate stages, winding up at a sophisticated, well-produced, well-constructed, and well-arranged spot. Together with Bob Dylan, they revolutionized contemporary music past, present, and future.

Albums/MEET THE BEATLES (1/64): *I Want to Hold Your Hand; I Saw Her Standing There; This Boy; It Won't Be Long; All I've Got to Do; All My Loving; Don't Bother Me; Little Child; Till There Was You; Hold Me Tight; I Wanna Be Your Man; Not a Second Time.* THE BEATLES' SECOND ALBUM (4/64): *Roll Over, Beethoven; Thank You Girl; Devil in Her Heart; You Really Got a Hold on Me; Money; You Can't Do That; Long Tall Sally; I Call Your Name; Please, Mr. Postman; I'll Get You; She Loves You.* A HARD DAY'S NIGHT (6/64): *A Hard Day's Night; I Should Have Known Better; If I Fell; I'm Happy Just to Dance with You; And I Love Her; Tell Me Why; Can't Buy Me Love; Any Time At All; I'll Cry Instead; Ringo's Theme (This Boy).* SOME-THING NEW (7/64): *I'll Cry Instead; Things We Said Today; Any Time At All; When I Get Home; Slow Down; Matchbox; Tell Me Why; And I Love Her; I'm Happy Just to Dance with You; If I Fell; Komm, Gib Mir Deine Hand.* AIN'T SHE SWEET (7/64): *Ain't She Sweet; Sweet Georgia Brown; Nobody's Child; Take Out Some Insurance on Me, Baby; other titles by a band called the*

Swallows. THE BEATLES' STORY (11/64): *On Stage with the Beatles; How Beatlemania Began; Beatlemania in Action; The Man behind the Beatles—Brian Epstein; John Lennon; Who's a Millionaire; The Beatles Look at Life; "Victims" of Beatlemania; Beatle Medley; Ringo Starr; Liverpool and All the World! Beatles Will Be Beatles; Man behind the Music—George Martin; George Harrison; A Hard Day's Night; Paul McCartney; Sneaky Haircuts.* BEATLES '65 (12/64): *No Reply; I'm a Loser; Baby's in Black; Rock and Roll Music; I'll Follow the Sun; She's a Woman; Mr. Moonlight; Honey, Don't; I'll Be Back; I Feel Fine; Everybody's Trying to Be My Baby.* THE EARLY BEATLES (3/65): *Love Me Do; Twist and Shout; Anna; Chains; Ask Me Why; Boys; Please Please Me; P.S. I Love You; Baby, It's You; Taste of Honey; Do You Want to Know a Secret.* BEATLES VI (6/65): *Kansas City; Eight Days a Week; You Like Me Too Much; Bad Boy; I Don't Want to Spoil the Party; Words of Love; Yes It Is; Dizzy Miss Lizzy; Tell Me What You See; Every Little Thing; What You're Doing.* HELP! (8/65): *Help; Night Before; From Me to You Fantasy; You've Got to Hide Your Love Away; I Need You; In the Tyrol; Another Girl; Another Hard Day's Night; Ticket to Ride; Bitter End; You're Gonna Lose That Girl; The Chase.* RUBBER SOUL (12/65): *I've Just Seen a Face; Norwegian Wood; You Won't See Me; Think for Yourself; The Word; Michelle; It's Only Love; Girl; I'm Looking through You; In My Life; Wait; Run for Your Life.* YESTERDAY AND TODAY (6/66): *Yesterday; Drive My Car; I'm Only Sleeping; Nowhere Man; Dr. Robert; Act Naturally; And Your Bird Can Sing; If I Needed Someone; We Can Work It Out; What Goes On; Day Tripper.* REVOLVER (8/66): *Yellow Submarine; Eleanor Rigby; Taxman; Love to You; Here, There and Everywhere; She Said She Said; Good Day Sunshine; For No One; I Want to Tell You; Got to Get You into My Life; Tomorrow Never Knows.* SERGEANT PEPPER'S LONELY HEARTS CLUB BAND (6/67): *Sergeant Pepper's Lonely Hearts Club Band; A Little Help from My Friends; Lucy in the Sky with Diamonds; Getting Better; I'm Fixing a Hole; She's Leaving Home; Being for the Benefit of Mr. Kite; Within You without You; When I'm Sixty-four; Lovely Rita; Good Morning Good Morning; Sergeant Pepper's Lonely Hearts Club Band Reprise; A Day in the Life.* MAGICAL MYSTERY TOUR (11/67): *Magical Mystery Tour; The Fool on the Hill; Flying; Blue Jay Way; Your Mother*

Should Know; I Am the Walrus; Strawberry Fields Forever; Penny Lane; Baby You're a Rich Man; All You 'Need Is Love; Hello Goodbye. THE BEATLES (their White Album; 11/68): *Back in the U.S.S.R.; Dear Prudence; Glass Onion; Ob-la-di, Ob-la-da; Honey Pie; The Continuing Story of Bungalow Bill; While My Guitar Gently Weeps; Happiness Is a Warm Gun; Martha, My Dear; I'm So Tired; Blackbird; Piggies; Rocky Raccoon; Don't Pass Me By; Why Don't We Do It in the Road; I Will; Julia; Birthday; Yer Blues; Mother Nature's Son; Everybody's Got Something to Hide except Me and My Monkey; Sexy Sadie; Helter Skelter; Long, Long, Long; Revolution 1; Savoy Truffle; Cry, Baby, Cry; Revolution 9; Good Night.* YELLOW SUBMARINE (1/69): *Yellow Submarine; Only a Northern Song; All Together Now; Hey Bulldog; It's All Too Much; All You Need Is Love; Pepperland Sea to Time and Sea of Holes; March of the Meanies; Sea of Monsters; Pepperland Laid to Waste; Yellow Submarine in Pepperland.* ABBEY ROAD (10/69): *Come Together; Something; Maxwell's Silver Hammer; Oh! Darling; Octopus's Garden; I Want You (She's So Heavy); Here Comes the Sun; You Never Give Me Your Money; Because; Sun King; Mean Mr. Mustard; Polythene Pam; She Came in through the Bathroom Window; Golden Slumbers; Carry That Weight; The End.* LET IT BE (2/70): *Two of Us; I Dig a Pony; Across the Universe; I Me Mine; Dig It; Let It Be; Maggie Mae; I've Got a Feeling; One After 909; The Long and Winding Road; For You Blue; Get Back.* THE BEATLES 1962–66 (4/73): *Love Me Do; Please Please Me; From Me To You; She Loves You; I Want to Hold Your Hand; All My Loving; Can't Buy Me Love; A Hard Day's Night; And I Lover Her; Eight Days a Week; I Feel Fine; Ticket to Ride; Yesterday; Help; You've Got to Hide Your Love Away; We Can Work It Out; Day Tripper; Drive My Car; Norwegian Wood; Nowhere Man; Michelle; In My Life; Girl; Paperback Writer; Eleanor Rigby; Yellow Submarine.* THE BEATLES 1967–70 (4/73): *Strawberry Fields Forever; Penny Lane; Sgt. Pepper's Lonely Hearts Club Band; With a Little Help from My Friends; Lucy in the Sky with Diamonds; A Day in the Life; All You Need Is Love; I Am the Walrus; Hello Goodbye; The Fool on the Hill; Magical Mystery Tour; Lady Madonna; Hey Jude; Revolution; Back in the U.S.S.R.; While My Guitar Gently Weeps; Ob-la-di, Ob-la-da; Get Back; Don't Let Me Down; The Ballad of John and Yoko; Old Brown Shoe; Here Comes the Sun;*

Come Together; Something; Across the Universe; The Long and Winding Road; Octopus's Garden. ROCK 'N' ROLL MUSIC (6/76): *Twist and Shout; I Saw Her Standing There; You Can't Do That; I Wanna Be Your Man; I Call Your Name; Boys; Long Tall Sally; Rock and Roll Music; Slow Down; Money; Kansas City; Bad Boy; Matchbox; Roll Over, Beethoven; Dizzy Miss Lizzie; Any Time At All; Drive My Car; Everybody's Trying to Be My Baby; The Night Before; I'm Down; Revolution; Back in the U.S.S.R.; Helter Skelter; Taxman; Got to Get You into My Life; Hey Bulldog; Birthday; Get Back.* THE BEATLES AT THE HOLLYWOOD BOWL (5/77): *Twist and Shout; She's a Woman; Dizzy Miss Lizzie; Ticket to Ride; Can't Buy Me Love; Things We Said Today; Roll Over, Beethoven; A Hard Day's Night; Help!; Long Tall Sally; She Loves You; All My Loving.* LIVE AT THE STAR-CLUB IN HAMBURG, GERMANY: 1962 (5/77): *I'm Gonna Sit Right Down and Cry over You; Hippy Hippy Shake; Roll Over, Beethoven; Sweet Little Sixteen; Lend Me Your Comb; Your Feets Too Big; Where Have You Been All My Life; Mr. Moonlight; A Taste of Honey; Besame Mucho; Till There Was You; Kansas City/Hey Hey Hey Hey; Hallelujah! I Love You So; Ain't Nothing Shaking Like the Leaves in the Trees; To Know Her Is to Love Her; Falling in Love Again; Be-Bop-a-Lula; Red Sails in the Sunset; Everybody's Trying to Be My Baby; Matchbox; Talkin' 'bout You; Shimmy Shake; Long Tall Sally; I Remember You.* LOVE SONGS (10/77): *Yesterday: I'll Follow the Sun; I Need You; Girl; In My Life; Words of Love; Here, There and Everywhere; Something; And I Love Her; If I Fell; I'll Be Back; Tell Me What You See; Yes It Is; Michelle; It's Only Love; You're Going to Lose That Girl; Every Little Thing; For No One; She's Leaving Home; The Long and Winding Road; This Boy; Norwegian Wood; You've Got to Hide Your Love Away; I Will; P.S. I Love You.*

Singles/*I Want To Hold Your Hand/I Saw Her Standing There* (1/64); *She Loves You* (1/64); *My Bonnie/Why* (2/64); *Please Please Me/From Me To You* (2/64); *Can't Buy Me Love/You Can't Do That* (3/64); *Do You Want To Know A Secret/Thank You Girl* (3/64); *Twist And Shout/There's A Place* (3/64); *Love Me Do/P.S. I Love You* (4/64); *Roll Over, Beethoven/All My Loving* (5/64); *A Hard Day's Night/I Should Have Known Better*

(7/64); *I'll Cry Instead/I'm Happy Just to Dance With You* (7/64); *And I Love Her/If I Fell* (7/64); *Slow Down/Matchbox* (8/64); *Sweet Georgia Brown/Take Out Some Insurance on Me Baby* (9/64); *I Feel Fine/She's A Woman* (11/64); *Honey Don't/I'm A Loser/Mr. Moonlight/Everybody's Trying To Be My Baby* (2/65); *Eight Days A Week/I Don't Want to Spoil the Party* (2/65); *Ticket To Ride/Yes It Is* (4/65); *Help!/I'm Down* (7/65); *Yesterday/Act Naturally* (9/65); *We Can Work It Out/Day Tripper* (12/65); *Nowhere Man/What Goes On* (2/66); *Paperback Writer/Rain* (5/66); *Yellow Submarine/Eleanor Rigby* (8/66); *Strawberry Fields Forever/Penny Lane* (2/67); *Baby You're A Rich Man/I Am The Walrus* (11/67); *Lady Madonna/The Inner Light* (3/68); *Hey Jude/Revolution* (8/68); *Get Back/Don't Let Me Down* (5/69); *The Ballad Of John And Yoko/Old Brown Shoe* (6/69); *Something/Come Together* (10/69); *Let It Be/You Know My Name* (3/70); *The Long And Winding Road/For You Blue* (5/70); *Got To Get You Into My Life/Helter Skelter* (5/76); *Ob-la-di, Ob-la-da* (11/76).

BEAU BRUMMELS/*Sal Valentino (vocals), Ron Meagher (bass), Ron Elliott (guitar), John Petersen (drums), Declan Mullican (bass and vocals).*
They started off in 1964 doing the same thing a lot of other groups did then—copying the Beatles. But what happened was the beginning of a new *American* sound, not British (although many of their fans thought they were part of that nation's musical invasion). Their single *Laugh, Laugh* was an exceptionally well-crafted song and, from that point onward, artistically the Beau Brummels could do no wrong. By the tail end of the sixties, however, their melodies got lost in the hard-rock shuffle. They faded from view, only to re-emerge in 1975 with a flawless long-player that attracted little or no attention. By 1976 the Beau Brummels had disappeared for a second time.
Albums/INTRODUCING THE BEAU BRUMMELS (4/65): *Laugh, Laugh; You Tell Me Why; Don't Talk to Strangers; other titles.* BEAU BRUMMELS '66 (7/66): *You've Got to Hide Your Love Away; Mr. Tambourine Man; Monday, Monday; other titles.* BEST OF THE BEAU BRUMMELS (1967): *Laugh, Laugh; Just a Little; You Tell Me Why; Sad Little Girl; Don't Talk to Strangers; other titles.* TRIANGLE (7/67): *Are You Happy; Only*

Dreaming Now; Painter of Women; Keeper of Time; It Won't Get Better; Nine-Pound Hammer; Magic Hollow; And I've Seen Her; Triangle; Wolf of Velvet Fortune; Old Kentucky Home. BRADLEY'S BARN (10/68): *Turn Around; Added Attraction; Cherokee Girl; Deep Water; Long Walking Down to Misery; Little Bird; I'm a Sleeper; Bless You, California; Loneliest Man in Town; Love Can Fall a Long Way Down; Jessica.* THE BEAU BRUM-MELS (5/75): *First in Line; Goldrush; Today by Day; Tennessee Walker; Gate of Hearts; Wolf; Down to the Bottom; You Tell Me Why; Singing Cowboy; The Lonely Side.*

Singles/*Laugh, Laugh* (12/64); *Just a Little* (3/65); *You Tell Me Why* (6/75); *Don't Talk To Strangers* (9/65); *Good Time Music* (11/65); *One Too Many Mornings* (5/66); *Lower Level/Magic Hollow* (8/67); *Are You Happy?/Lift Me* (5/68); *Long Walking Down to Misery/I'm a Sleeper* (10/68); *Cherokee Girl/Deep Water* (1/69); *You Tell Me Why/Down to the Bottom* (6/75).

JEFF BECK/Jeff Beck was one of those flashy young British guitarists who came into the spotlight in the mid-sixties, at the height of the "British invasion." When he played his lead licks with the Yardbirds, people used to take bets on who weighed more: Jeff or his guitar. He was young, wiry and exceedingly talented, but when he left the Yardbirds to embark on a career of his own, few people really thought he'd cut it. He did, and in a fairly bizarre way. The Surrey-born musician was only twenty-five back in '67 when he vaulted onto the British charts with two demented singles, *Hi-Ho Silver Lining* and *Love Is Blue.* One year later, Jeff formed the first Jeff Beck Group, featuring up-and-coming crouper Rod Stewart handling vocals "extraordinaire." Their sound was basically a ballsy slant on the blues-rock riff but Beck's unique phrasing and Stewart's macadam-like mumblings made them a truly outstanding unit.

Internal problems, alas, led to the collapse of the first mob after but two albums. As Beck made tentative plans to launch a second chapter in his advancing career, a series of events stopped him cold. Tim Bogert and Carmine Appice, two ex-Vanilla Fudgers whom Jeff was courting for his next band, abruptly decided to form Cactus—a lobotomy rock ensemble with the dubious distinction of making the Vanilla Fudge dirge style sound positively uptempo. A serious car accident then put Jeff out of commision for nearly two years.

The feisty Briton came back strong in '71, however, with a second Jeff Beck Group. Two albums later, the band broke up and Jeff finally joined Appice and Bogert (Cactus had, by then, proved a spiny dud) to record the only BBA album. It was underwhelming in all areas but guitar. Abandoning the group approach shortly thereafter, Jeff emerged as an axe grinder of the first magnitude with his nimble-fingered opus *BLOW BY BLOW* in 1975. His career firmly established, Jeff went on to display his prowess on *WIRED* and *WITH THE JAN HAMMER GROUP*. Today Jeff Beck is somewhat of an elder statesman of the realm of rock guitar. He dabbles in just about every style of music imaginable: rock, jass, blues and funk. He always leaves his fans satisfied.

Albums/TRUTH (8/68): *Shapes of Things; Let Me Love You; Morning Dew; You Shook Me; Old Man River; Greensleeves; Rock My Plimsoul; Beck's Bolero; Blues Deluxe; I Ain't Superstitious.* BECK-OLA (6/69): *All Shook Up; Spanish Boots; Girl from Mill Valley; Jailhouse Rock; Plynth; Hangman's Knee; Rice Pudding.* ROUGH AND READY (10/71): *Got the Feeling; Situation; Short Business; Max's Tune; I've Been Used; New Ways; Raynes Park Blues; Jody; Train Train.* THE JEFF BECK GROUP (4/72): *Ice Cream Cakes; Glad All Over; Tonight I'll Be Staying Here with You; Sugar Cane; I Can't Give Back; I Got to Have a Song; Definitely Maybe; Highways; Going Down; The Love I Have for You.* BECK, BOGERT AND APPICE (3/73): *Black Cat Moan; Lady; Oh to Love You; Superstition; Sweet, Sweet Surrender; Why Should I Care; Lose Myself; with You; Livin' Alone; I'm So Proud.* BLOW BY BLOW (3/75): *You Know What I Mean; She's a Woman; Constipated Duck; Air Blower; Scatterbrain; Cause We've Ended As Lovers; Thelonius; Freeway Jam; Diamond Dust.* WIRED (5/76): *Led Boots; Come Dancing; Goodbye Pork-Pie Hat; Head For a Backstage Pass; Blue Wind; Sophie; Play With Me; Love Is Green.* JEFF BECK WITH THE JAN HAMMER GROUP (3/77): *Freeway Jam; Earth (Still Our Only Home); She's a Woman; Full Moon Boogie; Darkness Earth in Search of a Sun; Scatterbrain; Blue Wind.*

Singles/Hi Ho Silver Lining/Beck's Bolero (3/67); *Tally Man/Rock My Plimsoul* (8/67); *Old Man River/Blues Deluxe*

(9/68); *Beck's Bolero/Hi Ho Silver Lining* (1/69);
Plynth/Jailhouse Rock (5/69); *Got the Feeling/Situation* (11/71);
Hi Ho Silver Lining/Definitely Maybe (12/72); *I'm So Proud/Oh
to Love You* (5/73); *Lady/Oh to Love You* (7/73); *You Know What
I Mean/Constipated Duck* (5/75); *Come Dance; Head for a
Backstage Pass* (9/76).

THE BEE GEES/*Robin Gibb (vocals), Barry Gibb (vocals),
Maurice Gibb (vocals). Former members: Colin Peterson (drums),
Vince Melouney (guitar).*
The Bee Gees are stars around the world, their ethereal (albeit
nasal) harmonies an easily recognizable trademark. Their career
started off on a high note over ten years ago and, now, continues
on the upward trend. The years in between, however, were racked
with dissention, defeat, and near-despair.

Prior to becoming global attractions, the Gibb Brothers were a
regional success in Australia. British-born but Australia-bred, the
Bee Gees ("B.G."—taken from Barry's initials) had their first hit
single in 1963 with the tune *Three Kisses of Love.* They quickly
followed it up with such early standards as *Spicks and Specks,
Wine and Women,* and *I Was a Lover and a Leader of Men.* The
number-one band in Australia, they were signed by Robert Stigwood and brought back to England for a frontal assault on the
music industry.

Their first album, recorded under the watchful eye of Stigwood
and produced by their Australian mentor Ossie Byrne was released in 1967. By that time, their first single, *The New York Mining Disaster 1941,* was a top-tenning hit. The public loved the Bee
Gees and disc jockeys had a lot of fun with the (then) unknown
band. They sounded like the Beatles. They came from England.
No one knew who they were. The Beatles were getting stranger
and more eccentric by the day. Could The Bee Gees *really* be the
Beatles?

For whatever reason, the single was a monster, as was their first
album. Subsequent long-players proved exceedingly popular and
singles such as·*Massachusetts, To Love Somebody,* and *Words
and World* assured the band hit status. Dissention soon flared
within the golden-throated ranks. Melouney left to start a group
of his own, a move that proved as intelligent as going for a dip
with a lead life-vest. As Melouney sank into the depths of music-

dom, Colin and the brothers Gibb had a verbal battle, which resulted in Colin's departing the Bee Gee cause in 1970. By that time, the brothers Gibb were a duo. In 1969 Robin had decided that he could be A Star without the benefit of family ties. A premier album and single *(ROBIN'S REIGN* and *Saved by the Bell)* inflated his dreams. Shortly thereafter, his dreams became nightmares and he found himself a star without an audience.

The two remaining Bee Gees split. Barry stagnated while Maurice attempted both an acting career and a marriage (to pop star Lulu)—both failures. With several unsuccessful albums behind them *(CUCUMBER CASTLE, SOUND OF LOVE, TRAFALGAR)*, the Bee Gees reunited in 1971 and promptly leaped back onto the charts with *How Can You Mend a Broken Heart?* This success was premature as the reformed brothers fell into a state of musical limbo, a maudlin existence that was destined to last four years. Their old fans had forgotten about the scintillating sounds of the sixties and the new fans were just not there.

In 1975, with the aid of genius producer Arif Mardin, the Bee Gees, the kings of British balladeering and sweet, sweet harmonies, became purveyors of disco dementia. The new kings of blue-eyed soul pummeled the competition with such backbeated bonanzas as *Jive Talkin'*, *Nights on Broadway*, and *Fanny*. With their crooning now crystalized into falsetto frenzy, the Bee Gees are enjoying a second long-lasting stab at fame—a rebirth that sounds as if it could stretch far into the future.

Albums/BEE GEES' FIRST (10/67): *Holiday; Turn of the Century; Red Chair, Fade Away; One Minute Woman Please; In My Own Time; Every Christian Lion-Hearted Man Will Show You; Craise Finton Kirk Royal Academy of Arts; New York Mining Disaster 1941; To Love Somebody; Cucumber Castle; I Close My Eyes; I Can't See Nobody; Please Read Me; Close Another Door.* HORIZONTAL (1/68): *World; And the Sun Will Shine; Lemons Never Forget; Really and Sincerely; Birdie Told Me; With the Sun in My Eyes; Harry Braff; Massachusetts; Day Time Girl; Earnest of Being George; Change Is Made; Horizontal.* IDEA (8/68): *Let There Be Love; Kitty Can; Indian Gin and Whiskey Dry; In the Summer of His Years; I Started a Joke; I Have Decided to Join the Air Force; Down to Earth; I've Gotta Get a Message to You; Idea;*

When the Swallows Fly; Kilburn Towers; Swan Song. RARE, PRECIOUS AND BEAUTIFUL (11/68): *What Are You; Spicks and Specks; Playdown; Big Chance; Glass House; How Many Birds; Second Hand People; I Don't Know Why I Bother with Myself; Monday's Rain; Tint of Blue; Jingle Jangle; Born a Man.* ODESSA (1/69): *Odessa (City on the Black Sea); You'll Never See My Face Again; Black Diamond; Marley Purt Drive; Edison; Melody Fair; Suddenly; Whisper Whisper; Lamplight; Sound of Love; Give Your Best; Seven Seas Symphony; With All Nations; I Laugh in Your Face; Never Say Never Again; First of May; The British Opera.* BEST OF THE BEE GEES (6/69): *Holiday; I've Gotta Get a Message to You; I Can't See Nobody; Words; I Started a Joke; Spicks and Specks; First of May; World; Massachusetts; To Love Somebody; Every Christian Lion-Hearted Man Will Show You; New York Mining Disaster 1941.* RARE, PRECIOUS AND BEAUTIFUL, VOLUME II (2/70): *I Was a Lover, a Leader of Men; Follow the Wind; Claustrophobia; Theme from Jamie McPheeters; Everyday I Have to Cry; Take Hold of That Star; Could It Be; To Be or Not to Be; Three Kisses of Love; Cherry Red; All of My Life; Don't Say Goodbye.* ROBIN'S REIGN (Solo Robin; 1970): *August October; Gone Gone Gone; The Worst Girl in This Town; Give Me a Smile; Down Came the Sun; Mother and Jack; Saved by the Bell; Weekend; Farmer Ferdinand Hudson; Lord Bless All; Most of My Life.* CUCUMBER CASTLE (4/70): *If Only I Had My Mind on Something Else; Io Io; Then You Left Me; The Lord; I Was the Child; I Lay Down and Die; Sweetheart; Bury Me Down by the River; My Thing; The Change of Love; Turning Tide; Don't Forget to Remember.* 2 YEARS ON (1/71): *2 Years On; Portrait of Louise; A Man for All Seasons; Sincere Relation; Back Home; The 1st Mistake I Made; Lonely Days; Alone Again; Tell Me Why; Lay It on Me; Every Second Every Minute; I'm Weeping.* TRAFALGER (10/71): *Trafalger; Remembering; When Do I; Dearest; Lion in Winter; Walking Back to Waterloo; How Can You Mend a Broken Heart; Isreal; Greatest Man in the World; It's Just the Way; Don't Wanna Live inside Myself; Somebody Stop the Music.* TO WHOM IT MAY CONCERN (10/72): *Run to Me; We Lost the Road; Never Been Alone; Paper Mache Cabbages and Kings; I Can Bring Love; I Help a Party; Please Don't Turn Out the Lights; Sea of Smiling Faces; Bad Bad Dreams; You Know It's for You; Alive;*

Road to Alaska; Sweet Song of Summer. LIFE IN A TIN CAN
(1/73): *Saw a New Morning; I Don't Wanna Be the One; South
Dakota Morning; Living in Chicago; While I Play; My Life Has
Been a Song; Come Home, Johnny Bride; Method to My Madness.*
BEST OF THE BEE GEES, VOLUME II (7/73): *How Can You
Mend a Broken Heart; Io Io; Don't Wanna Live inside Myself;
Melody Fair; My World; Let There Be Love; Saved by the Bell;
Lonely Days; Morning of My Life; Don't Forget to Remember;
And the Sun Will Shine; Run to Me; A Man for All Seasons; Alive.*
MR. NATURAL (7/74): *Charade; Throw a Penny; Down the
Road; Voices; Give a Hand, Take a Hand; Dogs; Mr. Natural;
Lost in Your Love; I Can't Let You Go; Heavy Breathing; Had a
Lot of Love Last Night.* MAIN COURSE (5/75): *Nights on
Broadway; Jive Talkin'; Wind of Change; Songbird; Fanny (Be
Tender with My Love); All This Making Love; Country Lanes;
Come On Over; Edge of the Universe; Baby As You Turn Away.*
CHILDREN OF THE WORLD (9/76): *Children of the World;
You Stepped into My Life; Love So Right; Lovers; Can't Keep a
Good Man Down; Boogie Child; Love Me; The Way It Was; You
Should Be Dancing; Subway.* BEE GEES GOLD (10/76): *How
Can You Mend a Broken Heart; Holiday; To Love Somebody;
Words; Lonely Days; Run to Me; Massachusetts; I've Gotta Get a
Message to You; My World; I Can't See Nobody; I Started a Joke;
New York Mining Disaster 1941.* ODESSA (re-issue on a single
record; 10/76). HERE AT LAST . . . LIVE (5/77): *I've Gotta Get
a Message to You; Love So Right; Edge of the Universe; Come On
Over; Can't Keep a Good Man Down; New York Mining Disaster
1941; Run to Me; World; Holiday; I Can't See Nobody; I Started
a Joke; Massachusetts; How Can You Mend a Broken Heart; To
Love Somebody; You Should Be Dancing; Boogie Child; Down the
Road; Words; Wind of Change; Nights on Broadway; Jive Talkin';
Lonely Days.*

Singles/*New York Mining Disaster 1941/I Can't See Nobody*
(5/67); *To Love Somebody/Close Another Door* (6/67);
Holiday/Every Christian Lion-Hearted Man Will Show You
(9/67); *Massachusetts/Sir Geoffrey Saved the World* (11/67);
Words/Sinking Ship (12/67); *Jumbo/Sing Sang His Song* (3/68);
I've Gotta Get a Message to You (8/68); *I Started a Joke/Kilburn
Towers* (12/68); *First of May* (2/69); *Tomorrow Tomorrow/In the*

Morning (5/69); *Don't Forget to Remember* (9/69); *If Only I Had My Mind on Something Else* (3/70); *Io Io* (7/70); *Lonely Days* (11/70); *How Can You Mend a Broken Heart* (5/71); *Don't Wanna Live inside Myself* (9/71); My World/On Time (1/72); *Run to Me/Road to Alaska* (7/72); *Alive/Paper Mache Cabbages and Kings* (10/72); *Saw a New Morning/My Life Has Been a Song* (2/73); *Run to Me/Jumbo* (3/73); *Wouldn't I Be Someone/Elisa* (5/73); *Mr. Natural/It Doesn't Matter Much to Me* (2/74); *Charade/Heavy Breathing* (10/74); *Jive Talkin'/Wind of Change* (4/75); *Nights on Broadway/Edge of the Universe* (9/75); *Fanny (Be Tender with My Love)/Country Lanes* (12/75); *You Should Be Dancing/Subway* (6/76); *Love So Right/You Stepped into My Life* (9/76); *Jive Talkin'/Come On Over* (7/77); *Boogie Child* (1977); *Edge of the Universe* (1977); *How Deep Is Your Love* (1977); Staying Alive (2/78).

CAPTAIN BEEFHEART/The notorious Captain Beefheart, a.k.a. Don Van Vliet, is infamous for his completely absurdist approach to rock. Beefheart came to the spotlight with his Magic Band via a blues group called the Blackouts. In 1964, Beefheart took his blues ideas into Rod Sterling territory and established the original Magic Band. Boasting slide guitars, vocal barking, and loose, funky rhythms, the band successfully stymied good-natured record executives who were perfectly willing to show the world that they were as far-out as the next cat (some even wore Nehru suits off hours, by god), but not quite *that* far-out. After an aborted start on A&M (one single: *Diddy Wah Diddy),* Beefheart finally found a place to hang his hat on Kama Sutra, a label best known for the Lovin' Spoonful. One album later, Beefheart found yet another place to doff his apparel, Blue Thumb. Another Album later and the controversial Captain seemed to have found the *ideal* place to hang his newfound trout mask, this time at friend Frank Zappa's Straight label.

Zappa and Beefheart were old cronies and, with Zappa in charge, Beefheart knew he could record an album with absolutely no concession made to commerciality. He did just that. The resulting LP, *TROUT MASK REPLICA,* was one of the most critically acclaimed financial disasters in the history of recording. Alternately ranting and raving and tearing his way through some brilliant passages of verbal surrealism (at times falling into the most captivating spoken rhythms heard since Lord Buckley), Beefheart and Zappa led the Magic Band into a realm of effective, uncoiling instrumentation.

When the album failed to make a splash, Zappa and Beefheart split (with a lot of subsequent finger-pointing over *who* was to blame for *this* turkey). Beefheart found another label. Reprise. Then another. Mercury. And all the while, the erratic Beefheart added and dropped members of his Magic troupe with marked regularity. (During their eleven-year career, the Magic Band had some twenty members.) In 1975, Beefheart broke up his group for the last time, patched up old differences with Zappa and recorded a collaborative effort: *BONGO FURY*. Record executives are still wondering how they ever let that one happen.

Albums/SAFE AS MILK (6/68): *Plastic Factory; Autumn's Child; Call on Me; Abba Zaba; Dropout Boogie; Zig Zag Wanderer; Sure 'Nuff 'n' Yes I Do; Electricity; Grown So Ugly; Yellow Brick Road; I'm Glad; Where There's Woman.* STRICTLY PERSONAL (12/68): *Ah Feel Like Ahcid; Safe As Milk; Trust Us; Son of Mirror Man—Mere Man; On Tomorrow; Beatle Bones 'n' Smokin' Stones; Gimme Dat Harp Boy; Kandy Korn.* TROUT MASK REPLICA (1/70); *Frownland; The Dust Blows Forward 'n' the Dust Blows Back; Dachau Blues; Ella Guru; Hair Pie; Bake 1; Moonlight on Vermont; Pachuco Cadaver; Bill's Corpse; Sweet Sweet Bulbs; Neon Meate Dream of a Octafish; China Pig; Dali's Car; My Human Gets Me Blues; Hair Pie; Bake 2; Pena; Well; When Big Joan Sets Up; Fallin' Ditch; Sugar 'n' Spikes; Ant Man Bee; Orange Claw Hammer; Wild Life; She's Too Much for My Mirror; Hobo Chang Ba; The Blimp; Steal Softly Thru Snow; Old Fart at Play; Veteran's Day Poppy.* LICK MY DECALS OFF, BABY (10/70); *Lick My Decals Off, Baby; Doctor Dark; I Love You, You Big Dummy; Peon; Bellerin' Plain; Woe-Is-uh-Me-Bop; Japan in a Dishpan; I Wanna Find a Woman That'll Hold My Big Toe Until I Have to Go; Petrified Forest; The Buggy Boogie Woogie; The Smithsonian Institute Blues (or the Big Dig); Space-Age Couple; Flash Gordon's Ape; The Clouds Are Full of Wine (Not Whiskey or Rye).* THE SPOTLIGHT KID (1/72): *Click Clack; Glider; Grow Fins; Alice in Blunderland; White Hane; Blabber 'n' Smoke; When It Blows Its Stack; I'm Gonna Boogarlize You, Baby; There Ain't No Santa on the Evening Stage.* CLEAR

SPOT (11/72): *Low Yo Yo Stuff; Nowadays a Woman's Gotta Hit a Man; Too Much Time; Circumstances; My Head Is My Only House Unless It Rains; Sun Zoom Spark; Clear Spot; Crazy Little Thing; Long-Neck Bottles; Her Eyes Are a Blue Million Miles; Big-Eyed Beans from Venus; Golden Birdies.* MIRROR MAN (1973). UNCONDITIONALLY GUARANTEED (3/74): *Upon the My-O-My; Sugar Bowl; New Electric Ride; Magic Be; Happy Love Song; Full Moon, Hot Sun; I Got Love on My Mind; This Is the Day; Lazy Music; Peaches.* BLUEJEANS AND MOON-BEAMS (10/74): *Same Old Blues; Observatory Chest; Pompadour Swamp; Captains Holiday; Rock 'n' Roll's Evil Doll; Further Than We've Gone; Twist Ah Luck; Bluejeans and Moonbeams.* BONGO FURY (with Zappa and the Mothers; 10/75): *Debra Kadabra; Carolina Hard-Core Ecstasy; Sam with the Showing-Scalp Flat-Top; Poofter's Froth Wyoming Plans Ahead; 200 Years Old; Cucamonga; Advance Romance; Man with the Woman Head; Muffin Man.*

Singles/*Upon the My-O-My/I Got Love on My Mind* (5/74).

CHUCK BERRY/Chuck Berry may be the single most important name in the history of rock. There is not a rock musician working today who has not consciously or unconsciously borrowed his sound, the sound that was to become the definitive sound of fifties rock. The Beach Boys made their national repuation with the Chuck Berry strains of *Surfin' U.S.A.,* and both the Beatles and the Stones started off in the sixties by reviving Chuck Berry's famous fifties songs. Berry's tunes were enormously popular at the height of the rock and roll era, only to be forgotten once the hard-rocking fifties style became more watered down. Like Elvis, Jerry Lee Lewis, and other giants of the decade, Berry was a raver. When the raving quieted down, it was supposedly a sign that rock was becoming acceptable, maturing. What, in fact, rock was doing was becoming pasteurized, palatable, dull. One of the reasons the Beatles and Stones and other British invasion groups made such a big dent in the music business is that they successfully recreated the kineticism, rave-up feeling that Berry and his peers had offered nearly a decade earlier.

Like most popular musicians of the fifties, Berry's style was fairly eclectic—encompassing licks of country, gospel, and rock. The Missouri-born giant first picked up a guitar while in high school in St. Louis. His music teacher encouraged the boy, and soon Chuck was leading a band of his own. After becoming a popular local act, Chuck journeyed to Chicago to visit the legendary blues capital. On that "vacation," he met and performed for blues staple Muddy Waters, who turned Chuck on to Chess Records. Chuck auditioned with a self-penned tune, *Ida Red*. The Contracts were signed and Chuck altered the name to *Maybelline* (inspired by a cow featured in a grammar-school reader).

Berry's immediate success at an R&B level cannot be denied. Unfortunately, he appeared during a time when the extent of one's success was often judged by the color of one's skin. And Chuck's skin was, by white standards, definitely the wrong color. As a result Chuck's tunes were often covered successfully by white artists, thus robbing him of national attention. By the late sixties, this racist trend had become somewhat passé and Berry finally emerged as a rock idol to a whole new breed of fan. His speeding-car lyricism and fast-paced duck walks won him a deserved spot in the hearts of millions and his performances in national rock revivals rejuvenated his career.

The music of Chuck Berry was, is, and always will be . . . genius.

Albums/AFTER SCHOOL SESSIONS (10/58): *School Days; Wee Wee Hours; Brown-Eyed Handsome Man; Too Much Monkey Business; Deep Falling; Rolli Polli; Berry Pickin'; Together No Omeny Down; Havanna Moon; Down Bound Train; Drifting Heart. ONE DOZEN BERRYS (1958): Sweet Little Sixteen; Reelin' and Rockin'; Rock and Roll Music; Blue Ceiling; Rock at the Philharmonic; Jaunda Español; Oh, Baby Doll; Guitar Boogie; In-Go; Low Ceiling; How You've Changed; I Don't Take but a Few.* CHUCK BERRY IS ON TOP: *Almost Grown; Carol; Maybelline; Johnny Be. Goode; Little Queenie; Anthony Boy; Sweet Little Rock and Roller; Jo Jo Gunne; Around and Around; Roll Over, Beethoven; Hey Pedro; Blues for Hawaiians.* ROCKIN' AT THE HOPS: *Bye Bye, Johnny; Worried Life Blues; Down the Road a Piece; Confessin' the Blues; Too Pooped to Pop; Mad Lad; I Got to Find My Baby; Betty Jean; Childhood Sweetheart; Broken Arrow; Driftin' the Blues; Let It Rock.* NEW JUKE BOX HITS: *I'm Talking about You; Diploma for Two; Rip It Up; Thirteen Questions Method; Way It Was Before; Away with You; Don't You Lie to*

Me; Little Star; Route 66; Sweet Sixteen; Stop and Listen; Run Around. TWIST: *Maybelline; Roll Over, Beethoven; Oh, Baby Doll; 'Round and 'Round; Come On; Let It Rock; Reelin' and Rockin'; School Days; Almost Grown; Sweet Little Sixteen; Thirty Days; Johnny B. Goode; Rock and Roll Music; Back in the U.S.A.* CHUCK BERRY ON STAGE (7/63): *Memphis; Sweet Little Sixteen; Rocking on the Railroad; Maybelline; Surfing Stella; Go Go Go; Brown-Eyed Handsome Man; Still Got the Blues; Jaguar and the Thunderbird; I Just Want to Make Love to You; All Aboard; Man and the Donkey; Trick or Treat.* CHUCK BERRY'S GREATEST HITS (4/64): *Roll Over, Beethoven; School Days; Rock and Roll Music; Too Much Monkey Business; Oh, Baby Doll; Johnny B. Goode; Nadine; Thirty Days; Memphis; Maybelline; Sweet Little Sixteen; Brown-Eyed Handsome Man.* ST. LOUIS TO LIVERPOOL (12/64): *Little Marie; You Never Can Tell; Go, Bobby Soxer; No Particular Place to Go; Merry Christmas Baby; Our Little Rendezvous; You Two; Night Beat; Promised Land; Things I Used to Do; Liverpool Beat; How Great Thou Art.* CHUCK BERRY IN LONDON (5/65): *My Little Love-Lights; She Once Was Mine; After It's Over; I Got a Booking; You Came a Long Way from St. Louis; Night Beat; St. Louis Blues; His Daughter Caroline; Dear Dad; Jamaica Farewell; Butterscotch; Song of My Love; Why Should We End This Way; I Want to Be Your Driver.* FRESH BERRY'S: *It Wasn't Me; Run, Joe; Every Day We Rock and Roll; One for My Baby; Welcome Back, Pretty Baby; It's My Own Business; Right Off Rampart Street; Vaya Con Dios; Merrily We Rock and Roll; My Mustang Ford; Ain't That Just Like a Woman; Wee Hour Blues.* GOLDEN DECADE (2/67); *Maybelline; Deep Feeling; Johnny B. Goode; Wee Wee Hours; Nadine; Thirty Days; Brown-Eyed Handsome Man; Roll Over, Beethoven; No Particular Place to Go; Havana Moon; Almost Grown; Baby Doll; Too Pooped to Pop; Reelin' and Rockin'; You Can't Catch Me; Bye Bye, Johnny; 'Round and 'Round; Sweet Little Sixteen; Rock and Roll Music; Anthony Boy; Back in the U.S.A.* GOLDEN HITS (2/67): *Sweet Little Sixteen; Memphis; Back·in the U.S.A.; School Days; Maybelline; Johnny B. Goode; Rock and Roll Music; Thirty Days; Oh, Carol; Club Nitty Gritty; Roll Over, Beethoven.* CHUCK BERRY IN MEMPHIS (8/67): *Back to Memphis; I Do Really Love You; My Heart Will Always Belong to You; Ramblin' Rose; Sweet Little Rock and*

Roller; Oh, Baby Doll; Check Me Out; It Hurts Me Too; Bring Another Drink; So Long; Goodnight, Well It's Time to Go. LIVE AT THE FILLMORE (9/67): *Driftin' Blues; Hoochie Coochie Man; Johnny B. Goode; See See Rider; Feelin' It; Flying Home; It Hurts Me Too; Fillmore Blues; Wee Baby Blues; medley.* FROM ST. LOUIS TO FRISCO (11/68): *Louie to Frisco; Ma Dear; The Love I Lost; I Love Her, I Love Her; Little Fox; Rock Cradle Rock; Soul Rockin'; I Can't Believe; Misery; My Tambourine; Oh Captain; Mum's the Word.* THE LONDON CHUCK BERRY SESSIONS (5/72). ST. LOUIS TO FRISCO TO MEMPHIS (10/72). SAN FRANCISCO DUES (1972). BIO (1973). CHUCK BERRY '75 (1975).

Singles/*Roll Over, Beethoven* (5/56); *School Day* (2/57); *Oh, Baby Doll* (6/57); *Sweet Little Sixteen* (1/58); *Johnny B. Goode* (3/58); *Beautiful Delilah* (6/58); *Carol* (8/58); *Sweet Little Rock and Roller/Jo Jo Gunne* (11/58); *Run Rudolph Run/Merry Christmas Baby* (11/58); *Anthony Boy* (1/59); *Almost Grown/Little Queenie* (3/59); *Back in the U.S.A.* (6/59); *Too Pooped to Pop/Let It Rock* (1/60); *Nadine* (2/64); *No Particular Place to Go* (4/64); *You Never Can Tell* (7/64); *Little Marie* (9/64); *Promised Land* (11/64); *Dear Dad* (3/65); *My Ding-a-Ling* (7/72); *Reelin' and Rockin'* (11/72).

THE BIG BOPPER/His real name was J. P. Richardson and he was nearly a major figure in the post-Elvis rock era. He wrote and recorded *Chantilly Lace,* a straight-talking rock tune that was the third-most-played record in America in 1958 and was released in thirty-seven other countries. On the night of February 2, 1959, with success at his heels and on leave from his job as a disc jockey and program director at station KTRM in Beaumont, Texas, the Bopper appeared before 1,100 fans at the Surf Ballroom in Mason City, Iowa. Early the next morning, with Buddy Holly and Ritchie Valens, he chartered a Beechcraft Bonanza to take them to Fargo, North Dakota. The plane went down five miles northwest of the airport; no one heard the crash. J. P. Richardson was dead at the age of twenty-four.

Album/CHANTILLY LACE (1958): *Chantilly Lace; Pink Petticoats; Walking through My Dreams; The Clock; Someone Watching Over You; Old Maid; Big Bopper's Wedding; Little Red*

*Riding Hood; Preacher and the Bear; It's the Truth, Ruth; White
Lightning; Strange Kiss.*

Singles/*Chantilly Lace* (7/58); *The Big Bopper's Wedding* (12/58);
Little Red Riding Hood (12/58).

BIG BROTHER AND THE HOLDING COMPANY/*Janis
Joplin (vocals), Peter Albin (bass, vocals), Sam Andrew (lead and
rhythm guitar, vocals), James Gurley (guitar, vocals), David Getz
(vocals).*

When the phenomenal Janis Joplin initially joined forces with
Big Brother and the Holding Company in 1966, the band was
already coming into its own on the San Francisco scene. A local
group, the band used to jam around Chet Helms, head adminis-
trator of the Family Dog (a group designed to organize the musical community in the area). Joplin was a Texan and so was Chet,
and it was he who thought Big Brother, one of the better bands of
the many that had sprung up there, might use a girl singer. Janis
had sung country music and blues with a bluegrass band, but
she's never had to sing as loud as she had to with Big Brother and
that battery of amplifiers; with all that Rhythm going, she found
herself moving and dancing like another rhythm instrument. That
was June of 1966 and magic was born.

Janis became a mean blues singer and began to look it, with her
trailing draperies and tangled hair. San Francisco fell in love with
her as if she were the first woman on earth. One year later, at the
Monterey Pop Festival of 1967, everyone else did too. The press,
the big music names from New York, everyone. The word was
out: Janis Joplin was it. Albert Grossman, dean of the rock managers, with Dylan, Peter, Paul and Mary, and other major talents
in his stable, snapped her and the band up on the spot. Soon
Joplin and the troupe became living legends, with the burden of
publicity falling on Janis. The first ballsy female rock star, Un-
heard of.

What a Jimi Hendrix or a Mick Jagger did to fainting girls,
Janis did to fainting men. She made her whole performance a
frantic, sweating, passionate, demanding sexual act. Janis soon
became a national star, the group in tow behind her. In the midst
of the celebrity whirlwind, problems arose. The band's first
album, recorded hastily for Mainstream Records, was a tribute to
bad producing and horrible sound. Their second album, for Co-

lumbia, was a vast improvement but still didn't match the band's in-concert kineticism. The publicity wave continued. Janis. Janis. Janis. The members of Big Brother grew unhappy. Janis grew unhappy. In late 1968, Big Brother and Janis Joplin parted company. Joplin went on to form the ill-fated Kozmic Blues Band. Big Brother reshuffled membership and enlisted the aid of rock maven Nick Gravenities. Two Joplin-less albums resulted before the band faded away. Without Joplin, they were a faceless working unit. Without Big Brother, Janis was a long figure on stage and on record, surrounded by lifeless musicians. And so it goes.

Albums/BIG BROTHER AND THE HOLDING COMPANY (1967): *Bye, Bye, Baby; Easy Rider; Intruder; Light Is Faster Than Sound; Call On Me; Women Is Losers; All Is Loneliness; Down On Me; Blind Man; Caterpillar.* CHEAP THRILLS (7/68): *Combination of the Two; I Need a Man to Love; Summertime; Piece of My Heart; Turtle Blues; Oh, Sweet Mary; Ball and Chain.* BEE A BROTHER (10/70): *Keep On; Joseph's Coat; Home on the Strange; Someday; Heartache People; Sunshine Baby; Mr. Natural; Funkie Jim; I'll Change Your Flat Tire, Merl; Be a Brother.* HOW HARD IT IS (7/71): *How Hard It Is; Black Widow Spider; Last Band on Side One; Shine On; Promise Her Anything but Give Her Argeggio; House On Fire; You've Been Talkin' 'bout Me, Baby; Nu Bugaloo Jam; Maui; Burried Alive in the Blues.*

Singles/*All Is Loneliness/Blind Man* (1968); *Bye, Bye, Baby/Intruder* (1968); *Piece of My Heart/Turtle Blues* (8/68); *Down On Me* (8/68); *The Coo Coo* (10/68); *Piece of My Heart/Kozmic Blues* (9/70); *Keep On/Home on the Strange* (1/71); *Black Widow Spider/Nu Bugaloo Jam* (11/71)

ELVIN BISHOP/Hootin' and hollerin' to fame proved a longtime plan for Tulsa-born guitarist Elvin Bishop. Bishop zipped to infamy in the mid-sixties as one of the two guitarists in the Paul Butterfield Blues Band. Bishop had met Butterfield in 1960 at the University of Chicago and was a member of the Blues brigade from the outset. He departed in 1968 to form his own band and recorded several albums of his own under the watchful eye of rock legend Bill Graham on Graham's ill-fated Fillmore Label. When the Fillmore label proved as big a stiff as Elvin's initial excursions into long-playerdom, Bishop jumped ship, landing on Fillmore's parent Epic label. Bishop wallowed in obscurity on Epic for an album before being dropped.

In 1973, he was introduced to Phil Walden, the wizard of Capricorn Records, which was known for its roster of top Southern bands including (at that time) the Allmans, Wet Willie, and Hydra. Bishop joined the tiny label and began recording once more. His third release, *STRUTTIN' MY STUFF,* proved to be the elusive breakthrough album he was looking for and a single, *Fooled Around and Fell in Love,* brought the curly-headed axe-grinder into the spotlight.

Albums/THE ELVIN BISHOP GROUP (10/69): *The Things I Used to Do; Tulsa Shuffle; Sweet Potatoe; How Much More; Dad Gum Ya Hide, Boy; Honey Bee; Prisoner of Love.* FEEL IT (10/70): *Don't Fight It (Feel It); I Just Can't Go On; So Good; Crazy 'bout You, Baby; So Fine; Party till the Cows Come Home; Hogbottom; Be with Me; As the Years Go Passing By.* ROCK MY SOUL (9/72): *Rock My Soul; Holler and Shout; Let It Shine; Don't Mind If I Do; Rock Bottom; Last Mile; Winds of a Bird; Have a Good Time; Old Man Trouble; Out behind the Barn; Storm.* LET IT FLOW (5/74): *Sunshine Special; Ground Hog; Honey Babe; Stealin' Watermelons; Travelin' Shoes; Fishin'; Let It Flow; I Can't Hold Myself in Line; Bourbon Saint; Hey, Good Lookin'.* JUKE JOINT JUMP (4/75); *Juke Joint Jump; Calling All Cows; Wide River; Rolling Home; Hold On; Arkansas Love; Sure Feels Good; Do Nobody Wrong; Crawling King Snake; Hold On.* CRABSHAW RISING/THE BEST OF ELVIN BISHOP (9/75): *Rock My Soul; So Fine; Holler and Shout; Hogbottom; Party till the Cows Come Home; Don't Fight It (Feel It); Stealin' Watermelons; Stomp; How Much More; Be with Me.* STRUTTIN' MY STUFF (12/75): *Struttin' My Stuff; Hey, Hey, Hey, Hey; My Girl; I Love the Life I Lead; Fooled Around and Fell in Love; Holler and Shout; Slick Titty Boom; Grab All the Love; Have a Good Time; Joy.* HOMETOWN BOY MAKES GOOD (10/76): *Sugar Dumplin'; Sidelines; Twist and Shout; Yes Sir; Spend Some Time; Give It Up; Keep It Cool; Graveyard Blues; Once in a Lifetime; Strut.* RAISIN' HELL (9/77): *Raisin' Hell; Rock My Soul; Sure Feels Good; Calling All Cows; Juke Joint Jump; Hey, Hey Hey; Joy; Stealin' Watermelons; Fooled Around and Fell in Love; Little Brown Bird; Yes Sir; Struttin' My Stuff; Give It Up; Travelin'*

Shoes; medley: Let the Good Times Roll, A Change Is Gonna Come, Bring It On Home to Me.

Singles/*So Fine/Sweet Potatoe* (3/70); *Don't Fight It (Feel It)/Dolores Park* (9/70); *I Just Can't Go On/Party till the Cows Come Home* (1/71); *Shout/Rock My Soul* (11/72); *Stealin' Watermelons/Last Mile* (6/73); *Travelin' Shoes/Fishin'* (7/74); *Let It Flow/Can't Go Back* (12/74); *Calling All Cows/Juke Joint Jump* (9/75); *Silent Night* (10/75); *Fooled Around and Fell in Love/Have a Good Time* (1/76); *Struttin' My Stuff/Grab All the Love* (5/76); *Spend Some Time/Sugar Dumplin'* (10/76); *Fooled Around and Fell in Love/Struttin' My Stuff* (12/76); *Keep It Cool/Yes Sir* (1/77).

BLACK SABBATH/*Ozzie Osbourne (vocals), Bill Ward (drums), Tony Iommi (guitar), Geezer Butler (bass).*

The Lord High Ministers of all that is sinister, Black Sabbath was a British foursome who slugged their way to the top brandishing a deafening style of rock that would reestablish the role of volume in popular music and help give birth to a new musical label: heavy metal. The Sabbath crew first united as Earth in Birmingham, England. By 1969 their name had been changed to Black Sabbath and their stage antics became firmly entrenched in menacing mysticism. Their first album totally revolted critics who saw them as one cut above terminal illness.

While the critics wretched on their typewriters, producing some of the vilest reviews ever, the public flocked to the ever-touring brigade like moths to a flame. Vocalist Ozzie Osbourne took great delight in outraging the public and the Sabbath fans enjoyed the insults. Sabbath's *PARANOID* and *MASTER OF REALITY* saw them enter supergroup status. The band's business interests, however, nearly wrecked their career. A tiff with a manager brought total cessation to Black Sabbath activities following the enormously successful *SABBATH BLOODY SABBATH*. The band made their way back to the studios some two years later for *SABOTAGE*, but by that time many of Sabbath's old fans had moved on to newer and more current rock items. In 1977, Sabbath faded from the rock and roll scene . . . a victim of changing times.

Albums/BLACK SABBATH (6/70): *The Wizard; Black Sabbath; NIB; Bassically; Behind the Wall of Sleep; Wasp; Wicked World;*

A Bit of Finger; Warning; Sleeping Village. PARANOID (9/70): *War Pigs; Luke's Wall; Iron Man; Paranoid; Planet Caravan; Rat Salad; Jack the Stripper; Hand of Doom.* MASTER OF REALITY (8/71): *Sweet Leaf; After Forever; Embryo; Orchid; Lord of This World; Solitude; Into the Void; Children of the Grave.* VOL. IV (9/72): *Wheel of Confusion; Under the Sun; Changes; Supernaut; Snowblind; St. Vitus Dance; Laguna Sunrise; Cornucopia; Tomorrow's Dream.* SABBATH BLOODY SABBATH (12/73): *Sabbath Bloody Sabbath; Fluff; Labbra Cadabra; A National Acrobat; Killing Yourself to Live; Who Are You; Looking for Today; Spiral Architect.* SABOTAGE (1975). WE SOLD OUR SOUL FOR ROCK AND ROLL (12/75): *Iron Band; Black Sabbath; Waranoid; The Wizard; War Pigs; Warning.* TECHNICAL ECSTASY (10/76): *Back Street Kids; You Won't Change Me; Gypsy; It's Alright; All Moving Parts; Rock and Roll Doctor; She's Gone; Dirty Woman.*

Singles/*Iron Man/Electric Funeral* (11/71); *Tomorrow's Dream/Laguna Sunrise* (9/72); *Sabbath, Bloody Sabbath/Charges* (12/73); *Iron Man/Electric Funeral* (3/74); *It's Alright/Rock and Roll Doctor* (1/77).

BLIND FAITH/*Eric Clapton (guitar, vocals), Ginger Baker (drums), Steve Winwood (keyboards, guitar, vocals), Rick Grech (bass, violin).*
A band that lived up to its name, Blind Faith was the short-lived super-group that evolved from the demise of Cream and the first demise of Traffic. When Cream split at the end of 1968, guitarist Clapton and demon drummer Baker started jamming with Winwood, an escapee from Traffic, much the same as three divorced husbands might get together for the occasional game of cards to while away the unfamiliar leisure of bachelorhood. The trio concept proved awkward and Grech, the bassist from the British cult band Family, was added.

The group made its English debut on June 7, 1969, at a free concert in London, and its American debut on July 11. Although their twenty-four-concert, eight-week maiden tour of the United States was expected to net over a million dollars, ticket sales were equaled by audience yawns. On stage, the band proved remarkably fragmented. The U.S. release of their debut LP was held up due to what American marketing mavens considered a racy cover (a barely teen bare maiden holding a model airplane). A suitable U.S. cover was hastily substituted and the album was released.

Shortly thereafter, the band called it quits.

Album/BLIND FAITH (1969): *Had to Cry Today; Can't Find My Way Home; Well All Right; Sea of Joy; Presence of the Lord; Do What You Like.*

BLOOD, SWEAT AND TEARS/*David Clayton Thomas (vocals), Bobby Colomby (drums), Bill Tillman (saxes), Ron McClure (bass), Dave Bargeron (trombone), George Wadenius (guitar), Larry Willis (keyboards).*
Credit whoever thought of the name with the sure gift of prophecy. Blood, sweat and tears was exactly what it took to get rock and jazz to meld in this nine- or eight- or seven- (depending on who shows up) man combination. The band grew out of an idea that Al Kooper (formerly of the Blues Project) had nursed for a long time: to augment the more or less traditional rock quartet with a strong new four-man horn section. Of course, others had thought of it as well, getting away from the predictable guitar-bass-and-occasional-organ combination of rock and roll. But enticing horn players away from jazz, the *right* horn players, helping them fit into the new format, and then getting the rock players to adjust—none of that was easy. It was no small triumph when Kooper, having tried and discarded a number of horn players, finally found what he wanted and unveiled, on what will be remembered as one of the weightiest rock and roll evenings of the sixties, his baby Big Band for all to see and hear.

Problems, however, nagged the band from the outset. By the time the original BS&T's first album, *CHILD IS FATHER TO THE MAN,* was out, Kooper had left to become a producer and the band looked like it was finished. At least, no one could seriously imagine it without Kooper, who was one of the giants of the 1967 music scene. But a miracle happened. Saxophone player Fred Lipsius breathed gently on the dying band and saw it revive. There was a little rearranging done among the horn personnel; David Clayton-Thomas, a Canadian blues singer, came to replace Kooper, and the new BS&T was hatched.

The new Blood, Sweat and Tears was a pleasant surprise to all concerned—from the scores of other bands who had seriously considered moving in a jazz direction to the New York fans who had missed having a band of their own since the demise of the Blues Project. There were, of course, those who thought that if 1968 was going to unite with jazz, it should be jazz of current vintage and not the "outdated" big-band style of Count Basie, which BS&T espoused. But that was a mere trifle. The thing was that Al Kooper's dream had come true . . . sort of.

By the time the new BS&T released their first album, two things were clear. One: They were exceedingly commercial, far more so than the original Kooper ensemble. Two: They were also fairly safe—totally enraging old fans who expected more from their heroes. Rock critics blasted the wishy-washy material as Bar Mitzvah soul. The record, however, did make the number-one slot on the charts and spawned a glut of singles. In 1969 many rock groups were hastily looking for a brass section in an effort to latch onto the "BS&T sound." The group was a huge financial success. Clayton-Thomas was a star. Everyone in the group was a star. So what if the theatrics were slickly programmed and the sound totally predictable? You couldn't have everything.

As it turned out, there wasn't much of anything for anybody. The singles-chart success of BS&T proved surprisingly short-lived and the band slowly drifted into an easy listening sound, relying on past success to push their career. Clayton-Thomas decided the group wasn't big enough for his talent and left to pursue a disastrous solo career on two different labels. During the same time period, BS&T as a working unit floundered, producing erratic albums with material that ranged from Ricki Ricardo re-treads to barroom blitzes. Eventually, Clayton-Thomas returned to the fold, but by that time, BS&T had lost their momentum, their image, and half of their original members. The band began to play musical chairs with its membership and appeared to be recruiting new musicians monthly. The reformed BS&T tried awfully hard at rekindling the spirit of '69 but failed. (To their credit, they threw in everything but the kitchen sink in this valiant effort.) They recorded. They took to the road (depending on where you saw them, Bobby Colomby either played with them onstage or remained at home, claiming that the rigors of road life were just too hard to handle.) Relations between the band and their long-time label, Columbia, grew strained and, eventually, BS&T joined a new company, ABC, where they presently look for better days.

Albums/CHILD IS FATHER TO THE MAN (2/68): *I Love You More Than You'll Ever Know; My Days Are Numbered; Morning Glory; Without Her; Just One Smile; I Can't Quit Her; House in the Country; Somethin' Goin' On; Meagan's Gypsy Eyes; Modern Adventures of Plato, Diogenes and Freud; So Much Love.* BLOOD, SWEAT AND TEARS (12/68): *Variations on a Theme By Eric Satie (First and Second Movements); Smiling Phases; Sometimes in the Winter; More and More; And When I Die; God Bless the Child; Spinning Wheel; You've Made Me So Very Happy; Blues—Part II.* BLOOD, SWEAT AND TEARS III (7/70): *Hi De Ho; The Battle; Lucretia MacEvil; Fire and Rain; Lonesome Suzie; Symphony for the Devil—Sympathy for the Devil; He's a Runner; Something's Comin' On; 40,000 Headmen.* BS&T 4 (6/71): *Go Down Gamblin'; Cowboys and Indians; John the Baptist; Redemption; Lisa, Listen to Me; Look to My Heart; High on a Mountain; Valentine's Day; Take Me in Your Arms; For My Lady; Mama Gets Me High.* GREATEST HITS (2/72): *You've Made Me So Very Happy; I Can't Quit Her; Go Down Gamblin'; Hi De Ho; Sometimes in Winter; And When I Die; Spinning Wheel; Lisa, Listen To Me; I Love You More Than You'll Ever Know; Lucretia MacEvil; God Bless the Child.* NEW BLOOD (9/72): *Down in the Flood; Touch Me; Alone; Velvet; I Can't Move No Mountain; Over the Hill; So Long Dixie; Snow Queen; Maiden Voyage.* NO SWEAT (7/73): *Roller Coaster; Save Our Ship; Ijamgo; Rosemary; Song for John; Almost Sorry; Back Up Against the Wall; Hip Pickles; My Old Lady; MT Pages; Many Miles; Inner Crises.* MIRROR IMAGE (7/74): *Tell Me That I'm Wrong; Look Up to the Sky; Love Looks Good on You; Hold on to Me; Thinking of You; Are You Satisfied; Mirror Image; She's Coming Home.* NEW CITY (4/75): *Ride, Captain, Ride; Life; No Show; I Was a Witness to a War; One-Room Country Shack; Applause; Yesterday's Music; Naked Man; Got to Get You into My Life; Takin' It Home.* MORE THAN EVER (6/76): *They; I Love You More Than Ever; Kathy Bell; Sweet Sadie the Saviour; Hollywood; You're the One; Heavy Blue; Saved by the Grace of Your Love.*

Singles/*I Can't Quit Her/House in the Country* (5/68); *You've Made Me So Very Happy/Blues Part II* (2/69); *More and More/Spinning Wheel* (/69); *And When I Die/Sometimes in Winter* (9/69); *You've Made Me So Very Happy/Spinning Wheel* (12/69); *Hi De Ho/The Battle* (7/70); *Lucretia*

MacEvil/Lucretia's Reprise (9/70); *And When I Die/Lucretia MacEvil* (2/71); *Go Down Gamblin'/Valentine's Day* (7/71); *Lisa, Listen to Me/Cowboys and Indians* (9/71); *So Long Dixie/Alone* (8/72); *I Can't Move No Mountain/Velvet* (12/72); *Roller Coaster/Inner Crises* (9/73); *Save Our Ship/Song for John* (11/73); *Tell Me That I'm Wrong/Rich Reprise* (5/74); *Spinning Wheel/You've Made Me So Very Happy* (9/74); *Got to Get You into My Life/Naked Man* (5/75); *You're the One/Heavy Blue* (9/76).

BLUE CHEER/*Original Members: Leigh Stephens (guitar), Dickie Peterson (bass and vocals), Paul Whaley (drums).*
During mid-1968, when most of the "acid-rock" bands were getting deeper and deeper into controlled psychedelia, the three members of Blue Cheer stepped forth with a sound that resembled the final reel of Godzilla vs. The Thing. Backed by a wall of Marshall amps, the band offered the musical equivalent of a bad trip, a five-car collision and Excedrin headache #975 all rolled into one. Their music was hard, uncontrolled, wild and . . . loud. Their hit version of *Summertime Blues* catapulted them into the limelight, but early personnel changes kept their effectiveness to a minimum. (Although their appearance on Dick Clark's *American Bandstand,* one of their rare excursions into television, must be considered one of the major sociological events of the decade. Ever see Clearasil shatter?)

Their second album wasn't nearly so inspired or raunchy as their first, and by their third and fourth releases, much of the pizzazz was gone, although the new, improved Blue Cheer band became quite proficient at easygoing, melodic rock. As the seventies spawned such bands as Dawn and Three Dog Night, the kinetic demon known as Blue Cheer found itself out of step with the times . . . and it faded away accordingly, leaving behind a legacy of frantic rhythms and thousands of nearly deaf fans.

Albums/VINCEBUS ERUPTUM (2/68): *Summertime Blues; Rock Me Baby; Dr. Please; Out of Focus; Parchment Farm; Second Time Around.* OUTSIDEINSIDE (10/68): *Feathers from Your Tree; Sun Cycle; Just a Little Bit; Gypsy Ball; Come and Get It; Satisfaction; The Hunter; Magnolia Caboose; Babylon.* NEW! IMPROVED! BLUE CHEER (3/69): *When It All Gets Old; West Coast Child of Sunshine; I Want My Baby Back; Aces 'n' Eights; As Long As I Live; It Takes a Lot to Laugh, It Takes a Train to*

Dry; Peace of Mind; Fruit and Iceburgs; Honey Butter Lover.
BLUE CHEER (12/69): *Fool; You're Gonna Need Someone;*
Hello L.A., Bye-Bye Birmingham; Saturday Freedom; Ain't That
the Way (Love's Supposed to Be); Rock and Rolle Queens; Natural
Man; Better When We Try; Lovin' You's Easy. THE ORIGINAL
HUMAN BEING (9/70): *Good Times Are So Hard to Find; Love*
of a Woman; Make Me Laugh; Pilot; Babji (Twilight Raga);
Preacher; Black Sun; Tears by My Bed; Man on the Run; Rest at
Ease Sandwich. OH! PLEASANT HOPE (4/71): *Hiway Man; Be-*
liever; Money Troubles; Traveling Man; Oh! Pleasant Hope; I'm
the Light; Ecological Blues; Lester the Arrester; Heart Full of
Soul.

Singles/*Summertime Blues/Out of Focus* (1/68); *Just a Little*
Bit/Gypsy Ball (6/68); *Sun Cycle/Feathers from Your Tree*
(10/68); *When It All Gets Old/West Coast Child of Sunshine*
(3/69); *All Night Long/Fortunes* (11/69); *Hello L.A., Bye-Bye*
Birmingham/Natural Man (2/70); *Fool/Ain't That the Way*
(Love's Supposed to Be) (7/70); *Pilot/Babaji* (10/70).

BLUE OYSTER CULT/*Eric Bloom (guitar and vocals), Albert*
Bouchard (drums and vocals), Joe Bouchard (bass and vocals), Allen
Lanier (keyboards), Donald Roeser (guitar and vocals).
Mutant heavy-metal gods from . . . gasp! . . . LONG ISLAND!
Strange, but true. These demonic denizens of phantasmagoric imagery actually started off, harmlessly enough, in and about the
peaceful vibes of 1967's Stony Brook College. In between bursts of
flower power, members of Blue Oyster Cult (BOC to their friends)
nearly made the big time via such groups as the Soft White Underbelly and Stalk Forest. (Soft White Underbelly was actually
signed to Elektra. An excellent debut LP was recorded but never
realeased. Who needed that hard rock stuff when you had Atomic
Rooster?) In 1970, Stalk Forest mutated into Blue Oyster Cult
and a demo was submitted to Columbia Record's Murray
Krugman by the band's truly visionary manager, Sandy
Pearlman. Krugman and Pearlman met, joined forces, and managed to get the band onto the label. This in itself was quite an
accomplishment because, at that time, the company's idea of
teen-oriented rock was Blood, Sweat and Tears and the Rowan
Brothers. Before long, the dangerous visions of BOC were unleashed on an unsuspecting public. The results were shattering.
Double guitar licks leaped from speaker to speaker, thunderous

rhythm patterns rumbled from below. Devilish vocals delved into nightmarish territory. Everybody and everything found a place in BOC's world: diz-busters, damnation, destruction, OD-ing on life, flower power, sado-masochism, corruption, urban blight, teen romance . . . even the Canadian mounted police. They were heavy-metal kids with a verbal clout. Their personalities were sheer Clockwork Orange with the best of World War II thrown in for good measure. The group's in-concert appearances—replete with oversized BOC flags, guitar duels (literal duels . . . as in Basil Rathbone vs. Errol Flynn), and torrid drum solos, wherein chains are used instead of the traditional pair of drum sticks—only served to heighten the band's sinister presence. At this point, the group is ready to explode. With countless gold albums and a hit single under their holster (*Don't Fear the Reaper* . . . it was a love song!), BOC is priming itself to take the country by storm. First the country . . . and then, the world!!

Albums/BLUE OYSTER CULT (1/72): *Transmanicon MC; I'm on the Lamb but I Ain't No Sheep; Then Came the Last Days of May; Stairway to the Stars; Before the Kiss. a Redcap; Screams; She's As Beautiful As a Foot; Cities on Flame with Rock and Roll; Workshop of the Telescopes; Redeemed.* BLUE OYSTER CULT PROMOTIONAL BOOTLEG (10/72): *The Red and the Black; Buck's Boogie; Workshop of the Telescopes; Cities on Flame with Rock and Roll.* TYRANNY AND MUTATION (2/73): *OD'd on Life Itself; Hot Rails to Hell; 7 Screaming Diz-Busters; Baby Ice Dog; Wings Wetted Down; Teen Archer; Mistress of the Salmon Salt (Quicklime Girl).* SECRET TREATIES (4/74): *Career of Evil; Subhuman; Dominance and Submission; ME 262; Cagey Cretins; Harvester of Eyes; Flaming Telepaths; Astronomy.* ON YOUR FEET OR ON YOUR KNEES (2/75): *Subhuman; Harvester of Eyes; Hot Rails to Hell; Before the Kiss, a Redcap; I Ain't Got You; Born to Be Wild.* AGENTS OF FORTUNE (5/76): *This Ain't the Summer of Love; True Confessions; Don't Fear the Reaper; ETI; The Revenge of Vera Gemini; Sinful Love; Tattoo Vampire; Morning Final; Tenderloin; Debbie Denise.* SPECTRES (11/77): *Godzilla; Golden Age of Leather; Death Valley Nights; Searchin' for Celine; Fireworks; R.U. Ready 2 Rock; Celestial the Queen; Goin' through the Motions; I Love the Night; Nosferatu.*

Singles/*Cities on Flame with Rock and Roll*/*Trust Me* (12/71); *Hot Rails to Hell*/*Screaming Diz-Busters* (7/73); *Cities on Flame with Rock and Roll*/*Before the Kiss, a Redcap* (11/73); *Career of Evil*/*Dominance and Submission* (10/74); *Born to Be Wild* (6/75); *Don't Fear the Reaper*/*Tattoo Vampire* (7/76); *This Ain't the Summer of Love*/*Debbie Denise* (5/77); *R.U. Ready 2 Rock* (11/77).

THE BONZO DOG BAND/*Vivian Stanshall (vocals), "Legs" Larry Smith (drums), Neil Innes (keyboards), Rodney Slater (reeds), Roger Ruskin Spear (reeds and explosions).*
Not only was the Bonzo Dog Band ahead of its time, it was ahead of everyone else's time as well. Begun as a college haven for strange artistes in 1966, the group originally brandished the name the Bonzo Dog Da Da Band with great élan. The Da Da was later changed to Do-dah in an attempt to make the band a bit more, er, accessible. Accessible they were never destined to be, with various members playing electronic legs, stuffed boards, and tubas. So the Do-dah was dispensed with as well. The Bonzos lampooned everything that vaguely resembled anything . . . often with brilliant results. They meshed rock with twenties ragtime and black humor –vaudeville, producing such winning propositions as *Can Blue Men Sing the Whites*, *My Pink Half of The Drainpipe*, and the bona-fide hit UK single *I'm the Urban Spaceman* (produced by Paul McCartney under the subtle pseudonym of Apollo C. Vermouth . . . the Bonzos just seemed to bring out the best in people).

The hapless happies were grossly misunderstood most of the time and the band dissolved amidst a sea of sour grapes. Neil Innes later went onto solo LPs before becoming Monty Python's resident musical maniac. Roger Ruskin Spear attempted a career with little or no financial reward. Viv Stanshall, after completing a successful nervous breakdown, rebounded with the truly classic *Men Opening Umbrellas Ahead* album, and Legs Larry carved a niche for himself in rock history as the tap-dancing ballerina on the 1974 Elton John world tour.

And who said there was no creativity in rock?

Albums/GORILLA (2/68): *Cool Britannia; Equestrian Statue; I Left My Heart in San Francisco; Jollity Farm; I'm Bored; Look Out, There's a Monster Coming; Jazz, Delicious Hot, Disgusting Cold; Deathcab for Cutie; Narcissus; Intro and the Outro; Mickey's Son and Daughter; Music for the Head Ballet; Piggy*

Bank Love; Sound of Music. I'M THE URBAN SPACEMAN (6/69): *I'm the Urban Spaceman; Postcard; Beautiful Zelda; Can Blue Men Sing the Whites?; Hello Mabel; Kama Sutra; Humanoid Boogie; Trouser Press; My Pink Half of the Drainpipe; Rockaliser Baby; Rhinocratic Oaths; Moustachioed Daughters; We Are All Normal.* TADPOLES (1969): *Hunting Tigers out in "Indiah"; Shirt; Tubas in the Moonlight; Doctor Jazz; Monster Mash; Ready-Mades; Ali-Baba's Camel; Laughing Blues; By a Waterfall; Mr. Apollo; Canyons of Your Mind.* KEYNSHAM (5/70): *You Done My Brain In; Keynsham; Quiet Talks and Summer Walks; Tent; We Were Wrong; Joke Shop Man; The Bride Stripped Bare by "Bachelors"; What Do You Do?; Mr. Slater's Parrot; Sport (the Odd Boy); I Want to Be with You; Noises for the Leg; Busted.* THE BEAST OF THE BONZOS (7/71): *Intro and the Outro; I'm the Urban Spaceman; Canyons of Your Mind;* other titles. LET'S MAKE UP AND BE FRIENDLY (4/72): *The Strain; Turkeys; King of Scurf; Waiting for the Wardrobe; Straight from My Heart; Rusty (Champion Thrust); Rawlinson End; Don't Get Me Wrong; Fresh Wound; Bad Blood; Slush.* HISTORY OF THE BONZOS (8/74): *Can Blue Men Sing the Whites?; The Intro and the Outro; Mr. Apollo; I'm the Urban Spaceman; Rockaliser Baby; Noises for the Leg; Labio Dental Fricative; Look at Me, I'm Wonderful; Laughing Blues; Hello Mabel; Suspicion; Bad Blood; Big Shot; Trouser Press; Sport (the Odd Boy); Mickey's Son and Daughter; We Are All Normal; My Pink Half of the Drainpipe; Hunting Tigers out in "Indiah"; Narcissus; Tent; Canyons of Your Mind; The Sound of Music; Rhinocratic Oaths; You Done My Brain In; Mr. Slater's Parrot; Blind Dates; Shirt; 9 to 5 Pollution Blues; Kind of Scurf; Kama Sutra; Jollity Farm; Slush; Please Release Me.*

Singles/*Mr. Apollo/Ready-Mades* (3/69); *Urban Spaceman/Canyons of Your Mind* (4/69); *Urban Spaceman/Canyons of Your Mind* (7/71); *Slush/King of Scurf* (8/72).

BOSTON/*Tom Scholz (guitars, keyboards), Brad Delp (vocals, guitar), Barry Goudreau (lead guitar), Fran Sheehan (bass), Sib Hashian (drums).*

A real rock rags-to-riches story, within one year's time, Boston went from total obscurity to the number-one position on the charts, becoming *the* hottest new group in America. Boston is the product of young mastermind Tom Scholz. An MIT graduate with a Masters in mechanical engineering, he was living a Jekyll and Hyde existence, working by day in the Product Design branch of Polaroid, slaving by night in a rock band. Building his own recording studio in his home, Tom recorded a demo tape of some of the songs that would wind up as Boston anthems. The tape was then submitted to several labels. After being passed on by one king company, the tape was scooped up by the same company's sister label. Tom quickly picked the best musicians around and formed Boston.

Once signed, Tom and his newly formed band went into a real live studio with Epic producer John Boylan and cut their monster debut album, including the single *More Than a Feeling*. The album went gold. The single went gold. The album went platinum and the melodic, guitar-oriented Boston sound became the cause célèbre of 1976.

Albums/BOSTON (6/76): *More Than a Feeling; Foreplay; Peace of Mind; Long Time; Rock and Roll Band; Smokin'; Hitch a Ride; Something About You; Let Me Take You Home Tonight.*

Singles/*More Than a Feeling/Smokin'* (8/76); *Long Time/Let Me Take You Home Tonight* (1/77); *Peace of Mind/Foreplay* (4/77).

THE BOSTON SOUND/After the San Francisco sound clicked commercially in 1967, some enterprising record executive sought to *create* a similar explosion on the East Coast. The target of the hype? Boston. The record biz thought the musical happenings of that city could be built up into a big Boss-town sound promotion. *Newsweek* was taken in to the extent of a long, favorable article. The trouble was that what was happening in Boston could not, even from the most optimistic viewpoint, be described in terms of the explosion that shook up San Francisco and the world. The Boston bands were simply not unified in concept. In essence, there was no *sound* to hype. The Boston promotion bombed painfully, leaving a lot of innocent groups out in the cold, victims of what the critics immediately caught on to as a hype, first class. The bands themselves had nothing to do with it all, but they were blamed for it nonetheless. Among the more notable victims were Orpheus, the Beacon Street Union, Ill Wind, Bagatelle, the Ultimate Spinach, Eden's Children, Phluph, and Earth Opera.

DAVID BOWIE/When David Bowie first slithered into the

limelight in the early seventies, the most obvious question plagu-
ing the critics was summed up in the epic utterance: "Huh?" Was
it a boy? Was it a girl? Was it . . . something else? No one knew.
No one cared. As far as most people were concerned, David
Bowie might as well have been from Mars. A few writers sus-
pected as much.

The cool, lithe singer-songwriter was born David Jones in 1947
and raised in a somewhat less than phantasmagorical section of
South London. A street brawl almost resulted in the loss of an eye
(his left) while he was still in his early teens. Subsequent surgery
left him with a paralyzed pupil. Even today the reflection of
strong light gives the eye an almost feline look. During the late
sixties, he dropped out of Bromley Technical High School and
formed David Jones and the Lower Third.

A hastily constructed album resulted, but when Davey Jones of
the Monkees attained notoriety, David Jones became David
Bowie. He joined the Lindsay Kemp Mime Troupe and later had
a hit with the slight, bizzarre single, *The Laughing Gnome,* a novelty tune that would have made Alvin and the Chipmunks blush.
Two albums, *MAN OF WORDS, MAN OF MUSIC* and *THE
MAN WHO SOLD THE WORLD,* earned him the beginnings of
a following in England but did not reach the States. His first U.S.
release, *HUNKY DORY,* earned him a sort of fame as being the
only male rock personality to look like Greta Garbo.

Cutting off his long blond hair and adopting a space-age stance
in 1972, Bowie released *THE RISE AND FALL OF ZIGGY
STARDUST.* Fame hit Bowie almost instantly. He produced Lou
Reed's *TRANSFORMER* album and Mott the Hooples *ALL
THE YOUNG DUDES.* His career blossomed with *ALADDIN
SANE* and *PINUPS,* but it was 1974's *DIAMOND DOGS* that
firmly established him as the George Orwell of rock and roll.
Filled with futuristic fables of death and decay, the *DIAMOND
DOGS* LP and coast-to-coast tour formed a science-fiction epic in
every possible sense.

David's initial unisex appearance on stage was, by this time, a
bit of a stereotype and, therefore, he resorted to a fairly Brechtian
stance. Smooth, suave, sleek. His obvious alienation with society
at large only served to enhance his position with his fans (a rather
unique lot who followed David through his various stages, at one
point showing up at his concerts gloriously covered in glued-on

glitter with hair dyed a rather horrid bright orange).

In the midst of his unusual musical stride (producing bizarre gold albums and singles), Bowie made a strong screen debut in Nicholas Roeg's *The Man Who Fell to Earth*. In this full-length motion picture, Bowie portrayed a visitor from space, trapped quite unceremoniously within the confines of commercial, make-a-buck earth. It may have been the most truthful, albeit unintentional, rock and roll story ever filmed.

Albums/DAVID BOWIE (5/67): *Rubber Band; Sell Me a Coat; Love You Till Tuesday; There Is a Happy Land; Uncle Arthur; When I Live My Dream; Join the Gang; Little Bombardier; Come and Buy My Toys; Silly Boy Blue; She's Got My Medals; Please, Mr. Gravedigger.* HUNKY DOREY (11/71): *Changes; Oh You Pretty Things; 8 Line Poem; Life on Mars?; Quicksand; Fell Your Heart; Andy Warhol; Song for Bob Dylan; Queen Bitch; The Bewlay Brothers.* THE RISE AND FALL OF ZIGGY STARDUST AND THE SPIDERS FROM MARS (5/72): *Five Years; Soul Love; Moonage Daydream; Starman; It Ain't Easy; Lady Stardust; Star; Hand On to Yourself; Ziggy Stardust; Suffragette City; Rock 'n' Roll Suicide.* SPACE ODDITY (10/72; recorded in 1969); *Space Oddity; Unwashed and Somewhat Slightly Dazed; Letter to Hermione; Cygnet Committee; Janine; An Occasional Dream; The Wild-Eyed Boy from Freecloud; God Knows I'm Good; Memory of a Free Festival.* THE MAN WHO SOLD THE WORLD (11/72; recorded in 1970): *The Width of a Circle; Black Country Rock; After All; Running Gun Blues; Saviour Machine; She Shook Me Cold; The Man Who Sold the World; The Supermen.* ALADDIN SANE (3/73): *Watch That Man; Aladdin Sane; Drive-In Saturday; Panic in Detroit; Cracked Actor; Time; The Prettiest Star; Let's Spend the Night Together; The Jean Genie; Lady Grinning Soul.* IMAGES (2/73): *Rubber Band; Maid of Bond Street; Sell Me a Coat; Love You Till Tuesday; There Is a Happy Land; the Laughing Gnome; Gospel According to Tony Day; Did You Ever Have a Dream; Uncle Arthur; We Are Hungry Men; When I Live My Dream; Join the Gang; Little Bombardier; Come and Buy My Toys; Silly Boy Blue; She's Got My Medals; Please, Mr. Gravedigger; London Boys; Karma Man; Let Me Sleep Beside You; In the Heat of the Morning.* PIN UPS (10/73): *Rosalyn; Here Comes the Night; I Wish You Would; See Emily Play; Where Have All the Good Times Gone; I Can't Explain; Sor-*

row; *Friday on My Mind; Anyway, Anyhow, Anywhere; Don't Bring Me Down; Everything's All Right; Shapes of Things.* DIAMOND DOGS (4/74): *Future Legend; Diamond Dogs; Sweet Thing; Candidate; Sweet Thing (reprise); Rebel Rebel; Rock 'n' Roll with Me; We Are the Dead; 1984; Big Brother; Chant of the Ever-Circling Skeletal Family.* LIVE (1/75): *1984; Rebel Rebel; Moonage Daydream; Sweet Thing; Changes; Suffragette City; Aladdin Sane; All the Young Dudes; Cracked Actor; Rock 'n' Roll with Me; Watch That Man; Knock on Wood; Diamond Dogs; Big Brother; Jean Genie; Width of a Circle; Rock 'n' Roll Suicide.* YOUNG AMERICANS (3/75): *Young Americans; Win; Fascination; Right; Somebody Up There Likes Me; Across the Universe; Fame; Can You Hear Me.* STATION TO STATION (1/76): *Station to Station; Golden Years; Word on A Wind; TVC 15; Stay; Wild Is the Wind.* CHANGES ONE (5/76): *Space Oddity; John, I'm Only Dancing; Changes; Ziggy Stardust; Suffragette City; Jean Genie; Diamond Dogs; Rebel Rebel; You Americans; Fame; Golden Years.* LOW (1/77): *Speed of Life; Breaking Glass; What in the World; A New Career; In a New Town; Be My Wife; Always Crashing in the Same Car; Weeping Wall; Subterranean; Sound and Vision; Warszawn; Art Decade.* HEROES (10/77): *Beauty and the Beast; Joe the Lion; Heroes; Sons of the Silent Age; Blackout; V-2 Schneider; Sense of Doubt; Moss Garden; Neukoin; The Secret Life of Arabia.*

Singles/*This Is a Happy Land/Rubber Band* (5/67); *Love You Till Tuesday/Did You Ever Have a Dream* (8/67); *Changes/Andy Warhol* (11/74); *Starman/Suffragette City* (5/72); *Jean Genie/Hang On to Yourself* (10/72); *Space Oddity/The Man Who Sold the World* (12/72); *Rebel Rebel/Lady Grinding Soul* (5/74); *1984/Queen Bitch* (7/74); *Rock 'n' Roll with Me/Panic in Detroit* (11/74); *Young Americans (1975); Fame/Right* (6/75); *Let's Spend the Night Together/Lady Grinding Soul* (7/75); *TVC 15/We Are the Dead* (4/76); *To My Wife/Speed of Life* (5/77); *Time/The Prettiest Star* (6/77).

THE BOXTOPS/*Alex Chilton (lead singer), Billy Cunningham (bass), Gary Talley (guitar), Danny Smythe (drums), John Evans (guitar, organ).*

No American group since the Righteous Brothers had looked whiter and sung blacker than the Boxtops on their sensational first single in 1967, *The Letter.* Alex Chilton's voice had more Memphis grit than was considered entirely proper for a white gentleman. The Memphis-based outfit continued cranking out the well-honed funk until 1970, when they faded from the scene. Leader of the pack Chilton brought forth another band shortly thereafter, Big Star. As critically acclaimed as this second unit was, it never lived up to its name and succumbed after a few LPs.

Albums/THE LETTER-NEON RAINBOW (10/67): *The Letter; Neon Rainbow; She Knows How; Trains and Boats and Planes; Break My Mind; I'm Your Puppet; White Shade of Pale; People Make the World; Everything I Am; Happy Time; Gonna Find Somebody; I Pray for Rain.* CRY LIKE A BABY (3/68): *Cry Like a Baby; Lost; Deep in Kentucky; Weeping Analeah; Trouble with Same; Fields of Clover; Good Morning, Dear; You Keep Me Hanging On; I'm the One for You; Every Time.* NON-STOP (10/68): *I'm Movin' On; She Shot a Hole in My Soul; People Gonna Talk; I Met Her in Church; Yesterday's Where My Mind; other titles.* SUPER HITS (11/68): *The Letter; Cry Like a Baby; Neon Rainbow, other titles.* DIMENSIONS (8/69): *You Keep Tightening Up on Me; Soul Deep; Turn On a Dream; other titles.*

Singles/*The Letter/Happy Times* (6/67); *Neon Rainbow/Everything I Am* (10/67); *Cry Like a Baby/Door You Closed to Me* (2/68); *Choo Choo Train/Fields of Clover* (5/68); *I Met Her in Church/People Gonna Talk* (8/68); *Sweet Cream Ladies, Forward March/See Only Sunshine* (12/68); *I Shall Be Released* (4/69); *Soul Deep* (6/69); *Turn On a Dream* (9/69); *You Keep Tightening Up on Me (2/70).*

BREAD/*David Gates (vocals, guitar, keyboards), James Griffin (vocals, guitar), Mike Botts (drums), Larry Knechtel (keyboards).* No great shakes artistically, Bread took the concept of whimp-rock and made it palatable for radio listeners of all ages. Veteran session musician and arranger Gates worked with Griffin in a group called Pleasure Faire with guitarist Rob Royer. In 1969, after Griffin had copped an Oscar for his tune *For All We Know* (from the film *Lovers and Other Strangers*), the threesome changed their name to Bread. Botts joined the entourage a year or so later. Eventually Royer left, to be replaced by Knechtel. Their sound was lightweight, homogenized, and totally geared for maximum airplay. Their success at designing hit singles seemed to ensure them a long-lasting career. In 1973, however, they suddenly disbanded. Gates sallied forth into a disastrous solo career, and the band reformed in 1976. This time around, however, the hits just haven't come their way.

Albums/BREAD (7/69): *Dismal Days; London Bridge; Could I; Look at Me; The Last Time; Any Way You Want Me; Don't Shut Me Out; Move Over; It Don't Matter to Me; Family Doctor; Friends and Lovers; You Can't Measure the Cost.* ON THE WATERS (7/70): *Why Do You Keep Me Waiting; Make It with You; Blue Satin Pillow; Look What You've Done; I Am That I Am; Been Too Long on the Road; I Want You with Me; Coming Apart; Easy Love; In The Afterglow; Call on Me; The Other Side of Life.* MANNA (3/71): *Let Your Love Go; Take Comfort; If; Too Much Love; Be Kind to Me; He's a Good Lad; She Was My Lady; Live in Your Love; What a Change; I Say Again; Come Again; Truckin'.* BABY I'M A WANT YOU (1/72): *Down on My Knees; Baby I'm a Want You; Everything I Own; Nobody Like You; Diary; Dream Lady; Daughter; Games of Magic; This Isn't What the Government meant; Just Like Yesterday; I Don't Love You.* THE GUITAR MAN (10/72): *Welcome to the Music; The Guitar Man; Make It by Yourself; Aubrey; Fancy Dancer; Sweet Surrender; Let Me Go; Yours for Life; Picture in Your Mind; Don't Tell Me No; Didn't Even Know Her Name;* THE BEST OF BREAD (3/73): *Make It with You; Everything I Own; Diary; Baby I'm a Want You; It Don't Matter to Me; Mother Freedom; Down on My Knees; Too Much Love; Let Your Love Go; Look What You've Done; Truckin'.* THE BEST OF BREAD 2 (4/74): *Sweet Surrender; Fancy Dancer; Guitar Man; Been Too Long on the Road; Friends and Lovers; Aubrey; Dream Lady; Daughter; Yours for Life; London Bridge; He's a Good Lad; Just Like Yesterday.* LOST WITHOUT YOUR LOVE (1/77): *Hooked on You; She's the Only One; Lost without Your Love; Change of Heart; Belonging; Fly Away; Lay Your Money Down; The Chosen One; Today's the First Day; Hold Tight; Our Lady of Sorrow.*

Singles/*Make It With You/Why Do You Keep Me Waiting* (5/70); *It Don't Matter to Me/Call on Me* (7/70); *Let Your Love Go/Too Much Love* (12/70); *If/Take Comfort* (3/71); *Baby I'm a Want You/Truckin'* (9/71); *Diary/Down on My Knees* (4/72); *The Guitar Man/Just Like* (6/72); *Sweet Surrender/Make It by Your-*

self (10/72); *Aubrey/Didn't Even Know Her Name* (1/73); *Lost Without Your Love/Change of Heart* (11/76); *Hooked on You/Our Lady of Sorrow* (3/77).

JACKSON BROWNE/Before becoming the proverbial Sad Sack of rock balladeering, Jackson Browne was a fairly faceless but highly respected songwriting force emanating from the West Coast. By the time he was seventeen, German-born, L.A.-raised Browne was playing guitar for ex-Velvet Underground crooner Nico at the Electric Circus in New York, penning three tunes for her debut album. Later, such artists as Tom Rush and the Nitty Gritty Dirt Band began recording his compositions. Gradually, his reputation as a writer par excellence spread. In 1972 he became part of the Asylum family of artists (The Eagles, Linda Ronstadt, J. D. Souther), and his first critically acclaimed album was released.

Jackson is fairly low-key on stage, although of late he has matured greatly in terms of performance. For the most part, he has gone on to fame as a song poet, each of his long-playing excursions into bemused melancholia becoming a much-anticipated event for his fans. His songs have been recorded by a host of artists, including the Eagles *(Take It Easy, James Dean)*, Joe Cocker *(Jamaica Say You Will)*, and Kiki Dee *(Song for Adam)*. His songwriting skills have betrayed him as being a literate, low-key rocker, something of an exception to the raucous rule of banal pop lyricism.

Albums/JACKSON BROWNE (1/72): *Jamaica Say You Will; A Child in These Hills; Song for Adam; Doctor My Eyes; From Silver Lake; Something Fine; Under the Falling Sky; Looking into You; Rock Me on the Water; My Opening Farewell.* FOR EVERYMAN (10/73): *Take It Easy; Our Lady of the Well; Colors of the Sun; I Thought I Was a Child; These Days; Redneck Friend; The Times You've Come; Ready or Not; Sing My Songs to Me; For Everyman.* LATE FOR THE SKY (9/74): *Late for the Sky; Fountain of Sorrow; Farther On; The Late Show; The Road and the Sky; For a Dancer; Walking Slow; Before the Deluge.* THE PRETENDER (11/76): *The Fuse; Your Bright Baby Blues; Linda Paloma; Here Come Those Tears Again; The Only Child; Daddy's Tune; Sleep's Dark and Silent Gate; The Pretender.*

Singles/*Looking into You/Doctor My Eyes* (2/72); *Rock Me on* *the Water/Something Fine* (7/72); *Redneck Friend/The Times You've Come* (8/73); *Ready or Not/Take It Easy* (1/74); *Fountain of Sorrow/The Late Show* (3/75); *Here Come Those Tears Again/Linda Paloma* (1/77).

BUBBLEGUM MUSIC/Why did records like *Chewy Chewy* and *Yummy, Yummy, Yummy* (10/68 and 7/68 respectively) dominate the charts during a period that is often described as the most sophisticated in rock? Because, statistically, there are more ten- and eleven-year-olds than ever; not only that, more ten- and eleven-year-olds are buying records than ever before. The most popular of the marching morons of bubblegum were such stellar bands as The Nineteen-Ten Fruitgum Company, The Ohio Express and, later on, Dawn. Bubblegum music died in the late sixties . . . in name. Today it is called great art or the Carpenters or something close to that.

THE BUCKINGHAMS/*Denny Tufano (vocals), Carl Giammarese (lead guitar), Jon-Jon Poulos (drums), Nick Fortune (bass), Marty Grebb (organ, replacing Dennis Miccoli).*
The Buckinghams were one of those sleek, expensively barbered, well-tailored, highly commercial rock groups beloved by record companies, adored by fans, and scorned by rock critics and rock intellectuals. They came out of Chicago at the height of the mid-sixties' rock boom and moved right into a hit formula, doing everything an efficient computer might recommend and never making a mistake—as far as singles were concerned. The albums were something else, with soon-to-be-Chicago-mentor James William Guercio taking over completely. Guercio's axiom seemed to be, "Be commercial with singles, experimental with albums." As a result, the Buckinghams unleashed a horde of schizoid long-players . . . catchy ditties surrounded by dross. The band never really dissolved—it just became easier and easier to ignore as the years went by.
Albums/KIND OF A DRAG (1967): *Kind of a Drag; I Call Your Name; I'll Go Crazy; Don't Want to Cry; Virginia Woolf; Beginners Love; Sweets for My Sweet; I've Been Wrong; Makin' Up and Breakin' Up; You Make Me Feel So Good; Summertime; Love Ain't Enough.* TIME AND CHARGES (7/67): *Don't You Care; And Our Love; Pitied Be the Dragon Hunter; Why Don't You Love Me; You Are Gone, I'll Be Back; Remember; Mercy, Mercy,*

Mercy; Married Life; Foreign Policy. PORTRAITS (3/68): *Susan, Hey Baby; C'mon Home; I Love All of the Girls; We Just Know; Inside Looking Out; Mail; Big Business Advisor; Have You Noticed You're Alive; Just Because I've Fallen Down; Any Place in Here.* IN ONE EAR AND GONE TOMORROW (9/68): *Back in Love Again; Simplicity; Can I Get a Witness; Our Wrong to Be Right; Can't Find the Words; Song of the Breeze; What Is Love; I Know I Think; Till the Sun Doesn't Shine; Are You There; Time of My Life.* GREATEST HITS (4/69): *Don't You Care; Lawdy Miss Clawdy; Back in Love Again; Why Don't You Love Me; I'll Go Crazy; Susan; Mercy, Mercy, Mercy; And Our Love; Hey Baby; Foreign Policy; Kind of a Drag.* MADE IN CHICAGO (2/75): *Don't You Care; Pitied Be the Dragon Hunter; And Our Love; Why Don't You Love Me; You're Gone; Married Life; Mercy, Mercy, Mercy; Susan; Foreign Policy; Remember; The Mail.*

Singles/*Don't Want to Cry/I'll Go Crazy* (1966); *Kind of a Drag/You Make Me Feel So Good* (11/66); *Lawdy Miss Clawdy/I Call Your Name* (2/67); *Don't You care/Why Don't You Move Me* (2/67); *Mercy, Mercy, Mercy/You Are Gone* (5/67); *Hey Baby/And Our Love* (8/67); *Susan/Foreign Policy* (11/67); *Don't You Care/Mercy, Mercy, Mercy* (12/67); *Back in Love Again/You Misunderstand Me* (5/68); *Hey Baby/Susan* (6/68); *Where Did You Come From/Song of the Breeze* (10/68); *This Is How Much I Love You/Can't Find the Words* (3/69); *Kind of a Drag/Back in Love Again* (5/69); *It's a Beautiful Day/Different or Opposite* (8/69); *I Got a Feeling/It Took Forever* (1/70).

BUFFALO SPRINGFIELD/*Richie Furay (rhythm guitar, vocals), Neil Young (lead guitar, vocals), Jim Messina (bass guitar, vocals, replacing Bruce Palmer), Dewey Martin (drums, vocals), Stephen Stills (lead guitar, vocals).*
The story of Buffalo Springfield is a sad one because they had all the markings of being *the* group of the sixties. One of the group's greatest assets was the multifaceted talents of its members. It started in the spring of '66 when two singing guitarists (Stills and Furay) ran into two Canadian musicians (Young and Palmer) in a Los Angeles traffic jam. The foursome recruited a Southern drummer, Martin (fresh from the Dillards), and shortly thereafter Buffalo Springfield was hatched.

From the outset, the fivesome radiated star potential. Their first national tour with the Beach Boys displayed their diversified sound effectively: a folk song here, a rocker there, a ballad tossed in for good measure, peppered with a few country licks. Their third single, written by Stills, *For What It's Worth,* gave the band the national exposure it needed and all seemed to be going well for the sure-to-be-stars. Their first album, however, was hindered from the start by lack of direction and embryonic personality clashes, with the overall sound being a bit thin. It was the old story of an essentially "live" group having to learn what to do in a studio.

Springfield's second long-player, BUFFALO SPRINGFIELD AGAIN, showed a marked change in the group, with a more sophisticated sound (enhanced by a group producing effort as well as help from Ahmet Ertegun, arranger Jack Nitzsche, and engineer Jim Messina). Arrangements were lush, totally overshadowing the band's former anemic efforts. Contained on the disc were such classics as *Blue Bird, Rock And Roll Woman,* and *Broken Arrow.* It was a giant step forward and the band was assured stardom. Then, in the midst of a third album, the band suddenly broke up. Friction between the two lead guitarists, Stills and Young, led to internal strife. The growing songwriting career of soft-spoken Furay only added fuel to the fire. This became the final album; *LAST TIME AROUND* was released "posthumously," with Jim Messina sitting in and handling producing chores.

Young set out on a solo career. Stills got together with ex-Hollie Graham Nash and Byrd David Crosby to form Crosby, Stills and Nash. Young later joined and the trio became a quartet but that old Stills-Young friction soon reduced it to a trio once more. In 1974, the trio called it quits, with Stills alternately going solo and performing with a home-grown group, Manassas. Nash and Crosby formed a duo. Today, the original Crosby, Stills and Nash troupe are recording a reunion album.

Richie Furay and Jim Messina went on to form the highly successful Poco. Messina left in 1971 to form Loggins and Messina, a kinetic concept which lasted until 1976. Furay split the Poco realm in 1975 to form the Souther-Hillman-Furay band. That little experiment lasted one year and two albums before Richie decided that he, too, preferred the solo route.

Albums/BUFFALO SPRINGFIELD (10/66): *For What It's*

*Worth; Burned; Nowadays Clancy Can't Even Sing; Flying on the
Ground Is Wrong; Hot Dusty Roads; Go and Say Goodbye; Sit
Down, I Think I Love You; Everybody's Wrong; Do I Have to
Come Right Out and Say It; Leave; Out of My Mind; Pay the
Price.* BUFFALO SPRINGFIELD AGAIN (10/67): *Mr. Soul;
Rock 'n' Roll Woman; Child's Claim to Fame; Everydays; Expect-
ing to Fly; Hung Upside Down; Sad Memory; Good Time Boy;
Broken Arrow; Bluebird.* LAST TIME AROUND (7/68): *Uno
Mundo; On the Way Home; It's So Hard to Wait; Pretty Girl
Why; Four Days Gone; Carefree Country Day; Special Care; In
the Hour of Not Quite Rain; Questions; I Am a Child; Merry Go
Round; Kind Woman.* THE BEST OF BUFFALO SPRING-
FIELD (1/69): *For What It's Worth; Sit Down, I Think I Love
You; Nowadays Clancy Can't Even Sing; Go and Say Goodbye; Pay
the Price; Burned; Out of My Mind; Mr. Soul; Bluebird; Broken
Arrow; Rock 'n' Roll Woman; Expecting to Fly; Hung Upside
Down; A Child's Claim to Fame; Kind Woman; On the Way Home;
I Am a Child; Pretty Girl Why; Special Care; Uno Mundo; In the
Hour of Not Quite Rain; Four Days Gone; Questions.*

Singles/*Go and Say Goodbye/Nowadays Clancy Can't Even Sing*
(8/66); *Burned/Everybody's Wrong* (10/66); *Do I Have to Come
Right Out and Say It/For What It's Worth* (12/66); *Bluebird/Mr.
Soul* (6/67); *Child's Claim to Fame/Rock 'n' Roll Woman* (9/67);
Expecting to Fly/Everydays (12/67); *Four Days Gone/Uno Mundo*
(3/68); *On the Way Home/Four Days Gone (9/68).*

PAUL BUTTERFIELD/Chicago-born Paul Butterfield almost
single-handedly spearheaded a white blues revival in the United
States in the 1960s. In 1965, when folk started going electric and
Dylan was upsetting a few folks by plugging in, Butterfield made
his own bid to shake the rafters of popular music by introducing
a blues-rock outfit, the all-electrified Paul Butterfield Blues Band.
Their debut album on Elektra records startled quite a few music
people, including executives at the label (it was the first *non*-folk
album, first electrified funk album the company ever produced).

The band (Butterfield, Mike Bloomfield on guitar, Elvin
Bishop on guitar, Sam Lay on drums, Jerome Arnold on bass and
soon, Mark Naftalin on piano) took blues-capital Chicago by
storm. Their second album, *EAST-WEST,* was a classic of that
decade, establishing the Blues Band as a perfect counterpoint for

the psychedelic era and vaulting Bloomfield into the guitar-super-
star spotlight. The popularity of the band mushroomed, although
they never cracked the singles market. They were respected by
rock, blues, and folk fans and were a big concert draw.

In 1966, Butterfield shook up a few fans by reshuffling his
members. Bloomfield had departed to try his hand at the Electric
Flag. Soon, Butterfield, Bishop, and Naftalin were the only original members left in the fold. A horn section (Gene Dinwiddie,
Dave Sanborn, and Keith Johnson) was added. Phil Wilson took
over drums and Bugsy Maugh assumed bass responsibilities.
From that point onward, the Blues Band showed much erraticism
and not much spark until its demise in 1971. Prior to its final note,
the Blues Band included such musicians as Billy Davenport
(drums), Buzzy Feiten (guitar), Rod Hicks (bass, cello, vocals),
Steve Madaio (trumpet), Big Black (congas), Ralph Wash (guitar,
vocals), Dennis Whitted (drums), George Davidson (drums),
Fred Beckmier (bass), Trevor Lawrence (sax), and Ted Harris
(keyboards). With the Blues Band behind him, Butterfield embarked on a new career.

Moving to Woodstock, New York, Paul joined the embryonic
Bearsville label and formed a fairly innocuous outfit, Better Days.
Never coming close to living up to their name, the group recorded
two albums before collapsing. Butterfield has since gone on to a
solo career, one of the best-kept secrets of rock and roll.

Albums/PAUL BUTTERFIELD BLUES BAND (10/65): *Born
in Chicago; Shake Your Money-Maker; Blues with a Feeling;
Thank You, Mr. Poohbah; I Got My Mojo Working; Mellow Down
Easy; Screamin'; Our Love Is Drifting; Mystery Train; Last Night;
Look Over Yonder Wall.* EAST-WEST (8/66): *East-West; Walk-
in' Blues; Get Out of My Life, Woman; I Got a Mind to Give Up
Living; All These Blues; Work Song; Mary, Mary; Two Trains
Running; Never Say No.* RESURRECTION OF PIGBOY
CRABSHAW (11/67): *One More Heartache; Driftin' and Drif-
tin'; Run Out of Time; Pity the Fool; Born under a Bad Sign;
Double Trouble; Drivin' Wheel; Droppin' Out; Tollin' Bells.* IN
MY OWN DREAM (7/68): *Last Hope's Gone; Mine to Love;
Just to Be with You; Get Yourself Together; Morning Blues; Drunk
Again; In My Own Dream.* KEEP ON MOVING (10/69): *Love
March; No Amount of Loving; Morning Sunrise; Losing Hand;
Walking by Myself; Except You; Love Disease; Where Did My*

Baby Go; All in a Day; So Far, So Good; Buddy's Advice; Keep On Moving. LIVE (12/70): *Everything's Going to Be Alright; Love Disease; The Boxer; No Amount of Loving; Driftin' and Driftin'; Intro; Number Nine; I Want to Be with You; Born under a Bad Sign; Get Together Again; So Far, So Good.* SOMETIMES I JUST FEEL LIKE SMILING (8/71). GOLDEN BUTTER (4/72): *Born in Chicago; Shake Your Money-Maker; Mellow Down Easy; Our Love Is Drifting; Mystery Train; Look Over Yonder Wall; East-West; Walking Blues; Get Out of My Life, Woman; Mary, Mary; Spoonful; One More Heartache; Last Hope's Gone; In My Own Dream; Love March; Driftin' and Driftin'; Blind Leading the Blind.* BETTER DAYS (12/72): *Walkin' Blues; Broke My Baby's Heart; Buried Alive in the Blues; Highway 28; Done a Lot of Wrong Things; Rule the Road; Nobody's Fault but Mine; Baby, Please Don't Go; Please Send Me Someone to Love.* IT ALL COMES BACK (10/73): *It's Getting Harder to Survive; If You Like; Win or Lose; Small Town Talk; It All Comes Back; Louisiana Flood; Poor Boy; Take Your Pleasure Where You Can; New Walking Blues.* PUT IT IN YOUR EAR (2/76): *Here I Go Again; I Don't Wanna Go; Day to Day; The Breadline; Ain't That a Lot of Love; The Flame; other titles.*

Singles/*I Got a Mind to Give Up Living/Come On In* (11/66); *New Walkin' Blues* (2/73).

THE BYRDS/*Original members: Roger McGuinn (guitar, lead vocals), Gene Clark (guitar, vocals), Chris Hillman (bass), Mike Clark (drums), David Crosby (guitar, vocals). Additional members: Kevin Kelly (drums), Gram Parsons (guitar, keyboards, vocals), Sneeky Pete (pedal steel), Doug Dillard (banjo on London '68 tour), Gene Parsons (drums, vocals), John York (bass, vocals), Clarence White (lead guitar, vocals), Skip Battin (bass, vocals), John Guerin (drums).*

Until the Byrds came along, the very notion of a group of folk singers strengthening their sound with rock devices was unthinkable. Folk was highminded, pure, and untouched by sordid commercial values. Rock was something you played for a quick buck. The most important thing the Byrds ever did was to recognize that rock could revitalize folk—with a finished product that was considerably more than the sum of its parts. Folk rock was officially born with the Byrds' early 1965 version of Dylan's *Mr.*

Tambourine Man, the classic model for ten thousand imitations that year as folk rock swept the West before snowballing toward the East. The Byrds were the first of the *thinking* musicians. And they were articulate at a time when the best that the Beatles could muster was a string of funny but not necessarily profound one-liners. The Byrds were the best innovators around. Folk and rock! It changed the face of American music and put them on the charts in a way that no one in the business had believed possible. At an early 1966 concert in New York, they were as mobbed and screamed over as the Beatles.

After the Byrds, it no longer was odd to find someone like poet Allen Ginsberg backstage at a rock concert, and when they opened at New York's Village Gate, Norman Mailer and Timothy Leary were among the ringsiders. The Byrds were not only musical. They were political and mystical. Later, acid rock would become commonplace. But the Byrds were the first acid rockers, the first head rockers, the first message rockers, the first outer-space rockers and the first country rockers. It was no wonder that, by the time everyone else had caught up with them in the late sixties, they had reverted back to the country sound that had been in the music from the start. From the outset, the quality that marked the Byrds as quite, quite different from the Beatles' imitators was a twangy, uniquely American country feel. No one since has been able to capture that feel, any more than they could capture the distinctive jangle of McGuinn's twelve-string Rickenbacker.

Everyone knew that the Byrds were one of the all-time great groups, but destiny was not in on the plan and a series of personnel changes constantly kept the band earthbound. They were five until Gene Clark left. Early in 1966, the foursome arrived in New York with a sound that was newer than folk-rock: raga-rock (although they cringed at that label). Dave Crosby came up with the idea of using sitar in rock and the whole craze began. Their *Eight Miles High* was immediately banned as a drug song (the Byrds said it was about jet planes). Their opening gig at the Village Gate during that period was the first light show in Manhattan. It gave the audience headaches. By March of '67, the American music scene was finally jumping and, in some ways, the innovative Byrds were being left behind. Their songs looked back in anger: *So You Want to Be a Rock and Roll Star* was downright caustic in a summer of good vibes and body paint.

During the '67–'68 period, their first wave of success receded. Mike Clarke and Crosby left. Gram Parsons eventually joined, bringing with him the spirit of sweet country music. By the time *DR. BYRDS AND MR. HYDE* rolled around, however, the only original Byrd left was McGuinn (Hillman and Parsons were with the Flying Burritos and Crosby was forming Crosby, Stills and Nash). Still, McGuinn carried on. Regrouping, rethinking. *THE BALLAD OF EASY RIDER* provided the Byrds with a needed shot in the arm. Skip Battin joined up for *UNTITLED* and the Byrds, once again, began to grow leaden. *FARTHER ALONG* and *BYRDMANIAX* were out-and-out duds and Roger, at last, saw the light. After a long and fruitful career, McGuinn and his last Byrds band called it quits. The lure of potential superstardom, however, reunited the original troupe in 1973 for what turned out to be an egomaniacal excursion that offered more unrealized potential than actual musical accomplishment. The group broke up (again). McGuinn then embarked on a rocky solo flight, leaving the history of the Byrds behind. As unstable as they were, the Byrds, in all of their various guises, had set the pace for country rock and, either directly (via former Byrds) or indirectly (via influence), caused the birth of such other folk-rock-countrified bands as Crosby, Stills and Nash, the Dillard and Clark Band, the Flying Burrito Brothers, the New Riders of the Purple Sage, and the Eagles.

Albums/MR. TAMBOURINE MAN (8/65): *Mr. Tambourine Man; You Won't Have to Cry; I'll Feel a Whole Lot Better; Here without You; Spanish Harlem Incident; Bells of Rhymney; All I Really Want to Do; I Knew I'd Want You; It's No Use; Don't Doubt Yourself, Babe; Chimes of Freedom; We'll Meet Again.* TURN TURN TURN (2/66): *Turn, Turn, Turn,; It Won't Be Wrong; Set You Free This Time; Lay Down Your Weary Tune; He Was a Friend of Mine; World Turns All Around Her; Satisfied Mind; If You're Gone; Times They Are a-Changin'; Wait and See.* FIFTH DIMENSION (9/66): *5D; Wild Mountain Thyme; Mr. Spaceman; I See You; What's Happening; I Come and Stand at Every Door; Eight Miles High; Hey Joe; Captain Soul; John Riley; 2-4-2 Fox Trot.* YOUNGER THAN YESTERDAY (4/67): *So You Want to Be a Rock and Roll Star; My Back Pages; Have You*

Seen Her Face; Why; C.T.A.-102; Renaissance Fair; Time Between; Mind Gardens; Girl with No Name; Thoughts and Words; Everybody's Been Burned. BYRDS' GREATEST HITS (10/67): *Mr. Tambourine Man; I'll Feel a Whole Lot Better; Bells of Rhymney; Turn, Turn, Turn; All I Really Want to Do; Mr. Spaceman; So You Want to Be a Rock and Roll Star; Eight Miles High; Chimes of Freedom; My Back Pages; 5D.* NOTORIOUS BYRD BROTHERS (3/68): *Goin' Back; Artificial Energy; Natural Harmony; Draft Morning; Wasn't Born to Follow; Get to You; Change Is Now; Old John Robertson; Tribal Gathering; Dolphins' Smile; Space Odyssey.* SWEETHEART OF THE RODEO (11/68): *You Ain't Going Nowhere; I Am a Pilgrim; Christian Life; You Don't Miss Your Water; You're Still on My Mind; Pretty Boy Floyd; Hickory Wind; One Hundred Years from Now; Blue Canadian Rockies; Life in Prison; Nothing Was Delivered.* DR. BYRDS AND MR. HYDE (2/69): *This Wheel's on Fire; Old Blue; Your Gentle Way of Loving Me; Child of the Universe; Nashville West; Drug Store Truck Drivin' Man; King Apathy III; Candy; Bad Night at the Whiskey; My Back Pages-B. J. Blues-Baby, What Do You Want Me to Do.* BALLAD OF EASY RIDER (10/69): *The Ballad of Easy Rider; Fido; Oil in My Lamp; Tulsa County; Jack Tarr the Sailor; Jesus Is Just Alright; It's All Over Now, Baby Blue; There Must Be Someone; Gunga Din; Deportee; Armstrong, Aldrin and Collins.* UNTITLED (9/70): *Lover of the Bayou; Positively 4th Street; Nashville West; So You Wanna Be a Rock and Roll Star; Mr. Tambourine Man; Hey, Mr. Spaceman; Chestnut Mare; Truck Stop Girl; All the Things; Yesterday's Train; Take a Whiff; You All Look Alike; Well Come Back Home; Hungry Planet.* BYRDMANIAX (6/71): *Glory, Glory; Pale Blue; I Trust; Tunnel of Love; Citizen Kane; I Wanna Grow Up to Be a Politician; Absolute Happiness; Green Apple Quick Step; My Destiny; Kathleen's Song; Jamaica Say You Will.* FARTHER ALONG (11/71): *Tiffany Queen; Get Down Your Line; Farther Along; BB Class Road; So Fine; Lazy Waters; Bristol Steam Convention Blues; Burglar; Antique Sandy; America's Great National Pastime; Precious Kate.* GREATEST HITS II (10/72): *The Ballad of Easy Rider; Wasn't Born to Follow; Jesus Is Just Alright; He Was a Friend of Mine; Chestnut Mare; Tiffany Queen; Drug Store Truck Drivin' Man; You Ain't Goin Nowhere; Citizen Kane; I Wanna Grow Up to Be a Politician.* THE BYRDS (3/73): *Full*

Circle; Sweet Mary; Changing Heart; For Free; Born to Rock and Roll; Things Will Be Better; Cowgirl in the Sand; Long Live the King; Borrowing Time; Laughing; Seè the Sky About to Rain. PREFLYTE (7/73): *You Showed Me; Here Without You; She Has a Way; The Reason Why; For Me Again; You Movin; Boston; The Airport Song; You Won't Have to Cry; I Knew I'd Want You; Mr. Tambourine Man.*

Singles/*Mr. Tambourine Man*/*I Knew I'd Want You* (4/65); *All I Really Want to Do*/*I'll Feel a Whole Lot Better* (6/65); *Turn, Turn, Turn*/*She Don't Care About You* (10/65); *Set You Free This Time*/*I Want to Be Wrong* (1/66); *Mr. Tambourine Man*/*All I Really Want to Do* (3/66); *Eight Miles High*/*Why* (3/66); *Mr. Spaceman*/*What's Happening* (4/66); *5D*/*Captain Soul* (6/66); *So You Wanna Be a Rock and Roll Star*/*Everybody's Been Burned* (1/67); *Back Pages*/*Renaissance Fair* (3/67); *Lady Friend; Old John Robertson* (7/67); *Going Back*/*Change Is Now* (10/67); *So You Wanna Be a Rock and Roll Star*/*My Back Pages* (12/67); *You Ain't Goin' Nowhere*/*Artificial Energy* (4/68); *I Am a Pilgrim*/*Pretty Boy Floyd* (9/68); *Drug Store Truck Drivin' Man*/*Bad Night at the Whiskey* (1/69); *Lay Lady Lay*/*Old Blue* (5/69); *Ballad Of Easy Rider*/*Wasn't Born to Follow* (10/69); *Jesus Is Just Alright*/*It's All Over Now, Baby Blue* (12/69); *Chestnut Mare*/*Just a Season* (10/70); *Glory, Glory*/*Citizen Kane* (8/71); *America's Great National Pastime*/*Farther Along* (11/71); *Full Circle*/*Long Live the King* (3/73); *Cowgirl in the Sand*/*Long Live the King* (5/73).*

CACTUS/*Tim Bogert (bass, vocals), Rusty Day (vocals, harmonica), Jim McCarty (guitar), Carmine Appice (guitar, vocals). Other members: Duane Hitchings (keyboards, vocals), Roland Robinson (bass, vocals), Mike Pinera (guitar, vocals), Jerry Norris (drums, vocals).*
One of the most unintentionally hysterical bands ever to arise from the ashes of the sixties, Cactus was an attempt by two ex–Vanilla Fudgers (Bogert and Appice) to carry on in the thunder-thudding tradition of rock and roll with an all-out hard rock group. The original Cactus sound was something of a cross between your average heavy metal outfit and the LaBrea tar pits. With numbers slowed in tempo to the point of catatonia and instrumentation searing through the leaden beats like red-hot bul-

lets, Cactus proved to be a mild success at best for the fresh-faced fans of the seventies. The group splintered, regrouped, and splintered again before reforming as The New Cactus Band in 1973 with none of the original foursome within the ranks.

Albums/CACTUS (6/70): *Parchman Farm; My Lady from South of Detroit; Bro. Bill; You Can't Judge a Book by Its Cover; Let Me Swim; No Need to Worry; Oleo; Feel So Good.* ONE WAY . . . OR ANOTHER (2/71): *Rockout, Whatever You Feel Like; Rock 'n' Roll Children; Big Mama's Boogie (Parts I and II); Hometown Bust; One Way . . . or Another; Long Tall Sally; Song for Aries; Feel So Bad.* NO RESTRICTIONS (9/71): *Restrictions; Token Chokin'; Guiltless Glider; Evil; Alaska; Sweet Sixteen; Bag Drag; Mean Night in Cleveland.* OT 'N' SWEATY (8/72): *Bad Mother Boogie; Our Li'l Rock-n-Roll Thing; Bad Stuff; Swim; Bringing Me Down; Bedroom Mazurka; Telling You; Underneath the Arches.* SON OF CACTUS (4/73): *It's Getting Better; I Can't Wait; Hook, Line and Sinker; It's Just a Feelin'; Lady; Ragtime Suzy; Blue Gypsy Woman; Senseless Rebel; Man Is a Boy; Daddy Ain't Gone; Hold On to My Love.*

CANNED HEAT/*Adolfo De La Parra (drums), Bob "The Bear" Hite (lead vocals), Larry Taylor (bass), Henry Vestine (lead guitar), Alan "Blind Owl" Wilson (guitar, vocals). Additional members: Gene Taylor (keyboards), Joel Scott Hill (guitar), Frank Cook (drums), Harvey Mandel (guitar), Antonio De La Barreda (bass), Richard Hite (guitar).*
Canned Heat was one of the most erratic, enjoyable surprises to emerge from 1967's Monterey Pop Festival. Formed in 1966, the California group specialized in blues and blues alone. The original troupe (Hite, Wilson, Cook, Vestine and Taylor) recorded their most successful album blues-wise, *CANNED HEAT,* in 1967. Their biggest commercial success proved to be the single *On the Road Again* pulled from that album a year after its release.

By 1968, personnel changes in the band were already going on. Canned Heat never quite made it to superstar status, although everyone in the world respected Blind Owl Wilson, the soft-spoken bluesologist who sang like an angel and played a mean harmonica and guitar. Blind Owl died in September of 1970, setting the stage for the stagnation of Canned Heat.

Albums following his death lacked spirit and, with a family of musicians that came and went on a revolving-door basis, it wasn't long before Canned Heat dissolved.

Albums/CANNED HEAT (8/67): *Rollin' and Tumblin'; Bullfrog Blues; Evil Is Going On; Goin' Down Slow; Catfish Blues; Dust My Broom; Help Me; Big Road Blues; The Story of My Life; The Road Song; Rich Woman.* BOOGIE WITH CANNED HEAT (1/68): *Evil Woman; My Crime; On the Road Again; World in a Jug; Turpentine Moan; Whiskey-Headed Woman No. 2; Amphetamine Annie; An Owl Song; Marie Laveau; Fried Hockey Boogie.* LIVIN' THE BLUES (10/68): *Pony Blues; My Mistake; Sandy's Blues; One Kind Favor; Going Up The Country; Walking by Myself; Boogie Music; Parthenogenesis; Refried Boogie (2 Parts).* HALLELUJAH (7/69). VINTAGE (11/69). COOK BOOK (11/69): *On the Road Again; Amphetamine Annie; Going Up the Country; Rollin' and Tumblin'; other titles.* FUTURE BLUES (8/70): *Sugar Bee; Shake It and Break It; That's All Right, Mama; My Time Ain't Long; Skat; Let's Work Together; London Blues; So Sad (The World's in a Tangle); Future Blues.* CANNED HEAT CONCERT RECORDED LIVE IN EUROPE (6/71). LIVING THE BLUES (9/71). HISTORICAL FIGURES AND ANCIENT HEADS (2/72). NEW AGE (1973). ONE MORE RIVER TO CROSS (1/74): *One More River to Cross; L.A. Town; I Need Someone; Bagful of Boogie; I'm a Hog for You, Baby; You Am What You Am; Bright Times Are Comin'; Shake, Rattle and Roll; Highway 401; We Remember Fats (medley).* THE VERY BEST OF CANNED HEAT (1975): *Going Up the Country; Bullfrog Blues; Refried Boogie Part I; Let's Work Together; An Owl Song; On the Road Again; Amphetamine Annie; Change My Ways; Rollin' and Tumblin'.*

Singles/*Rollin' and Tumblin' Bullfrog Blues* (6/67); *Evil Woman/World in a Jug* (10/67); *On the Road Again/Boogie Music* (4/68); *One Kind Favor/Going Up the Country* (12/68); *Time Was* (2/69); *Let's Work Together* (9/70); *Rockin' with the King* (2/72); *One More River to Cross/Highway 401* (1/74); *The Harder They Come/Rock 'n' Roll Show* (12/74).

THE CAPTAIN AND TENNILLE/The rise to stardom for Toni Tennille and Daryl Dragon, collectively known as the Captain and Tennille, is nothing short of a pop overnight miracle. The husband and wife duo first met during a run of *Mother Earth,* a rock ecology musical presented by the South Coast Repertory Theatre in San Francisco. Toni, an Alabama-born file clerk turned vocalist, was a cast member and Daryl a member of the house band. Dragon, the son of conductor Carmen Dragon, was an L.A. sessionman who toured once or twice with the Beach Boys. After their fateful meeting, Toni and Daryl *both* toured with the aforementioned kings of Hollywood surf. During the tour, Daryl, the possessor of a truly nifty captain's hat, was christened "Captain Keyboard" by Beach Boy Mike Love. The name stuck and, after the tour, Daryl and Toni teamed up, calling themselves the Captain and Tennille. (Quite logical when you think about it.) Fate intervened via A&M Records who brought the up-and-coming pair a Neil Sedaka tune to record, *Love Will Keep Us Together.* The song not only kept them together, it won them a Grammy in 1975 as Record of the Year, selling over 2 ½ million copies worldwide and earning the pair a shot at a nationwide television series. After a few years of the usual bar and sleezoid club circuit, the Captain and Tennille found themselves major pop stars. Bemused and more than a little bit stunned, the twosome went on to record such top-tenning singles as *The Way I Want to Touch You, Muskrat Love,* and *Come In from the Rain.*

Albums/LOVE WILL KEEP US TOGETHER (5/75): *Love Will Keep Us Together; Disney Girls; The Way I Want to Touch You; Cuddle Up; The Good Songs; God Only Knows; Honey Come Love Me; Broddy Bounce; Gentle Stranger; I Write the Songs.* POR AMOR VIVIREMOS (1/76): *Por Amor Viviremos; Mi Mundo Irreal; Como Yo Quiero; Sentirte; Vivir Asi; Mis Canciones; Lo Sabe Dios; No Te Levantes; Sentir Senor; El Rebote de Broddy; Dulce Extrano; Es la Cancion.* SONG OF JOY (2/76): *Song of Joy; Lonely Night; Smile for Me One More Time; Shop Around; Going Bananas; Butterscotch Castle; Muskrat Love; Thank You, Baby; Wedding Song; 1954 Boogie Blues; Mind Your Love.* COME IN FROM THE RAIN (3/77): *Come In from the Rain; Sad Eyes; Let Mama Know; Easy Evil; Can't Stop Dancin'; Don't Be Scared; Circles; Ladybug; Happier Than the Morning Sun; Ka-Ding-Dong; We Never Really Say Goodbye.* GREATEST HITS (11/77): *Love Will Keep Us Together; The Way I Want to Touch You; Shop Around; Lonely Nights; Muskrat Love; Circles; Come In from the Rain; I Write the Songs; Disney Girls; Can't Stop Dancin'; We Never Really Say Goodbye.*

Singles/*The Way I Want to Touch You*/*Disney Girls* (9/74); *Love Will Keep Us Together*/*Gentle Stranger* (2/75); *Por Amor Viviremos*/*Dulce Extrano* (7/75); *The Way I Want to Touch You*/*Broddy Bounce* (9/75); *Sentirte*/*El Rebote de Broddy* (12/75); *Lonely Nights*/*Smile for Me One More Time* (1/76); *Shop Around*/*Butterscotch Castle* (4/76); *Muskrat Love*/*Honey Come Love Me* (9/76); *Can't Stop Dancing*/*Mis Canciones* (3/77); *Come In from the Rain*/*We Never Really Say Goodbye* (5/77); *Circles*/*1954 Boogie Blues* (8/77).

THE CARPENTERS/The original exponents of "tooth power," smiling Karen and Richard Carpenter almost singlehandedly revolutionized AM radio with their fresh-as-a-daisy pop antics in the early seventies. *We've Only Just Begun, Close to You, Top of the World,* and *Solitaire* are only a few of the tunes that have led the duo to more than thirty million singles and albums sold, three Grammy Awards, seventeen gold records, and thousands of packed concerts throughout the world.

Born in New Haven, Connecticut, the borther-and-sister team started their musical careers when still in their teens. Richard began studying piano at the age of twelve, increasing his knowledge at Yale, where he enrolled at the age of sixteen. While in high school, Karen began futzing with a drum kit. The two plucky teens joined with friend and bassist Wes Jacobs and formed a jazz trio that placed first in a Hollywood Bowl Battle of the Bands. The Carpenter family, who had recently moved to Downey, California, where Richard continued his musical education at U.S.C. and Cal State, found themselves faced with two semi-professional musicians. Richard and Karen then formed Spectrum, a six-piece pop-rock ensemble that enraged hard rock fans throughout California.

The group disbanded, and Karen and Richard recorded a demo-tape with an overdubbed nature that would soon be a trademark of the Carpenters. The tape found its way to A&M's Herb Alpert who, offering the duo both encouragement and a contract, unleashed the spic-and-span Carpenters on an unsuspecting world. Karen's voice has become a trademark, as has Richard's amazing musical arrangements. In an oft-quoted remark, Richard credits his musical influences as "the three B's: the Beach Boys, the Beatles, and Burt Bacharach."

Albums/ TICKET TO RIDE (11/69): *Invocation; Your Wonderful Parade; Someday; Get Together; All of My Life; Turn Away; Ticket to Ride; Don't Be Afraid; What's the Use; All I Can Do; Eve; Nowadays Clancy Can't Even Sing; Benediction.* CLOSE TO YOU (8/70): *We've Only Just Begun; Love Is Surrender; Maybe It's You; Reason to Believe; Help; Close to You; Baby, It's You; I'll Never Fall in Love Again; Crescent Moon; Mr. Guder; I Kept On Loving You; Another Song.* CARPENTERS (5/71): *Rainy Days and Mondays; Saturday; Let Me Be the One; Hideaway; For All We Know; Superstar; Druscilla Penny; One Love; Bacharach-David medley: Knowing When to Leave, Make It Easy on Yourself, Always Something There to Remind Me, I'll Never Fall in Love Again, Walk On By, Do You Know the Way to San Jose.* A SONG FOR YOU (6/72): *A Song for You; Top of the World; Hurting Each Other; It's Going to Take Some Time; Goodbye to Love; Intermission; Bless the Beasts and Children; Flat Baroque; Piano Picker; I Won't Last a Day without You; Crystal Lullaby; Road Ode; A Song for You (Reprise).* NOW AND THEN (5/73): *Sing; This Masquerade; Heather; Jambalaya; I Can't Make Music; Yesterday Once More; medley: Fun, Fun, Fun, The End of the World, Da Doo Ron Ron, Deadman's Curve, Johnny Angel, The Night Has a Thousand Eyes, Our Day Will Come, One Fine Day; Yesterday Once More (reprise).* THE SINGLES 1969–1973 (11/73): *We've Only Just Begun; Top of the World; Ticket to Ride; Superstar; Rainy Days and Mondays; Goodbye to Love; Yesterday Once More; It's Going to Take Some Time; Sing; For All We Know; Hurting Each Other; Close to You.* HORIZON (6/75): *Aurora; Only Yesterday; Desperado; Please, Mr. Postman; I Can Dream, Can't I; Solitaire; Happy; Goodbye and I Love You; Love Me for What I Am; Eventide.* A KIND OF HUSH (6/76): *There's a Kind of Hush; You; Sandy; Goofus; Can't Smile without You; I Need to Be in Love; One More Time; Boat to Sail; I Have You; Breaking Up Is Hard to Do.* PASSAGE (9/77): *B'wana She No Home; All You Get from Love Is a Love Song; I Just Fall in Love Again; On the Balcony of the Casa Rosada—Don't Cry for Me, Argentina; Sweet, Sweet Smile; Two Sides; Man Smart, Woman Smarter; Calling Occupants of Interplanetary Craft.*

Singles/ *Ticket to Ride* (11/69); *I Kept on Loving You* (5/70); *We've Only Just Begun* (8/70); *Merry Christmas, Darling* (11/70);

For All We Know (1/71); *Rainy Days and Mondays* (4/71); *Super-star* (8/71); *Hurtin' Each Other* (12/71); *It's Going to Take Some Time* (4/72); *Goodbye to Love* (6/72); *Sing* (1/73); *Yesterday Once More* (5/73); *Top of the World* (9/73); *I Won't Last a Day without You* (3/74); *Please, Mr. Postman* (11/74); *Santa Claus Is Coming to Town* (11/74); *Only Yesterday* (3/75); *Solitaire* (7/75); *There's a Kind of Hush* (2/76); *I Need to Be in Love* (5/76); *Goofus* (8/76); *All You Get from Love Is a Love Song* (5/77); *Calling Occupants of Interplanetary Craft* (9/77).

CHAD AND JEREMY/How could two polite, well-bred, long-haired, lean-faced English gentlemen with nice California tans possibly go wrong with the fans in that early 1964 post-Beatle period when just to be English was practically all you needed for a number-one record? (Relax, they didn't go wrong . . . it would have taken them years even if they had tried to mess up.) Their second album was still English but mixed with Dylan and folk rock; and how could you go wrong with *that* in the fall of '65 when the strains of *Mr. Tambourine Man* were heard everywhere from concert halls to manholes? By 1966, Chad Stuart and Jeremy Clyde were well established in a style they would later dismiss as Muzak. During their Muzak period, their sound was Beatles-Everly harmonies with Byrds-Beach Boys overtones, exactly what California teenyboppers wanted from these two tame Eng-lishmen. And tame they were, hitting the talk show circuit and staring incredulously at Merv Griffin as they spoke in awe of the recorded no-no's they despised, i.e., the Stones' *Let's Spend the Night Together.* ("But surely they mean they're married, right?" said Merv in shock, fondly remembering a bunch, *any* bunch of coconuts.) Then, in 1967, came the realization that there had to be more to life than this, or at least that's the way Chad & Jeremy explained it afterwards. The Beatles had just unleashed *SER-GEANT PEPPER,* so Chad and Jeremy put out *their* serious album, *OF CABBAGES AND KINGS,* with most of the songs by Jeremy, arrangement and scoring by Chad, and an entire side de-voted to a five-movement *Progress Suite.* The critics marveled. My goodness, there certainly was more to Chad and Jeremy than *Muzak!* Hot on the heels of this musical breakthrough, Chad and Jeremy retired. Life sometimes is like that.

Albums/BEFORE AND AFTER (5/64): *Before and After; Why*

Should I Care; For Lovin' Me; I'm in Love Again; Little Does She Know; Tell Me Baby; What Do You Want to Know. I DON'T WANNA LOSE YOU BABY (9/65): *I Don't Want to Lose You Baby; Should I; Mr. Tambourine Man; Girl Who Sang the Blues; Funny How Love Can Be; The Woman in You; I Have Dreamed; Don't Think Twice, It's All Right; Baby Don't Go; There but for Fortune; These Things You Don't Forget.* THE BEST OF CHAD AND JEREMY (3/66): *Summer Song; What Do You Want with Me; Too Soon; Only Those in Love; Like I Love You Today; If I Loved You; Willow Weep for Me; My, How the Time Goes By; Yesterday's Gone; If You've Got a Heart; From a Window.* MORE CHAD AND JEREMY (6/66): *September in the Rain; Girl from Ipanema; It was a Very Good Year; Lemon Tree; No Tears for Johnny; Truth Often Hurts the Heart; Dirty Old Town; My Coloring Book; Four Strong Winds; Now and Forever; Donna, Donna.* DISTANT SHORES (8/66): *Distant Shores; Ain't It Nice; Homeward Bound; The Way You Look Tonight; Morning; You Are She; Everyone's Gone to the Moon; I Won't Cry; Early Morning Rain; Don't Make Me Do It.* CABBAGES AND KINGS (9/67): *Rest in Peace; Gentle Cold of Dawn; Busman's Holiday; Can I See You; Family Way; I'll Get Around to It When and If I Can; Progress Suite (five movements).* THE ARK (9/68): *The Emancipation of Mr. X; Sunstroke; The Ark; The Raven; Imagination; Painted Dayglow Smile; Pipe Dream; Transatlantic Trauma; Sidewalk Requiem; Los Angeles, June Fifth and Sixth; Pantheistic Study for Guitar and Large Bird; Paxton Quigley's Had the Course; You Need Feet (you Need Hands).* CHAD AND JEREMY (9/69): *Mr. Tambourine Man; Homeward Bound; Early Morning Rain; Pipe Dream; Say It Isn't True; I Won't Cry; These Things You Don't Forget; I Have Dreamed; Should I.*

Singles/*Before and After/Fare Thee Well* (4/65); *I Don't Wanna Lose You Baby/Pennies* (7/65); *Teenage Failures/Early Morning Rain* (7/65); *I Have Dreamed/Should I* (9/65); *Distant Shores/Last Night* (6/66); *Summer Song/Willow Weep for Me* (7/66); *You Are She/I Won't Cry* (9/66); *Rest in Peace/The Family Way* (5/67); *Painted Dayglow Smile/Editorial* (11/67); *Sister Marie/Rest in Peace* (4/68); *You Need Feet (You Need Hands)/Paxton Quigley's Had the Course* (10/68).

THE CHAMBERS BROTHERS/ *George Chambers (bass),*

Willie Chambers (guitar, vocals), Joe Chambers (guitar, vocals),
Brian Keenan (drums), Lester Chambers (percussion, vocals).

An explosive soul-rock group that became a musical mainstay
of the sixties New York discotheque circuit, the Chambers
Brothers band was one of the first black units to attain status in
the hard rock field (pre-dating Sly and the Family Stone). At the
height of their popularity, the band was composed of four black
musicians and one white drummer. Mississippi-born and -bred,
the Chambers Brothers went professional in 1961 as a gospel entourage and continued doing inspirational music until 1965. Unlike most gospel groups, the Chambers boys played all their own
instruments (they added a drummer when they discovered that
they were too busy playing to have time for the traditional hand-
clapping.) Their main claim to fame, *Time Has Come Today,* was
described by one critic as Afro-psychedelic-rock, and featured
screaming electric guitars and an African cowbell. It ran from
fifteen to thirty minutes when performed live, eleven on their
chart-busting album. (*Time Has Come Today,* by the way, was
one of the first tunes to fall into the FM radio "album
version"/"AM version" snob-appeal category. One of the big
pluses of the then-embryonic FM radio world was to advertise the
fact that FM djs played only the "album"—or long—versions of
hit songs, as opposed to the shorty AM-oriented edits.) The instant hysteria created by *Time Has Come Today* was never quite
equaled by the Chambers Brothers, and they eventually succumbed to post-sixties arthritis, changing members frequently
and getting more and more repetitive with each ensuing album.
After being dropped by one major label, the band soon disappeared into the ranks of small-label rosterdom.

Albums/NOW: *High Heel Sneakers; Baby Please Don't Go;*
What'd I Say; Long Tall Sally; Bony Baronie; It's Groovin' Time;
You Don't Have to Go; See See Rider; So Fine. PEOPLE GET
READY (1967): *People Get Ready; Call Me; Hook Tooka; Yes,*
Yes, Yes; Tore Up; Reconsider Baby; You've Got Me Running;
Money; You Can Run; Summertime; Your Old Lady; It's All Over
Now. TIME HAS COME TODAY (10/67): *All Strung Out over*
You; People Get Ready; I Can't Stand It; Romeo and Juliet; In the
Midnight Hour; So Tired; Uptown; Please Don't Leave Me; What
the World Needs Now Is Love; Time Has Come Today. SHOUT
(9/68): *Johnny B. Goode; Blues Get off My Shoulder; I Got It;*

Shout; There She Goes; Seventeen; Pretty Girls; Rain the Day You Left; So Fine; Love Me Like the Rain. NEW TIME—A NEW DAY *(10/68): I Can't Turn You Loose; Guess Who; Do Your Thing; Where Have All the Flowers Gone; Love Is All I Have; You Got the Power—to Turn Me On; I Wish It Would Rain; Rock Me Mama; No, No, No, Don't Say Goodby; Satisfy You; A New Time —A New Day.* LOVE, PEACE AND HAPPINESS (11/69): *Have a Little Faith; Let's Do It; To Love Somebody; If You Want Me to; Wake Up; Love, Peace and Happiness (three movements); Wade in the Water; Everybody Needs Somebody; I Can't Turn You Loose; People Get Ready; Bang Bang; You're So Fine; medley: Undecided, Love, Love, Love.* NEW GENERATION (1/71): *Are You Ready; Young Girl; Funky; When the Evening Comes; Practice What You Preach; Reflections; Pollution; New Generation; Going to the Mill.* GREATEST HITS (10/71): *Funky; Midnight Hour; Time Has Come Today; I Can't Turn You Loose; People Get Ready; All Strung Out over You; Are You Ready; Let's Do It; Love, Peace and Happiness.* OH MY GOD! (1/72): *Mean Old World; Which Side of the Fence; Heaven; Any Old Time; Man Did It; Old Doggone Devil; This Little Piece of Land; Celebration of Life; By the Hair of My Chinny Chin Chin.* TIME HAS COME TODAY/A NEW TIME—A NEW DAY (9/75): re-issue in double-album form of two earlier albums.

Singles/ *All Strung Out over You/Falling in Love* (12/66); *I Can't Stand It/Summer Days and Summer Nights* (4/67); *Please Don't Leave Me/I Can't Stand It* (5/67); *Uptown/Love Me Like the Rain* (9/67); *Time Has Come Today/People Get Ready* (12/67); *Call Me/Seventeen; Pretty Girls Everywhere/Love Me Like the Rain* (1968); *Can't Turn You Loose/Do Your Thing* (10/68); *Shout Part I/Shout Part II* (11/68); *Time Has Come Today/Can't Turn You Loose* (2/69); *Are You Ready/You Got the Power* (2/69); *Wake Up/Everybody Needs Someone* (5/69); *Have a Little Faith/My Baby Takes Care of Business* (9/69); *Merry Christmas, Happy New Year/Did You Stop to Pray This Morning* (11/69); *Love, Peace and Happiness/If You Want Me To* (1/70); *Let's Do It/To Love Somebody.* (4/70); *Funky/Love, Peace and Happiness* (11/70); *New Generation/When the Evening Comes* (5/71); *By the Hair on My Chinny Chin Chin/Heaven* (10/71); *Merry Christmas, Happy New Year/Did You Stop to Pray This Morning* (11/71); *Boogie/You Make the Magic* (4/73).

HARRY CHAPIN/Harry Chapin's fans consider him the Faulkner of Pop. His critics, on the other hand, hear him as a cross between *Search for Tomorrow* and Merv Griffin. Chapin, who has gained fame in the United States as a painter of moody, if somewhat turgid, word pictures, began his musical career as an orthodox folkie. Turning from classical trumpet to acoustic guitar, he eventually grew good enough to join his brothers in a band called the Chapin Brothers. They caused a stir back in 1964 for being the first electric band to appear at the Bitter End in Manhattan. With the dawning of the Vietnam era, however, Chapins Tom and Steve saw the true value of a college education (as opposed to an all-expenses-paid, scenic tour of Hanoi) and went off in search of sheepskins. Strumming Harry was left as a solo. Abandoning music momentarily, Harry plunged headfirst into filmmaking, working on over three hundred productions in one capacity or another. A film he edited, wrote and directed, *Legendary Champions,* was nominated for an Oscar for Best Feature Documentary. In 1970, Tom and Steve Chapin, now educated, returned to the music world. Harry began writing for the reformed Chapin ensemble. His rekindled musical inklings, however, instilled in him the urge to go it alone. In 1971, he formed a backing band and made the rounds in New York. A contract with Elektra Records that fall was the end result. Harry's story-songs, beginning with *Taxi,* assured him a long career. His subsequent sketches, *WOLD, Cat's in the Cradle,* and *What Made America Famous?,* did wonders on the charts, establishing Harry as a force to be reckoned with in the realm of easy-listening rock.

Albums/HEADS AND TALES (2/72); *Could You Put Your Lights On, Please; Any Old Kind of Day; Dogtown; Same Sad Singer; Greyhound; Everybody's Lonely; Sometime, Somewhere Wife; Empty; Taxi.* SNIPER AND OTHER LOVE SONGS (9/72); *Sunday Morning Sunshine; Sniper; And the Baby Never Cries; Burning Herself; Barefoot Boy; Better Place to Be; Circle; Woman Child; Winter Song.* SHORT STORIES (11/73): *Short Stories; WOLD; Song for Myself; Song Man; Changes; They Call Her Easy; Mr. Tanner; Mail Order Annie; There's a Lot of Lonely People Tonight; Old College Avenue.* VERITIES AND BALDERDASH (8/74): *Cat's in the Cradle; I Wanna Learn a Love Song; Shining Star; 30,000 Pounds of Bananas; She Sings Songs without Words; What Made America Famous?; Vacancy;*

Halfway to Heaven; Six String Orchestra. PORTRAIT GAL-
LERY (9/75): *The Rock; Sandy; Dirt Gets under the Fingernails;
Bummer; Stop Singing These Sad Songs; Someone Keeps Calling
My Name; Babysitter; Tangled-Up Puppet; Star Tripper; Dreams
Go By.* GREATEST STORIES LIVE (4/76): *Dreams Go By;
WOLD; Saturday Morning; I Wanna Learn a Love Song; Mr.
Tanner; A Better Place to Be; Let Time Go Lightly; Cat's in the
Cradle; Taxi; Circle; 30,000 Pounds of Bananas; Love Is Just An-
other Word; The Shortest Story.* ON THE ROAD TO KING-
DOM COME (10/76): *On the Road to Kingdom Come; The
Parade's Still Passing By; The Mayor of Candor Lied; Laugh
Man; Corey's Coming; If My Mary Were Here; Fall in Love with
Him; Roll Down the River; Caroline.* DANCE BAND ON THE
TITANIC (9/77): *There Only Was One Choice; Dance Band on
the Titanic; My Old Lady; Why Should People Stay the Same; We
Grew Up a Little Bit; Bluesman; Country Dreams; I Do It for You,
Jane; I Wonder What Happened to Him; Paint a Picture of Your-
self (Michael); Mismatch; Mercenaries; Manhood; One Light in a
Dark Valley (An Imitation Spiritual).*

Singles/*Taxi/Empty* (2/72); *Could You Put Your Lights on,
Please/Any Old Kind of Day* (6/72); *Sunday Morning
Sunshine/Burning Herself* (9/72); *Better Place to Be/Winter Song*
(11/72); *WOLD/Short Stories* (11/73); *What Made America
Famous?/Old College Avenue* (5/74); *Cat's in the Cradle/Vacancy*
(8/74); *I Wanna Learn a Love Song/She Sings Songs without
Words* (2/75); *Dreams Go By/Stop Singing Those Sad Songs*
(7/75); *Tangled-Up Puppet/Dirt Gets under the Fingernails*
(10/75); *The Rock/Star Tripper* (1/76); *A Better Place to Be*
(6/76); *Corey's Coming/If My Mary Were Here* (11/76).

RAY CHARLES/Ray Charles' unique combination of gospel.
rhythm and blues, and pop virtually defined the term "soul" during the fifties and early sixties. He has been accorded every com-
plimentary title in existence, yet the one that comes to mind the
most is "genius." The genius of Ray Charles.

Georgia-born Ray began singing in his pre-teen years, at that
time inspired by the late Nat King Cole. Blinded at the age of six
and orphaned at the age of fifteen, Ray turned to music as a
means of expression. His first band, formed while Ray was only
seventeen, began working the club and bar circuit along the West

Coast, attracting the attention of many minor, independent labels. In 1957, Ahmet Ertegun of Atlantic Records was impressed enough with the twenty-seven-year-old musician to buy his contract from a smaller label and set him loose on Atlantic. Within months, Ray was on the charts with *Swanee River Rock*.

From that point onward, there was no stopping the talented Mr. Charles. His style broadened, his vocals left pop far behind and strayed into the coarse, rich warbling that became his trademark. His brand of soul encompassed all elements: jazz, rock, gospel, traditional R&B. The sound was fluid and almost off the cuff but uncompromising when it came to power. His first top-ten record, in 1959, became a rock standard: *What'd I Say?* And subsequent singles, *One Mint Julep* and *Georgia on My Mind,* showed a mellower, more subtly arranged side of Ray.

In 1961, Ray moved to ABC Records, whence some of his finest tunes emerged. *Hit the Road Jack, Ruby,* and *Unchain My Heart* quickly established Ray as a steady, driving force in the rock world despite the growing influx of British-oriented talent. In 1962, Ray sent his fans reeling with the announcement that his next long-playing release would be entitled *MODERN SOUNDS IN COUNTRY AND WESTERN.* The music world was shocked. Surely, this was musical suicide. The rocking king of R&B sacrificing everything for a brief fling at C&W.

Ray's fans should have known better. The genius of Ray Charles was simply expanding its musical scope, widening its horizons. Ray's version of the Hank Williams tune *I Can't Stop Loving You* remained on the top charts for eighteen weeks, eventually reaching the coveted number-one spot. Ray's powerful artistry remained a crowd-pleaser throughout the remainder of the sixties. When flower power, psychedelia, and saccharine soul dominated the airwaves, Ray resorted to his natural versatility in order to stay on top. *Busted, Crying Time, Let's Go Get Stoned, Here We Go Again,* and *Yesterday* all made it to the top-twenty with a combined total of fifty-five weeks on the charts.

Unfortunately, his professional wisdom was marred by a few incidents of personal despair. A flirtation with heroin led to a brief prison sentence, during which Charles kicked the habit. But during the seventies, Ray has expanded his career even further via a horde of personal appearances, both live and on television (encompassing comedy as a guest host on NBC's truly bizarre *Satur-*

day Night Live), taking part in pre-recorded concert events (a taped concert of Ray was picked up by the national television cable network, and a special concert version of Gershwin's *Porgy and Bess* was released on RCA, featuring Ray and Cleo Laine) and founding his own label, Crossover. In 1975, Ray's *Living for the City* single earned a Grammy. In 1977, his Crossover label left ABC to return to Ray's first home, Atlantic.

By anyone's standards, Ray Charles is something more than mere genius. He was, and is, a galvanizing force in contemporary music, prodding others onward with each progressive success. Ray Charles' raspy vocalizing and syncopated piano style is now a standard used to judge the work of others. There is no higher compliment in the pop realm.

He is that rare breed of musician known as "an original."

Albums/HALLELUJAH I LOVE HER SO (6/57): *Ain't That Love; Drown in My Own Tears; Come Back, Baby; Sinner's Prayer; Funny (But I Still Love You); Losing Hand; A Fool for You; Hallelujah I Love Her So; Mess Around; This Little Girl of Mine; Mary Ann; Greenbacks; Don't You Know; I Got a Woman.* THE GREAT RAY CHARLES (8/57): *The Ray; My Melancholy Baby; Black Coffee; There's No You; Doodlin'; Sweet Sixteen Bars; I Surrender, Dear; Undecided.* YES INDEED (10/58): *What Would I Do without You; It's All Right; I Want to Know; Yes Indeed; Get on the Right Track, Baby; Talkin' 'bout you; Swanee River Rock; Lonely Avenue; Blackjack; The Sun's Gonna Shine Again; I Want a Little Girl; Heartbreaker; Leave My Woman Alone.* CHARLES AT NEWPORT (10/58): *The Right Time; In a Little Spanish Town; I Got a Woman; Blues Waltz; Hot Rod; Talkin' 'bout You; Cherry; A Fool for You.* WHAT'D I SAY (9/59): *What'd I Say (Parts 1 and 2); Jumpin' in the Morning; You May Be My Baby; Tell Me How Do You Feel; What Kind of Man Are You; Rockhouse (Parts 1 and 2); Roll with Me, Baby; Tell All the World about You; My Bonnie; That's Enough.* THE GENIUS OF RAY CHARLES (10/59): *Let the Good Times Roll; It Had to Be You; Alexander's Rag Time Band; Two Years of Torture; When Your Lover Has Gone; 'Deed I Do; Just for a Thrill; You Won't Let Me; Tell Me You'll Wait for Me; Don't Let the Sun Catch You Crying; Am I Blue; Come Rain or Come Shine.* IN PERSON (5/60): *The Right Time; What'd I Say; Yes Indeed; The Spirit-*

Feel; Frenesi; Drown in My Own Tears; Tell the Truth. GENIUS
HITS THE ROAD (7/60): *Alabamy Bound; Georgia on My Mind;
Basin Street Blues; Mississippi Mud; Moonlight in Vermont; New
York's My Home; California, Here I Come; Moon over Miami;
Deep in the Heart of Texas; Carry Me Back to Old Virginny; Blue
Hawaii; Chattanooga Choo-Choo.* DEDICATED TO YOU
(1/61): *Hardhearted Hannah; Nancy; Margie; Ruby; Rosetta;
Stella by Starlight; Josephine, Cherry; Candy; Marie, Diane;
Sweet Georgia Brown.* GENIUS PLUS SOUL EQUALS JAZZ
(2/61): *From the Heart; I've Got News for You; Moanin'; Let's Go;
One Mint Julep; I'm Gonna Move to the Outskirts of Town; Stomp-
in' Room Only; Mister "C"; Strike Up the Band; Birth of the
Blues.* THE GENIUS AFTER HOURS (6/61): *The Genius after
Hours; Ain't Misbehavin'; Dawn Ray; Joy Ride; Hornful Soul; The
Man I Love; Charlesville; Music, Music, Music.* RAY CHARLES
AND BETTY CARTER (7/61): *Ev'ry Time We Say Goodbye;
You and I; Intro: Goodbye; We'll Be Together; People Will Say
We're in Love; Cocktails for Two; Side by Side; Baby, It's Cold
Outside; Together; For All We Know; Takes Two to Tango; Alone
Together; Just You, Just Me.* THE GENIUS SINGS THE
BLUES (9/61): *Early in the Mornin'; Hard Times; The Midnight
Hour; The Right Time; Ray's Blues; Feelin' Sad; I'm Movin' On;
I Believe to My Soul; Nobody Cares; Mr. Charles' Blues; Some
Day Baby; I Wonder Who.* THE GREATEST RAY CHARLES
(11/61): *Tell Me How Do You Feel; I Got a Woman; Heart-
breaker; Tell the Truth; What'd I Say; Talkin' 'bout You; You Be
My Baby; Leave My Woman Alone; I'm Movin' On.* MODERN
SOUNDS IN COUNTRY AND WESTERN MUSIC (1/62):
*Hey, Good Looking; Just a Little Lovin'; Makes No Difference
Now; Careless Love; Bye Bye Love; Move It On Over; Who Cares;
Half As Much; I Can't Stop Loving You; You Don't Know Me;
Born to Lose; I Love You So Much It Hurts.* THE RAY
CHARLES STORY (7/62): *The Sun's Gonna Shine Again; Losing
Hand; Mess Around; It Should've Been Me; Don't You Know;
Come Back, Baby; I've Got a Woman; A Fool for You; Hallelujah
I Love Her So; This Little Girl of Mine; Mary Ann; Lonely Ave-
nue; Doodlin'; Sweet Sixteen Bars; Ain't That Love; Rockhouse;
Swanee River Rock; Talkin' 'bout You; What Kind of Man Are
You; Yes Indeed; My Bonnie; Tell All the World about You; The
Right Time; What'd I Say; Just For a Thrill; Come Rain or Come*

Shine; Drown in My Own Tears; Let the Good Times Roll; I'm
Movin' On. THE RAY CHARLES STORY, VOL. 1 (7/62): The
Sun's Gonna Shine Again; Losing Hand; Mess Around; It
Should've Been Me; Don't You Know; Come Back, Baby; I've Got
a Woman; A Fool for You; This Little Girl of Mine; Mary Ann;
Hallelujah I Love Her So; Lonely Avenue; Doodlin'; Sweet Sixteen
Bars; Ain't That Love. THE RAY CHARLES STORY, VOL. 2
(7/62): Rockhouse; Swanee River Rock; Talkin' 'bout You; What
Kind of Man Are You; Yes Indeed; My Bonnie; Tell All the World
about You; The Right Time; What'd I Say; Just For A Thrill;
Come Rain or Come Shine; Drown in My Own Tears; Let the Good
Times Roll; I'm Movin' On. GREATEST HITS (7/62): Them That
Got; Georgia on my Mind; Unchain My Heart; I'm Gonna Move to
the Outskirts of Town; The Danger Zone; I've Got News for You;
Hit the Road, Jack; Ruby; I Wonder; Sticks and Stones; But on the
Other Hand, Baby; One Mint Julep. SOUL MEETIN'—RAY
CHARLES AND MILT JACKSON (11/62): Hallelujah I Love
Her So; Blue Genius; X-Ray Eyes; Soul Meetin'; Love on My
Mind; Bags of Blues. MODERN SOUNDS IN COUNTRY
AND WESTERN, VOL. 2 (1/63): You Are My Sunshine; No Let-
ter Today; Someday; Don't Tell Me Your Troubles; Midnight; Oh,
Lonesome Me; Take These Chains from My Heart; Making Be-
lieve; I'll Never Stand in Your Way; Teardrops in My Heart; Hang
Your Head in Shame. THE RAY CHARLES STORY, VOL. 3
(6/63): Sinner's Prayer; Funny; Feelin' Sad; Hard Times; What
Would I Do without You; I Want to Know; Leave My Woman
Alone; It's All Right; Get on the Right Track, Baby; That's
Enough; I Want a Little Girl; You Be My Baby; I Had a Dream;
Tell the Truth. INGREDIENTS FOR A RECIPE FOR SOUL
(7/63): Busted; Where Can I Go?; Born to Be Blue; That Lucky
Old Sun; Ol' Man River; In the Evening (When the Sun Goes
Down); A Stranger in Town; Over the Rainbow; You'll Never Walk
Alone. SWEET AND SOUR TEARS (1/64): I Cried for You; I
Cried a River; Willow, Weep for Me; Baby, Don't You Cry;
Teardrops from My Eyes; Don't Cry, Baby; A Tear Fell; No One
to Cry To; You Got Me Crying Again; Guess I'll Have to Hang Out
My Tears to Dry; After My Laughter Came Tears. HAVE A
SMILE WITH ME (6/64): Smack Dab in the Middle; Feudin' And
Fightin'; Two Ton Tessie; I Never See Maggie Alone; Move It On
Over; Ma; The Thing; The Man with the Weird Beard; The Naugh-

ty Lady of Shady Lane; Who Cares (for Me). GREAT HITS
(6/64): *Tell Me How Do You Feel; I Had a Dream; Carrying That
Load; Tell All the World about You; I Believe to My Soul; What'd
I Say; I'm Movin' On; You Be My Baby; The Right Time; Yes
Indeed; Tell the Truth; My Bonnie; Early in the Mornin'.* THE
RAY CHARLES STORY, VOL. 4 (6/64): *Blackjack;
Alexander's Ragtime Band; I Believe to My Soul; A Bit of Soul;
Greenbacks; Undecided; When Your Lover Has Gone; It Had to Be
You; Early in the Mornin'; Heartbreaker; Music, Music, Music;
Tell Me How Do You Feel; You Won't Let Me Go; In a Little
Spanish Town.* LIVE IN CONCERT (1/65): *Swing a Little Taste;
I Got a Woman; Margie; You Don't Know Me; Hide nor Hair;
Baby, Don't You Cry; Makin' Whoopee; Hallelujah I Love Her So;
Don't Set Me Free; What'd I Say; Finale.* COUNTRY AND
WESTERN MEETS RHYTHM AND BLUES (8/65): *Together
Again; I'd Like to Hear It Sometime; I've Got a Tiger by the Tail;
Please Forgive and Forget; I Don't Care; Next Door to the Blues;
Blue Moon of Kentucky; Maybe It's Nothing At All; All Night
Long; Light Out of Darkness; Watch It, Baby; Don't Let Her
Know.* CRYING TIME (1/66): *Crying Time; No Use Crying;
Let's Go Get Stoned; Peace of Mind; Going Down Slow; Tears;
Drifting Blues; We Don't See Eye to Eye; You're In for a Big Sur-
prise; You're Just About to Lose Your Clown; Don't You Think I
Ought to Know; You've Got a Problem.* RAY'S MOODS (7/66):
*What-Cha Doing in There; Please Say You're Fooling; By The
Light of the Silvery Moon; You Don't Understand; Maybe It's Be-
cause of Love; Chitlins with Candied Yams; Granny Wasn't Grin-
ning That Day; She's Lonesome Again; Sentimental Journey; A
Born Loser; It's a Man's World; A Girl I Used to Know.* A MAN
AND HIS SOUL (1/67): *I Can't Stop Loving You; What'd I Say;
Ol' Man River; Crying Time; Makin' Whoopee; Takes Two to
Tango; Let's Go Get Stoned; Cry; Unchain My Heart; Georgia on
My Mind; Baby, It's Cold Outside; Worried Mind; I Chose to Sing
the Blues; Busted; Ruby; I Don't Need No Doctor; Born to Lose;
Hit the Road, Jack; You Are My Sunshine; From the Heart;
Teardrops from My Eyes; No Use Crying; Chitlins with Candied
Yams.* TOGETHER AGAIN (re-issue of COUNTRY AND
WESTERN MEETS WITH RHYTHM AND BLUES; 4/67).
RAY CHARLES INVITES YOU TO LISTEN (6/67): *She's
Funny That Way; How Deep Is the Ocean; Yesterday; I'll Be*

Seeing You; Here We Go Again; All for You; Love Walked In; Gee, Baby, Ain't I Good to You; People. A PORTRAIT OF RAY (3/68): *Never Say Naw; The Sun Died; Am I Blue; Yesterday; When I Stop Dreamin'; I Won't Leave; A Sweet Young Thing Like You; The Bright Lights and You, Girl; Understanding; Eleanor Rigby.* I'M ALL YOURS, BABY (3/69): *Yours; I Didn't Know What Time It Was; Memories of You; Till the End of Time; I Had the Craziest Dream; Someday; Indian Love Call; I Dream of You; Gloomy Sunday.* DOING HIS THING (5/69): *The Same Things That Can Make You Laugh; Finders Keepers, Losers Weepers; Baby Please; Come and Get It; We Can Make It; I'm Ready; That Thing Called Love; If It Wasn't for Bad Luck; I Told You So.* MY KIND OF JAZZ (4/70): *Golden Boy; Booty Butt; This Here; I Remember Clifford; Sidewinder; Bluesette; Pas-se-o-ne Blues; Zig Zag; Angel City; Senior Blues.* LOVE COUNTRY STYLE (6/70): *If You Were Mine; Ring of Fire; Your Love Is So Doggone Good; Don't Change on Me; Till I Can't Take It Anymore; You've Still Got a Place in my Heart; I Keep It Hid; Sweet Memories; Good Morning, Dear; Show Me the Sunshine.* VOLCANIC ACTION OF MY SOUL (4/71): *See You Then; What Am I Living For; Feel So Bad; The Long and Winding Road; The Three Bells; All I Ever Need Is You; Wichita Lineman; Something; I May Be Wrong; Down in the Valley.* 25TH ANNIVERSARY IN SHOW BUSINESS SALUTE TO RAY CHARLES (11/71): *Hit the Road, Jack; Mary Ann; Hallelujah I Love Her So; Unchain My Heart; Don't Let the Sun Catch You Cryin'; Georgia on My Mind; What'd I Say; I Got a Woman; One Mint Julep; Busted; If You Were Mine; I Can't Stop Lovin' You; Cryin' Time Again; Yesterday; Born to Lose; Eleanor Rigby; Don't Change on Me; It Should've Been Me; The Mess Around; Don't You Know, Baby; You Are My Sunshine; Drown in My Own Tears; Ain't That Love; Swanee River Rock; I Believe to My Soul; Lonely Avenue; Ruby; Rock House; Just for a Thrill; Night Time Is the Right Time; Yes Indeed; Understanding; Booty Butt; Feel So Bad.* A MESSAGE FROM THE PEOPLE (5/72): *Lift Every Voice and Sing; Seems Like I Gotta Do Wrong; Heaven Help Us All; Hey Mister; There'll Be No Peace without All Men as One; What Have They Done to My Song, Ma; Abraham, Martin and John; Take Me Home, Country Roads; Every Saturday Night; America the Beautiful.* THROUGH THE EYES OF LOVE (8/72): *My First Night Alone*

Without You; I Can Make It thru the Days but Oh Those Lonely Nights; Someone to Watch over Me; A Perfect Love; You Leave Me Breathless; Never Ending Song of Love; Rainy Night in Georgia. JAZZ NUMBER II (1/73): *Our Suite; A Pair of Threes; Morning of Carnival; Going Home; Kids Are Pretty People; Togetherness; Brazilian Skies.* COME LIVE WITH ME (1/74): *Till There Was You; If You Go Away; It Takes So Little Time; Somebody; Come Live with Me; Problems, Problems; Louise; Where Was He?; Everybody Sing.* RENAISSANCE (8/75): *Living for the City; Then We'll Go Home; My God and I; We're Gonna Make It; Sunshine; It Ain't Easy Being Green; Sail Away.* MY KIND OF JAZZ, PART THREE (10/75): *I'm Gonna Go Fishin'; For Her; Sister Sadie; Of the Time; Ray Minor Ray; Samba de Elencia; Metamorphosis; Nothing Wrong; Project "S".* PORGY AND BESS (with Cleo Laine 1976): *Summertime; My Man's Gone Now; A Woman Is a Sometime Thing; They Pass By Singin'; What You Want Wid Bess; I Got Plenty of Nuttin; Bess, You Is My Woman; Oh, Doctor Jesus; Crab Man; Here Come de Honey Man; Strawberry Woman; It Ain't Necessarily So; There's a Boat Dat's Leaving Soon for New York; I Loves You, Porty; Oh Lord, I'm on My Way.* TRUE TO LIFE (11/77): *I Can See Clearly Now; The Jealous Kind; Oh, What a Beautiful Mornin'; How Long Has This Been Going On; Be My Love; Anonymous Love; Heavenly Music; Game Number Nine; Let It Be Me.*

Singles/*Baby, Let Me Hold Your Hand* (2/51); *Kiss Me, Baby* (2/52); *The Midnight Hour/Roll with Me, Baby* (12/52); *The Sun's Gonna Shine Again/Jumpin' in the Morning* (1953); *Mess Around/Funny* (7/53); *Feelin' Sad/Heartbreaker* (1953); *It Should've Been Me/Sinner's Prayer* (3/54); *Losing Hand/Don't You Know* (7/54); *I've Got a Woman/Come Back, Baby* (12/54); *A Fool for You/This Little Girl of Mine* (5/55); *Black Jack/Greenbacks* (9/55); *Mary Ann/Drown in My Own Tears* (1/56); *Halleulujah I Love Her So/What Would I Do without You* (5/56); *Lonely Avenue/Leave My Woman Alone* (9/56); *I Want to Know/Ain't That Love* (1/57); *It's All Right/Get on the Right Track, Baby* (5/57); *Swanee River Rock/I Want a Little Girl* (9/57); *Talkin' 'Bout You/What Kind of Man Are You* (1958); *Yes, Indeed/I Had a Dream* (1958); *You Be My Baby/My Bonnie* (1958); *Rockhouse (Parts 1 and 2)* (1/58); *I'm Movin' On/I Believe to My Soul* (10/59); *Let the Good Times Roll/Don't Let the Sun*

Catch You Crying (12/59); *My Baby/Who You Gonna Love* (1/60); *Just for a Thrill/Heartbreaker* (3/60); *Tell the Truth/Sweet Sixteen Bars* (1960); *Sticks and Stones/Worried Life Blues* (5/60); *Georgia on My Mind/Carry Me Back to Old Virginny* (8/60); *Tell Me You'll Wait for Me/Come Rain or Come Shine* (11/60); *Ruby/Hard Hearted Hannah* (11/60); *A Bit of Soul/Early in the Morning* (2/61); *One Mint Julep/Let's Go* (2/61); *I've Got News for You/I'm Gonna Move to the Outskirts of Town* (6/61); *Am I Blue/It Should've Been Me* (6/61); *Ray's Blues/Hard Times* (8/61); *Hit the Road, Jack/The Danger Zone* (8/61); *Talkin' 'bout You/In a Spanish Town* (1961); *Unchain My Heart/But on the Other Hand, Baby* (11/61); *Doodlin' (Parts 1 and 2)* (1961); *Baby, It's Cold Outside* (with Betty Carter) */We'll Be Together Again* (with Betty Carter) (1/62); *At the Club/Hide nor Hair* (3/62); *I Can't Stop Loving You/Born to Lose* (4/62); *You Don't Know Me/Careless Love* (7/62); *You Are My Sunshine/Your Cheating Heart* (11/62); *Don't Set Me Free/The Brightest Smile in Town* (2/63); *Take These Chains from My Heart/No Letter Today* (3/63); *No One/Without Love* (5/63); *Busted/Making Believe* (8/63); *That Lucky Old Sun/Ol' Man Time* (11/63); *Baby, Don't You Cry/My Heart Cries for You* (2/64); *My Baby Don't Dig Me/Something's Wrong* (5/64); *No One to Cry To/A Tear Fell* (6/64); *Smack Dab in the Middle/I Wake Up Crying* (9/64); *Makin' Whoopee* (11/64); *Cry/Teardrops from My Eyes* (1/65); *I Got a Woman (2 Parts)* (3/65); *Without a Song (2 Parts)* (4/65); *I'm a Fool to Care/Love's Gonna Live Here* (6/65); *The Cincinatti Kid/That's All I Am to You* (9/65); *Crying Time/When My Dreamboat Comes Home* (10/65); *Together Again/You're Just About to Lose Your Clown* (3/66); *Let's Go Get Stoned/The Train* (5/66); *I Chose to Sing The Blues/Hopelessly* (8/66); *Please Say You're Fooling/I Don't Need No Doctor* (10/66); *I Want to Talk about You/Something Inside Me* (2/67); *Here We Go Again/Somebody Ought to Write a Book about It* (4/67); *In the Heat of the Night/Something's Got to Change* (8/67); *Never Had Enough of Nothing Yet* (10/67); *Go On Home/That's a Lie* (1/68); *Understanding/Eleanor Rigby* (5/68); *Sweet Young Thing Like You/Listen, They're Playing My Song* (8/68); *If It Wasn't for Bad Luck/When I Stop Dreaming* (11/68); *I'll Be Your Servant/I Didn't Know What Time It Was* (2/69); *Let Me Love You/I'm Satisfied* (4/69); *We Can Make It/I Can't Stop Loving You* (8/69);

Claudie Mae/Someone to Watch Over Me (11/69); *Laughin' and Clownin'/That Thing Called Love* (1./70); *If You Were Mine/Till I Can't Take It Anymore* (8/70); *Don't Change Me/Sweet Memories* (2/71); *Feel So Bad/Your Love Is So Doggone Good* (7/71); *What Am I Living For/Tired Of My Tears* (12/71); *Look What They've Done to My Song, Ma* (6/72); *I Can Make It thru the Days/Ring of Fire* (1973); *Come Live with Me/Everybody Sing* (6/73); *Louise/Somebody* (3/74); *Living in the City/Then We'll Be Home* (7/75); *America the Beautiful/Sunshine* (2/76); *I Can See Clearly* (12/77).

CHUBBY CHECKER/Ernest Evans was a Philadelphia boy, a good dancer and singer who, by 1960, had launched himself into a modest career. It was Mrs. Dick Clark who took one look at him and, thinking he looked like a young Fats Domino, named him Chubby Checker. When he first recorded a Hank Ballard number called *The Twist* in 1960, he had no idea it would set off not just a national but an international craze, which would put him in the Copacabana, make him a household world, and earn him close to a million dollars in one year. Kids were already doing the twist at high school dances. When the fad spread to the sleazy little Peppermint Lounge, just off Times Square in New York, it attracted the news media and adults began to take an interest in the dance. Suddenly, the lounge was *in,* as was Chubby Checker in a way that no single performer had been since the early days of Elvis.

Once the Jet Set took it up (and that included Elsa Maxwell, the Duke and Duchess of Windsor, and Greta Garbo), people at every conceivable level started twisting just to keep up. Chubby found himself with a daily show instructing would-be twisters on the latest steps. Other twist touters, such as Joey Dee, hit the singles charts. What Chubby and the Twist did was move into a very stale musical season of a very stale year with something so catchy it was irresistible.

The Twist brought about a renaissance in terms of disco dancing in the sixties. Once the craze was over, Chubby turned to the Pony and the Limbo before fading from view. In the late sixties and early seventies, Chubby made the rock-revival route, twisting into the sunset while offering a few self-penned rock ballads for good measure.

Albums/TWIST WITH CHUBBY CHECKER (10/60): *Twistin' U.S.A.: Cooh-Poo-Pah-Doo Shimmy; C. C. Rider Stroll; The Strand; The Chicken; Hucklebuck; The Twist; The Madison; Love Is Strange; Calypso; Mexican Hat Twist; The Slop; The Pony.* IT'S PONY TIME (/61): *Pone Time; Watusi; Stroll; Hully Gully; Shimmy; Hi Ho Silver; Mashed Potatoes; We Like Birdland; Let's Dance, Let's Dance, Let's Dance; Charleston; Mess Around.* LETS TWIST AGAIN (9/61); *Let's Twist Again; I Could Have Danced All Night, It Takes Two to Tango; Ballin' the Jack; Quarter to Three; Fishin'; Continental Walk; Peanut Butter; The Jet; I Almost Lost My Mind; Dance Along.* FOR TWISTERS ONLY (11/61): *The Fly; Peppermint Twist; Your Lips and Mine; Dear Lady Twist; Twist Along; Shout; Lose Your Inhibitions Twist; Slow Twistin'; Love Is Like a Twist; Runaround Sue; Twistin' Blues; Twistin' Bones.* YOUR TWIST PARTY (11/61): *Twist; Let's Twist Again; Hucklebuck; Rock Around the Clock; Twisting U.S.A.; Whole Lotta Shakin' Goin' On; Ballin' the Jack; I Could Have Danced All Night; Blueberry Hill; Hound Dog; Mr. Twister; Mexican Hat Twist.* CHUBBY CHECKER AND BOBBY RYDELL (11/61): *Jingle Bell Rock; Swingin' Together; Teach Me to Twist; Side by Side; Jingle Bells Imitations; What Are You Doing New Year's Eve; My Baby Cares for Me; Voodoo; Walkin' My Baby Back Home; Medley; other selections.* FOR TEEN TWISTERS ONLY (3/62). TWISTIN' ROUND THE WORLD (4/62): *Twistin' Round the World; Alouette; O Sole Mio; Twist Marie; Paloma; Miserlou; Let's Twist Again; Twist Mit Mir; Twistin' Matilda; Tea for Two; Hava Nagila; Never on Sunday.* DON'T KNOCK THE TWIST (5/62): *Twistin'; Bristol Stomp; Paloma Twist; Bo Diddley; I Love to Twist; Don't Know the Twist; Do the New Continental; Salome Twist; The Fly; Mashed Potatoes; Slow Twistin'; Mashed Potato Time.* ALL THE HITS (10/62). CHUBBY CHECKER AND DEE DEE SHARP (10/62); TWIST IT UP; *Twist It Up; Kansas City; Ript It Up; Don't Let Go; Slow Twistin'; Twist; Don't You Just Know It; I'm Walkin'; Johnny B. Goode; Let's Twist Again; Maybelline; Hi-Ho Silver.* LIMBO PARTY (11/62): *Man Smart, Woman Smarter; Mary Ann Limbo; Bossa Nova; Desafinado; La La Limbo; Baby, Come Back; Somebody Bad Stole the Wedding Bell; Limbo Rock; When the Saints Go Limbo In; Jamaica Farewell; Banana Boat Song; La Bamba.* BIGGEST HITS (12/62): *Popeye; Slow*

Twistin'; Let's Twist Again; Limbo Rock; Hucklebuck; The Fly;
Pony Time; Dance the Mess Around; The Twist; Dancin' Party;
Good Good Lovin'. LET'S LIMBO SOME MORE (3/63): Let's
Limbo Some More; Manana; Cindy, Oh Cindy; Twenty Miles;
How Low Can You Go; Girl with the Swingin' Derriere; Peanut
Vendor; Rum and Coca Cola; Lotta Limbo; Run Chico Run; Mama
Look a Boo Boo; Mother. BEACH PARTY (7/63): Birdland;
Limbo Side by Side; Twist It Up; Mashed Potato Love; Surf Party;
Killer; Oo-Kook-A-Boo; Surfin'; She Said; Nothin' but the Twist;
She's a Hippy; Let's Surf Again. CHUBBY CHECKER IN PER-
SON (11/63); CHUBBY CHECKER'S FOLK ALBUM (2/64):
Loddy Lo; Hooka Tooka; Everybody Loves Saturday Night; Sip-
pin' Cider through a Straw; Go Tell My Baby; Hey, Bobba Needle;
Doodang; Ole Anna; Ah Si Mon Moine; Tzena Tzena; 6-0-9;
Doncha Get Tired. GREATEST HITS (11/72): The Twist; Pony
Time; Let's Twist Again; Popeye; other titles.

Singles/The Class (4/59); The Twist (7/60); The
Hucklebuck/Whole Lotta Shakin' Goin' On (9/60); Pony Time
(1/61); Dance the Mess Around/Good, Good Lovin' (3/61); Let's
Twist Again (6/61); The Fly (9/61); The Twist/Twistin' U.S.A.
(10/61); Let's Twist Again (10/61); Slow Twistin'/La Palmao
Twist (2/62); Dancin' Party (6/62); Limbo Rock/Popeye (The
Hitchhiker) (8/62); Twenty Miles/Let's Limbo Some More (1/63);
Birdland/Black Cloud (5/63); Twist It Up/Surf Party (7/63); Lod-
dy Lo/Hooka Tooka (10/63); Hey Bobba Needle (2/64); Lazy
Elsie Molly (5/64); She Wants t'Swim (8/64); Lovely, Lovely
(12/64); Let's Do the Freddie (3/65); Hey You! Little Boog-Ga-
Loo (6/66); Back in the U.S.S.R. (3/69.).

CHER/Cherilyn Sakisian became the idol of millions during the
1960s both as a solo performer and as one-half of the Nick-and-
Nora-Charles-with-a-backbeat team of Sonny and Cher. Following their split in 1974, Cher embarked on a full-fledged career,
moving to a new label (from MCA to Warners). At her newfound
musical home, she encountered problems relaunching herself as a
viable recording entity. Her TV show floundered and, in 1975, she
received sympathetic but negative news coverage due to her marriage to laid-back, low-down rock 'n' roller Gregg Allman. The
marriage, which was going to be annulled after a week, has been
a rocky one, and Cher's career has followed suit.

Her biggest successes came in the late sixties when most of her smash tunes were either written or produced (mostly both) by nasal-voiced hubby Sonny.

Albums/ALL I REALLY WANT TO DO (11/65): *All I Really Want to Do; I Got to Sleep; She Thinks I Still Care; Needles and Pins; Don't Think Twice; Dream Baby; Bells of Rhymney; Girl Don't Come; See See rider; Come and Stay with Me; Cry Myself to Sleep; Blowin' in the Wind.* SONNY SIDE OF CHER (6/66): *Our Day Will Come; Bang Bang; Girl from Ipanema; Elusive Butterfly; It's Not Unusual; Like a Rolling Stone; Time; Where Do You Go; Come to My Window; Old Man River; Milord; Young Girl.* CHER (3/67): *Alfie; Sunny; You Don't Have to Say You Love Me; Homeward Bound; Catch the Wind; Until It's Time for You to Go; I Want You; Cruel War; Twelfth of Never; Will You Love Me Tomorrow; Pied Piper; Magic in the Air.* WITH LOVE (1/68): *You Better Sit Down, Kids; But I Can't Love You More; Hey Joe; Mama (When My Dollies Have Babies); Behind the Door; Sing for Your Supper; Look at Me; There but for Fortune; I Will Wait for You; Times They Are a-Changin'.* BACK STAGE (8/68): *Go Now; Carnival; It All Adds Up Now; Take Me for a Little While; Reason to Believe; Masters of War; Do You Believe in Magic; I Wasn't Ready; A House Is Not a Home; Click Song; Impossible Dream; Song Called Children.* GOLDEN GREATS (10/68): *You Better Sit Down, Kids; Sunny; Come and Stay with Me; Alfie; Take Me for a Little While; All I Really Want to Do; Needles and Pins; Bang Bang; Dream Baby; Where Do You Go; Elusive Butterfly; Hey Joe.* CHASTITY (1969; original soundtrack): *Chastity's Song; Chastity Overture; Motel 1; Chastity Walk; Flowers (Love of a Family); Chastity Love Theme; Chastity Titles; Motel II; Chastity Carousel; Mexico; Chastity (Closing Theme).* 3614 JACKSON HIGHWAY (1969): *For What It's Worth; Just Enough to Keep Me Hangin' On; Dock of the Bay; Tonight I'll Be Staying Here with You; I Walk on Guided Splinters; Lay Baby Lay; Please Don't Tell Me; Cry Like a Baby; Do Right Woman, Do Right Man; Save the Children.* CHER (8/71): *The Way of Love; Gypsys, Tramp and Thieves; He'll Never Know; Fire and Rain; When You Find Out Where You're Goin', Let Me Know; He Ain't Heavy, He's My Brother; I Hate to Sleep Alone; I'm in the Middle; Touch and Go; Honest Man.* CHER (12/71): *All I*

Really Want to Do; The Bells of Rhymney; Girl Don't Come; Come and Stay with Me; Blowin' in the Wind; Needles and Pins; Bang Bang; Elusive Butterfly; Time; Where Do You Go; Until It's Time for You to Go; Will You Still Love Me Tomorrow; Alfie; Homeward Bound; Catch the Wind; Reason to Believe; A House Is Not a Home; You Don't Have to Say You Love Me; You Better Sit Down, Kids; Sunny; There but for Fortune; Do You Believe in Magic; Mama; Click Song. FOXY LADY (7/72): *The First Time; Let Me Down Easy; If I Knew Then; Don't Hide Your Love; Never Been to Spain; Living in a House Divided; It Might as Well Stay Monday; Song For You; Down, Down, Down; Don't Ever Try to Close a Rose.* SUPERPACK VOL. II (8/72): *Our Day Will Come; The Times They Are a-Changin'; Come to Your Window; I Wasn't Ready; Hey Joe; Milord; Don't Think Twice; She Thinks I Still Care; The Cruel War; A Young Girl; Song Called Children; Girl from Ipanema; Old Man River; The Impossible Dream; Cry Myself to Sleep; Carnival; Twelfth of Never; Like a Rolling Stone; It's Not Unusual; I Want You; I Will Wait for You; Take Me for a Little While; Sing for Your Supper; Go Now.* BITTERSWEET WHITE LIGHT (3/73): *Jolson medley: Sonny Boy, Mammy, Rock-A-Bye Your Baby with a Dixie Melody; More Than You Know; Why Was I Born; The Man That Got Away; By Myself; I Got It Bad and That Ain't Good; Am I Blue; How Long Has This Been Going On; The Man I Love.* HALF BREED (9/73): *David's Song; Melody; The Long and Winding Road; This God-Forsaken Day; Chastity's Sun; My Love; Two People Clinging to a Thread; Half Breed; The Greatest Son I Ever Heard; How Can You Mend a Broken Heart; Carousel Man.* DARK LADY (5/74): *Train of Thought; Dixie Girl; I Saw a Man and He Danced with His Wife; I Hate to Sleep Alone, other titles.* GREATEST HITS (10/74): *Dark Lady: The Way of Love; Don't Hide Your Love; Half Breed; Train of Thought; Gypsys, Tramps and Thieves; I Saw a Man and He Danced with His Wfie; Carousel Man; Living in a House Divided; Melody.* THE VERY BEST OF CHER (1/75): *All I Really Want to Do; Needles and Pins; Hey Joe; Come and Stay with Me; Where Do You Go; Sunny; Bang Bang; Will You Love Me Tomorrow; Mama; The Cruel War; You Better Sit Down, Kids.* STARS *(3/75): Stars; Geronimo's Cadillac; These Days; other titles.* I'D RATHER BELIEVE IN YOU (8/76): *Long Distance Love Affair;*

I'd Rather Believe in You; Spring, Knock on Wood; Flashback; It's a Crying Shame; Borrowed Time; I Know; Silver Wings and Golden Rings. CHERISHED (6/77): *Pirate; He Was Beautiful; War Paint and Soft Feathers; Love the Devil out of Ya; She Loves to Hear the Music; L.A. Plane; Dixie; Again; Send the Man Over; Thunderstorm.*

Singles/*All I Really Want to Do/Dream Baby* (6/65); *Where Do You Go* (9/65); *Bang Bang/Needles and Pins* (2/66); *Alfie* (6/66); *Behind the Door* (10/66); *Hey Joe* (8/67); *You Better Sit Down, Kids* (9/67); *Classified 1A/Don't Put It on Me* (3/71); *Gypsys, Tramps and Thieves* (8/71); *Will You Love Me Tomorrow/Reason to Believe* (11/71); *The Way of Love/Don't Put It on Me* (1/72); *Living in a House Divided/One Honest Man (4/72); Don't Hide Your Love/The First Time* (8/72); *Our Day Will Come/Ol' Man River* (10/72); *All I Really Want to Do/Where Do You Go* (1/73); *Bang Bang/You Better Sit Down, Kids* (1/73); *You Better Sit Down, Kids/Sunny* (1/73); *All I Really Want to Do/Dream Baby* (1/73); *Bang Bang/Alfie* (1/73); *Am I Blue/How Long Has This Been Going On* (4/73); *Half Breed/Melody* (7/73); *Train of Lady/Two People Clinging to a Thread* (12/73); *Train of Thought/Dixie Girl* (5/74); *I Saw a Man and He Danced with His Wife/I Hate to Sleep Alone* (7/74); *Alfie/Sunny* (8/74); *Carousel Man/When You Find Out Where You're Goin', Let Me Know* (10/74); *Rescue Me/Dixie Girl* (3/75); *Geronimo's Cadillac/These Days* (4/75); *Long Distance Love Affair/Borrowed Time* (8/76); *Pirate/Send the Man Over* (12/76).

CHICAGO/*Robert Lamm (keyboards), James Pankow (trombone), Daniel Seraphine (drums), Lee Loughnane (trumpet), Walt Parazaider (woodwinds), Terry Kath (guitar), Peter Cetera (bass), Laudir De Oliveria (percussion; joined in 1974).*
One of the most controversial bands in the rock-pop realm, Chicago has to be considered a mainstay of modern music of both the sixties and the seventies. The eight-man recording group is one of the most popular bands of all time, both onstage and on record, earning ten gold album awards for ten albums released and selling out concert halls from New York to Tokyo. Pop music fans consider them jazz, jazz fans consider them rock, and heavy-metal freaks don't want any part of them. Meanwhile, the brass-laden

Chicago rolls along, picking up gold and platinum records like they were going out of style.

The group first got off the ground during the mid-sixties in the Windy City itself. Several weddings, sock hop, and bar mitzvah bands (The Missing Links, the Exceptions, the Majestics, and the Big Thing) decided the time was right to stop playing other peoples' material and form a band so they could perform their own. Chicago Transit Authority (or CTA) was the initial result. And their brand of music? Well, after one or two practices, the members realized that they had something different on their hands. Some of the musicians were into jazz, others into rock, still others into rhythm and blues. Playing together, they produced a sound that was exciting and *new*.

The hastily formed CTA, however, found the going tough in the Chicago area. Most clubs just weren't interested in innovative bands. They wanted to hear the hits. Period. Jobs were few and far between. "In the city at that time," recalls Cetera, "that was known as paying your dues." The discouraged ensemble packed up their horns and moved to L.A. at the request of producer James Guercio. Guercio had attended a few music classes at De-Paul University with several members of CTA and had gone on to some degree of commercial success on the West Coast, as bass player for both Dick Clark's road band and the original Mothers of Invention, and as producer for the Buckinghams. Guercio placed the band in a small house located precariously close to the Hollywood freeway and told them not to worry about the bills, just about developing their unique sound.

The net result was a cult following in L.A., a few choice gigs at the Whiskey-A-Go-Go and, finally, a recording contract. Their premier disc, *CHICAGO TRANSIT AUTHORITY,* was a milestone in pop music, featuring a fistful of jazzed-up rock tunes, the introduction of the now-famous Chicago logo, and the debut of an opulent type of album packaging that soon became the band's trademark. (Many fans feel that this style peaked with Chicago's three-record *CARNEGIE HALL* package, commonly referred to as the "kitchen sink" album. As in "everything but, etc." The album even included a floor plan of the building.)

With horns blaring, rhythm section churning, and vocal harmonies floating dreamily across the airwaves, Chicago gallops forward unchallenged after a full decade in the music business.

Albums/CHICAGO TRANSIT AUTHORITY (4/69): *Introduction; Does Anybody Really Know What Time It Is?; Beginnings; Questions 67 and 68; Listen; Poem 58; Free Form Guitar; South California Purples; I'm a Man; Prologue, August 29, 1968; Someday (August 29, 1968); Liberation.* CHICAGO II (1/70): *Moving In; The Road; Poem for the People; In the Country; Wake Up Sunshine; (Ballet for a Girl in Buchannon): 1.Make Me Smile, 2.So Much to Say—So Much to Give, 3.Anxiety's Moment, 4.West Virginia Fantasies, 5.Colour My World, 6.To Be Free, 7.More Than Ever; Fancy Colours; 25 or 6 to 4; Prelude; 1 AM Mourning; 2 PM Mourning; Memories of Love; It Better End Soon; Where Do We Go from Here?* CHICAGO III (1/71): *Sing a Mean Tune Kid; Loneliness Is Just a Word; I Don't Want Your Money; What Else Can I Say? Travel Suite: 1.Flight 601, 2.Motorboat to Mars, 3.Free, 4.Free Country, 5.At the Sunrise, 6.Happy Cause I'm Going Home; Mother; Lowdown; An Hour in the Shower; A Hard Risin' Morning without Breakfast; Off to Work; Fallin Out; Dreamin Home; Morning Blues Again; Elegy; When All the Laughter Dies in Sorrow; Canon; Once upon a Time; Progress; The Approaching Storm; Man vs. Man; The End.* CHICAGO AT CARNEGIE HALL (10/71): *In the Country; Fancy Colours; Does Anybody Know What Time It Is?; Free Form Intro; Does Anybody Really Know What Time It Is?; South California Purples; Questions 67 and 68; Sing a Mean Tune Kid; Beginnings; It Better End Soon (Movements One through Five); Introduction; Mother; Lowdown; Flight 601; Motorboat to Mars; Free; Where Do We Go From Here?; I Don't Want Your Money; Happy Cause I'm Going Home; (Ballet for a Girl in Buchannon); Make Me Smile, So Much to Give, Anxiety's Moment, West Virginia Fantasies, Colour My World, To Be Free, More Than Ever; A Song for Richard and His Friends; 25 or 6 to 4; I'm a Man.* CHICAGO V (6/73): *A Hit of Varese; All Is Well; Now That You're Gone; Dialogue (Part One and Two); While the City Sleeps; Saturday in the Park; State of the Union; Good-bye; Alma Mater.* CHICAGO VII (3/74): *Prelude to Aire; Aire; Devil's Sweet; Italian from New York; Hanky Panky; Life Saver; Happy Man; Wishing You Were Here; Call on Me; Woman Don't Want to Love Me; Skinny Boy; I've Been Searchin' So Long; Mongonucleosis; Song of the Evergreens; Byblos.* CHICAGO VIII (3/75): *Anyway You Want; Brand New Love Affair (Parts One and Two); Never Been in Love Before; Hideaway; Till*

We Meet Again; Harry Truman; Oh, Thank You Great Spirit; Long Time No See; Ain't It Blue; Old Days. CHICAGO'S GREATEST HITS (11/75): *25 or 6 to 4; Does Anybody Really Know What Time It Is?; Colour My World; Just You 'n' Me; Saturday in the Park; Feelin' Stronger Every Day; Make Me Smile; Wishing You Were Here; Call on Me; I've Been Searchin' So Long; Beginnings.* CHICAGO X (6/76): *Once or Twice; You Are on My Mind; Skin Tight; If You Leave Me Now; Another Rainy Day in New York City; Mama Mama; Scrapbook; Gently I'll Wake You; You Get It Up; Hope for Love.* CHICAGO XI (9/77): *Mississippi Delta City Blues; Baby, What a Big Surprise; Till the End of Time; Policeman; Take Me Back to Chicago; Vote for Me; Takin' It on Uptown; This Time; The Inner Struggles of a Man Prelude (Little One); Little One.*

Singles/*Questions/Listen* (6/69); *Beginnings/Poem 58* (10/69); *Make Me Smile/Colour My World* (3/70); *25 or 6 to 4/Where Do We Go From Here?* (6/70); *Does Anybody Really Know What Time It Is?/Listen* (10/70); *Free/Free Country* (2/71); *Make Me Smile/25 or 6 to 4* (2/71); *Lowdown/Loneliness Is Just a Word* (4/71); *Beginnings/Colour My World* (6/71); *Does Anybody Really Know What Time It Is?/Free* (7/71); *Questions/I'm a Man* (9/71); *Beginnings/Questions* (2/72); *Colour My World/I'm a Man* (5/72); *Saturday in the Park/Alma Mater* (7/72); *Dialogue (Parts One and Two) /Now That You've Gone* (10/72); *Saturday in the Park/Dialogue* (4/73); *Feeling Stronger Every Day/Jenny* (6/73); *Just You'n' Me/Critic's Choice* (9/73); *I've Been Searchin' So Long/Blybos* (2/74); *Just You'n' Me/Feeling Stronger Every Day* 4/74); *Call on Me/Prelude to Aire* (5/74); *Wishing You Were Here/Life Saver* (10/74); *Harry Truman/Till We Meet Again* 2/75); *Old Days/Hideaway* (4/ 75); *Brand New Love Affair/Hideaway* (8/75); *I've Been Searchin' So Long/Call on Me* (11/ 75); *Harry Truman/Old Days* (11/75); *Another Rainy Day in New York City/Hope for Love* (6/76); *If You Leave Me Now/Together Again* (7/76); *Old Days/Brand New Love Affair* (11/76).

ERIC CLAPTON/"Old slow-hand." The King of British Guitarists. Eric Clapton. Eric Clapton's meteoric rise to fame in the 1960s was a well-deserved phenomenon that completely revolutionized the concept of rock guitar playing during that period.

Along with Jimi Hendrix, Clapton stands as being the finest guitar technician to emerge from the decade of re-fried blues and overdone psychedelia.

Clapton started playing guitar while in his mid-teens, a student at Kingston Art School. Records by past masters of blues and rock and roll from Muddy Waters to Chuck Berry led him to start his first band, the Roosters, in 1963, at the age of eighteen. The Roosters led to a few other gigs before Clapton found himself replacing Top Topham in the infamous Yardbirds later that same year. His stint with the band led to critical acclaim, but when the Yardbirds began to pursue commercial goals, Clapton opted for musical ones. He departed the troupe in '65 and teamed with John Mayall and his Bluesbreakers. Before the year was out, "Clapton Is God!" was a popular cry around London music handouts.

In July of 1966, Clapton left Mayall to form the first real supergroup of the post-Beatles/Stones years. Cream. Cream, as a working unit, was both powerful and unpredictable, swinging precariously from rock to blues to bizarre jamming. They helped bring back a rebirth of blues in both England and the States but, commercially, enjoyed the most success via rock singles such as *Sunshine of Your Love* and *Anyone for Tennis?*

When Cream disbanded at the end of 1968, Clapton's career took on a nomadic quality that would plague him clear into the mid-seventies. He became a fairly misanthropic figure, either by design or circumstances, and his attempts at keeping a low profile nearly made him faceless. His next musical venture, Blind Faith, proved fairly disastrous. Clapton, shying away from the responsibilities of playing "star," embarked on a journey of session gigs. He appeared briefly on the Mothers of Invention's *WE'RE ONLY IN IT FOR THE MONEY* album (reciting "God. I See God"). He recorded and toured with Delaney and Bonnie. And, in 1970, purloined many of the Delaney and Bonnie troupe (including D&B) for his first solo album, *ERIC CLAPTON,* an enjoyably low-keyed affair.

With the solo album not doing much on the charts, Clapton returned to session work before forming the fabulous Derek and the Dominos. *LAYLA AND OTHER ASSORTED LOVE SONGS* was a classic double album that, unfortunately, went unnoticed by most until over a year later, when a disgusted Clapton was already dissolving the band. A tardily re-released single,

Layla, smashed through the stateside top ten.

The years following *Layla* were not kind to Eric. Plagued by the memory of Duane Allman's untimely death (Eric and Duane had become close friends, the two guitarists culminating their friendship on the album *Layla),* a heroin addiction, and a troubled personal life, Clapton withdrew from the music world he so dearly loved. Apparently, the music world loved his company just as much. Many of his rock peers rallied around the floundering guitarist, including the Who's Pete Townshend, who egged Clapton out of retirement and urged him to hold the now famous "comeback" gig at the Rainbow in London, January 1973.

Clapton slowly made his way back to a normal lifestyle, kicking both his physical and emotional crutches. With the support of super-manager Robert Stigwood, Clapton began a successful solo career in 1974 with the release of the heralded *461 OCEAN BOULEVARD.* After that, both the hit albums and singles began coming regularly. Singles-wise, *I SHOT THE SHERIFF* threw Clapton firmly in the arms of AM radio, and LPs like *THERE'S ONE IN EVERY CROWD* and *NO REASON TO CRY* endeared him to new FM-oriented audiences who were too young to remember Eric's Cream days.

In the 1970s as in the 1960s, Eric Clapton remains the guitarist's guitarist. He influences the styles and ideas of countless young musicians and continues to do so with each subsequent recording.

Albums/ERIC CLAPTON (6/70): *Slunky; Bad Boy; Lonesome and a Long Way from Home; After Midnight; Easy Now; Blues Power; Bottle of Red Wine; Lovin' You Lovin' Me; Told You for the Last Time; Don't Know Why; Let It Rain.* HISTORY OF ERIC CLAPTON (3/72): *I Ain't Got You; Tribute to Elmore; I Want to Know; Sunshine of Your Love; Crossroads; Spoonful; Badge; Sea of Joy; I Don't Want to Discuss It; Only You Know and I Know; Teasin'; Blues Power; Tell the Truth; Layla.* AT HIS BEST (9/72): *Bottle of Red Wine; Anyday; I Looked Away; Let It Rain; Lonesome and a Long Way from Home; Sea of Joy; Layla; Blues Power; Bell Bottom Blues; After Midnight; Keep On Growing; Little Wing; Presence of the Lord; Why Does Love Have to Be So Sad?; Easy Now; Slunky; Key to the Highway.* CLAPTON (1973): *Told You for the Last Time; Don't Know Why; Have You*

Ever Loved a Woman; Nobody Knows You When You're Down and Out; Lovin' You Lovin' Me; Tell the Truth; Bad Boy; Bell Bottom Blues. RAINBOW CONCERT (8/73): *Badge; Roll It Over; Presence of the Lord; Pearly Queen; After Midnight; Little Wing.* 461 OCEAN BOULEVARD (7/74): *Motherless Children; Give Me Strength; Willie and the Hand Jive; Get Ready; I Shot the Sheriff; I Can't Hold Out; Please Be with Me; Let It Grow; Steady Rollin' Man; Mainline Florida.* THERE'S ONE IN EVERY CROWD (3/75): *We've Been Told (Jesus Coming Soon); Swing Low, Sweet Chariot; Little Rachel; Don't Blame Me; The Sky Is Crying; Singin' the Blues; Better Make It through Today; Pretty Blue Eyes; High; Opposites.* E.C. WAS HERE (8/75): *Have You Ever Loved a Woman; Presence of the Lord; Drifting Blues; Can't Find My Way Home; Rambling on My Mind; Farther On up the Road.* NO REASON TO CRY (10/76): *Beautiful Thing; Carnival; Sign Language; County Jail Blues; All Our Past Times; Hello, Old Friend; Double Trouble; Innocent Times; Hungry; Black Summer Rain.*

Singles/*After Midnight* (9/70); *Let It Rain* (9/72); *Bell Bottom Blues* (1/73); *I Shot the Sheriff/Give Me Strength* (7/74); *Willie and the Hand Jive/Mainline Florida* (10/74); *Swing Low, Sweet Chariot/Pretty Blue Eyes* (4/75); *Knockin on Heaven's Door/Someone Likes You* (7/75).

THE DAVE CLARK FIVE/*Dave Clark (drums), Lenny Davidson (guitar), Rick Huxley (guitar, banjo), Denis Payton (sax, guitar, reeds), Mike Smith (lead vocals, keyboards, vibes).*

It's hard to describe exactly what the Dave Clark Five was all about. They made a lot of money and there were plenty of groups back in England (whence the Clark group vaulted) who resented Clark's success bitterly, particularly enraged over the group's lack of musical creativity. They self-righteously pointed out that Clark would never had made it in England the way he did in the States. Perhaps not, but the Dave Clark Five—who first met in a gym and originally played together to raise money for Dave's football club—managed to be in America in 1964, hot on the heels of the Beatles. They were armed with all you needed at that time. English haircuts and English accents. The whole key to the five was that Clark was not so much a musician as a businessman and that his whole operation, from the start, was run as a very efficient corporation. The group played uncomplicated rock and borrowed freely from Motown R&B. Mike Smith, the lead vocalist, looked like a salesman at Harrods but sounded like a black bluesman.

When the group finally did make it in England, they were elated but didn't have any pretensions about what they were doing. They weren't trailblazers. They created music that was needed during a certain musical time and place. When the hits stopped coming and their time was over, they went their separate ways, with Clark fading out of the rock limelight into the business world and Mike Smith later resurfacing in a British group, Smith-D'Abo.

Albums/GLAD ALL OVER (4/64): *Glad All Over; All of the Time; Chaquita; I Know You; Stay; Do You Love Me; No Time to Lose; Bits and Pieces; Doo Dah; Time; She's All Mine.* AMERICAN TOUR (9/64): *Because; Who Does He Think He Is; Move On; Whenever You're Around; I Want You Still; Long Ago; Come On Over; Blue Monday; Any Time You Want Love; Sometimes; I Cried over You; Ol' Sol.* DAVE CLARK FIVE RETURN (10/64): *Can't You See That She's Mine; I Need You, I Love You; Forever and a Day; Theme Without a Name; On Broadway.* DAVE CLARK FIVE—COAST TO COAST (3/65): *Any Way You Want It; Give Me Love; I Can't Stand It; I'm Left without You; Everybody Knows (I'm Still in Love with You); Crying over You; Say You Want Me; When; Don't You Know; It's Not True; To Me.* HAVING A WILD WEEKEND (6/65): *Having a Wild Weekend; New Kind of Love; Dum-Dee-Dee-Dum; I Said I Was Sorry; No Stopping; Don't Be Taken In; When I'm Alone; Catch Us If You Can; If You Come Back On the Move; Sweet Memories; Don't You Realize.* I LIKE IT LIKE THAT (1/66): *I Like It Like That; Pumping; I Need Love; I Am on My Own; Maybe It's You; That's How Long Our Love Will Last; Little Bit of Love; I'll Be Yours, My Love; Please Love Me; You Know You're Lying; Goodbye My Friends; She's a Loving Girl.* DAVE CLARK FIVE'S GREATEST HITS (4/66): *Over and Over; Glad All Over; Catch Us If You Can; Bits and Pieces; I Like It Like That; Can't You See That She's Mine; Everybody Knows (I Still Love You); Because; Any Way You Want It; Do You Love Me.* TRY TOO HARD (8/66): *Try Too Hard; Today; I Never Will; Looking In; Ever Since You've Been Away; Somebody Find a New Love; I Really*

Love You; It Don't Feel Good; Scared of Falling in Love; I Know.
SATISFIED WITH YOU (9/66): *Satisfied with You; Do You Still
Love Me; Go On; I Meant You; Look Before You Leap; Please
Tell Me Why; You Never Listen; I Still Need You; Good Lovin';
It'll Only Hurt For a Little While.* MORE GREATEST HITS
(12/66): *Try Too Hard; Come Home; I'm Thinking; All Night
Long; Look Before You Leap; Please Tell Me Why; Don't Let Me
Down; Reelin' and Rockin'; At the Scene; Satisfied with You.* 5 BY
5 (5/67): *Nineteen Days; Something I've Always Wanted; Little Bit
Strong; Bernedette; Sitting Here Baby; You Don't Want My Lov-
ing; How Can I Tell You; Picture of You; Small Talk; Pick Up
Your Phone.* YOU GOT WHAT IT TAKES (8/67): *You've Got
What It Takes; I've Got to Have a Reason; You Don't Play Me
Around; Thinkin' of You Baby; Lovin' So Good; Doctor Rhythm;
Play with Me; Let Me Be; Blueberry Hill; Tabatha Twitchit.* EV-
ERYBODY KNOWS (3/68): *Everybody Knows; Little Bit Now;
At the Place; Inside and Out; Red and Blue; You Must Have Been
a Beautiful Baby; Good Love Is Hard to Find; Concentration Baby;
Lost in His Dreams; I'll Do the Best I Can; Hold On Tight.*
WEEKEND IN LONDON (5/68): *Come Home; We'll Be Run-
ning; I'm Thinking; Blue Suede Shoes; Hurting Inside; I'll Never
Know; 'Till the Right One Comes Along; Your Turn to Cry; Little
Bitty Pretty One; Remember, It's Me; Mighty Good Loving.* THE
DAVE CLARK FIVE (9/71): *Glad All Over; Can't You See That
She's Mine; I Need Love; Good Love Is Hard to Find; Try Too
Hard; Because; 'Till the Right One Comes Along; Having a Wild
Weekend; Sitting Here Baby; Concentration Baby; Please Tell Me
Why; Inside and Out; Come Home; Forever and a Day; Bernedette;
Hurting Inside; I'll Be Your Love.* ALL-TIME GREATEST HITS
(4/75): *Glad All Over; Bits and Pieces; Can't You See That She's
Mine; Catch Us If You Can; Because; Any Way You Want It; Try
Too Hard; At the Scene; Everybody Knows; Come Home; Do You
Love Me; Reelin' and Rockin'; I Like It Like That; Over and Over;
You Got What It Takes; Nineteen Days; Good Time Woman;
Forget; I've Got to Have a Reason; Here Comes Summer.*

Singles/*Do You Love Me/Because* (7/64); *Glad All Over/Bits and
Pieces* (9/64); *Everybody Knows/I Like It Like That* (9/64); *Catch
Us If You Can/On the Move* (8/65); *Can't You See That She's
Mine/Any Way You Want It* (10/65); *Over and Over/I'll Be Yours*

(10/65); *At the Scene/I Miss You* (1/66); *Try Too Hard/All Night Long* (4/66); *Satisfied with You/Don't Let Me Down* (7/66); *You've Got What It Takes/Doctor Rhythm* (3/67); *You Must Have Been a Beautiful Baby/Man in the Pin Stripe Suit* (5/67); *A Little Bit Now/You Don't Play Around* (7/67); *Red and Blue/Concentration Baby* (10/67); *Forget/Please Stay* (4/68); *Red Balloon/Maze of Love* (8/68); *Paradise/34–06* (5/69); *If Somebody Loves You/Best Day's Work* (7/69); *Bring It on Home to Me/Darling, I Love You* (10/69); *Here Comes Summer/Five By Five* (6/70); *If Somebody Loves You/Bring It on Home to Me* (7/70); *One Night/Lawdy Miss Clawdy* (11/70); *Southern Man/If You Want to See Me Cry* (2/71); *Won't You Be My Lady/Into Your Life* (7/71); *Rub It In/I'm Sorry Baby* (7/72); *Can't You See That She's Mine/I Like It Like That* (4/73); *You Got What It Takes/Come Home* (4/73).

JIMMY CLIFF/Most famous for his starring role, both as an actor and a singer, in the epic reggae film *The Harder They Come,* Jimmy Cliff is yet another talent to get bogged down in the on-again, off-again romance between the world at large and reggae music. Touted as being "the next big thing" in pop for the last five years, reggae has never quite caught on in a global sense and, as a result, several bona fide artists' careers have been hampered.

Cliff began his vocalizing in 1962 while a resident of Kingston, Jamaica. The Jamaican-born talent cut a few sides for local labels and became a well-known personality on a regional level. Chris Blackwell of Island Records was impressed enough with Cliff's vocal skills to talk him into both moving to the United Kingdom and signing with the label. After several years of just missing his mark in England, Cliff finally hit the charts with *Wonderful World, Beautiful People.* Success, however, seemed forever beyond his grasp. Cliff decided to abandon his reggae roots and embark on a career as an R&B performer. The resulting album, *ANOTHER CYCLE,* nearly cost him his professional life.

Fortunately, fate intervened in the form of the motion picture *The Harder They Come.* Cast as a reggae star caught between the law and the underworld, Cliff soon became synonymous with the term "reggae" to most of the world media. This association proved something of a drawback to Cliff, who never really considered himself a reggae purist. His music has always bounded around the nebulous R&B-pop-reggae area, never quite falling into one identifiable pigeonhole. As a result, on one hand, Cliff's career has been hampered by its association with reggae in that the Jamaican style has never achieved true popularity. Conversely, his association with pop and R&B have kept his record sales to a minimum in strict reggae quarters. Despite his constant brushes with various rock versions of "Catch-22," Cliff has succeeded in recording several excellent long-players, showcasing his strong, crystal-clear vocals.

Albums/WONDERFUL WORLD, BEAUTIFUL PEOPLE (1/70): *Many Rivers to Cross; You'll Never Walk Alone; Moon River; One Woman; I've Been Trying; La, La, Always Stay; Wild World; Here Today, Gone Tomorrow; Cousin of Mine; Come into My Life; My Ancestors.* THE HARDER THEY COME (soundtrack; 1972): *You Can Get It if You Really Want; Draw Your Brakes; Rivers of Babylon; Many Rivers to Cross; Sweet and Dandy; The Harder They Come; Johnny Too Bad; Shanty Town; Pressure Drop; Sitting in Limbo; You Can Get It if You Really Want; The Harder They Come.* UNLIMITED (8/73): *Born to Win; Poor Slave; World of Peace; Black Queen; Be True; Oh, Jamaica; Commercialization; The Price of Peace; On My Life; I See the Light; Rip Off; Fundamental Reggae; Under the Sun Moon and Stars.* STRUGGLING MAN (1974): *Struggling Man; When You're Young; Better Days Are Coming; Sooner or Later; Those Good Good Old Days; Can't Stop Worrying, Can't Stop Loving You; Let's Seize the Time; Can't Live without You; Going Back West.* MUSIC MAKER (9/74): *Brother; I Want to Know; House of Exile; Foolish Pride; No. 1 Rip-off Man; Long Time No See; Music Maker; My Love Is Solid as a Rock; You Can't Be Wrong and Get It Right; Look What You Dont to My Life, Devil Woman; Money Won't Save You; I've Been Dead 400 Years.* FOLLOW MY MIND (9/75): *Look at the Mountains; The News; I'm Gonna Live, I'm Gonna Love; Going Mad; Dear Mother; Who Feels It, Knows It; Remake the World; No Woman, No Cry; Wahjahka Man; Hypocrites; If I Follow My Mind; You're the Only One.* REGGAE SPECTACULAR (4/76): *Wonderful World, Beautiful People; Viet Nam; Time Will Tell; Sitting in Limbo; plus other titles by various artists.* IN CONCERT (10/76): *You Can Get It if You Really Want; Viet Nam; Wonderful World, Beautiful People; Fountain of Life; Wild World; Under the Sun Moon and Stars;*

Sitting in Limbo; The Harder They Come; Struggling Man; Many Rivers to Cross.

Singles/*Wonderful World, Beautiful People* (11/69); *Viet Nam* (2/70); *Wild World* (8/70); *Goodbye Yesterday* (6/71); *The Harder They Come* (1972); *Born to Win/Black Queen* (8/73); *Music Maker/You Can't Be Wrong and Still Get It Right* (11/74); *The Harder They Come/Viet Nam* (12/76).

EDDIE COCHRAN/Guitarist Eddie Cochran was only twenty-one when he died in a car accident on April 17, 1960. He had just completed a tour of Britain with Gene Vincent and was on his way to the airport and a plane home when the accident occurred. Although overlooked in some circles, Cochran's contributions to rock were vast. He was one of the first of the rock and roll over-dubbers (*Summertime Blues* featured Eddie handling every instrumental and vocal chore) and his rebellious rockabilly style became a staple of the fifties' and sixties' rock diet. His guitar-playing style can be witnessed (albeit briefly) in the film *The Girl Can't Help It*, and his performances on such tunes as *C'mon Everybody* and *Hallelujah, I Love Her So* are considered classic.

Albums/SUMMERTIME BLUES (8/58): *Summertime Blues; Proud of You; One Kiss; Tell Me Why; other titles.* EDDIE COCHRAN (2/60): *C'mon Everybody; Three Steps to Heaven; Cut Across Shorty; Have I Told You Lately That I Love You; Hallelujah, I Love Her So; Sittin' in the Balcony; Summertime Blues; Lovin' Time; Somethin' Else; Tell Me Why; Teenage Heaven; Drive-In Show.* NEVER TO BE FORGOTTEN (12/63): *Weekend; Long Tall Sally; Lonely; Nervous Breakdown; Cherished Memories; Love Again; Twenty Flight Rock; Boll Weevil; Milk Cow Blues; Little Angel; Sweetie Pie; Blue Suede Shoes.* EDDIE COCHRAN (1/71): *Skinny Jim; Let's Get Together; Eddie's Blues; Little Lou; Pink Pegged Slacks; Jeannie Jeannie Jeannie; Something Else; Pretty Little Devil; Who Can I Count On; Thinkin' about You; Opportunity; Latch On; I'm Ready; Three Stars; Cotton Picker; Summertime Blues; Cut Across Shorty; Milk Cow Blues; My Way; Blue Suede Shoes; Nervous Breakdown; Come On, Everybody; Sittin' in the Balcony; Twenty Flight Rock; Teenage Cutie; Hallelujah, I Love Her So; Fourth Man Theme; Bo Weevil; Weekend; Long Tall Sally.*

Singles/*Sittin' in the Balcony* (2/57); *Drive-In Show* (8/57); *Jean-*

nie Jeannie Jeannie/Pocketful of Hearts (1/58); *Teresa/Pretty Girl* (5/58); *Summertime Blues/Love Again* (6/58); *C'mon Everybody/Don't Ever Let Me Go* (10/58); *Teenage Heaven/I Remember* (1/59); *Hallelujah, I Love Her So/Little Angel* (10/59); *Three Steps to Heaven/Cut Across Shorty* (3/60); *Lonely/Sweetie Pie* (8/60); *Weekend/Lonely* (10/61).

JOE COCKER/One of the most-oft-asked questions during the sixties' more pretentious moments was the epic "Can white men sing the blues?" Well, the answer presented itself as a loud affirmative in 1969 with the appearance of John Robert Cocker's first long-player, *WITH A LITTLE HELP FROM MY FRIENDS*. The growling, gutsy Englishman injected a double dose of rhythm and blues into every rock rhythm he touched from Lennon and McCartney standards to old-fashioned epics such as *Bye Bye Blackbird.* For Joe Cocker, blues had no color. Blues was emotion. Blues was power.

Cocker's childhood was spent in Sheffield, England, not exactly a hotbed of musical activity. After attending a local technical school, young Joe went on to become a gas fitter. During this time, however, Joe developed a taste for R&B, especially the sound of Ray Charles. His first band experience was as a drummer in a group called the Cavaliers. By the time the group mutated into the Avengers, Cocker was lead singer and the band was well known in local pubs as a fine R&B revue, with Joe vocalizing to the strains of Ray Charles and the Four Tops, among others.

An initial stab at recording fame ended in failure in 1964 when Cocker cut *I'll Cry Instead,* a Beatle tune. Cocker returned to his gas-fitting trade and weekend gigs in bars. He formed a new band, the Grease Band, which featured his long-time musical partner Chris Stainton. The band enjoyed a healthy life, playing every popular Motown tune in existence. After a year or two, Stainton arranged for Cocker and the band to meet with producer Denny Cordell. A single, *Marjorine,* resulted (based on a puppet-show character) and, although the single did not do well commercially, it convinced Cordell that Cocker was a major talent.

He was right, of course, and soon the career of Joe Cocker was launched in earnest. A single, *With a Little Help from My Friends,* soon brought Joe fame on both sides of the Atlantic, reaching the

number-one spot in England and breaking the top forty in the
States. The album of the same name and subsequent tours established Cocker as a star on the horizon. Many critics compared
him to Janis Joplin. Both were white blues interpreters, both
wrenched every ounce of emotion possible from their lyrics, and
both exuded lethal doses of sheer rock energy. Cocker, however,
got so physically involved with his music that he often appeared
grotesque to some fans. With arms flailing like a jitterbugging
epileptic and face contorted into a lifemask of agony/ ecstasy, the
bellowing newcomer became the cause célèbre of the 1968–69 music scene.

He appeared at the major American music festivals, a shot on
the *Ed Sullivan Show* ensured him national recognition, hit singles
like *Delta Lady, The Letter,* and *She Came Through the Bathroom
Window* seemed to assure him long-lasting success. Then a chain
of events occurred which earned Cocker the label of rock's "tragic
hero." Cocker, a shy but likeable individual, began having problems with some of his musical and business associates. He split
with the Grease Band and came to America in 1970 for a well-
earned rest.

Unfortunately, a tour for Cocker had already been booked.
Committed to the dates, Cocker found himself without the benefit
of band. Enter Leon Russell, an American musician, arranger,
and producer who had aided Cocker on his second album, *JOE
COCKER.* Russell assembled the gigantic Mad Dogs and Englishman outfit, a few dozen musicians and hangers-on who
backed Cocker on the tour. The resulting album, *MAD DOGS
AND ENGLISHMEN,* is one of the finest "live" albums ever released. It also marked the beginning of a downhill slide for the
singer.

Cast in the middle of the musical sideshow, Cocker appeared a
bit befuddled. Ultimately, the tour did more for the careers of
Russell and the sidemen than it did for Joe. On the brink of a
physical breakdown and allegedly relying on drugs and alcohol to
bolster his sagging spirits, Joe returned home to his parents. Two
years later, he attempted a brief comeback, which ended in failure. A bout with a manager over legal matters cost him nearly all
his earnings. Several singles stiffed. Disillusioned, Cocker once
again retreated from the limelight.

In 1974, with the aid of Jim Price, Cocker again attempted a comeback. An album, *I CAN STAND A LITTLE RAIN* was the result. A live touring situation ended in disaster with Cocker, now unused to performing in public, drinking heavily in a vain attempt to gain confidence. It was an embarrassment to all concerned. Fortunately, a single, *You Are So Beautiful,* took Cocker to the top ten and, for the first time in nearly five years, success seemed definite.

Joe's live antics, unfortunately, became more and more bizarre. With each subsequent concert, his self-destructive presence onstage overshadowed his superb vocal skills. Audiences assumed a ghoulish demeanor with many fans flocking to the concert halls just to see whether the star would remain on his feet. Eventually, his concerts approached legendary status, with inane tales working their way into print. Despite whatever insecurities Cocker demonstrated onstage, he more than compensated for his weaknesses on record. His voice a bit more gravelly, his delivery slightly slower, Cocker succeeded (and still succeeds) in delivering some of the most poignant blues-rock melodies ever heard on wax.

Recent albums such as *JAMAICA SAY YOU WILL* and *STINGRAY* have proven that, although his career has had its share of ups and downs, Joe Cocker will always be an immense talent capable of producing more feeling in one quivering note than most performers can scrounge up with ten amplifiers.

Albums/WITH A LITTLE HELP FROM MY FRIENDS (4/69): *Feeling Alright; Bye Bye Blackbird; Change in Louise; Marjorine: Just Like a Woman; Do I Still Figure in Your Life?; Sandpaper Cadillac; Don't Let Me Be Misunderstood; With a Little Help from My Friends; I Shall Be Released.* JOE COCKER! (10/69); *Dear Landlord; Bird on the Wire; Lawdy Miss Clawdy; She Came in through the Bathroom Window; Hitchcock Railway; That's Your Business; Something; Delta Lady; Hello, Little Friend; Darling, Be Home Soon.* MAD DOGS AND ENGLISHMEN (8/70): *Blue Medley: I'll Drown in My Own Tears/ When Something Is Wrong with My Baby, I've Been Loving You Too Long; Girl from the North Country; Please Give Peace a Chance; She Came In Thru the Bathroom Window; Space Captain; The Letter; Delta Lady; Honky Tonk Women; Sticks and Stones; Cry Me a River; Bird on the Wire; Feelin' Alright; Superstar; Let's Go Get Stoned.* JOE COCKER (11/72): *Pardon Me, Sir; High Time We Went; She Don't Mind; Black-Eyed Blues; Something to*

Say; Midnight Rider; Do Right Woman; Woman to Woman; St. James Infirmary Blues. I CAN STAND A LITTLE RAIN (8/74): *Put Out the Light; I Can Stand a Little Rain; I Get Mad; Sing Me a Song; The Moon Is a Harsh Mistress; Don't Forget Me; You Are So Beautiful; It's a Sin When You Love Somebody; Performance; Guilty.* JAMAICA SAY YOU WILL (8/75): *(That's What I Like) In My Woman; Where Am I Now; I Think It's Going to Rain To-day; Forgive Me Now; Oh Mama; Lucinda; If I Love You; Jamaica Say You Will; It's All Over but the Shoutin'; Jack-a-Diamonds.* STINGRAY (4/76): *The Jealous Kind; I Broke Down; You Came Along; Catfish; Moon Dew; The Man in Me; She Is My Lady; Worrier; Born thru Indifference; A Song for You.* JOE COCKER'S GREATEST HITS (12/77): *With a Little Help from My Friends; Woman to Woman; The Jealous Kind; Black-Eyed Blues; I Think It's Going to Rain; Cry Me a River; You Are So Beautiful; Feeling Alright; Delta Lady; Darling, Be Home Soon; High Time We Went; The Letter.*

Singles/*Marjorine* (4/68); *With a Little Help from My Friends/Something's Coming On* (10/68); *Feeling Alright* (4/69); *She Came In Thru the Bathroom Window* (11/69); *The Letter/Space Captain* (3/70); *Cry Me a River* (9/70); *Black-Eyed Blues/High Time We Went* (4/71); *Woman to Woman/Midnight Rider* (8/72); *Pardon Me, Sir* (1/73); *Put Out the Light/If I Love You* (5/74); *I Can Stand a Little Rain* (9/74); *You Are So Beautiful/It's a Sin When You Love Somebody* (11/74); *The Jealous Kind* (6/76); *I Broke Down* (8/76).

LEONARD COHEN/Poet. Novelist. Singer-songwriter. These are all descriptions of monotoned Canadian Leonard Cohen. With two novels and countless poems to his credit, Cohen turned to music in the mid-sixties. Judy Collins was the first to record a Cohen song, *Suzanne,* on her *IN MY LIFE* album in 1966. In the summer of '67, when she did a concert in New York's Central Park, she brought him up on the stage with her. He was diffident, handsome, very vulnerable—and his voice was thin. When his first album was released in 1968, every one of those qualities worked for him. His face stared out compellingly from a picture he'd taken himself in a photo machine. His thin voice made for a realism that seemed to bring him right into the room with the listener. The songs were in the same mood as his novels and poems had been; the lyrics were always those of a poet. You'd never call the tunes *funky,* but there was a hypnotic repetitiousness that made the album a calming antidote for loneliness.

Before long, Cohen became *the* artist to listen to if you were lonely, deep, heavy, intellectual, female, college bound and/or literate. For a time, Cohen's albums packed the same clout as the best paragraphs from *The Prophet* or the Herman Hesse book of one's choice. His rather maudlin lyricism, full of introspective meanderings and self-doubt, caught on faster than a speeding J. L. Seagull. He was, simply, all things to all people. In a rock world populated by budding flower children and soon-to-be acid casualties, Cohen's mature, somewhat anachronistic appearance only added to his charismatic stance.

He toured very little and therefore did not attain superstardom. But his cult was (and still is) strong and his devoted flock jammed concert halls wherever he played. During the seventies, he emerged as a bona fide *star* in Europe and he has embarked on several critically acclaimed stateside tours. Among Cohen's most famous compositions are *Suzanne, Famous Blue Raincoat,* and *Bird on the Wire.*

Albums/SONGS OF LEONARD COHEN (1/68): *Suzanne; Master Song; Winter Lady; Stranger Song; Sisters of Mercy; So Long, Marianne; Hey, That's No Way to Say Goodbye; Stories of the Street; Teachers; One of Us Cannot Be Wrong.* SONGS FROM A ROOM (4/69): *Bird on the Wire; Story of Isaac; A Bunch of Lonesome Heroes; The Partisan; Seems So Long Ago, Nancy; The Old Revolution; The Butchers; You Know Who I Am; Lady Midnight; Tonight Will Be Fine.* SONGS OF LOVE AND HATE (3/71): *Avalanche; Last Year's Man; Dress Rehearsal Rag; Diamonds in the Mine; Love Calls You by Your Name; Famous Blue Raincoat; Sing Another Song, Boys; Joan of Arc.* LIVE SONGS (4/73): *Seems So Long Ago, Nancy; Prologue; Passing Through; Bird on the Wire; Story of Isaac; Queen Victoria; You Know Who I Am; Tonight Will Be Fine; Please Don't Pass Me By.* NEW SKIN FOR THE OLD CEREMONY (10/74): *Is This What You Wanted; Chelsea Hotel Number Two; Lover Lover Lover; I Tried to Leave You; Who by Fire; Take This Longing; Leaving Greensleeves; Field Commander Cohen; Why Don't You Try; There Is a War; A Singer Must Die.* THE BEST OF LEONARD COHEN (2/76): *Suzanne; Sisters of Mercy; So Long, Marianne;*

Bird on the Wire; Lady Midnight; Partisan; Hey, That's No Way to Say Goodbye; Famous Blue Raincoat; Last Year's Man; Chelsea Hotel Number Two; Who by Fire; Take This Longing. DEATH OF A LADIES' MAN (11/77): *True Love Leaves No Traces; Iodine; Paper-Thin Hotel; Memories; I Left a Woman Waiting; Don't Go Home with Your Hard-On; Fingerprints; Death of a Ladies' Man.*

Singles/*Suzanne/Hey, That's No Way to Say Goodbye* (1/68); *Bird on the Wire/Seems So Long Ago, Nancy* (4/69); *Suzanne/Bird on the Wire* (9/70); *Avalanche/Dress Rehearsal Rag* (5/71); *Passing Through/Seems So Long Ago, Nancy* (4/73).

JUDY COLLINS/Judy Collins started in the days when what a girl needed most was a trusty guitar, a soulful expression, a formidable repertoire of songs from other times and other places, and a fine clear voice to sing them in. There were a lot of them around in the folk boom of the late fifties and early sixties— soulful ladies singing *John Riley* and *I Know Where I'm Going*— but Judy was one of the few to survive that whole sweet, sad, gentle, unrealistic period. Who could mourn one long, lost love in 1963 when a whole world looked as if it were about to go up in flames? Once the gentle maid from Denver heard what Bob Dylan, Phil Ochs, and Tom Paxton sang and wrote about the troubled, changing times, she knew that for her, anyway, there would be no more *John Riley's*. This was the beginning of her Stage Two, and if it seemed then, on *JUDY COLLINS NO. 3,* that she was just about the first to sing those songs of protest, it was because she was one of the first to sing them with conviction. When others saw that protest-folk worked musically and aesthetically, as well as socially and commercially, they followed, and soon so many folk and pop-folk albums had their mandatory track of angry Dylan or ironic Ochs that it was easy to forget that Judy had been one of those who made it possible.

With her point made, she was now able to move into Stage Three and return to lyricism and romance, introducing the new poetics of Leonard Cohen, Joni Mitchell, Donovan, Randy Newman and, of course, Judy Collins. Within this framework she has done a lot of moving: classical musicians onstage with her for some concerts; the songs from *Marat/Sade* and *A Little Night Music;* a hard-rocking single that was in the jukebox at the old

Blue Cue of Berkeley for a whole summer; her own three-piece traveling electric band; even, in 1969, a stint in the theater as Peer Gynt's Solveig.

During the seventies, her career has shown no signs of slowing down. If anything, the scope of her talent has broadened. Aside from her habit of turning *any* type of music into beautiful and accessible recordings (her more recent hits range from *Amazing Grace* to *Send in the Clowns*), she has displayed deftness as a writer (*The Judy Collins Songbook* and articles for *Ms.* and *Redbook*), and has even dabbled in film, co-directing a motion-picture documentary on the life of her former classical piano teacher, Antonia Brico. The production, *Antonia: A Portrait of the Woman,* was released in 1974 and was chosen to open the American Filmmakers Series at New York's Whitney Museum. It was named one of the Ten Best by *Time* magazine and was nominated for an Oscar. In 1977, Judy Collins celebrated her fifteenth year as a recording artist. From the looks of things, there will be many more such celebrations.

Albums/A MAID OF CONSTANT SORROW (1962): *Maid of Constant Sorrow; Prickilie Bush; Wild Mountain Thyme; Tim Evans; Sailor's Life; Bold Fenian Men; Wars of Germany; O Daddy Be Gay; I Know Where I'm Going; John Riley; Pretty Saro; Rising of the Moon.* GOLDEN APPLES OF THE SUN (1962): *Golden Apples of the Sun; Bonnie Ship the Diamond; Crow on the Cradle; Fannerio; Tell Me Who I'll Marry; Christ Child Lullaby; Great Selchie of Shule Skerry; House Carpenter; Little Brown Dog; Minstrel Boy; Twelve Gates to the City; Lark in the Morning; Shule Aroon; Sing Hallelujah.* JUDY COLLINS NO. 3 (10/63): *Anathea; Bullgine Run; Farewell; Dove; Hey Nellie; Town Crier; Masters of War; Hills of Shiloh; Bells of Rhymney; Deportees; Settle Down; Come Away Melinda; Turn, Turn, Turn.* JUDY COLLINS IN CONCERT (8/64): *Winter Sky; That Was the Last Thing on My Mind; Tear Down the Walls; Bonnie Boy Is Young; Me and My Uncle; Wild Rippling Water; Lonesome Death of Hattie Carrol; Ramblin' Boy; Red-Winged Blackbird; Coal Tattoo; Cruel Mother; Bottle of Wine; Medgar Evers Lullaby; Hey, Nellie, Nellie.* JUDY COLLINS 5TH ALBUM (10/65): *Pack Up Your Sorrows; Coming of the Roads; So Early, Early in the Spring; Daddy You've Been on My Mind; Thirsty Boots; Carry It On; Early*

Morning Rain; Tomorrow Is a Long Time; Lord Gregory; In the Heat of the Summer; Mr. Tambourine Man; It Isn't Nice. IN MY LIFE (11/66): *Just Like Tom Thumb's Blues; Hard Lovin' Loser; Pirate Jenny; Suzanne; La Colombe; Marat/Sade; I Think It's Going to Rain Today; Sunny Goodge Street; Liverpool Lullaby; Dress Rehearsal Rag; In My Life.* WILDFLOWERS (11/67): *Albatross; Michael from Mountains; Hey, That's No Way to Say Goodbye; Sisters of Mercy; Chanson Des Vieux Amants; Both Sides Now; Sky Fell; Since You Asked; Priests; Ballata of Francesco Landini.* WHO KNOWS WHERE THE TIME GOES (11/68): *Hello Hooray; Story of Isaac; My Father; Someday Soon; Who Knows Where the Time Goes; Poor Immigrant; First Boy I Loved; Bird on the Wire; Pretty Polly.* RECOLLECTIONS (10/69): *Pack Up Your Sorrows; Tomorrow Is A Long Time; Early Morning Rain; Anathea; Turn, Turn, Turn; Daddy, You've Been on My Mind; Mr. Tambourine Man; Winter Sky; The Last Thing on My Mind/Bells of Rhymney; Farewell.* WHALES AND NIGHT-INGALES (10/70): *Song for David; Sons of: The Patriot Game; Prothalamium; Oh, Had I A Golden Thread; Gene's Song; Farewell to Tarwathie; Time Passes Slowly; Marieke; Nightingale I and II; Simple Gifts; Amazing Grace.* LIVING (11/71): *Joan of Arc; Four Strong Winds; Vietnam Love Song; Innisfree; Song for Judith; All Things Are Quite Silent; Easy Times; Chelsea Morning; Blue Raincoat; Just Like Tom Thumb's Blues.* COLORS OF THE DAY/ THE BEST OF JUDY COLLINS (5/72): *Someday Soon; Since You Asked; Both Sides Now; Sons Of; Suzanne; Farewell to Tarwathie; Who Knows Where the Time Goes; Sunny Goodge Street; My Father; Albatross; In My Life; Amazing Grace.* TRUE STORIES AND OTHER DREAMS (1/73): *Cook with Honey; So Begins the Task; Fishermen Song; The Dealer; Secret Gardens; Holly Ann; The Hostage; Song for Martin; Che.* JUDITH (3/75): *The Moon Is a Harsh Mistress; Angel, Spread Your Wings; Houses; The Loving of the Game; Song for Duke; Send in the Clowns; Salt of the Earth; Brother, Can You Spare a Dime; City of New Orleans; I'll Be Seeing You; Pirate Ships; Born to the Breed.* BREAD AND ROSES (8/76): *Bread and Roses; Everything Must Change; Special Delivery; Out of Control; Come Down in Time; Plegaria a Un Labrador; Spanish is the Loving Tongue; I Didn't Know about You; Marjorie; King David; Love Hurts; Take This Longing.* THE FIRST 15 YEARS (7/77): *Pretty Polly; So Early,*

Early in the Spring; Pretty Saro; Golden Apples of the Sun; Bonnie Ship the Diamond; Farewell to Tarwathie; The Hostage; La Colombe; Coal Tattoo; Carry It On; The Lovin; Of the Game; Bread and Roses; Marat/Sade; Special Delivery; Since You've Asked; Born to the Breed; Holly Ann; Houses; Secret Gardens; My Father; Bird on the Wire; Send in the Clowns; Marieke; Both Sides Now.

Singles/*I'll Keep It With Mine/Thirsty Boots* (11/65);*Hard Lovin' Loser/I Think It's Going to Rain Today* (1/67); *Both Sides Now/ Who Knows Where the Time Goes* (10/68); *Amazing Grace/Nightingale II* (11/70); *Open the Door (Song for Judith)/ Innisfree* (10/71); *Someday Soon/Suzanne* (6/72); *In My Life/Sunny Goodge Street* (9/72); *Cook with Honey/So Begins the Task* (1/73); *Secret Gardens/The Hostage* (4/73);*Send in the Clowns/Houses* (5/75); *Bread and Roses/Out of Control* (10/76); *Everything Must Change/Special Delivery* (1/77).

RITA COOLIDGE/The voice of Rita Coolidge is a perfect combination of fire and ice. Laidback and languid in style, Coolidge is a songstress who has risen from the ranks of background performer to superstar with apparent ease. Part Cherokee, Rita began singing at the age of two, with both the blessing and encouragement of her Baptist minister father, Richard. Learning the ropes of the vocal trade in her dad's choir, Rita turned to vocalizing as a way of paying her tuition while studying at Florida State, working on a Master's in Fine Arts. Soon the college student found music more attractive than homework and an embryonic career was begun. Rita's initial work was mostly commercial oriented, with most of the TV and radio spots cut in Memphis. A single, *Turn Around And Love You,* recorded between jingles, became a regional hit.

It was at this time that she came to the attention of Delaney and Bonnie, who asked her to join them for a national tour. The D&B and Friends exposure gave a nice boost to Rita's career. The session work began to pour in. Delaney and Bonnie's first album, sessions with Clapton, Booker T., Graham Nash, Stephen Stills, and the now-historic Joe Cocker Mad Dogs and Englishmen tour were among the many.

In 1971, Rita embarked on a solo career with the release of her first album. It was in 1971 that she met Kris Kristofferson as well.

Kris and Rita later married and currently live in California with daughter Casey. The twosome have become the seventies' idea of the ideal musical couple, with two successful musical careers in the house and an occasional duet both on wax and on the concert stage.

Albums/RITA COOLIDGE (2/71): *That Man Is My Weakness; Second Story Window; Crazy Love; The Happy Song; Seven Bridges Road; Born under a Bad Sign; Ain't That Peculiar; Mountains; Mud Island; I Believe in You.* NICE FEELIN' (11/71): *Family Full of Soul; You Touched Me in the Morning; If You Were Mine; Nice Feelin'; Only You Know and I Know; I'll Be Here; Better Days; Lay My Burden Down; Most Likely You Go Your Way; Journey thru the Past.* THE LADY'S NOT FOR SALE (10/72): *My Crew; Fever; Bird on the Wire; I'll Be Your Baby Tonight; A Woman Left Lonely; Whiskey, Whiskey; Everybody Loves a Winner; Donut Man; Inside of Me; The Lady's Not for Sale.* FULL MOON (8/73): *Hard to be Friends; It's All Over; I Never Had It So Good; From the Bottle to the Bottom; Take Time to Love; Tennessee Blues; Part of Your Life; I'm Down; I Heard the Bluebirds Sing; After the Fact; Loving Arms; A Song I'd Like to Sing.* FALL INTO SPRING (4/74): *Love Has No Pride; That's What Friends Are For; Cowboys and Indians; Hold an Old Friend's Hand; We Had It All; Mama Lou; Heaven's Dream; Desperados Waiting for the Train; A Nickel for the Fiddler; The Burden of Freedom; Now Your Baby Is a Lady; I Feel Like Going Home.* IT'S ONLY LOVE (11/75): *Born to Love Me; I Wanted It All; Keep the Candle Burning; Don't Let Love Pass You By; It's Only Love; Star; Late Again; My Rock and Roll Man; Mean to Me; Am I Blue.* ANYTIME . . . ANYWHERE (3/77): *Higher and Higher; The Way You Do the Things You Do; We're All Alone; I Feel the Burden Being Lifted Off My Shoulders; I Don't Want to Talk about It; Words; Good Times; Who's to Bless and Who's to Blame; Southern Lady; The Hungry Years.*

Singles/*Crazy Love* (3/71); *I Believe in You* (6/71); *Nice Feelin'* (1/72); *A Song I'd Like to Sing* (10/72); *Fever* (1/73); *Whiskey, Whiskey* (2/73); *Loving Arms* (1/74); *Hold an Old Friend's Hand* (7/74); *Love Has No Pride* (11/74); *Star* (1/76); *Keep the Candle Burning* (4/76); *Higher and Higher* (3/77).

ALICE COOPER/Generally regarded as the father of rock's Grand Guignol movement, Alice Cooper is the man who brought rock theater to the extreme of its nadir, introducing boa constrictors, ten-foot cyclops beasts, and titanic teeth and towering toothbrushes to the concert stage. En route to performing a complete concert set, Alice was beheaded, electrocuted, hung, and finally tormented by the devil himself within the confines of hell. Such is the price of rock fame.

Alice, born Vincent Furnier in Detroit, actually was bitten by the R&R bug while still in high school. The son of a minister, Vinnie formed the Earwigs with fellow classmates Michael Bruce, Neal Smith, Dennis Dunaway, and Glen Buxton. Playing the popular hits of the day, the Earwigs became the Spiders and then Nazz before leaving hometown Phoenix, Arizona, in search of fame and fortune in Los Angeles. Eventually, the band was signed by Frank Zappa's Straight label, a recording operation that specialized in the bizarre. The Alice Cooper band's initial two albums, *PRETTIES FOR YOU* and *EASY ACTION,* were essentially routine exercises in ear-shattering rock.

The band's big break came when one of their concerts in the Michigan area was broadcast, coast to coast, on a syndicated rock TV "special." Suddenly, Alice Cooper, now headquartered in the Detroit area, became an underground cause célèbre. Was it a boy? A girl? What were they doing? As Alice and the band covered themselves with white sheets and groped around the stage area playing deranged solos, several rock business notables reevaluated the band's potential. Among those who thought Alice could make it was spunky producer Bob Ezrin, who took a chance and dragged the band into the studio for a third crack at album-making. The resulting long-player, *LOVE IT TO DEATH,* was a smash, launching Alice successfully to superstardom via a hit single, *I'm 18.* The follow-up albums, *KILLER* and *SCHOOL'S OUT* along with Alice's unique theatrical approach to the concert trail, firmly established the band as America's number-one attraction.

Problems arose after the release of *BILLION DOLLAR BABIES,* wherein Alice seemed to step back from the spotlight and caricature his own efforts to attain fame. He parted ways with the original group (who resurfaced in 1977 as Billion Dollar Babies) and gathered unto himself top session players Whitey

Glan, Josef Chirowsky, Dick Wagner, John Prakash, and Steve Hunter. That combo proved effective on *MUSCLE OF LOVE* and on Alice's TV special/soundtrack album *WELCOME TO MY NIGHTMARE.*

By 1977, it was clear that Alice was growing tired of the rock business proper. Frequent television guest spots, both as a talk-show personality and as a budding actor, began to take up most of his time. In 1977 the talented singer-songwriter-performer fended off an alcoholic exile successfully. The same year found Alice completing a role in the motion picture *SGT. PEPPER'S LONELY HEARTS CLUB BAND.*

Albums/PRETTIES FOR YOU (1/70): *Titanic Overture; 10 Minutes before the Worm; Sing Low, Sweet Cherio; Today Mueller; Living; Fields of Regret; No Longer Umpire; Levity Ball; B.B. on Mars; Reflected; Apple Bush; Earwigs to Eternity; Changing Arranging.* EASY ACTION (3/70): *Mr. and Misdemeanor; Blow Your Means; Still No Air; Shoe Salesman; Return of the Spiders; Laughing at Me; Lay Down and Die, Goodbye; Beautiful Flyaway Refrigerator Heaven.* LOVE IT TO DEATH (2/71): *Caught in a Dream; I'm Eighteen; Hallowed Be My Name; Long Way to Go; Black Juju; Is It My Body; Second Coming; Ballad of Dwight Frye; Sun Arise.* SCHOOL'S OUT (2/71): *School's Out; Alma Mater; Blue Turk; Grande Finale; My Stars; Public Animal; Gutter Cat vs. the Jets; Luney Tunes.* KILLER (11/71): *Under My Wheels; Be My Lover; Killer; Desperado; Halo of Flies; You Drive Me Nervous; Yeah, Yeah, Yeah; Dead Babies.* BILLION DOLLAR BABIES (4/73): *Elected; I Love the Dead; Sick Things; Billion Dollar Babies; Hello! Hurray!; Raped and Freezin'; Unfinished Sweet; No More Mister Nice Guy; Generation Landslide; Mary-Ann.* MUSCLE OF LOVE (9/73): *Big Apple Dreamin'; Never Been Sold Before; Woman Machine; Teenage Lament '74; Man with the Golden Gun; Crazy Little Child; Hard-Hearted Alice.* GREATEST HITS (8/74): *I'm Eighteen; Is It My Body; Desperado; Under My Wheels; Be My Lover; School's Out; Hello! Hooray!; Elected; No More Mister Nice Guy; Billion Dollar Babies; Teenage Lament '74; Muscle of Love.* WELCOME TO MY NIGHTMARE (2/75): *Welcome to my Nightmare; Devil's Food; The Black Widow; Some Folks; Only Women Bleed; Department of Youth; Cold Ethyl; Years Ago; Steven; The Awakening;*

Escape. ALICE COOPER GOES TO HELL (6/76): *Give the Kid a Break; Guilty; Wake Me Gently; Wish You Were Here; I'm Always Chasing Rainbows; Going Home; Go To Hell; I'm the Coolest; Didn't We Meet; I Never Cry.* LACE AND WHISKEY (3/77): *Damned If You Do; My God; It's Hot Tonight; Lace and Whiskey; Road Rats; Love at Your Convenience; Ubangi Stomp; You and Me; I Never Wrote Those Songs.* THE ALICE COOPER SHOW (9/77): *Under My Wheels; Eighteen; Only Women Bleed; Sick Things; I Never Cry; Is It My Body; Billion Dollar Babies; Devil's Food/The Black Widow; You and Me; I Love the Dead/ Go to Hell/Wish You Were Here; School's Out.*

Singles/*Shoe Salesman/Return of the Spiders* (5/70); *I'm Eighteen/Is It My Body* (11/70); *Caught in a Dream/Hallowed Be My Name* (5/71); *Under My Wheels/Desperado* (10/71); *Be My Lover/Yeah, Yeah, Yeah* (2/72); *School's Out/Gutter Cat vs. the Jets* (5/72); *Be My Lover/Under My Wheels* (9/72); *Hello! Hooray!/Alma Mater* (1/73); *Raped and Freezin'/No More Mister Nice Guy* (3/73); *Billion Dollar Babies/Mary-Ann* (6/73); *Teenage Lament '74/Hard-Hearted Alice* (11/73); *Muscle of Love/I'm Eighteen* (8/74); *Department of Youth/Some Folks* (1/75); *Only Women Bleed/Cold Ethyl* (3/75); *Welcome to My Night-mare/Cold Ethyl* (9/75); *Only Women Bleed/Welcome to My Nightmare* (2/76); *I Never Cry/Go To Hell* (5/76); *You and Me/It's Hot Tonight (3/77).*

CREAM/*Eric Clapton (guitar), Ginger Baker (drums), Jack Bruce (bass, harmonica, vocals).*

Cream was the first of the supergroups. Born of the musician's perennial dream of bringing together the cream of the current musical crop into one mind-boggling all-star group, Cream united Ginger Baker, master drummer, Eric Clapton, king of the British blues guitarists, and Jack Bruce, superbassist. This was early 1967, when those who had outgrown early Beatles and early Beatles imitators were ready to get their teeth into some adult and substantial music, so Cream's timing was perfect.

Prior to their emergence as a trio, the three Cream musicians had accumulated a devoted following in their own right. Bruce, who started off singing Scots folk songs, was in the Graham Bond Organization, an organ group with jazz and blues influences, with which jazz-oriented Ginger Baker also played. Bruce also played with the highly commercial Manfred Mann group for a while and with the bloozey John Mayall Bluesbreakers, the group Eric Clapton went to after starting the Yardbirds. Clapton was a living legend prior to Cream for both the aforementioned Yardbirds and Mayall's roots-oriented band.

With Cream, rock finally grew up and Clapton became an all-time rock hero, edging Lennon and Jagger from their pedestals. Although there had been plenty of blues-playing around, it took Cream to fully tune a whole new generation into that kind of music. Cream was one of the prime movers behind the blues revival of 1968 and the great interest in the roots of the new blues-rock. Clapton and fellow guitarist Mike Bloomfield (the American wonder from the Electric Flag and the Paul Butterfield Blues Band) continually gave credit where it was due. talking of roots and sources, bringing up the names of blues originals like Muddy Waters, Howlin' Wolf, Elmore James, and B. B. King. It worked two ways for them, for once some of the more astute heard the originals, they were less impressed by what the Cream and Bloomfield bands were doing. But that was irrelevant because Cream conquered like no other band did, so that by the end of 1968, when they called it quits, they were able to sell out New York's enormous Madison Square Garden weeks before their farewell concert (and this was in the days when "monster" concerts were *not* a regular event).

Cream's music was essentially interpretive blues and rock, with all kinds of personal versatility but very little cheap flash and virtually no help from musical friends. There were no stars, just the music. Clapton's guitar was as lean and melancholy as his face. Jack Bruce was the quintessential musician. Ginger Baker was the devil with drumsticks. Once the pressures of success got to all three members, there was nowhere to go but o-u-t.

Following Cream's demise, Clapton and Baker reunited briefly for their Blind Faith stumble. Jack Bruce embarked on an erratic solo career that has yet to take hold. Baker went on to form the nearly disastrous Ginger Baker's Airforce. This ensemble was quickly followed by a few commercially wanting solo albums and a still existent Baker-Guervitz Army. Clapton, of course, has achieved fame both as a solo guitarist and as the leader of the short-lived but phenomenal Derek and the Dominoes.

Albums/FRESH CREAM (1/67): *I Feel Free; N.S.U.; Sleepy Time Time; I'm So Glad; Toad; Dreaming; Sweet Wine; Cat's Squirrel; Four Until Late; Rollin' and Tumblin'.* DISRAELI GEARS (12/67): *Strange Brew; Sunshine of Your Love; Blue Condition; World of Pain; Dance the Night Away; Tales of Brave Ulysses; Swlabr; We're Going Wrong; Outside Woman Blues; Take It Back; Mother's Lament.* WHEELS OF FIRE (6/68): *White Room; Sitting on Top of the World; Passing the Time; As You Said; Pressed Rat and Warthog; Politician; Those Were the Days; Born under a Bad Sign; Deserted Cities of the Heart; Crossroads; Spoonful; Traintime; Toad.* GOODBYE (1/69): *Sitting on Top of the World; Badge; Doing That Scrapyard Thing; What a Bringdown; I'm So Glad; Politician.* THE BEST OF CREAM (6/69): *Sunshine of Your Love; I'm So Glad; Strange Brew; White Room, other titles.* LIVE CREAM (4/70). LIVE CREAM, VOL. II (3/72): *Deserted Cities of the Heart; White Room; Politician; Tales of Brave Ulysses; Sunshine of Your Love; Hideaway.* HEAVY CREAM (10/72): *Strange Brew; White Room; Badge; Spoonful; Rollin' and Tumblin'; I Feel Free; Born under a Bad Sign; Passing the Time; As You Said; Deserted Cities of the Heart; Cat's Squirrel; Crossroads; Sitting on Top of the World; Swlabr; What a Bringdown; Tales of Brave Ulysses; Take It Back; Politician; I'm So Glad; Sunshine of Your Love; Those Were the Days; Doing That Scrapyard Thing.* OFF THE TOP (1973): *Dance the Night Away; Four Until Late; Toad; World of Pain; N.S.U.; Dreaming; Mother's Lament; Sweet Wine; Traintime; Outside Woman Blues; Sleepy Time Time.*

Singles/*I Feel Free/N.S.U.* (1/67); *Strange Brew/Tales of Brave Ulysses* (5/67); *Spoonful* (9/67); *Sunshine of Your Love/Swlabr* (12/67); *Pressed Rat and Warthog/Anyone for Tennis* (3/68); *White Room/Those Were the Days* (9/68); *Crossroads* (1/69); *Badge* (3/69).

CREEDENCE CLEARWATER REVIVAL/*John Fogerty (guitar, vocal), Tom Fogerty (guitar, vocal), Stu Cook (bass), Doug Clifford (drums).*
The original Cro-Magnon men of sixties rock, the Creedence brigade first assaulted the airwaves with their bare-boned sound during a period when rock sophistication was THE concept to strive for. They played low down and nasty, simplistic R&B-rock

that made many an Anglophile cringe as, one by one, their singles shot to the top of the charts. (Quite uncouth of them.) The foursome actually got started a few years before their 1968 debut when, known as the Blue Velvets, the band signed with a local San Francisco-based label, Fantasy. The band later evolved into the Golliwogs and proceeded to release a slew of stiff singles, much to everyone's chagrin; including Fantasy's. Fantasy began harping at the boys to change their name and, eventually, Creedence Clearwater Revival emerged.

Led by John Fogerty's brash guitar style and agonized vocals, the band chugged its way into the hearts and stereo speakers of music fantatics world-wide for over three years. Trouble eventually reared its head and brother Tom left the band in a huff. CCR continued as a trio for a while, but nothing much came of it. The problem was that John felt that he was the important factor in the band's success. As it turned out, he was; and once he stopped caring about what he was doing, Creedence skidded to a stop. They disbanded in 1972 but, by that time, their fans, their music and their popularity had long since passed them by.

Albums/CREEDENCE CLEARWATER REVIVAL (6/68):*I Put a Spell on You; The Working Man; Ninety Nine and a Half (Won't Do); Suzie Q; Get Down Woman; Porterville; Gloomy; Walk on the Water.* BAYOU COUNTRY (1/69): *Born on the Bayou; Bootleg; Graveyard Train; Good Golly Miss Molly; Penthouse Pauper; Proud Mary; Keep on Choogin.* GREEN RIVER (8/69): *Green River; Commotion; Tombstone Shadow; Wrote a Song for Everyone; The Night Time Is the Right Time; Bad Moon Rising; Lodie; Cross Tie Walker; Sinister Purpose.* WILLY AND THE POORBOYS (11/69): *Down on the Corner; It Came out of the Sky; Cotton Fields; Poorboy Shuffle; Feelin' Blue; Fortunate Son; Don't Look Now (It Ain't You or Me); Midnight Special; Side O The Road; Effigy.* COSMOS FACTORY (7/70): *Ramble Tamble; Before You Accuse Me; Ooby Dooby; Lookin' out My Back Door; Run through the Jungle; Up around the Bend; My Baby Left Me; Who'll Stop the Rain; I Heard It through the Grapevine; Long As I Can See the Light.* MARDI GRAS (4/72): *Tearin' up the Country; Someday Never Comes; Lookin' for a Reason; Take It Like a Friend; Need Someone to Hold; What Are You Gonna Do; Sail Away; Hello Mary Lou; Door to Door; Sweet Hitch-Hiker.* PENDULUM (12/70): *Pagan Baby; Sailor's Lament; Chameleon;*

Have You Ever Seen the Rain?; Wish I Could Hide Away; Born to Move; Hey Tonight; It's Just a Thought; Molina; Rude Awakening #2. CHRONICLE (4/76): *Susie Q: I Put a Spell on You; Proud Mary; Bad Moon Rising; Lodi; Green River; Commotion; Down on the Corner; Fortunate Son; Travelin' Band; Have You Ever Seen the Rain?; Up around the Bend; Run through the Jungle; Lookin' out My Back Door; Long As I Can See the Light; I Heard It through the Grapevine; Hey Tonight; Sweet Hitch Hiker; Someday Will Never Come; Who'll Stop the Rain.*

Singles/*Susie Q* (6/68); *I Put a Spell on You/Walk on the Water* (1968); *Proud Mary/Born on the Bayou* (1/69); *Bad Moon Rising/Lodi* (4/69); *Green River/Commotion* (7/69); *Down on the Corner/FortunateSon* (10/69); *Travelin' Band/Who'll Stop the Rain* (1/70); *Up around the Bend/Run through the Jungle* (4/70); *Lookin' Out My Back Door/Long As I Can See the Light* (7/70); *Have You Ever Seen the Rain?/Hey Tonight* (1/71); *Sweet Hitch-Hiker/Door to Door* (7/71); *Someday Never Comes/Tearin' up the Country* (3/72); *I Heard It through the Grapevine* (1/76).

JIM CROCE/A working man's hero, Jim Croce was the lumber-jack figure with the porcelain voice. Philadelphia-born Jim first got a taste of music in his college years at Villanova, where he spent his free hours alternately playing guitar and playing disc jockey on the local station. While making the rounds in New York's mid-sixties folk-rock jungle, Jim was given some heart-to-heart advice by friend Tommy West (soon to hit with Cashman, Pistilli and West, later with Cashman and West, and still later as a producer/owner of Lifesong Records). Gig all you can and let your reputation grow naturally was the essence of the message. Jim did just that, and soon he and his wife, Ingrid, were signed to Capitol Records for a folkie album. It proved a much-ignored effort.

A bit disheartened, Croce took to manual labor, doing odd jobs and driving a truck. By the time he ran into West again, Tommy was part of a producing duo with Cashman and Jim was loaded with songs. Cashman and West were impressed, so Jim (aided by sideman–best friend Maury Muehleisen) recorded his first album, *YOU DON'T MESS AROUND WITH JIM*. The album hemmed and hawed around the charts for the first few months of its existence, but two singles, *You Don't Mess Around with Jim* and

Operator eventually sent the album to the top ten. Croce's next album, *LIFE AND TIMES,* went gold, with *Leroy Brown* topping the singles charts. Croce was clearly a talent to be reckoned with. He was alternately rough-and-tumble and touching with his melodies. Onstage he was everyone's big brother, open and warm and wise. His lyrics were simplistic yet subtle, wry yet heart-wrenching.

At the height of his popularity, both Croce and friend Muehleisen (who shared in all of Jim's triumphs) were killed when their chartered plane went down immediately after takeoff in Louisiana on September 20, 1973. Four years later, his widow, Ingrid, successfully proved in court that the pilot (who also died in the crash) was unfit for duty at the time. A tragic blunder in job scheduling brought about the loss of one of America's most promising artists.

Croce's song poetics were to be heard in full flower one more time—on his final studio album, *I GOT A NAME,* completed shortly before the accident and released posthumously.

Albums/YOU DON'T MESS AROUND WITH JIM (5/72): *You Don't Mess Around with Jim; Tomorrow's Gonna Be a Brighter Day; New York's Not My Home; Hard Time Losin' Man; Photographs and Memories; Walkin' Back to Georgia; Operator (That's Not the Way It Feels); Time in a Bottle; Rapid Roy (The Stock Car Boy); Box #10; A Long Time Ago; Hey Tomorrow.* LIFE AND TIMES (1/73): *One Less Set of Footsteps; Roller Derby Queen; Dreamin' Again; Careful Man; Alabama Rain; A Good Time Man Like Me Ain't Got No Business (Singin' the Blues); Next Time, This Time; Bad, Bad Leroy Brown; Speedball Tucker; These Dreams; It Doesn't Have to Be That Way.* I GOT A NAME (12/73): *I Got a Name; Lover's Cross; Five Short Minutes; Age; Workin' at the Car Wash Blues; I'll Have to Say I Love You in a Song; Salon and Saloon; Thursday; Top Hat Bar and Grille; Recently; The Hard Way Every Time.* PHOTOGRAPHS AND MEMORIES (9/74): *Bad, Bad Leroy Brown; Operator (That's Not the Way It Feels); Photographs and Memories; Rapid Roy (The Stock Car Boy); Time in a Bottle; New York's Not My Home; Workin' at the Car Wash Blues; I Got a Name; I'll Have to Say I Love You in a Song; You Don't Mess Around with Jim; Lover's Cross; One Less Set of Footsteps; Roller Derby Queen; These Dreams.*

Singles/ *You Don't Mess Around with Jim* (1972); Operator/Rapid Roy (8/72); *One Less Set of Footsteps/It Doesn't Have to Be That Way* (1/73); *Bad, Bad Leroy Brown/A Good Time Man Like Me Ain't Got No Business (Singin' the Blues)* (3/73); *Alabama Rain/I Got a Name* (8/73); *Hard Time Losin' Man/Time in a Bottle* (10/73); *Roller Derby Queen/It Doesn't Have to Be That Way* (11/73); *I Got a Name/Alabama Rain* (1/74); Time in a Bottle/It Doesn't Have to Be That Way (3/74); *Workin' at the Car Wash Blues/Thursday* (5/74); *Workin' at the Car Wash Blues/Thursday* (2/75).

CROSBY AND NASH/ *David Crosby (vocals and guitar), Graham Nash (vocals and guitar).*
Easygoing L.A. cowboy David Crosby paired with Britisher Graham Nash in 1972, during a lull in the productivity of Crosby, Stills, Nash and Young. Crosby, a former New Christy Minstrel and Byrds member, dabbled briefly in a solo career with his LP, *IF I COULD ONLY REMEMBER MY NAME.* The album proved the point. Nash's work as a single artist was similarly uninspiring. This twosome's on-again, off-again teaming has proved remarkably fruitful, yielding three solid albums and such singles as *Carry Me* and *Foolish Man.* With Crosby, Stills and Nash spurting back to life again of late, it looks as if the Crosby and Nash duet will be put on ice for a while.

Albums/ GRAHAM NASH AND DAVID CROSBY (4/72): *Southbound Train; Whole Cloth; Blacknotes; Strangers Room; Where Will I Be; Page; Frozen Smiles; Games; Girl to Be on My Mind; The Wall Song; Immigration Man.* WIND ON THE WATER (9/75): *Carry Me; Mama Lion; Bittersweet; Take the Money and Run; Naked in the Rain; Love Work Out; Low Down Payments; Cowboy of Dreams; Homeward through the Haze; Fieldworker; Critical Mass/Wind on the Water.* WHISTLING DOWN THE WIRE (8/76): *Spotlight; Broken Bird; Time After Time; Dancer; Mutiny; J.B.'s Blues; Marguerita; Taken At All; Foolish Man; Out of the Darkness.* **Singles**/ *Carry Me/Mama Lion* (10/75); *Bittersweet/Love Work Out* (4/76); *Out of the Darkness/Broken Bird* (6/76); *Spotlight/Foolish Man* (8/76).

CROSBY, STILLS, NASH AND YOUNG/ The syrupy sweet sounds of Crosby, Stills, Nash and Young first came into being during the summer of '68 when Byrd-on-the-wing David Crosby joined forces with ex–Buffalo Springfielder Stephen Stills and disgruntled Hollie Graham Nash. Nash soon left his group too and in 1969, the original group, Crosby, Stills and Nash was born. Their debut album was one of the biggest hits of the year, spawning two gold singles: *Marrakesh Express* and *Suite: Judy Blue Eyes.*

Seeking to form a backup band to allow them to play adequately live, the trio became a quartet the following year with the addition of ex–Buffalo Springfield member Neil Young. Greg Reeves on bass and Dallas Taylor on drums joined the fold in time for *DEJA VU,* the second top-tenning album by the entourage. Differences of musical opinion, however, began to surface within the band as all four members began to pursue different directions.

By the time *FOUR-WAY STREET* appeared, it was clear that the band's days were numbered. A subsequent "live" fiasco, concerning the release of cuts appearing on the Woodstock album sets, brought about rumors that various members could no longer perform live "in the right key."

For whatever reason, the band split in 1972. Immediately thereafter, the talk of the music industry was where and when a reunion was about to take place. It never happened. In 1976, Stephen Stills and Neil Young got together for the short-lived Stills-Young Band, and in 1977 Crosby, Stills and Nash got together for a thoroughly comatose long-player.

Crosby and Nash have had much success as a duo, Stills has achieved a niche for himself as a solo artist, and the quicksilver Neil Young has topped the albums and singles charts both as a solo artist and as a frontman with the classic Crazy Horse band.

Albums/ CROSBY, STILLS AND NASH (5/69): *Suite: Judy Blue Eyes; Marrakesh Express; Guinnervere; You Don't Have to Cry; Pre-Road Downs; Wooden Ships; Lady of the Island; Helplessly Hoping; Long Time Gone; 49 Bye-Byes.* DEJA VU (3/70): *Carry On; Teach Your Children; Almost Cut My Hair; Helpless; Woodstock; Deja Vu; Our House; 4+20; Country Girl; Everybody I Love You.* FOUR-WAY STREET (3/71): *On the Way Home; Teach Your Children; Triad; All Along the Lee Shore; Chicago; Right between the Eyes; Cowgirl in the Snad; Don't Let It Bring You Down; 49 Bye-Byes; America's Children; Love the One You're With; Pre-Road Downs; Long Time Gone; Southern Man; Ohio;*

Carry On; Find the Cost of Freedom. SO FAR (8/74): *Deja Vu; Helplessly Hoping; Wooden Ships; Teach Your Children; Ohio; Find the Cost of Freedom; Woodstock; Our House; Helpless; Guinnevere; Suite: Judy Blue Eyes.* CSN (6/77): *Shadow Captain; See the Changes; Carried Away; Fair Game; Anything at All; Dark Star; Just a Song before I Go; Run from Tears; Cold Rain; In My Dreams; I Give You Give Blind.*
Singles/ *Marrakesh Express* (6/69); *Suite: Judy Blue Eyes* (11/69); *Woodstock* (2/70); *Teach Your Children* (5/70); *Ohio* (6/70); *Our House* (8/70); *Just a Song before I Go* (6/77); *I Give You Give Blind* (11/77).

ROGER DALTRY/ The flaming-maned lead singer of the Who chose to go solo early in 1973, during one of the Who's frequent breathers. As well as journeying into the rock-pop field, Daltry ventured into acting, first assuming the lead role in Ken Russel's film version of *Tommy* and then in Russel's *Lisztomania.* Along his soloing way, Daltry has managed to give a substantial life to the career of Leo Sayer, who co-penned a few of the tunes on Roger's *DALTRY* album.

Albums/DALTRY (5/73); *One Man Band; The Way of the World; You Are Yourself; Thinking; You and Me; Hard Life; Giving It All Away; The Story So Far; When the Music Stops; Reasons; One Man Band: Reprise.* RIDE A ROCK HORSE (7/75): *Come and Get Your Love; Heart's Right; Oceans Away; Proud; World Over; Proud; Near to Surrender; Feeling; Walking the Dog; Milk Train; I Was Born to Sing Your Song.* ONE OF THE BOYS (6/77): *Parade; Single Man's Dilemma; Avenging Annie; The Prisoner; Leon; One of the Boys; Giddy; Say It Ain't So, Joe; Satin and Lace; Doing It All Again.*

Singles/*Giving It All Away/Way of the World* (4/73); *Thinking/There Is Love* (7/73); *Come and Get Your Love/Heart's Right* (8/75); *Oceans Away/Feeling* (1/76).

THE SPENCER DAVIS GROUP/*Spencer Davis (guitar, harmonica, vocals), Steve Winwood (keyboards, vocals, guitar), Muff Winwood (bass, vocals), Peter York (drums). Other members: Ray Fenwick (guitar, vocals), Dee Murray (bass), Dave Hynes (drums), Eddie Hardin (keyboards), Phil Sawyer (guitar), Charlie Mc-Cracken (bass), Nigel Olsson (drums).*

Formed in 1963, the original Spencer Davis group was a high-spirited, keyboard-oriented rock and roll band that featured the extremely talented sixteen-year-old Stevie Winwood. Steve's high-pitched vocals and helter-skelter organ soloing brought the band a healthy amount of fame via such singles as *I'm a Man* and *Gimme Some Lovin'*. Vaulting from the British pub circuit to the international top ten, the Spencer Davis Group seemed assured a long career when Winwood decided to split (circa 1967) to form Traffic. Davis' attempts to salvage the band were futile with various members embarking on various careers. Muff Winwood became a record company executive. Nigel Olsson and Dee Murray would stick together until finding Elton John. The band finally fell apart in 1969 with Davis pursuing a solo career as an acoustic performer.

Albums/GIMME SOME LOVIN' (3/67): *Gimme Some Lovin'; Keep On Running; Nobody Knows You When You're Down and Out; Hammer Song; When I Come Home; It Hurts Me So; Here Right Now; Somebody Help Me; Midnight Special; Sittin' and Thinkin'; Goodbye, Stevie.* I'M A MAN (6/67): *I'm a Man; Every Little Bit Hurts; Searchin'; I Can't Stand It; Dimples; Look Away; My Babe; Georgia on My Mind; Stevie's Blues; I Can't Get Enough of It; On the Green Light.* SPENCER DAVIS' GREATEST HITS (2/68): *Gimme Some Lovin'; I'm a Man; Keep On Running; Somebody Help Me; On the Green Light; Time Seller; Don't Want You No More; Midnight Special; Blues in F; Searchin'.* WITH THEIR NEW FACES ON (6/68): *Time Seller; With His New Face On; Don't Want You No More; Alec in Transitland; Mr. Second Class; Morning Sun; Feel Your Way; Sanity Inspector; Stop Me, I'm Falling; One Time, Some Time or Never.* VERY BEST OF (1975): *Gimme Some Loving; Dimples; Don't Want You No More; I'm a Man; I Was Looking Back; Keep On Running; Searchin'; Somebody Help Me; Stevie's Blues; Jay's Tune (Mountain Girl).*

Singles/*Keep On Running/High Time Baby* (1/66); *Stevie's Blues/Somebody Help Me* (4/66); *Gimme Some Lovin'/Blues in F* (12/66); *After Tea/Looking Back* (1967); *I'm a Man/Can't Get Enough* (2/67); *Somebody Help Me/On the Green Light* (5/67); *Time Seller/Don't Want You No More* (8/67); *After Tea/Looking Back; Short Change/Picture Heaven* (11/68).

DEATH ROCK/(or neck-rock-philia). From the Shangri-La's

Leader of the Pack and Mark Dinning's *Teen Angel* to the Righteous Brothers' *Rock and Roll Heaven,* songs about death and dying tend to sell well on the charts. Oddly enough, once a live rock artist dies, his or her recordings usually do spectacularly well post mortem, as well. On the charts, death is the hottest commodity to come along since unrequited love. Come to think of it, a song about unrequited love between two recently deceased rock stars sung by a potential suicide victim could probably make a mint and start a new, albeit brief, trend.

KIKI DEE/Elton John's favorite songstress, Kiki Dee, actually began her career back in the dark ages of mod-dom when, in 1964, she metamorphosed from Pauline Matthews to Kiki Dee for a debut single, *Early Night.* A five-year career with Phillips Records and scads of unrealized dreams ensued, culminating in a contract from Motown and a confused album, *GREAT EXPEC-TATIONS.* After wallowing in the doldrums a bit, she emerged victorious in 1974 with a debut Rocket Records long-player, *LOVING AND FREE.* Her next album, *I'VE GOT THE MUSIC IN ME,* provided her with her biggest success to that date. Later, her Elton John duet, *Don't Go Breakin' My Heart,* firmly established Ms. Dee in the hearts and minds of music lovers everywhere. Her main problem in establishing herself permanently seems to lie in the failure to tour on a regular basis. At present, her career is going great guns and, on the rare occasion when she does do concert work, she scores heavily with the audience.

Albums/LOVING AND FREE (4/74): *Loving and Free; If It Rains; Lonnie and Josie; Travelin' in Style; You Put Something Better inside Me; Supercool; Rest My Head; Amoureuse; Song for Adam; Sugar on the Floor.* I'VE GOT THE MUSIC IN ME (10/74); *I've Got the Music in Me; Someone to Me; Step by Step; Water; Out of My Head; Do It Right; Little Frozen One; Heart and Soul; You Need Help.* KIKI DEE (4/77); *How Much Fun; Sweet Creation; Into Eternity; Standing Room Only; Bad Day Child; Chicago; Night Hours; Keep Right On; In Return; Walking; First Thing in the Morning.*

Singles/*Lonnie and Josie/The Last Good Man in My Life* (7/73); *Amoureuse/Rest My Head* (11/73); *Supercool/Loving and Free* (5/74); *I've Got the Music in Me/Simple Melody* (8/74); *Step by Step/Amoureuse* (2/75); *How Glad I Am/Peter* (4/75); *Once a*

Fool/Someone to Me (1/76); *Don't Go Breakin' My Heart (with Elton John)/Snow Queen (with Elton John)* (6/76); *Chicago/Bad Day Child* (5/77).

DEEP PURPLE/*Rod Evans (vocals), Jon Lord (organ), Nick Simper (bass), Ritchie Blackmore (lead guitar), Ian Paice (drums). Additional members: Glenn Hughes (bass, vocals), Tommy Bolin (lead guitar), David Coverdale (vocals), Ian Gillan (vocals), Roger Glover (bass).*
Deep Purple firmly established themselves as kings of heavy metal in the early 1970s. Beginning in Germany in 1968 as the refuge of five British musicians on tour, Deep Purple made a triumphant return home via a hit single, *Hush.* Subsequent releases charted fairly well, but it was apparent to all concerned that Deep Purple would have to reevaluate their musical stance if they were to succeed in the quicksilver musical transition of decades. A major reshuffling occurred in 1970 with original members Simper and Evans being replaced by Gillan and Glover. The "new" Deep Purple sound was born and the searing, guitar–keyboard-dominated sound of the band achieved status worldwide with such albums as *DEEP PURPLE IN ROCK* and *FIREBALL.*

Intramural dissention reared its head in '73 and saw Gillan and Glover leaving the fold, being replaced by Huges and Coverdale. The new group carried on with such popular LPs as *MACHINE HEAD* and *DEEP PURPLE: MADE IN JAPAN.* But the lack of harmony continued. Blackmore jumped ship in '75, eventually to begin anew with Ritchie Blackmore's Rainbow. Tommy Bolin stepped in for *COME TASTE THE BAND,* but within a year he was off for a brief fling at solo stardom before his drug-related death a few months after his first solo tour. Nineteen seventy-six saw Deep Purple bite the dust, with Jon Lord and Ian Paice forming Ashton, Paice and Lord, and Hughes joining the re-formed British band Trapeze.

Albums/SHADES OF DEEP PURPLE (10/68): *Hush; Help; Hey Joe; Mandrake Root; And the Address; Love, Help Me; One More Rainy Day; Prelude; Happiness; I'm So Glad.* BOOK OF TALIESYN (12/68): *Listen, Learn, Read On; Hard Road; Kentucky Woman; Exposition; We Can Work It Out; The Shield; Anthem; River Deep, Mountain High.* DEEP PURPLE (6/69): *Chasing Shadows; The Bird Has Flown; Why Didn't Rosemary?; Em-*

meretta; April. DEEP PURPLE AND THE ROYAL PHILHARMONIC (5/70): *First Movement; Second Movement; Third Movement.* IN ROCK (9/70): *Speed King; Bloodsucker; Child in Time; Flight of the Rat; Hard Lovin' Man; Into the Fire; Living Wreck.* FIREBALL (8/71): *The Mule; Fools; No One Came; Anyone's Daughter; No. 3; Strange Kind of Woman; Fireball.* MACHINE HEAD (2/72): *Highway Star; Maybe I'm a Leo; Pictures of Home; Never Before; Smoke on the Water; Lazy; Space Truckin'.* PURPLE PASSAGES (9/72): *And the Address; Hey Joe; Hush; Emmeretta; Chasing Shadows; The Bird Has Flown; Why Didn't Rosemary?; Hard Road (Wring That Neck); The Shield; Mandrake Root; Kentucky Woman; April.* WHO DO WE THINK WE ARE? (12/72): *Woman From Tokayo; Mary Long; Super Trooper; Rat Bat Blue; Smooth Dancer; Place in Line; Our Lady.* MADE IN JAPAN (3/73): *Highway Star; Child in Time; The Mule; Smoke on the Water; Space Truckin'; Lazy; Strange Kind of Woman.* BURN (2/74): *Burn; Might Just Take Your Life; Lay Down, Stay Down; Sail Away; A 200; You Fool No One; Mistreated; What's Going On Here?* STORMBRINGER (11/74): *The Gypsy; Lady Double Dealer; High Ball Shooter; Holy Man; Hold On; Love Don't Mean a Thing to You; You Can't Do It Right; Stormbringer; Soldier of Fortune.* COME TASTE THE BAND (11/75): *Comin' Home; Lady Luck; Gettin' Tighter; Dealer; I Need Love; Drifter; Love Child; This Time Around; Owed to 'G'; You Keep on Moving.* MADE IN EUROPE (10/76): *Burn, Mistreated; Lady Double Dealer; You Fool No One; Stormbringer.*

Singles/*Hush/One More Rainy Day* (6/68); *Kentucky Woman/Hard Road* (10/68); *River Deep, Mountain High* (1/69); *Black Night/Into the Fire* (6/70); *Black Night* (11/70); *Strange Kind of Woman/I'm Alone* (5/71); *Fireball/I'm Alone* (10/71); *Never Before/When a Blind Man Cries* (3/72); *Lazy/When a Blind Man Cries* (4/72); *Highway Star* (9/72); *Hush/Kentucky Woman* (9/72); *Smoke on the Water* (3/73); *Woman from Tokayo/Super-Trooper* (8/73); *Might Just Take Your Life* (1/74); *Burn/ Coronarias Redig* (4/74); *You Can't Do It Right/High Ball Shooter* (10/74); *Stormbringer/Love Don't Mean a Thing to You* (1/75).

DELANEY AND BONNIE/The concept of rock as "family" was pioneered in the late 1960s by Delaney and Bonnie Bramlett. Their roadshow idea of "live" rock and roll was an energetic if haphazard affair that produced some of rock's loftier instrumental moments and united, on one stage, some of the finest session musicians and superstars in the world. Delaney's first major claim to fame was as part of the nationally televised *Shindig* ensemble on ABC-TV. The show, in an attempt to siphon off some of the fan response from NBC-TV's highly touted *Hullabaloo,* featured Bramlett as half of the rock-in-residence duo, the Shindogs.

Bonnie Lynn was a session singer who specialized in R&B before joining the Ike and Tina Turner Review as one of the gyrating Ikettes. The two met in 1967 and one week later were married. They were immediately signed to Stax/Volt, but dissatisfaction on both the duo's and the record company's parts led to a parting of the ways. One record for Elektra followed before Delaney and Bonnie moved to Atlantic Records for their halcyon years. Eventually, Columbia Records wooed them away with promises of megabucks and a long-lived career. Delaney and Bonnie joined the Columbia roster of artists and then promptly divorced each other. Their careers as solo artists have subsequently floundered.

The genius of Delaney and Bonnie at their prime rested in their powerful and seemingly off-the-cuff approach to intense blue-eyed soul. Their concept of Delaney and Bonnie "and Friends" proved to be both innovative and musically stimulating, in that their "friends" varied from album to album and tour to tour, providing a fresh musical shot in the arm for each session.

Among the horde of musicians that sat in with the duo were Eric Clapton, Leon Russell, George Harrison, Rita Coolidge, Duane Allman, Dave Mason, Jim Keltner, Bobby Keyes, Jim Price, Carl Radle, and Bobby Whitlock. Eventually the informal approach grew tiresome and D&B's rock family found itself outnumbered and outclassed by Joe Cocker's rock army, Mad Dogs and Englishmen (half of which was culled from D&B alumni).

Albums/DOWN HOME (1969). ACCEPT NO SUBSTITUTE— THE ORIGINAL DELANEY AND BONNIE (1969). ON TOUR—WITH ERIC CLAPTON (3/70): *Things Get Better; Poor Elijah and Tribute to Robert Johnson; Only You Know and I Know; Don't Want to Discuss It; That's What My Man Is For; Where There's a Will There's a Way; Comin' Home; Little Richard.* TO BONNIE FROM DELANEY (9/70): *Hard Luck and*

Troubles; God Knows I Love You; Lay Down My Burden; medley: Come in My Kitchen, Mama, He treats Your Daughter Mean, Going Down the Road Feeling Bad; The Love of My Man; They Call It Rock and Roll Music; Soul Shake; Miss Anne; Alone Together; Living on the Open Road; Sweet Dreams; Free the People. MOTEL SHOT (3/71): *Come on in My Kitchen; Never-Ending Song of Love; Sing My Way Home; Going Down the Road Feeling Bad; Lonesome and a Long Way from Home; Where the Soul Never Dies; Will the Circle Be Unbroken; Rock of Ages; Long Road Ahead; Faded Love; Talkin' about Jesus; Don't Deceive Me.* COUNTRY LIFE (3/72): *Only You Know and I Know; Sound of the City; I'm on Fire; Superstar-Groupie Song; Well, Well; I know Something Good about You; Coming Home; Country Life; Big Change Comin'; Wade in the River Jordan; Your Kind of Kindness; Try a Little Harder.* THE BEST OF DELANEY AND BONNIE (10/72): *When the Battle Is Over; Dirty Old Man; Only You Know and I Know; We've Got To Get Ourselves Together; Where There's a Will, There's a Way; Never-Ending Song of Love; Coming Home; The Love of My Man; Soul Shake; Medley: Come on in My Kitchen, Mama, He Treats Your Daughter Mean, Goin' Down the Road Feeling Bad; Free the People.*

Singles/*Comin' Home/Groupie* (1/70); *Free the People/Soul Shake* (4/70); *Miss Anne/Lay Down My Burden* (10/70); *Never-Ending Song of Love/Don't Deceive Me* (4/71); *Only You Know and I Know/God Knows I Love You* (9/71); *Move 'Em Out/Sing My Way Home* (12/71); *Where There's a Will, There's a Way/Lonesome and a Long Way from Home* (3/72).

JOHN DENVER/His ardent fans see him as being as pure as the mountain snow . . . a breath of fresh air in a stagnant music industry . . . a ray of sunshine in a polluted society. His detractors call him everything from "The Pollyanna of Pop" and "The Mickey Mouse of Rock" to "Glen Campbell with a coat hanger in his mouth." The chap in question is, of course, smiling John Denver, the ageless mountain cherub who has strummed his way into the hearts of millions via his good-natured, sing-songish ballads of peace, love, pinecones, and assorted visions of rural splendor. Born in New Mexico (John Henry Deutschendorf, Jr.), the son of an Air Force pilot, young John led a fairly nomadic existence, traveling with his family from Air Force base to Air

Force base. Since the life of an Air Force brat can be a fairly lonely one, flitting from school to school and peer group to peer group before having time to really fit in, young John turned to music.

Picking up a guitar at the age of ten, Denver began strumming both to occupy his time and to make friends at whatever new school he was about to enter. By the time he entered college in Lubbock, Texas, Denver was quite an accomplished balladeer. He began playing solo at local coffee houses between classes, gaining both experience and confidence as he progressed.

Emigrating to L.A., he joined the Chad Mitchell Trio in 1964. It was then that John dropped the Deutschendorf and picked up the Denver. During his first year with the trio, he penned what was to be his first step toward fame. *Leaving on a Jet Plane.* Peter, Paul and Mary recorded the song in 1967 for their *1700* album but it wasn't until 1969 that the song was released as a single. It was a smash.

By that time, John had parted ways with the Trio and was a struggling unknown. He had been married for nearly two years to Annie Martell (who inspired *Annie's Song)* and he was nearly broke. The success of *Jet Plane* led to bigger and better bookings and eventually garnered John a powerful new manager, Jerry Weintraub and, later still, an audition with John's producer-to-be, Milt Okun of RCA. Soon Denver was a neophyte recording artist. After one or two truly underwhelming albums, he hit upon his country comfort stride and the rest, they say, is gold record history.

Probably the oddest thing about Denver's career to date has been his ability to enrapture and enrage the public simultaneously with the very same innocuous tunes. His simplistic odes to nature, such as *Rocky Mountain High* and *Sunshine on My Shoulder,* have sent the rock press intelligentsia into *grand mal* seizures. The most potent line in either song is probably "Sunshine on my shoulder gets me high." Phrases like this have killed thousands of rock critics . . . but have sold millions of records.

Of late, smiling John has branched out to nightclub work and frequent television appearances, both on his own series of specials and as guest host on such staple TV fare as the *Tonight Show.*

Albums/RHYMES AND REASON (9/69): *The Love of the Com-*

mon People; Catch Another Butterfly; Daydream; The Ballad of
Spiro Agnew; Circus; When I'm Sixty-Four; The Ballad of Richard
Nixon; Rhymes and Reasons; Yellow Cat; Leaving on a Jet Plane;
My Old Man; (You Dun Stomped) My Heart; Today Is the First
Day of the Rest of My Life; I Wish I Knew How It Would Feel to
Be Free. TAKE ME TO TOMORROW (4/70): Take Me to
Tomorrow; Isabel; Follow Me; Forest Lawn; Aspenglow; Amster-
dam; Anthem-Revelation; Carolina on My Mind; Sticky Summer
Weather; Jimmy Newman; Molly. WHOSE GARDEN WAS
THIS (9/70): Tremble If You Must; Sail Away Home; The Night
They Drove Old Dixie Down; Mr. Bojangles; I Wish I Could Have
Been There (Woodstock); The Game Is Over; Eleanor Rigby; Old
Folks; Medley: Golden Slumbers, Sweet Sweet Life, Tremble If
You Must, Jungle Bells. POEMS, PRAYERS & PROMISES
(3/71): Poems, Prayers & Promises; Let It Be; My Sweet Lady;
Wooden Indian; Junk; Gospel Changes; Take Me Home, Country
Roads; I Guess He'd Rather Be in Colorado; Sunshine on My
Shoulders; Around and Around; Fire and Rain; The Box. AERIE
(11/71): Starwood in Aspen; Everyday; Casey's Last Ride; City of
New Orleans; Friends with You; 60-Second Song for a Bank, with
the Phrase "May We Help You Today"; Blow Up Your TV
(Spanish Pipe Dream); All of My Memories; She Won't Let Me
Fly; Readjustment Blues; The Eagle and the Hawk; Tools.
ROCKY MOUNTAIN HIGH (8/72): Rocky Mountain High;
Mother Nature's Son; Paradise; For Baby (for Bobbi); Darcy Far-
row; Prisoners; Good-Bye Again; Season Suite. FAREWELL AN-
DROMEDA (3/73): I'd Rather Be a Cowboy; Berkeley Woman;
Please, Daddy; Angels from Montgomery; River of Love; Rocky
Mountain Suite (Cold Nights in Canada); Whiskey Basin Blues;
Sweet Misery; Zachary and Jennifer; We Don't Live Here No
More; Farewell Andromeda (Welcome to My Morning).
GREATEST HITS (11/73): Leaving on a Jet Plane; Take Me
Home, Country Roads; Poems, Prayers & Promises; For Baby (for
Bobbi); Starwood in Aspen; Rhymes and Reasons; Follow Me; The
Eagle and the. Hawk; Goodbye Again; Sunshine on My Shoulders.
BACK HOME AGAIN (6/74): Back Home Again; On the Road;
Grandma's Feather Bed; Matthew; Thank God I'm a Country Boy;
The Music Is You; Annie's Song; It's Up to You; Cool an' Green
an' Shady; Eclipse; Sweet Surrender; This Old Guitar. AN EVE-
NING WITH JOHN DENVER (2/75): The Music Is You;

Farewell Andromeda (Welcome to My Morning); Mother Nature's Son; Today; Summer; Saturday Night in Toledo, Ohio; Matthew; Rocky Mountain Suite (Cold Nights in Canada); Sweet Surrender; Grandma's Feather Bed; Annie's Song; The Eagle and the Hawk; My Sweet Lady; Annie's Other Song; Boy from the Country; Rhymes and Reasons; Forest Lawn; Pickin' the Sun Down; Thank God I'm a Country Boy; Take Me Home, Country Roads; Poems, Prayers & Promises; Rocky Mountain High; This Old Guitar. WINDSONG (9/75): *Windsong; Cowboy's Delight; Spirit; Looking for Space; Shipmates and Cheyenne; Late Nite Radio; Love Is Everywhere; Two Shots; I'm Sorry; Calypso; Fly Away; Song of Wyoming.* ROCKY MOUNTAIN CHRISTMAS (10/75): *Rudolph, the Red-Nosed Reindeer; Silver Bells; Silent Night; The Christmas Song; Christmas for Cowboys; Oh Holy Night; Please, Daddy; A Baby Just Like You; Away in a Manger; Coventry Carol; What Child Is This?* SPIRIT (7/76): *Come and Let Me Look in Your Eyes; Eli's Song; Wrangle Mountain Song; Hitchhiker; In the Grand Way; Polka Dots and Moonbeams; It Makes Me Giggle; Baby, You Look Good to Me Tonight; Like a Sad Song; San Antonio Rose; Pegasus; The Wings That Fly Us Home.* GREATEST HITS VOLUME II (2/77): *Like a Sad Song; Calypso; Fly Away; Looking for Space; I'm Sorry; Thank God I'm a Country Boy; This Old Guitar; My Sweet Lady; Annie's Song' Grandma's Feather Bed; Farewell Andromeda (Welcome to My Morning).*

Singles/*Daydream* (10/69); *Sail Away Home* (8/70); *Take Me Home, Country Roads/Poems, Prayers & Promises* (2/71); *Friends with You/Starwood in Aspen* (10/71); *Everyday/City of New Orleans* (2/72); *Rocky Mountain High/Spring* (10/72); *Whiskey Basin Blues/Farewell Andromeda (Welcome to My Morning)* (8/73), *Please, Daddy/Rocky Mountain High* (11/73); *Sunshine on My Shoulders/Around and Around* (1/74); *Back Home Again/It's Up to You* (9/74); *Sweet Surrender/Summer* (12/74); *Thank God I'm a Country Boy/Sweet Lady* (3/75); *I'd Rather Be a Cowboy/Sunshine on My Shoulders* (4/75); *I'm Sorry/Calypso* (7/75); I'm Sorry (9/75); *Fly Away/Two Shots* (11/75); *Looking for Space/Windsong* (2/76); *Like a Sad Song/Pegasus* (8/76); *Baby You Look Good to Me Tonight/Wrangle Mountain Song* (11/76).

DEREK AND THE DOMINOES/*Eric Clapton (guitars and vo-*

*cals), Bobby Whitlock (keyboards, vocals, acoustic guitar), Jim
Gordon (drums, piano), Carl Radle (bass and percussion), Duane
Allman (guitars).*
Derek and the Dominoes was the would-be supergroup formed by
Eric Clapton in 1971. Clapton had never really reestablished
himself since the demise of Cream and this five piece lineup seemed
to suit the bill perfectly. Clapton's good friend, American guitarist
Duane Allman, consented to guest on the first double LP and the
results were nothing short of scintillating. The release of *LAYLA
AND OTHER LOVE SONGS* was greeted with indifference, at
best, in the United States in 1971. Clapton was shocked, to say the
least. He had crafted what he believed was (and was indeed) an
epic two-album set of guitar-oriented rock and blues songs. The
performances were spontaneous but refined, the production
without fault.

Discouraged by the lack of response, Clapton brought a second
studio recording of the band to an abrupt halt in 1972. A live
album was released instead. Ironically, a single version of *Layla,*
re-released stateside in 1972, almost twelve months after its initial
appearance, proved to be a top-ten item. By that time, however,
Clapton was in the depths of despair. Friend Duane had died in
a freak motorcycle accident the previous October and Clapton's
career showed no signs of real musical life.

Happily for Clapton, the lull after the Dominoes' breakup was
temporary.

Albums/LAYLA AND OTHER ASSORTED LOVE SONGS
(11/70): *I Looked Away; Bell-Bottom Blues; Keep on Growing;
Nobody Knows You When You're Down and Out; I Am Yours;
Anyday; Key to the Highway; Tell the Truth; Why Does Love Got
to Be So Sad?; Have You Ever Loved a Woman; Little Wing; It's
Too Late; Layla; Thorn Tree in the Garden.* IN CONCERT
(1/73): *Why Does Love Got to Be So Sad; Got to Get Better in a
Little While; Let It Rain; Presence of the Lord; Tell the Truth;
Bottle of Red Wine; Roll It Over; Blues Power; Have you Ever
Loved a Woman.*

Singles/ *Tell the Truth/Roll It Over* (8/70); *Bell-Bottom
Blues/Keep On Growing* (1/71); *Layla* (2/71); *Layla* (4/72); *Why
Does Love Have to Be So Sad/Presence of the Lord* (2/73).

RICK DERRINGER/Edgar and Johnny Winter's main man,

producer-guitarist-songwriter Rick Derringer began his career back in Union City, Indiana, in 1962 when, at the ripe old age of fifteen, he and brother Randy joined with friends Randy Hobbs and Bobby Peterson to form the McCoys. Three years later, Rick (known at that time as Rick Zehringer) was in New York with the band, recording his first penned song, *Hang on Sloopy*. It was a smash, and so were the McCoys . . . for a while. After a series of catchy tunes, the McCoys changed labels and direction, attempting to expand their musical scope. A few experimental rock albums later, the McCoys found themselves young has-beens, playing regularly at Steve Paul's Scene in New York City. In 1969, Paul took over their career and brought them into the Johnny Winter project, as Johnny's new backup band. At this point, Rick became Derringer . . . producer, writer *(Rock and Roll Hoochi Coo)*, guitarist, singer. After Johnny quit the performing circuit, Rick joined brother Edgar Winter's White Trash and, still later, the Edgar Winter Group. Rick has, more or less, remained with Edgar for the past five years, taking extended leaves of absence to promote his own solo band.

Albums/ALL AMERICAN BOY (10/73): *Rock and Roll Hoochie Coo; Joy Ride; Teenage Queen; Cheap Tequila; Uncomplicated; Hold; The Airport Giveth; It's Raining; Time Warp; Slide on Over Slinky; Jump, Jump, Jump; Teenage Love Affair.* SPRING FEVER (3/75): *Gimme More; Tomorrow; Don't Ever Say Goodbye; Still Alive and Well; Rock; Hang on Sloopy; Roll with Me; Walkin' the Dog; He Needs Some Answers; Skyscraper Blues.* DERRINGER (1976): *Let Me In; You Can Have Me; Loosen Up Your Grip; Envy; Comes a Woman; Sailor; Beyond the Universe; Goodbye Again.* LIVE (5/77): *Let Me In; Teenage Love Affair; Sailor; Beyond the Universe; Sitting by the Pool; Uncomplicated; Still Alive and Well; Rock and Roll Hoochie Coo.*

Singles/*Teenage Love Affair/Slide Over Slinky* (10/73); *Rock and Roll Hoochie Coo/Time Warp* (12/73); *Uncomplicated/Jump, Jump, Jump* (4/74); *It's Raining/Cheap Tequila* (6/74); *Don't Ever Say Goodbye/Gimme More* (6/75); *Rock and Roll Hoochie Coo/Hang On Sloopy* (9/75; *Let Me In* (1976).

NEIL DIAMOND/Considered by his fans to be the crème de la crème of singer-songwriters, Neil Diamond first achieved fame as the composer of the hit Monkee tunes *I'm a Believer* and *A Little*

Bit Me, A Little Bit You. The Brooklyn-born writer then ventured
forth as a solo performer, while penning a glut of hit tunes including *Solitary Man, Cherry, Cherry, I Got the Feelin, Sweet
Caroline,* and *Cracklin' Rosie.* A successful singles artists (one of
the top sellers of the mid-to-late-sixties), Diamond was considered somewhat of a "nerd" by serious music buffs in the
psychedelia-laden, FM-oriented period, a fact which annoyed
Diamond no end.

Surrounded by *Sgt. Pepper* melodies, Dylanesque imagery, and
song-poetry galore, Diamond took his hit style one step further
and attempted to carve a career for himself as a "respectable"
song craftsman. He succeeded somewhat with a series of tunes
that expanded the Diamond style lyrically. His fandom
mushroomed, although it never did include the rock segment in
its ranks. Diamond grew more and more "heavy" as the years
rolled by and, by the time he jumped labels for a few million
dollars in 1973, his legions considered him the Kahlil Gibran of
pop.

One of his first new projects was a long-playing soundtrack of
the film *Jonathan Livingston Seagull.* His career has hovered in
that water-logged area since then.

Albums/FEEL OF NEIL DIAMOND (9/66): *Cherry, Cherry;
Solitary Man; Monday, Monday; Red Rubber Ball; Hanky Panky;
New Orleans; La Bamba; Do It; I Got The Feelin'; I'll Come Run-
ning; Love to Love.* JUST FOR YOU (7/67): *I'm a Believer; It's
Such a Pretty World Today; Walk through This World with Me;
Detroit City; My Cup Runneth Over; Get Out of My Life; You
Pushed Me Too Far; Cryin' Time; Lonesome Out Tonight; You
Should Live My Life; Don't Hurt Me Anymore; Bridge I Have
Never Crossed.* NEIL DIAMOND'S GREATEST HITS (6/68):
*Cherry, Cherry; I Got the Feelin'; New Orleans; Do It; Girl, You'll
Be a Woman Soon; You Got to Me; Solitary Man; Kentucky Wom-
an; Red Red Wine; Thank the Lord for the Nighttime; Hanky Pan-
ky; Boat That I Row.* VELVET GLOVES AND SPIT (11/68):
*Sunday Sun; A Modern-Day Version of Love; Honey-Drippin'
Times; The Pot Smokers Song; Brooklyn Roads; Two-Bit
Manchild; Holiday Inn Blues; Practically Newborn; Knackelflerg;
Merry-Go-Round.* SWEET CAROLINE (4/69): *Brother Love's
Travelling Salvation Show; Dig In; River Runs, New-Grown Plums;
Juliet; Long Gone; And the Grass Won't Pay No Mind; Glory*

Road; Deep in the Morning; If I Never Knew Your Name; Memphis Streets; You're So Sweet Horseflies Keep Hangin' 'Round Your Face; Hurtin' You Don't Come Easy; Sweet Caroline. TOUCH-ING YOU, TOUCHING ME (11/69): *Everybody's Takin'; Mr. Bojangles; Smokey Lady; Holly Holy; Both Sides Now; And the Singer Sings His Songs; Ain't No Way; New York Boy; Until It's Time for You to Go.* GOLD (7/70): *Lordy; Both Sides Now; Solitary Man; Holly Holy; Cherry, Cherry; Kentucky Woman; Sweet Caroline; Thank the Lord for the Nighttime; And the Singer Sings His Songs; Brother Love's Travelling Salvation Show.* TAP ROOT MANUSCRIPT (11/70): *Cracklin Rosie; Free Life; Cold-water Morning; Done Too Soon; He Ain't Heavy, He's My Brother; Childsong; I am the Lion; Madrigal; Soolaimon; Missa; African Trilogy; Childsong Reprise.* STONES (11/71): *I Am I Said; The Last Thing on My Mind; Husbands and Wives; Chelsea Morning; Crunchy Granola Suite; Stones; If You Go Away; Suzanne; I Think It's Gonna Rain Today.* MOODS (6/72): *Song Sung Blue; Porcupine Pie; High Rollin' Man; Canta Libre; Cap-tain Sunshine; Play Me; Gitchy Goomy; Walk on Water; Theme; Prelude in E Major; Morningside.* HOT AUGUST NIGHT (11/72): *Play Me; Canta Libre; Morningside; Song Sung Blue; Cracklin' Rosie; Porcupine Pie; You're So Sweet; Red Red Wine; Soggy Pretzels; And the Grass Won't Pay No Mind; Shilo; Girl, You'll Be a Woman Soon; Holly Holy; I Am I Said; Walk Off; Soolaimon; Brother Love's Travelling Salvation Show; Encore; Crunchy Granola Suite; Done Too Soon; Solitary Man; Cherry Cherry; Sweet Caroline.* RAINBOW (8/73): *Everybody's Talkin'; Both Sides Now; Husbands and Wives; Chelsea Morning; Until It's Time for You to Go; The Last Thing on My Mind; Suzanne; Mr. Bojangles; If You Go Away; Think It's Gonna Rain Today; He Ain't Heavy, He's My Brother.* JONATHAN LIVINGSTON SEAGULL (10/73): *Prologue; Be; Flight of the Gull; Dear Father; Skybird; Lonely Looking Sky; The Odyssey; Anthem; Be; Skybird; Dear Father; Be.* GREATEST HITS (5/74): *Sweet Caroline; Brother Love's Travelling Salvation Show; Holly Holy; Brooklyn Roads; Cracklin' Rosie; Play Me; Done Too Soon; Stones; Brooklyn Roads; I Am I Said.* SERENADE (10/74): *I've Been This Way Before; Rosemary's Wine; Lady Magdeline; The Last Picasso; Longfellow Serenade; Yes I Will; Reggae Strut; The Gift of Song.* BEAUTIFUL NOISE (6/76): *Beautiful Noise;*

Stargazer; Lady-Oh; Don't Think . . . Feel; Surviving the Life; If You Know What I Mean; Street Life; Home Is a Wounded Heart; Jungletime; Signs; Dry Your Eyes. AND THE SINGER SINGS HIS SONG (9/76): *Captain Sunshine; Free Life; Hurtin' You Don't Come Easy; Coldwater Morning; Walk on Water; Stones; And the Grass Won't Pay No Mind; If I Never Knew Your Name; Merry-Go-Round; Juliet; Brooklyn Roads; And the Singer Sings His Song.* LOVE AT THE GREEK (2/77): *Street Life; Kentucky Woman; Sweet Caroline; The Last Picasso; Longfellow Serenade; Beautiful Noise; Lady-Oh; Stargazer; If You Know What I Mean; Surviving the Life; Song Song Blue; Holly Holy; Glory Road; Brother Love's Travelling Salvation Show; Be; Dear Father; Lonely Looking Sky; Sanctus; Sky Bird; Be; I've Been This Way Before.* I'M GLAD YOU'RE HERE WITH ME TONIGHT (11/77): *Desiree; Free Man in Paris; God Only Knows; Let the Little Boy Sing; I'm Glad You're Here with Me Tonight; Lament in D Minor; Dance of the Sabres; You Don't Bring Me Flowers; Once in a While; As If; Let Me Take You in My Arms Again.*

Singles/*Solitary Man/Do It* (3/66); *Cherry, Cherry/I'll Come Running* (7/66); *I Got the Feelin'/Boat That I Row* (10/66); *Someday Baby/You Got Me* (1/67); *Girl, You'll Be a Woman Soon/You'll Forget* (3/67); *Thank the Lord for The Nighttime/Long Way Home* (6/67); *Kentucky Woman/The Time Is Now* (10/67); *Hanky Panky/New Orleans* (12/67); *Red Rubber Ball/Red Red Wine* (3/68); *Brookyn Roads/Holiday Inn Blues* (4/68); *Sunday Sun/Honey Drippin' Times* (8/68); *Brother Love's Travelling Salvation Show/A Modern-Day Version of Love* (1/69); *Sweet Caroline/Dig In* (5/69); *Holly Holy/Hurtin' You* (10/69); *Until It's Time for You to Go/And the Singer Sings His Song* (2/70); *Soolaimon/And the Grass Won't Pay No Mind* (4/70); *Cracklin' Rosie/Lordy* (7/70); *He Ain't Heavy, He's My Borther/Free Life* (10/70); *I Am I Said/Done Too Soon* (3/71); *Stones/Crunchy Granola Suite* (10/71); *Song Sung Blue/Gitchy Goomy* (4/72); *Play Me/Porcupine Pie* (7/72); *Walk on Water/High Rolling Man* (10/72); *Cherry, Cherry/Morningside* (2/73); *Cracklin' Rosie/He Ain't Heavy, He's My Brother* (4/73); *Sweet Caroline/Brother Love's Travelling Salvation Show* (4/73); *Holly Holy/Soolaimon* (6/73); *Canta Libre/Last Thing on My Mind* (7/73); *Be/Flight of the Gull* (10/73); *Skybird/Lonely Look-*

ing Sky (2/74); *Longfellow Serenade/Rosemary's Wine* (9/74); *I've Been This Way Before/Reggae Strut* (1/75); *The Last Picasso/The Gift of Song* (4/75); *Be/Longfellow Serenade* (11/75); *If You Know What I Mean/Street Life* (6/76); *Don't Think . . . Feel/Home Is a Wounded Heart* (8/76); *Beautiful Noise/Signs* (11/76);

THE DICTATORS/*Handsome Dick Manitoba (lead vocals, half-nelsons), Ross the boss (guitar), Top ten (rhythm guitar), Adny Shernoff (keyboards, vocals), Ritchie Teeter (drums, vocals), Mark the Animal Mendoza (bass).*
When the Dictators released their first album in 1975, no one at their record company knew what to do with them. They were, in a word, crude. In two words: crude and vile. All this in an era when punk rock was still a dream of the future and the nearest thing to nasty on wax was Alice Cooper. Lead singer Handsome Dick looked and sang like a pro wrestler. Writer Adny Shernoff was known for writing lyrics that were, um, not quite right. After debating as to the viability (read: salability) of the band, Epic Records dropped them posthaste and made a concerted effort to forget they ever existed.

Two years later, the band resurfaced as a six-piece entourage with a new label (Asylum) and a record that had to be considered the *SGT. PEPPER* of Punk. Handsome Dick still bellowed his brains out, but newcomer Ritchie Teeter smoothed things over with his pure and simple vocalizing. The guitar licks were mild but melodic, the tunes, demented but catchy. The whole album brimmed with infectious musical hooks. The Dictators may not be destined for the rock and roll hall of fame; they are still quite unorthodox . . . but if they don't get voted in, you can be sure they'll smash their way inside through a skylight.

Albums/THE DICTATORS GO GIRL CRAZY (3/75): *The Next Big Thing; I Got You Babe*; Back to Africa; Master Race Rock; Teengenerate; California Sun*; Two Tub Man; Weekend; (I Live for) Cars and Girls.* MANIFEST DESTINY (4/77): *Exposed; Heartache; Sleepin' with the TV On; Disease; Hey Boys; Steppin' Out; Science Gone Too Far; Young, Fast and Scientific; Search and Destroy.*

Single/*Hey Boys* (7/77)
*These songs have *got* to be *heard* to be *believed!*

DION (AND THE BELMONTS)/Bronx-born Dion Dimucci exploded on the singles charts in 1958, backed by the legendary New Yawk Band, the Belmonts, with *I Wonder Why*. Throughout the remainder of that decade, Dion, Angelo D'Aleo, Carlo Mastangelo, and Fred Milano were regular residents in the top ten of rock and roll hitdom. The quartet parted ways in 1960 with Dion going on to a meteoric solo career which boasted such hits as *The Wanderer* and *Runaround Sue*. The British Invasion of the early sixties and the advent of progressive rock brought his career grinding to a complete halt and, by 1964, he was a has-been.

In 1968, a new, improved Dion fought his way into the limelight as a sensitive singer of semi-folk. An initial offering, *Abraham, Martin and John* seemed to portend greater things to come, but Dion's career as a singles artist during the flower-powered sixties never equaled his efforts of ten years previously. Several folkie albums on Warners sold well but not spectacularly so and, when the rock and roll revival of the early seventies took place, Dion was ready to ride the crest of the wave. A few recordings with mastercraftsman of the fifties, Phil Spector, caused some noise on the charts and a *REUNION* album with the Belmonts sent chills up and down the spine of vintage rock and rollers. The reunited entourage hit the concert stage between the strobe lights and Dion once again was a star.

With the rock revival over, it's time for Dion to find a new niche for himself in the world of rock. Knowing the singer-songwriter's persistence in the past, it's safe to say that it's only a matter of time before he's on top once again.

Albums/PRESENTING DION AND THE BELMONTS. DION AND THE BELMONTS (4/60). WHEN YOU WISH UPON A STAR (10/60). DION ALONE. RUNAROUND SUE (11/61). LOVERS WHO WANDER (6/62). DION SINGS HIS GREATEST HITS (11/62): *Teenager in Love; Teen Angel; Where or When; Don't Pity Me; That's My Desire; No One Knows; I Wonder Why; In the Still of the Night; When You Wish upon a Star; Little Miss Blue; Lonely Teenager.* RUBY BABY (2/63). DION SINGS TO SANDY (5/63). LOVE CAME TO ME. TOGETHER WITH THE BELMONTS (10/66). 15 MILLION SELLERS (10/66): *Teenager in Love; Runaround Sue; Lovers Who Wander; The Wanderer; other titles.* TOGETHER AGAIN

(3/67): *Movin' Man; Berimbau; Come to My Side; All I Wanna Do; But Not for Me; New York Town; Loserville; For Bobbie; Jump Back, Baby; My Girl, the Month o' May; Baby, You've Been on My Mind.* DION (11/68): *Abraham, Martin and John; He Looks a Lot Like Me. Purple Haze; From Both Sides Now; other Titles.* I WONDER WHERE I'M BOUND (12/68): *I Can't Help But Wonder Where I'm Bound; Baby Blue; A Sunday Kind of Love; Knowing I won't Go Back There; 900 Miles; Now; Southern Train; Seventh Son; Farewell; Wake Up, Baby; Baby, Please Don't Go.* SIT DOWN, OLD FRIEND (1/70): *Natural Man;King Con Man; If We Only Have Love; Little Pink Pony; Sit Down, Old Friend; Just a Little Girl; Let Go, Let Go; Sweet Pea; Jammed Up Blues; I Don't Believe My Race Is Over; Can't Judge a Book by Its Cover.* YOU'RE NOT ALONE (1/71): *Close to It All; The Visitor; Josie; Blackbird; Let It Be; The Stuff I Got; Peaceful Place; Windows; Attraction Works Better Than Promotion; Sunniland.* SANCTUARY (11/71): *Sanctuary; Abraham, Martin and John; Ruby Baby; Almond Joy; Brand New Morning; Wanderer; Gotta Get Up; Sunshine Lady; Take a Little Time; Please Be My Friend.* SUITE FOR LATE SUMMER (10/72): *Sea Gull; Wedding Song; Jennifer Knew; It All Fits Together; To Dream Tomorrow; Didn't You Change; Tennessee Madonna; Traveler in the Rain; Running Close behind You.* DION AND THE BELMONTS REUNION (1/73): *The Wanderer; No One Knows; I Wonder Why; Teenager in Love; Ruby Baby; That's My Desire; Drip Drop; Where or When; Runaround Sue; Little Diane.* GREATEST HITS (2/73): *Teenager in Love; Where or When; Runaround Sue; A Lover's Prayer; Lovers Who Wander; I Wonder Why; No One Knows; When You Wish Upon a Star; Lonely Teenager; The Wanderer.* STREETHEART (6/76): *Runaway Man; Streetheart; Hey My Love; Oh the Night; Lover Boy Supreme; Queen of '59; You Showed Me What Love Is; More To You; If I Can Just Get through the Night.*

Singles/*Lonely Teenager/Little Miss Blue* (9/60); *Havin' Fun* (1/61); *Kissin' Game* (4/61); *Runaround Sue* (9/6.); *The Wanderer/The Majestic* (11/61); *Lovers Who Wander/Born To Cry* (3/62); *Little Diane* (6/62); *Love Came to Me* (10/62); *Ruby Baby* (12/62); *Sandy* (2/63); *This Little Girl* (3/63); *Come Go with Me* (5/63); *Be Careful of Stones That You Throw* (6/63); *Donna the Prima Donna* (8/63); *Drip Drop* (10/63); *Johnny B. Goode*

(7/64); *Abraham, Martin and John* (9/68); *Purple Haze* (12/68); *Both Sides Now* (3/69); *If We Only Have Love/Natural Man* (11/69); *Your Own Back Yard/Sit Down, Old Friend* (6/70); *Sunniland/Josie* (5/71); *Sanctuary/Brand New Morning* (11/71); *New York City Song/Richer Than a Rich Man* (3/74); *Hey, My Love/Lover Boy Supreme* (8/76); *Queen of '59/Oh, the Night* (10/76); *Young Virgin Eyes/Oh, the Night* (6/77).

DISCOTHEQUE/By 1961 music had the most kinetic beat since tom-toms. In France, clubs found they didn't need live musicians to get people to dance—just a *disquaire* who "programmed" dance records and moods for the evening. Such a place was called a discotheque. The first one in New York, a private place called La Club, was a raging success. Dozens and then thousands followed in the wake of the biggest dance craze of the decade, the Twist. By 1964–65 there were five thousand in America alone. The dawning of the age of flower power sent discos reeling. By the late sixties they were as au courant as saber-toothed tigers. In 1973–74, however, discos started to flourish again. Indeed, by 1977, discos and disco music were *the* rage around the globe. To best imagine the sound of disco, picture a steamer trunk, filled to the brim, being dragged down a spiral staircase into infinity.

DR. JOHN/Before emerging as the mysterious king of gris-gris in 1968, Dr. John was known as the consummate sessionman. New Orleans–born and –bred, Malcolm John Rebennack got into music in a big way during his teenage years; most of his education occurred at the local R&B recording studios, where he picked up the musical tricks of the trade from the local talent, including Fats Domino's band and legendary New Orleans star Professor Longhair.

Before the fifties drew to a close, "Mac" had established himself as both an ace backing musician for live dates and a reliable sessionman for recording. He even dabbled in producing for several of the local labels. The sixties brought Mac to the music-mania of Los Angeles where he quickly began session work with Sam Cooke and Sonny and Cher. Sessions with Phil Spector and the gradual burgeoning of the L.A. rock scene injected a heavy dose of rock vitality into Rebennack's New Orleans–based R&B roots. By the time he made his big career move in 1968, Mac's music was a mixture of traditional New Orleans funk, voodoo-oriented chants, and rock. Dr. John, replete with feathers and ceremonial outfits, was born.

With his Creole influence a visual delight for rock addicts, Dr. John was soon an underground sensation. By the early seventies, he had even managed to worm his way onto the pop charts with such funk-rock ditties as *In the Right Place*. By the mid-seventies, however, the gris-gris was all but gone, replaced with a lackluster rock approach. An album, *TRIUMVIRATE*, with John Hammond and Mike Bloomfield, was a highly touted dud, and a changing rock audience soon found the onstage gumbo getups passe. A switch to a less-distinguished label brought the night-tripper a taste of anonymity in 1975. At present, the good doctor concentrates mostly on session work.

Albums/GRIS GRIS (7/68): *Gris-Gris Gumbo Ya Ya; Croker Courthbouillon; I Walk on Gilded Splinters; Danse Flambeaux; Mama Roux; Jump Sturdy; Danse Kalida Ba Doom.* BABYLON (1969): *Babylon; Black Widow Spider; Glowin'; Barefoot Lady; Twilight Zone; The Patriotic Flag Waver; The Lonesome Guitar Strangler.* REMEDIES (1971): *Loop Garoo; What Goes Around Comes Around; Wash, Mama, Wash; Chippy Chippy; Mardi Gras Day; Angola Anthem.* THE SUN, MOON & HERBS (7/71): *Black John the Conqueror; Where Yaa'at Mule; Craney Crow; Familiar Reality Opening Cadenza; Pots on Fiyo (File Gumbo)/Who I Got to Fall On (if the Pot Get Heavy); Zu Zu Mamou; Familiar Reality Chaser.* GUMBO (4/72): *Iko Iko; Blow Wind Glow; Big Chief; Somebody Changes the Lock; Mess Around; Let the Good Times Roll; Junko Partner; Satck-a-Lee; Tipitina; Hueye Smith medley; High Blood Pressure, Don't You Just Know It, Well I'll Be John Brown; Little Liza Jane; Those Lonely Lonely Nights.* IN THE RIGHT PLACE (2/73): *Right Place Wrong Time; Same Old Same Old; Just the Same; Qualified; Traveling Mood; Peace Brother Peace; Life; Such a Night; Shoo Fly Marches On; I Been Hoodood; Cold Cold Cold.* DESITIVELY BONNAROO (1974): *Quitters Never Win; Stealin'; What Comes Round (Goes Around); Me-You=Loneliness; Mos' Scocious; (Everybody Wanna Get Rich) Rite Away; Let's Make a Better World; R/U/4/Real; Sing Along Song; Go Tell the People; Desitively Bonnaroo.* HOLLYWOOD BY THY NAME (1975): *New Island Soiree; Reggae Doctor; The Way You Do the Things You Do; Swanee River Boogie; Yesterday; Babylon; Back by the River; medley: It's All Right with*

Me, Blue Skies, Will the Circle Be Unbroken; Hollywood Be Thy Name; I Wanna Rock.

Singles/*Jump Sturdy*/*Mama Roux* (12/68); *Iko Iko* (3/72); *Right Place Wrong Time* (3/73); *Such a Night* (8/73); *Everybody Wanna Get Rich Rite Away* (4/74).

FATS DOMINO/Born Antoine Domino, this New Orleans denizen achieved worldwide fame in the 1950s via a string of piano-pounding R&B rock tunes. One of his finest songs, *Ain't That a Shame,* was successfully covered by Pat Boone and a top-tenner was born in the mid-fifties. The success rubbed off on the fat man, who had a number of top-tenners himself ranging from *Blueberry Hill* to *I'm Walkin'.* As the rock scene progressed, Fats, like so many of his fifties' peers, fell into obscurity. The great rock revival of the late nineteen sixties, however, brought Fats into the limelight once again. A series of SRO concert dates and semi-successful records followed until ill-health forced the music giant to curtail his professional activities.

Albums/ROCK AND ROLLIN' (1950): *Tired of Crying; Rose Mary; All By Myself; You Said You Love Me; Ain't It a Shame; Fat Man; Poor Me; Bo Weevil; Don't Blame It on Me; Goin' Home; Going to the River; Please Don't Leave Me.* ROCK AND ROLLIN': *My Blue Heaven; Swanee River Hop; Second Line Jump; Goodbye; I Love Her; I'm in Love Again; When My Dreamboat Comes Home; My Heart Is in Your Hands; Careless Love; Are You Going My Way; If You Need Me; Fats' Frenzy.* THIS IS FATS DOMINO: *Blueberry Hill; Blue Monday; Poor Poor Me; Honey Chile; What's the Reason I'm Not Pleasing You; So Long; La La; Troubles of My Own; You Done Me Wrong; Reeling and Rocking; Fat Man's Hop; Trust Me.* HERE STANDS FATS DOMINO: *Detroit City Blues; Hide Away Blues; She's My Baby; New Baby; Cheatin'; Little Bee; I'm Walkin'; Every Night about This Time; You Can Pack Your Suitcase; I'm in the Mood for Love; Hey Fat Man; I'll Be Gone.* THIS IS FATS (9/58): *As Time Goes By; Hey, La Bas; Rooster Song; My Happiness; Valley of Tears; It's You I Love; Love Me; Don't You Hear Me Calling You; Where Did You Stay; Baby Please; You Know I Miss You; Thinking of You.* FABULOUS MR. D. (9/58): *Big Beat; I'll Be Glad When You're Dead, You Rascal You; Barrel House; What Will I Tell My Heart; Little Mary; Sick and Tired; I Want You to Know;*

44'; Mardi Gras in New Orleans; I Can't Go On; Long Lonesome Journey; Young School Girl. LET'S PLAY FATS DOMINO: *I'm Gonna Be a Wheel; Someday; When the Saints Go Marchin' in; Margie; Li'l Liza Jane; I Want to Walk You Home; You Left Me; Ain't It Good; Howdy, Podner; Stack and Billy; Would You; Hands across the Table.* MILLION RECORD HITS: *You Said You Loved Me; I Still Love You; Be My Guest; Country Boy; If You Need Me; I Want to Walk You Home; It's You I Love; I've Been Around; Margie; I'm Gonna Be a Wheel Someday; I'm Ready; I Want You to Know.* 12,000,000 RECORDS (8/59). I MISS YOU SO: *I Miss You So; It Keeps Rainin'; Ain't That Just Like a Woman; Once in a While; I Hear You Knocking; Isle of Capri; What a Price; When I Was Young; Fell in Love on Monday; My Bleeding Heart; Easter Parade; I'll Always Be in Love with You.* FATS DOMINO SWINGS: *Fat Man; Blue Monday; Blueberry Hill; I'm Walkin'; I'm in Love Again; Going to the River; My Blue Heaven; Bo Weevil; Please Don't Leave Me; Goin' Home; Ain't It a Shame; Whole Lotta Loving.* MILLION SELLERS BY FATS (7/62): *Walking to New Orleans; My Real Name; My Girl Josephine; Three Nights a Week; Ain't Gonna Do It; Shu Rah; Natural Born Lover; What a Price; Let the Four Winds Blow; My Heart Is Bleeding; Jambalaya; You Win Again.* LOTS OF DOMINOS: *Put Your Arms around Me, Baby; Three Nights a Week; Shu Rah; Rising Sun; My Girl Josephine; Sheik of Araby; Walking to New Orleans; How Can I Be Happy; One of These Days; So Glad; Lazy Woman; My Love for Her; What's Wrong; Little Mama; I Guess I'll Be on My Way.* LET'S DANCE WITH DOMINO: *Ain't It a Shame; I Don't Want to Walk without You; I Lived My Life; Someday; Telling Lies; When I See You; Just a Little While; Oh Ba-a-by; When You're Smiling; Don't You Know I Love You; Yes, My Darling; True Confession.* HERE HE COMES AGAIN: *Goin' Home; Trouble in Mind; Every Night; I Can't Give You Anything but Love; When I See You; Oh Ba-a-by; Ain't Gonna Do It; Li'l Liza Jane; Your Cheatin' Heart; Along the Navajo Trail; South of the Border; Telling Lies.* HERE COMES FATS DOMINO (7/63): *When I'm Walking; I've Got a Right to Cry; There Goes My Heart Again; Just a Lonely Man; Red Sails in the Sunset; Bye Baby, Bye Bye; Forever, Forever; I'm Livin' Right; Can't Go On without You; Land of 1,000 Dances; Tell Me the Truth, Baby.* FATS ON FIRE: *I Don't Want to Set the World On Fire; You*

Know I Miss You; Fat's on Fire; Land of Make Believe; Old Man Trouble; Love Me; Mary, Oh Mary; Gotta Get a Job; Fat Man; Valley of Tears; Fats' Shuffle; I'm a Fool to Care. GETAWAY WITH FATS DOMINO (2/66): When My Dreamboat Comes Home; Trouble in Mind; Wigs; Man That's All; Kansas City; Reelin' and Rockin'; Slow Boat to China; Girl I'm Gonna Marry; Monkey Business; Heartbreak Hill; Why Don't You Do Right; Ballin' the Jack. FATS DOMINO (6/66): One Night; Goin' Home; I Just Cry; I've Been Calling; six other titles. STOMPIN' FATS DOMINO (7/67): Every Night; She's My Baby; Domino Stomp; Don't Blame It on Me; other titles. TROUBLE IN MIND: South of the Border; I Know; Hold Hands; Coquette; Trouble in Mind; other titles. FATS IS BACK (9/68): My Old Friend; I'm Ready; So Swell When You're Well; Wait till It Happens to You; I Know; Lady Madonna; Honest Papas Love Their Mamas Better; Make Me Belong to You; One for the Highway; Lovely Rita; One More Song for You. COOKIN' WITH FATS (1973): My Girl Josephine; Jambalaya; Honey Chile; One Night; Little Mama; Shu Rah; Ain't That Just Like a Woman; What's the Reason I'm Not Pleasin' You; Bo Weevil; You Done Me Wrong; What a Price; Rose Mary; When I See You; So Long; Three Nights a Week; Sick and Tired; Are You Going My Way; What Will I Tell My Heart; La La; Ain't Gonna Do It.

Singles/The Fat Man (1/50); Every Night about This Time (11/50); Rockin' Chair (12/51); Goin' Home (4/52); How Long (12/52); Goin' to the River (4/53); Please Don't Leave Me (7/53); Rose Mary (10/53); Something's Wrong (12/53); You Done Me Wrong (3/54); Don't You Know (5/55); Ain't It a Shame (5/55); All By Myself (9/55); Poor Me (11/55); Bo Weevil (2/56); I'm in Love Again/My Blue Heaven (4/56); When My Dreamboat Comes Home/So Long (6/56); Blueberry Hill (9/56); Blue Monday/What's the Reason I'm Not Pleasin' You (12/56); I'm Walkin' (2/57); Valley of Tears/It's You I Love (5/57); When I See You/What Will I Tell My Heart (7/57); Wait and See/I Still Love You (9/57); The Big Beat/I Want You to Know (12/57); Yes, My Darling (2/58); Sick and Tired/No, No (4/58); Little Mary/Young School Girl (6/58); Whole Lotta Loving/Coquette (11/58); When the Saints Go Marchin' In/Telling Lies (2/59); I'm Ready/Margie (5/59); I Want to Walk You Home/I'm Gonna Be a Wheel Some-

day (7/59); *Be My Guest/I've Been Around* (10/59); *Country Boy/If You Need Me* (1/60); *Tell Me That You Love Me/Before I Grow Too Old* (4/60); *Walking to New Orleans/Don't Come Knockin'* (6/60); *Three Nights a Week/Put Your Arms around Me, Honey* (9/60); *My Girl Josephine/Natural Born Lover* (10/60); *What a Price/Ain't That Just Like a Woman* (12/60); *Shu Rah/Fell in Love on Monday* (3/61); *It Keeps Raining/Let the Four Winds Blow* (5/61); *What a Party/Rockin' Bicycle* (10/61); *Jambalaya/I Hear You Knocking* (11/61); *You Win Again/Ida Jane* (2/62); *My Real Name* (4/62); *Nothing New/Dance with Mr. Domino* (6/62); *Did You Ever See a Dream Walking* (9/62); *There Goes My Heart Again* (5/63); *Red Sails in the Sunset* (9/63); *Who Cares* (12/63); *Lazy Lady* (2/64); *Sally Was a Good Old Girl* (8/64); *Heartbreak Hill* (10/64); *Lady Madonna/One for the Highway* (8/68); *Lovely Rita/Wait Till It Happens to You* (1968).

DONOVAN/What does an aging flower child do when the harvest is over? Well, if you're Donovan Leitch, you just keep on making music. The Glasgow-born troubadour first made waves across the Atlantic in 1965 when he suddenly appeared on the music scene in a very Dylanesque manner: clad in an oversized denim cap with harmonica stand fixed securely to his neck and acoustic guitar perched nicely on his knee. His regular appearances on the vintage British TV-er, *Ready Steady Go,* made him an instant celebrity in England but, in the states, he was resented by many musicologists as a Dylan-come-lately clone.

No matter what his appearance, Donovan quickly established himself as a songwriter in his own right penning both *Catch the Wind* and *Colours* during his first year on wax. Gradually his folkie image faded and Donovan became a soft peddler of psychedelia first class, offering such flower-powered epics as *Sunshine Superman* and *Mellow Yellow.* Even the American doubters rallied around these toe-tappers. When TM came into vogue, Donovan donned the sandals and spoke in hushed tones of the Maharishi . . . offering up his humble *Gift from a Flower to a Garden.* This lighter-than-air side of the songwriter, however, slackened the momentum of his career, which, commercially, never fully revved up again. Glimpses of the Donovan of old resurfaced in *Jennifer Juniper* and *Atlantis* but, for the most part, as the sixties sputtered to a close, so did Donovan's career.

The plucky Scot has made all types of comeback attempts, wallowing into rock and roll, folk retreading, and pop (covering Bowie's *When You Rock and Roll with Me)* but nothing, to date, has worked. Regardless of his lack of clout in the seventies, Donovan remains one of the most prolific and pastoral song poets of the past decade of youth.

Albums/CATCH THE WIND (12/65): *Josie; Catch the Wind; The Alamo; Cuttin' Out; Car Car; Keep On Truckin'; Goldwatch Blues; To Sing for You; You're Gonna Need Somebody on Your Bond; Tangerine Puppet; Donna Donna; Ramblin' Boy.* SUNSHINE SUPERMAN (8/66); *Sunshine Superman; Legend of a Girl Child Linda; Three King Fishers; Ferris Wheel; Fat Angel; Bert's Blues; Season of the Witch; The Trip; Guinevere; Celeste.* FAIRY TALES (12/66); *Universal Soldiers; Colours; Sunny Goodge Street; Jersey Thursday; To Try for the Sun; Circus of Sour; Summerday Reflection Song; Candy Man; Belated Forgiveness Please; Ballad of the Crystal Man; Little Tin Soldier; Battle of Geraldine.* REAL DONOVAN (12/66): *Turquoise; Oh Deed I Do; Catch the Wind; Remember the Alamo; Ballad of the Crystal Man; Colours; Hey Gyp; Belated Forgiveness Please; Ramblin' Boy; The War Drags On; Josie; To Try for the Sun.* LIKE IT IS (1/67): *Colours; Josie; Catch the Wind; Sunny Goodge Street; Universal Soldier; Summer Day Reflection Song; Do You Hear Me Now; Why Do You Treat Me the Way You Do; To Try for the Sun; Hey Gyp; The War Drags On.* MELLOW YELLOW (1/67): *Mellow Yellow; Writer in the Sun; Sand and Foam; The Observation; Bleak City Woman; House of Jansch; Young Girl Blues; Museum; Hampstead Incident; Sunny South Kensington.* GIFT FROM A FLOWER TO A GARDEN (11/67): *RECORD ONE: WEAR YOUR LOVE LIKE HEAVEN: Wear Your Love Like Heaven; Mad John's Escape; Skip-a-Long Sam; Sun; There Was a Time; Oh Gosh; Little Boy Corduroy; Under the Greenwood Tree; Land of Doesn't Have To Be; Someone's Singing. RECORD TWO: FOR LITTLE ONES: Song of the Naturalist's Wife; Enchanted Gypsy; Voyage into the Golden Screen; Isle of Islay; The Mandolin Man and His Secret; Lay of the Last Tinker; Tinker and the Crab; Widow with Shawl; Lullaby of Spring; The Magpie; Starfish-on-the-Toast; Epistle to Derrol.* DONOVAN IN CONCERT (7/68): *Isle of Islay; Young Girl Blues; There Is a Moun-*

tain; Poor Cow; Celeste; Fat Angel; Guinevere; Widow with Shawl; Preachin' Love; Lullaby of Spring; Writer in the Sun; Pebble and the Man; Rules and Regulations; Mellow Yellow. HURDY GURDY MAN (10/68): *Hurdy Gurdy Man; Peregrine; Entertaining of a Shy Girl; As I Recall It; Get Thy Bearings; Hi It's Been a Long Time; West Indian Lady; Jennifer Juniper; River Song; Tangier; Sunny Day; The Sun Is a Very Magic Fellow; Teas.* DONOVAN'S GREATEST HITS (1/69): *Epistle to Dippy; Sunshine Superman; There Is a Mountain; Jennifer Juniper; Wear Your Love Like Heaven; Season of the Witch; Mellow Yellow; Colours; Hurdy Gurdy Man; Catch the Wind; Lalena.* BARABAJAGEL (9/69): *Barabajagel; Superlungs My Supergirl; Happiness Runs; Where Is She; I Love My Shirt; The Love Song; To Susan on the West Coast Waiting; Trudi; Pamela Jo.* OPEN ROAD (7/70): *Song for John; Curry Lard; Joe Bean's Theme; People Used To; Celtic Rich; Riki Tiki Tavi; Clara Clairvoyant; Roots of Ooh; Season of Farewell; Poke at the Pope; New Year's Resolution.* THE WORLD OF DONOVAN (9/72): *Barabajagel; Fat Angel; Riki Tiki Tavi; Mad John's Escape; Sunshine Superman; Isle of Islay; Song of the Wandering Gypsy; Sand and Foam; Celia of the Seas; Celeste; To Susan on the West Coast Waiting; Guinevere; Hi It's Been a Long Time; Lalena; Wear Your Love Like Heaven; The Mandolin Man and His Secret; Changes; Hurdy Gurdy Man; Atlantis.* COSMIC WHEELS (3/73): *Cosmic Wheels; Earth Sign Man; Sleep; Maria Magenta; Wild Witch Lady; The Music Makers; Intergallactic Laxative; Only the Blues; Appearances.* ESSENCE TO ESSENCE (1/74): *Operating Manual for Spaceship Earth; Lazy Daze; Life Goes On; There Is an Ocean; The Dignity of Man; Yellow Star; Devin the Boy for Every Girl; Saint Valentine Angel; Life Is a Merry-Go-Round; Sailing Homeward.* 7 TEASE (11/74): *Rock and Roll Souljer; Your Broken Heart; Salvation Stomp; The Ordinary Family; Ride a Mile; Sadness; Moon Rock; Love of My Life; Voice of Protest; How Silly; The Great Song of the Sky; Quest.* SLOW DOWN WORLD (5/76): *Cryin' Shame; The Mountain; Children of the World; My Love Is True; A Well-Known Has-Been; Dark-Eyed Blue Jean Angel.* DONOVAN (9/77): *Local Boy Chops Wood; Astral Angel; The Light; Dare To Be Different; Brave New World; Lady Of The Stars; International Man; Sing My Song; Maya's Dance; Kalifornia Kiddies.*

Singles/*Sunshine Superman*/*The Trip* (7/66); *Catch the Wind*/*Why Do You Treat Me the Way You Do* (10/66); *Little Tin Soldier*/*You're Gonna Need Somebody on Your Bond* (10/66); *Summer Day Reflection*/*Sunny Goodge Street* (11/66); *Hey Gyp*/*The War Drags On* (11/66); *Do You Hear Me Now*/*Why Do You Treat Me Like You Do* (11/66); *Do You Hear Me Now*/*Universal Soldier* (1/67); *Mellow Yellow*/*Sunshine Superman* (5/67); *There Is a Mountain*/*Sand and Foam* (7/67); *Jennifer Juniper*/*Poor Cow* (2/68); *Wear Your Love Like Heaven*/*There Is a Mountain (4/68); Teen Angel*/*Hurdy Gurdy Man* (5/68); *Lalena*/*Aye My Love* (9/68); *Atlantis*/*To Susan on the West Coast Waiting* (1/69); *Barabajagel*/*Trudi* (7/69); *I Like You*/*Earth Sign Man* (4/73); *Sailing Homeward*/*Yellow Star* (3/74); *Rock and Roll with Me*/*Divine Daze of deathless Delight* (8/74); *Rock and Roll Souljer*/*How Silly* (2/75); *A Well-Known Has-Been*/*Dark-Eyed Blue Jean Angel* (5/76).

THE DOOBIE BROTHERS/*Tom Johnston (vocals, guitars, keyboards), John Hartman (drums), Dave Shogren (bass), Pat Simmons (guitar). Additional members: Jeff Baxter (guitar, vocals), Tiran Porter (bass), Keith Knudsen (drums), Greg Murph (bass), Mike Hossack (drums), Mike McDonald (keyboards).*
One of the true phenomena of the seventies, the Doobie Brothers could be called, historically speaking, the Son of Pud. Pud was the original group whence the band arose, consisting of Murph, Johnston, and Hartman. Jamming in 1970, the lineup soon became Johnston, Hartman, Simmons, and Shogren. A demo tape fell into the hands of Moby Grape genius–former Jefferson Airplane drummer–San Francisco crazy–all-around music maven Skip Spence, who brought it to the right people's attention.

The band was signed in 1971 by Warners. After an initial album, Shogren was out and Tiran Porter was in, as was Hossack. The Doobies' second long-player, *TOULOUSE STREET,* brought them instant fame via a repetitious single, *Listen to the Music.* The single went gold. The album went gold. From that point onward, the Doobies would be regular bullet-wearers on both albums and singles charts.

Nineteen seventy-four saw another change for the popular band: the addition of Steely Dan guitarist Jeff "Skunk" Baxter.

Although insisting, at first, that it was only a "part-time" gig, Skunk was soon a full-time Doobie and an ex–Steely Dan. In 1975 former Lee Michaels skin-pounder Knudson joined the fold, as did keyboard player McDonald. The Doobies have continued to grow since that time, with horn and string arrangements augmenting their rock antics on their various gold albums.

Albums/THE DOOBIE BROTHERS (4/71): *Nobody; Slippery Saint Paul; Travelin' Man; It Won't Be Right; The Master; Beehive State; Closer Every Day; Chicago; Feelin' Down Farther; Greenwood Creek.* TOULOUSE STREET (7/72): *Listen to the Music; Don't Start Me to Talkin'; Mamaloi; Toulouse Street; Rockin' Down the Highway; Jesus Is Just Alright; White Sun; Cotton Mouth; Disciple; Snake Man.* THE CAPTAIN AND ME (3/73): *Natural Thing; Long Train Runnin'; China Grove; Without You; Uhiah; The Captain and Me; Evil Woman; Clear As the Driven Snow; Dark-Eyed Cajun Woman; Busted Down around O'Connely Corners.* WHAT WERE ONCE VICES . . . (2/74): *Road Angel; Flying Cloud; Daughters of the Sea; Tell Me What You Want; Down in the Track; You Just Can't Stop It; Song to See You Through; Spirit; Pursuit on 53rd Street; Black Water; Eyes of Silver.* STAMPEDE (4/75): *Sweet Maxine; Neal's Fandango; Music Man; Texas Lullabye; Precise; I Been Workin' on You; Double Dealin' Four Flusher; Slat Key Soquel Rag; Take Me in Your Arms; I Cheat the Hangman; Rainy Day Crossroad Blues.* TAKIN' IT TO THE STREETS (4/76): *Losin' End; Turn It Loose; Carry Me Away; Wheels of Fortune; Rio; For Someone Special; Takin' It to the Streets; 8th Avenue Shuffle; It Keeps You Runnin'.* THE BEST OF THE DOOBIE BROTHERS (10/76): *China Grove; Long Train Runnin'; Takin' It to the Streets; Jesus Is Just Alright; Listen to the Music; Without You; Take Me in Your Arms; Black Water; Rockin' Down the Highway; South City Midnight Lady.* LIVIN' ON THE FAULT LINE (7/77): *Nothin' but a Heartache; Little Darling (I Need You); Livin' on the Fault Line; Larry the Logger Two-Step; Echoes of Love; There's a Light; You Belong to Me; Chinatown; Need a Lady; You're Made That Way.*

Singles/*Nobody/Slippery Saint Paul* (5/71); *Feelin' Down Farther/Travelin' Man* (9/71); *Beehive State/Closer Every Day* (12/71); *Listen to the Music/Toulouse Street* (8/72); *Jesus Is Just Alright/Rockin' Down the Highway* (11/72); *Long Train*

Runnin'/Without You (3/73); *China Grove/Evil Woman* (8/73); *Black Water/Another Park, Another Sundown* (3/74); *Eyes of Silver/You Just Can't Stop It* (6/74); *Nobody/Flying Cloud* (9/74); *Black Water/Song to See You Through* (11/74); *Take Me in Your Arms/Slat Key Soquel Rag* (3/75); *Sweet Maxine/Double Dealin' Four Flusher* (7/75); *I Cheat the Hangman/Music Man* (11/75); *Takin' It to the Streets/For Someone Special* (3/76); *Wheels of Fortune/Slat Key Soquel Rag* (7/76); *Little Darling (I Need You)* (7/77).

THE DOORS/*Jim Morrison (vocals), Ray Manzarek (organ), Robbie Krieger (guitar), John Densmore (drums)*
Jim Morrison had the right idea about the rock "tastemaker" pecking order. He didn't give a good goddamn about it. When the rock world called for anger, he gave them black humor. When they called for sex, he gave them violence. When the underground gourmets craved hidden meaning, he gave them AM singles. When the critics looked to him for guidance, he gave them the Bronx cheer. The Doors just didn't play by the rules. As a result, the critics, the cliques, and the professional rock pollsters wrung their hands and rolled their eyes. They were just SO uncool.

What Morrison and company were practicing on them was something that the Doors had always toyed with . . . the concept of rock guerilla theater. Morrison, the son of a rear admiral, met Manzarek at UCLA, where Morrison was majoring in film. They joined forces in 1965, Morrison seeing a band as something more than just a normal playing unit. Manzarek, a veteran of the bluesy Rick and the Ravens, caught sight of a band called the Psychedelic Rangers about that time. Krieger and Densmore were part of the group. The Doors were subsequently formed and, after gigging around L.A. for a while, they were signed by Elektra. They began to seep in through the West Coast underground in early '67, a time when no one could have possibly predicted that a group that sang about the evil and the reptilian and the bloody was about to become not just the number-one group in America but the number-one *singles* group in America.

Their first album punched a hole through the closed-minded guitar-oriented psychedelic school of thought. The sound of the Doors originated with the rumbling keyboard antics of Manzarek. There was a violent, hypnotic quality to it that couldn't be ignored. It wasn't. Their first album shook the album charts by the rafters. *The End* became an FM standard, as did the longer version of *Light My Fire*. A shorter version of the latter stormed up the singles charts. Soon, the Doors had the best of both worlds at their disposal. Their albums always pleased the LP-oriented crowd, and singles like *Hello, I Love You* and *Touch Me* sent chills up and down the spines of countless thirteen-year-old girls. But as the Doors mastered the art of being an all-around band, the tastemakers started to worry.

It was impossible for a group to have hit singles and still be legitimate. A Doors backlash began in earnest. Morrison began to take his surly rock-star stance more and more to heart, behaving erratically both onstage and off. In New Haven, in 1969, he was first maced by police while in his dressing room with a female fan and then was pulled off the stage for telling the audience about it (the police figuring that this would incite a riot). Later that year he was issued six warrants for "lewd and lascivious behavior in public by exposing his private parts and by simulating masturbation and oral copulation" and for alleged public profanity and drunkenness during a March 2, 1969, concert.

As Morrison's problems mounted, the Doors' popularity soared. Manzarek's organ soloing still thrilled crowds, Krieger's riffing and Densmore's drumming still packed a wallop and Morrison . . . was Morrison. The arrests began to irritate the singer, although they pleased the critics (the more marrow-headed thinking it was sure to please the long-lost "hip" Doors audience). Depressed, Morrison quit the band in 1971. Leaving for an extended R&R period in Europe with his young wife, Pamela, Morrison left the rock world behind. He died of a heart attack on July 3, 1971. His widow died of a heroin overdose in May of '74.

The rock community, stunned by the sudden demise of this angry young poet, quickly shifted into reverse and praised his gallant stand against the forces of *them*. The remaining Doors tried valiantly to keep the band afloat, but two post-Morrison releases proved fairly anemic. Manzarek has done both solo and group work since that time and Krieger and Densmore have been involved with the Butts Band, with Krieger also offering a guitar solo effort.

Albums/THE DOORS (1/67): *Break On Through; Soul Kitchen;*

Crystal Ship; Twentieth Century Fox; Alabama Song (Whiskey Bar); Light My Fire; Back Door Man; I Looked at You; End of the Night; Take It As It Comes; The End. STRANGE DAYS (10/67): *People Are Strange; Strange Days; You're Lost, Little Girl; Love Me Two Times; Unhappy Girl; Horse Latitudes; Moonlight Drive; My Eyes Have Seen You; I Can't See Your Face in My Mind; When the Music's Over.* WAITING FOR THE SUN (7/68): *Hello, I Love You; Love Street; Summer's Almost Gone; Not to Touch the Earth; Five to One; Wintertime Love; Unknown Soldier; Spanish Caravan; My Wild Love; Yes, the River Knows; We Could Be So Good Together.* THE SOFT PARADE (10/69): *Tell All the People; Touch Me; Shaman's Blues; Do It; Easy Ride; Wild Child; Runnin' Blue; Wishful Sinful; The Soft Parade.* MORRISON HOTEL (2/70): *Roadhouse Blues; Waiting for the Sun; You Make Me Real; Peace Frong; Blue Sunday; Ship of Fools; Land Ho!; The Spy; Queen of the Highway; Indian Summer; Maggie M'Gill.* ABSOLUTELY LIVE (7/70): *Who Do You Love; Medley: Alabama Song, Back Door Man, Love Hides, Five to One; Build Me a Woman; When the Music's Over; Close to You; Universal Mind; Break On Through #2; The Celebration of the Lizard; Soul Kitchen.* 13 (11/70): *Light My Fire; People Are Strange; Back Door Man; Moonlight Drive; The Crystal Ship; Roadhouse Blues; Touch Me; Love Me Two Times; You're Lost, Little Girl; Land Ho!; Wild Child; Hello, I Love You; The Unknown Soldier.* L.A. WOMAN (4/71): *The Changeling; Love Her Madly; Been Down So Long; Cars Hiss by My Window; L.A. Woman; L'America; Crawling King Snake; The WASP (Texas Radio and the Big Beat); Riders on the Storm.* OTHER VOICES (11/71): *In the Eye of the Sun; Variety Is the Spice of Life; Ships Sails; Tightrope Ride; Down on the Farm; I'm Horny, I'm Stoned; Wandering Musician; Hang On to Your Life.* WEIRD SCENES INSIDE THE GOLD MINE (1/72): *Break On Through; Strange Days; Shaman's Blues; Love Street; Peace Frong; Blue Sunday; The Wasp; End of the Night; Love Her Madly; Spanish Caravan; Ship of Fools; The Spy; The End; Take It As It Comes; Running Blue; L.A. Woman; Five to One; Who Scared You; (You Need Meat) Don't Go No Further; Riders on the Storm; Maggie McGill; Horse Latitudes; When the Music's Over.* FULL CIRCLE (7/72): *Get Up and Dance; 4 Billion Souls; Verdilac; Hardwood Floor; Good Rockin'; The Peking King and the New York Queen; It Slipped My Mind; The*

Mosquito; The Piano Bird. THE BEST OF THE DOORS (8/73):
*Who Do You Love; Soul Kitchen; Hello, I Love You; People Are
Strange; Riders on the Storm; Touch Me; Love Her Madly; Love
Me Two Times; Take It As It Comes; Moonlight Drive; Light My
Fire.*

Singles/*Break On Through/End of the Night* (1/67); *Light My
Fire/Crystal Ship* (4/67); *People Are Strange/Unhappy Girl*
(9/67); *Love Me Two Times/Moonlight Drive* (11/67); *Unknown
Soldier/We Could Be So Good Together* (3/68); *Hello, I Love
You/Love Street* (6/68); *Touch Me/Wild Child* (1/69); *You Make
Me Real/Roadhouse Blues* (3/70); *Love Her Madly/Don't Go No
Further* (3/71);*Riders on the Storm/Changeling* (6/71); *Tightrope
Ride/Variety Is the Spice of Life* (11/71); *Ships w/ Sails/In the
Eye of the Sun* (2/72); *Get Up and Dance/Fleetrunk* (7/72); *The
Mosquito/It Slipped My Mind* (8/72); *Piano Bird/Good Rockin'*
(11/72).

BOB DYLAN/Born Robert Allen Zimmerman, Bob Dylan successfully and single-handedly altered the concept of popular music in the early sixties. He is one of those rarities known as "living
legends." Born in Duluth, Minnesota, he started playing guitar in
his pre-teen years in Hibbing. He attended Minnesota U., where
he adopted the surname of Dylan, linking him permanently with
the imagery of Dylan Thomas. He dropped out of college to embark on a folksinging career.

Fall 1960: Dylan arrives in New York from Minnesota, to visit
the ailing Woody Guthrie, his idol. He hangs out in Greenwich
Village—Gerde's Folk City, the Gaslight, Izzy Young's Folklore
Center—and sings like Guthrie, but he soon discovers that that's
not what is making money in the winter of 1960.

1961: Dylan survives the winter. He is writing a lot of songs.
Robert Shelton hears him at Folk City and on September 29
writes in the New York *Times* that this boy who looks like "a
cross between a choirboy and a beatnik" is "bursting with talent." John Hammond, Sr., producer, signs the young (twenty-
year-old) unknown to Columbia. He cuts his first album, *BOB
DYLAN,* and gives his first concert in Carnegie Recital Hall . . .
to fifty-three people.

1962: The first album is released. Dylan writes more songs—
among them, *Blowin' in the Wind,* which becomes the unofficial

anthem of the Civil Rights Movement. Eventually something like sixty people record that song—not just Peter, Paul and Mary, who take it to the top of the charts, but such unlikely people as Sam Cooke, Marlene Dietrich, Duke Ellington, Percy Faith, and the New Christy Minstrels.

1963: Dylan's first solo concert at Town Hall, April 12, makes him a star. *FREEWHEELIN' BOB DYLAN* is released. He's invited to sing on the *Ed Sullivan Show,* May 12, but CBS bans his *Talking John Birch Society Blues* and he refuses. He meets Joan Baez at the Monterey Folk Festival. That summer, Baez and Dylan are the stars of the Folk Festival. Peter, Paul and Mary have a hit with *Blowin' in the Wind.*

1964: The Times They Are A-Changin' is the song of 1964. Dylan makes his way into *Life* and *Newsweek.* Dylan, whose songs have made a whole generation political *(Masters of War, Talking World War III Blues),* is slowly starting to move out of politics. *ANOTHER SIDE OF BOB DYLAN,* out that summer, seemed like a betrayal to the protest movement. The Beatles and the Rolling Stones come to America.

1965: Dylan uses electric instrumentation on *BRINGING IT ALL BACK HOME,* released in March. He and Baez do a successful tour of London. In America, the Byrds do *Mr. Tambourine Man* with electric guitars and amplifiers and folk-rock is born. On July 25, Dylan appears on stage in Newport with an electric guitar and is booed and hissed. He loses many of the folk people, but already there is a rock generation growing up who understands him. *HIGHWAY 61 REVISITED* reaches them, reaches more people than any previous Dylan record. Forest Hills Stadium, August 28: thousands find the new Dylan unbearable; millions have a new hero. Elsewhere, especially in California, folk-rock takes over and wins over some of Dylan's harshest critics. Some, of course, are never won over.

1966: The furor has settled down. Rock is respectable. *BLONDE ON BLONDE* is released and is superb. Everyone is playing Dylan and singing him *(Don't Think Twice, It's All Right,* from the second album is eventually recorded by more than thirty names, including Lawrence Welk and the Four Seasons). The twenty-five-year-old troubadour is now writing a novel, *Tarantula.*

1967: Dylan is involved in his legendary motorcycle accident. How bad was it really? More rumors. Was he crippled? Disfigured? A mindless veggie? Or hurt just enough to have an excuse to take some time off? He hides out in Woodstock with wife and children. The novel is dropped. *BOB DYLAN'S GREATEST HITS* is released but no new album. Nor will there be one for eighteen months.

1968: JOHN WESLEY HARDING gives some clues as to what happened in Woodstock, reflecting its rustic calm. He appears at a Memorial to Woody Guthrie in Carnegie Hall. He sings (with The Band) rockabilly. The acid generation is somewhat disappointed by *HARDING,* but there are plenty more who welcome the new tranquility. After *JWH,* both the Beatles and the Rolling Stones put out albums that are significantly simple. Later in the year, Dylan turns up at a Johnny Cash concert. Wee doggies.

1969: NASHVILLE SKYLINE is released early in the year, and all the people who had acquired a taste for that harsh Dylan voice now have to get used to the new voice. The album is very country and a continuation of the direction he took with *HARDING,* only warmer and more personal. Almost sexy. Even so, the change costs him a few friends. He appears on the Johnny Cash TV show, singing with him *Girl from the North Country.* He makes a surprise appearance in St. Louis at a concert for The Band (introduced as Elmer Johnson) and sings four songs. As usual, he speaks best to his audience through his work. They love him.

1970: Dylan returns to a non-country sound with the release of *NEW MORNING.* He then retreats from public life. A single, *Copper Kettle,* stiffs, as does the subsequent *Fool Such As I.* He was never a top-forty act, anyway.

1971: Dylan comes out of seclusion in time for the mammoth concert for Bangla Desh along with George Harrison, Ravi Shankar, and Leon Russell. *BOB DYLAN'S GREATEST HITS, VOL. II* is released. No new album is to be heard during that year although a single, *Watching the River Flow,* is released, to general apathy. A second single, *George Jackson,* appears in November. It does not soar up the charts.

1972: Bob takes a creative break this year, producing no new releases whatsoever, although he does play on sessions with Steve Goodman and John Prine.

1973: Dylan shakes up the music industry on two fronts. He appears in the Sam Peckinpah feature-length motion picture dud,

Pat Garrett and Billy the Kid. As a character named Alias, Dylan's biggest scene finds him reading the labels of canned goods aloud off a grocery store shelf. No matter, the soundtrack album provides him with a hit single: *Knocking on Heaven's Door.* He stuns musicologists by leaving Columbia Records after more than a decade and jumping to the Asylum label.

1974: Now an Asylum artist, Dylan embarks on a highly touted tour of the country backed by The Band. His first Asylum release, *PLANET WAVES,* is a near disaster, selling as many albums as a gold record should but leaving an equal number of unsold LPs in the stores. An in-concert LP with the band, *BEFORE THE FLOOD,* fares somewhat better. Nevertheless, by the end of the year, he is off Asylum and back on Columbia.

1975: In January, Dylan celebrates his homecoming with the epic *BLOOD ON THE TRACKS* LP, a very controversial long-player. By December, he has a *second* LP, *DESIRE,* in the stores as well. During the interim, a special double-LP issue of Bob Dylan and The Band's historic *BASEMENT TAPES* is released. To keep all his fans happy, the revitalized Dylan begins the Rolling Thunder Revue, a barn-storming coast-to-coast tour featuring Mick Ronson, Joan Baez, Roger McGuinn, Joni Mitchell, and Ronnee Blakley.

1976: Dylan's Rolling Thunder troupe tickles the video airwaves via an "in-concert" special. Yet another new album, *HARD RAIN,* takes the charts by storm. A single, *Mozambique,* nearly makes it.

1977: Not a vintage year by any means. Dylan and his wife Sara start a very messy series of divorce proceedings. Custody of their children is a sore point and, at one point, Mrs. D. is alleged to have abducted her children from their father. Dylan regularly makes the scandal sheets because of his marital problems. To make matters worse, his opulent home in California is reported to be sinking in marshy earth.

1978: Dylan releases a film version of his Rolling Thunder Revue tour entitled *Renaldo and Clara,* a three hour and fifty-two minute production released by Dylan's own film company, Circuit Films. The $1,250,000 film boasts no soundtrack so as not to lead the audience into believing it's a concert film. Dylan prefers to think of it as a documentary. Period.

Albums/BOB DYLAN (3/62): *You're No Good; Talkin' New York; See That My Grave Is Kept Clean; In My Time of Dyin'; Man of Constant Sorrow; Fixin' to Die; Song to Woody; Pretty Peggy-O; Highway 51; House of the Risin' Sun; Gospel Plow; Baby, Let Me Follow You Down; Freight Train Blues.* FREE-WHEELIN' BOB DYLAN (5/63): *Blowin' in the Wind; Down the Highway; Bob Dylan's Blues; Hard Rain's Gonna Fall; I Shall Be Free; Don't Think Twice, It's All Right; Oxford Town; Corrin, Corrina; Honey, Just Allow Me One More Chance; Girl from the North Country; Masters of War; Talking World War III Blues; Bob Dylan's Dream.* THE TIMES THEY ARE A-CHANGIN' (1/64): *Times They Are A-Changin'; Ballad of Hollis Brown; With God on Our Side; One Too Many Mornings; North Country Blues; When the Ship Comes In; Only a Pawn in Their Game; Boots of Spanish Leather; Lonesome Death of Hattie Carroll; Restless Farewell.* ANOTHER SIDE OF BOB DYLAN (8/64): *All I Really Want to Do; Black Crow Blues; Spanish Harlem Incident; Chimes of Freedom; I Shall Be Free; To Ramona; My Back Pages; Motorpsycho Nitemare; I Don't Believe You; Ballad in Plain D; It Ain't Me, Babe.* BRINGING IT ALL BACK HOME (3/65): *Subterranean Homesick Blues; On the Road Again; Bob Dylan's 115th Dream; Gates of Eden; Mr. Tambourine Man; It's Alright, Ma (I'm Only Bleeding); It's All Over Now, Baby Blue; medley.* HIGHWAY 61 REVISITED (8/65): *Like a Rolling Stone; Tombstone Blues; It Takes a Lot to Laugh, It Takes a Train to Cry; From a Buick 6; Ballad of a Thin Man; Queen Jane Approximately; Desolation Row; Highway 61 Revisited; Just Like Tom Thumb's Blues.* BLONDE ON BLONDE (5/66): *Rainy Day Women No. 12 & 35; Pledging My Time; Visions of Johanna; One of Us Must Know (Sooner or Later); I Want You; Memphis Blues Again; Just Like a Woman; Most Likely You Go Your Way and I'll Go Mine; Temporary Like Achilles; Absolutely Sweet Marie; 4th Time Around; Obviously 5 Believers; Sad-Eyed Lady of the Lowlands.* GREATEST HITS (3/67): *Rainy Day Women No. 12 & 35; Blowin' in the Wind; Subterranean Homesick Blues; Like a Rolling Stone; Positively 4th Street; Times They Are A-Changin'; It Ain't Me, Babe; Mr. Tambourine Man; I Want You; Just Like a Woman.* JOHN WESLEY HARDING (12/67): *John Wesley Harding; As I Went Out One Morning; I Dreamed I Saw St. Augustine; All Along the Watchtower; Ballad of Frankie Lee and Judas Priest;*

Drifter's Escape; Dear Landlord; I Am a Lonesome Hobo; I Pity the Poor Immigrant; Wicked Messenger; Down Along the Cove; I'll Be Your Baby Tonight. NASHVILLE SKYLINE (4/69): *Girl from the North Country (with Johnny Cash); Nashville Skyline Rag; To Be Alone with You; I Threw It All Away; Peggy Day; Lay, Lady, Lay; One More Night; Tell Me That It Isn't True; Country Pie; Tonight I'll Be Staying Here with You.* SELF PORTRAIT (6/70): *All the Tired Horses; Alberta #1; I Forgot More Than You'll Ever Know; Days of '49; Early Mornin' Rain; In Search of Little Sadie; Let It Be Me; Little Sadie; Woogie Boogie; Belle Isle; Living the Blues; Like a Rolling Stone; Copper Kettle; Gotta Travel On; Blue Moon; The Boxer; The Mighty Quinn (Quinn the Eskimo); Take Me As I Am; Take a Message to Mary; It Hurts Me Too; Minstrel Boy; She Belongs to Me; Wigwam; Alberta #2.* NEW MORNING (10/70): *If Not for You; Day of the Locusts; Time Passes Slowly; Went to See the Gypsy; Winterlude; If Dogs Run Free; New Morning; Sign on the Window; One More Weekend; The Man in Me; Three Angels; Father of the Night.* GREATEST HITS VOL. II (11/71): *Watching the River Flow; Don't Think Twice, It's All Right; Lay, Lady, Lay; Stuck Inside of Mobile with the Memphis Blues Again; I'll Be Your Baby Tonight; All I Really Want to Do; My Back Pages; Maggie's Form; Tonight I'll Be Staying Here with You; She Belongs to Me; All Along the Watchtower; The Mighty Quinn (Quinn the Eskimo); Just Like Tom Thumb's Blues; A Hard Rain's A-Gonna Fall; It's All Over Now, Baby Blue; Tomorrow Is a Long Time; When I Paint My Masterpiece; I Shall Be Released; You Ain't Goin' Nowhere; Down in the Flood.* PAT GARRETT AND BILLY THE KID (soundtrack; 7/73): *Main Title Theme (Billy); Cantina Theme (Working for the Law); Billy 1; Bunkhouse Theme; River Theme; Turkey Chase; Knockin' on Heaven's Door; Final Theme; Billy 4; Billy 7.* DYLAN (11/73): *Lily of the West; Can't Help Falling in Love; Sarah Jane; Ballad of Ira Hayes; Mr. Bo Jangles; Mary Ann; Big Yellow Taxi; A Fool Such As I; Spanish Is the Loving Tongue.* PLANET WAVES (1/74): *On a Night Like This; Going Going Gone; Tough Mama; Hazel; Something There Is about You; Forever Young; Dirge; You Angel You; Never Say Goodbye; Wedding Song.* BEFORE THE FLOOD (6/74): *Most Likely You Go Your Way (and I'll Go Mine); Lay, Lady, Lay; Rainy Day Women #12 & 35; Knockin' on Heaven's Door; It Ain't Me, Babe; Ballad of a Thin Man; Up on Cripple Creek; I Shall Be Released; Endless Highway; The Night They Drove Old Dixie Down; Stage Fright; Don't Think Twice, It's All Right; Just Like a Woman; It's Alright, Ma (I'm Only Bleeding); The Shape I'm In; When You Awake; The Weight; All Along the Watchtower; Highway 61 Revisited; Like a Rolling Stone; Blowin' in the Wind.* BLOOD ON THE TRACKS (1/75): *Tangled Up in Blue; Simple Twist of Fate; You're a Big Girl Now; Idiot Wind; You're Gonna Make Me Lonesome When You Go; Meet Me in the Morning; Lily, Rosemary and the Jack of Hearts; Shelter from the Storm; Buckets of Rain.* THE BASEMENT TAPES (6/75): *Odds and Ends; Orange Juice Blues (Blues for Breakfast); Million Dollar Bash; Yazoo Street Scandal; Goin' to Acapulco; Katie's Been Gone; Lo and Behold!; Clothes Line Saga; Bessie Smith; Apple Suckling Tree; Please, Mrs. Henry; Tears of Rage; Too Much of Nothing; Yea! Heavy and a Bottle of Bread; Ain't No More Cane; Crash on the Levee (Down in the Flood); Ruben Remus; Tiny Montgomery; You Ain't Goin' Nowhere; Don't Ya Tell Henry; Nothing Was Delivered; Open the Door, Homer; Long Distance Operator; This Wheel's on Fire.* DESIRE (12/75): *Hurricane; Isis; Mozambique; One More Cup of Coffee; Oh, Sister; Joey; Romance in Durango; Black Diamond Bay; Sara.* HARD RAIN (9/76): *You're a Big Girl Now; Shelter from the Storm; Lay, Lady, Lay; Maggie's Farm; Stuck Inside of Mobile with the Memphis Blues Again; I Threw It All Away; One Too Many Mornings; Oh, Sister; Idiot Wind.*

Singles/*Mixed Up Confusion/Corrina, Corrina* (11/62); *Subterranean Homesick Blues/She Belongs to Me* (3/65); *Like a Rolling Stone/Gates of Eden* (6/65); *From a Buick 6/Positively 4th Street* (9/65); *Can You Please Crawl Out Your Window/Highway 61 Revisited* (12/65); *One of Us Must Know (Sooner or Later)* (2/66); *Rainy Day Women #12 & 35/Pledging My Time* (3/66); *I Want You/Just Like Tom Thumb's Blues* (6/66); *Just Like a Woman/Obviously 5 Believers* (8/66); *Rainy Day Women #12 & 35/Like a Rolling Stone* (9/66); *Just Like a Woman/I Want You* (1/67); *Leopard-Skin Pill-Box Hat/Most Likely You Go Your Way and I'll Go Mine* (3/67); *I Threw It All Away/Drifter's Escape* (4/69); *Lay, Lady, Lay/Peggy Day* (7/69); *Tonight I'll Be Staying Here with You/Country Pie* (10/69); *Lay, Lady, Lay/I Threw It All Away; Copper Kettle/Wigwam* (7/70); *A Fool Such*

As I/Lily of the West (11/70); *Watching the River Flow/Spanish Is the Loving Tongue* (6/71); *George Jackson (big band version)/George Jackson (acoustic version)* (11/71); *Positively 4th Street/Subterranean Homesick Blues* (4/73); *Knockin' on Heaven's Door/Turkey Chase* (8/73); *On a Night Like This/You Angel You* (1/74); *Something There Is about You/Tough Mama* (4/74); *Knockin' on Heaven Door/A Fool Such As I* (4/74); *Most Likely You Go Your Way (and I'll Go Mine)/Stage Fright* (7/74); *It Ain't Me, Babe/All Along the Watchtower* (9/74); *Hurricane (Parts I and II)* (10/75); *Hurricane (Part I)/Mozambique* (11/75); *Tangled Up in Blue/If You See Her, Say Hello* (11/75); *Stuck Inside of Mobile with the Memphis Blues Again/Rita May* (11/76).

THE EAGLES/*Glen Frey (guitar, vocals), Don Felder (guitars), Don Henley (drums, vocals), Randy Meisner (bass, vocals), Joe Walsh (guitar, vocals—replaced original member Bernie Leadon).* In the 1960s, it was the Byrds who brought the influences of country music into mainstream rock and roll, profoundly influencing the charts and spawning a host of imitators. During the seventies, the Eagles have performed a similar feat, unleashing both an avalanche of distinctive-sounding hit tunes and an army of laid-back L.A.-cowboy sound-alikes. All of their albums have gone gold and they show no signs of slowing down the pace.

1971. The Eagles get together as an offshoot of Linda Ronstadt's newly formed touring band. Glenn Frey and Don Henley are plucked from the entourage by Linda's manager, John Boylan, who teams them with Randy Meisner and Bernie Leadon. Randy was a veteran of Poco and Rick Nelson's band. Bernie was formerly with the Burritos and Dillard and Clark. Once signed with Asylum, they're assigned producer Glyn (the Who, the Stones) John for their first album.

1972. *THE EAGLES* is released. *Take It Easy, Witchy Woman* and *Peaceful Easy Feeling* storm the charts.

1973. *DESPERADO* is released. A hit album and tour are the results. The Eagles antagonize a few Anglophile members of the rock press with their earthy humor, dropping a few choice remarks about a famous British "art-rock" troupe. By year's end, they are the beloved misanthropes of rock.

1974. Don Felder, a slide guitarist, becomes the fifth Eagle during *ON THE BORDER.* Irv Azoff becomes their new manager and *Best Of My Love* reestablishes the band on the singles charts.

1975. *ON THE BORDER* surpasses a million in sales, earning the Eagles a platinum record (their first but not their last). *ONE OF THESE NIGHTS* goes gold both as an album and a single. *Lyin' Eyes* is yet another hit. Bernie Leadon quits the band late in the year in reaction to the dehumanizing road life. Long-time buddy and ex–James Gang-er Joe Walsh is enlisted.

1976. *GREATEST HITS* goes platinum instantly, becoming the third album in history to go platinum upon release. Later in the year, *HOTEL CALIFORNIA* is released. It too goes platinum.

1977. *Life in the Fast Lane,* featuring Walsh's off-the-wall guitar licks, becomes the new Eagles anthem.

Albums/THE EAGLES (6/72): *Take It Easy; Witchy Woman; Chug All Night; Most of Us Are Sad; Train Leaves Here This Morning; Take the Devil; Earlybird; Peaceful Easy Feeling; Trying; Nightingale.* DESPERADO (4/73): *Doolin' Daltons; Twenty-One; Out of Control; Tequila Sunrise; Desperado; Certain Kind of Fool; Outlaw Man; Saturday Night; Bitter Creek; Doolin' Daltons Reprise; Desperado Reprise.* ON THE BORDER (3/74): *Already Gone; You Never Cry Like a Lover; Midnight Flyer; My Man; On the Border; James Dean; Ol' 55; Is It True; Good Day in Hell; The Best of My Love.* ONE OF THESE NIGHTS (6/75): *One of These Nights; Too Many Hands; Hollywood Waltz; Journey of the Sorcerer; Lyin' Eyes; Take It to the Limit; Visions; After the Thrill Is Gone; I Wish You Peace.* THEIR GREATEST HITS (2/76): *Take It Easy; Witchy Woman; Lyin' Eyes; Already Gone; Desperado; One of These Nights; Take It to the Limit; Tequila Sunrise; Peaceful Easy Feeling; Best of My Love.* HOTEL CALIFORNIA (12/76): *Hotel California; New Kid in Town; Life in the Fast Lane; Wasted Time; Wasted Time Reprise; Victim of Love; Pretty Maids All in a Row; Try and Love Again; The Last Resort.*

Singles/*Take It Easy/Get You in the Mood* (5/72); *Witchy Woman/Early Bird* (8/72); *Peaceful Easy Feeling/Tryin'* (12/72); *Tequila Sunrise/Twenty-One* (5/73); *Outlaw Man/Certain Kind of Fool* (8/73); *Already Gone/Is It True?* (4/74); *James Dean/Good Day in Hell* (8/74); *Best of My Love/Ol' 55* (11/74); *One of These Nights/Visions* (5/75); *Lyin' Eyes/Too Many Hands* (9/75); *Take*

It to the Limit/After the Thrill Is Gone (12/75); *New Kid in Town/Victim of Love* (12/76); *Hotel California/Pretty Maids All in a Row* (2/77); *Life in the Fast Lane/The Last Resort* (5/77).

EARTH, WIND AND FIRE/*Maurice White (vocals, drums, kalimba), Verdine White (vocals, bass), Philip Bailey (vocals, bass), Larry Dunn (piano, oberheim, moog synthesizer), Al McKay (guitar), Ralf Johnson (drums), Fred White (drums), Johnny Graham (guitar), Andrew Woolfolk (tenor sax), Donald Myrick (alto, tenor, baritone sax), Louis Satterfield (trombone), Michael Harris (trumpet). Previous members: Ronnie Laws (guitar), Ronald Bautista (guitar), Jessica Cleaves (vocals).*

Formed in 1971 by former Ramsey Lewis Group-member Maurice White, Earth, Wind and Fire was one of the first black rock-and-soul bands to appeal to both a black- and a rock-oriented white audience. White's initial musical message was, and continues to be, one of intense positive direction. Brandishing a harsh, optimistic brand of brassy rock, the original Earth, Wind and Fire toiled for two albums unsuccessfully.

Signed by Columbia Records in 1972, Earth, Wind and Fire reshuffled its membership slightly as fame loomed close at hand. In 1973, original members Law and Bautista were replaced by Al McKay and Johnny Graham. Andrew Woolfolk also joined that year. In 1974, Jessica Cleaves left the band and, in 1975, Fred White joined.

EW&F's initial success came strong with the release of their *HEAD TO THE SKY* album. Their albums began going gold, spawning hit singles. *OPEN YOUR EYES* and *THAT'S THE WAY OF THE WORLD* were chart phenomenas, with the latter giving birth to the hit single *Shining Star*. The single was awarded a Grammy for Best R&B Performance by a Vocal Group. The live *GRATITUDE* LP of 1975 spawned an avalanche of EW&F awards, including the Favorite R&B Group title in the American Music Awards of that year.

Nineteen seventy-six saw the death of EW&F's long-time co-producer and mentor, Charles Stepney. The group's *SPIRIT* album is dedicated to their late musical leader. *ALL IN ALL* shot the group back up the charts in 1977 in time for a Merry Christmas rush.

Onstage, the band has earned a reputation, over their seven-years, of being one of the most kinetic ensembles ever to hit the spotlights. Pianos levitate and twirl, singers vault through the air, and pillars of smoke and fire punctuate each downbeat of their raucous rhythms.

Albums/EARTH, WIND AND FIRE (2/71): *Help Somebody; Moment of Truth; Love Is Life; Fan the Fire; C'mon Children; Bad Time; This World Today.* NEED OF LOVE (11/71): *Energy; Beauty; I Can Feel It in My Bones; I Think about Lovin' You; Everything Is Everything.* LAST DAYS AND TIME (10/72): *Time Is on Your Side; They Don't See; Make It with You; Power; Mom; Remember the Children; Where Have All the Flowers Gone; I'd Rather Have You.* HEAD TO THE SKY (5/73): *Evil; Keep Your Head to the Sky; Build Your Nest; The World's a Masquerade; Clover; Zanzibar.* OPEN OUR EYES (2/74): *Mighty Mighty; Devotion; Fair but So Uncool; Feelin' Blue; Kalimba Story; Drum Song; Tee Nine Chee Bit; Spasmodic Movements; Caribou; Open Our Eyes.* ANOTHER TIME (5/74): *Fan the Fire; Moment of Truth; Love Is Life; Help Somebody; C'mon Children; Beauty; Energy; Bad Time; This World Today; Handwriting on the Wall; other titles.* THE WAY OF THE WORLD (2/75): *Shining Star; That's the Way of the World; Happy Feelin'; All about Love; Yearnin' Learnin'; Reasons; Africano; See the Light.* GRATITUDE (11/75): *Shining Star; New World Symphony; Sunshine; Singasong; Gratitude; Celebrate; Can't Hide Love; Introduction; Africano; Yearnin' Learnin'; Power; Devotion; Sun Goddess; Reasons; Sing a Message to You.* SPIRIT (9/76): *Getaway; On Your Face; Imagination; Spirit; Saturday Night; Earth, Wind and Fire; Departure; Biyo; Burnin' Bush.* ALL 'N ALL (11/77): *Jupiter; Be Ever Wonderful; Magic Mind; Serpentine Fire; I'll Write a Song for You; Runnin'; Love's Holiday; Fantasy.*

Singles/*Love Is Life/This World Today* (4/71); *Fan the Fire/This World Today* (4/71); *I Think about Lovin' You/C'mon Children* (12/71); *Mom/Power* (11/72); *Where Have All the Flowers Gone/Time Is on Your Side .(2/73); Evil/Clover* (6/73); *Keep Your Head to the Sky/Build Your Nest* (10/73); *Mighty Mighty/Drum Song* (2/74); *Keep Your Head to the Sky/Evil* (4/74); *Kalimba Story/Tee Nine Chee Bit* (6/74); *Fair but So Uncool/Devotion* (8/74); *Hot Dawgit/Tambura* (10/74); *Shining Star/Yearnin' Learnin'* (1/75); *Sun Goddess* (with Ramsey Lewis)/*Jungle Strut*

(2/75); *That's the Way of the World/Africano* (6/75); *Reasons/Happy Feeling* (7/75); *Mighty Mighty/Devotion* (11/75); *Singasong/Singasong* (instrumental; 11/75); *Saturday Nite/Departure* (10/76); *Shining Star/That's the Way of the World* (11/76); *Hot Dawgit/Sun Goddess* (11/76); *Serpentine Fire* (10/77).

THE ELECTRIC FLAG/*Original members: Mike Bloomfield (guitar), Harvey Brooks (bass), Buddy Miles (drums), Marcus Doubleday (trumpet), Herbie Rich (baritone and tenor sax), Peter Strazza (tenor sax), Nick Gravenities (vocals), Barry Goldberg (keyboards). Additional member: Roger Troy (bass and lead vocals).*

Formed in 1967 by a disgruntled Michael Bloomfield (late of the Paul Butterfield Blues Band) and Barry Goldberg (a top sessionist), the high-stepping Electric Flag was the first big rock-outfit to employ a horn section. The musicianship was superb, the sound was brassy blues-rock. After two albums and less than two years, the band called it quits. Bloomfield drifted from project to project, as did Goldberg. Buddy Miles formed the successful Buddy Miles Express before settling into rock limbo. Harvey Brooks was instrumental in forming the Fabulous Rhinestones, a slick band largely overlooked by the music industry. Gravenities tried to keep Big Brother and the Holding Company intact.

In 1974, Bloomfield, Miles, Gravenities, and Goldberg took a shot at reforming the Flag. Roger Troy was chosen to replace Brooks. The experiment produced one solid albeit uninspired album and a hastily put-together concert tour. The band collapsed. Bloomfield and Goldberg went on to form KGB, a fairly mindless rock and roll band, which saw Bloomfield jumping ship within months of his joining.

Albums/A LONG TIME COMIN' (7/68): *Killing Floor; Groovin' Is Easy; Over-Lovin' You; She Should Have Just; Wine; Texas; Sittin' in Circles; You Don't Realize; Another Country; Easy Rider.* AN AMERICAN MUSIC BAND (12/68): *Sunny; With Time There Is Change; Nothing to Do; See to Your Neighbor; Qualified; Hey, Little Girl; Mystery; My Woman That Hangs around the House; Soul Searchin'.* THE BEST OF THE ELECTRIC FLAG (6/71): *Killing Floor; Sunny; Over-Lovin' You; You Don't Realize; Soul Searchin'; Groovin' Is Easy; Mystery; Another Country.* THE BAND KEPT PLAYING (1974): *Sweet Soul Mu-*

sic; Every Now and Then; Sudden Change; Earthquake Country; Doctor, Oh Doctor (Massive Infusion); Lonely Song; Make Your Move; Inside Information; Talkin' Won't Get It; The Band Kept Playing.

Singles/*Groovin' Is Easy*/*Over-Lovin' You* (9/67); *Sunny*/*Soul Searchin'* (1/69); *Sweet Soul Music* (1974).

ELECTRIC LIGHT ORCHESTRA/*Bev Beven (drums); Jeff Lynne (vocals, guitars), Kelly Croucutt (bass), Hugh McDowell (cello), Melvyn Gale (cello), Mik Kaminski (violin), Richard Tandy (keyboards).*
If the London Philharmonic collided head-on with a rock and roll band, the survivors would be named ELO. Combining classical instrumentation with lavishly produced rock and roll, they are one of the finest progressive rock outfits around today. Originally started in 1971 as an offshoot of the Move by prime Movers Roy Wood, Jeff Lynne, and Bev Beven, the band soon became an entity of its own. Roy Wood moved on to form Wizzard in 1972, leaving the young band to progress on its own accord. The group owes a lot to Wood's initial inspiration (a Beatles-phile of the first magnitude, Roy wanted to emulate the fab four in terms of orchestrating rock à la *Strawberry Fields*), but the main thrust of ELO has long come from Lynne and Beven. They have taken the group from its original, one-dimensional concept, and journeyed into worlds of sheer fantasy *(Eldorado)* and good old rock 'n' roll *(Do Ya)*. There is practically nothing that ELO cannot incorporate into its brazen realm (hard-as-nails guitar solos and syrupy cellos are no strange bedfellows in this topsy-turvy outfit) and the band's in-concert performances always combine the expertise of classical music with the down-and-out lunacy of rock. They are, in short, one of the most inventive bands to come along in quite a while.

Albums/NO ANSWER (3/72): *10538 Overture; Nellie Takes Her Vow; Battle of Marston Moor (July 2nd, 1644); Look at Me Now; 1st Movement; Queen of the Hours; Manhattan Rumble; Mr. Radio; Whistler in the Night.* ELECTRIC LIGHT ORCHESTRA II (2/73): *In Old England Town (Boogie #2); Mama; Roll Over Beethoven; Kuiama; From the Sun to the World (Boogie #1).* ON THE THIRD DAY (11/73: *Ocean Breakup; King of the Universe; Bluebird Is Dead; Oh No, Not Susan; New World Rising; Ocean*

Breakup Reprise; Showdown; Daybreaker; Ma-Ma-Ma Belle; Dreaming of 4000; In the Hall of the Mountain King. ELDORADO (9/74); *Eldorado Overture; Can't Get It Out of My Head; Boy Blue; Laredo Tornedo; Poor Boy (The Greenwood); Mister Kingdom; Nobody's Child; Illusions in G Minor; Eldorado; Eldorado Finale.* FACE THE MUSIC (9/75); *Fire on High; Waterfall; Evil Woman; Nightrider; Poker; Strange Magic; One Summer Dream; Down Home Town.* OLE ELO (6/76): *10538 Overture; Kuiama; Roll Over Beethoven; Showdown; Ma-Ma-Ma Belle; Can't Get It Out of My Head; Boy Blue; Evil Woman; Strange Magic.* A NEW WORLD RECORD (10/76): *Tightrope; Telephone Line; Rockaria; Mission (A New World Record); So Fine; Livin' Thing; Above the Clouds; Do Ya; Shangri-La.* OUT OF THE BLUE (10/77): *Turn to Stone; It's Over; Sweet Talkin' Woman; Across the Border; Night in the City; Starlight; Jungle; Believe Me Now; Steppin' Out; Standin' in the Rain; Big Wheels; Summer and Lightning; Mr. Blue Sky; Sweet Is the Night; The Whale; Birmingham Blues; Wild West Hero.*

Singles/*10538 Overture/Battle of Marston Moor* (5/72); *Queen of the Hours/Mr. Radio* (not released); *Roll Over Beethoven/Queen of the Hours* (2/73); *Showdown/In an Old England Town* (10/73); *Ma-Ma-Ma-Belle/Daybreaker* (2/74); *Showdown/Roll Over Beethoven* (8/74; *Can't Get It Out of My Head/Illusion in G Major* (11/74); *Boy Blue/Eldorado* (4/75); *Evil Woman/10538 Overture* (10/75); *Strange Magic/New World Rising* (2/76); *Showdown/Daybreaker* (7/76); *Livin' Thing/Ma-Ma-Ma Belle* (10/76); *Do Ya/Night Rider* (1/77); *Telephone Line/Poorboy* (5/77).

THE ELECTRIC PRUNES/*Ron Morgan (guitar), Mark Kincaid (guitar, vocals), Richard Whetstone (drums, guitar, vocals), Brad Wade (bass, flute, vocals). Previous members: John Herren (keyboards), Jim Lowe (vocals), Weasel (guitar), Quent (drums), Ken Williams (lead guitar), Mark Tulin (bass).*
I Had Too Much to Dream (Last Night,) the first successful single of this South California band, was a minor psychedelic classic. Their *MASS IN F MINOR* album (complete with rosary on the cover), sung in Latin, was described by one critic as sounding like "tone-deaf monks singing Gregorian chants." Nonetheless, the piece was one of the first examples of God Rock . . . and also one of the last. The rosary would have come in handy by the late

sixties, when the band hit the skids and faded away.

Albums/ELECTRIC PRUNES (2/67): *I Had Too Much to Dream (Last Night); Are You Lovin' Me More (But Enjoying It Less); Bangles; Onie; Train for Tomorrow; Sold to the Highest Bidder; Get Me to the World on Time; About a Quarter to Nine; King in the Counting House; Luvin'; Try Me On for Size; Tunerville Trolley.* UNDERGROUND (7/67): *Great Banana Hoax; Children of Rain; Wind-Up Toys; Antique Doll; It's Not Fair; Big Captain Glory; Long Day's Fight.* MASS IN F MINOR (11/67): *Kyrie Eleison; Gloria; Credo; Sanctus; Angus Dei; Benedictus.* THE RE-LEASE OF AN OATH (9/68): *Kol Nidre; Holy Are You; General Confessional; Individual Confessional; Our Father; Our King; The Adoration; Closing Hymn.* JUST GOOD OLD ROCK AND ROLL (5/69): *Sell; 14 Year Old Funk; Love Grows; So Many People to Tell; Giant Sunhorse; Thorjon; Tracks; Sing to Me; Silver Passion Mine; Violent Rose.*

Singles/*I Had Too Much to Dream (Last Night)* (11/66); *Get Me to the World on Time* (3/67); *Dr. Do-Good/Hideaway* (5/67); *Great Banana Hoax/Wind-Up Toys* (7/67); *Everybody Knows You're Not in Love/You Never Had It Better* (1/68).

EMERSON, LAKE AND PALMER/*Keith Emerson (keyboards), Greg Lake (bass, vocals, guitar), Carl Palmer (drums).*
Emerson, Lake and Palmer (ELP to their fans) are the Mount Rushmore of popular music. Brandishing haughty, heavy sounds, this thunderous trio has brought forth songs of durability and stature that trip delightfully from rock to classical with marked regularity. Their wall of sound may strike some as being preten-tious, but onstage ELP is wont to shatter that impression by breaking up the musical interludes with fits of knife-throwing, organ-throttling, piano-jumping and general outbursts of sado-masochism directed at their equipment. In short, they are three quite intellectual and adventuresome loons.

Emerson, resident madman from Nice, was watching his band sink slowly to its knees when he ran into Greg Lake, vocalist of King Crimson, and Carl Palmer of Atomic Rooster. The three wanted to explore rock in an involved direction and all felt stifled in their present bands. They formed a triumvirate, and soon ELP had transcended their initial slot of "cult status" band to dwell in the high reaches of superstardom.

The group's popularity peaked and began to recede by 1975 when they suddenly disappeared from view. They re-emerged triumphant in 1977 with a best-selling album, *WORKS*.

Albums/EMERSON, LAKE AND PALMER (1/71): *The Barbarian; Take a Pebble; Knife-Edge; The Three Fates—Clotho, Lachesis, Atropos; Tank; Lucky Man.* TARKUS (6/71): *Eruption; Stones of Years; Iconoclast; Mass; Manticore; Battlefield; Aquatarkus; Jeremy Bender; Bitches Crystal; The Only Way; Infinite Space; A Time and a Place; Are You Ready Eddy?* PICTURES AT AN EXHIBITION (1/72): *The Great Gates of Kiev; Promenade; The Curse of Baba Yaga; The Hut of Baba Yaga; The Old Castle; The Sage; The Gnome; Pictures at an Exhibition; Blues Variation.* TRILOGY (6/72): *The Endless Enigma (Parts I and II); Fugue; From the Beginning; The Sheriff; Hoedown; Trilogy; Living in Sin; Abaddon's Bolero.* BRAIN SALAD SURGERY (1/73): *Jerusalem; Toccata; Still . . . You Turn Me On; Benny the Bouncer; Karn Evil; 1st Impression (Parts I and II); 2nd Impression; 3rd Impression.* WELCOME BACK MY FRIENDS TO THE SHOW THAT NEVER ENDS, LADIES AND GENTLEMEN, EMERSON LAKE AND PALMER (8/74): *Hoedown; Jerusalem; Toccata; Takus; Tarkus (conclusion); Take a Pebble (Still . . . You Turn Me On/Lucky Man); Piano Improvisations; Take a Pebble; Jeremy Bender/The Sheriff; Karn Evil 9 (1st Impression); Karn Evil 9 (2nd and 3rd Impressions).* WORKS (3/77): *Piano Concerto No. 1 (Three Movements); Lend Your Love to Me Tonight; C'est la Vie; Hallowed Be Thy Name; Nobody Loves You Like I Do; Closer to Believing; The Enemy God; L.A. Nights; New Orleans; The Two-Part Invention In D Minor; Tank; Food for Your Soul; Fanfare for the Common Man; Pirates.*

Singles/*Lucky Man* (2/71); *Nutrocker* (2/72); *From the Beginning* (7/72); *Lucky Man* (11/72); *I Believe in Father Christmas/Humbug* (11/75); *Fanfare for the Common Man/Brain Salad Surgery* (5/77).

ENGLAND DAN AND JOHN FORD COLEY/After a false start in the early seventies, the songwriting-performing duo of England Dan and John Ford Coley staged a remarkable comeback in 1976 with a hit single, *I'd Really Love to See You Tonight,* and a top album, *I HEAR THE MUSIC.* The duo's lilting, easy-listening sound bombed circa '72 and was on the way to deep-sixing it once again four years later when, after being rejected by several major record company executives, it came to the attention of an enterprising young A&R man at the Atlantic Records family of labels. The duo was signed to a subsidiary distributed by the label, and soon their first comeback single was top-tenning it across the country.

Albums/FABLES (6/72): *Simone; Casey; Free the People; What I'm Doing; Carolina; Tomorrow; Candles of Our Lives; Matthew; Stay by the River.* NIGHTS ARE FOREVER (7/76): *I'd Really Love to See You Tonight; I'll Stay; Westward Wind; Long Way Home; There'll Never Be Another for Me; Nights Are Forever without You; Showboat Gambler; The Prisoner; Lady; Everything's Gonna Be Alright.* I HEAR THE MUSIC (11/76): *Used to You; Tell Her Hello; New Jersey; Idolizer; Mud and Stone; I hear the Music; Legendary Captain; Miss Me; The Pilot; Carry On.* DOWDY FERRY ROAD (4/77): *Dowdy Ferry Road; It's Sad to Belong; Soldier in the Rain; Love Is the One Thing We Hide; Gone Too Far; Where Do I Go from Here; Falling Stars; You Know We Belong Together; Don't Feel That Way No More; Holocaust.*

Singles/*New Jersey* (7/71); *Simone* (4/72); *Free the People* (8/72); *I Hear the Music* (8/73); *I'd Really Love to See You Tonight/It's Not the Same* (5/76); *Nights Are Forever without You/Showboat Gambler* (9/76); *Simone* (1/77); *It's Sad to Belong/The Time Has Come* (4/77).

THE EVERLY BROTHERS/The duo of Don and Phil Everly was one of the few original rock and roll acts to live through the English invasion and the psychedelic era without disappearing entirely from the pop scene. Unlike Conway Twitty and Jerry Lee Lewis, who both left rock to make their fortunes in the country and western world, Don and Phil Everly never missed a beat during their years together. When the rock revival mania of the late sixties exploded, they were waiting in the wings as if nothing had happened.

The Kentucky-born singer-songwriters cut their first record in 1956, but it wasn't until 1957 that they became top-tenners with such epic singles as *Bye Bye Love* and *Wake Up Little Susie.*

And the hits kept coming until the early nineteen sixties—gold records like *Bird Dog, Problems, Cathy's Clown, All I Have to Do Is Dream,* and *Ebony Eyes.* A stint in the Marine Corps, however, completely shattered their meteoric rise. Civilians again, on tour in 1963, the Everly Brothers encountered a further setback to their professional lives when Don suffered a nervous breakdown in Great Britain. From that point onward, the recorded works of the Everly Brothers proved erratic and were passively received by the general public.

They managed to survive the sixties, however, dabbling in rock and a bit of pop and taking part in the rock revivalism movement. In 1970 they signed with RCA Records in hopes of a comeback. Artistic differences between Don and Phil brought the duo to an end in 1973, with both brothers then pursuing solo careers. They left behind a legacy of recordings that influenced dozens of contemporary rock bands, from Simon Garfunkel to the Mamas and the Papas. The sound of the Everly Brothers—sweet, slick and joyous—is truly timeless.

Albums/THE EVERLY BROTHERS (1/58). SONGS OUR DADDY TAUGHT US (1959). IT'S EVERLY TIME (4/60). THE FABULOUS STYLE OF THE EVERLY BROTHERS (7/60). A DATE WITH THE EVERLY BROTHERS (11/60): *Made to Love; That's Just Too Much; Stick with Me, Baby; Baby, What You Want Me Do Do; Sigh; Cry, Almost Die; Always It's You; So How Come; Love Hurts; Lucille; Donna, Donna; Change of Heart; Cathy's Clown.* BOTH SIDES OF AN EVENING (11/51): *My Mammy; Muskrat; My Gal Sal; Bully of the Town; Chlo-E; In Sheboygan; Hi-Lili, Hi-Lo; Wayward Wind; Don't Blame Me; Little Old Lady; When I Grow Too Old to Dream; Love Is Where You Find It.* INSTANT PARTY (3/62): *Step It Up and Go; Theme from "Carnival"; Bye Bye Blackbird; Jezebel; True Love; When It's Nighttime in Italy, It's Wednesday over Here; Oh Mein Papa; Trouble in Mind; Long Lost John; Autumn Leaves; Party's Over; Ground Hawg.* VERY BEST OF (4/62): *Bye Bye Love; Till I Kissed You; Wake Up Little Susie; Crying in the Rain; Walk Right Back; Cathy's Clown; Lucille; Bird Dog; All I Have to Do Is Dream; Devoted to You; So Sad (to Watch a Good Love Go Bad); Ebony Eyes.* GOLDEN HITS (6/62): *That's Old Fashioned; How Can I Meet Her; Crying in the Rain; I'm Not Angry; Muskrat; Don't Blame Me; Ebony Eyes; Cathy's Clown; Walk Right Back; Lucille; So Sad; Temptation.* EVERLY BROTHERS SING GREAT COUNTRY HITS (10/63): *Oh, Lonesome Me;*

Born to Lose; Just One Time; Send Me the Pillow You Dream On; I'm So Lonesome I Could Cry; Release Me; Sweet Dreams; Please Help Me; I'm Falling; I Walk the Line; Lonely Street; Silver Threads and Golden Needles; This Is the Last Song I'm Ever Going to Sing. GONE, GONE, GONE (1/65): *Donna, Donna; Lonely Island; Facts of Life; Ain't That Lovin' You, Baby; Love Is All I Need; Torture; Drop Out; Radio and TV; Ferris Wheel; Honolulu; It's Been a Long Dry Spell; Gone, Gone, Gone.* TWO YANKS IN ENGLAND (3/65): *Somebody Help Me; So Lonely; Kiss Your Man Goodbye; Signs That Will Never Change; Like Every Time Before; Pretty Flamingo; I've Been Wrong Before; Have You Ever Loved Somebody; The Collector; Don't Run and Hide; Fifi the Flea; Hard Hard Year.* ROCK 'N' SOUL (3/65): *That'll Be the Day; So Fine; Maybelline; I'm Gonna Move to the Outskirts of Town; Susie Q; Dancing in the Street; Kansas City; I Got a Woman; Love Hurts; Slippin' and Slidin'; Hound Dog; Lonely Weekends.* BEAT 'N' SOUL (8/65): *Love Is Strange; Money; What Am I Living For; Hi-Heel Sneakers; See See Rider; My Baby; Lonely Avenue; Man with Money; Girl Can't Help It; People Get Ready; Walking the Dog; I Almost Lost My Mind.* IN OUR IMAGE (3/66): *Leave My Girl Alone; Chained to a Memory; I'll Never Get Over You; Doll House Is Empty; Glitter and Gold; Power of Love; Price of Love; It's All Over; I Used to Love You; Lovely Kravezit; June Is As Cold As December; It Only Costs a Dime.* HIT SOUNDS (2/67): *Blueberry Hill; Devil's Child; I'm Movin' On; Trains and Boats and Planes; Sea of Heartbreak; Oh Boy; Legend in My Time; Let's Go Get Stoned; Sticks and Stones; House of the Rising Sun; She Never Smiles Anymore; Good Golly Miss Molly.* EVERLY BROTHERS SING (7/67): *Bowling Green; Voice Within; I Don't Want to Love You; It's All Over; Deliver Me; I'm Finding It Rough; Talking to the Flowers; Mary Jane; Do You; Somebody Help Me; Mercy, Mercy, Mercy; Whiter Shade of Pale.* ROOTS (11/68): *Mama Tried; Less of Me; T for Texas; You Done Me Wrong; I Wonder If I Care As Much; Ventura Blvd.; Shady Grove; Illinois; Living Too Close to the Ground; Sing Me Back Home; Turn Around.* THE EVERLY BROTHERS SHOW (1970). ORIGINAL GREATEST HITS (6/70). STORIES WE CAN TELL (2/72): *All We Really Want to Do; Breakdown; Green River; Mandolin Wind; Up in Mabel's Room; Del Rio Dan; Ridin'*

High; Brand New Tennessee Waltz; Stories We Can Tell; Christmas Eve Can Kill You; I'm Tired of Singing My Songs In Las Vegas. PASS THE CHICKEN AND LISTEN (10/72): *Ladies Love Outlaws; Not Fade Away; Paradise; Lay It Down; other titles.*

Singles/*Bye Bye Love* (5/57); *Wake Up Little Susie* (9/57); *This Little Girl of Mine* (1/58); *All I Have to Do Is Dream/Claudette* (3/58); *Bird Dog/Devoted to You* (7/58); *Problems/Love of My Life* (10/58); *Take a Message to Mary/Poor Jenny* (3/59); *(Til') I Kissed You* (7/59); *Let It Be Me* (1/60); *Cathy's Clown/Always It's You* (3/60); *When Will I Be Loved/Be Bop A-Lula* (5/60); *So Sad/Lucille* (8/60); *Like Strangers* (10/60); *Walk Right Back/Ebony Eyes* (1/61); *Temptation/Stick with Me, Baby* (5/61); *All I Have to Do Is Dream* (6/61); *Don't Blame Me/Muskrat* (9/61); *Crying in the Rain* (12/61); *That's Old Fashioned/How Can I Meet Her* (4/62); *Don't Ask Me to Be Friends* (9/62); *I'm Here to Get My Baby out of Jail* (9/62); *The Ferris Wheel* (5/64); *Gone, Gone, Gone* (9/64); *Bowling Green* (4/67); *Mary Jane/Talking to the Flowers* (7/67); *Love of the Common People/Voice Within* (8/67); *Milk Train/Lord of the Manor* (8/68); *Carolina in My Mind/My Little Yellow Bird* (9/69); *Lay It Down/Paradise* (11/72); *Ladies Love Outlaws/Not Fade Away* (1/73).

THE FACES/*Ron Wood (guitar), Ronnie Lane (bass), Ian MacLagan (keyboards), Kenny Jones (drums), Rod Stewart (vocals), Tetsu Yamauchi (bass).*
After Steve Marriott formed Humble Pie at the tail end of the sixties, his former peers, the remainder of the Small Faces, decided to have a go at the rock whirl. Their "go" was to be erratically successful and their six-year career was to be a stormy one—plagued by rumors of splits, egocentricities, and general backbiting. In 1969, Small Faces Lane, Jones, and MacLagan joined with Stewart and Wood and formed the (just plain) Faces. At the time, Stewart was a hot commodity in the making, having just embarked on a post–Jeff Beck Group solo career. As his solo antics rose in popularity, his Faces activity followed a similar route.

Faces albums were helter-skelter affairs, being both energy-laden and sloppy. Excellently constructed songs would be followed by throwaway riffs, and entire LPs often gave one the impression that they were recorded in a gin mill. Riding on the crest of a bona fide hit single, *Stay with Me,* the Faces came to blows, artistically, with lead singer Rod Stewart, who was rapidly becoming a solo superstar. Stewart's activities with the Faces were regarded by many as being something of a hobby and the Faces were justifiably annoyed at their lead singer being more popular than the band as a unit.

A few choice remarks by Rod about his lack of enthusiasm for the Faces' material (circa *OOH LA LA*) seemed to put a capper on the band. Terse statements by various members *about* other members began to surface in print. Lane departed in 1973 in pursuit of a solo route, replaced by ex-Free thunderthudder Tetsu. Wood released two solo albums (stiffs) before joining the Rolling Stones full-time in 1975. Stewart gave up his duties with the band later that same year.

Without Stewart, the Faces stumbled to a complete halt. By 1977, several members of the original Small Faces had begun putting together the groundwork for a comeback attempt.

Albums/FIRST STEP (4/70): *Wicked Messenger; Stone; Around the Plynth; Devotion; Shake, Shudder, Shiver; Flying; Nobody Knows; Pineapple and the Money; Three Button Hand Me Down; Looking out the Window.* LONG PLAYER (2/71): *Had Me a Real Good Time; On the Beach; I Feel So Good; Jerusalem; Bad 'n' Ruin; Tell Everyone; Sweet Lady Mary; Richmond; Maybe I'm Amazed.* A NOD IS AS GOOD AS A WINK TO A BLIND HORSE (11/71): *Miss Judy's Farm; You're So Rude; Stay with Me; Love Lives Here; Last Orders Please; Debris; Memphis; Too Bad; That's All You Need.* OOH LA LA (4/73): *Silicone Grown; Cindy Incidentally; Flags and Banners; My Fault; Borstal Boys; Fly in the Ointment; If I'm on the Late Side; Glad and Sorry; Just Another Honky; Ooh La La.* FACES LIVE: COAST TO COAST, OVERTURE AND BEGINNERS (1974): *It's All Over Now; Cut Across Shorty; Too Bad; Every Picture Tells a Story; Angel; Stay with Me; I Wish It Would Rain; I'd Rather Go Blind; Borstal Boys;*

Amazing Grace; Jealous Guy. SNAKES AND LADDERS (THE BEST OF THE FACES) (11/76): *Pool Hall Richard; Cindy Incidentally; Ooh La La; Sweet Lady Mary; Pineapple and the Monkey; You Can Make Me Dance, Sing or Anything; Had Me a Real Good Time; Stay with Me; Miss Judy's Farm; Silicone Grown; Around the Plynth.*

Singles/*Around the Plynth/Wicked Messenger* (4/70); *Had Me a Real Good Time/Rear Wheel* (10/70); *Maybe I'm Amazed/O Lord I'm Browned Off* (4/71); *Stay with Me* (12/71); *Cindy Incidentally* (2/73); *Ooh La La/Borstal Boys* (5/73); *You Can Make Me Dance/As Long As You Tell Him* (1/75).

THE FIFTH DIMENSION/*Ron Townson (vocals), Lamonte Lemore (vocals), Marilyn McCoo (vocals), Florence LaRue (vocals), Billy Davis (guitar, vocals).*
If white singers like Mick Jagger and Steve Winwood had the right to sing black, then black singers like the Fifth Dimension certainly had all the right in the world to sing white. They used to be known in L.A. as the Versatiles, and later as the Hi-Fi's, and they sang nothing but blues before arriving in 1966 as the Fifth Dimension. By the end of that year they had the white Californian male-female vocal harmonies of a revved-up Mamas and Papas and, significantly, their first hit, *Go Where You Wanna Go,* was a Papa John Phillips composition.

They began earning gold records shortly thereafter, spotlighting songs by Jimmy Webb *(Up Up and Away)* and Laura Nyro *(Stoned Soul Picnic).* Their careers soared until the early seventies when their slick, commercial sound faltered under the barrage of heavy-metal popularity, David Bowie-ism, and glitter. They attempted a comeback in 1975–76, but their recordings were overshadowed by the success of husband and wife duo, McCoo and Davis, as a solo act.

Albums/UP UP AND AWAY (4/67): *Up Up and Away; Another Day, Another Heartache; Which Way to Nowhere; California My Way; Misty Roses; Go Where You Wanna Go; Never Gonna Be the Same; Pattern People; Rosecrans Blvd.; Learn How to Fly; Poor*

Side of Town. THE MAGIC GARDEN (11/67): *Prologue; The Magic Garden; Summer's Daughter; Dreams; Carpet Man; Ticket to Ride; Requiem; 820 Latham; The Girls' Song; The Worst That Could Happen; Orange Air; Paper Cup; Epilogue.* STONED SOUL PICNIC (7/68): *The Sailboat Song; Sweet Blindness; It'll Never Be the Same Again; It's a Great Life; Stoned Soul Picnic; California Soul; Lovin' Stew; Broken Wing Bird; Good News; Bobbie's Blues; The Eleventh Song.* THE AGE OF AQUARIUS (4/69): *Aquarius; Let the Sun Shine In; Working on a Groovy Thing; Wedding Bell Blues; other titles.* GREATEST HITS (4/70): *Up Up and Away; Paper Cup; Carpet Man; Stoned Soul Picnic; Aquarius/Let the Sun Shine In; Sweet Blindness; other titles.* PORTRAIT (5/70); *Puppet Man; Save the Country; A Change Is Gonna Come & The People Gotta Be Free; The Declaration; On the Beach (In the Summertime); other titles.* THE JULY 5TH ALBUM (7/70). LOVE'S LINES, ANGLES AND RHYMES (2/71): *Love's Lines, Angles and Rhymes; Light Sings; Never My Love; other titles.* LIVE!! (9/71). REFLECTIONS (10/71). INDIVIDUALLY AND COLLECTIVELY (3/72): *Last Night I Didn't Get to Sleep at All; If I Could Reach You; other titles.* GREATEST HITS ON EARTH (8/72): *Last Night I Didn't Get to Sleep at All; Stoned Soul Picnic; One Less Bell to Answer; medley: Aquarius/Let the Sun Shine In; Wedding Bell Blues; Save the Country; Love's Lines, Angles and Rhymes; Up Up and Away; Puppet Man; Never My Love; Together Let's Find Love.* LIVING TOGETHER, GROWING TOGETHER (1973): *Open Your Window; Ashes to Ashes; Everything's Been Changed; Day by Day; There's Nothin' Like Music; What Do I Need to Be Me; There Never Was a Day; Let Me Be Lonely; Woyaya.* SOUL AND INSPIRATION (11/74): *Soul and Inspiration; Harlem; The Best of My Love; My Song; Hard Care Poetry; No Love in the Room; House for Sale; Salty Tears; I Don't Know How to Look for Love.* EARTHBOUND (8/75).

Singles/*I'll Be Lovin' You Forever/Train, Keep On Movin'* (10/66); *Go Where You Wanna Go/Too Poor to Die* (12/66); *Another Day, Another Heartache/Rosecrans Blvd.* (3/67); *Up Up and Away/Which Way to Nowhere* (5/67); *Paper Cup/Poor Side of*

Town (10/67); *Carpet Man* (1/68); *Stoned Soul Picnic/The Sailboat Song* (5/68); *Sweet Blindness/Bobby's Blues* (9/68); *California Soul/It'll Never Be the Same* (12/68); *Aquarius/Let the Sun Shine In* (2/69); *Workin' on a Groovy Thing* (6/69); *Wedding Bell Blues* (8/69); *Blowing Away* (12/69); *A Change Is Gonna Come & The People Gotta Be Free/The Declaration* (1/70); *Save the Country* (5/70); *On the Beach (in the Summertime)* (7/70); *One Less Bell to Answer* (9/70); *Love's Lines, Angles and Rhymes* (1/71); *Light Sings* (4/71); *Never My Love* (8/71); *Together Let's Find Love* (12/71); *Last Night I Didn't Get to Sleep at All* (3/72); *If I Could Reach You* (8/72); *Living Together, Growing Together* (12/72); *Everything's Been Changed* (3/73); *Ashes to Ashes* (7/73); *Flashback* (11/73).

FLEETWOOD MAC/*Mick Fleetwood (drums), John McVie (bass), Christine McVie (keyboards, vocals), Stevie Nicks (vocals), Lindsey Buckingham (guitar, vocals). Previous members: Peter Green (guitar, vocals), Jeremy Spencer (guitar, vocals), Danny Kirwan (guitar), Bob Welch (guitar, vocals), Bob Weston (guitar), Dave Walker (vocals, harmonica).*
The remarkable "overnight" success of Fleetwood Mac is, in reality, a ten-year tale of talent, dedication, and endurance. Begun in 1967, the original Fleetwood group was a British blues band, one of the best. Begun by ex-members of John Mayall's Bluesbreakers, Peter Green (guitar) and John McVie (drums), the first lineup included Fleetwood on drums and Jeremy Spencer on guitar and vocals. This initial membership tore into the British popularity polls with a passion, being touted in some circles as *the* next big British blues band to happen.

Their first LP, a hard-as-nails blues extravaganza, completely baffled pop musicologists by embedding itself on the best-seller list for over a year. Encouraged by this success, Green added a third guitarist to the band, young Danny Kirwan. Fleetwood Mac then began to experiment a bit, getting into lusher, richer guitar sounds that were not necessarily related to blues. All three guitarists composed, and soon Fleetwood Mac was a mainstay in the top-ten singles charts.

However, American success was hard to come by. The band began to develop musical differences of opinion. In 1970, founder-member Peter Green abruptly left. The remainder of the band (together with "guest" member Christine McVie, ex–Chicken Shack pianist and wife of John McVie), recorded *KILN HOUSE,* an LP that showed the band moving toward new musical horizons.

Before those horizons could be reached, however, the band endured yet another trauma while touring the United States. In Los Angeles, Jeremy Spencer disappeared, joining the religious group the Children of God and promptly renouncing his godless ways as a Fleetwood Mac member. Peter Green stepped in to flesh out the band for the remainder of the tour, but Fleetwood remained shaken. A needed shot in the arm came in the person of California guitarist-singer-composer Bob Welch, who promptly set the band on the right track on *FUTURE GAMES.*

A new, "mellow" Fleetwood Mac was emerging, winning them the much-sought-after popularity in the States but costing them their blues buffs in Britain. In 1972, Danny Kirwan left the band, being replaced briefly by Bob Weston and Dave Walker. Within a year, however, both had been ousted and Fleetwood Mac came very near to splintering. Plagued by financial difficulties, intramural arguments, and assorted traumas, the band was even subject to the total indignity of having their manager form a *second* group called Fleetwood Mac and having *them* tour instead of the genuine article.

Fleetwood and McVie promptly obtained a court injunction barring the bogus band from playing. In the suit that followed, Fleetwood Mac was effectively barred from playing for over twelve months, until all litigation was finished. Happily, they emerged with a key album in their career, *HEROES ARE HARD TO FIND,* in 1974. With Christine McVie handling many of the key vocals, the album brought the band to the attention of a lot of FM-radio programmers.

Bob Welch exited the band shortly after the release of the disc, nearly tossing a monkey wrench into the plans for fame and fortune. Fortunately, the band came across the much-overlooked singing-songwriting team of Buckingham-Nicks (one album on Polydor stiffed) and a new, improved Fleetwood Mac was well on its way to stardom.

Their first album with this lineup produced the phenomenal *FLEETWOOD MAC* album, which stayed in the top five for over six months, went platinum, spawned a host of singles (including *Over My Head* and *Rhiannon*) and shot the band into the number-one-group slot in the United States. In the midst of their new-found success, the band found their personal lives in less than exceptional shape. The McVies were having a hard time with their marriage and the Buckingham-Nicks team was rapidly becoming two solos.

The band managed to keep their emotions in check and re-bounded in 1977 with *RUMORS*, a six-month number-one platinum album, laden with hit-singles. A '77 SRO tour of the States proved that Fleetwood Mac could be as magical in concert as they could be on record, and the talented band that had toiled ten years to make it was acknowledged an "overnight sensation."

Fleetwood Mac today is one of the top five bands in the world.

Recently, Bob Welch rejoined the Fleetwood fold, in a business sense. Fleetwood has been managed by Mick Fleetwood since the court injunction against their former manager. After Welch left the band, he formed the short-lived Paris group before going solo. He is now being managed and produced by Mick. Jeremy Spencer still renounces his sinful Mac days from time to time, causing a bit of embarrassment to all concerned. He recorded two solo LPs, the second with members of the Children of God tribe. Danny Kirwan recorded one overlooked LP on his own.

Albums/FLEETWOOD MAC (8/68): *My Heart Beat Like a Hammer; Merry Go Round; Long Grey Mare; Hellbound on My Trail; Shake Your Moneymaker; Looking for Somebody; No Place to Go; My Baby's Good to Me; If I Loved Another Woman; Cold Black Night; The World Keeps On Turning; Got to Move.* ENGLISH ROSE (1/69): *Stop Messin' 'round; Jigsaw Puzzle Blues; Doctor Brown; Something inside of Me; Evenin' Boogie; Love That Burns; Black Magic Woman; I've Lost My Baby; One Sunny Day; Without You; Coming Home; Albatross.* PLAY ON (9/69): *Oh Well; other titles.* KILN HOUSE (9/70): *This Is the Rock Station Man; Blood on the Floor; Hi Ho Silver; Jewel-Eyed Judy; Buddy's Song; Earl Grey; One Together; Tell Me All the Things You Do; Mission Bell.* BLACK MAGIC WOMAN (double album re-package of FLEETWOOD MAC and ENGLISH ROSE; 7/71). FUTURE GAMES (10/71): *Woman of a Thousand Years; Morn-*

ing Rain; What a Shame; Future Games; Sands of Time; Sometimes; Lay It All Down; Show Me a Smile. BARE TREES (3/72): *Child of Mine; The Ghost; Homeward Bound; Sunny Side of Heaven; Bare Trees; Sentimental Lady; Danny's Chant; Spare Me a Little of Your Love; Dust; Thoughts on a Gray Day.* PENGUIN (3/73): *Remember Me; Bright Fire; Dissatisfied; Road Runner; The Derelict; Revelation; Did You Ever Love Me; Night Watch; Caught in the Rain.* MYSTERY TO ME (10/73): *The City; Miles Away; Somebody; The Way I Feel; Why; For Your Love; Emerald Eyes; Believe Me; Hypnotize; Keep On Going; Forever.* HEROES ARE HARD TO FIND (10/74): *Heroes Are Hard to Find; Coming Home; Angel; Bermuda Triangle; Come a Little Bit Closer; She's Changing Me; Bad Loser; Silver Heels; Prove Your Love; Born Enchanter; Safe Harbour.* FLEETWOOD MAC (7/75): *Monday Morning; Warm Ways; Blue Letter; Rhiannon; Over My Head; Crystal; Say You Love Me; Landslide; World Turning; Sugar Daddy; I'm So Afraid.* RUMOURS (1/77): *Second-Hand News; Dreams; Never Going Back Again; Don't Stop; Go Your Own Way; Songbird; The Chain; You Make Loving Fun; I Don't Want to Know; Oh Daddy; Gold Dust Woman.* ENGLISH ROSE (yet another clever repackage of FLEETWOOD MAC AND ENGLISH ROSE; 9/75). THE ORIGINAL FLEETWOOD MAC (11/77): *Drifting; Leaving Town Blues; Watch Out; A Fool No More; Mean Old Fireman; Can't Afford to Do It; Fleetwood Mac; Worried Dream; Love That Woman; Allow Me One More Show; First Train Home; Rambling Pony No. 2.*

Singles/*Black Magic Woman/Long Gray Mare* (6/68); *Need Your Love So Bad/Stop Messin' 'round* (8/68); *Oh Well* (11/69); *Sands of Time/Lay It All down* (11/71); *Jewel-Eyed Judy/Station Man* (1/71); *Oh Well/The Green Manalishi* (3/72); *Sentimental Lady/Sunny Side of Heaven* (5/72); *Remember Me/Dissatisfied* (5/73); *Did You Ever Love me/Revelation* (8/73); *For Your Love/Hypnotized* (12/73); *Heroes Are Hard to Find/Born Enchanter* (11/74); *Over My Head/I'm So Afraid* (9/75); *Rhiannon/Sugar Daddy* (1/76); *Say You Love Me/Monday Morning* (5/76); *Go Your Own Way/Silver Springs* (11/76); *Dreams/Songbird* (3/77); *Don't Stop/Never Going Back Again* (7/77); *You Make Lovin' Fun* (9/77).

THE FLYING BURRITO BROTHERS/*Chris Hillman (guitar,*

vocals), Chris Ethridge (bass), Gram Parsons (guitar, vocals), Sneaky Pete Kleinow (pedal steel guitar). Additional members: Michael Clarke (drums), Bernie Leadon (guitar, vocals), Rick Roberts (guitar, vocals), Al Perkins (pedal steel), Byron Berline (fiddle), Kenny Wertz (guitar), Roger Bush (bass), Erick Dalton (drums), Don Beck (pedal steel), Alan Munde (guitar), Gib Guilbeau (guitar, fiddle), Gene Parsons (drums), Joel Scott Hill (guitar), Skip Battin (bass).

The Flying Burrito Brothers was one of the first bands, if not *the* first, to try to bring legitimate country music to rock audiences. Formed by ex-Byrds Hillman and Parsons in 1968, the Flying Burritos enlisted the aid of sessionists Kleinow and Ethridge before finally drafting the drumming services of ex-Byrd Michael Clarke. The Burritos never did achieve the commercial success they sought and deserved. As a result, the membership fluctuated wildly, as did the quality of the band.

Ethridge was the first to leave, being replaced by not-yet-Eagle Leadon. Parsons was the next to depart, amidst a flurry of internal difficulties. With his departure, much of the initial magic of the Burritos disappeared along with Parsons' playing and songwriting skills. Rick Roberts next entered the scene, briefly instilling a new life in the band via his own songwriting and singing. talents (he penned and sang the beautiful *Colorado*). By that time, however, the band was showing signs of stress. Kleinow left, to be replaced by Perkins. Leadon left to be an Eagle.

With a tour of Europe in the works and an album to be completed, the depleted Burrito roster was given a lift by the hasty addition of three members of United Artists Records' country troupe, Country Gazette. Wertz, Berline, and Bush. Briefly, the Burritos became the Hot Burrito Review featuring Country Gazette. During this formation, however, Hillman and Perkins left to join Stephen Stills and Manassas, and Michael Clarke either quit or was fired, depending on which ex-Burrito you get the story from.

At this point, the original troupe was gutted, with Roberts being the only "old" hand, a veteran of less than two years. Dalton, Munde, and Beck were added and the European tour was completed. Roberts then embarked on a solo career before becoming a member of Stephen Stills' band circa '75 and, ultimately, forming Firefall.

The Burritos were legally dead, leaving behind them a legacy of erratic but often brilliant music. Compilation albums were released by A&M Records and all was right with the world. . .

. . . until 1974–75, when Kleinow and Ethridge decided to do it all over again. Guilbeau, Hill, and Parsons were recruited and a 1975 Flying Burrito Brothers proved nothing short of a travesty. Ethridge had the good sense to leave in 1976, replaced by Skip Battin, who left the band by 1977. During the first half of 1977, the Flying Burrito Brothers disappeared from the roster of their record label, Columbia, leaving their future up in the air.

Albums/THE GILDED PALACE OF SIN (2/69): *Christine's Tune; Sin City; Do Right Woman; Dark End of the Street; My Uncle; Wheels; Juanita; Hot Burrito #2; Do You Know How It Feels; Hippie Boy.* BURRITO DELUXE (4/70): *Lazy Days; Image of Me; High Fashion Queen; If You Gotta Go; Man in the Fog; Farther Along; Older Guys; Cody, Cody; God's Own Singer; Down in the Churchyard; Wild Horses.* THE FLYING BURRITO BROTHERS (5/71); *White Line Fever; Colorado; Hand to Mouth; Tried So Hard; Just Can't Be; To Ramona; Four Days of Rain; Can't You Hear Me Calling; All Alone; Why Are You Crying?* THE LAST OF THE RED HOT BURRITOS (4/72); *Devil in Disguise; Six Days on the Road; My Uncle; Dixie Breakdown; Don't Let Your Deal Go Down; Orange Blossom Special; Ain't That a Lot of Love; High Fashion Queen; Don't Fight It; Hot Burrito #2; Losing Game.* CLOSE UP THE HONKY TONKS (6/74); *Close Up the Honky Tonks; Sing Me Back Home; Bony Maronie; To Love Somebody; Break My Mind; Beat the Heat; Did You See; Here Tonight; Money Honey; Roll Over, Beethoven; Wake Up, Little Susie.* FLYING AGAIN (9/75): *Easy to Get On; Wind and Rain; Why, Baby, Why; Dim Lights, Thick Smoke; You Left the Water Running; Building Fires; Sweet Desert Childhood; Bon Soir Blues; River Road; Hot Burrito #3.* SLEEPLESS NIGHTS—GRAM PARSONS AND THE FLYING BURRITO BROTHERS (4/76): *Brand New Heartache; Tonight the Bottle Let Me Down; Sing Me Back Home; Crazy Arms; Your Angel Steps Out of Heaven; Sleepless Nights; Close Up the Honky Tonks; Together Again; Honky Tonk Women; Green, Green Grass of Home; Dim Lights; The Angels Rejoiced Last Night.* AIRBORNE (5/76): *Out of Control; Waitin' for Love to Begin; Toe-Tappin' Music; Quiet Man; Northbound Bus; Big Bayou; Walk on*

*the Water; Linda Lu; Border Town; She's a Sailor; Jesus Broke the
Wild Horses.*

Singles/*The Train Song* (5/69); *If You Gotta Go* (1/70); *Older
Guys* (5/70); *White Line Fever* (7/71); *Building Fires/Hot Burrito
#3* (10/75); *Bon Soir Blues/Hot Burrito #3* (2/76); *Waitin' for Love
to Begin/Big Bayou* (7/76).

DAN FOGELBERG/Singer-songwriter Dan Fogelberg's career
almost died before it had a fighting chance to be hatched. After
serving an apprenticeship as a sessionman working out of Los
Angeles (where he met Van Morrison, subsequently becoming
part of Van's touring band), Fogelberg moved to Nashville. A
contract with Columbia Records resulted. Fogelberg's first masterpiece, *HOME FREE,* was regarded by the company as something closely akin to leprosy. The album died a horrible death and
the soft, lilting voice of Dan Fogelberg fell on deaf ears as he was
dropped from the label's roster into oblivion.

Fate intervened a year or so later when Epic picked up the
struggling performer, a stroke of business luck which resulted in
the gold LP, *SOUVENIRS.* Managed by Eagles mentor Irving
Azoff, Fogelberg strutted his newfound stuff for his new label
with style, backed by such other Azoff boosters as Joe Walsh and
members of the Eagles. *SOUVENIRS* catapulted Fogelberg firmly into the rock spotlight. He still basks in its glow.

Albums/HOME FREE (11/72): *To the Morning; Stars; More
Than Ever; Be on Your Way; Hickory Grove; Long Way Home
(Live in the Country); Looking for a Lady; Anyway I Love You;
Wisteria; The River.* SOUVENIRS (10/74): *Part of the Plan; Illi-
nois; Changing Horses; Better Change; Souvenirs; The Long Way;
As the Raven Flies; Song from Half Mountain; Morning Sky;
Someone's Been Telling You Stories; There's a Place in the World
for a Gambler.* CAPTURED ANGEL (11/75): *Aspen/These
Days; Comes and Goes; Captured Angel; Old Tennessee; Next
Time; Man in the Mirror/Below the Surface; Crow; The Last Nail.*
NETHERLANDS (5/77): *Nether Lands; Once upon a Time;
Dancing Shoes; Lessons Learned; Loose Ends; Love Gone By;
Promises Made; Give Me Some Time; Scarecrow's Dream;
Sketches; False Faces.*

Singles/*Anyway I Love You/Looking for a Lady* (12/72); *Part of
the Plan/Song from Half Mountain* (11/74); *Next Time/Captured
Angel* (10/75); *Below the Surface/Comes and Goes* (1/76); *Chang-*

The Beatles

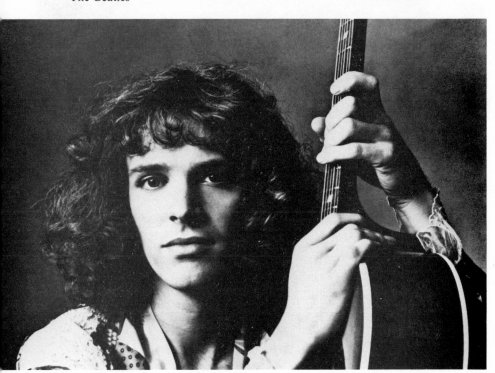

Peter Frampton

Linda Ronstadt

John Denver

David Crosby and Graham Nash

Arlo Guthrie

Jim Morrison of The Doors

Eric Clapton

Lynyrd Skynyrd

Courtesy MCA Records

The Moody Blues

Courtesy London Records

Helen Reddy

Courtesy Capitol Records

Bachman-Turner Overdrive

Courtesy Mercury Records

Ian Anderson of Jethro Tull

Paul McCartney of Wings

Patti Smith

The Beach Boys

ing Horses/Morning Sky (5/76); *Old Tennessee/Crow* (5/76); *Love Gone By/Scarecrow's Dream* (6/77).

FOGHAT/*Original members: Lonesome Dave Peverett (guitar, vocals), Roger Earl (drums), Rod Price (slide guitar), Tony Stevens (bass). Other members: Nick Jameson (bass, keyboards), Craig MacGregor (bass, vocals).*
The two-fisted rock and roll stance of Foghat has its roots in an older, more blues-oriented troupe of low-down zanies, Savoy Brown. Leaving Savoy founder-member Kim Simmons to reorganize his brood in 1971, Savoy members Peverett, Early, and Stevens joined with Price to form the original Foghat. This lineup lasted until 1975 when Stevens left, replaced by Jameson, who also served as the band's guiding light in the production area. Jameson left the stage in 1977, replaced by Craig MacGregor. That year, the band released the phenomenal "live" set, *FOGHAT LIVE,* on which Jameson was producer and Craig was showcased as a formal Foghatter.

Albums/FOGHAT (5/72): *I Just Want to Make Love to You; Trouble Trouble; Leavin' Again (Again!); Fool's Hall of Fame; Sarah Lee; Highway (Killing Me); A Hole to Hide In; Gotta Get to Know You.* ROCK AND ROLL (FOGHAT) (3/73): *Ride, Ride, Ride; Feel So Bad; Long Way to Go; It's Too Late; What a Shame; Helpin' Hand; Road Fever; She's Gone; Couldn't Make Her Stay.* ENERGIZED (11/73): *Honey Hush; Step Outside; Fly by Night; That'll Be the Day; Wild Cherry; Nothing I Won't Do; Home in My Hand; Golden Arrow.* ROCK AND ROLL OUTLAWS (10/74): *Eight Days on the Road; Hate to See You Go; Dreamer; Trouble in My Way; Rock and Roll Outlaw; Shirley Jean; Blue Spruce Woman; Chateau Lafitte '59 Boogie.* FOOL FOR THE CITY (9/75): *Fool for the City; Save Your Loving (for Me); Drive Me Home; Take It or Leave It; Terraplane Blues; My Babe; Slow Ride.* NIGHT SHIFT (8/76): *Night Shift; Drivin' Wheel; I'll Be Standing By; Burning the Midnight Oil; Take Me to the River; Hot Shot Love; New Place to Call Home; Don't Run Me Down.* FOGHAT LIVE (8/77): *Fool for the City; Home in My Hand; I Just Want to Make Love to You; Road Fever; Honey Hush; Slow Ride.* STONE BLUE (5/78): *Stone Blue; Sweet Home Chicago; Easy Money; Midnight Madness; It Hurts Me Too; High on Love; Chevrolet; Stay With Me.*

Singles/*I Just Want to Make Love to You/A Hole to Hide In*

(6/72); *What a Shame/Helping Hand* (3/73); *Ride, Ride, Ride/It's Too Late* (7/73); *That'll Be the Day/Wild Cherry* (1/74); *Step Outside/Maybelline* (4/74); *Slow Ride/I Just Want to Make Love to You* (12/76).

FOREIGNER/*Lou Gramm (lead vocals), Mick Jones (lead guitar, vocals), Ian McDonald (guitars, keyboards, horns, vocals), Al Greenwood (keyboards, synthesizer), Dennis Eliott (drums).*
Anglo-American rock and rollers of the first magnitude, Foreigner hit the States by storm in early 1977 with a smash album *(FOREIGNER)* and single *(Feels Like the First Time)*. They took audiences coast to coast with all the grace and finesse exhibited by King Kong during his wooing of Faye Wray. With teeth-gnashing drum and bass combinations offset by searing guitar solos and thunderous keyboard antics, Foreigner cut people to the quick via Lou Gramm's plaintive vocalizing. The sound was new and vibrant, but with roots tracing back to the crotch-rocking days of the late sixties.

Jones had served well with the thunder thudding Spooky Tooth entourage during their finer hours. McDonald has survived both King Crimson and McDonald and Giles. Elliot served time with If and Gram spearheaded the Free-sounding American band Black Sheep. By the time they got together, they were all ready to let loose with raunchy rock power. Which they have . . . in large doses.

Albums/FOREIGNER (1/77): *Feels Like the First Time; Cold As Ice; Starrider; Headknocker; The Damage Is Done; Long, Long Way from Home; Woman, Oh Woman; At War with the World; Fool for You Anyway; I Need You.*

Singles/*Feels Like the First time/Woman, Oh Woman* (3/77); *Cold as Ice* (7/77).

THE FOUR SEASONS/*Frankie Valli (vocals), Bob Gaudio (vocals, Tommy DeVito (vocals), Joe Long (vocals). Other members: Gerry Polci (vocals, drums), Don Ciccone (bass), Lee Shapiro (keyboards), John Paiva (guitar), Nick Massi (vocals).*
Arising from the Italian community of Newark, New Jersey, the original Four Seasons (Valli, Nick DeVito and brother Tommy, and Hank Magenski) were known as the Four Lovers when they

signed and stiffed with RCA records in the mid-fifties. By the sixties, the Seasons were the Seasons and subtle rearrangements within the ranks had been made. Songwriter Bob Gaudio was unofficial writer-arranger and producer Bob Crewe was the power behind the scenes.

A spate of falsetto-dominated classics *(Big Girls Don't Cry, Sherry, Walk Like a Man, Rag Doll,* and *Dawn)* kept the unique vocal group in the top ten even after the beginning of the trend-setting British invasion. Clinging to their squeaky-clean sound in the face of menacing psychedelia, the Seasons continued to score with *Let's Hang On* and *Working My Way Back to You.* By 1969, however, the band felt obligated to Sgt. Pepper, along with the rest of the rock world. The resulting album, *GENUINE IMITA-TION LIFE GAZETTE,* truly grossed out their die-hard fans. It stiffed and, in effect, the foursome had split their professional throats.

Floundering into the seventies, the Four Seasons eventually wound up on a Motown-distributed label that effectively hid them from the public eye until 1975 when, after successfully re-grouping and triumphing "live" during the rock revival years, they emerged on Warner Brothers Records with a smash single, *Who Loves You.* The group is still going strong, with Valli curtailing performing activities because of ear problems and Gaudio becoming the chief writer and nonperforming in-concert Season.

Albums/SHERRY (9/62). BIG GIRLS DON'T CRY (2/63). AIN'T THAT A SHAME (6/63). GOLDEN HITS OF THE FOUR SEASONS (8/63): *Sherry; Big Girls Don't Cry; Candy Man; Ain't That a Shame; other titles.* STAY AND OTHER GREAT HITS (5/64). BORN TO WANDER (1/64): *Born to Wander; Don't Cry, Elena; Ballad for Our Time; Where Have All the Flowers Gone; Cry Myself to Sleep; Silence Is Golden; New Town; Golden Ribbons; Little Pony Get Along; No Surfin' Today; Searching Wind; Millie.* DAWN (3/64): *Big Man's World; You Send Me; Life Is but a Dream; Mountain High; Church Bells May Ring; Dawn; Only Yesterday; Don't Let Go; Sixteen Candles; Breaking Up Is Hard to Do; Earth Angel; Do You Want to Dance.* RAG DOLL (6/64): *Save It for Me; Touch of You; Danger; Rag Doll; No One Cares; Marcie; Angel Cried; Funny Face; Huggin' My Pillow; On Broadway Tonight; Setting Sun; Ronnie.* MORE

GOLDEN HITS OF THE FOUR SEASONS (8/64). FOUR SEASONS ENTERTAIN YOU (3/65): *Show Girl; Where Is Love; One Clown Cried; My Prayer; Little Darlin'; Bye Bye Baby; Betrayed; Somewhere; Living Just for You; Little Angel; Big Man in Town; Sunday Kind of Love.* FOUR SEASONS SING BIG HITS: HAL DAVID . . . BOB DYLAN (11/65): *What the World Needs Now Is Love; Anyone Who Had a Heart; Always Something There to Remind Me; Make It Easy on Yourself; Walk on By; What's New, Pussycat; Queen Jane Approximately; Mr. Tambourine Man; All I Really Want to Do; Blowin' in the Wind; Like a Rolling Stone; Don't Think Twice.* FOUR SEASONS GOLD VAULT OF HITS (11/65): *Let's Hang On; Rag Doll; Ronnie; Big Man in Town; Silence Is Golden; Bye Bye Baby; Dawn; Save It for Me; Girl Come Running; Betrayed; Toy Soldier; Cry Myself to Sleep.* WORKING MY WAY BACK TO YOU (12/65): *Working My Way Back to You; Pity; I Woke Up; Living Just for You; Beggars Parade; One Clown Cried; Can't Get Enough of My Baby; Sundown; Too Many Memories; Show Girl; Comin' Up in the World; Everybody Knows My Name.* LOOKING BACK (11/66): *Silhouettes; Sincerely; Yes Sir, That's My Baby; Why Do Fools Fall in Love; Long Lonely Nights; Lucky Lady Bug; Since I Don't Have You; Teardrops; Tonight; Honey Love; Happy, Happy Birthday Baby; Goodnight My Love.* FOUR SEASONS CHRISTMAS ALBUM (11/66). SECOND VAULT OF HITS (1/67); *Sherry; Walk Like a Man; Candy Girl; Stay; Alone; Marlena; I've Got You under My Skin; Big Girls Don't Cry; Working My Way Back to You; Opus 17 (Don't Worry 'bout Me); Connie-O; Peanuts.* NEW GOLD HITS (6/67): *C'mon Marianne; Let's Ride Again; Beggin'; Around and Around; Goodbye Girl; I'm Gonna Change; Tell It to the Rain; Body; Puppet Song; Lonesome Road.* GENUINE IMITATION LIFE GAZETTE (12/68): *American Crucifixion Resurrection; Mrs. Stately's Garden; Look Up, Look Over; Somebody's on Her Mind; Saturday's Father; Wall Street Village; Day Genuine Imitation Life; Idaho; Wonder What You'll Be; Soul of a Woman.* HALF AND HALF (5/70). CHAMELEON (1972). WHO LOVES YOU? (11/75): *Storybook Lovers; Silver Star; Harmony, Perfect Harmony; Emily's (Salle de Danse); Mystic Mr. Sam; December, 1963 (Oh, What a Night); Slip Away; Who Loves You.* HELICON (12/76).

Singles/Sherry (7/62); *Big Girls Don't Cry* (9/62); *Santa Claus Is Coming to Town* (11/62); *Walk Like A Man* (12/62); *Ain't That a Shame/Soon (I'll Be Home Again)* (3/63); *Candy Girl/Marlena* (6/63); *New Mexican Rose/That's the Only Way* (9/63); *Stay* (1/64); *Dawn* (1/64); *Ronnie* (3/64); *Alone* (5/64); *Rag Doll* (5/64); *Sincerely* (7/64); *Save It for Me* (7/64); *Big Man in Town* (10/64); *Little Boy (in Grown-Up Clothes)* (11/64); *Bye Bye Baby* (12/64); *Toy Soldier* (3/65); *Girl Come Running* (5/65); *Let's Hang On* (11/65); *Working My Way Back to You* (12/65); *Opus 17* (4/66); *I've Got You under My Skin* (8/66); *Tell It to the Rain* (11/66); *Beggin'* (2/67); *C'mon Marianne* (5/67); *Watch the Flowers Grow* (11/67); *Will You Love Me Tomorrow* (1/68); *Electric Stories* (11/68); *Idaho/Something's on Her Mind* (2/69); *And That Reminds Me* (8/69); *Patch of Blue* (4/70); *Who Loves You* (7/75); *Silver Star/Mystic Mr. Sun* (4/76); *Down These Halls/I Believe in You* (6/77).

THE FOUR TOPS/*Levi Stubbs (lead vocals), Renaldo "Obie" Benson (vocals), Abdul "Duke" Fakir (vocals), Lawrence Payton (vocals).*
Formed in 1954 in Detroit, the Four Tops have had a two-and-a-half-decade career chock-full of top-tenning hits. They recorded for Chess, Columbia, Riverside, and Singular until 1964, when they signed with Motown Records; the Four Tops became one of that label's biggest-selling acts (the other being the Supremes). Spurred by the quality songwriting of the Holland-Dozier-Holland team, the Tops cracked the top ten over and over again with such tunes as *Baby, I Need Your Loving, I Can't Help Myself, It's the Same Old Song,* and *Seven Rooms of Gloom.* Other Four Tops hits include *Bernadette* and *Reach Out, I'll Be There.*

With the popularity of freer, psychedelic-oriented rock in the late sixties, the slick, well-produced sound of the Tops began to slide down the popularity charts. A brief flurry of activity with a re-activated Supremes in the early seventies kept the band alive at Motown. By 1972, however, it was clear that the label and the group were not seeing eye to eye artistically. A switch to ABC provided the foursome with a much-needed comeback single, *Keeper of the Castle.* Hits have been inconsistent since that time.

Albums/FOUR TOPS (1/65): *Baby, I Need Your Loving; Without* *the One You Love; Where Did You Go; Ask the Lonely; Sad Souvenirs; Your Love Is Amazing; Don't Turn Away; Tea House in Chinatown; Left with a Broken Heart; Love Has Gone; Call on Me.* FOUR TOPS SECOND ALBUM (10/65); *Something about You; I Can't Help Myself; It's the Same Old Song; Love Feels Like a Fire; Is There Anything I Can Do; Helpless; Just As Long As You Need Me; I Like Everything about You; Since You've Been Gone; Stay in My Lonely Arms; I'm Grateful.* ON TOP (7/66): *Shake Me, Wake Me; Michelle; I Got a Feeling; Brenda; Loving You Is Sweeter Than Ever; Until You Love Someone; There's No Love Left; Matchmaker; In the Still of the Night; Bluesette; Quiet Nights of Quiet Stars; Then.* LIVE! (11/66): *Reach Out, I'll Be There; You Can't Hurry Love; It's the Same Old Song; It's Not Unusual; Baby, I Need Your Loving; I'll Turn to Stone; I Left My Heart in San Francisco; I Can't Help Myself; Ask the Lonely; Climb Every Mountain; If I Had a Hammer; I Like Everything about You.* ON BROADWAY (3/67): *On the Street Where You Live; What Did I Have That I Don't Have; Make Someone Happy; Hello Broadway; Maria; Climb Every Mountain; Mame; I Want to Be with You; Sound of Music; For Once in My Life; My Way; Nice 'n' Easy.* REACH OUT (7/67): *Reach Out, I'll Be There; Standing in the Shadows of Love; Bernadette; Seven Rooms of Gloom; If I Were a Carpenter; Walk Away Renee; Last Train to Clarksville; I'll Turn to Stone; I'm a Believer; Cherish; What Else Is There to Do; Wonderful Baby.* GREATEST HITS (8/67): *Shake Me, Wake Me; I Can't Help Myself; Ask the Lonely; Loving You Is Sweeter Than Ever; Baby, I Need Your Loving; Seven Rooms of Gloom; Bernadette; Something about You; It's the Same Old Song; Without the One You Love; Standing in the Shadows of Love; Reach Out, I'll Be There.* YESTERDAY'S DREAMS (8/68): *Yesterday's Dreams; Can't Seem to Get You Out of My Mind; I'm in a Different World; We've Got a Strong Love on Our Side; By the Time I Get to Phoenix; Remember When; Sonny; Never My Love; Daydream Believer; Once Upon a Time; The Sweetheart Tree; A Place in the Sun.* NOW! (6/69): *What Is a Man; Don't Let Him Take Your Love From Me; other titles.* SOUL SPIN (11/69). STILL WATERS RUN DEEP (3/70): *It's All in the Game; Still Water (Love); other titles.* CHANGING TIMES (10/70): *Just Seven Numbers; In These Changing Times; MacArthur Park; other titles.* GREATEST HITS. VOL. 2 (8/71). NATURE

PLANNED IT (4/72). KEEPER OF THE CASTLE (10/72):
*Keeper of the Castle; Ain't No Woman; Put a Little Love Away;
Turn on the Light of Your Love; When Tonight Meets Tomorrow;
Love Music; Remember What I Told You to Forget; Love Makes
You Human; Keeper of the Castle (reprise); Dreaming; The Good
Lord Knows; Jubilee with Soul.* MAIN STREET PEOPLE (8/73):
*Main Street People; I Just Can't Get You Out of My Mind; It
Won't Be the First Time; Sweet Understanding Love; Am I My
Brother's Keeper; Are You Man Enough; Whenever There's Blue;
Too Little, Too Late; Peace of Mind; One Woman Man; Main
Street People.* THE FOUR TOPS (1973): *Baby, I Need Your Lov-
ing; Without the One You Love; Ask the Lonely; I Can't Help My-
self; It's the Same Old Song; Something about You; I'll Turn to
Stone; You Keep Running Away; Walk Away Renee; If I Were a
Carpenter; Yesterday's Dreams; I'm in a Different World; Shake
Me, Wake Me; Loving You Is Sweeter Than Ever; Reach Out, I'll
Be There; Standing in the Shadows of Love; Bernadette; Seven
Rooms of Gloom; It's All in the Game; Just Seven Numbers;
MacArthur Park; Still Water (Love); It's the Way Nature Planned
It.* MEETING OF THE MINDS (3/74): *One Chain Don't Make
No Prison; Midnight Flower; The Well Is Dry; Love Ain't Easy to
Come By; No Sad Songs; Right On, Brother; Tell Me You Love
Me; All My Love; I Found the Spirit; Meeting of the Minds.* LIVE
(9/74). NIGHT LIGHTS HARMONY (5/75): *Seven Lonely
Nights; Is This the Price?; We All Gotta Stick Together; I've Got
What You Need; I Can't Hold On Much Longer; Drive Me Out of
My Mind; I'm Glad You Walked into My Life; Let Me Know the
Truth.* CATFISH (9/76): *Catfish; Feel Free; You Can't Hold Back
on Love; I Know You Like It; Love Don't Come Easy; Disco Dad-
dy; Look at My Baby; Strung Out for Your Love.*

Singles/*Baby, I Need Your Loving* (7/64); *Without the One You
Love* (10/64); *Ask the Lonely* (1/65); *I Can't Help Myself* (4/65);
It's the Same Old Song (6/65); *Ain't That Love* (6/65); *Something
about You* (10/65); *Shake Me, Wake Me* (1/66); *Loving You Is
Sweeter Than Ever* (4/66); *Reach Out, I'll Be There* (8/66); *Stand-
ing in the Shadows of Love* (11/66); *Bernadette* (2/67); *Seven
Rooms of Gloom* (4/67); *You Keep Running Away* (8/67); *Walk
Away Renee* (1/68); *If I Were a Carpenter* (3/68); *Yesterday's
Dreams* (6/68); *I'm in a Different World* (11/68); *What Is a Man*

(4/69); *Don't Let Him Take Your Love from Me* (11/69); *It's All in the Game* (3/70); *Still Water (Love)* (7/70); *Just Seven Numbers* (12/70); *In These Changing Times* (6/71); *MacArthur Park (Part II)* (8/71); *A Simple Game* (1/72); *It's the Way Nature Planned It* (8/72); *Keeper of the Castle/Jubilee with Soul* (10/72); *Ain't No Woman/The Good Lord Knows* (1/73); *Guardian de Tu Castillo/Jubilee with Soul* (1/73); *Are You Man Enough/Peace of Mind* (5/73); *Marie/I Gambled with Love* (6/73); *Ain't No Woman/The Good Lord Knows* (8/73); *Sweet Understanding Love/Main Street People* (9/73); *Am I My Brother's Keeper/I Just Can't Get You Out of My Mind* (12/73); *One Chain Don't Make No Prison/Sweet Understanding Love* (9/74); *Seven Lonely Nights/I Can't Hold On Much Longer* (4/75); I'm Glad You Walked into My Life/Mama, You're All Right with Me (12/75); *Catfish/Look at My Baby* (8/76).

PETER FRAMPTON/Peter Frampton is the biggest superstar to emerge during the seventies. His fluid guitar style and plaintive vocals have brought out the beast in countless teenage girls who flock to concert halls worldwide for a glimpse of their newfound idol. For the second time in his young life, Peter Frampton is a pinup of rock. Frampton first set hearts a-flutter over a decade ago when, at the age of sixteen, he achieved national status with a bopper band in Britain, the Herd. His little-boy looks made him the teenyboppers' numero-uno star. This status, however, made Frampton something less than easy as it effectively obscured his legitimate talent for guitar playing.

Frampton allowed the Herd to disband before forming Humble Pie, a band which originally hovered effortlessly between hard and lyrical rock and roll. Eventually, Frampton's intricacies clashed head-on with the ballsy approach of Pie's co-founder, Steve Marriot. Frampton left after Pie's famous *ROCK ON* album and, at twenty-one, became a much-sought-after session guitarist. Playing on recordings by George Harrison, John Entwistle, and Harry Nilsson, Frampton bolstered his confidence enough to seek a solo career. His first effort, *WINDS OF CHANGE,* received favorable notices in 1972 but was anything but a runaway success. Peter later formed a loose-knit band to record *FRAMPTON'S CAMEL* (in 1973), which also assured him a low profile.

Frampton trudged along for three years, releasing politely accepted records. His success story is really one of faith. Faith in an artist by his record company (A&M) and his manager (Dee Anthony). After months of near-obscurity, Frampton released *FRAMPTON COMES ALIVE,* a perfectly swell live recording that unexpectedly shot up to the top of the album charts in 1976. An unheard-of string of "live" singles *(Show Me the Way, Baby I Love Your Way, Do You Feel Like We Do)* kept the album in the number-one position for seventeen weeks, making it the biggest-selling double album of all time.

In 1977, he continued his vault in the top of pop with his instant Gold Record, *I'M IN YOU.* In his mid-twenties, Frampton is now one of the most popular rock guitarists ever to grace the stage, offering an easy-going sound that was very much in evidence back in his early Humble Pie days.

Albums/WIND OF CHANGE (6/72): *Fig Tree Bay; Wind of Change; Lady Lieright; Jumping Jack Flash; It's a Plain Shame; Oh, for Another Day; All I Want to Be; The Lodger; Hard; Alright.* FRAMPTON'S CAMEL (5/73): *I Got My Eyes on You; All Night Long; Lines on My Face; Which Way the Wind Blows; I Believe (When I Fall in Love with You It Will Be Forever); White Sugar; Don't Fade Away; Just the Time of Year; Do You Feel Like We Do.* SOMETHING'S HAPPENING (2/74): *Doobie Wah; Golden Goose; Underhand; I Wanna Go to the Sun; Baby (Somethin's Happening); Waterfall; Magic Moon; Sail Away.* FRAMPTON (3/75): *Day's Dawning; Show Me the Way; One More Time; The Crying Clown; Fanfare; Nowhere's Too Far; Nassau; Baby, I Love Your Way; Apple of Your Eye; Penny for Your Thoughts; Money.* FRAMPTON COMES ALIVE (1/76): *Penny for Your Thoughts; Money; Shine On; Jumping Jack Flash; Lines on My Face; Do You Feel Like We Do; Something's Happening; Doobie Wah; Show Me the Way; It's a Plain Shame; All I Want to Be (Is By Your Side); Wind of Change; Baby, I Love Your Way; I Wanna Go to the Sun.* I'M IN YOU (6/77): *I'm in You; Heart on the Line; St. Thomas; Won't You Be My Friend; You Don't Have to Worry; Tried to Love; Rocky's Hot Club; Road Runner; Signed, Sealed, Delivered.*

Singles/*Jumping Jack Flash* (9/72); *Somethin's Happening* (4/74); *Show Me the Way* (5/75); *Baby, I Love Your Way* (8/75); *(I'll Give*

You) Money (11/75); *Show Me the Way* (2/76); *Baby, I Love Your Way* (6/76); *Do You Feel Like We Do* (9/76); *I'm in You* (5/77); *Signed, Sealed, Delivered* (8/77).

ARETHA FRANKLIN/In an age of cool, Aretha Franklin made it cool to be hot. Exploding in the late sixties with such soulful hit singles as *Respect, Baby, I Love You,* and *I Never Loved a Man the Way I Loved You,* Aretha quickly carved a niche for herself in the pop world, becoming the country's leading female vocalist and earning the title "Lady Soul."

Born in Detroit, one of five children of the Reverend C. L. Franklin, Aretha received musical encouragement at an early age from her father, a highly regarded gospel singer. She joined her father's choir while in her early teens. By the age of eighteen, she had expanded her musical horizons to include popular R&B material and, moving to New York, auditioned for and was signed by Columbia's greatest A&R man, John Hammond, Sr. Her years at Columbia Records were frustrating, with Aretha constantly stymied by record producers and banal material. Trapped by middle-of-the-road music, she opted for a new label and a new start in 1966.

The new label was Atlantic and the new start came in the person of famed producer Jerry Wexler. Wexler took Aretha to Muscle Shoals. The music world wasn't the same afterward. *I NEVER LOVED A MAN (THE WAY I LOVED YOU)* was a huge album and single and Aretha's career was launched immediately. Her career soared during the latter part of the sixties, slowing down somewhat in the seventies due to personal problems and general introspection.

After a brief hiatus at the turn of the decade, she quickly resumed her career full force, although leaning more toward intricate instrumental arrangements of late than she did ten years ago.

Albums/ARETHA (3/61): *Won't Be Long; Over the Rainbow; Love Is Long; Who Needs You; Right Now; Are You Sure; Maybe I'm a Fool; It Ain't Necessarily So; By Myself; Today I Sing the Blues.* ELECTRIFYING ARETHA FRANKLIN (1962): *You Made Me Love You; I Told You So; Rockabye Your Baby with a Dixie Melody; Nobody Like You; Exactly Like You; It's So Heartbreakin'; Rough Lover; Blue Holiday; Just for You; That Lucky*

Old Sun; I Surrender, Dear; Ac-Cent-Tchu-Ate the Positive. TEN-
DER, MOVING, SWINGING—ARETHA FRANKLIN
(8/62): *Don't Cry, Baby; Try a Little Tenderness; I Apologize;
Without the One You Love; Look for the Silver Lining; I'm Sitting
on Top of the World; Just for a Thrill; God Bless the Child; I'm
Wandering; How Deep Is the Ocean; I Don't Know You Anymore;
Lover Come Back to Me.* LAUGHING ON THE OUTSIDE
(8/63); *Skylark; For All We Know; Make Someone Happy; I Won-
der (Where Are You Tonight); Solitude; Laughing on the Outside;
Say It Isn't So; Until the Real Thing Comes Along; If Ever I Would
Leave You; Where Are You; Mr. Ugly; I Wanna Be Around.* UN-
FORGETTABLE (3/64): *Unforgettable; Cold, Cold Heart; What
a Difference a Day Made; Drinking Again; Evil Gal Blues; Nobody
Knows the Way I Feel This Morning; Don't Say You're Sorry
Again; This Bitter Earth; If I Should Lose You; Soulville.* SONGS
OF FAITH (9/64): *There Is a Fountain Filled with Blood; You
Grow Closer; Precious Lord; Day Is Past and Gone; Never Grow
Old; He Will Wash You White as Snow; While the Blood Runs
Warm; Yield Not to Temptation.* RUNNIN' OUT OF FOOLS
(11/64); *Mockingbird; How Glad I Am; Walk On By; My Guy;
Every Little Bit Hurts; Shoop Shoop Song; You'll Lose a Good
Thing; I Can't Wait Until I See My Baby's Face; It's Just a Matter
of Time; Runnin' Out of Fools; Two Sides of Love; One-Room Par-
adise.* YEAH (5/65): *This Could Be the Start of Something; If I
Had a Hammer; Once in a Lifetime; More; Misty; There Is No
Greater Love; Love for Sale; Muddy Water; Today I Love Ev-
erybody; Without the One You Love; Trouble in Mind; Impossible.*
SOUL SISTER (5/66): *Until You Were Gone; You Made Me Love
You; Follow Your Heart; Ol' Man River; Sweet Bitter Love;
Mother's Love; Swanee; I'm Losing You (No, No); Take a Look;
Can't You Just See Me; Cry Like a Baby.* I NEVER LOVED A
MAN (3/67): *I Never Loved a Man; Do Right Woman—Do Right
Man; Respect; Drown in My Own Tears; Soul Serenade; Don't Let
Me Lose This Dream; Baby, Baby, Baby; Dr. Feelgood; Good
Times; Save Me; Change Is Gonna Come.* ARETHA
FRANKLIN'S GREATEST HITS (4/67): *Running Out of Fools;
Rock-a-Bye Your Baby with a Dixie Melody; Today I Sing the
Blues; Cry Like a Baby; Without the One You Love; One Step
Ahead; Evil Gal Blues; Try a Little Tenderness; Sweet Bitter Love;
God Bless the Child; If Ever I Would Leave You.* TAKE IT LIKE

YOU GIVE IT (5/67): *Why Was I Born; I May Never Get to Heaven; Tighten Up Your Tie; Button Up Your Jacket; Lee Cross; Her Little Heart Went to Loveland; Take It Like You Give It; Only the One You Love; Deeper; Remember Me; Land of Dreams; Little Bit of Soul.* ARETHA ARRIVES (7/67): *Baby, I Love You; Satisfaction; You Are My Sunshine; 96 Tears; Prove It; Night Life; I Wonder; That's Life; Ain't Nobody; Going Down Slow.* ARETHA FRANKLIN'S GREATEST HITS, VOLUME II (2/68): *Lee Cross; Say It Isn't So; Skylark; Take It Like You Give It; Take a Look; Mockingbird; Soulville; Every Little Bit Hurts; Don't Cry, Baby; Just for a Thrill.* LADY SOUL (2/68): *Chain of Fools; Natural Woman; Come Back, Baby; Money Won't Change You; People Get Ready; Niki Hokey; Since You've Been Gone; Good to Me as I Am to You; Groovin'; Ain't No Way.* ARETHA NOW (6/68): *Think; You Send Me; I Say a Little Prayer for You; See Saw; Night Time Is the Right Tine; You're a Sweet Sweet Man; I Take What I Want; Hello Sunshine; A Change; I Can't See Myself Leaving You.* ARETHA IN PARIS (10/68): *Satisfaction; Don't let Me Lose This Dream; Soul Serenade; Night Life; Baby, I Love You; Groovin'; Natural Woman; Come Back, Baby; Dr. Feelgood; Since You've Been Gone; I Never Loved a Man; Chain of Fools; Respect.* SOUL 69 (1/69): *Ramblin'; Today I Sing the Blues; River's Invitation; Pitiful; Crazy He Calls Me; Bring It On Home to Me; Tracks of My Tears; If You Gotta Make a Fool of Somebody; Gentle on My Mind; So Long; I'll Never Be Free; Elusive Butterfly.* ARETHA'S GOLD (6/69): *I Never Loved a Man; Do Right Woman—Do Right Man; Respect; Dr. Feelgood; Baby, I Love You; A Natural Woman; Chain of Fools; Since You've Been Gone; Ain't No Way; Think; You Send Me; The House That Jack Built; I Say a Little Prayer for You; See Saw.* THIS GIRL'S IN LOVE WITH YOU (1/70). SPIRIT IN THE DARK (8/70): *Don't Play That Song; The Thrill Is Gone; Pullin'; You and Me; Honest I Do; Spirit in the Dark; When the Battle Is Over; One Way Ticket; Try Matty's; That's All I Want from You; Oh No, Not My Baby; Why I Sing the Blues.* LIVE AT THE FILLMORE WEST (5/71): *Respect; Love the One You're With; Bridge over Troubled Water; Eleanor Rigby; Make It with You; Don't Play That Song; Dr. Feelgood; Spirit in the Dark; Spirit in the Dark (reprise with Ray Charles); Reach Out and Touch.* GREATEST HITS (9/71): *Spanish Harlem; Chain of Fools; Don't Play That Song; I Say a*

Little Prayer; Dr. Feelgood; Do Right Woman—Do Right Man; Bridge over Troubled Water; Respect; Baby, I Love You; A Natural Woman; You're All I Need to Get By; Call Me. YOUNG, GIFTED AND BLACK (1/72): *Oh Me, Oh My; Day Dreaming; Rock Steady; Young, Gifted and Black; All the King's Horses; A Brand New Me; April Fools; I've Been Loving You Too Long; First Snow in Kokomo; The Long and Winding Road; Didn't I; Border Song.* AMAZING GRACE (6/72): *How I Got Over; What a Friend We Have in Jesus; Amazing Grace; Precious Memories; Climbing Higher Mountains; God Will Take Care of You.* HEY NOW HEY (THE OTHER SIDE OF THE SKY) (1973): *Hey Now Hey; Somewhere; So Swell When You're Well; Angel; Sister from Texas; Mister Spain; That's the Way I Feel about Cha; Moody's Mood; Just Right Tonight.* LET ME IN YOUR LIFE (1974): *Let Me in Your Life; Every Natural Thing; Oh Baby; I'm in Love; Until You Come Back to Me; The Masquerade Is Over; With Pen in Hand; A Song for You; If You Dont Think; Ain't Nothing Like the Real Thing; Eight Days on the Road.* WITH EVERYTHING I FEEL IN ME (11/74): *Without Love; Don't Go Breaking My Heart; When You Get Right Down to It; You'll Never Get to Heaven; With Everything I Feel in Me; I Love Every Little Thing about You; Sing It Again—Say It Again; other titles.* YOU (10/75): *Mr. D.J.; It Only Happens; I'm Not Strong Enough to Love You; Walk Softly; You Make My Life; Without You; The Sha-La Bandit; You; You Got All the Aces; As Long As You Are There.* SPARKLE (5/76): *Sparkle; Look into Your Heart; Hooked on Your Love; Rock with Me; Something He Can Feel; Jump; Get High; Loving You, Baby.* TEN YEARS OF GOLD (11/76): *I Never Loved a Man; Respect; Baby, I Love You; A Natural Woman; Think; See Saw; Spanish Harlem; Rock Steady; Day Dreaming; Until You Come Back to Me; Angel; Something He Can Feel.* SWEET PASSION (5/77): *Break It to Me Gently; When I Think about You; What I Did for Love; No One Could Ever Love You More; Sweet Passion; A Tender Touch; Touch Me Up; Mumbles; Sunshine Will Never Be the Same; Meadows of Springtime.*

Singles/*Today I Sing the Blues* (9/60); *Won't Be Long* (1/61); *Operation Heartbreak* (9/61); *Rock-a-Bye Your Baby with a Dixie Melody* (9/61); *I Surrender, Dear* (1/62); *Rough Lover* (1/62); *Don't Cry, Baby* (6/62); *Try a Little Tenderness* (9/62); *Trouble in*

Mind (11/62); *Runnin' Out of Fools* (9/64); *Can't You Just See Me* (1/65); *One Step Ahead* (5/65); *Cry Like a Baby/Runnin' Out of Fools* (10/66); *I Never Loved A Man* (2/67); *Respect/Dr. Feelgood* (3/67); *Lee Cross* (7/67); *Baby, I Love You/Going Down Slow* (7/67); *A Natural Woman/Baby Baby Baby* (9/67); *Take a Look/Follow Your Heart* (9/67); *Mockingbird/Mother's Love* (11/67); *Chain of Fools/Prove It* (11/67; *Soulville* (1/68); *Ain't No Way/Since You've Been Gone* (2/68); *I Say a Little Prayer/House That Jack Built* (7/68); *Think/You Send Me* (8/68); *See Saw/My Song* (11/68); *The Weight/Tracks of My Tears* (1/69); *I Can't See Myself Leaving You/Gentle on My Mind* (3/69); *Share Your Love with Me* (7/69); *Eleanor Rigby* (10/69); *Call Me/Son of a Preacher Man* (1/70); *Spirit in the Dark* (5/70); *Don't Play That Song* (7/70); *Border Song/You and Me* (10/70); *You're All I Need to Get By* (1/71); *Bridge over Troubled Water/Brand New Me* (3/71); *Spanish Harlem* (7/71); *Rock Steady* (10/71); *Oh Me, Oh My* (1/72); *Day Dreaming* (2/72); *All the King's Horses* (5/72); *Wholy Holy* (7/72); *Master of Eyes* (1/73); *Angel* (6/73); *Until You Come Back* (10/73); *I'm in Love* (3/74); *Ain't Nothing Like the Real Thing* (7/74); *Without Love/Don't Go Breaking My Heart* (10/74); *With Everything I Feel in Me/Sing It Again—Say It Again* (1/75); *Mr. D.J./As Long As You Are There* (8/75); *You/Without You* (12/75); *Something He Can Feel/Loving You, Baby* (5/76); *Jump/Hooked on Your Love* (9/76); *Break It to Me Gently/Meadows of Springtime* (4/77).

FREE/*Paul Rodgers (vocals), Andy Fraser (bass), Simon Kirke (drums), Paul Kossoff (guitar). Additional members: Wendell Richardson (guitar), Snuffy (guitar), Tetsu Yamauchi (bass), Rabbit (keyboards).*
Free was one of the finest bands ever to emerge from Great Britain during the sixties. They were one of the most influential in terms of style and one of the most underrated in terms of airplay. The crisp, fluid guitar licks of Paul Kossoff can be heard today, echoed in dozens of rock bands, and the terse, no-holds-barred spirit of Free can be discerned in the current musical antics of Bad Company, whose residents include former Free agents Paul Rodgers and Simon Kirke.

The band came about in 1968, when all four members were in their mid-to-late teens. Kossoff and Kirke toiled in a British blues

band called Black Cat Bones—a band that didn't exactly stimu-
late their creative juices. Seeking to form a band of their own,
they began to scout for members. About the same time, bassist
extraordinaire Andy Fraser (a mere fifteen) was having problems
within the John Mayall Bluesbreakers entourage, a rocking-blues
outfit that was rapidly assuming jazz overtones. Paul Rodgers,
then a singer with an outfit called Brown Sugar, was seen by Koss
and Kirke and asked to join the soon-to-be band. Fraser was con-
tacted by a mutual friend and the foursome came together and
jammed. During the course of the first evening, Free wrote the
foundations of four songs. It was clear there was something big in
the works.

One of Free's most ardent supporters was legendary music figure Alexis Korner, who supported the band in its early months
and subsequently gave them the name Free, from a band he'd
called Free At Last when working with Ginger Baker and
Graham Bond. The plucky foursome began gigging around England and, with Korner's support, amassed quite a following.
Eventually they encountered Island Records main man Chris
Blackwell, who took them on and gave them a six-month recording deal. That deal later was extended when their debut LP,
TONS OF SOBS, caused quite a ruckus throughout U.K. music
circles. Their second album, FREE, got rave reviews on both sides
of the Atlantic, and a stellar Rolling Stone piece started a cult
following in America. By the time HIGHWAY and FIRE AND
WATER arose, Free was looking like the Next Big Thing.

A single, All Right Now, shot the band to the top ten worldwide. And then the problems started. The Free style was remarkably bareboned. Each member carried a precise sense of responsibility. The bass and drum patterns hovered in one musical
location, while the vocals shot across another. When there was a
lull in the activity, Koss' searing guitar lines filled the void. This
exacting nature began to cause frustration within the ranks as the
individual members began to grow and expand. Fraser became a
truly distinctive bassist and an accomplished songwriter, cul-
tivating a vocal delivery of his own that, at times, could rival
Rodgers'. Rodgers, during his stay with Free, went from a tentative delivery to a masterful swagger, bursting with brilliant
flares of soulful rock. Kirke developed an anvil-chorus drumming
style and Kossoff, feeling hemmed in by the Free patterns, offered

some of the most tasteful and clean guitar-playing ever heard on record.

Following the recording of *HIGHWAY*, the band split up. Various solo projects never got off the ground. Rodgers' band Peace collapsed shortly after being formed, as did Fraser's Toby. Kossoff and Kirke fared somewhat better united with Japanese bassist Tetsu Yamauchi and Texas keyboard-player Rabbit Bundrick for the album *KOSSOFF, KIRKE, TETSU AND RABBIT*.

Shortly thereafter, however, Free attempted a comeback and united for *FREE AT LAST*. While producing a fine album, the foursome did little to reestablish old friendships. Rodgers and Fraser were at odds for leadership responsibilities. Kossoff's drug use caught up with him physically and a subsequent tour proved a travesty with Kossoff too ill to perform or too drained even to travel to the dates. Koss left for the States and Fraser left the group for good. The remaining dates were filled by Rodgers, Kirke, Tetsu, and Rabbit. This new foursome went on to record *HEARTBREAKER*, with additional help from Kossoff on guitar and Snuffy (an American friend of Rabbit)) on some lead guitar riffs.

Yet another tour was scheduled (a single, *Wishing Well*, garnering the new Free a lot of attention) with Kossoff in the ranks. Illness again forced him to withdraw and his position was hastily filled by ex-Osibisa member Wendell Richardson. With the American tour dates completed, the masters of below-the-belt rock and roll called it quits for good. Fraser went on to form several versions of the Andy Fraser Band, none of them to last more than six months. Kossoff began Back Street Crawler, a rollicking rock troupe he helmed until his death from a heart attack in 1976, and Kirke and Rodgers formed the enormously successful Bad Company in 1974.

Fringe Free members Tetsu and Rabbit also went on to bigger and better things. Tetsu became a regular member of the Faces during their infamous Rod Stewart and the Faces years, and Rabbit, after sitting in with Johnny Nash and the Sutherland Brothers and Quiver, eventually joined Kossoff's revamped band, Crawler.

Albums/TONS OF SOBS (7/69): *Over the Green Hills (Parts I and II); Worry; Walk in My Shadow; Wild Indian Woman; Goin' Down Slow; I'm a Mover; The Hunter; Moonshine; Sweet Tooth.*

FREE (2/70): *I'll Be Creepin'; Songs of Yesterday; Lying in the Sunshine; Trouble in Double Time; Mouthful of Grass; Woman; Free Me; Broad Daylight; Mourning Sad Morning.* FIRE AND WATER (8/70): *Fire and Water; Oh I Wept; Remember; Heavy Load; Mr. Big; Don't Say You Love Me; All Right Now.* HIGH-WAY (1/71): *The Highway Song; The Stealer; On My Way; Be My Friend; Sunny Day; Ride On Pony; Love You So; Bodie; Soon I Will Be Gone.* FREE LIVE! (8/71): *All Right Now; I'm a Mover; Be My Friend; Fire and Water; My Brother Jake; Ride On Pony; The Hunter; Mr. Big; Get Where I Belong.* HEARTBREAKER (1/73): *Wishing Well; Come Together in the Morning; Travellin' In Style; Heartbreaker; Muddy Water; Common Mortal Man; Easy on My Soul; Seven Angels.* THE BEST OF FREE (4/75): *Fire and Water; The Highway Song; Little Bit of Love; Mouthful of Grass; My Brother Jake; The Hunter; All Right Now; Woman; Catch a Train; I'm a Mover; The Stealer; Goodbye.*

Singles/*I'm a Mover* (7/69); *I'll Be Creepin'* (2/70); *All Right Now* (6/70); *Stealer* (11/70); *I'll Be Creepin'* (5/71); *My Brother Jake* (7/71); *Little Bit of Love* (4/72); *Wishing Well* (1973).

THE FUGS/*Ed Sanders (vocals), Ken Weaver (vocals, drums), Tuli Kupferberg (vocals), Ken Pine (vocals, guitar), Bill Wolf (bass), Bob Mason (drums).*

Someone once referred to the Fugs as the Lenny Bruces of rock. Certainly, right from the start they went out of their way to be "offensive," particularly on such musically taboo subjects and explicit physical sex and drugs. Songs like *I Couldn't Get High* and *Coca Cola Douche* proved the rule, not the exception. Like Bruce, they were comics and satirists, except that their literary leanings led to the creation of some beautiful lyrics on both beautiful and outrageous subjects. The Fugs never claimed to be rock musicians. They were, first and foremost, poets.

Starting out in the mid-sixties, in a small theater on New York's St. Mark's Place, they came together: a team of East Village poets and artists who decided to sing some of the poetry they were writing. At that stage, it was unthinkable for poets to form a rock group, and especially for freaky-looking poets to form a freaky rock group. The sixties' freedom was burgeoning, however, and soon the Fugs had garnered an adoring (albeit microscopic) following.

An "underground" New York record label, ESP (a company that catered to freeform music and poetry), signed the band, and soon the Fugs were on wax. A leap for the "big time" in 1968 led to a contract with Warner/Reprise Records. The fates were not kind to the Fugs on their commercial venture and, by 1969, the group was off the label and, indeed, off the face of the Earth—disbanding that same year.

In a sense, the outrageous verbal and physical activities of the Fugs paved the way for the more refined insanity of such artists as Zappa, Cheech and Chong, and the punk rockers.

Albums/THE FUGS FIRST ALBUM (1965): *Slum Goddess; Sunflower Weary of Time; Supergirl; Swineburne Stomp; I Couldn't Get High; How Sweet I Roamed from Field to Field; Seize the Day; My Baby Done Left Me; Boobs a Lot; Nothing.* VIRGIN FUGS (FOR ADULT MINDS ONLY) (1965): *We're the Fugs; New Amphetamine Shriek; Saran Wrap; The Ten Commandments; Hallucination Horrors; I Command the House of the Devil; CIA Man; Coca-Cola Douche; My Bed Is Getting Crowded; Caca Rock; I Saw the Best Minds of My Generation Rot.* THE FUGS (1966): *Frenzy; I Want to Know; Skin Flowers; Group Grope; Dirty Old Man; Kill for Peace; Morning, Morning; Doin' All Right; Virgin Forest.* TENDERNESS JUNCTION (11/67): *Turn On/Tune In/Drop Out; Knock Knock; The Garden Is Open; Wet Dream; Hare Krishna; Exorcising the Evil Spirits from the Pentagon; October 21, 1967; War Song; Dover Beach Fingers of the Sun; Aphrodite Mass.* IT CRAWLED INTO MY HAND, HONEST (10/68): *Crystal Liaison; Ramses II Is Dead, My Love; Burial Waltz; Wide Wide River; Life Is Strange; Johnny Pissoff Meets the Red Angel; Marijuana; Leprechaun; When the Mode of the Music Changes; Whimpers from the Jellow; The Divine Toe (Part I); We're Both Dead Now, Alice; Life Is Funny; Grope Need (Part I); Tuli, Visited by the Ghost of Plotimus; More Grope Need (Grope Need Part II); Robinson Crusoe; Claude Pelliu and J.J. Lebel Discuss Early Verlaine Bread Crust Fragments; The National Haiku Contest; The Divine Toe (Part I); Irene.* THE BELLE OF AVENUE A (6/69): *Bum's Song; Dust Devil; Chicago; Four Minutes to Twelve; Mr. Mack; The Belle of Avenue A; Queen of the Nile; Flower Children; Yodeling Yippie; Children of the Dream.* GOLDEN FILTH (2/70): *Slum Goddess; How Sweet I Roamed from Field to Field; I Couldn't Get High; Saran Wrap; I Want to*

Know; Homemade; Coca Cola Douche; Supergirl; Nothing.

PETER GABRIEL/For years the focal point of the group Genesis, ex-art student, Peter Gabriel departed the infamous band in 1975. Gabriel, a singer-songwriter, was one of the founding members of the group and left after a stay of nearly seven years. Well-known for his outrageous theatricals while with Genesis, he went into relative artistic seclusion for over eighteen months, emerging in 1977 with a premier solo album. The LP was a splendid first effort, brimming with songs demonstrating Gabriel's unique, surreal approach to rock and roll. The long-player proved too esoteric for some. A single, *Salsbury Hill,* proved uneventful in the United States but secured a goodly amount of airplay in Gabriel's homeland, England.

Albums/PETER GABRIEL (2/77): *Moribund the Burgermeister; Salsbury Hill; Modern Love; Excuse Me; Humdrum; Slowburn; Waiting for the Big One; Down the Dolce Vita; Here Comes the Flood.*

Single/*Salsbury Hill/Moribund the Burgermeister* (3/77).

RORY GALLAGHER/Guitarist extraordinaire Rory Gallagher is one of the best-kept secrets of rock and roll today. Born and raised in Ireland, he picked up the guitar at the ripe old age of nine and hasn't seen fit to put it down yet . . . which is all the better for his fans. A versatile musician from the outset, Gallagher paid his dues by performing as a teen in various rock, blues, and show bands. In 1965, he formed the nucleus of Taste, with bassist Charles McCarcken and drummer John Wilson. By 1969, Taste was the big power-trio on the horizon of the London music scene. Unfortunately, their potential was never fully realized. By 1971, after moderate success, Taste folded and Gallagher went on to a solo career.

As a guitarist-singer-songwriter, Gallagher has achieved tremendous success on the Continent, delivering a hard-nosed mixture of electric and Delta blues and good old rock and roll. His albums are always exceedingly well played and his concert sets are without peer. Unfortunately, stateside status has eluded the plucky Irishman for a number of reasons. After the fall of Taste, that band's U.S. distributor (Atlantic) saw fit to release Gallagher's initial records with a great deal of apathy. A subsequent switch to Polydor U.S. assured Rory instant anonymity.

However, despite his lack of overt commercial success, Gallagher has proven himself to be an extraordinary "in-concert" draw across the United States, especially in college towns. His 1975 jump to the Chrysalis label, both in the United Kingdom and the United States, bodes well for the future success of the rip-roaring axe wielder.

Albums/RORY GALLAGHER (9/71): *Laundromat; Just the Smile; I Fall Apart; Wave Myself Goodbye; Hands Up; Sinner Boy; For the Last Time; It's You; I'm Not Surprised; Can't Believe It's True.* DEUCE (2/72): *Used to Be; I'm Not Awake Yet; Don't Know Where I'm Going; Maybe I Will; Whole Lot of People; In Your Town; Should've Learnt My Lesson; There's a Light; Out of My Mind; Crest of a Wave.* LIVE (7/72): *Messin' with the Kid; Laundromat; I Could've Had Religion; Pistol Slapper Blues; Going to My Home Town; In Your Town; Bullfrog Blues.* BLUEPRINT (1973): *Walk on Hot Coals; Daughter of the Everglades; Banker's Blues; Hands Off; Race the Breeze; The Seventh Son of a Seventh Son; Unmilitary Two-Step; If I Had a Reason.* TATOO (10/73): *Tatoo'd Lady; Cradle Rock; 20:20 Vision: They Don't Make Them Like You Anymore; Livin' Like a Trucker; Sleep on a Clothes-Line; Who's That Coming; A Million Miles Away; Admit It.* IRISH TOUR '74 (1974): *Cradle Rock; I Wonder Who (Who's Gonna Be Your Sweet Man); Tatoo'd Lady; Too Much Alcohol; As the Crow Flies; A Million Miles Away; Walk on Hot Coals; Who's That Comin'; Back on My (Stompin' Ground); Just a Little Bit.* SINNER (1975): *Used to Be; Sinner Boy; For the Last Time; Hands Up; Just the Smile; Crest of a Wave; There's a Light; I Fall Apart; Don't Know Where I'm Going.* AGAINST THE GRAIN (10/75): *Let Me In; Cross Me Off Your List; Ain't Too Good; Souped-Up Ford; Bought and Sold; I Take What I Want; Lost at Sea; All-Around Man; Out on the Western Plain; At the Bottom.* CALLING CARD (9/76): *Do You Read Me; Country Mile; Moonchild; Calling Card; I'll Admit You're Gone; Secret Agent; Jackknife Beat; Edged in Blue; Barley and Grape Rag.*

ART GARFUNKEL/When Simon and Garfunkel split in 1970, silken-voiced crooner Art temporarily abandoned music to pursue a short-lived career in acting. Following up his role in *Catch 22* (1969) with the critically acclaimed portrayal of Jack Nicholson's straight-as-an-arrow buddy in *Carnal Knowledge*

(1970), Art was definitely considered an upstart to watch when he abandoned the thespian realm quite suddenly. Three years later, he returned to music with a lavish, middle-of-the-road album, *ANGEL CLARE*. It was the kind of album you could play in St. Patrick's Cathedral and not get yelled at. Heavenly choirs, lighter-than-air strings and ethereal melody lines all joined forces to create a cumulative sound that was sheer, uh, froth. In spite of two collections of such music, Art has never really made it big on the pop charts as a lone artist, with irregular releases and non-existent concert dates.

Albums/ANGEL CLARE (&/73): *Traveling Boy; Down in the Willow Garden; I Shall Sing; Old Man; Feuilles—Oh Do Space Men Pass Dead Souls on the Way to the Moon; All I Know; Mary Was an Only Child; Woyaya; Barbara Allen; Another Lullaby.* BREAKAWAY (9/75): *I Believe When I Fll in Love It Will Be Forever; Rag Doll; Break Away; Disney Girls; Waters of March; My Little Town; I Only Have Eyes for You; Looking for the Right One; 99 Miles from L.A.; The Same Old Tears on a New Background.* WATERMARK (1/78); *Crying in My Sleep; Marionette; Shine It on Me; Watermark; Saturday Suit; All My Love's Laughter; (What a) Wonderful World; Mr. Shuck 'n' Jive; Paper Chase; She Moved through the Fair; Someone Else (1958); Wooden Planes.*

Singles/*All I Know/Mary Was an Only Child* (8/73); *I Shall Sing/Feuilles* (12/73); *Traveling Boy/Old Man* (3/74); *Second Avenue/Woyaya* (8/74); *All I Know/I Shall Sing* (9/74); *I Only Have Eyes for You/Looking for the Right One* (7/75); *Break Away/Disney Girls* (12/75); *I Only Have Eyes For You/Second Avenue* (11/76); *My Little Town/Gone at Last* (11/76).

J. GEILS BAND/*J. Geils (guitar), Magic Dick (harmonica), Peter Wolf (vocals), Danny Klein (bass), Seth Justman (keyboards), Stephen Bladd (percussion).*
During the mid-sixties, the musical world reverberated with the epic question: Can white men sing the blues? (As if anyone really cared.) Well, by 1969, no one was really thinking about the blues much. Long hair, psychedelia, *2001,* and *Easy Rider* were in. Going against the mainstream, however, was the cantankerous J. Geils Band, which was formed in Boston that year. From the outset, Geils and his gonzos were oddities. They played rough-

and-tumble blues in a musical era when flower power was still
being preached by Woodstockian merchants everywhere.

They were high-energy musicians who didn't seem to care
about rules or regulations. They greased their hair back, dressed
in leather jackets, outraged audiences, played flawlessly and, in
spite of themselves, won over a huge following in the Boston area.
A recording contract with Atlantic was signed and Geils began a
cross-country assault on the radio airwaves with such tunes as
Looking for a Love, Hard-Driving Man, and *House Party.* Over
the years, the fellows mellowed a little (they de-Criscoed their
hair, for instance, put on shirts and actually looked like counterculture crossovers) but their style remained hard, crude, and
fascinating.

Their career began to slide around 1975 when the rocking blues
approach to music began to wear thin on some fans. In 1977 they
revamped their image with a new album and a new name, simply
Geils.

Albums/THE J. GEILS BAND (11/70): *Wait; Ice Breaker;
Crusin' for a Love; Hard-Drivin' Man; Serves You Right to Suffer;
Homework; First I Look at the Purse; What's Your Hurry; On
Borrowed Time; Back Fair and Square; Sno-Cone.* THE MORN-
ING AFTER (10/71): *I Don't Need You No More; Whammer
Jammer; So Sharp; The Usual Place; Gotta Have Your Love;
Looking for a Love; Gonna Find Me a New Love; Cry One More
Time; Floyd's Hotel; It Ain't What You Do (It's How You Do It!).*
FULL HOUSE (9/72): *First I Look at the Purse; Homework;
Back Fair and Square; Whammer Jammer; Hard-Drivin' Man;
Serves You Right to Suffer; Cruisin' for a Love; Looking for a
Love.* BLOODSHOT (4/73): *House Party; Make Up Your Mind;
Back to Get Ya; Struttin' with My Baby; Don't Try to Hide It;
Southside Shuffle; Hold Your Loving; Start All Over Again; Give It
to Me.* LADIES INVITED (11/73). NIGHTMARES . . . AND
OTHER TALES FROM THE VINYL JUNGLE (9/74): *Detroit
Breakdown; Givin' It All Up; Must of Got Lost; Look Me in the
Eye; Nightmares; Stoop Down #39; I'll Be Coming Home; Funky
Judge; Gettin' Out.* HOTLINE (9/75): *Love-itis; Easy Way Out;
Think It Over; Be Careful (What You Do); Jealous Love; Mean
Love; Orange Driver; Believe in Me; Fancy Footwork.* LIVE:
BLOW YOUR FACE OUT (4/76): *Southside Shuffle; Back to
Get Ya; Shoot Your Shot; Musta Got Lost; Where Did Our Love*

Go; Truck-Drivin Man; Love-Itis; Intro/Lookin' for a Love; Houseparty; So Sharp; Detroit Breakdown; Chimes; Sno-Cone; Wait; Raise Your Hand; Start All Over. MONKEY ISLAND (6/77): *Surrender; I Do; You're the Only One; Somebody; I'm Not Rough; I'm Falling; Monkey Island; Wreckage.*

Singles/*Homework/First I Look at the Purse* (1/71); *Cruisin; for a Love/Wait* (4/71); *Looking for a Love/Whammer Jammer* (10/71); *I Don't Need You No More/Dead Presidents* (2/72); *Hard-Drivin' Man/Whammer Jammer* (11/72); *Give It to Me/Hold Your Loving* (3/73); *Make Up Your Mind/Southside Shuffle* (7/73); *Did You No Wrong/That's Why I'm Thinking of You* (1/74); *Looking for a Love/Give It to Me* (1/74); *Give It All Up/Gettin' Out* (1/75); *Love-itis/Think It Over* (10/75); *Where Did Our Love Go/What's Your Hurry* (2/76); *Houseparty/Give It to Me* (7/76); *Must of Got Lost/Funky Judge* (10/76); *Peanut Butter/Magic's Mood* 12/76).

GRAND FUNK RAILROAD/*Mark Farner (guitar, vocals), Mel Schacher (bass), Don Brewer (drums), Craig Frost (organ).*
Arising from the depths of Michigan, Grand Funk was one of the first rock bands to be labeled a total "hype" by the critics at large. Originating as a threesome (Mark, Don, and Mel), the band was formed in 1968 by Don (formerly of Terry Knight and the Pack) and Mark. Mel was then auditioned and the embryonic Funk was born. The band was given an added boost by buddy Terry Knight, who saw the band's "marketability" and quickly became their manager, wielding complete creative control over the trio. Terry's move from pop star to pop-star manager was an easy one; the brash, business-minded former DJ felt that he knew what the rock fans wanted and, to many rock intellectuals' chagrin, delivered unto them the lowest common denominator . . . Grand Funk. He cashed in.

Funk first scored in a big way at the Atlanta Pop Festival in July of '69. The trio performed a set of loud but uninspired riff-rock and the crowds went wild. A contract with Capitol was signed and *ON TIME,* the first of an avalanche of Grand Funk records, was released the same year. The LP was the laughing stock of the music press, but in spite of the mirth displayed toward the band, both their popularity and album sales soared, with *ON TIME* going gold. As Funk's presence grew, so did their image of the ultimate hype. Eventually it began to get to the band and, in 1971, they sought to sever their relationship with Knight (their mentor or hypester, depending on whose side you were on). They decided to ally themselves with manager/lawyer John Eastman (Paul McCartney's brother-in-law and business confidant). Knight countersued Eastman and the entire court procedure proved a messy affair, with Knight eventually losing in a business sense but the band suffering in terms of image. Did Terry Knight make them? Were they a hype? Were they now egomaniacs? What would they do on their own? Were they has-beens? Would they survive the seventies?

With their career beginning to slide swiftly, the threesome became a foursome as Craig Frost joined them for their *PHOENIX* album (heavy symbolism there, mythology buffs). Funk scored a few points with the critics on that one but still got the cold shoulder *BAND* set the world straight and, once again, Funk reaped gold. They began to enlist the aid of such top-flight producers as Todd Rundgren and Frank Zappa to further establish themselves as legitimate, hypeless artists. What seems to have happened, however, is that their concentrated effort to create a positive image led to creative exhaustion. By 1976, their popularity was once again fizzling. They jumped labels in search of greener pastures and met with concrete. Mark Farner took a sabbatical and attempted to put a solo career together. He's still working on it. Suddenly, Funk was no more. Grand Funk, one of the first groups to pursue the bareboned sound of cretinous heavy metal, passed away without anyone's even noticing.

Albums/ON TIME (9/69): *Are You Ready; Anybody's Amswer; Time Machine; High on a Horse; T.N.U.C.; Into the Sun; Heartbreaker; Call Yourself a Man; Can't Be Too Long; Ups and Downs.* GRAND FUNK (12/69); *Got This Thing on the Move; Please Don't Worry; High Falootin' Woman; Mr. Limousine Driver; In Need; Winter and My Soul; Paranoid; Inside Looking Out.* CLOSER TO HOME (6/70): *Sin's a Good Man's Brother; Aimless Lady; Nothing Is the Same; Mean Mistreater; Get It Together; Hooked on Love; I Don't Have to Sing the Blues; I'm Your Captain.* LIVE ALBUM (11/70): *Are You Ready; Paranoid; In Need; Into the Sun; Heartbreaker; Inside Looking Out; Words of Wisdom; Mean Mistreater; Mark Says Alright; T.N.U.C.* SUR-

VIVAL (4/71): *Country Road; All You've Got Is Money; Comfort Me; Feelin' Alright; I Want Freedom; I Can Feel Him in the Morning; Gimme Shelter.* E PLURIBUS FUNK (11/71): *Footstompin' Music; People, Let's Stop the War; Upsetter; I Come Tumblin'; Save the Land; No Lies; Loneliness.* MARK, DON AND MEL (4/72): *Time Machine; Into the Sun; Heartbreaker; Feelin' Alright; Inside Looking Out; Closer to Home; Footstompin' Music; Paranoid; Loneliness; Are You Ready; Mean Mistreater; T.N.U.C.* PHOENIX (9/72): *Flight of the Phoenix; Trying to Get Away; Someone; She Gotta Move Me; Rain Keeps Fallin'; I Just Gotta Know; So You Won't Have to Die; Freedom Is for Children; Find Me a Better Day; Rock 'n' Roll Soul.* WE'RE AN AMERICAN BAND (7/73): *We're an American Band; Stop Lookin' Back; Creepin'; Black Licorice; The Railroad; Ain't Got Nobody; Walk Like a Man; Loneliest Rider.* SHININ' ON (3/74): *Shinin' On; To Get Back In; The Locomotion; Carry Me Through; Please Me; Mr. Pretty Boy; Gettin' Over You; Little Johnny Hooker.* ALL THE GIRLS IN THE WORLD BEWARE! (12/74): *Responsibility; Runnin'; Life; Look at Granny Run Run; Memories; All the Girls in the World Beware; Wild; Good and Evil; Bad Time; Some Kind of Wonderful.* CAUGHT IN THE ACT (8/75): *Intro; Foot Stompin' Music; Rock 'n' Roll Soul; Closer to Home; Inside Looking Out; Gimme Shelter; Heartbreaker; Some Kind of Wonderful; Shinin' On; The Locomotion; Black Licorice; The Railroad; We're an American Band; T.N.U.C.* BORN TO DIE (1/76): *Born to Die; Dues; Sally; I Fell for Your Love; Talk to the People; Love Is Good Things; Genevieve; Take Me; Good Things.* GRAND FUNK HITS (10/76); *Rock 'n' Roll Soul; We're an American Band; Walk Like a Man; Bad Time; Shinin' On; Take Me' To Get Back In; Some Kind of Wonderful; The Locomotion.*

Singles/*Time Machine/High on a Horse* (8/69); *Mr. Limousine Driver/High Falootin' Woman* (12/69); *Heartbreaker/Please Don't Worry* (2/70); Sin's a Good Man's Brother/Nothing is The Same (5/70); *Closer to Home/Aimless Lady* (7/70); *Mean Mistreater/Mark Says Alright* (11/70); *Feelin' Alright/I Want Freedom* (4/71); *Gimme Shelter/I Can Feel Him in the Morning* (8/71); *People, Let's Stop the War/Save the Land* (11/71); *Footstompin' Music/I Come Tumblin'* (12/71); *Upsetter/No Lies* (4/72); *Rock 'n' Roll Soul/Flight of the Phoenix* (8/72); *We're An American Band/Creepin'* (7/73); *Walk Like a Man/The Railroad*

(10/73); *The Loco-Motion/Destitute and Losin'* (2/74); Shinin'
On/Mr. Pretty Boy (6/74); *Some Kind of Wonderful/Wild*
(12/74); *Bad Time/Good and Evil* (3/75); *Take Me/Genevieve*
(1/76); *Sally/Love Is Dyin'* (3/76).

THE GRATEFUL DEAD/*Jerry Garcia (guitar, vocals), Donna
Godchaux (vocals), Mickey Hart (percussion), Keith Godchaux (piano), Bill Kreutzmann (drums), Phil Lesh (bass), Bob Weir (rhythm
guitar). Previous members: Ron "Pig Pen" McKernan (organ,
mouthharp, vocals), Tom Constanten (keyboards).*
Prior to the formation of the Warlocks, which would evolve into
the Dead, the various members and friends of members drifted in
and out of the San Francisco troupes of the early 1960s. Jerry
Garcia's initial entrance into the world of bluegrass was with the
Wildwood Boys, along with Bob Hunter (future Dead lyricist)
and David Nelson (future New Riders of the Purple Sager). Another, later, group was the Mother McCree's Uptown Jug Champions band featuring Garcia, Pig Pen, Bob Weir, Bob Matthews,
John "Marmaduke" Dawson (future NRPS) and, occasionally,
David Parker on washboard. The Jug Band went electric in 1965,
with the lineup being Lesh, Kreutzmann, and the above-men-
tioned members. The band then became the Warlocks, featuring
Lesh, Kreutzmann, Garcia, Pigpen, and Weir.

Playing a combination blues, bluegrass, and rock and roll, the
band became fairly popular. After experimenting with LSD, however, the group's music expanded into never-before-reached territories—territories already inhabited by a lot of their mushrooming fans. In 1966, in a state of drug nirvana, they changed their
name to the Grateful Dead. By 1967, they were on Warner
Brothers Records where their first long-player, *THE GRATEFUL
DEAD,* promptly died. Their second, more psychedelic, effort,
ANTHEM OF THE SUN, gained them critical attention, and the
Grateful Dead became a bona fide cult band.

Mickey Hart and Constanten were enlisted; their band's
albums slowly began to sell. *AOXOMOXOA, LIVE DEAD,* and
WORKINGMAN'S DEAD gradually took them out of debt.
With the latter album, Garcia began to take the band away from
long, drawn-out compositions and back into his early love; country. A subsequent album, *AMERICAN BEAUTY,* offered the
world a hit single, *Truckin'.* The group's career soared, with concert dates selling out and record stores demanding more LPs.

Constanten left the band for religious reasons and Mickey Hart left the band for a short spell because of a legal row involving the band and his father, the group's manager. In 1971, *GRATEFUL DEAD,* a double-live album, went gold and the Dead were a definite money-making proposition for their label.

But that year brought strife as well. Pigpen, plagued by a serious liver ailment, was forced to leave the band, replaced by the Godchauxes. The following year, a triple-live LP, *EUROPE '72* went gold, although some fans got the sneaky suspicion that they had heard it all before. In 1973, Pigpen died of a stomach hemorrhage. That same year, the band severed ties with Warners, opting for their own label, to be distributed by United Artists. It was not a very smart move.

A flurry of Dead solo albums had come out the year before, all doing somewhat less than splendidly well. The New Riders of the Purple Sage, a Dead spinoff group formed in 1970, was floundering on their Columbia label, despite the blanket endorsement of the Dead. Since the creation of the Grateful Dead label, the Dead have retained their popular cult status but have not impressed the music community as a whole. Further solo efforts by various band members have not fared well, although the group is a major concert draw around the world.

In 1977, the Grateful Dead signed with Arista Records.

Albums/THE GRATEFUL DEAD (3/67): *The Golden Road; Beat It On Down the Line; Good Morning, Little School Girl; Cold Rain and Snow; Sitting on Top of the World; Cream Puff War; Morning Dew; New, New Minglewood Blues; Viola Lee Blues.* ANTHEM OF THE SUN (8/68): *That's It for the Other One; Cryptical Envelopment; Quadlibet for Tenderfeet; The Faster We Go the Rounder We Get; New Potato Caboose; Born Cross-Eyed; Alligator; Caution (Do Not Stop on the Tracks).* AOXOMOXOA (6/69): *St. Stephen; Dupree's Diamond Blues; Rosemary; Doin' That Rag; Mountains of the Moon; China Cat Sunflower; What's Become of the Baby; Cosmic Charley.* LIVE DEAD (1/70): *Dark Star; St. Stephen; The Eleven; Turn On Your Love Light; Death Don't Have No Mercy; Feedback; And We Bit You Goodnight.* WORKINGMAN'S DEAD (7/70): *Uncle John's Band; High Time; Dire Wolf; New Speedway Boogie; Cumberland Blues; Black Peter; Easy Wind; Casey Jones.* AMERICAN BEAUTY 11/70): *Box of Rain; Friend of the Devil; Sugar Magnolia; Opera-*

tor; Candyman; Ripple; Brokedown Palace; Till the Morning Comes; Attics of My Life; Truckin'. GRATEFUL DEAD (9/71): *Bertha; Mama Tried; Big Railroad Blues; Playing in the Band; The Other One; Me and My Uncle; Big Boss Man; Me and Bobby McGee; Johnny B. Goode; Wharf Rat; Not Fade Away; Goin' Down the Road Feelin' Bad.* EUROPE '72 (10/72): *Cumberland Blues; He's Gone; One More Saturday Night; Jack Straw; You Win Again; China Cat Sunflower; I Know You, Rider; Brown-Eyed Woman; It Hurts Me, Too; Ramble On Rose; Sugar Magnolia; Mr. Charlie; Tennessee Jed; Truckin'; Epilogue; Prelude; Morning Dew.* HISTORY OF THE GRATEFUL DEAD, VOL. I (6/73): *Katie Mae; Dark Hollow; I've Been All around This World; Wake Up, Little Susie; Black Peter; Smokestack Lightnin'; Hard to Handle.* WAKE OF THE FLOOD (10/73): *Mississippi Half-Step Uptown Toodeloo; Let Me Sing Your Blues Away; Row, Jimmy; Stella Blue; Here Comes Sunshine; Eyes of the World; Weather Report Suite.* GRATEFUL DEAD FROM THE MARS HOTEL (6/74): *U.S. Blues; China Doll; Unbroken Chain; Loose Lucy; Scarlet Begonias; Pride of Cucamonga; Money Money; Ship of Fools.* BLUES FOR ALLAH (8/75): *Help on the Way/Slipknot!; Franklin's Tower; King Solomon's Marbles; Stronger Than Dirt or Milkin' the Turkey; Crazy Fingers; The Music Never Stopped; Sage and Spirit; Blues for Allah; Sand Castles and Glass Camels; Unusual Occurrences in the Desert.* STEAL YOUR FACE (8/76): *The Promised Land; Cold Rain and Snow; Around and Around; Stella Blue; Mississippi Half-Step Uptown Toodeloo; Ship of Fools; Beat It On down the Line; Big River; Black-Throated Wind; U.S. Blues; El Paso; Sugaree; It Must Have Been the Roses; Casey Jones.* TERRAPIN STATION (6/77): *Lady with a Fan; Terrapin Station; Terrapin; Terrapin Transit; At a Siding; Terrapin Flyer; Refrain; Estimated Prophet; Dancin' in the Streets; Passenger; Samson and Delilah; Sunrise.* THE BEST OF THE GRATEFUL DEAD (9/77): *Truckin'; St. Stephen; Jack Straw; Dark Star; Born Cross-Eyed; Me and My Uncle; Black Peter; Brown-Eyed Woman; Cumberland Blues; Cosmic Charlie; New, New Minglewood Blues; Doin' That Rag; Ripple; High Time; Ramble On Rose; Tennessee Jed; New Speedway Boogie; Playing in the Band.*

Singles/*Dark Star/Born Cross-Eyed* (4/68); *Dupree's Diamond Blues/Cosmic Charlie* (8/69); *Uncle John's Band/New Speedway*

Boogie (7/70); _Truckin'/Ripple_ (1/71); _Johnny B. Goode/So Fine_
(8/72); _Truckin'/Johnny B. Goode_ (9/72); _Sugar Magnolia/Mr._
Charlie (12/72); _The Music Never Stopped/Help On The Way_
(9/75); _Franklin's Tower/Help On The Way_ (1/76).

AL GREEN/After achieving brief status in 1966 with a single,
Back Up Train, prefab soul-rocker Al Green hovered in limbo
until 1969, when producer Will Mitchell signed him to Hi
Records. By 1970, Green's sky-high vocals and Mitchell's slick
commercial arrangements were at the top of the charts. The
Arkansas-born gospel-turned-pop singer remained at the top until 1974, when the momentum began to fade from his sound-alike
series of soulful songs.

A well-publicized accident stemming from an argument with a
lady friend (he was scalded with hot grease, she shot herself) and
a dud movie venture _(Mimi)_ caused Green to retreat from the
public eye somewhat at the end of 1974. Currently, Green is getting his vocal chords in high gear for a return to hit-making.

Albums/GREEN IS BLUE (6/69): _One Woman; Talk to Me; My_
Girl; The Letter; I Stand Accused; Gotta Find a New World; What
Am I Gonna Do With Myself?; Tomorrow's Dream; Get Back,
Baby; Summertime. GETS NEXT TO YOU (12/70): _I Can't Get_
Next To You; Are You Lonely for Me, Baby; God Is Standing By;
Tired of Being Alone; I'm a Ram; Driving Wheel; Light My Fire;
You Say It; Right Now, Right Now; All Because. LET'S STAY
TOGETHER (1/72): _Let's Stay Together; La-La for You; So_
You're Leaving; What Is This Feeling; Old Time Lovin'; I've Never
Found a Girl; How Can You Mend a Broken Heart; Judy; It Ain't
No Fun For Me. I'M STILL IN LOVE WITH YOU (9/72): _I'm_
Still in Love with You; I'm Glad You're Mine; Love and Happiness;
What a Wonderful Thing Love Is; Simply Beautiful; Oh, Pretty
Woman; For the Good Times; Look What You Done for Me; One
of Those Good Old Days. CALL ME (4/73): _Call Me; Have You_
Been Making Out OK; Stand Up; I'm So Lonesome I Could Cry;
Your Love Is Like the Morning Sun; Here I Am; Funny How Time
Slips Away; You Ought to Be with Me; Jesus Is Waiting. LIVIN'
FOR YOU (11/73): _Living for You; Home Again; Free at Last;_
Let's Get Married; So Good to Be Here; My Sixteen; Unchained
Melody; My God Is Real; Beware. AL GREEN EXPLORES
YOUR MIND (10/74): _Sha-La-La; Take Me to the River; God_

*Blessed Our Love; The City; One Nite Stand; I'm Hooked on You;
Stay with Me Forever; Hangin' On; School Days.* GREATEST
HITS (2/75): *Tired of Being Alone; Call Me; I'm Still in Love with
You; Here I Am; How Can You Mend a Broken Heart; Let's Stay
Together; I Can't Get Next to You; You Ought to Be with Me;
Look What You Done for Me; Let's Get Married.* AL GREEN IS
LOVE (10/75): *Love; Rhymes; The Love Sermon; There Is Love;
Could I Be the One; Love Ritual; I Didn't Know; Oh Me, Oh My;
I Gotta Be More; I Wish You Were Here.* FULL OF FIRE (2/76):
*Glory Glory; That's the Way It Is; Always; There's No Way; I'd
Fly Away; Full of Fire; Together Again; Soon As I Get Home; Let
It Shine.*

Singles/*I Want to Hold Your Hand/What Am I Gonna Do* (4/69);
One Woman/Tomorrow's Dreams (6/69); *You Say It/Gotta Find a
New World* (12/69); *Mister Man/Right Now, Right Now* (5/70);
Drivin' Wheel/True Love (2/71); *Tired of Being Alone/Get Back,
Baby* (7/71); *Let's Stay Together/Tomorrow's Dream* (10/71);
Look What You Done for Me/La-La For You (4/72); *I'm Still in
Love with You/Old Time Lovin'* (6/72); *You Ought to Be with
Me/What Is This Feeling?* (9/72); *Call Me/What a Wonderful
Thing Love Is* (1/73); *Here I Am/I'm Glad You're Mine* (6/73);
Livin' for You/It Ain't No Fun to Me (11/73); *Let's Get
Married/So Good to Be Here* (3/74); *Sha-La-La/School Days*
(9/74); *Love/I Wish You Were Here* (2/75); *Oh Me, Oh
My/Strong As Death* (6/75); *Full of Fire/Could I Be the Way*
(10/75); *Let It Shine/There's No Way* (4/76); *Keep Me
Cryin'/There Is Love* (9/76); *I Tried to Tell Myself/Something*
(1/77); *Love and Happiness/Glory, Glory* (6/77).

GRIN/*Nils Lofgrin (vocals, guitar), Bob Gordon (bass, vocals), Bob
Berberich (drums, vocals).*
At seventeen, Nils Lofgrin was playing guitar behind Neil Young
and Crazy Horse. By the time he was eighteen, his band, Grin,
was signed to a label and his career seemed to be on the upswing.
Appearances proved deceiving, however, and this cheerful entourage from Washington, D.C., bit the dust after three albums
filled with melodic, joyful rockers and sweet-as-candy ballads.
The first, *1+1,* is considered one of Lofgrin's finest works (a real
cult artist, this Nils), and the second and third proved interesting
as well. Playing sleezoid clubs and bottom-billed concert dates got

to the band and, in 1973, Lofgrin departed to play with Neil Young on tour. Subsequently he signed with A&M records as a solo artist.

Albums/GRIN (3/71): *See What a Love Can Do; Everybody's Missin' the Sun; 18-Faced Lover; Outlaw; We All Sung Together; If I Were a Song; Take You to the Movies Tonight; Direction; Pioneer Mary; Open Wide; I Had Too Much.* 1+1 (11/71): *White Lies; Please Don't Hide; Slippery Fingers; Moon Tears; End Unkind; Sometimes; Just a Number; Hi, Hello Home; Just a Poem; Soft Fun.* ALL OUT (12/72): *Sad Letter; Heavy Chevy; Don't Be Long; Love Again; She Ain't Right; Love or Else; Ain't Love Nice; Heart on Fire; Rusty Gun.* GONE CRAZY (11/73): *You're the Weight; Boy & Girl; What About Me; One More Time; True Thrill; Beggar's Day; Nightmare; Believe; Ain't for Free.* THE BEST OF GRIN (10/76): *Like Rain; White Lies; Direction; Moon Tears; See What a Love Can Do; Take You to the Movies Tonight; Sad Letter; Heavy Chevy; Love or Else; We All Sung Together.*

Singles/*We All Sung Together/See What a Love Can Do* (9/70); *Like Rain/See What a Love Can Do* (3/71); *If I Were a Song/See What a Love Can Do* (4/71); *White Lies/Just to Have You* (12/71); *End Unknown/Slippery Fingers* (4/72); *Ain't Love Nice/Love or Else* (2/73).

GROUPIES/In the kindest terminology, groupies are the ultimate in fandom—selfless young men and women who give their all (constantly) for and, more often than not, *to* the rock star of their choice for the sheer hedonistic pleasure of it and the right to brag about it the following day. *Classic Groupie of the Sixties Award:* To the young lady who calmly wore one of Jimi Hendrix's actual guitar strings around her neck, supposedly awarded to her for valor above and beyond etc., etc., etc. Only one problem, the string was taken from a bass guitar. Hendrix played lead.

THE GUESS WHO/*Burton Cummings (vocals, keyboards), Don McDougall (guitar), Billy Wallace (bass), Domenic Trojano (guitar), Garry Paterson (drums).*
If ever there was a band who needed an ACLU lawyer to defend them from overt discrimination, it was the Guess Who. The band first came to light in the late sixties, in the days when a good rock band wasn't supposed to have catchy hit singles. (Remember? If

you did cop out and have an AM radio hit, you were supposed to have a longer, FM radio version on your album. If you didn't, they took away your mustache or something equally as important.) The Guess did, of course, have hit singles—lots of them. As a result, they just never caught on with the "serious" music crowd. (Ya know, "Not tonight Monique, I'm reading *Rolling Stone.*")

The band actually started off north of the border in the early sixties when Randy Bachman and Chad Allan split from a local outfit and formed what turned out to be the first Guess Who. Allan left in 1965 and Bachman became the leader of the pack; the pack being Garry Paterson, Burton Cummings and Jim Cale. Chunky Cummings took over the lead vocal spot and did his best to be a teen heart throb (the angry young counter-culture cat). Bachman, meanwhile, played his butt off on guitar. The combination clicked and after a dozen or so Canadian singles, they finally struck paydirt with *These Eyes.*

RCA latched onto the Guess Who in 1969 and the hits started coming. By 1970, however, Bachman (a Mormon) decided that the grinding wheel existence of road life just wasn't his cup of tea. A feud developed within the ranks, resulting in both bad feelings and Bachman leaving to start a group called Brave Belt (which eventually evolved into Bachman Turner Overdrive). Two Canadian guitarists, Kurt Winter and Greg Kewkiw joined the band and Cummings assumed leadership. This new lineup worked for a short period, but by 1972, the Guess Who was in a shaky position careerwise. Their image still wasn't all that respectable at the FM radio level and the band was having trouble coming up with those dyno-mite-hit-bound-smash-widda-bullet tunes. At this point, Leskiw and bassist Jim took a walk and Don McDougall and Billy Wallace entered the picture.

The Guess Who still didn't crank 'em out like in days of yore and, soon, McDougall was out and James Gang pinch-hitter Domenic Trojano was in. At this point, the group assumed nearly a parody stance, going through the motions; playing old tunes listlessly and new compositions that could only be termed "mild." During this low point, Cummings and crew had to swallow the earthshattering beginnings of Bachman-Turner; watching their old comrade rocket to the top of the charts with riff-rocking songs not too far removed from the Guess Who's earlier *American Woman,* a song penned by Bachman.

Billy Wallace left the band in 1975 and the rest of the troupe simply called it quits. Burton Cummings has gone on to a fairly successful solo career and Bachman-Turner-Overdrive is still cranking out those head-bashing anthems. And the Guess Who? Well, they've left behind a legacy of gold singles, tons of them, but little else. Unlike most of their peers of the late sixties and early seventies, they never made an impression on the concert-going public. They started off and wound up as being a uniquely faceless band.

Albums/WHEATFIELD SOUL (4/69): *These Eyes; Pink Wine Sparkles in the Glass; I Found Her in a Star; Friends of Mine; When You Touch Me; A Wednesday in Your Garden; Lightfoot; Love and a Yellow Rose; Maple Fudge; We're Coming to Dinner.* CANNED WHEAT (9/69): *Laughing; No Time; Minstral Boy; 6 AM or Nearer; Undun; Old Joe; Key; Fair Warning; A Dropping Pin.* AMERICAN WOMAN (1/70): *No Time; American Woman; Talisman; No Sugar Tonight; New Mother Nature; 969; When Friends Fall Out; 8:1; Proper Stranger; Humpty's Blues.* SHARE THE LAND (10/70): *Bus Rider; Do You Miss Me Darlin?; Hand Me Down World; More for You Joe; Share the Land; Hang on to Your Life; Coming down off the Money Bug; Song of the Dog; Three More Days.* THE BEST OF THE GUESS WHO (1971): *These Eyes; Laughing; Undun; No Time; American Woman; No Sugar Tonight; New Mother Nature; Hand Me down World; Bus Rider; Do You Miss Me Darlin?; Hang on to Your Life; Bus Rider; Share the Land.* SO LONG BANNATYNE (8/71): *Rain Dance; Pain Train; Goin' a Little Crazy; Fiddlin'; One Divided; She Might Have Been a Nice Girl; Grey Day; Sour Suite; Life in the Blood Stream; One Man Army.* ROCKIN' (3/72): *Heartbroken Bopper; Guns, Guns, Guns; Get Your Ribbons Out; Running Bear; Hi Rockers; Herbert's a Loser; Smoke Big Factory; Arrivarderci Girl; Your Nashville Sneakers.* ARTIFICIAL PARADISE (9/72): *Bye Bye Babe; Samantha's Living Room; Rock and Roller Steam; Follow Your Daughters Home; Those Show Biz Shoes; All Hashed Out; Orly; Lost and Found Town; Hamba Gahle-Usalang Gahle; The Watcher.* LIVE AT THE PARAMOUNT (1/73): *Albert Flasher; New Mother Nature; Glace Bay Blues; Runnin' back to*

Saskatoon; Pain Train; American Woman; Truckin' off across the Sky. NUMBER TEN (7/73): *Take it off My Shoulders; Musicione; Glamour Boy; Miss Frizzy; Cardboard Empire; Lie Down; Just Let Me Sing; Self Pity.* GREATEST HITS VOL. II (11/73): *Broken down World; Albert Flasher; Rain Dance; Sour Suite; Guns, Guns, Guns; Heartbroken Bopper; Orly; Life in the Bloodstream; Running Back to Saskatoon; Follow Your Daughters Home.* ROADFOOD (4/74): *Star Baby; Attilla's Blues; Straight Out; Don't You Want Me; One Way Road to Hell; Clap for the Wolfman; Pleasin' for a Reason; Roadfood; Ballad of the Last Five Years.* FLAVORS (9/74): *Dancin' Fool; Hoe Down Time; Nobody Knows His Name; Diggin' Yourself; Seems Like I Can't Live without You; Dirty Eye; Loves Me Like a Brother; Long Gone.* POWER IN THE MUSIC (6/75): *Down and out Woman; Women; When the Band Was Singin' Shakin' All Over; Dreams; Rich World-Poor World; Shopping Bag Lady; Coors for Sunday; Rosanne; Power in the Music.* THE WAY THEY WERE (5/76): *Silver Bird; Species Hawk; Miss Frizzy; The Answer; Take the Long Way Home; Palmyra; other titles.*

Singles/*These Eyes*/*Lightfoot* (1/69); *Laughing*/*Undun* (6/69); *No Time*/*Proper Stranger* (11/69); *American Woman*/*No Sugar Tonight* (3/70); *Hand Me Down World*/*Runnin' Down the Street* (6/70); *Laughin'*/*Undun* (12/70); *These Eyes*/*No Time* (12/70); *Hang on to Your Life*/*Do You Miss Me Darlin?* (1/71): *Albert Flasher*/*Broker* (3/71); *Rain Dance*/*One Divided* (7/71); *Sour Suite*/*Life in the Bloodstream* (11/71); *Heartbroken Bopper; Arriverderci Girl* (2/72); *Guns, Guns, Guns* (5/72); *Follow Your Daughters Home*/*Bye Bye Baby* (12/72); *Glamour Boy*/*Lie Down* (5/73); *Star Baby*/*Musicione* (1/74); *Clap for the Wolfman*/*Roadfood* (6/74); *Dancin' Fool* (11/74); *New World in the Morning*/*Rosanne* (7/75); *Silver Bird*/*Runnin' Down the Street* (6/76).

JO JO GUNNE/*Jay Ferguson (vocals, keyboards), Mark Andes (bass, vocals), Matt Andes (guitar, vocals), Curly Smith (drums).*
After leaving the much-overlooked but highly touted Spirit in 1971, Jay Ferguson and Mark Andes were anxious to form a group of their own—a group that would, perhaps, suceed in commercial areas where Spirit had failed to conquer. The resulting band, Jo Jo Gunne, was an excellent hard-rock gathering. Un-

fortunately, it too failed to spark the masses . . . although the critics fell head over heels for the foursome's carefree teeth-gnashing sound.

After some success with their first LP, Jo Jo Gunne began shifting membership. Mark Andes departed, to be replaced by Jim Randell. Brother Matt left the band two years later, replaced by John Staehely, a guitarist who had entered Spirit during its eleventh hour as well. After four albums, the band called it quits, with the Andes brothers joining Spirit for an album, Ferguson going solo, and Curly Smith joining the short-lived Ian Hunter Overnight Angels touring band.

Albums/JO JO GUNNE (1/72): *Run Run Run; Shake That Fat; Babylon; I Make Love; Barstow Blue Eyes; 99 Days; Academy Award; Take It Easy; Flying Home.* BITE DOWN HARD (2/73): *Ready Freddy; Roll over Me; 60 Minutes to Go; Rock around the Symbol; Broken-Down Man; Special Situations; Take Me Down Easy; Wait a Lifetime; Rhoda.* JUMPIN' THE GUNNE (11/73): *Neon City; I Wanna Love You; other titles.* SO . . . WHERE'S THE SHOW? (11/74): *Where Is the Show?; I'm Your Shoe; Single Man; She Said Alright; S&M Blvd.; Falling Angel; Big, Busted Bombshell from Bermuda; Into My Life; Around the World.*

Singles/*Take It Easy/Run Run Run* (2/72); *Shake That Fat/I Make Love* (7/72); *Take Me Down Easy/Rock around the Symbol* (7/73); *I Wanna Love You/Neon City* (1/74).

ARLO GUTHRIE/Son of folksinging legend Woody Guthrie, Arlo Guthrie was born in Coney Island, New York, and lived a decidedly urban lifestyle before embarking on a bluegrass-tinged career similar to his father's. Nineteen sixty-seven saw Arlo catapulted into the limelight with the epic recording of *Alice's Restaurant,* a monumental tale of black humor-laced woe based on a true experience. Guthrie's puckish delivery and wide-eye mannerisms made him an "in-concert" crowd pleaser as well as a recording star. The song was subsequently made into a motion picture in 1970 and starred Arlo, displaying his remarkable versatility as both a singer-songwriter and a deft comedian.

During the seventies, Arlo has maintained a somewhat low profile in musical circles, emerging every now and then with a tour linked to a release of a new hit album *(HOBO'S LULLABY, ARLO GUTHRIE)* or a top-tenning single *(City of New Orleans).*

A genius at both penning slice-of-life song portraits and interpreting the works of other composers, Guthrie stands as being one of the few remaining great troubadours in America.

Albums/ALICE'S RESTAURANT (9/67): *Alice's Restaurant Massacre; Chilling of the Evening; Ring-around-a-Rosy Rag; Now and Then; I'm Going Home; Motorcycle Song; Highway in the Wind.* ARLO (10/68): *The Motorcycle Song; Wouldn't You Believe It; Try Me One More Time; John Looked Down; Mediation (Wave upon Wave); Standing at the Threshold; The Pause of Mr. Claus.* RUNNING DOWN THE ROAD (9/69): *Oklahoma Hello; Every Hand in the Lord; Creole Belle; Oh, in the Morning; Wheel of Fortune; Coming into Los Angeles; Stealin'; My Front Pages; Running Down the Road; Living in the Country.* WASHINGTON COUNTY (8/70): *Fence Post Blues; Gabriel's Mother's Hiway Ballad #16 Blues; Washington County; Lay Down, Little Doggies; Valley to Pray; I Could Be Singing; If You Would Just Drop By; Percy's Song; I Want to Be Around.* HOBO'S LULLABY (5/72): *Anytime; The City of New Orleans; Lightning Bar Blues; Shackles and Chains; 1913 Massacre; Somebody Turned On the Light; Ukelele Lady; When the Ship Comes In; Mapleview (20%) Rag; Days Are Short; Hobo's Lullaby.* LAST OF THE BROOKLYN COWBOYS (3/73): *Farewell, Davy; This Troubled Mind of Mine; Week on the Rag; Miss the Mississippi and You; Lovesick Blues; Uncle Jeff; Gates of Eden; Last Train; Cowboy Song; Sailor's Bonnett; Cooper's Lament; Ramblin' Round.* ARLO GUTHRIE (5/74): *Bling Blang; Presidential Rag; Won't Be Long; Deportees; Nostalgia Rag; When the Cactus Is in Bloom; Go Down, Moses; Children of Abraham; Me and My Goose; Hard Times; Last to Leave.* AMIGO (8/76): *Guabi Guabi; Darkest Hour; Massachusetts; Victor Jara; Patriot's Dream; Grocery Blues; Walking Song; My Love; Manzanillo Bay; Ocean Crossing; Connection.* GREATEST HITS (11/77): *Alice's Restaurant Massacre; Gabriel's Mother's Hiway Ballad #16 Blues; Cooper's Lament; Motorcycle; Coming into Los Angeles; Last Train; City of New Orleans; Darkest Hour; Last to Leave.*

Singles/*Motorcycle Song/Now and Then* (9/67); *Motorcycle Song (Parts I and II) (11/68); Alice's Rock and Roll Restaurant* (11/69); *Valley to Pray/Gabriel's Mother's Hiway Ballad #16 Blues* (9/70); *The Ballad of Tricky Fred/Shackles and Chains* (2/71); *The City of New Orleans/Days Are Short* (6/72); *Cooper's Lament/Ukelele*

Lady (12/72); *Gypsy Davy/Week on the Rag* (5/73); *Presidential Rag/Nostalgia Rag* (6/74); *Patriot's Dream/Ocean Crossing* (6/76); *Guabi /Grocery Blues* (11/76); *Massachusetts/My Love* (3/77).

BILL HALEY/Detroit-born Bill Haley's band, the Comets, was originally a country band (the Saddlemen) and later what must have been the first white instrumental rhythm and blues band. Bill Haley himself was probably the first white face on what was still, in 1954, a basically black rock and roll scene. He recorded Jimmy DeKnight's *Rock around the Clock* during that year but the record never took off. Then, a whole year later, it turned up again as the theme song of the film *The Blackboard Jungle,* and a star was born. *Rock around the Clock,* in the context of the film, took on a whole new meaning. It became the first song to have a special, secret, defiant meaning for teenagers only. It was the first inkling white teenagers had that they might be a force to be reckoned with, in numbers alone. If there could be one song, there could be others; there could be a whole world of songs, and then, a whole world.

Unwittingly, Bill Haley, basically a down-home sort, had opened up a Pandora's box of acne-scarred emotion. He was always apologizing for the social monster he had created. Musically, however, he was proud. Proud that as far back as 1951 (with songs like *Crazy Mama)* he was combining R&B, country and western, and pop in what was to become one of the basic rock and roll sounds. He always said that he had developed rock and roll, while Alan Freed, the disc jockey, had only *named* it and *exploited* it.

Haley and his Comets continued to soar during the fifties with such tunes as *Shake, Rattle and Roll* and *See You Later, Alligator.* As the sound of rock progressed in the late fifties, however, Haley and his crew's two-dimensional, unison-vocaled approach took a back-seat position to syrupy, nasal, harmonied teen epics. Haley's comet fizzled as quickly as it had exploded. His career was destined to smolder anew during the rock-and-roll-revival period of the late sixties and early seventies.

Albums/BILL HALEY AND HIS COMETS: *Caldonia; ABC Rock; Fool Such As I; Dragon Rock; Walkin' Beat, seven other titles.* ROCK AND ROLL STAGE SHOW: *Calling All Comets;*

Rockin' through the Rye; Hook, Line and Sinker; Rudy's Rock; Rocking Little Tune; Hide and Seek; Choo Choo Ch'Boogie; Blue Comet Blues; Hey Then, There Now; Goofin' Around; Hot Dog Buddy Buddy; Tonight's the Night. ROCK AROUND THE CLOCK (12/55): *Razzle-Dazzle; Two Hound Dogs; Burn That Candle; Rock-a-Beatin' Boogie; Rock around the Clock; Shake, Rattle and Roll; Thirteen Women; ABC Boogie; Dim, Dim the Lights; Happy Baby; Birth of the Boogie; Mambo Rock.* ROCKIN' THE JOINT: *New Rock the Joint; Move It On Over; It's a Sin; Rock Lommond; How Many; Beak Speaks; See You Later, Alligator; Forty Cups of Coffee; Saints Rock and Roll; Sway with Me; Burn That Candle; Rip It Up.* GREATEST HITS (6/68): *Rock around the Clock; Thirteen Women; See You Later, Alligator; Sway with Me; Choo Choo Ch'Boogie; Razzle-Dazzle; Burn That Candle; Shake, Rattle and Roll; Skinny Minnie; Saints Rock 'n' Roll; Joe's Song.* GOLDEN HITS (1972): *Rock around the Clock Burn That Candle; Forty Cups of Coffee; Two Hound Dogs; Tonight's the Night; Dim, Dim the Lights; See You Later, Alligator; R-O-C-K; Skinny Minnie; Razzle-Dazzle; ABC Boogie; Shake, Rattle and Roll; Don't Knock the Rock; Rip It Up; (You Hit the Wrong Note) Billy Goat; Rockin' Rollin' Rover; Rock-a-Beatin' Boogie; Thirteen Women; Saints Rock 'n' Roll; Corrine, Corrina; Calling All Comets; Rockin' thru the Rye.*

Singles/*Crazy Man, Crazy* (5/53); *Shake, Rattle and Roll* (7/54); *Dim, Dim the Lights* (10/54); *Mambo Rock* (2/55); *Birth of the Boogie* (3/55); *Rock around the Clock* (4/55); *Razzle-Dazzle/Two Hound Dogs* (7/55); *Burn That Candle/Rock-a-Beatin' Boogie* (9/55); *See You Later, Alligator* (12/55); *R-O-C-K/Saints Rock 'n' Roll* (3/56); *Hot Dog Buddy Buddy/Rockin' through the Rye* (5/56); *Rip It Up/Teenager's Mother* (7/56); *Rudy's Rock* (10/56); *Forty Cups of Coffee* (3/57); *(You Hit the Wrong Note) Billy Goat* (5/57); *Skinny Minnie* (3/58); *Lean Jean* (8/58); *Joey's Song* (10/59); *Skokiaan* (1/60).

HALL AND OATES/Two modern-day saints of the church of blue-eyed soul, Daryl Hall and John Oates are a twosome who worked nearly a decade together before hitting it big with their 1975 smash single, *Sara Smile.* The two met in Philadelphia where, in 1967, Hall was picking up work at various soul sessions at Sigma Sound and Oates was studying journalism. The two began writing songs together. Hall, however, was momentarily sidetracked with the one-album band Gulliver (the semi-whimp-rock Elektra band also featured Tim Moore on guitar). Once that group folded, Hall and Oates joined forces as songwriter-performers full time.

After gigging around Philly for a while, they were spotted and signed to Atlantic Records. A series of critically acclaimed albums ensued but when the hits didn't start coming, the band and the label parted ways. A short hop to RCA proved fruitful for the duo. *Sara Smile* was the first of a series of hit singles for the team.

Albums/WHOLE OATS (10/72): *I'm Sorry; All Our Love; Georgie; Fall in Philadelphia; Waterwheel; Lazyman; Goodnight and Goodmorning; They Needed Each Other; Southeast City Window; Thank You For . . .; Lilly (Are You Happy).* ABANDONED LUNCHEONETTE (10/73): *When the Morning Comes; Had I Known You Better Then; Las Vegas Turnaround (The Stewardess Song); She's Gone; I'm Just a Kid (Don't Make Me Feel Like a Man); Abandoned Luncheonette; Lady Rain; Laughing Boy; Everytime I Look at You.* WAR BABIES (9/74): *Can't Stop the Music (He Played It Much Too Long); Is It a Star; Beanie G. and the Rose Tattoo; You're Much Too Soon; 70's Scenario; War Baby Son of Zorro; I'm Watching You (A Mutant Romance); Better Watch Your Back; Screaming through December; Johnny Gore and the "C" Eaters.* HALL AND OATES (8/75): *Camellia; Sara Smile; Alone Too Long; Out of Me, Out of You; Nothing at All; Gino (The Manager); (You Know) It Doesn't Matter Anymore; Ennui on the Mountain; Grounds for Separation; Soldering.* BIGGER THAN BOTH OF US (8/76): *Rich Girl; Kerry; Crazy Eyes; Back Together Again; Do What You Want, Be What You Are; London, Luck and Love; Room to Breathe; Falling; You'll Never Learn.* NO GOODBYES (2/77): *It's Uncanny; I Want to Know You for a Long Time; Can't Stop the Music (He Played It Much Too Long); Love You Like a Brother; Las Vegas Turnaround (The Stewardess Song); She's Gone; Lilly (Are You Happy); When the Morning Comes; Beanie G. and the Rose Tattoo.* BEAUTY ON A BACK STREET (8/77); *Don't Change; Why Do Lovers Break Each Other's Heart?; You Must Be Good for Something; Love Hurts (Love Heals); The Emptiness; Bigger Than Both of Us; Bad Habits and Infections; Winged Bull; The Girl Who Used to Be.*

Singles/*Goodnight and Good Morning/All Our Love* (11/72); *I'm Sorry/Lilly (Are You Happy)* (2/73); *She's Gone/I'm Just A Kid* (11/73); *When the Morning Comes/Lady Rain* (4/74); *Can't Stop the Music/70's Scenerio* (12/74); *She's Gone/I'm Just a Kid* (8/75); *Camellia/Ennui on the Mountain* (8/75); *Alone Too Long/Nothing at All* (10/75); *Rich Girl* (6/76); *She's Gone/When the Morning Comes* (8/76); *Do What You Want, Be What You Are/You'll Never Learn* (10/76); *Back Together Again/Room to Breathe* (4/77).

HARD ROCK/Originally coined to describe the totally joyous and uncomplicated antics of Elvis Presley and Bill Haley in the fifties, the term "hard rock" later resurfaced in the late sixties to apply to such raucous bands as Spooky Tooth and Free who didn't really fit into the psychedelic area and were not deranged enough for heavy metal. The term has survived since that time and is today often applied to such artists as Bob Seger and Ted Nugent.

GEORGE HARRISON/Ex-Beatle George Harrison's solo career has been one fraught with erraticism. Before the Beatles' split-up, Harrison began dabbling with outside projects via *WONDER-WALL* (a soundtrack album) and the avant-garde *ELEC-TRONIC SOUNDS*. Both were tremendous commercial failures. After the demise of the Beatles, the resourceful guitarist emerged with his finest recording to date, the triple album *ALL THINGS MUST PASS*. Brimming with overt religious lyricism, uplifting moralizing, and hard-as-nails guitar work, the album made its way into the top ten, spawning Harrison's biggest single ever, *My Sweet Lord*. Several music critics at the time pointed out the similarities between Harrison's tune and the old Chiffon's ditty, *He's So Fine*—a point that was not lost on the songwriter's publisher, Bright Music, but which would not come to light until 1976.

Nineteen seventy's *ALL THINGS MUST PASS* kept Harrison's fans happy until 1972's release of *THE CONCERT FOR BANGLA DESH,* which featured George and a host of his musical cronies (Ravi Shankar, Leon Russell, Badfinger, and Ringo Starr) in a live set recorded during 1971's epic concert for famine victims in Bangladesh, organized by George and held in Madison Square Garden.

If *BANGLA DESH* proved George an altruist first class, 1973's

LIVING IN THE MATERIAL WORLD proved him a solo musician in trouble. With *MATERIAL WORLD* and *DARK HORSE,* George fell victim to a fickle audience, a barrage of personal problems, and a lack of positive inspiration. Singles failed to get past the middle of the charts, Harrison's wife, Patti, left with close friend Eric Clapton, and a Harrison tour of the United States proved a bona fide disaster, with the shaky star fighting off hoarseness and audience boredom simultaneously.

In 1974, Harrison founded his own label, Dark Horse. In the States, it was distributed by A&M. Unfortunately, George was distributed by Capitol, and the guitar genius found himself working in one capacity or another for two very different companies. During this hectic period, the spectre of *My Sweet Lord* began to rear its head and, within eighteen months, George would find himself in court.

Meanwhile, the Dark Horse releases on A&M proved to be commercial duds, in spite of Harrison's endorsements. Harrison's prize band, Splinter, fared miserably stateside although they charted in the United Kingdom. In 1976, George left Capitol and opted for Dark Horse Records. In a move which rankled the loyal following at A&M, Harrison also took his entire label operation to the Warner Brothers family. While A&M fumed, Capitol acted quickly to cull the best of George Harrison for a quick post-mortem release.

Harrison, meanwhile, was not doing well in his battle with Bright over who really wrote *My Sweet Lord.* In the end, George was found guilty of lifting three of the song's notes, although not "intentionally." In 1977, the case still dragged on. The verdict, initially delivered in 1976, inspired Harrison to write one of his wittiest and certainly most commercial songs since *My Sweet Lord,* entitled *This Song* (boasting the lyrics "This song . . . has nothing Bright about it"). The single sold moderately well.

Despite his helter-skelter scrambling for a sane stance, both musically and personally, Harrison has retained his unique flare for composing and his intrinsic sense of humor. His antics with various members of the British comedy troupe Monty Python's Flying Circus are near legend, and a series of Python commercials touting a new Harrison album with the dismal exclamation "Oh, no, not *him* again!" are rock promotion classics.

Albums/WONDERWALL (12/68): *Microbes; Red Lady Too;*

*Tabla and Pacavaj; In the Park; Drilling a Home; Guru Vandana;
Greasy Legs; Dream Scene; Ski-ing and Gat Kirwani; Party
Seacombe; Love Scene; Crying; Cowboy; Museum; Fantasy Se-
quins; Glass Box; On the Bed; Wonderwall to Be Hear; Singing
Om.* ELECTRONIC SOUND (5/69): *Under the Mersey Wall; No
Time or Space.* ALL THINGS MUST PASS (11/70): *I'd Have
You Anytime; My Sweet Lord; Wah-Wah; Isn't It a Pity (Versions
One and Two); What Is Life; If Not for You; Behind That Locked
Door; Let It Down; Run of the Mill; Beware of Darkness; Apple
Scruffs; Ballad of Sir Frankie Crisp (Let It Roll); Awaiting on You;
All Things Must Pass; I Dig Love; Art of Dying; Hear Me Lord;
Out of the Blues; Congratulations; Plug Me In; I Remember Jeep;
Thanks for the Pepperoni.* THE CONCERT FOR BANGLA
DESH (12/71): *Introduction; Bangla Dhun; Wah-Wah; My Sweet
Lord; Awaiting You All; That's the Way God Planned It; It Don't
Come Easy; Beware of Darkness; Intro; While My Guitar Gently
Weeps; Jumpin' Jack Flash; Youngblood; Here Comes the Sun; A
Hard Rain's Gonna Fall; It Takes a Lot to Laugh, It Takes a Train
to Cry; Blowin' in the Wind; Mr. Tambourine Man; Just Like a
Woman; Something; Bangla Desh.* LIVING IN THE MATERI-
AL WORLD (5/73): *Give Me Love (Give Me Peace on Earth); Sue
Me, Sue You Blues; The Light That Had Lighted the World; Don't
Let Me Wait Too Long; Who Can See It; Living in the Material
World; The Lord Loves the One (That Loves the Lord); Be Here
Now; Try Some Buy Some; The Day the World Gets Round; That
Is All.* DARK HORSE (12/74): *Hari's on Tour; Express; Simply
Shady; So Sad (No Love of His Own); Dark Horse; Maya Love;
Bye Bye, Love; Ding Dong, Ding Dong; Far East Man; It Is He
(Jai Sri Krishna); (You Know That I Love You).* EXTRA TEX-
TURE (9/75): *You; The Answer's at the End; This Guitar (Can't
Keep from Crying); Ooh Baby (You Know That I Love You); World
of Stone; A Bit More of You; Tired of Midnight Blue; Grey Cloud
Lies; His Name is Legs (Ladies and Gentlemen).* THE BEST OF
GEORGE HARRISON (11/76): *Something; If I Need Someone;
Here Comes the Sun; Taxman; Think for Yourself; For You Blue;
While My Guitar Gentle Weeps; My Sweet Lord; Give Me Love
(Give Me Peace on Earth); You; Bangla Desh; Dark Horse; What Is
Life.* 33⅓ (12/76): *Woman Don't You Cry for Me; Dear One;
Beautiful Girl; This Song; See Yourself; It's What You Value; True
Love; Pure Smokey; Crackerbox Palace; Learning How to Love.*

Singles/*My Sweet Lord/Isn't It a Pity?* (11/70); *What Is Life/Apple Scruffs* (2/71); *Bangla Desh/Deep Blue* (7/71); *Give Me Love (Give Me Peace on Earth)/Miss O'Dell* (5/73); *Dark Horse/I Don't Care Anymore* (11/74); *Ding Dong, Ding Dong/Hari's on Tour* (12/74); *You/World of Stone* (9/75); *This Guitar (Can't Keep from Crying)/Maya Love* (12/75); *This Song/Learning How to Love You* (11/76); *Crackerbox Palace/Beautiful Girl* (12/76).

HEAD MUSIC/During the late sixties, in its most common usage, head music was defined as music that enhanced the marijuana experience—gentle, soothing, calm, but the same time with enough happening to engage heightened perceptions. A "head's" (drug user's) idea of "head music" was any cut on *SERGEANT PEPPER*. A newspaper reporter's idea of "head music" was the Association's *Along Comes Mary*. As soon as the media found out about the possible connection between rock music and drugs, any and all songs were accused of being "head" inspired. Most remarkable candidate as head music: *Puff, the Magic Dragon.*

HEAVY METAL/Guitar-oriented rock, the logical successor to hard rock. Heavy metal, with its brash, ringing, distorted guitar sounds really came into being during the late sixties with the emergence of such bands as Led Zepplin and, in the seventies, Deep Purple. The phrase began dying out in '75–'76 when heavy-metal bands either started moving on to more sophisticated territory or splintering up under the weight.

JIMI HENDRIX/To a lot of rock fans during the nineteen sixties, Jimi Hendrix was an electric god. James Marshall Hendrix virtually invented a school of rock, harnessing all the furies of feedback, distortion, wah-wah pedals, and fuzz boxes into a cohesive, extraterrestrial sound. His infectious brand of R&B-laden psychedelia became a global phenomenon. He was probably the only performer in rock and roll history to turn the *Star-Spangled Banner* into a counterculture anthem. Played at Woodstock, the song featured rockets bursting, shells howling, and the dawn breaking . . . all courtesy of Jimi's magical guitar.

Born in Seattle, Washington, Hendrix first bumped into the blues while in his teens, listening to the popular records of the day. A stint in the paratroopers in the early sixties brought him in touch with bassist Billy Cox, who would later play with Jimi in one of his last bands. Discharged because of a back injury in 1963, Hendrix began the hand-to-mouth life of a session guitarist, playing for everyone and anyone, including Little Richard, Jackie Wilson, and the Isley Brothers. Playing under the name of Jimmy James, he sought (and got) a back-up spot with Curtis Knight's band.

While playing at the Cafe What in Greenwich Village, Hendrix was spotted by Animal Chas Chandler who was, at that point, leaving his performing days behind for a career in management. He quickly snatched Hendrix up and brought him to England where a career was fashioned for the talented black guitarist in the lily-white world of British rock. Guitarist Noel Redding was auditioned and given the chore of bassist for Jimi's troupe and Mitch Mitchell was brought in on drums. The Jimi Hendrix Experience was formed.

The Experience's success in the United Kingdom was instantaneous. Signed to Track records, they broke the top ten with their first single, *Hey Joe*. Rock musicians such as Eric Clapton and Peter Townsend rallied behind the cosmic blues man, increasing his stature credibility-wise. Paul McCartney brought Jimi to the attention of the powers-that-be at the Monterey Pop Festival in 1967 and the Experience made their United States debut (captured on film) in a fairly explosive manner. After stunning the audience with his guitar gymnastics for an entire spaced-out set, Hendrix set his guitar on fire and did it in onstage while Mitchell and Redding roared onward and upward on drums and bass. The crowd went wild. The media coverage was historic. Hendrix's time was at hand.

His first concert tour made him a star in the States, although he really didn't get a chance to play. Booked as an opening act for the Monkees, he was subsequently yanked off the bill when outraged mothers complained about the sexual overtones of his stage act. From that point onward, Hendrix was a living legend. His albums got spacier and spacier and his fandom mushroomed. By the time his third album, *ELECTRIC LADYLAND,* appeared, it was clear that there was trouble afoot in Hendrix's musical realm.

The cover art of the double LP had to be changed for stateside audiences. A fairly surreal scene populated by a dozen or so naked women holding a photo of Hendrix was altered drastically in an attempt to placate the U.S. audience. In the end, the cover design was scrapped, replaced by a two-year-old color photo of the Experience and a photo of Jimi himself. In addition, Hendrix was getting tired of his reputation as a psychedelic guitar-juggler. He wanted to be known as a musician. Period.

A fight with Noel Redding landed him in jail. His jams with other musicians pleased him more than his recording with his band. In 1969, he broke up the Experience, resurfacing that summer at the Newport Jazz Festival and Woodstock with a new trio consisting of Mitchell and buddy Billy Cox. That entourage proved short-lived and on New Year's Eve of that year he unveiled his Band of Gypsies at the Fillmore East—his first black rock band, consisting of Cox and screaming drummer Buddy Miles. An album of that evening's songs was released, much to Hendrix's dismay. At the end of that concert set, he put his guitar aside and walked offstage disgusted.

Hendrix was undergoing a rough time. His music was a course of frustration. A drug bust in 1969 led to constant run-ins with local authorities. Beginning his next album, *CRY OF LOVE,* he reverted to the Cox and Mitchell lineup. Abandoning much of his psychedelic trappings for plain old hard R&B, Hendrix was beginning to soar once more. In August, however, he appeared a bit out of it during a concert set at the Isle of Wight Festival. On September 18 of that year, he died in London. He died in his sleep, choking on vomit caused by a barbiturate overdose.

Following his death, Hendrix's career began a fairly ghoulish second stage. Repackages, bootlegs, and re-repackages were produced. One of the most bizarre occurrences in terms of long-players was the discovery of over 1,000 hours of Hendrix material by producer Alan Douglas. After working out permission from the Hendrix estate, Douglas began to re-produce and re-record the sessions, using new drummers and bassists. In essence, years after his death, Hendrix is still making music with some of the nation's best sidemen.

Albums/ARE YOU EXPERIENCED (9/67): *Purple Haze; Manic Depression; Hey Joe; I Don't Live Today; Love or Confusion; May This Be Love; The Wind Cries Mary; Third Stone from the Sun; Fire; Foxey Lady; Are You Experienced.* GET THAT FEELING (A Curtis Knight album featuring Hendrix as resident guitarist;): *How Would You Feel; Simon Says; Get That Feeling; Hush Now; Welcome Home; Gotta Have a New Dress; No Business; Strange Things.* AXIS: BOLD AS LOVE (3/68): *Up from the Skies; Little Miss Lover; Spanish Castle Magic; Wait until Tomorrow; Ain't No Telling; Little Wing; If 6 Was 9; You Got Me Floatin'; Castles Made of Sand; One Rainy Wish; So Fine; Bold As Love.* ELECTRIC LADY LAND (9/68): *And The Gods Made Love; Have You Ever Been; Crosstown Traffic; Still Raining, Still Dreaming; Voodoo Chile; All Along the Watchtower; House Burning Down; Voodoo Child Reprise; Little Miss Strange; Long Hot Summer Night; Come On; Gypsy Eyes; Burning of the Midnight Lamp; Rainy Day, Dream Away; 1983; Moon, Turn the Tides.* SMASH HITS (7/69): *Purple Haze; Fire; The Wind Cries Mary; Can You See Me; Hey Joe; Stone Free; Manic Depression; Foxey Lady; All Along the Watchtower; Red House; Remember.* BAND OF GYPSYS (4/70): *Who Knows; Machine Gun; Changes; Power to Love; Message of Love; We Gotta Live Together.* MONTEREY INTERNATIONAL POP FESTIVAL: OTIS REDDING/THE JIMI HENDRIX EXPERIENCE (8/70): *Like a Rolling Stone; Rock Me, Baby; Can You See Me; Wild Thing.* Otis Redding songs: *Shake; Respect; Satisfaction; Try a Little Tenderness; I've Been Loving You Too Long.* CRY OF LOVE (1/71): *Freedom; Drifting; Easy Rider; Night Bird Flying; My Friend; Straight Ahead; Astro Man; Angel; In from the Storm; Belly Button Window.* RAINBOW BRIDGE (soundtrack; 9/71): *Dolly Dagger; Earth Blues; Pali Gap; Room Full of Mirrors; Star-Spangled Banner; Look Over Yonder; Hear My Train a-Comin'; Hey Baby.* HENDRIX IN THE WEST (2/72): *Lover Man; Johnny B. Goode; Blue Suede Shoes; Red House; The Queen; Sgt. Pepper's Lonely Hearts Club Band; Little Wing; Voodoo Chile.* WAR HEROES (11/72): *Bleeding Heart; Highway Chile; Tax Free; Peter Gunn; Catastrophe; Stepping Stone; Midnight; 3 Little Bears; Beginning; Isabella.* JIMI HENDRIX (sound track recordings from the film; 7/73): *Hey Joe; Red House; Purple Haze; Johnny B. Goode; Like a Rolling Stone; Star-Spangled Banner; Rock Me; Wild Thing; Machine Gun; In from the Storm; Hear My Train a-Comin'; Machine Gun II.* CRASH LANDING (2/75): *Message to Love; Somewhere over the Rainbow; Crash Landing; Come Down Hard on Me; Peace in Mississippi; With the Power; Stone Free Again; Captain Coconut.* MIDNIGHT LIGHTNING (10/75): *Trash*

Man; Midnight Lightning; Hear My Train; Gypsy Boy; Blue Sude Shoes; Machine Gun; Once I Had a Woman; Beginnings. JIMI HENDRIX (1975): *Go Go Shoes; Bring My Baby Back; Wipe the Sweat; Psycho; Voice in the Wind; Goodbye, Bessie Mae; All I Want.*

Singles/*Hey Joe/51st Anniversary* (5/67); *The Wind Cries Mary/Purple Haze* (6/67); *Foxey Lady/Hey Joe* (11/67); *One Rainy Wish/Up from the Skies* (1/68); *All Along the Watchtower/Burning of the Midnight Lamp* (9/68); *Crosstown Traffic/Gypsy Eyes* (10/68); *Stepping Stone/Isabella* (4/70); *Freedom/Angel* (3/71); *Dolly Dagger/Star-Spangled Banner* (9/71); *Johnny B. Goode/Love Man* (3/72); *The Wind Cries Mary/Little Wing* (9/72).

THE HOLLIES/*Original members: Eric Haydock (bass), Allan Clarke (lead vocals), Bobby Elliot (drums), Tony Hicks (lead guitar, vocals), Graham Nash (guitar, vocals). Present members: Allan Clarke (vocals), Tony Hicks (lead guitar), Terry Sylvester (guitar), Bobby Elliott (drums), Bernie Calvert (bass).*
The Hollies have been around since 1963 which, in rock terminology, qualifies them for Medicare. The band has constantly been on the charts since that time, picking up and dropping members along the way but always retaining the clean-cut, choir-boy sound that has become their trademark. The band started in Manchester during the beginning of the Beatles era. From their inception, the Hollies proved a popular item on the British charts, although American success didn't really come until 1965. The band was recognized more for their style than for their faces so, early in their career, they were able to reshuffle their membership without any real repercussions.

Eric Haydock was the first to go, in 1966, replaced by Bernie Calvert. Graham Nash was next to leave, in 1968. Graham had a case of the blues. The Hollies just never did make it on the album charts and, at that time, *serious* bands were *album* bands. He made the album charts in a big way later that year with Crosby, Stills and Nash. Terry Sylvester was picked as Graham's replacement and the Hollies weathered the storm.

In 1971, during one of the band's low points, Allan Clarke decided to pack up his tonsils and move out. Swedish Michael Rickfors was tapped for the lead singer slot but after a Clarke-performed tune, *Long Cool Woman,* shot to number one, Rickfors was un-tapped and Clarke returned to the fold, where he has remained since. The Hollies' career has been patterned pretty much after the lifestyle of a roller coaster. After a mountain of hits they seem to plummet from view. But just when you think they're out of sight forever, this band of the sixties jumps right back up the charts.

Albums/HEAR, HERE (12/65): *I'm Alive; Very Last Day; You Must Believe Me; Put Yourself in My Place; Down the Line; That's My Desire; Look through Any Window; Lawdy Miss Clawdy; When I Go Home to You; Lonely; I've Been Wrong; Too Many People.* HERE I GO AGAIN (12/65): *Memphis; Stay; Just One Look; Talkin' 'bout You; You Better Move On; Keep off That Friend of Mine; Rockin' Robin; It's Only Make Believe.* BEAT GROUP (6/66): *I Can't Let Go; That's How Strong My Love Is; Running throughThe Night; Oriental Sadness; A Taste of Honey; Mr. Moonlight; Don't You Ever Care; Hard Hard Year; Take Your Time; Fifi the Flea; I Take What I Want.* BUS STOP (10/66): *Bus Stop; Candy Man; That's All; I Am a Rock; Sweet Little Sixteen; We're Through; Don't Run and Hide; Mickey's Monkey; Little Lover; You Know He Did; Whatcha Gonna Do 'bout It.* STOP, STOP, STOP (2/67): *Stop Stop Stop; What's Wrong with the Way I Live; Pay You Back with Interest; Tell Me to My Face; Clown; Suspicion; Look in Your Eyes; It's You; High Classed; Peculiar Situation; What Went Wrong; Crusader; Don't Ever Think about Changing.* HOLLIES' GREATEST HITS (4/67): *On a Carousel; Bus Stop; Pay You Back with Interest; Here I Go Again; Tell Me to My Face; I'm Alive; Look through Any Window; Stop Stop Stop; Whatcha Gonna Do 'bout It; Just One Look; Memphis; I Can't Let Go.* EVOLUTION (6/67): *Carrie-Anne; Stop Right There; Rain on the Window; Then the Heartaches Begin; Ye Olde Toffee Shoppe; You Need Love; Heading for a Fall; Games We Play; Lullaby Have You Ever Loved Somebody.* DEAR ELOISE/KING MIDAS IN REVERSE (12/67): *Dear Eloise; Wishyouawish; Charlie and Fred; Butterfly; Leave Me; Postcard; King Midas in Reverse; Would You Believe; Away Away Away; Maker, Step Inside.* WORDS AND MUSIC BY BOB DYLAN (7/69): *When the Ship Comes In; I'll Be Your Baby Tonight; I Want You; This Wheel's on Fire; I Shall Be Released; Blowin' in the Wind; Quit Your Lowdown Ways; Just*

Like a Woman; The Times They Are a-Changing; All I Really Want to Do; My Back Pages; Mighty Quinn. HE AIN'T HEAVY, HE'S MY BROTHER (2/70): *Why Didn't You Believe; Don't Give Up Easily; Look at Life; Please Sign Your Letters; My Life Is Over without You; Please Let Me Please; Do You Believe in Love; He Ain't Heavy, He's My Brother; You Love 'Cos You Like It; Reflections of a Time Long Past; Goodbye Tomorrow.* MOVING FINGER (12/70): *Survival of the Fittest; Confessions of a Minx; Lady Please; Little Girl; Too Young to be Married; Man without a Heart; Isn't It Nice; Frightened Lady; Marigold Gloria Swansong; Perfect Lady; House Wife; Gasoline Alley Breed.* DISTANT LIGHT (6/72): *Look What We've Got; Life I've Led; Hold On; Pull Down the Blind; To Do with Love; Promised Land; Long Cool Woman in a Black Dress; You Know the Score; Cable Car; Little Things Like Love; Long Dark Road.* ROMANY (12/72): *Magic Woman Touch; Words Don't Come Easy; Won't We Feel Good That Morning; Down River; Slow Down; Delaware Taggett and the Outlaw Boys; Jesus Was a Cross Maker; Romany; Blue in the Morning; Courage of Your Convictions.* GREATEST HITS (9/73): *Bus Stop; Carrie Anne; Step 3; Look through Any Window; Dear Eloise; Long Cool Woman; He Ain't Heavy, He's My Brother; Just One Look; King Midas in Reverse; Pay You Back with Interest; Long Dark Road; On a Carousel.* THE HOLLIES (2/74): *Fallin' Calling; It's a Shame, It's a Game; Don't Let Me Down; Out on the Road; The Air That I Breathe; Rubber Lucy; Transatlantic Westbound Jet; Pick Up the Pieces Again; Down on the Run; Love Makes the World Go Round; The Day That Curly Bill Shot Down Crazy Sam McGee.* ANOTHER NIGHT (2/75): *Sandy; Another Night; Lonely Hobo Lullabye; Second-Hand Hang-Ups; Time Machine Jive; I'm Down; Look Out Johnny; Give Me Time; You Gave Me Life; Lucy.* THE HOLLIES (5/77): *Sandy: 48-Hour Parole; Thanks for the Memories; My Love; Star; Russian Roulette; Draggin' My Heels; Love Is the Thing; I Won't Move Over; Write On.*

Singles/*Just One Look* (5/64); *Look Through Any Window/I'm Alive* (10/65); *I Can't Let Go* (3/66); *Stop Stop Stop/I Can't Let Go* (10/66); *On a Carousel* (3/67); Carrie Anne/Signs That Will Never Change (5/67); *Pay You Back with Interest* (6/67); *Just One Look* (9/67); *King Midas in Reverse; Water on the Brain* (9/67);

Jennifer Eccles/Try It (2/68); *Do the Best You Can/Elevated Observation* (7/68); *Listen to Me/Everything Is Sunshine* (9/68); *Sorry Suzanne/Not That Way At All* (3/69); *He Ain't Heavy, He's My Brother/'Cos You Like To Love* (9/69); *I Can't Tell the Bottom from the Top/Mad Professor Blyth* (4/70); *Gasoline Alley Bred/Dandelion Wine* (10/70); *He Ain't Heavy, He's My Brother/Carrie Anne* (12/70); *Survival of the Fittest/Man without a Heart* (3/72); *Hey Willy/Row the Boat Together* (7/71); *The Baby/Oh Granny* (3/72); *Long Dark Road/Indian Girl* (10/72); *Magic Woman Touch/Blue in the Morning* (1/73); *Jesus Was a Cross Maker/I Had a Dream* (4/73); *Long Cool Woman/Long Dark Road* (4/73); *Slow Down/Won't We Feel Good* (7/73); *Curly Billy/Born a Man* (10/73); *The Air That I Breathe/No More Riders* (3/74); *Don't Let Me Down/Lay into the Music* (8/74); *Sandy/Time Machine Jive* (2/75); *Another Night/Time Machine Jive* (4/75); *I'm Down/Look Out, Johnny* (8/75); *Write On/Crocodile Woman* (2/76); *The Air That I Breathe/Jennifer Eccles* (11/76); *Sandy/Second-Hand Hang-Ups* (3/77).

BUDDY HOLLY/Charles Hardin Holly was one of the giants of early rock—a figure so important in the history of popular music that it is impossible to hear a song on the charts today that does not owe something to the tall, slim, bespectacled boy from Lubbock, Texas. He started off in 1956 as a country singer, as so many of those early rock figures did, but from the summer of 1957 until his death in 1959, he recorded scores of rock songs—the great classics *Peggy Sue, That'll Be the Day, Maybe Baby, Oh Boy, Early in the Morning.* Just how prolific he was in a career that was only a matter of months came to light during the great rock revival in England in 1968 when four albums (forty-seven songs) of his were released under the title *THE IMMORTAL BUDDY HOLLY.* More than any other singer of that era, he brings back a time when music was fun, when rock was fun, when no one was trying to push it as an art form, and when sheer animal exuberance was what counted.

As well as his own material (co-written with manager Normal Petty), Buddy did all the standards of the day: *Shake Rattle and Roll, Blue Suede Shoes, Rip It Up.* Like a lot of country boys of that time who automatically headed for country music, he was sidetracked by the success other country musicians—Elvis Presley, Bill Haley, Johnny Cash, Jerry Lee Lewis, Carl Perkins—were having in the new field of rock. Once he got going, he became one of rock's greatest hitmakers, brandishing an infectious rock-a-billy sound that was both powerful and lightweight.

You only have to listen to those hits to know where a lot of the early Beach Boys and Beatles come from, not to mention the hundreds of other bands that would not have been possible without him.

Albums/THE BUDDY HOLLY STORY (2/57): *Raining in My Heart; Early in the Morning; It Doesn't Matter Anymore; Heartbeat; Peggy Sue; Maybe Baby; Everyday; Rave On; That'll Be the Day; Think It Over.* BUDDY HOLLY (3/58); *I'm Gonna Love You Too; Peggy Sue; Listen to Me; Everyday; Look at Me; Valley of Tears; Ready Teddy; Mailman; Bring Me No More Blues; Words of Love; You're So Square, Baby; Rave On; Little Baby.* THAT'LL BE THE DAY (5/58); *Rock Around with Ollie Vee; Ting-a-Ling; I'm Changing All Those Changes; Girl on My Mind; That'll Be the Day; other titles.* THE BUDDY HOLLY STORY VOL. 2 (3/60): *Oh Boy; It's So Easy; Peggy Sue Got Married; Crying, Waiting, Hoping; Learning the Game; That Makes It Touch; Well Alright; Now We're One; What to Do; Take Your Time; True Love Ways; Little Baby; Moondreams; That's What They Say.* BUDDY HOLLY AND THE CRICKETS (4/62): *Oh, Boy; Not Fade Away; You've Got Love; Maybe Baby; It's Too Late; Tell Me How; I'm Lookin' for Someone to Love; That'll Be the Day; Empty Cup; Send Me Some Lovin'; Last Night; Rock Me Baby.* REMINISCING (2/63): *Reminiscing; Slippin' and Slidin'; Bo Diddley; Wait Till the Sun Shines Nellie; It's Not My Fault; Baby, Won't You Please Come Home; Brown-Eyed Handsome Man; Because I Love You; I'm Gonna Set My Foot Down; Rock-a-Bye Rock; Changing All Those Changes.* BUDDY HOLLY SHOWCASE (5/64): *Shake, Rattle and Roll; Rock Around with Ollie Vee; Honky Tonk; I Guess I Was Just a Fool; Ummm, Oh Yea; You're the One; Blue Suede Shoes; Come Back, Baby; Rip It Up; Love's Made a Fool of You; Gone; Girl on My Mind.* HOLLY IN THE HILLS (1/65): *I Wanna Play House with You; Door to My Heart; Fool's Paradise; Gotta Get You Near Me Blues; I Gambled with My Heart; What to Do; Wishing; Down the Line; Soft Place in My Heart; Lonesome Tears; Flower of My Heart;*

You and I Are Through. BEST OF BUDDY HOLLY (4/66): *Peggy Sue; Blue Suede Shoes; Learning the Game; Brown-Eyed Handsome Man; Everyday; Maybe Baby; Early in the Morning; Ready Teddy; It's Too Late; What To Do; Rave On; True Love Ways; It Doesn't Matter Anymore; Crying, Waiting, Hoping; Moondreams; Rock Around with Ollie Vee; Raining in My Heart; Bo Diddley; That'll Be the Day; I'm Gonna Love You Too; Peggy Sue Got Married; That Makes It Tough; Shake, Rattle and Roll; Wishing.* GREATEST HITS (3/67): *Peggy Sue; True Love Ways; Bo Diddley; What to Do; Learning the Game; It Doesn't Matter Anymore; That'll Be the Day; Oh, Boy; Early in the Morning; Brown-Eyed Handsome Man; Everyday; Maybe Baby.* GREAT BUDDY HOLLY (10/67): *Blue Days, Black Nights; Girl on My Mind; That'll Be the Day; Love Me; other titles.* A ROCK AND ROLL COLLECTION (1972): *Rave On; Tell Me How; Peggy Sue Got Married; Slippin' and Slidin'; Oh Boy; Not Fade Away; Bo Diddley; What to Do; Heartbeat; Well All Right; Words of Love; Love's Made a Fool of You; Reminiscing; Lonesome Tears; Listen to Me; Maybe Baby; Down the Line; That'll Be the Day; Peggy Sue; Brown-Eyed Handsome Man; You're So Square; Crying, Waiting, Hoping; Ready Teddy; It Doesn't Matter Anymore.*
Singles/*Peggy Sue/Everyday* (9/57); *Rave On* (5/58); *Early in the Morning* (7/58); *Heartbeat* (1/59); *It Doesn't Matter Anymore* (2/59); *Raining in My Heart* (2/59); *Bo Diddley/True Love Ways* (4/63); *Brown-Eyed Handsome Man/Wishing* (9/63); *I'm Gonna Love You Too/Rock Around with Ollie Vee* (1/64); *Love Is Strange/You're the One* (3/69).

HOT ROD MUSIC/California started with surf music in 1963, but in 1965, with the discovery that a teenager's first love is his car, came hot-rod music. The Beach Boys did a whole album of it. No hot rod was more famous than the one driven by Jan and Dean's *Little Old Lady from Pasadena,* a drag-racing spinster. *Dead Man's Curve* was about teenage lovers who total their car. The hot-rod sound was quite similar to the surf sound, very California and summery and, naturally, easy to drive to.

HOT TUNA/*Jack Casady (bass), Jorma Kaukonen (guitar), vocals), Bob Steeler (drums).*
Any band with the name Hot Tuna has got to be good to survive,

and Hot Tuna has survived for nearly a decade. The exotic, eccentric, and helter-skelter sounds of Tuna began in late 1969 when, faced with a low period during their stay in the Jefferson Airplane, Jorma Kaukonen and Jack Casady began getting together to play music that just didn't fit into the Jefferson Airplane formula. Initially, it was an ensemble that included Joey Covington, Peter Kaukonen, and Mary Balin, but by the time a first album was recorded, Hot Tuna was an acoustic trio featuring Jorma, Jack, and Will Scarlett on harmonica.

For the first few years, the Kaukonen-Casady duo alternately played with both the Airplane and Tuna. But as the faces within the Tuna changed, Jorma and Jack grew more and more involved with their embryonic band. Sammy Piazza was added on drums and Tuna went electric. Papa John Creach was added on electric fiddle. Will Scarlett dropped out. By 1972, the duo were full-time Tunaphiles and ex-Airplaners. Plans were made for Hot Tuna to take off first class. For one reason or another, the band never made it past solid cult status, however. Drummer Piazza said, "Sorry, Charlie," in '74 and Tuna was, once again, acoustic. In '75, the band became an electric trio with Bob Steeler joining in on drums.

It's hard to describe the sound of Hot Tuna because, depending on what day, hour or mood you catch them in, they'll either be dishing out heaping fistfuls of pastoral imagery or refried psychedelia-blooze.

Albums/HOT TUNA (9/70): *Hesitation Blues; How Long Blues; Uncle Sam Blues; Don't You Leave Me Here; Death Don't Have No Mercy; Know You Rider; Oh Lord, Search My Heart; Winin' Boy Blues; New Song; Mann's Fate.* FIRST PULL UP, THEN PULL DOWN (7/71): *John's Other; Candy Man; Been So Long; Want You to Know; Keep Your Lamps Trimmed and Burning; Never Happen No More; Come Back Baby.* BURGERS (3/72): *True Religion; Highway Song; 99 Year Blues; Keep on Truckin'; Water Song; Ode for Billy Dean; Let Us Get Together Right Down Here; Sunny Day Strut.* PHOSPHORESCENT RAT (1/74): *I See the Light; Letter to the North Star; Easy Now; Corners without Exits; Day to Day out the Window Blues; In the Kingdom; Seaweed Strut; Living Just for You; Soliloquy For 2; Sally, Where'd You Get Your Liquor From?* QUAH (9/74): *Genesis; I'll Be All Right; I'll Let*

You Know Before I Leave; Flying Clouds; Another Man Done Gone; I Am the Light of This World; Police Dog Blues; Blue Prelude; Sweet Hawaiian Sunshine; Hamar Promenade. AMERICA'S CHOICE (4/75): *Sleep Song; Funky; Walkin' Blues; Invitation; Hit Single #1; Serpent of Dreams; I Don't Wanna Go; Great Divide: Revisited.* HOPPKORV (10/76): *Santa Claus Retreat; Watch the North Wind Rise; It's So Easy; Bowlegged Woman, Knock-Kneed Man; Drivin' Around; I Wish You Would; I Can't Be Satisfied; Talkin' 'bout You; Extrication Love Song; Song from the Stainless Cymbal.*

Singles/*Keep on Truckin'*/*Watersong* (2/72); *Hot Jelly Roll Blues* (11/75); *It's So Easy* (10/76).

HUMBLE PIE/*Steve Marriott (vocals, guitar), Jerry Shirley (drums), Greg Ridley (bass), Dave Clempson (guitar, vocals; replacing original member Peter Frampton).*

Hard-rocking, head-knocking, teeth-gnashing Humble Pie was touted as a supergroup from its inception in 1968, and that label almost did the band in prematurely. By the late sixties, it was clear that England was the place to be for hard-rock bands. In 1968, the Small Faces' lead voice and face, Steve Marriott, and the Herd's teenybopper idol, Peter Frampton, joined forces with Spooky Tooth's Greg Ridley and with Jerry Shirley. Humble Pie was born.

From the outset, Humble Pie was a band torn by lack of unified direction. Frampton, a songwriting guitarist, had an ear for lightweight rockers with a distinctly melodic flair. Marriott, on the other hand, was about as subtle as a sledgehammer, preferring his music to hit the listener around the crotch area as opposed to the eardrums. In spite of their erratic, style-less approach, Humble Pie managed to release two very popular albums; *AS SAFE AS YESTERDAY IS* and *TOWN AND COUNTRY*. The two longplayers proved to be underground hits but didn't score too well on the almighty American pop charts. Pie managed to keep their buzz alive by staging a well-received tour of the States.

Their struggling career, however, was soon done in—temporarily—by their record company, Immediate, which chose that time to go out of existence due to lack of funds. Humble Pie was down for the count. American manager Dee Anthony (who later spurred on such performers as Alvin Lee, Peter Frampton, and Gary Wright), urged the band onward and onward they did go.

Marriott's hard-nosed, gut-busting style eventually over-shadowed Frampton pastoral visions of truth and beauty. The band adapted a swaggering stance, and soon Frampton parted ways with the Pie. Dave Clempson was adopted from Coloseum. The growing popularity of Humble Pie, which began with such albums as *ROCK ON* and *ROCKIN' AT THE FILLMORE,* climaxed with the hot and nasty *SMOKIN'.* For the first time, Humble Pie was a legitimate gold-record-selling act.

Shortly thereafter, the band began to falter. Marriott's devotion to soul-screeching R&B proved his undoing and subsequent albums such as *EAT IT* and *THUNDERBOX* proved excessive and rather overdone, in a "y'all heah now" sort of way. Marriott's erratic stage performance and his on-again, off-again vocal prowess did nothing to enhance the band's sagging presence. By the time the Pie recorded their last long-player, *STREET RATS* (an amiable little fistful of retreaded rock), it was clear that the magic was over. The swagger had become a grimace, the cockiness had lost its clout.

Following the band's demise in 1975, Marriott embarked on an ill-fated blue-eyed-soul revue with Steve Marriot's All Stars. An LP, featuring an "American" side and a "British" side, nearly severed Anglo-American musical relations. In 1977, Marriott and several members of the original Small Faces staged a reunion with a recording career in mind.

Albums/AS SAFE AS YESTERDAY IS (6/69): *Desperation; Stick Shift; Buttermilk Boy; Growing Closer; As Safe As Yesterday; Bang?; Alabama '69' I'll Go Alone; A Nifty Little Number Like You; What You Will.* TOWN AND COUNTRY (12/69): *Take Me Back; The Sad Bag of Shaky Jake; The Light of Love; Cold Lady; Down Home Again; Ollie Ollie; Every Mother's Son; Heartbeat; Only You Can Say; Silver Tongue; Home and Away.* HUMBLE PIE (8/70): *Live with Me; Only a Roach; One-Eyed Trouser-Snake Rhumba; Earth and Water Song; I'm Ready;* theme from *Skint—See You Later, Liquidator; Red Light Mama; Red Hot!; Sucking on the Sweet Vine.* ROCK ON (3/71): *Shine On; Sour Grain; 79th and Sunset; Stone Cold Fever; Rollin' Stone; A Song for Jenny; The Light; Big George; Strange Days; Red Neck Jump.* PERFORMANCE—ROCKIN' THE FILLMORE (10/71): *Four Day Creep; I'm Ready; Stone Cold Fever; Hallelujah (I Love Her So); I Don't Need No Doctor; I Walk on Gilded Splinters; Rol-*

lin' Stone. SMOKIN (5/72): *Hot 'n' Nasty; The Fixer; You're So Good for Me; C'mon Everybody; Old Time Feelin'; 30 Days in the Hole; Road Runner; Road Runners "G" Jam; I Wonder; Sweet Peace and Time.* LOST AND FOUND (Re-issues of *AS SAFE AS YESTERDAY* and *TOWN AND COUNTRY* 8/72). EAT IT (3/73): *Say No More; Oh, Bella; Summer Song; Becton Dumps; Up Our Sleeve; Honky Tonk Woman; Road Runner; Get Down to It; Good Booze and Bad Women; Is It for Love?; Drugstore Cowboy; Black Coffee; I Believe in My Soul; Shut Up and Don't Interrupt Me; That's How Strong My Love Is.* THUNDERBOX (2/74): *Thunderbox; Groovin' with Jesus; I Can't Stand the Rain; Anna; No Way; Rally with Ali; Don't Worry, Be Happy; Ninety-Nine Pounds; Every Single Day; No Money Down; Drift Away; Oh Le-De-Da.* STREET RATS (3/75): *Street Rat; Rock and Roll Music; We Can Work It Out; Scored Out; Road Hog; Rain; There 'Tis; Let Me Be Your Lovemaker; Countryman Stomp; Drive My Car; Queens and Nuns.*

Singles/*I Don't Need No Doctor* (7/71); *Hot 'n' Nasty* (4/72); *30 Days in the Hole* (7/72); *Black Coffee* (2/73); *Get Down to It* (4/73); *Ninety-Nine Pounds.* (4/74); *Rock and Roll Music* (6/75).

IAN HUNTER/One of the most underrated rock influences of the nineteen sixties. Britisher Ian Hunter influenced a generation of rock fans with his terse, halting poetics as lead singer with Mott the Hoople. Joining the already-formed Mott during the mid-sixties (replacing lead singer Stan Tippen, soon to be Mott's manager), Hunter originally planned a career as a folkie à la Bob Dylan. His rambling, erratic sense of poetic style seemingly clashed with Mott's hard-driving stance but, magically, on wax, it clicked magnificently.

Departing from Mott in 1974 after a breakdown and a verbal tag-team match with a few of the members, Hunter embarked on a critically acclaimed, commercially dismal solo career. An initial partnership with wandering rock soul Mick Ronson (guitarist pal of David Bowie) was shortlived. Two solo albums, *IAN HUNTER* and *ALL-AMERICAN ALIEN BOY,* led to his settling in New York State. A third LP, *OVERNIGHT ANGELS,* was produced by Queen producer Roy Thomas Baker. It was released early in 1977 in the United Kingdom, but just prior to release stateside on the Columbia label, both Ian and his long-player were given the axe rather unceremoniously.

One of rock's most literate composers, Hunter is the author of the wondrously bizarre *Diary of a Rock 'n' Roll Star,* a behind-the-scenes look at one of Mott the Hoople's more interesting tours. Currently hunting for a label, Hunter took time to co-write one of the finest cuts on 1977's Blue Oyster Cult album, *SPEC-TRES,* entitled *Going through the Motions.*

Albums/IAN HUNTER (4/75): *Once Bitten Twice Shy; Who Do You Love; Lounge Lizard; Boy; 3,000 Miles from Here; The Truth, the Whole Truth, Nuthin' but the Truth; It Ain't Easy When You Fall; Shades Off; I Get So Excited.* ALL-AMERICAN ALIEN BOY (4/76): *Letter to Brittania from the Union Jack; All-American Alien Boy; Irene Wilde; Restless Youth; Rape; You Nearly Did Me In; Apathy 83; God (Take 1).* OVERNIGHT ANGELS (U.K. only; 4/77): *Golden Opportunity; Shallow Crystals; Overnight Angels; Broadway; Justice of the Peace; (Miss) Silver Dime; Wild 'n' Free; The Ballad of Little Star; To Love a Woman.*

Single/*Once Bitten Twice Shy/3,000 Miles from Here* (6/75).

JANIS IAN/At the age of fifteen, Janis Ian was a singer-songwriter familiar to New York folk audiences. By the age of sixteen, she was appearing on in-concert shows on rock with Leonard Bernstein and being touted by WOR-FM *(the* underground station in New York) dj Murry the K as being the finest new singer-songwriter to come along in years. She shook the music industry to its rafters with *Society's Child,* a composition about a white girl and a black boy who are kept apart by an unfeeling society. At the time, Janis was four feet seven inches tall and a high school sophomore.

Janis was born in New York and educated in New Jersey. By the time she was fourteen, she was beginning to come into her own as a young folksinger in the then–folk singing heaven of Greenwich Village. Signed by Elektra, she was dropped before she ever got into the studio. She was then picked up by Verve Records, a division of MGM which often guided its artists into oblivion. Her first album, *JANIS IAN,* featured the controversial single and sold exceedingly well. Not so successful were subsequent records.

Young Janis quietly grew disillusioned with the business aspects of the record world. Leaving Verve in the late sixties, she moved to Philadelphia to attempt to restructure her priorities. She emerged in 1971 on Capitol Records with a country-oriented album, *PRESENT COMPANY*. By that time, however, Janis was considered yesterday's news. A child star too old for modern music. She was twenty.

Undaunted, Janis retreated inward, composing, reworking, rearranging. In 1974 she staged a much-overlooked comeback via her long-player *STARS*, a critically acclaimed album that went unnoticed in some quarters because of its lack of hit singles. Then, something strange began to happen. FM-radio stations around the country began to play the title track. Although it wasn't a "hit" single, *Stars* soon was heard coast to coast on radio stations. Sales of the album built slowly. Janis began to tour. The wheels were moving again.

Her following album, *BETWEEN THE LINES*, boasted the hit single *At Seventeen*, a maudlin slice-of-life tale that apparently touched a common nerve with every teenager in the country. The song soared to number one. Thousands of publications printed the headline "Society's Child Grows Up" (much to Janis' dismay). With success hers for the second time, Janis began to take her musical stance even further. Lyrically, her compositions remained steadfastly introspective and yet somehow universal. The pain, the joy, the everyday bittersweet experiences continued to be present, but soon they were surrounded by touches of jazz, of rock, of orchestration. Janis began producing her albums as well, working twelve-/and eighteen-hour recording shifts with her talented sidemen.

At this stage in her career, Janis Ian is a top attraction at college campuses and music venues around the country. In 1977, she embarked on an SRO tour of Japan, completely dazzling both the fans and the press. Does anyone know the Japanese version of "Society's Child Grows Up"?

Albums/JANIS IAN (3/67): *Society's Child; Go 'Way, Little Girl; Hair of Spun Gold; The Tangles of a Mind; I'll Give You a Stone If You'll Throw It; Pro-Girl; New Christ Cardiac Hero; Younger Generation Blues; Lover Be Kindly; Mrs. McKenzie; Janey's Blues.* FOR ALL THE SEASONS OF YOUR MIND (1/68): *Insanity Comes Quietly to the Structured Mind; And I Did, Ma; Honey, D'Ya Think; Bahimsa; Sunflakes Fall, Snowrays Call; Lonely One; Queen Merkin and Me; There Are Times; Shady Acres; Evening*

Star. THE SECRET LIFE OF J. EDDY FINK (8/68): *Everybody Knows; Mistaken Identity; Friends Again; 42nd Street Psycho Blues; She's Made of Porcelain; Sweet Misery; When I Was a Child; What Do You Think of the Dead; Look to the Rain; Son of Love; Baby's Blue.* WHO REALLY CARES (1969): *Time on My Hands; Snowbird; Love You More Than Yesterday; Orphan of the Wind; Sea and Sand; Galveston; Do You Remember; Month of May; Calling You Names.* PRESENT COMPANY (2/71): *The Seaside; Present Company; See My Grammy Ride; Here in Spain; On the Train; He's a Rainbow; Weary Lady; Nature's at Peace; See the River; Let It Run Free; Alabama; Liberty; My Land; Hello, Jerry; Can You Reach Me; The Sunlight.* STARS (2/74): *The Man You Are in Me; Sweet Sympathy; Stars; Page Nine; Thankyous; Dance with Me; Without You; Jesse; You've Got Me on a String; Applause.* BETWEEN THE LINES (2/75): *When the Party's Over; At Seventeen; From Me to You; Bright Lights and Promises; In the Winter; Watercolors; Between the Lines; The Come-On; Light a Light; Tea and Sympathy; Lover's Lullabye.* AFTERTONES (12/75): *Aftertones; I Would Like to Dance; Love Is Blind; Roses; Belle of the Blues; Goodbye to Morning; Boy, I Really Tied One On; This Must Be Wrong; Don't Cry, Old Man; Hymn.* MIRACLE ROW (1/77): *Party Lights; I Want to Make You Love Me; Sunset of Your Life; Take to the Sky; Candlelight; Let Me Be Lonely; Slow Dance Romance; Will You Dance?; I'll Cry Tonight; Miracle Row/Maria.*

Singles/*Younger Generation Blues/I'll Give You a Stone If You'll Throw It* (2/67); *Society's Child* (4/67); *Insanity Comes Quietly to the Structured Mind/Sunflakes Fall, Snowrays Fall* (11/67); *Song for All the Seasons of Your Mind/Lonely One* (1/68); *Society's Child/Letter to John* (8/68); *Jesse/The Man You Are in Me* (5/74); *When the Party's Over/Bright Lights and Promises* (3/75); *At Seventeen/Stars* (5/75); *In the Winter/Thankyous* (10/75); *Boy, I Really Tied One On/Aftertones* (2/76); *I Would Like to Dance/Goodbye to Morning* (4/76); *Roses/Love Is Blind* (8/76); *At Seventeen/When the Party's Over* (11/76); *Miracle Row/Take to the Sky* (1/77); *I Want to Make You Love Me/Candlelight* (4/77).

THE INCREDIBLE STRING BAND/Robin Williamson and Mike Heron led, for nearly a decade, one of the most unique musical ensembles ever to worm its way into the pop spotlight.

The Incredible String Band was never "a band" in the traditional sense of the word. An ever-changing collection of modern-day minstrels, the String Band came to represent the British answer to "flower power" during the sixties. Clad in flowing robes and strumming exotic instruments, the String Band conjured up visions of eternal pastoral bliss.

The original group consisted of Williamson, Heron, and Clive Palmer. Williamson and Palmer were two Scottish folkies who joined forces with Britisher Heron in 1965. Their first LP and *THE 5,000 SPIRITS (THE LAYERS OF THE ONION SKIN)* quickly established them as viable force for change within the weakening ranks of folkdom. Palmer left, allowing Williamson and Heron to continue their wondrous ways. At one point or another, the String Band numbered two, three, four, and five members with such musical friends as Rose Simpson (bass), Licorice McKenzie (violin), Gerald Dott (keyboards), and Malcolm LeMaistre (bass and vocals) joining the troupe along the way.

As the ethereal pastoral strains of flower power bit the dust in the dawning of the seventies, the String Band found themselves afloat in a wilted musical sea. Electrifying their sound somewhat, they changed labels (from Elektra to Warner Reprise) and attempted to redefine their melodic direction. Alas, the band did not survive the transition; in 1974, they disbanded. Heron attempted to carry on with Mike Heron's Reputation but, in terms of stateside success, did not travel very far.

Albums/THE INCREDIBLE STRING BAND (4/67): *Maybe Someday; October Song; When the Music Starts to Play; Schaeffer's Jig; How Happy I Am; Womankind; The Tree; Whistle Tune; Dandelion Blues; Empty Pocket Blues; Smoke Shovelling Song; Can't Help Me Here; Good as Gone; Footsteps of the Heron; Niggertown; Everything's Fine Right Now.* THE 5,000 SPIRITS (THE LAYERS OF THE ONION SKIN) (10/67): *Way Back in the 1960's; Painting Box; Eyes of Fate; Blues for the Muse; Chinese White; No Sleep Blues; Mad Hatter's Song; Little Cloud; Hedgehog's Song; First Girl I Loved; You Know What You Could Be; My Name Is Death; Gently Tender.* HANGMAN'S BEAUTIFUL DAUGHTER (5/68): *Koeeoaddi There; Minotaur's Song; Witches Hat; Very Cellular Song; Mercy I Cry City; Waltz of the New Moon; Water Song; Three Is a Green Crown; Swift As* *the Wind; Nightfall.* WEE TAM/BIG HUGE (3/68): *Job's Tears; Puppies; Beyond the Sea; The Yellow Snake; Log Cabin Home in the Sky; You Get Brighter; The Half-Remarkable Question; Air; Ducks on a Pond; Maya; Greatest Friend; The Sons of Noah's Brother; Lordly Nightshade; The Mountain of God; Cousin Caterpillar; The Iron Stone; Doughals Traherne Harding; The Circle Is Unbroken.* CHANGING HORSES (1969): *Big Ted; White Bird; Dust Be Diamonds; Sleepers Awake; Creature; Mr. and Mrs.* I LOOKED UP (5/70): *Black Jack Davy; The Letter; Pictures in a Mirror; This Moment; When You Find Out Who You Are/Fair As You.* U (11/70): *El Wool Suite; The Juggler's Song; Time; Bad Sadie Lee; Queen of Love; Partial Belated Overture; Light in Time of Darkness/Glad to See You; Walking Along with You; Hirem Pawnitof/Fairies' Hornpipe; Bridge Theme; Bridge Song; Astral Plane Theme; Invocation; Robot Blues; Puppet Song; Cutting the Strings; Rainbow; I Know You.* RELICS (10/71): *Everything's Right Now; October Song; Painting Box; First Girl I Loved; Way Back in the 1960's; Hedgehog's Song; No Sleep Blues; Koeeodaddi There; My Name Is Death; The Minotaur's Song; Air; Cousin Caterpillar; Job's Tears; Log Cabin Home in the Sky; Maya; Big Ted; The Letter; This Moment; My Name Is Death.* LIQUID ACROBAT AS REGARDS THE AIR (1972): *Adam and Eve; Red Hair; Here Till Here Is There; Tree; Jigs; Darling Belle; Painted Chariot; Evolution Rag; Words They Rise and Fall; Cosmic Boy; Dear Old Battlefield; Talking of the End.* EARTHSPAN (10/72): *Black Jack Davy; Bands of Sweet Italy; The Actor; Moon Hang Low; Sunday Song; Restless Night; Antoine; My Father Was a Lighthouse Keeper; Seagull.* NO RUINOUS FEUD (3/73): *Explorer; Second Fiddle; My Blue Tears; Little Girl; Weather the Storm; Circus Girl; Jigs; Old Buccaneer; Saturday Maybe; At the Lighthouse Dance; Down before Cathay; Turquoise Blue.* HARD ROPE AND SILKEN TWINE (6/74): *Ithkos; Dumb Kate; Dreams of No Return; Maker of Islands; Cold February; Glancing Love.*

IRON BUTTERFLY/*Original members: Doug Ingle (keyboards, vocals), Ron Bushy (drums), Jerry Penrod (guitar), Danny Weiss (guitar), Darryl DeLoach (bass). Later members: Erik Braunn (guitar), Lee Dorman (bass), Larry Reinhardt (guitar), Mike Pinera (guitar), Phil Kramer (bass), Bill DeMartines (keyboards).*

Iron Butterfly were the original heavy-metal Cro-Magnons. Their low-browed, jutting-jawed sound conjured up visions of steamer trunks being dropped down several flights of stairs. The group started in San Diego in '66–'67 and, by '68, was killing the nation with their epic, grunting dirge *In-A-Gadda-Da-Vida,* a primordial chant that, to many music afficionados, simply meant: "Stop me before I play it again!" The song was one of the longest album cuts ever recorded until then (1968) and shot the album of the same name up the charts like a Nike Zeus missile. The album was the first rock LP ever to go platinum.

The band subsequently endured many personality conflicts but nothing seemed to slow the lumbering giant down. The seventies found Iron Butterfly bogged down in their own pretentiousness and the group dissolved. They resumed their careers briefly in 1975 for a few ill-fated albums that are best forgotten.

Albums/HEAVY (1/68): *Possession; Unconscious Power; Get Out of My Life, Woman; Gentle As It May Seem; You Can't Win; So-Lo; Look for the Sun; Iron Butterfly Theme; Fields of the Sun; Stamped Ideas.* IN-A-GADDA-DA-VIDA (7/68): *Most Anything You Want; Flowers and Beads; My Mirage; Termination; Are You Happy; In-A-Gadda-Da-Vida.* BALL (1/69): *In the Time of Our Lives; Soul Experience; Lonely Boy; Real Fright; In the Crowds; It Must Be Love; Her Favorite; Filled with Fear; Belda-Beast.* LIVE (4/70): *In the Time of Our Lives; Filled with Fear; Soul Experience; You Can't Win; Are You Happy; In-A-Gadda-Da-Vida.* METAMORPHOSIS (8/70): *Free Flight; New Day; Shady Lady; Best Years of Our Life; Slower Than Cows; Stone Believer; Soldier in Our Town; Easy Rider (Let the Wind Pay the Way); Butterfly Bleu.* EVOLUTION (11/71): *Iron Butterfly Theme; Possession; Unconscious Power; Flowers and Beads; Termination; In-A-Gadda-Da-Vida; Soul Experience; Stone Believer; Belda-Beast; Easy Rider; Slower Than Guns.* SCORCHING BEAUTY (1/75): *1975 Overture; Hard Miseree; High on a Mountain Top; Am I Down; People of the World; Searchin' Circles; Pearly Gates; Lonely Hearts; Before You Go.* SUN AND STEEL (10/75): *Sun and Steel; Lightnin'; Beyond the Milky Way; Free; Scion; Get It Out; I'm Right, I'm Wrong; Watch the World Goin' By.*

Singles/*Unconscious Power/Possession* (4/68); *In-A-Gadda-Da-Vida/Iron Butterfly Theme* (7/68); *Soul Experience/In the Crows* (1/69); *In the Time of Our Lives/It Must Be Love* (4/68); *I Can't*

Help but Deceive You, Little Girl/To Be Alone (9/69); *Easy Rider/Soldier in Our Town* (9/70); *Silly Sally/Stone Believer* (4/71); *In-A-Gadda-Da-Vida/Soul Experience* (10/72); *Searchin' Circles/Pearly Gates* (3/75); *Beyond the Milky Way/Get It Out* (11/75).

THE JAMES GANG/*Dale Peters (bass, vocals), Richard Shack (guitar), Bubba Keith (guitar, vocals), Jimmy Fox (drums, vocals). Original Members: Joe Walsh (guitar), Tom Kriss (bass), Jimmy Fox (drums).*
The James Gang never became a bona fide superstar group but guitarist Joe Walsh, now an Eagle, was always regarded as a musician's musician. Admired by Pete Townshend of the Who, the Gang was given the opening act slot on a Who tour in the late sixties. Stardom seemed to be theirs.

The Gang arose from the Cleveland, Ohio area in 1968 and, moving to the West, attained quite a cult status before attempting to capture the hearts of all America. That ambush just never came off, for a number of reasons. Many of the Gang's albums were pretty understated and they lacked true personality on stage. The membership, after a while, looked like a revolving-door-inspired comedy.

In 1970, Kriss left and Dave Peters took his place. Walsh, after watching the band attain gold-record status with *RIDES AGAIN* and *LIVE IN CONCERT,* quit in 1971 to embark on a solo career. Domanic Troiana and Roy Kenner, on guitar and vocals, were subsquently drafted as replacements. In 1973, Troiano split for the floundering Guess Who and Tommy Bolin appeared. But Bolin's erratic behavior saw him leave, along with Kenner, that same year. The band folded. A year later, it *un*folded with two new members, Keith and Shack. At this point, even the Gang's stalwart fans need a score card to keep track of what's going on.

At their best, the James Gang was a high-powered, guitar-oriented rock band. At their worst, they were just another rock and roll band . . . and there are always enough of those to go around without adding any new ones.

Albums/YER ALBUM (1969): *Lost Woman; Collage; Bluebird; Funk #48; Stop; other titles.* JAMES GANG RIDES AGAIN (6/70): *Funk #49; The Bomber; Garden Gate; There I Go Again; Ashes, the Rain and I; Woman; other titles.* THIRDS (3/71): *Walk*

Away; Yadig?; Things I Could Be; Dreamin' in the Country; It's All the Same; Midnight Man; Again; White Man/Black Man; Live My Life Again. LIVE IN CONCERT (8/71). STRAIGHT SHOOTER (2/72): *Madness; Kick Back Man; Get Her Back Again; Looking for My Lady; Getting Old; I'll Tell You Why; Hairy Hypochondriac; Let Me Come Home; My Door Is Open.* PASSIN' THRU (8/72): *Ain't Seen Nothin' Yet; One Way Street; Had Enough; Up to Yourself; Everybody Needs a Hero; Run, Run, Run, Run; Things I Want to Say to You; Out of Control; Drifting Girl.* BEST OF THE JAMES GANG (1/73): *Funk #48; Walk Away; Midnight Man; Take A Look Around; Funk #49; Woman; The Bomber; Ashes, The Rain and I; Yadig?; Stop.* 16 GREATEST HITS (9/73). BANG (12/73): *Standing in the Rain; The Devil Is Singing Our Song; Must Be Love; Alexis; Ride the Wind; Got No Time for Trouble; Rather Be Alone with You; Mystery; From Another Time.* MIAMI (8/74): *Cruisin Down the Highway; Do It; Wildfire; Sleepwalker; Miami Two-Step; Praylude; Red Skies; Spanish Lover; Summer Breezes; Head above the Water.* NEWBORN (4/75): *Merry-Go-Round; Gonna Get By; Earthshaker; All I Have; Watch It; Driftin' Dreamer; Should'a Seen Your Face; Come with Me; Heartbreak Hotel; Red Satin Lover; Cold Wind.* JESSE COME HOME (9/76): *I Need Love; Another Year; Feelin' Alright; Peasant Song; Hollywood Dream; Love Hurts; Pick Up the Pizzas; Stealin' the Show; When I Was a Sailor.*

Singles/*Funk #49* (7/70); *Walk Away/Yadig?* (4/71); *Midnight Man/White Man—Black Man* (8/71); *Had Enough/Kick Back Man* (9/72); *Must Be Love/Got No Time for Trouble* (12/73); *Funk #49/Had Enough* (1/74); *Standing in the Rain/From Another Time* (4/74); *Cruisin' Down the Highway/Miami Two-Step* (10/74); *Merry Go-Round/Red Satin Lover* (6/75).

JAN AND DEAN/To hear Jan Berry and Dean Torrence in 1963 was to see the world as one big California where life revolved around the beach, the sea, and the California freeways. Jan and Dean were around before the Beach Boys but they didn't really make their name until they moved into the Beach Boys' turf— surf. Having introduced their public to the pleasures of Surf City ("Two girls to every boy"), they explored another phenomenon: the love of a man for his car. And *Dead Man's Curve* showed just

where it could finish. Like the Beach Boys and other lesser-known
California groups, they became as obsessed with speed as they
had been with H²O, the subject changing but the sound—high
surfy harmonies—as familiar as ever. You only had to hear *The
Little Old Lady from Pasadena* to know that riding the highway
wasn't that different from riding the waves.

Probably the most appealing aspect of Jan and Dean's approach to music was their genuine amusement with the entire
rock scene. While the Beach Boys grasped for nirvana on their
post-surf records, Jan and Dean simply refused to take the oo-
soo-heavy-psychedelia thing seriously. They were out for a good
time. Music, to them, was fun. If it hadn't been music, it would
certainly have been something else. It was such a goof. But the
laughter stopped suddenly for the team when, in 1966, handsome
Jan Berry, who was using a large portion of his recording
payments to further his studies in medicine, totaled his car on
L.A.'s Whittier Blvd. Nearly dead, he was rushed to a nearby
hospital with extensive brain damage. To this day, he has yet to
recover fully, although producer Lou Adler has demoed him now
and again as therapy. Dean Torrence, after an aborted attempt at
solo work, began Kittyhawk Graphics, one of the most inventive
crews to get involved with album-cover work in a while. The
twosome attempted a reunion in 1973, but the live appearance
served only to make one long for the memories of yesterday's
music.

And so, it ended. The two boys who met in high school on the
football team, who recorded their first single in a garage in 1958,
and who worked their way through college by puttering around
the nation's top-ten charts called it quits. Their legacy? A mountain of hits and a whole lotta fun.

Albums/JAN AND DEAN TAKE LINDA SURFIN' (5/63):
*Linda; Walk Like a Man; Surfin' USA; Mr. Bass Man; Let's Tur-
key Trot; Rhythm of the Rain; Walk Right In; Best Friend I Ever
Had; The Gypsy Cried; My Foolish Heart; When I Learn How to
Cry; Surfin' Safari.* SURF CITY AND OTHER SWINGIN'
CITIES (6/63): *Surf Cities; Memphis; Detroit City; Manhattan;
Philadelphia, Pa.; Way Down Yonder in New Orleans; Honolulu
Lulu; Kansas City; I Left My Heart In San Francisco; You Came
a Long Way from St. Louis; Tallahassee Lassie; Soul City.* DRAG

CITY (11/63): *Drag City; I Gotta Drive; Drag Strip Girl; Surfin' Hearse; Dead Man's Curve; Schlock Rods Parts 1 and 2; Popsicle Truck; Surf Route 101; Sting Ray; Little Deuce Coupe; Hot Stocker.* DEAD MAN'S CURVE/THE NEW GIRL IN SCHOOL (5/64): *Dead Man's Curve; Three Window Coupe; Bucket "T"; Rockin' Little Roadster; "B" Gas Rickshaw; My Mighty GTO; The New Girl in School; Linda; Barons, West L.A.; School Day; As Easy as 1,2,3; Hey Little Freshman.* RIDE THE WILD SURF (8/64); *Ride the Wild Surf; Tell 'Em I'm Surfin; Waimea Girl; She's My Summer Girl; The Restless Surfer; Skateboarding Part 1; Sidewalk Surfin; Surfin' Wild; Down at Malibu Beach; A Surfer's Dream; Walk on the Wet Side; The Submarine Races.* THE LITTLE OLD LADY FROM PASADENA (9/64): *The Little Old Lady from Pasadena; Memphis; When It's Over; Horace, the Swingin' School Bus Driver; Old Ladies Seldom Power Shift; Sidewalk Surfin'; The Anaheim, Azusa and Cucamonga Sewing Circle, Book Review and Timing Association; Summer Means Fun; It's As Easy As 1,2,3; Move Out Little Mustang; Skateboarding Part 2; One-Piece Topless Bathing Suit.* COMMAND PERFORMANCE—LIVE IN PERSON (1/65): *Surf City; Little Honda; Dead Man's Curve; I Get Around; All I Have to Do Is Dream; Theme from the* Tami *Show; Rock and Roll Music; The Little Old Lady from Pasadena; Do Wah Diddy; I Should Have Known; Sidewalk Surfin'; Louie Louie.* GOLDEN HITS (8/65): *Baby Talk; Heart and Soul; Jennie Lee; We Go Together; Tennessee; Palisades Park; Who Put the Bomp; Sunday Kind of Love; Queen of My Heart; In a Turkish Town; Poor Little Puppet; Barbara Ann.* GOLDEN HITS VOL. II (9/65): *Linda; Surf City; Honolulu Lulu; Drag City; Dead Man's Curve; The New Girl in School; The Little Old Lady from Pasadena; The Anaheim, Azusa and Cucamonga Sewing Circle, Book Review and Timing Association; Ride the Wild Surf; Sidewalk Surfin'; From All Over the World; You Really Know How to Hurt a Guy.* FOLK 'N' ROLL (11/65): *I Found a Girl; Hang On Sloopy; I Can't Wait to Love You; Eve of Destruction; It's a Shame to Say Goodbye; Where Were You When I Needed You; A Beginning from an End; Yesterday; The Universal Coward; It Ain't Me Babe; Folk City; Turn! Turn! Turn!* JAN AND DEAN MEET BATMAN (3/66): *Batman; The Origin of Captain Jan and Dean the Boy Blunder; Robin the Boy Wonder; A Vi-Ta-Min a Day; Mr. Freeze; The Doctor's*

Dilemma; A Stench in Time; Batman Theme; A Hank of Hair and a Banana Peel; The Fireman's Flaming Flourish; The Joker Is Wild; Tiger Tiger, Burning; Flight of the Batmobile; A Hot Time in the Old Town Tonight. FILET OF SOUL (4/66): *Norwegian Wood; 1–2–3; Lightin' Strikes; You've Got to Hide Your Love Away; Let's Hang On; Hang On, Sloopy; Honolulu Lulu; Gonna Hustle You; Dead Man's Curve; Michelle; I Found a Girl; Everybody Loves a Clown.* POPSICLE (6/66): *Popsicle; The Restless Surfer; She's My Summer Girl; Down at Malibu Beach; Summer Means Fun; Tennessee; Norwegian Wood; A Surfer's Dream; Surf Route 101; Surfin' Wild; Waimea Bay; One-Piece Topless Bathing Suit.* JAN AND DEAN'S GOLDEN HITS VOL. III (8/66): *Batman; Do What Diddy; Detroit City; Eve of Destruction; 1–2–3; Hang On Sloopy; Little Deuce Coupe; Louie Louie; Memphis; Yesterday; Walk Right In; Everybody Loves a Clown.* SAVE FOR A RAINY DAY (3/67): *Yellow Balloon; Here Comes the Rain; Like Summer Rain; Lullaby in the Rain; Pocketful of Rainbows; When Sunny Gets Blue; Rain on the Roof; Raindrops; Cryin' in the Rain; Save for a Rainy Day Theme.* LEGENDARY MASTERS (1/72): *Jenny Lee; Baby Talk; Clementine; Heart and Soul; Tennessee; Barbara Ann; Linda; Surfin' Safari; Surf City; Honolulu Lulu; Drag City; Little Deuce Coupe; The New Girl in School; Dead Man's Curve; The Little Old Lady from Pasadena; The Anaheim, Azusa and Cucamonga Sewing Circle, Book Review and Timing Association; Ride the Wild Surf; Sidewalk Surfin'; One-Piece Topless Bathing Suit; Popsicle; Vegetables; Pigeon Joke; Brass Section Intro; Beatle Part of Our Portion; You've Got to Hide Your Love Away; Let's Hang On; Hang On Sloopy.* VERY BEST OF VOL. I (6/75): *Jenny Lee; Baby Talk; Heart and Soul; Surf City; Honolulu Lulu; Drag City; Little Deuce Coupe; Dead Man's Curve; Little Old Lady from Pasadena; Ride the Wild Surf.* VERY BEST OF VOL. II (9/75): *We Go Together; Linda; New Girl in School; The Anaheim, Azusa and Cucamonga Sewing Circle, Book Review and Timing Association; Sidewalk Surfin'; Here They Come from All Over the World; You Really Know How to Hurt a Guy; I Found a Girl; Batman; Popsicle.*

Singles/*A Sunday Kind of Love/Poor Little Puppet* (11/61); *Tennessee Your Heart Has Changed Its Mind* (4/62); *My Favorite Dream/Who Put the Bomp* (8/62); *Baby Talk/Jeanette Get Your*

Hair Done (9/62); *Frosty/She's Still Talking Baby Talk* (11/62);
When I Learn How to Cry/Linda (1/63); *The New Girl in
School/Dead Man's Curve* (2/63); *She's My Summer Girl/Surf
City* (5/63); *Honolulu Lulu/Someday* (8/63); *Drag City/Schlock
Rod* (11/63); *The Little Old Lady from Pasadena/My Mighty
GTO* (6/64); *Ride the Wild Surf/The Anaheim, Azusa and
Cucamonga Sewing Circle, Book Review and Timing Association*
(8/64); *Sidewalk Surfin'/When It's Over* (10/64); *Freeway
Flyer/From All Over the World* (2/65); *You Really Know How to
Hurt a Guy/It's As Easy As 1,2,3* (3/65); *It's a Shame to Say
Goodbye/Folk City* (9/65); *A Beginning from an End/Folk City*
(12/65); *Batman/Bucket "T"* (2/66); *Norwegian Wood/Popsicle*
(5/66); *A Surfer's Dream/Fiddle Around* (10/66); *Love and
Hate/Only a Boy* (2/68); *I Know My Mind/Laurel and Hardy*
(6/68); *The Still of the Night/Girl, You're Blowing My Mind*
(10/68); *Jennie Lee/Baby Talk; Linda/The New Girl in School;
Surf City/Ride the Wild Surf; Dead Man's Curve/Drag City; Hon-
olulu Lulu/Sidewalk Surfin; The Little Old Lady from
Pasadena/Popsicle* (all re-released 1/73); *Sidewalk Surfin'/Gonna
Hustle You* (6/75).

JAY AND THE AMERICANS/*Jay Black (lead vocals), Kenny
Vance (vocals), Sandy Dean (vocals), Marty Sanders (guitar). Additional member: Howie Kane.*
These four Brooklyn boys gave the Four Seasons a run for their
money in the shoo-wop style of the sixties' race. With a vocal style
slightly reminiscent of Roy Orbison in his prime, Jay Black led his
group on a rampage through the charts which lasted until the
dawning of psychedelia in the sixties. The band never made it into
the seventies, although Black is currently mulling a comeback. In
1977, he appeared with Frank Sinatra in the TV film *Contract on
Cherry Street.*

Albums/SHE CRIED (5/63): *Drums; Kansas City; My Clair de
Lune; Save the Last Dance for Me; Dawning; She Cried; Yes;
Stand by Me; Moon River; Tonight; Other Girls; Spanish Harlem.*
AT THE CAFE WHA? (7/63): *Gypsy in My Soul; I Hear Music;
Song Is You; Certain Smile; This Land Is Your Land; Lot of Living
to Do; Percolator Song; Riddle; Girls, Girls, Girls; Gonna Build
Me a Mountain; Lawrence; Golden Vanity; Kansas City; Baby,
That Is Rock 'n' Roll; For All We Know.* COME A LITTLE BIT

CLOSER (11/64): *Come a Little Bit Closer; She Doesn't Know It; Strangers Tomorrow; What's the Use; To Wait for Love; Only in America; Look in My Eyes, Maria; Friday; This Is It; Come Dance with Me; Tomorrow; Goodbye, Boys, Goodbye.* BLOCK-BUSTERS (5/65): *When It's All Over; Something in My Eye; Cara Mia; Think of the Good Times; Somebody's Gonna Cry; If You Were Mine, Girl; Run to My Lovin' Arms; Let's Lock the Door; Twenty-four Hours from Tulsa; Please Let Me Dream; Silly Girl, Silly Boy; Hang Around.* GREATEST HITS (10/65): *Some Enchanted Evening; Come a Little Bit Closer; Only in America; When It's All Over; Think of the Good Times; Goodbye, Boys, Goodbye; Cara Mia; Something in My Eye; Girl; Let's Lock the Door; If You Were Mine; Run to My Lovin' Arms; Through This Doorway.* SUNDAY AND ME (2/66): *Sunday and Me; Granada; Crying; Til; I Miss You; I Don't Need a Friend; Why Can't You Bring Me Home; Maria; Baby, Stop Your Cryin'; Chilly Winds; She's the Girl (That's Messin' Up My Mind).* LIVIN' ABOVE YOUR HEAD (8/66): *Livin' Above Your Head; Grass Will Sing; Too Many Times; Diana; Over the Mountain; I'll Remember; Sun Ain't Gonna Shine Anymore; Reason for Living; Monday, Monday; Baby, Come Home; Stop the Clock; Look at Me—What Do You See.* GREATEST HITS, VOLUME II (11/66); *Crying; Sunday and Me; Stop the Clock; Hang Around; Granada; Til; Twenty-four Hours from Tulsa; Monday, Monday; Livin' Above Your Head; Maria; Why Can't You Bring Me Home; Silly Girl, Silly Boy.* TRY SOME OF THIS (3/67): *You Ain't As Hip As All That, Baby; Always Something There to Remind Me; Where's the Girl; Show Must Go On; Truly Julie's Blues; Where Is the Village; Nature Boy; Here, There, and Everywhere; He's Raining in My Sunshine; What to Do with Laurie; It's a Big, Wide, Wonderful World.* SANDS OF TIME (2/69): *This Magic Moment; When You Dance; Hushabye; other titles.* WAX MUSEUM (2/70).

Singles/*She Cried/Tonight* (2/62); *Only in America/My Clair de Lune* (7/63); *Come Dance with Me* (10/63); *Come a Little Bit Closer/Goodbye, Boys, Goodbye* (8/64); *Let's Lock the Door/I'll Remember You* (11/64); *Think of the Good Times* (2/65); *Cara Mia/When It's All Over* (5/65); *Some Enchanted Evening* (8/65); *Sunday and Me* (10/65); *Why Can't You Bring Me Home* (1/66); *Crying* (4/66); *Livin' above Your Head* (6/66); *He's Raining on My Sunshine* (10/66); *This Magic Moment* (11/68); *When You Dance*

(3/69); *Hushabye* (4/69); *Walkin' in the Rain* (10/69); *Capture the Moment* (2/70).

THE JEFFERSON AIRPLANE/THE JEFFERSON STARSHIP/*AIRPLANE members: Signe Anderson (vocals), replaced after one album by Grace Slick (vocals). Marty Balin (vocals), Skip Spence (drums), replaced after one album by Spencer Dryden, who was replaced in turn by Joey Covington in 1971, Paul Kantner (guitar, vocals), Jorma Kaukonen (lead guitar), Jack Casady (bass) —Kaukonen and Casady later left the band to form Hot Tuna— David Freiberg (vocals). STARSHIP members: Paul Kantner (guitar, vocals), Grace Slick (piano, vocals), David Freiberg (bass, keyboards, vocals), Craig Chaquico (lead guitar), John Barbata (drums, percussion), Papa John Creach (violin), Pete Sears (bass, keyboards), Marty Balin (vocals).*

To a lot of music fans in the 1960s, the Jefferson Airplane was the closest thing you could get to God. They were the BIG San Francisco band and, as such, touched the nation with surrealistic visions of life, love, politics, and the beyond. Their instrumentation was delicate yet powerful and exceedingly spacey, yet it never got in the way of the strong vocal lines and ethereal harmonies.

The Airplane got its start during the dark ages of the mid-sixties ('65, actually). While Gary Lewis was whining about diamond rings and Donovan was getting famous for his Dondi caps, Marty Balin (a member of an SF group called the Town Criers) met Paul Kantner at a club named the Drinking Gourd. The two decided to form a folk-rock band, which evolved into the first Airplane. The embryonic band would go on to include Balin on vocals, Kantner on rhythm guitar and vocals, Jorma Kaukonen on lead guitar, Signe Anderson handling the vocalizing and Bob Harvey on bass. Harvey bailed out almost immediately and was replaced by Jack Casady. By August of 1965, the Airplane was playing at the Matrix Club; a few months later they were signed to RCA. A first album was recorded but most felt that it was a bit . . . anticlimactic. Anderson left, as did Spence. (Spence, switching to guitar, became the resident battery in Moby Grape.) Spencer Dryden entered the fold on drums and a young lady named Grace Slick took over the chore of vocalizing. Grace had a nice reputation coming into the Airplane, having proven to be an exceptionally strong vocalist with a popular local band, the Great Society.

This lineup went on to change the music industry both musically and lyrically. The band caused quite a stir with such singles as "White Rabbit" and "Volunteers," garnering airplay despite the controversial (at that time) lyrics. Their controlled use of guitar distortion opened up the AM-radio airwaves for more progressive-sounding bands. Success was there, even as the inner workings of the band got more and more bizarre. The Airplane was always known as being a musical family composed of unique and spirited individuals. It was only natural that some did not see eye-to-eye on occasion. And they did not see eye-to-eye quite a bit. When the Airplane wasn't discussing artistic direction within the confines of the group, they often discussed it rather blatantly with their record label. At times, it was clear that RCA did not know what to do with the innovative troupe. Legend has it that every time a new Airplane album was released, the corporation's interest in aspirin stock increased a hundredfold.

As success followed success for the Airplane, and the sixties slid into the seventies, several of the members began to grow bored within the musical confines of the band. In 1970, Spencer Dryden left the band to join the New Riders of the Purple Sage; by the following year, Joey Covington was a group mainstay. Paul and Grace's shipboard romance saw the birth of their daughter, China, in 1971. The same year spawned the departure of Marty Balin, who embarked on a short-lived solo career. Shortly after Marty's exit, the Airplane formed their own label, Grunt, which served as a clearinghouse for both their own music and that of their closest friends.

In a free concert in New York's Central Park in August, 1972, the Airplane introduced their newest member, former Quicksilver founder David Freiberg, on vocals and keyboards. That same month, however, Jorma and Jack jumped ship to form Hot Tuna. After their departure, The Airplane glided to a stop, the only album to arise subsequent to Jorma and Jack's leaving being the live *WINTERLAND* set. As the Airplane drifted into the sunset, a host of solo albums emerged. Kantner, Slick, and Frieberg released their *BARON VON TOLLBOOTH* in June of 1973 and Grace's solo *MANHOLE* LP appeared in January of 1974. By

1974, it was clear that the Airplane would never take off again. But loyal Jefferson fans were not desolate for long.

THE JEFFERSON STARSHIP

In February of 1974, the Jefferson Starship debuted, featuring Slick, Kantner, Freiberg, Papa John Creach, Craig Chaquico, ex-Turtle John Barbata, and Peter Kangaroo (Kaukonen). The sound was honed from the core of the Airplane but, overall, it was modernized, amplified—and it possessed a free-flowing feel that the Airplane had seldom known during the 70's. By June of that year, Kangaroo had hopped away and Pete Sears had slithered in. Marty Balin came out of the woodwork to contribute a classic song, *Caroline,* to the recording sessions that led to *DRAGON-FLY.* He joined the band permanently the following year (in January) and has remained with them since.

Proving that you can't keep a spaced-up Airplane down, the Starship has gone on to garner three gold albums in three years, a gold single, a platinum album, and a solid number-one status on the Billboard charts four times in three months. The music of the Jefferson Starship remains as integral a part of the seventies as the celestial droning of the Jefferson Airplane was of the sixties.

Albums/THE JEFFERSON AIRPLANE TAKES OFF (8/66): *Blues from an Airplane; Let Me In; It's No Secret; Bringing Me Down; Tobacco Road; Come Up the Years; Run Around; Let's Get Together; Don't Slip Away; Chauffeur Blues; And I Like It.* SUR-REALISTIC PILLOW (2/67): *She Has Funny Cars; Somebody to Love; My Best Friend; Today; Comin' Back to Me; How Do You Feel; 3/5 of a Mile in Ten Seconds; Embryonic Journey; D.C.B.A.-25; White Rabbit; Plastic Fantastic Lover.* AFTER BATHING AT BAXTER'S (1/68): *Ballad of You and Me and Pooneil; Two Heads; Last Wall of the Castle; Rejoyce; Watch Her Ride; Spare Chaynge; Won't You Try/Saturday Afternoon; Wild Tyme; Martha; Small Package of Value Will Come to You, Short-ly; Young Girl Sunday Blues.* CROWN OF CREATION (9/68): *Lather; In Time; Triad; Star Track; Share a Little Joke; Chus-ingura; If You Feel; Ice Cream Phoenix; Crown of Creation; Greasy Heart; House at Pooneil Corners.* BLESS ITS POINTED LITTLE HEAD (3/69): *Clergy; 3/5 of a Mile in Ten Seconds; Somebody to Love; Fat Angel; Rock Me Baby; The Other Side of This Life; It's No Secret; Plastic Fantastic Lover; Turn Out the Lights; Bear Melt.* VOLUNTEERS (11/69): *We Can Be Togeth-*

er; Good Shepherd; The Farm; Hey Fredrick; Turn My Life Down; Wooden Ships; Eskimo Blue Day; A Song for All Seasons; Meadowlands; Volunteers. PAUL KANTNER—JEFFERSON STARSHIP: BLOWS AGAINST THE EMPIRE (a Kantner solo album featuring musician friends such as Jerry Garcia, Grace Slick, Joey Covington, Jack Casady, David Crosby, Graham Nash, Peter Kaukonen, David Freiberg, and Mickey Hart performing in a loose unit named after a *Star Trek* term; 11/70): *Mau Mau; The Baby Tree; Let's Go Together; A Child Is Coming; Sunrise; Hijack; Home; Have You Seen the Stars Tonight; XM; Starship.* THE WORST OF THE JEFFERSON AIRPLANE (11/70): *It's No Secret; Blues from an Airplane; Somebody to Love; Today; White Rabbit; Embryonic Journey; Martha; Ballad of You and Me and Pooneil; Crown of Creation; Lather; Crushingura; Plastic Fantastic Lover; Good Shepherd; We Can Be Together; Volunteers.* BARK (9/71): *When the Earth Moves Again; Feel So Good; Crazy Miranda; Pretty As You Feel; Wild Turkey; Law Man; Rock and Roll Island; Third Week in Chelsea; Never Argue with a German; Thunk; War Movie.* KANTNER/SLICK: SUNFIGHTER (12/71): *Silver Spoon; Diana; Sunfighter; Titanic; Look at the World; When I Was a Boy I Watched the Wolves; Million; China; Earth Mother; Diana 2; Universal Copernican Mumbles; Holding Together.* LONG JOHN SILVER (7/72): *Long John Silver; Aerie (Gang of Eagles); Milk Train; Song of Jesus; Twilight Double Lead; Easter?; Trial by Fire; Alexander the Medium; Eat Starch, Mom.* THIRTY SECONDS OVER WINTERLAND (the final Airplane album; 4/73): *Have You Seen the Saucers; Feel So Good; Crown of Creation; When the Earth Moves Again; Milk Train; Trial by Fire; Twilight Double Leader.* KANTNER, SLICK AND FREIBERG: BARON VON TOLLBOOTH AND THE CHROME NUN (6/73): *Ballad of the Chrome Nun; Fat; Flowers of the Night; Walkin'; Your Mind Has Left Your Body; Across the Board; Harp Tree Lament; White Boy; Fishman; Sketches of China.* MARTY BALIN: BODACIOUS (10/73): *Drifting; Good Folks; The Witcher; Roberta; Second-Hand Information; Driving Me Crazy; Twixt Two Worlds.* GRACE SLICK: MANHOLE (1/74): *Jay; Come Again Toucan; It's Only Music; Betty Lying Down; Epic (#38).* JEFFERSON AIRPLANE EARLY FLIGHT (4/74): *High Flyin' Bird; Runnin' 'Round This World; It's Alright; In the Morning; J.P.P. McStep B. Blues; Up or Down; Mexico; Have You Seen the Saucers; Go to*

Her. DRAGON FLY (the first Starship album; 10/74): *Ride the Tiger; That's for Sure; Be Young You; Caroline; Devil's Den; Come to Life; All Fly Away; Hyperdrive.* RED OCTOPUS (6/75); *Fast Buck Freddie; Miracles; Git Fiddler; Ai Garimasu (There Is Love); Sweeter Than Honey; Play on Love; Tumblin; I Want to See Another World; Sandalphon; There Will Be Love.* SPITFIRE (6/76): *Hot Water; Big City; Switchblade; Cruisin'; Love Lovely Love; St. Charles; Dance with the Dragon; With Your Love; Song to the Son—Ozymandias, Don't Let It Rain.* FLIGHT LOG (2/77): *Come Up the Years; White Rabbit; Comin' Back to Me; Won't You Try Saturday Afternoon; Greasy Heart; If You Feel; Silver Spoon; Feel So Good; Pretty As You Feel; Milk Train; Ja Da; Somebody to Love; Wooden Ships; Volunteers; Hesitation Blues; Have You Seen the Stars Tonight; Come Again Toucan; Sketches of China; Genesis; Ride the Tiger; Please Come Back.* EARTH (3/78): *Love Too Good; Count on Me; Take Your Time; Crazy Feelin'; Skateboard; Fire; Show Yourself; All Nite Long; Runaway.*

Singles/*It's No Secret/Runnin' 'Round This World* (2/66); *Come Up the Years/Blues from an Airplane* (5/66); *Bringing Me Down/Let Me In* (9/66); *My Best Friend/How Do You Feel* (12/66); *Somebody to Love/She Has Funny Cars* (2/67); *White Rabbit/Plastic Fantastic Lover* (6/67); *Ballad of You and Me and Pooneil/Two Heads* (8/67); *Watch Her Ride/Martha* (11/67); *Greasy Heart/Share a Little Joke* (3/68); *White Rabbit/Somebody to Love* (9/68); *Crown of Creation/Lather* (10/68); *Other Side of This Life/Plastic Fantastic Lover* (5/69); Kantner: *A Child Is Coming/Let's Go Together* (2/71); *Volunteers/We Can Be Together; Been So Long/Candy Man* (9/71); *Pretty As You Feel/Wild Turkey* (10/71); Kantner-Slick: *China/ Sunfighter* (2/72); *Long John Silver/Milk Train* (7/72); *Trial by Fire/Twilight Double Leader* (12/72); Slick-Kantner-Freiberg: *Sketches of China/Ballad of the Chrome Nun* (7/73); Slick: *Theme from MANHOLE/Come Again Toucan* (3/74); *Ride the Tiger/Devil's Den* (10/74); *Caroline* (1/75); *Miracles/Ai Garimasu* (7/75); *Play on Love/I Want to See Another World* (11/75); *With Your Love* (6/76); *St. Charles/Love Lovely Love* (10/76).

ELTON JOHN/Elton John is a superstar in the truest sense of the word. That may sound corny, but Elton is one of the few rock performers not only to survive the seventies but actually to blossom during their fickle years. Unlike most "stars" of this decade who have a nasty habit of disappearing within the span of three albums, John has risen from total obscurity to the top of the heap—outselling just about all the current competition. He is to the children of the seventies what the Beatles and the Stones were to the sixties' generation.

Elton, born Reginald Kenneth Dwight in Middlesex, England, began his show-business career while still a teen. A chubby, shy lad, he was exceedingly ambitious and ran after his show-biz goal like a man possessed. Both his mother and stepfather encouraged his quest but began to worry when Reg began holding down two and three jobs at a time—working as a messenger during the day and doubling as both a rock musician and a saloon piano player at night. Eventually, Reg was able to quit the barroom brigade and concentrate all his efforts on rock. The band was Bluesology and Dwight was the keyboard player par excellence. Dragging a compact electric piano with him from gig to gig, he and Bluesology made the rounds, both playing gigs and backing visiting headliners such as Patti Labelle and the Bluebelles and Major Lance.

The band might have remained in backup limbo for an unbearably long time were it not for the efforts of veteran British bloozer Long John Baldry. After spotting the boys at a local club, Baldry (who was attempting a kamikaze comeback on the pop charts) used the group on his shlocky hit single *Let the Heartaches Begin*. It soared to number one and, in 1967, Reggie Dwight had his first taste of fame. During his stay with Baldry, Dwight changed his name to Elton John: a title culled from Baldry's monicker and sax player Elton Dean's.

As Baldry became increasingly popular with the cabaret crowd, it was clear that Bluesology's days were numbered as his raunchy backup unit. Elton, out of work, answered a "new talent" ad taken out by Liberty Records in a British music publication. He auditioned as a singer-pianist, which was a first in that he had never crooned a note in Bluesology. He underwhelmed all present. One quick-thinking executive, however, remembered the name of Bernie Taupin, a teen who had submitted lyrics in the talent search, without the benefit of melodies. John was given Taupin's lyrics and told to compose. Compose he did. But by the time he was through, Liberty was no longer interested.

Over six months later, Taupin and John finally met and got jobs as "hit" songwriters with Dick James Music, a publishing company. For two years they labored, turning out shlock tunes like mad. Elton supplemented his income by playing on numerous bogus "greatest hits" LPs, on which unknown bands performed the hits of established bands for a discount retail price. He even wangled a session or two as a keyboard player for the Hollies.

Fairly discouraged, the twosome was given a shot in the arm by the arrival of Steve Brown in James' office. Brown told them to forget the top-forty stuff and write what they wanted to. They did. In 1969, Elton's first single, *Lady Samantha,* was released. It was a well-received stiff. By the time Elton's first album, *EMPTY SKY,* was released, the world was aware of his presence. The record, unreleased stateside until 1975, was fairly crude, produced on a four-track tape deck by Brown. But it proved that Taupin-John had talent. Brown allowed Gus Dudgeon to take over for the following LP and the hit single *Your Song.* Elton's career had started in earnest.

From that point onward, Elton and Bernie continued to grow in every musical respect. The hits kept on coming. The albums improved both material- and production-wise. The sound expanded, taking in aspects of rock, reggae, MOR, R&B, and autobiography. John's frantic stage antics (a mild-mannered lad offstage, he became a mini Jerry Lee Lewis onstage, on piano, and on anything that didn't move too quickly). By 1972, it was clear that Elton John had transcended the ranks of rockdom and was a rock institution unto himself, incapable of doing wrong. In 1973, he formed Rocket Records, a company co-owned by his manager, John Reid. Rock has launched, or re-launched, the careers of Kiki Dee and Neil Sedaka, as well as serving as a showcase for bands like Longdancer.

At this point in his career, there is no stopping the elfish pianist. He has dabbled in film, playing a role in the motion picture *Tommy.* He is now represented in Madame Toussaud's Wax Museum in London; right up there with the Beatles, Winston Churchill, JFK, and other prime movers. And the records just keep on coming. In less than a decade, he has racked up nine gold singles, thirteen gold albums and twelve platinum long-players. In 1977, he announced his retirement from live performing. A few months later, a greatest hits album went gold upon the day of its release.

One really shouldn't be amazed, though, at Elton's seemingly impossible musical feats. A few years back, Reggie Dwight had his name changed, legally, to Elton John. And his new middle name? Hercules, of course.

Albums/ELTON JOHN (7/70): *Your Song; I Need You to Turn To; Take Me to the Pilot; No Shoestrings on Louise; First Episode at Heinton; Sixty Years On; Border Song; The Greatest Discovery; The Cage; The King Must Die.* TUMBLEWEED CONNEC-TION (1/71): *Ballad of a Well-Known Gun; Talking Old Soldiers; Son of Your Father; Country Comfort; Amoreena; Burn Down the Mission; Love Song; My Father's Gun; Come Down in Time; Where to Now, St. Peter?* 11-17-70 (5/71): *Take Me to the Pilot; Honky Tonk Woman; Sixty Years On; Can I Put You On; Bad Side of the Moon; Burn Down the Mission.* MADMAN ACROSS THE WATER (11/71): *Tiny Dancer; Levon; Razor Face; Madman across the Water; Indian Sunset; Holiday Inn; Rotten Peaches; All the Nasties.* HONKY CHATEU (5/72); *Honky Cat; Mellow; I Think I'm Going to Kill Myself; Susie (Dramas); Rocket Man (I Think It's Going to Be a Long, Long Time); Salvation; Slave; Army; Mona Lisas and Mad Hatters; Hercules.* DON'T SHOOT ME, I'M ONLY THE PIANO PLAYER (1/73): *Daniel; Teach I Need You; Elderberry Wine; Blues for Baby and Me; Midnight Creeper; Crocodile Rock; Have Mercy on the Criminal; I'm Going to Be a Teenage Idoll Texas Love Song; High Flying Bird.* GOODBYE YELLOW BRICK ROAD (10/73): *Funeral for a Friend; Love Lies Bleeding; Candle in the Wind; Bennie and the Jets; Goodbye Yellow Brick Road; This Song Has No Title; Grey Seal; Jamaica Jerk-Off; I've Seen That Movie Too; Sweet Painted Lady; The Ballad of Danny Baily (1909–34); Dirty Little Girl; All the Girls Love Alice; Your Sister Can't Twist (But She Sure Can Rock and Roll); Saturday Night's Alright for Fighting; Roy Rogers; Social Disease; Harmony.* CARIBOU (6/74): *The Bitch Is Back; Pinky; Grimsby; Dixie Lily; Sola Restige a Gammon; You're So Static; I've Seen the Saucers; Stinker; Don't Let the Sun Go Down on Me; Ticking.* GREATEST HITS (11/74): *Your Song; Daniel; Honky Cat; Rocket Man; Goodbye Yellow Brick Road; Saturday Night's Alright for Fighting; Bennie and the Jets; Don't Let the Sun Go Down on Me; Border Song; Crocodile Rock.* EMP-TY SKY (1/75): *Empty Sky; Valhalla; Western Ford Gateway; Hymn 2000; Lady; What's Tomorrow; Sails; The Scaffold; Skyline*

Pigeon; Gulliver ... Hey Chewed. CAPTAIN FANTASTIC AND THE BROWN DIRT COWBOY (5/75): *Captain Fantastic and the Brown Dirt Cowboy; Tower of Babel; Bitter Fingers; Tell Me When The Whistle Blows; Someone Saved My Life Tonight; Gotta Get a Meal Ticket; Better Off Dead; Writing; We All Fall in Love Sometimes; Curtains.* ROCK OF THE WESTIES (10/75); *Island Girl; Sugar on the Floor; Grow Some Funk of Your Own; I Feel Like a Bullet (in the Gun of Robert Ford); other titles.* HERE AND THERE (5/76): *Skyline Pigeon; Border Song; Honky Cat; Love Song; Crocodile Rock; Funer for a Friend; Love Lies Bleeding; Rocket Man; Bennie and the Jets; Take Me to the Pilot.* BLUE MOVES (10/76): *Your Starter For . . .; Tonight; One Horse Town; Chameleon; Boogie Pilgrim; Cage the Songbird; Crazy Water; Shoulder Holster; Sorry Seems to Be the Hardest Word; Out of the Blue; Between Seventeen and Twenty; The Wide-Eyed and Laughing; Someone's Final Song; Where's the Shoorah?; If There's a God in Heaven (What's He Waiting For?); Idol; Theme from a Non-Existent TV Series; Bite Your Lip (Get Up and Dance).* GREATEST HITS, VOLUME II (11/77): *The Bitch Is Back; Lucy in the Sky with Diamonds; Sorry Seems to Be the Hardest Word; Don't Go Breaking My Heart; Someone Saved My Life Tonight; Philadelphia Freedom; Island Girl; Grow Some Funk of Your Own; Levon; Pinball Wizard.*

Singles/*Lady Samantha*/*It's Me That You Need* (2/70); *Border Song*/*Bad Side of the Moon* (4/70); *Your Song*/*Take Me to the Pilot* (10/70); *Friends*/*Honey Roll* (3/71); *Levon*/*Goodbye* (11/71); *Tiny Dancer*/*Razor Face* (2/72); *Rocket Man*/*Suzie* (4/72); *Honky Cat*/*Slave* (7/72); *Crocodile Rock*/*Elderberry Wine* (11/72); *Daniel*/*Skyline Pigeon* (3/73); *Saturday Night's Alright for Fighting*/*Jack Rabbit*—*Whenever You're Ready* (7/73); *Goodbye Yellow Brick Road*/*Young Man's Blues* (10/73); *Step into Christmas*/*Ho Ho Ho (Who'd Be a Turkey at Christmas)* (11/73); *Bennie and the Jets*/*Harmony* (2/74); *Don't Let the Sun Go Down on Me*/*Sick City* (6/74); *The Bitch Is Back*/*Cold Highway* (9/74); *Lucy in the Sky with Diamonds*/*One Day at a Time* (11/74); *Philadelphia Freedom*/*I Saw Her Standing There* (featuring John Lennon) (2/75); *Someone Saved My Life Tonight*/*House of Cards* (6/75); *Island Girl*/*Sugar on the Floor* (9/75); *Grow Some Funk of Your Own*/*I Feel Like a Bullet (in the Gun of Robert Ford)* (1/76); *Don't Go Breaking My Heart* (with Kiki Dee)/*Snow Queen* (with

Kiki Dee) (6/76); *Sorry Seems to Be the Hardest Word/Shoulder Holster* (11/76).

JANIS JOPLIN/Onstage, Janis Joplin shone brighter than any star in the sky. On record, she gave off more energy than a nuclear power plant. She was one of the most powerful personalities to emerge from the sixties and her banshee approach to blues-rock was totally unique, one hundred percent of her own.

Born and raised in Port Arthur, Texas, Joplin trudged through a childhood brimming with hurt and resentment. An ordinary-looking, introverted girl, Joplin read poetry and attempted to find her way into the mainstream of society through the beat generation. She also tried her hand at folk singing. The small city of Port Arthur, however, considered both actions high intolerable.

At the age of seventeen, Janis ran away from home. She dropped in and out of four colleges, held assorted odd jobs, collected unemployment, and cultivated her folk-singing career. A chance encounter with a Leadbelly record led to an all-consuming fascination with the blues idiom. Bessie Smith and Odetta records soon found their way into Janis' collection. "One night I was at this party," Joplin once recalled, "and I did an imitation of Odetta. I'd never sung before, and I came out with this huge voice."

Janis began singing in clubs and bars along the coast of California. Still very much the folk singer, she introduced a very pleasant sounding blues into her act. Eventually, she went back to the local clubs in Austin, Texas. An acquaintance told her that San Francisco was the place for her and, soon, Joplin was face to face with SF figure Chet Helms, who promptly introduced her to a singerless band, Big Brother and the Holding Company.

She auditioned with the band and, finding that her demure vocaling was no match for the hard-rocking high volume behind her, really cut loose. Helms was impressed. Big Brother was impressed. Joplin was stunned. Her career as a rock artist had begun.

The band cut a fairly grotesque record for a small label on the West Coast—it sounded as if it had been produced with an electric can opener. The LP did please Big Brother's growing legion of regional devotees, however, and the reputation of the plucky lead singer spread like wildfire. By the time the Monterey Pop Festival of 1967 happened, so did Big Brother. A bit out of tune (as always), a little ragged and very raunchy, the group erupted with a classic set, showcasing the rasping ranting of Joplin on Bessie Smith's standard *Ball and Chain*. In the audience was Columbia Records president Clive Davis, out music shopping in the psychedelic supermarket. He signed the band and, in 1968, their first Columbia LP, *CHEAP THRILLS,* was released. It was also their last.

Not long after the release of the LP, Big Brother and Janis parted company, the victims of two years of trying too hard to make it. Stagnation had set in. What were new tunes to new audiences in 1968 were old stuff to the band who had been playing them for eighteen months, sometimes six nights a week.

But Joplin emerged a star. Her rowdy, cackling, hooch-drinking personality coupled with her overall projection of total vulnerability made her one of rock's biggest (and different) sex symbols. Guys liked her because she was ballsy and energetic. Girls liked her because she was one outspoken woman. Although Joplin enjoyed a meteoric rise with Big Brother, she was destined to have difficult times with her groups to come.

Her first unit, unveiled in 1969, was the loosely knit Kozmic Blues Band, aka Squeeze. By December of that year, the Blues Band was considered anything but kosmic, Squeeze had been squoze, and Joplin was without a band once more. Her personal life plagued by hangers-on, bouts with depression, loneliness, critics, and recording deadlines, she disappeared into the jungles of Rio de Janeiro to get away from it all. Emerging in April, Joplin seemed totally recovered from the traumas that had beset her and, after appearing with Big Brother for a brief reunion gig at the Fillmore West, she formed her finest band ever: Full Tilt. Unveiled in June, the band consisted of John Till (guitar), Brad Campbell (bass), Richard Bell (piano), and Clark Pierson (drums).

The band met with instant success. A guest appearance on the ABC-TV *Dick Cavett Show* (where Joplin was getting to be a semi-regular) showed the band to be a tightly knit organization capable of tasteful, albeit raucous, rhythms. An album was soon begun. But by the time *PEARL* was released, the phenomenal career of Janis Joplin had come to an end. Her body was found in a Hollywood motel on October 4, 1970, the victim of a drug overdose. The latter circumstance puzzled all of her close personal and business friends.

Janis Joplin was more than a rock star. She was an art form, a source of energy, a way of life in the sixties. She literally personified what the hard-rocking San Francisco sound was all about. She once remarked about her frenzied stage antics, which constantly galvanized her audiences to the point of eruption: "It used to make me very unhappy, all that feeling. I just didn't know what to do with it, but now I've learned how to make feelings work for me. I'm full of emotion and I want a release. And if you're onstage and if it's really working and you've got the audience with you, it's a *oneness* you feel. I'm into me, plus they're into me, and everything comes together. . . . It's what soul is all about."

I GOT DEM OL' KOZMIC BLUES AGAIN, MAMA (8/69): *Try; Maybe; One Good Man; As Good As You've Been to This World; To Love Somebody; Kozmic Blues; Little Girl Blues; Work Me, Lord.* PEARL (1/71): *Move Over; Cry Baby; A Woman Left Lonely; Half Moon; Buried Alive in the Blues; My Baby; Me and Bobby McGee; Mercedes Benz; Trust Me; Get It While You Can.* JOPLIN IN CONCERT (4/72): *Down on Me; Bye-Bye, Baby; All Is Loneliness; Piece of My Heart; Road Block; Flower in the Sun; Summertime; Ego Rock; Half Moon; Kosmic Blues; Move Over; Try; Get It While You Can; Ball and Chain.* GREATEST HITS (6/73): *Me and Bobby McGee; Down on Me; Piece of My Heart; Try; Bye-Bye, Baby; Sumertime; Ball and Chain; Move Over; Cry Baby; Get It While You Can.* JANIS (soundtrack; 4/75): *Mercedes Benz; Ball and Chain; Rap on Try; Try; Summertime; Albert Hall Interview; Cry Baby; Trouble in Mind; What Good Can Drinkin' Do?; Silver Threads and Golden Needles; Mississippi River; Stealin'; No Reason for Livin'; Black Mountain Blues; Walk Right In; Move Over; Dick Cavett TV Interview; Piece of My Heart; Port Arthur High School Reunion; Maybe; Me and Bobby McGee; River Jordan; Mary Jane; Kansas City Blues; Daddy, Daddy, Daddy; C.C. Rider; San Francisco Bay Blues; Winin' Boy; Careless Love; I'll Drown in My Old Tears.*

Singles/*Kozmic Blues*/*Little Girl Blue* (10/69); *Try*/*One Good Man* (1/70); *Maybe*/*Work Me, Lord* (3/70); *Piece of My Heart*/*Kozmic Blues* (9/70); *Me and Bobby McGee*/*Half Moon* (1/71); *Cry Baby*/*Mercedes Benz* (4/71); *Get It While You Can*/*Move Over* (8/71); *Me and Bobby McGee*/*Get It While You Can* (2/72); *Cry Baby*/*Mercedes Benz* (5/72); *Down on Me*/*Bye-Bye, Baby* (6/72).

JOURNEY/*Gregg Rolie (vocals, keyboards, guitar), Neal Schon (guitar), George Tickner (bass), Aynsley Dunbar (drums).*
Rising Phoenix-like from the ashes of the Santana troupe, Journey is a hard-rocking San Francisco outfit made up of ex-Santanaites (Rolie and Schon), a primo session musician (Dunbar, late of Bowie, Zappa, Jeff Beck, and Flo and Eddie) and local talent (Tickner). The group made their debut in 1973 before a crowd of ardent music freaks at Winterland's New Year's Eve party. That gig launched their career with a bang. Since that time, however, they really haven't been able to shift to second gear. Their albums have all been well played but fairly unmemorable, hindered by underproduction and uninspired arranging. Still, Journey does have a grassroots following that's hot to trot. One spark from this band is all that's needed.

Albums/JOURNEY (4/75): *Of a Lifetime; In the Morning Day; Kohoutek; To Play Some Music; Topaz; In My Lonely Feeling; Conversations; Mystery Mountain.* LOOK INTO THE FUTURE (12/75): *On a Saturday Night; It's All Too Much; Anyway; She Makes Me (Feel Alright); You're on Your Own; Look into the Future; Midnight Dreamer; I'm Gonna Leave You.* NEXT (12/76): *Spaceman; People; I Would Find You; Here We Are; Hustler; Next; Nickel and Dime; Kama; Look into the Future.* INFINITY (1/78): *Wheel in the Sky; Somethin' to Hide; La Do Da; Open the Door; Feeling That Way; Winds of March; Lights; Patiently; Can Do; Anytine.*

Singles/*Kohoutek/Topaz* (5/75); *To Play Some Music/Topaz* (6/75); *On a Saturday Night/To Play Some Music* (3/76); *She Makes Me (Feel Alright)/It's All Too Much* (6/76); *Spaceman/Nickel and Dime* (4/77).

KANSAS/*Phil Ehart (drums), Dave Hope (bass), Kerry Livgren (guitar, keyboards), Robby Steinhardt (violin, vocals), Steve Walsh (keyboards, vibes, vocals), Rich Williams (guitar).*
Rock-mastermind Don Kirshner (the man who spawned both the Monkees and the Archies) brought Kansas to light a few years back—his first legitimate rock venture. Kansas is a combination of American rhythms and progressive British flavoring. Lead guitarist/composer Kerry Livgren is a rabid classical music buff, while fellow songwriter Steve Walsh digs Pink Floyd and Stevie Wonder. Put it all together and it spells strangeness but successful

strangeness, as the band gathers up its gold records and hit-single awards.

Albums/KANSAS (3/74): *Can I Tell You; Bringing It Back; Lonely Wind; Belexes; Journey from Mariabronn; The Pilgrammage; Death of Mother Nature Suite.* SONG FOR AMERICA (2/75): *Down the Road; Song for America; Lamplight Symphony; Lonely Street; The Devil Game; Incomudro-Hymn to the Atmar.* MASQUE (11/75): *It Takes a Woman; Two Cents Worth; Icarus —Borne on Wings of Steel; All The World; Child of Innocence; It's You; Mysteries and Mayhem; The Pinnacle.* LEFTOVERTURE (9/76): *Carry On, Wayward Son; The Wall; What's on My Mind; Miracles out of Nowhere; Opus Insert; Questions of My Childhood; Cheyenne; Anthem; Magnum Opus; It Takes a Woman's Love (to Make a Man).* POINT OF KNOW RETURN (10/77): *Point of Know Return; Paradox; The Spider; Portrait (He Knew); Closet Chronicles; Lightning's Hand; Sparks of the Tempest; Dust in the Wind; Hopelessly Human.*

Singles/*Can I Tell You/The Pilgrammage* (5/74); *Lonely Wind/Bringing It Back* (9/74); *Song for America* (4/75); *It's You* (3/76); *Carry On, Wayward Son/Questions of My Childhood* (11/76); *What's on My Mind/Lonely Street* (5/77).

B.B. KING/Riley King was born in Itta Bena, Mississippi, in 1925. For blues buffs, that was a good year for guitar magic, because in the world of electric blues there is only one real wizard and that's B.B. King. When Riley was old enough, he moved to Memphis where he ran into Sonny Boy Williamson. Sonny Boy was the host of the King Biscuit Boy radio show. He was impressed with the young man from Mississippi and gave him a spot as a dj, nicknaming him Blues Boy . . . B.B. B.B. started from there, absorbing, experimenting, playing.

He was well known among primarily black audiences when, in the late sixties, while British rock musicians came forth with blues licks. It was only a matter of time before laid-back, ultra-powerful B.B. was onstage playing rings around the best of them. They acknowledged the presence of their master, so, ten years ago, B.B. King brought the blues to rock audiences, to white audiences, for the first time in his career. And, although the blues-rock furor has died down of late, B.B. is still there, wielding his ageless guitar, Lucille, and producing some of the sweetest, most soul-searing notes ever to be heard in the blues world.

Albums/MR. BLUES (6/63): *Young Dreamers; By Myself; Chains of Love; A Mother's Love; Blues at Midnight; Sneakin' Around; On My Word of Honor; Tomorrow Night; My Baby's Coming Home; Guess Who; You Ask Me; I'm Gonna Sit In 'Til You Give In.* "LIVE" AT THE REGAL (1/65): *Every Day I Have the Blues; Sweet Little Angel; It's My Own Fault; How Blue Can You Get; Please Love Me; You Upset Me, Baby; Worry, Worry; Woke Up This Mornin; You Done Lost Your Good Thing Now; Help the Poor.* CONFESSIN' THE BLUES (10/65): *See See Rider; Do You Call That a Buddy; Wee Baby Blues; I'd Rather Drink Muddy Water; In the Dark; Confessin' the Blues; Goin' to Chicago Blues; I'm Gonna Move to the Outskirts of Town; World of Trouble; How Long; How Long Blues; Cherry Red; Please Send Me Someone to Love.* BLUES IS KING (1/67): *Waitin' on You; Gambler's Blues; Tired of Your Jive; Night Life; Buzz Me; Don't Answer the Door; Blind Love; I Know What You're Puttin' Down; Baby Get Lost; Gonna Keep On Loving You.* THE ELECTRIC B.B. KING—HIS BEST (1968, re-issued 3/75); *Tired of Your Jive; Don't Answer the Door; The B.B. Jones; All Over Again; Payin' the Cost to Be the Boss; Think It Over; I Done Got Wise; Meet My Happiness; Sweet Sixteen; You Put It on Me; I Don't Want You Cuttin' Off Your Hair.* BLUES ON TOP OF BLUES (1/68): *Heartbreaker; Losing Faith in You; Dance with Me; That's Wrong, Little Mama; Having My Say; I'm Not Wanted Anymore; Worried Dream; Paying the Cost to Be the Boss; Until I Found You; I'm Gonna Do What They Do to Me; Raining in My Heart; Now That You've Lost Me.* INDIANOLA MISSISSIPPI (9/70): *Nobody Loves Me but My Mother; You're Still My Woman; Ask Me No Questions; Until I'm Dead and Cold; King's Special; Ain't Gonna Worry My Life Anymore; Chains and Things; Go Underground; Hummingbird.* LIVE IN COOK COUNTY JAIL (2/71) *Intro; Everyday I Have the Blues; How Blue Can You Get; Worry, Worry, Worry; medley: Three O'Clock Blues—Darlin' You Know I Love You; Sweet Sixteen; The Thrill Is Gone; Please Accept My Love.* B.B. KING IN LONDON (9/71): *Caledonia; Blue Shadows; Alexis' Boogie; We Can't Agree; Ghetto Woman; Wet Hayshark; Part-Time Love; Power of the Blues; Ain't Nobody Home.* "LIVE" AT THE REGAL (re-issued 9/71).

L.A. MIDNIGHT (2/72). GUESS WHO (8/72): *Summer in the City; Just Can't Please You; Any Other Way; You Don't Know Nothin' about Love; Found What I Need; Neighborhood Affair; It Takes a Young Girl; Better Lovin' Man; Guess Who; Shouldn't Have Left Me; Five Long Years.* THE BEST OF B.B. KING (1/73). TO KNOW YOU IS TO LOVE YOU (7/73): *I Like to Live the Love; Respect Yourself; Who Are You; Love; I Can't Leave; To Know You Is to Love You; Thank You for Loving the Blues.* HIS BEST (3/75). LIVE AND WELL (3/75). COMPLETELY WELL (3/75): *The Thrill Is Gone; So Excited; Confessin' the Blues; Key to My Kingdom; You're Losin'; You're Mean; other titles.* BACK IN THE ALLEY (THE CLASSIC BLUES OF B.B. KING) (3/75). BLUES IS KING (3/75). LUCILLE (3/75). FRIENDS (7/75): *Friends; I Got Them Blues; Baby I'm Yours; Up at 5 A.M.; Philadelphia; When Everything Else Is Gone; My Song.* LUCILLE TALKS BACK (10/75): *Lucille Talks Back; Breaking Up Somebody's Home; Reconsider Baby; Don't Make Me Pay for His Mistakes; When I'm Wrong; I Know the Price; Have Faith; Everybody Lies a Little.* BEST OF B.B. KING: *Walking Dr. Bill; Hold That Train; You're Breaking My Heart; Did You Ever Love a Woman; Going Down Slow; Sneaking Around; Sweet Sixteen; Partin' Time; You Upset Me; My Own Fault, Baby; Bad Luck; Three O'Clock Blues; Woke Up This Morning; Every Day I Have the Blues; Ten Long Years; Sweet Little Angel.* ROCK ME BABY: *You Know I Love You; Bad Case of Love; You Upset Me Baby; Rock Me Baby; Woke Up This Morning; Three O'Clock Blues; When My Heart Beats Like a Hammer; Sweet Sixteen; Ten Long Years; Sneakin' Around; Every Day I Have the Blues; Sweet Little Angel.* LET ME LOVE YOU: *You're Gonna Miss Me; I'm Gonna Quit My Baby; Come By Here; Whole Lot of Lovin'; I've Got a Right to Love My Baby; I Can't Explain; Walkin' Dr. Bill; Hold That Train; Let Me Love You; Driving Wheel; Did You Ever Love a Woman; Troubles Don't Last.* B.B. KING LIVE ON STAGE: THE SOUL OF B.B. KING: *Good Man Gone Bad; Beautician's Blues; You Won't Listen; Someday Baby; Please Remember Me; Long Nights; You Never Know; You Shouldn't Have Left; Partin' Time; Ruby Lee; What a Way to Go; Come Back Baby.* THE JUNGLE: *The Jungle; Eyesight to the Blind; Ain't Nobody's Business; Five Long Years; Blue*

Shadows; Worst Thing in My Life; Blues Stay Away; Beautician's Blues; I Stay in the Mood; I Can Hear My Name; Got 'Em Bad; It's a Mean World.

Singles/*Three O'Clock Blues* (12/51); You *You Know I Love You* (9/52); *Story from My Heart and Soul* (12/52); *Woke Up This Morning* (3/53); *Please Love Me* (6/53); *Please Hurry Home* (10/53); *You Upset Me Baby* (10/54); *Whole Lotta Lovin'* (11/54); *Every Day I Have the Blues* (1/55); *Sneakin' Around* (1/55); *Ten Long Years* (9/55); *Crying Won't Help You* (1/56); *Bad Luck/Sweet Little Angel* (8/56); *On My Word of Honor* (10/56); *Troubles, Troubles, Troubles/I Want to Get Married* (5/57); *You've Been an Angel* (11/58); *Please Accept My Love* (11/58); *Sweet Sixteen* (1/60); *Got a Right to Love My Baby* (6/60); *Partin' Time* (7/60); *Walking Dr. Bill* (10/60); *Someday* (6/61); *Peace of Mind* (6/61); *My Sometimes Baby* (2/62); *I'm Gonna Sit In Till You Give In/You Ask Me* (3/62); *Blues at Midnight/My Baby's Comin' Home* (6/62); *Sneakin' Around/Chains of Love* (3/63); *Mother's Love/Tomorrow Night* (3/63); *Guess Who/By Myself* (4/63); *Young Dreams/On My Word of Honor* (6/63); *How Do I Love You/Slowly Losing My Mind* (10/63); *How Blue Can You Get/Please Accept My Love* (1/64); *Help the Poor/I Wouldn't Have It Another Way* (4/64); *The Hurt/Whole Lotta Lovin'* (7/64); *Never Trust a Woman/Worryin' Blues* (10/64); *Please Send Me Someone to Love/Stop Leading Me On* (1/65); *Every Day I Have the Blues/It's My Own Fault* (3/65); *Night Owl/Tired of Your Jive* (5/65); *Blue Shadows* (6/65); *All Over Again/The Things You Put Me Through* (8/65); *I'd Rather Drink Muddy Water/Goin' to Chicago Blues* (10/65); *Eyesight to the Blind* (2/66); *Tormented/You're Still a Square* (4/66); *I Stay in the Mood* (9/66); *Don't Answer the Door* (10/66); *Night Life/Waitin' on You* (12/66); *I Don't Want You Cuttin' Off Your Hair/Think It Over* (4/67); *Heartbreaker/Raining in My Heart* (12/67); *Paying the Cost to Be the Boss/Having My Say* (2/68); *I'm Gonna Do What They Do to Me/Losing Faith in You* (6/68); *You Put It On Me* (10/68); *Dance with Me/Please Send Me Someone to Love* (12/68); *Why I Sing the Blues* (5/69); *I Want You So Bad* (8/69); *Get Off My Back, Woman* (8/69); *Just a Little Love* (11/69); *The Thrill Is Gone* (1/70); *So Excited* (5/70); *Hummingbird* (6/70); *Worried Life* (8/70); *Chains and Things* (9/70); *Chains and Things/Hummingbird* (12/70); *Nobody Loves Me but My*

Mother/Ask Me No Questions (1/71); *That Evil Child* (3/71); *Help the Poor/Lucille's Granny* (5/71); *I Believe I've Been Blue Too Long* (1/72); *Ghetto Woman/Ain't Nobody Home* (1/72); *Guess Who/Better Lovin' Man* (6/72); *Five Long Years/Summer in the City* (10/72); *I Like to Live the Love/Love* (10/73); *Who Are You/Oh to Me* (3/74); *Philadelphia/Up at 5 A.M.* (8/74); *Friends/When Everything Else Is Gone* (12/74).

KING CRIMSON/*Original members: Robert Fripp (guitar, mellotron), Greg Lake (bass, vocals), Mike Giles (drums), Ian McDonald (reeds, keyboards), Peter Sinfield (synthesizer, lyrics).*
King Crimson was the most impressive marriage of intelligence and musical adventure to arise out of the "art-rock" period of 1967–72. Not only was it the quintessential British experimental band but Crimson also served as a training ground for some of the finest rock musicians to come out of the United Kingdom during that time period. Passing through the King's court at one time or another were such mainstay Britons as Greg Lake (of Emerson, Lake and Palmer), Ian McDonald and Mike Giles (who formed McDonald and Giles), Boz Burrell (Bad Company), Mel Collins (Kokomo), Bill Bruford (Yes), and John Wetton (of Family).

Crimson was largely the realization of the dream of guitar genius Robert Fripp, an erratic rock intellect who could slide from rock-oriented tunes to classically inspired numbers with the wink of a bespectacled eye. Fripp had begun his career in 1967 as one-third of the short-lived pop troupe Giles, Giles and Fripp, which featured Robert along with brothers Mike and Peter Giles. The band's recording career was disastrous and Peter left show business altogether.

Fripp and Giles, however, went on to form King Crimson. By January of 1969, the five members were busily rehearsing. By the time Crimson played the Speakeasy in London (in April), word had spread that this band was *the* next underground hit. In July, the well-honed King devastated a crowd of over fifty thousand at the Rolling Stones' Hyde Park freebie. With the subsequent release of their first LP, *IN THE COURT OF THE CRIMSON KING,* the group firmly established themselves as being the big newcomer of 1969.

Their sound was ambitious, stark, lyrically mesmerizing, and powerful. As the band's following mushroomed, the constant re-shuffling of members began in earnest. Giles and McDonald decided to leave during Crimson's first United States tour. Lake left to join ELP shortly thereafter. With Fripp at the reins, Crimson's second album, *IN THE WAKE OF POSEIDON,* was completed with the help of a lot of friends and transient Crimson members. When a new group finally did emerge in some sort of solidified state, it consisted of Fripp, Mel Collins (reeds), Marc Charig (cornet), Keith Tippett (piano), Andy McCulloch (drums), Pete Sinfield and Gordon Haskell (vocals). Haskell was out by the time the third Crimson album was released . . . and the rest of the band was jettisoned as well.

Boz Burrell, a singer who couldn't play bass at all, was hired by Fripp as a bassist. Fripp actually taught him how to play. Ian Wallace appeared on drums. This Crimson was short-lived and the introspective, progressive Fripp found himself being a one-man band, literally. Going into hibernation for nearly a year, Fripp returned with a new, improved King Crimson that proved, musically, to be the strongest ensemble to date. Ex-Yesman Bill Bruford was handling the drumming chores. David Cross was on keyboards. John Wetton played bass and sang and Jaimie Muir offered percussion. Muir soon fled the music scene and Crimson continued as a foursome, producing some of the most enigmatic, wondrous rock-jazz-folk meanderings ever recorded.

Crimson was going strong in this reincarnation when Fripp, in 1974, decided to allow the band to dissolve. Thus, one of the most anarchistic, creative, and revered bands in rock's history floated away amidst a sea of confusion.

Albums/IN THE COURT OF THE CRIMSON KING (11/69): *21st-Century Schizoid Man; I Talk to the Wind; Epitaph; Moonchild; The Court of the Crimson King.* IN THE WAKE OF POSEIDON (8/70): *Peace—A Beginning; Pictures of a City; Cadence and Cascade; In the Wake of Poseidon; Peace—A Theme; Cat Food; The Devil's Triangle; Peace—An End.* LIZARD (2/71): *Cirkus; Indoor Games; Happy Family; Lady of the Dancing Water; Prince Rupert Awakes; Bolero—The Peacock's Tale; The Battle of the Glass Tears.* ISLANDS (1/72): *Formentera Lady; Sailor's Tale; The Letters; Ladies of the Road; Prelude: Song of the Gulls; Islands.* LARKS' TONGUES IN ASPIC (11/73): *Larks' Tongues in Aspic, Part One; Book of Saturday; Exiles; Easy Money; The*

Talking Drum; Larks' Tongues in Aspic, Part Two. STARLESS
AND BIBLE BLACK (4/74): *The Great Deceiver; Lament; We'll
Let You Know; The Night Watch; Trio; The Mincer; Starless and
Bible Black; Fracture.* RED (10/74). USA (4/75): *Larks' Tongues
in Aspic; Lament; Exiles; Asbury Park; Easy Money; 21st-Century
Schizoid Man.*
Singles/*The Court of the Crimson King, Parts I and II* (12/69); *The
Night Watch/The Great Deceiver* (4/74).

THE KINKS/*Original members: Ray Davis (vocals, guitar), Dave
Davis (guitar, vocals), Mick Avory (drums), Peter Quaife (bass, vocals). Additional members: John Dalton (bass), John Gosling (keyboards), John Beecham (trombone), Alan Holmes (saxophone),
Laurie Brown (trumpet).*
Before becoming known as bearers of wry rock, the Kinks were
just another rock band out of the United Kingdom, playing cover
versions of classic R&R tunes. Formed in 1964, the band released
two stiff singles before hitting it big with *You Really Got Me.* It
was released in the United States in August of 1964—a time when
music, even the Beatles' music, was fairly simplistic—yet it was an
incredibly complex number for its day, with the vocal harmonies
going through calisthenics unheard-of until the arrival of the lush
Beach Boys sound. The Kinks instinctively blended all the com-
plexities of post-*Good Vibrations* music, meshing fairly ambitious
vocalizing with tooth-and-nails guitar work. The hits continued
to flow with *All Day and All of the Night, Set Me Free,* and *Tired
of Waiting for You.*
    After an initial period of rollicking rock, however, the true tal-
ents of songwriting Ray Davis began to emerge. His powers of
observation, his sense of slightly black humor, could be discerned
in such seemingly delicate ditties as *A Well-Respected Man, Waterloo Sunset,* and *Dedicated Follower of Fashion.* As this new style
proved just as successful as their raunchier one, the Kinks saw no
reason not to continue onward, brandishing Davis' rapier wit.
The sarcasm grew more overt, the lyrics more praiseworthy and,
soon, the Kinks were one of the most lauded rock groups in the
world.
    Oddly enough, however, as their musical and lyrical prowess
grew, their commercial success faltered. By 1970 the band had
suffered a period of nearly three years without a hit, when sudden-

ly they struck with *Lola,* a deceptively simplistic tune about a guy/girl and problems he/she causes with his/her lover. The song tossed the Kinks back into the rock spotlight. However, by now the band's spirits were sagging. Plagued by business woes and the loss of an original member (Quaife), they vainly tried to extricate themselves from the mire known as rock biz. Eventually, they found themselves a new manager and a new stateside label, RCA. More problems ensued.

Their RCA releases were greeted favorably in critical circles but did not fare at all well on the charts. The Kinks' British fans lost interest in the band almost completely, and Ray and Dave turned their attention to the States where the college concert scene was blooming. The Kinks attacked the youth market ferociously and, as a result, became a major live American act. Their albums, however, still did not fare very well and the hits stopped coming.

By 1977, it was clear that the Kinks and RCA were fairly incompatible. Joining Clive Davis' Arista label, they released *SLEEP WALKER* and made both the concert and the television rounds dutifully.

Despite their recent lack of mass appeal, the Kinks stand as one of the most literate and thought-provoking bands ever to cross rockdom's threshold. Their lyrics have been witty, yet powerfully and unabashedly honest, and their music has been something of a triumph when compared to their lesser, more popular peers. The Kinks still have a strong following in the United States, and with good reason. Live, they are amazingly charismatic. Perhaps with the backing of a new and enthusiastic label, the Kinks will win back their rightful place on the pop charts.

Albums/YOU REALLY GOT ME (11/64): *Beautiful Delilah; So Mystifying; Long Tall Shorty; Just Can't Go to Sleep; You Really Got Me; Cadillac; Bald-Headed Woman; Too Much Monkey Business; I've Been Driving on Bald Mountain; Stop Your Sobbing; Got Love If You Want It.* KINKS-SIZE (3/65): *Tired of Waiting for You; Louie, Louie; Come On Now; I've Got That Feeling; Revenge; I'm a Lover Not a Fighter; I Gotta Move; Things Are Getting Better; I Gotta Go Now; All Day and All of the Night.* KINDA KINKS (7/65): *Look for Me, Baby; Dancing in the Street; So Long; Got My Feet on the Ground; Don't Ever Change; Nothin' in the World Can Stop Me Worrying 'bout That Girl; Wonder Where My Baby Is Tonight; Set Me Free; Ev'rybody's Gonna Be Happy;*

You Shouldn't Be Sad; Something Better Beginning. KINKS KINKDOM (11/65): *A Well-Respected Man; Such a Shame; Wait 'til the Summer Comes Along; Naggin' Woman; Never Met a Girl Like You Before; See My Friends; Who'll Be the Next in Line; Don't You Fret; I Need You; It's All Right; Louie, Louie.* KONTROVERSY (3/66): *Milk Cow Blues; Ring the Bells; Gotta Get the First Plane Home; You Can't Win; I Am Free; World Keeps Going Round; It's Too Late; Till the End of the Day; I'm on an Island; Where Have the Good Times Gone; What's in Store For Me; When I See That Girl of Mine.* KINKS' GREATEST HITS (7/66): *Dedicated Follower of Fashion; Tired of Waiting for You; All Day and All of the Night; You Really Got Me; Well-Respected Man; Who'll Be the Next in Line; Till the End of the Day; Set Me Free; Something Better Beginning.* FACE TO FACE (1/67): *Fancy; Party Line; Rosy, Won't You Please Come Home; Dandy; Too Much on My Mind; Session Man; Rainy Day in June; House in the Country; Holiday in Waikiki; Most Exclusive Residence for Sale; Little Miss Queen of Darkness; You're Lookin' Fine; Sunny Afternoon; I'll Remember.* LIVE KINKS (8/67): *Well-Respected Man; Till the End of the Day; You're Looking Fine; Sunny Afternoon; Dandy; I'm on an Island; Come On Now; You Really Got Me; medley; Milk Cow Blues; Batman Theme; Tired of Waiting for You.* SOMETHING ELSE (2/68): *David Watts; Death of a clown; Two Sisters; No Return; Harry Rag; Tin Soldier Man; Love Me till the Sun Shines; Situation Vacant; End of the Season; Lazy Old Sun; Afternoon Tea; Funny Face; Waterloo Sunset.* FOUR MORE WELL-RESPECTED GENTLEMEN (11/68): *She's Got Everything; Days; Polly Monica; Mr. Songbird; Johnny Thunder; Animal Farm; Berkeley Mews; Picture Book; Phenomenal Cat; Misty Water.* VILLAGE GREEN PRESERVATION SOCIETY (3/69): *The Village Green Preservation Society; Do You Remember Walter; Picture Book; Johnny Thunder; Last of the Steam-Powered Trains; Big Sky; Sitting by the Riverside; Animal Farm; Village Green; Starstruck; Phenomenal Cat; All of My Friends Were There; Wicked Annabella; Monica; People Take Pictures of Each Other.* ARTHUR (OR THE DECLINE AND FALL OF THE BRITISH EMPIRE) (8/69): *Victoria; Yes Sir, No Sire; Some Mother's Son; Drivin'; Brainwashed; Australia; Shangri-La; Mr. Churchill Says; She Bought a Hat Like Princess Marina; Arthur; Nothing to Say; Young and Innocent Days.* LOLA

VS. POWERMAN AND THE MONEYGOROUND (11/70): *The Contenders; Strangers; Denmark Street; Get Back in Line; Lola; Top of the Pops; The Moneygoround; This Time Tomorrow; A Long Way from Home; Rats; Apeman; Powerman; Got to Be Free.* MUSSWELL HILLBILLIES (11/71): *20th Century Man; Holiday; Skin and Bone; Alcohol; Complicated Life; Here Comes the People in Grey; Have a Cuppa Tea; Hollaway Jail; Oklahoma, USA; Uncle Son; Musswell Hillbilly; Acute Schizoid Paranoid Blues.* KRONIKLES (4/72): Victoria; Village Green Preservation Society; Berkeley Mews; Holiday in Waikiki; This Is Where I Belong; Waterloo Sunset; Lola; Polly Monica; Mindless Child of Motherhood; Big Black Smoke; Susannah's Still Alive; Days; She's Got Everything; Wonderboy; David Watts; Fancy; King Kong; Mr. Pleasant; God's Children; Death of a Clown; Sunny Afternoon; Autumn Almanac; Dead End Street; Shangri-La; Did You See His Name. EVERYBODY'S IN SHOW-BIZ (8/72); *Here Comes Yet Another Day; Celluloid Heroes; Hot Potatoes; other titles.* GREAT LOST KINKS ALBUM (1/73); *Till Death Do Us Part; This Is No Life without Love; Mr. Songbird; Misty Water; Rosemary Rose; Groovy Movies; Lavender Hill; When I Turn Out the Living Room Lights; The Way Love Used to Be; This Man He Weeps Tonight; Pictures in the Sand; Where Did the Spring Go; I'm Not Like Everybody Else.* PRESERVATION ACT 1 (9/73): *Morning Songs; Daylight; Sweet Lady Genevieve; There's a Change in the Weather; Where Are They Now?; One of the Survivors; Cricket; Money and Corruption/I Am Your Man; Here Comes Flash; Sitting in the Midday Sun; Demolition.* PRESERVATION ACT 2 (2/74): *Announcement: Introduction to Solution; When a Solution Comes; Shepherds of the Nation; Money Talks; Announcement; Scum of the Earth; Second-hand Car Spiv; He's Evil; Mirror of Love; Announcement; Nobody Gives; Oh Where Oh Where Is Love?; Flash's Dream (The Final Elbow); Flash's Confession; Nothing Lasts Forever; Announcement; Artificial Man; Scrapheap City; Announcement; Salvation Road.* SOAP OPERA (4/75): *Everybody's a Star (Starmaker); Ordinary People; Rush Hour Blues; Nine to Five; When Work Is Over; Have Another Drink; Underneath the Neon Sign; Holiday Romance; You Make It All Worthwhile; Face in the Crowd; You Can't Stop the Music.* SCHOOLBOYS IN DISGRACE (9/75): *Schooldays; Jack the Idiot Dunce; Education; The First Time We Fall in Love; I'm in Dis-*

grace; Headmaster; The Hard Way; The Last Assembly; No More Looking Back; Finale. THE KINKS (1975): You Really Got Me; I'm Not Like Everybody Else; So Mystifying; Set Me Free; The World Keeps Going Round; Dedicated Follower of Fashion; Sunny Afternoon; I Took My Baby Home; I Gotta Move "Gotta Move"; Long Tall Shorty; Where Have All the Good Times Gone; Till the End of the Day. CELLULOID HEROES (5/76): Everybody's a Star (Starmaker); Sitting in My Hotel; Here Comes Yet Another Day; Holiday; Musswell Hillbilly; Celluloid Heroes; 20th Century Man; Sitting in the Midday Sun; One of the Survivors; Alcohol; Skin and Bone; Face in the Crowd. SLEEPWALKER (2/77): Life on the Road; Mr. Big Man; Sleepwalker; Brother; Juke Box Music; Sleepless Night; Stormy Sky; Full Moon; Life Goes On.

Singles/You Really Got Me/It's Alright (8/64); All Day and All of the Night (11/64); Tired of Waiting for You (2/65); Set Me Free (5/65); Who'll Be the Next in Line (7/65); A Well-Respected Man (11/65); Till the End of the Day (2/66); Dedicated Follower of Fashion (4/66); Sunny Afternoon (7/66); Dead End Street (12/66); Mr. Pleasant (6/67); Victoria/Brainwashed (10/69); Lola/Mindless Child of Motherhood (10/70); Apeman/Rats (12/70); God's Children/The Way Love Used to Be (7/71); 20th Century Man/Skin and Bone (12/71); King Kong/Waterloo Sunset (5/72); Celluloid Heroes (11/72); One of the Survivors/Scrapheap City (4/73); Sitting in the Midday Sun/Sweet Lady Genevieve (8/73); Money Talks/Here Comes Flash (4/74); Mirror of Love/He's Evil (7/74); Preservation/Salvation Road (12/74); Starmaker/Ordinary People (3/75); I'm in Disgrace/The Hard Way (1/76); Sleepwalker (3/77); Juke Box Music (5/77).

KISS/Ace Frehley (guitar), Paul Stanley (guitar), Gene Simmons (bass, vocals), Peter Criss (drums).
The band that music sophisticates love to hate, Kiss, is not only laughing their way to the bank, but they are growling, prancing, and spitting fire on their way to the vault. The foursome began in deepest New York in 1973 when glitter was king and Bowie and Lou Reed packed the kaleidoscopic-faced kids into halls like sardines (or lemmings, as the case may be). The members of Kiss openly admit that they actively designed their outrageous image (a combination of Kabuki Theater and the final reel of The Curse of Frankenstein) in an attempt to convey a sense of being larger

than life. Their songs bordered on fantasy and they felt, logically enough, that their stage show, their persona, should mirror their music. Hence the wild makeup, the flame-breathing bassist, the high-heeled dragon boots, and the pussycat whiskers.

When Kiss first started to play, the rock press had a collective attack of the dry heaves. Bowie they could take—but *this?* It was Disneyland on acid. Undaunted, Kiss began to tour . . . and tour . . . and tour. They literally worked seven nights a week for most of their first year and a half together. As a result, the public knew what the press didn't, and their first two albums sold over a quarter million copies each. With the groundwork firmly in place, the boys came back with three monsters in a row: *DRESSED TO KILL, ALIVE,* and *DESTROYER.* The albums shot up the charts with all three going gold, the latter two going platinum (over a million copies sold). By 1976, Kissmania was sweeping the country. The band didn't need to court the press anymore—it was the press that pursued Kiss. *ROCK AND ROLL OVER* and *LOVE GUN* were both platinum LPs and '76–'77 saw Kiss firmly entrenched on the singles charts, for the first time, with *Beth* and *Calling Dr. Love.*

In 1977, the Kiss army (as their legion of fanatics are called) got their ultimate wish and their heroes became the *first* rock band to get their own Marvel superhero comic book. The first issue of Kiss comics appeared on the stands in the summer of '77, fictionally tracing the super careers of the four Kiss members as they joined forces with such other Marvel heroes as the Hulk and Spider-Man in staving off the forces of evil.

Larger than life.

Fantasy-laden.

More than mortal.

Those are just some of the attractions inherent in the hard-rocking mutant quartet known as Kiss.

Now if only Superman could get his band off the ground.

Albums/KISS (2/74): *Strutter; Nothin' to Lose; Cold Gin; Let Me Know; Deuce; Love Them from Kiss; 100,000 Years; Black Diamond; Kissin' Time.* HOTTER THAN HELL (10/74): *Got to Choose; Parasite; Goin' Blind; Hotter Than Hell; Let Me Go, Rock 'n' Roll; All the Way; Mainline; Comin' Home; Watchin' You; Strange Ways.* DRESSED TO KILL (3/75): *Room Service; Two Timer; Ladies in Waiting; Rock Bottom; C'mon and Love Me;*

Anything for My Baby; Love Her All I Can; Rock and Roll All Nite. ALIVE (9/75): *Deuce; Strutter; Got to Choose; Hotter Than Hell; Firehouse; Nothin' to Lose; C'mon and Love Me; She; Watchin' You; 100,000 Years; Parasite; Black Diamond; Rock Bottom; Cold Gin; Rock and Roll All Nite; Let Me Go, Rock and Roll.* DESTROYER (3/76): *Detroit Rock City; King of the Night Time World; God of Thunder; Great Expectations; Flaming Youth; Shout It Out Loud; Sweet Pain; Do You Love Me; Beth.* THE ORIGINALS (Re-issue, in triple-LP format, of KISS, HOTTER THAN HELL, and DRESSED TO KILL; 7/76). ROCK AND ROLL OVER (11/76): *I Want You; Take Me; Calling Dr. Love; Ladies Room; Baby Driver; See You in Your Dreams; Hard Luck Woman; Makin' Love; Love 'Em and Leave 'Em.* LOVE GUN (6/77): *Love Gun; Got Love for Sale; Tomorrow and Tonight; Christine Sixteen; Almost Human; Plaster Caster; Shock Me; Then She Kissed Me; I Stole Your Love; Hooligan.* KISS ALIVE II (11/77): *Detroit Rock City; King of the Night Time World; Ladies Room; Makin' Love; Love Gun; Calling Dr. Love; Christine Sixteen; Shock Me; Hard Luck Woman; Tomorrow and Tonight; I Stole Your Love; Beth; God of Thunder; I Want You Out; Shout It Out Loud; All American Man; Rockin' in the USA; Larger Than Life; Rocket Ride; Any Way You Want It.*

Singles/*Let Me Go, Rock 'n' Roll* (1/75); *Rock and Roll All Night* (4/75); *C'mon and Love Me* (7/75); *Rock and Roll All Nite* (10/75); *Shout It Out Loud* (3/76); *Flaming Youth* (4/76); *Beth* (7/76); *Detroit Rock City* (7/76); *Hard Luck Woman* (12/76); *Calling Dr. Love* (3/77).

AL KOOPER/Originally singer and organist with the Blues Project and later with Blood, Sweat & Tears (founder-member), Kooper became a star in his own right with *SUPER SESSION,* an album of instrumental jams with guitarist Mike Bloomfield (Paul Butterfield Blues Band, Electric Flag) and Steve Stills (Buffalo Springfield, CSN&Y). He also recorded a live album with Bloomfield, *THE LIVE ADVENTURES OF MIKE BLOOMFIELD AND AL KOOPER.* Prior to emerging as a rock personality, Kooper had been an active side musician beginning as a keyboard player for the Royal Teens *(Short Shorts).* He later penned *This Diamond Ring* for Gary Lewis and the Playboys, jammed on Moby Grape's *GRAPE JAM* LP, contributed to

Hendrix's *ELECTRIC LADYLAND* album and played keyboards on Dylan's historic *BLONDE ON BLONDE*. Once established as an underground sensation in the late sixties, Kooper
branched out into producing, but with lop-sided results.

At first he limited his production to his own solo albums; slightly overblown affairs with massive arrangements successfully
weighing down his own compositions. This style later afflicted
the albums he produced for other artists, such as Sweet Linda
Devine. By the time the seventies rolled around, Kooper was regarded as an artifact from the Peace and Love days. Still, his solo
albums kept on coming. To his credit, Kooper often wrote splendid songs for the mostly overlooked long-players, and he performed them well. Kooper the performer, however, always suffered at the hands of Kooper the producer. After years without a
legitimate "hit," he began to devote more and more time to producing; handling chores for Lynyrd Skynyrd (they didn't like the
album). The Tubes (they didn't like the album), and Nils Lofgrin
(not too many people liked the album).

These days, Al is still quite a controversial figure on the music
scene; a much revered musician, a presently active recording artist
and a controversial producer.

Albums/I STAND ALONE (12/68): *Overture; I Stand Alone;
Camille; One; Coloured Rain; Soft Landing on the Moon; I Can
Love a Woman; Blue Moon of Kentucky; Toe Hold; Right Now for
You; Hey, Western Union Man; Song and Dance for the Unborn,
Frightened Child.* YOU NEVER KNOW WHO YOUR
FRIENDS ARE (8/69): *Magic in My Socks; Lucille; Too Busy
Thinking about My Baby; First Time Around; Loretta; Blues Part
IV; Morning Glory Story; Anna Lee; I'm Never Gonna Let You
Down; The Great American Marriage; Nothing; Don't Know Why
I Love You.* KOOPER SESSIONS (introducing Shuggie Otis)
(11/69): *Bury My Body; Double or Nothing; One Room Country
Shack; Lookin' for a Home; 12:15 Glow Goonbash Blues;
Shuggie's Old Time Slide Boogie; Shuggie's Shuffle.* EASY DOES
IT (7/70): *Brand New Day; Piano Solo Intro; I Got a Woman;
Country Road; I Bought You the Shoes (You're Walking Away In);
Intro; Easy Does It; Buckskin Boy; Love Theme From "The Land-
lord"; Sad Sad Sunshine; Let the Duchess Know; She Gets Me
Where I Live; A Rose for Baby Ruth; Baby Please Don't Go; God
Sheds His Grace on Thee.* AL KOOPER (5/71): *New York City*

(You're a Woman); John The Baptist; Can You Hear It Now (500 Miles); The Ballad of the Hard Rock Kid; Going Quietly Mad; Medley: Oowie Baby, I Love You; Love Is A Man's Best Friend; Back on My Feet; Come Down in Time; Dearest Darling; Nightmare #5; The Warning (Someone's on the Cross Again). A POSSIBLE PROJECTION OF THE FUTURE (3/72): *Bended Knees; Childhood's End; The Man in Me; Please Tell Me Why; Love Trap; The Monkey Time; Let Your Love Shine; Swept for You Baby.* NAKED SONGS (11/72): *(Be Yourself) Be Real; As The Years Go Passing By; Jolie; Blend Baby; Been and Gone; Sam Stone; Peacock Lady; Touch The Hem of His Garment; Where Were You When I Needed You; Unrequited.* AL'S BIG DEAL (3/75): *I Can't Quit Her; I Love You More Than You'll Ever Know; My Days Are Numbered; Without Her; So Much Love; Underture; Albert's Shuffle; Season of The Witch; If Dogs Run Free; The 59th Street Bridge Song; The Weight; Bury My Body; I Stand Alone; Brand New Day; Same Stone; New York (You're a Woman); I Got a Woman.*

Singles/*You Never Know Who Your Friends Are/Soft Landing on the Moon* (1/69); *I Stand Alone/Hey, Western Union Man* (3/69); *Bury My Body/One Room Country Shack* (2/70); *She Gets Me Where I Live/God Sheds His Grace on Thee* (4/70); *Brand New Day/Love Them From "The Landlord")* (6/70); *I Got a Woman/Easy Does It* (9/70); *John The Baptist/Back on My Feet* (6/71); *Medley/Dearest Darling* (12/71); *Monkey Time/Bended Knees* (2/71); *Be Yourself (Be Real)/Sam Stone* (9/72); *Jolie/Be Yourself (Be Real)* (11/72).

LEO KOTKE/When Leo Kotke takes the stage, armed only with his lone guitar and a wry smile, audiences pay attention. In spite of the fact that his music owes more to Mississippi John Hurt than to the Rolling Stones, Kotke has garnered quite a following in a rock era renowned more for its fad following than its taste. Born in Georgia to a musical family, Leo first picked up a guitar while in his teens, influenced by Delta blues singers and players. While in high school, he began playing in backup ensembles with blues legends like Sun House. Once he had his high school diploma, he sought adventure in the U.S. Navy Submarine service, which resulted in an ill-fated training maneuver and the permanent impairment of his hearing. Upon his discharge, Kotke began recording for local labels. Two albums, *CIRCLE ROUND*

THE SUN (1970) and *SIX AND TWELVE STRING GUITAR)* (on John Fahey's Takoma Records) were released before Kotke made the move from record-packer at Takoma to musical hopeful on Capitol Records. With each subsequent release, Kotke's following grew. Eventually he moved over to the Chrysalis label, bringing with him his unique guitar style—a combination of dexterity and bemusement.

Albums/MUDLARK (5/71): *Cripple Creek; Eight Miles High; June Bug; The Ice Miner; Bumblebee; Stealing; Monkey Lust; Poor Boy; Lullaby; Machine #2; Hear the Wind Howl; Bourree; Room 8; Standing in My Shoes.* GREEN HOUSE (1/72): *Bean Time; Owls; In Christ There Is No East or West; Last Steam Engine Train; The Song of the Swamp; The Spanish Entomologist; Lost John; Tiny Island; Louise; From the Cradle to the Grave; You Don't Have to Need Me.* MY FEET ARE SMILING (3/73): *Introduction; Hear the Wind Howl; Busted Bicycle; Easter; Louise; The Blue Dot; Stealing; Living in the Country; June Bug; Standing in My Shoes; The Fisherman; Bean Time; Eggtooth; medley: Crow River Waltz, Jesu—Joy of Man's Desiring, Jack Fig.* ICE WATER (1/74): *Morning Is the Long Way Home Pamela Brown; A Good Egg; Tilt Billings and the Student Prince; All through the Night; Short Stories; You Tell Me Why; You Know I Know You Know; Born to Be With You; A Child Should Be a Fish.* DREAMS AND ALL THAT STUFF (10/74): *Mona Ray; When Shrimps Learn to Whistle; Twilight Property; Bill Cheatham; Vertical Trees; medley: San Antonio Rose, America the Beautiful; Constant Traveler; Why Ask Why?; Taking a Sandwich to a Feast; Hole in the Day; Mona Ray.* CHEWING PINE (9/75): *Standing on the Outside; Power Failure; Venezuela There You Go; Don't You Think; Regards from Chuck Pink; Money Money; Grim to the Brim; The Scarlatti Rip-Off; Wheels; Rebecca; Trombone; Can't Quite Put It into Words.* DID YOU HEAR ME? (10/76): *Morning Is the Long Way Home; June Bug; When Shrimps Learn to Whistle; Room 8; Cripple Creek; Pamela Brown; Standing on the Outside; Grim to the Brim; Power Failure; You Tell Me Why; Why Ask Why?; Open Country Joy (Constant Traveler); All through the Night; The Scarlatti Rip-Off.* LEO KOTKE (1/77): *Buckarro; The White Ape; Haysee Suede; Rio Leo; Range; Airproofing; Maroon; Waltz; Death by Reputation; Up Tempo; Shadowland.*

Singles/*Pamela Brown*/*A Child Should Be a Fish* (3/74); *Pamela Brown*/*A Child Should Be a Fish* (5/75); *Power Failure*/*Can't Quite Put It into Words* (11/75).

LABELLE/*Patti Labelle, Sarah Dash, Nona Hendryx (vocals).*
Culled from the remnants of the sixties' vocal group Patti La Belle and the Bluebelles, LaBelle was one of the biggest female groups to top the charts in the seventies. After floundering during the psychedelic late sixties, the Bluebelles turned to nightclubs and bars for work. Enlisting a new manager, Vicki Wickham, in 1970, the Bluebelles began to revamp both their image and their name, emerging as LaBelle.

Two albums on Warner Brothers proved uneventful and the trio moved on to RCA, where a third album was released with little commercial success. A third label, Epic, proved the launching pad for the girls' meteoric careers as the Allen Toussaint–produced *NIGHTBIRDS* spawned the global number-one disco single, *Lady Marmalade*. To match their sensual sound, the trio began appearing in concert in equally sensual plumage. Their fandom grew by leaps and bounds. A special concert at the New York Metropolitan Opera House was a sold-out affair.

The seeds of discontent, however, appeared shortly after their million-selling furor died down. A followup album, *PHOENIX,* failed to live up to expectations and subsequent singles fared well, but not as well as *Marmalade*. By 1977, LaBelle decided that, as a group, they had exhausted their creativity. The trio disbanded quietly, with Hendryx and LaBelle emerging as solo artists.

Albums/LABELLE (9/71): *You've Got a Friend; Time; Wild Horses; When the Sun Comes Shining Through; Heart, Be Still; Running Out of Fools; Too Many Days; Time and Love; Baby's Out of Sight; Morning Much Better; Shades of Difference.* MOONSHADOW (7/72): *Won't Get Fooled Again; Sunday's News; Peace with Yourself; Ain't It Sad When It's All Over; Moon Shadow; Touch Me All Over; If I Can't Have You; I Believe That I've Finally Made It Home; People Say They Are Changing.* PRESSURE COOKIN' (8/73): *Pressure Cookin'; Hollywood; Sunshine; Something in the Air; The Revolution Will Not Be Televised; Mr. Music Man; Last Dance; Open Up Your Heart; Goin' on a Holiday; Let Me See You in the Light.* NIGHTBIRDS (9/74): *Lady Marmalade; Somebody Somewhere; Are You Lonely?; It*

Took a Long Time; Don't Bring Me Down; What Can I Do for You?; Night Bird; Space Children; You Turn Me On; All-Girl Band. PHOENIX (8/75): *Phoenix; Slow Burn; Black Hole in the Sky; Good Intentions; Far As We Felt Like Goin'; Messin' with My Mind; Chances Go Round; Cosmic Dancer; Take the Night Off; Action Time.* CHAMELEON (8/76): *Get You Somebody New; Come into My Life; Isn't It a Shame; Who's Watching the Watcher; Chameleon; Gypsy Moth; A Man in a Trenchcoat; Going Down Makes Me Shiver.*

Singles/*Morning Much Better/Shades of Difference* (7/71); *Moon Shadow/If I Can't Have You* (3/72); *Ain't It Sad When It's All Over/Touch Me All Over* (8/72); *Open Up Your Heart/Going on a Holiday* (4/73); *Sunshine/Mr. Music Man* (11/73); *Lady Marmalade/Space Children* (11/74); *What Can I Do for You/Nightbird* (4/75); *Messin' with My Mind/Take the Night Off* (8/75); *Far As We Felt Like Goin'/Slow Burn* (10/75); *Who's Watching the Watcher/Get You Somebody New* (9/76); *Lady Marmalade/What Can I Do for You?* (11/76); *Isn't It a Shame/Gypsy Mothers* (11/76).

LED ZEPPELIN/*Jimmy Page (guitar), Robert Plant (vocals), John Paul Jones (bass, keyboards), John Bonham (drums).*
Led Zeppelin. The name betrays the music. Loud. Grinding. Ponderous, thunderous rock and roll. Rumbling bass and drums. Piercing vocals. Whiplash guitar riffs. A musical institution whose albums are dubbed gold upon release. Whose concert tours are constantly sold out. Whose every move finds its way to their legions of fans. Yet, very few Led Zep buffs know that the group came about quite by accident.

In 1968, Jimmy Page found himself the only Yardbird remaining in that band. He had joined the group in 1966 as a replacement for the departing Eric Clapton. Now he found himself without a troupe but with a host of concert dates to fulfill. Page began a hasty search for fill-in Yardbirds for a new band, tentatively called the New Yardbirds. Friend John Paul Jones was ready to offer his skills; Procol's B. J. Thomas and vocalist Terry Reid had prior commitments, so, Robert Plant and John Bonham rounded out the touring unit.

The Continental antics of the New Yardbirds delighted the old YB fans and impressed an entire army of new ones. The band cooked onstage with the riffing taking more ominous, hard-rock-ing directions than before. Keith Moon, ever the punster, in-vented a bizarre joke about the band and the name Led Zeppelin was the offshoot. Led Zep signed a contract and recorded their first album in a few weeks' time. It was a monster. It went gold in the States and a U.S. debut tour proved devastating. Zep's second opus, *LED ZEPPELIN II,* spawned the heavy-metal hymn *Whole Lotta Love.* Escaping as a single, the song put the young band safely within the top-tenning 45's ranks.

From there on in, there was no stopping Zeppelin. Their tours became more eventful with their music vying neck and neck with their performance and stage effects. Their chugging, guitar-ori-ented style began to expand, intertwining fleeting glimpses of fantasy-laden pastoral splendor within its riffing. Acoustic num-bers saw the light of day. The melodic, ethereal *Stairway to Heaven* surpassed *Whole Lotta Love* in popularity, and Zeppelin found themselves masters of both heavy-metal and iron-coated balladeering. Touches of reggae, R&B, and blues materialized. Album jackets became more and more surreal.

By 1976, with the release of their first full-length film, *THE SONG REMAINS THE SAME,* Led Zeppelin was secure in their position of primo heavy-metal exponents.

Albums/LED ZEPPELIN (1/69): *Good Times Bad Times; Babe, I'm Gonna Leave You; You Shook Me; Dazed and Confused; Your Time Is Gonna Come; Black Mountain Side; Communications Breakdown; I Can't Quit You Baby; How Many More Times.* LED ZEPPELIN II (10/69): *Whole Lotta Love; What Is and What Should Never Be; The Lemon Song; Thank You; Heartbreaker; Ramble On; Moby Dick; Bring It On Home; Living Loving Maid.* LED ZEPPELIN III (10/70): *Immigrant Song; Friends; Celebra-tion Day; Since I've Been Loving You; Out on the Tiles; Gallows Pole; Tangerine; That's the Way; Bron-Y-Aur Stomp; Hats Off to (Roy) Harper.* LED ZEPPELIN (11/71): *Black Dog; Rock and Roll; The Battle of Evermore; Stairway to Heaven; Misty Moun-tain Hop; Four Sticks; Going to California; When the Levee Breaks.* HOUSES OF THE HOLY (3/73): *The Song Remains The Same; The Rain Song; Over the Hills and Far Away; The Crunge; Dancing Days; D'Yer Mak'er; No Quarter; The Ocean.* PHYSI-CAL GRAFFITI (2/75): *Custard Pie; The Rover; In My Time of Dying; Houses of the Holy; Trampled Under Foot; Kashmir; In the*

Light; Bron-Y-Aur; Down by the Seaside; Night Flight; The Wanton Song; Boogie with Stu; Black Country Woman; Sick Again. PRESENCE (3/76): *Nobody's Fault but Mine; Candy Store Rock; Hots on for Nowhere; Tea for One; Archilles Last Stand; For Your Life; Royal Orleans.* THE SONG REMAINS THE SAME (10/76): *Rock and Roll; Celebration Day; The Song Remains the Same; Rain Song; Dazed and Confused; No Quarter; Stairway to Heaven; Moby Dick; Whole Lotta Love.*

Singles/*Good Times Bad Times/Communications Breakdown* (3/69); *Whole Lotta Love/Living Loving Maid* (11/69); *Immigrant Song/Hey Hey What Can I Do* (11/70); *Black Dog/Misty Mountain Hop* (12/71; *Rock and Roll/Four Sticks* (2/72; *Whole Lotta Love/Living Loving Maid* (1/73); *Black Dog/Misty Mountain Hop* (3/73); *Immigrant Song/Hey Hey What Can I Do* (3/73); *Rock and Roll/Four Sticks* (3/73); *Over the Hill and Far Away/Dancing Days* (5/73); *D'Yer Mak'er/The Crunge* (9/73); *Trampled Under Foot/Black Country Woman* (3/75); *Candy Store Rock/Royal Orleans* (6/76).

THE LEFT BANKE/*Original members: Rick Brand (banjo, mandolin), Steve Martin (vocals), Tom Finn (bass), Mike Brown (organ, piano, harp, clavichord), George Cameron (drums).*
For every hundred groups getting by on little more than nose and effrontery in the late-1967 rock boom, there was one group whose members performed on their instruments as if they had just walked out of music school—which was indeed the case with the Left Banke. Their songs (especially *Pretty Ballerina* and *Walk Away Renee,* replete with chamber strings and classical discipline), were almost too delicate for rock and roll. This New York–based group was among the first, as early as 1966, to try to combine rock and classical instrumentation. As a result, although they made truly beautiful music, a lot of the musical trend–setters overlooked the band while searching for the new Mick Jagger, Young Rascals, or Bubblegum artist of the month. Problems arose within the Banke's ranks with lead composer Brown allegedly the egomaniacal factor (although no one disputed the fact that he was the prime mover). A second album, *TOO,* showed the band fragmenting. *Desiree,* a single from the album, proved too sophisticated for the mass market, and a few more singles, with new members appearing for every session, did little to enhance the

struggling band's image. The Left Banke lost their recording contract and drifted off to the second-string circuit, playing clubs and
dances with a lot of pick-up members (including Aerosmith's
Steve Tyler on drums). Mike Brown went on to found the band
Stories, but left that band in a huff after their first release.

Albums/WALK AWAY RENEE/PRETTY BALLERINA
(2/67): *Pretty Ballerina; She May Call You Up Tonight; Bar-
tenders and Their Wives; I've Got Something on My Mind; Let Go
of You, Girl; Evening Gown; Walk Away Renee; What Do You
Know; Shadows Breaking over My Head; I Haven't Got the Nerve;
Lazy Day.* THE LEFT BANKE TOO (12/68): *Goodbye Holly;
There's Gonna Be a Storm; Sing Little Bird Sing; Nice to See You;
Give the Man a Hand; Bryant Hotel; Desiree; Dark Is the Bark; In
the Morning Light; My Friend Today.*

Singles/*Walk Away Renee/I Haven't Got the Nerve* (5/66); *Pretty
Ballerina/Lazy Day* (12/66); *Walk Away Renee/I Haven't Got the
Nerve* (3/67); *Ivy, Ivy/And Suddenly* (4/67); *Desiree/I've Got
Something on My Mind* (9/67); *Dark Is the Bark/My Friend To-
day* (5/68); *Goodbye Holly/Sing Little Bird Sing* (11/68); *Bryant
Hotel/Give the Man a Hand* (2/69); *Nice to See You/There's Gon-
na Be a Storm* (6/69); *Myrah/Pedestal* (10/69).

JOHN LENNON/During his stay with the Beatles, John Lennon
always seemed the most controversial, the most outspoken,
perhaps the most politically "aware" of the group. It was therefore no surprise that, once the Beatles called it quits, Lennon went
on to become one of the most inventive and certainly most controversial figures in popular music. Forming a very loose musical
relationship called the Plastic Ono Band (dubbed for his wife,
Japanese artist Yoko Ono), John began releasing solo work while
still an active member of the Beatles.

After the split of the fab four, John took the Plastic Ono Band on
tour and began recording some of the most jarring, eclectic
albums ever beheld by man or fan. His first single release, *Give
Peace a Chance,* became the anthem of the post-Woodstock poli-
ticos. Lennon recorded the song in a Canadian hotel room during
a marathon "bed-in" wherein John and Yoko remained in their
beds for the cause of peace. The event became a media field day
and Lennon was promptly labeled an eccentric—a tag which
would hinder his musical success for a few years.

Lennon did not exactly go out of his way to discourage his critics. His first two solo long-players aroused a storm of controversy. His premier discs with Yoko Ono, *UNFINISHED MUSIC NO. 2: LIFE WITH THE LIONS* and *WEDDING ALBUM,* evoked howls of amazement from the legions of Beatles buffs. The former was musically inaccessible to most and the latter's cover (John and Yoko in the buff for the buffs) caused the album to be heavily censored in some record stores until an alternate cover design could be found.

Somehow, Lennon managed to weather the storm quite well and achieved commercial success with such unorthodox singles as *Cold Turkey, Instant Karma, Mother, Power to the People,* and *Woman Is the Nigger of the World.* What was once considered musical eccentricity was eventually recognized as sheer genius and Lennon's stark, sometimes bitter, always emotionally wrenching LPs (such as *IMAGE* and *MIND GAMES)* were duly recognized as being minor masterpieces.

In 1975, it looked as if John was in for a personal trauma when it was revealed that Yoko and he were on the way to permanent separation. Happily, the split was easily reconciled and Lennon emerged unscathed. Lennon's recording activities have slowed down recently. His *ROCK 'N' ROLL* album was a project that had been worked on for two years and his *SHAVED FISH* was a compilation piece showcasing his past successes. The literate ex-Beatle seems to have found inner peace for the time being.

Albums/UNFINISHED MUSIC NO. 2: LIFE WITH THE LIONS (with Yoko Ono; 5/69): *Cambridge 1969; Son for John; Cambridge 1969; Let's Go On Flying; Snow Is Falling All the Time; Don't Worry Kyoko (Mummy's Only Looking for Her Hand in the Snow); No Bed for Beatle John; Baby's Heartbeat; Two Minute Silence; Radio Play.* WEDDING ALBUM (with Yoko Ono; 10/69): *John and Yoko; Amsterdam.* THE PLASTIC ONO BAND LIVE PEACE IN TORONTO (with the Plastic Ono Band; 12/69): *Intro; Money; Dizzy Miss Lizzy; Blue Suede Shoes; Yer Blues; Cold Turkey; Give Peace a Chance; Don't Worry Kyoko (Mummy's Only Looking for Her Hand in the Snow); John, John (Let's Hope for Peace).* PLASTIC ONO BAND (12/70): *Mother; Hold On John; I Found Out; Working Class Hero; Isolation; Remember; Love; Well Well Well; Look at Me; God; My Mummy's Dead.* IMAGINE (9/71): *Imagine; Crippled Inside; Jealous Guy;*

It's So Hard; I Don't Want to Be a Soldier; Give Me Some; Oh My Love; How Do You Sleep; How?; Oh Yoko! SOME TIME IN NEW YORK CITY (with Elephants Memory, Yoko Ono, and Invisible Strings; 6/72): *Woman Is the Nigger of the World; Sisters, O Sisters; Attica State; Born in a Prison; New York City; Sunday Bloody Sunday; Luck of the Irish; John Sinclair; Angela; We're All Water; Cold Turkey; Don't Worry Kyoko; Well (Baby Please Don't Go); Jam Rag; Scumbag; Au.* MIND GAMES (10/73): *Mind Games; Tight A$; Aisumasen (I'm Sorry); One Day (at a Time); Bring On the Lucie (Freeda People); Nutopian International Anthem; Intuition; Out of the Blue; Only People; I Know (I Know); You Are Here; Meat City.* WALLS AND BRIDGES (9/74): *Going Down on Love; Whatever Gets You through the Night; Old Dirt Road; What You Got; Bless You; Scared; #9 Dream; Surprise, Surprise (Sweet Bird of Paradox); Steel and Glass; Beef Jerky; Nobody Loves You (When You're Down and Out); Ya Ya.* ROCK 'N' ROLL (2/75): *Be-Bop-A-Lula; Stand By Me; medley: Ready Teddy, Rip It Up; You Can't Catch Me; Ain't That a Shame; Do You Want to Dance; Sweet Little Sixteen; Slippin' and Slidin'; Peggy Sue; medley: Bring It On Home to Me; Send Me Some Lovin'; Bony Moronie; Ya Ya; Just Because.* SHAVED FISH (with the Plastic Ono Band; 10/75): *Give Peace a Chance; Cold Turkey; Instant Karma; Power to the People; Mother; Woman Is the Nigger of the World; Imagine; Whatever Gets You Thru the Night; Mind Games; #9 Dream; medley: Happy Xmas (War Is Over), Give Peace a Chance (Reprise).*

Singles/*Give Peace a Chance/Remember Love* (Plastic Ono; 7/69); *Cold Turkey/Don't Worry Kyoko* (Plastic Ono; 11/69); *Instant Karma/Who Has Seen the Wind* (B side by Yoko and Plastic Ono Band; 3/70); *Mother/Why* (Plastic Ono, B side by Yoko and Plastic Ono; 1/71); *Power to the People/Touch Me* (Plastic Ono, B side by Yoko and Plastic Ono; 4/71); *God Save Us/Do the Oz* (A side by Bill Elliott and the Elastic Oz Band; B side by Lennon and Elastic Oz; 7/71); *Imagine/It's So Hard* (Plastic Ono and the Flux Fiddlers; 10/71); *Happy Xmas (War Is Over)/Listen, the Snow Is Falling* (Yoko, Plastic Ono, Harlem Community Choir; (B side by Yoko and Plastic Ono; 12/71); *Woman Is the Nigger of the World/Sisters O Sisters* (Plastic Ono, Elephants Memory, Invisible Strings; B side by Ono, Plastic Ono, Elephants Memory, Invisible Strings; 5/72); *Mind Games/Meat City* (10/73); *What-*

ever Gets You Thru the Night/Beef Jerky (Plastic Ono Nuclear Band, Little Big Horns, Booker Table and the Maitre D's; 9/74); *#9 Dream/What You Got* (12/74); *Stand by Me/Move Over Mrs. L.* (3/75).

LIGHT SHOWS/"At last, music for the deaf!" exclaimed one rock fan of the sixties, on seeing his first light show. Conceivably, the light show *could* have translated sound into color, line, shape, pattern, image, and movement but, more often than not, the show did not replace the sound but merely enhanced it. Light shows emerged as public entertainment in late 1965, along with dance halls and acid rock, both of which involved rock audiences more than they had ever been involved before. Light shows employed all kinds of mechanics—films, slides, strobe lights, spotlights, oil paints swirling in saucers of water—in all sorts of combinations that commented on the content and even the lyrics of the music, and throbbed and pulsated with the beat like another instrument. As the music played, so did the light and the color, usually on a large screen above and behind the players, often on the players themselves, and on the audience and walls and ceiling, breaking down yet another barrier between the spectacle and the spectator. As the psychedelic sounds faded from the music scene in the early seventies, so did the hallucinogenic light-show phenomenon.

LITTLE FEAT/*Roy Estrada (bass), Lowell George (vocals, guitar), Paul Barrere (guitar, vocals), Kenn Gradney (bass), Sam Clayton (congas), Richard Hayward (drums, vocals), Bill Payne (keyboards, vocals).*
The lowdown funkiness of Little Feat first came about in 1970 when ex-Mothers George and Estrada decided to have a go of it sans the rest of the Invention crew. Payne, Hayward, Estrada, and George were subsequently signed by Warner Brothers. Their first two albums were exceedingly well received at critical levels but were not exactly hot stuff in the record store. Warner complicated matters by treating the band like a well-developed case of leprosy.

Discouraged, the group began to think about the future. One of the busiest thinkers was Estrada, who jumped ship, eventually showing up in Captain Beefheart's Magic Band (a move comparable to leaving a leaky lifeboat for a first-class berth on the *Titanic).* Undaunted, George enlisted Barrere, Gradney, and

Clayton, and the Feats kept plodding on. Fortunately, their success began to grow, albeit in small doses. Their third LP, *DIXIE CHICKEN,* was embraced universally by the rock establishment. Unfortunately, this enthusiasm was never translated into sales. The band broke up.

They regrouped to cut the contractually owed *FEATS DON'T FAIL ME NOW,* which proved enormously successful. A tour of the United Kingdom quickly garnered them a grassroots following in Britain and that occurrence sparked renewed interst in the States. Subsequent American tours established the band as masters of off-the-cuff funk. At present, Little Feat isn't a superstar status band but they are admired and respected by a growing legion of fans, fans that attend concerts and buy records. The fact that Little Feat weathered their lean years to emerge victorious and musically inventive is a tribute to both their determination and creativity. No small feat, that.

Albums/LITTLE FEAT (11/70): *Hamburger Midnight; Snakes on Everything; Strawberry Flats; Truck-Stop Girl; Willing; Brides of Jesus; Crack in Your Door; Takin' My Time; Crazy Captain Gunboat Willie; I've Been the One; Forty-Four Blues; How Many More Years.* SAILIN' SHOES (2/72): *Easy to Slip; Willin'; A Political Blues; Tripe-Face Boogie; Trouble; Cold Cold Cold; Teenage Nervous Breakdown; Texas Rose Cafe; Cat Fever.* DIXIE CHICKEN (1/73): *Dixie Chicken; Two Trains; On Your Way Down; Kiss It Off; Fool Yourself; Walkin' All Night; Fat Man in the Bathtub; Juliette; Lafayette Railroad.* FEATS DON'T FAIL ME NOW (8/74): *Rock and Roll Doctor; Oh Atlanta; Long Distance Love; Front Page News; Feats Don't Fail Me Now; Wait till the Shit Hits the Fan; Skin It Back; Cold Cold Cold/Tripe-Face Boogie.* THE LAST RECORD ALBUM (10/75): *Down below the Borderline; Somebody's Leaving; All That You Dream; Mercenary Territory; One-Love Stand; Romance Dance; Day or Night; Long-Distance Love.* TIME LOVES A HERO (3/77); *Time Loves a Hero; Hi Roller; New Delhi Freight Train; Old Folks Boogie; Red Streamliner; Keepin' Up with the Joneses; Rocket in My Pocket; Missin' You; Day at the Dog Races.*

Singles/*Hamburger Midnight/Strawberry Flats* (9/70); *Easy to Slip/Cat Fever* (1/72); *Dixie Chicken/Lafayette Railroad* (2/73); *Atlanta/Down the Road* (10/74); *Spanish Moon/Down the Road* (3/75); *Long-Distance Love/Romance Dance* (1/76).

LITTLE RICHARD/Richard Penniman was born on Christmas Day in Macon, Georgia. During the fifties, he proved a big gift indeed for the embryonic realm of rock and roll. After singing in choirs and traveling in revival shows during his teens, he showed up in the recording studios in the early fifties as a gospel singer. By 1955, however, the brilliant singer-pianist emerged full throttle as a screamer extraordinaire with such tunes as *Tutti Frutti, Keep a-Knockin',* and *Good Golly Miss Molly.* His machine-gun piano style and wham-bam-thank-you-ma'am delivery as a crooner completely revolutionized modern music, setting the stage for a horde of performers from Otis Redding to Mitch Ryder.

He left the rock industry in 1957 to pursue religion but the rocking minister returned to his original fold in 1963. His career in the sixties remained in neutral gear until the rock revival toward the end of the decade. A new recording contract with Warner Reprise and quite a few guest appearances on nationwide television launched his career into a brilliant second stage. With outrageous makeup, penciled-in eyebrows, and hands and feet pounding away on the piano, Little Richard quickly re-established himself as one of rockdom's most joyfully crazed denizens.

Of late he has confined himself to a few session dates on other artists' recordings and playing across the country in traveling rock-and-roll-revival outfits.

Albums/HERE'S LITTLE RICHARD (6/57): *Long Tall Sally; Miss Ann; She's Got It; Can't Believe You Wanna Leave; Slippin' and Slidin'; Ready Teddy; Oh Why; Baby; Tutti-Frutti; Rip It Up; True, Fine Mama; Jenny Jenny.* LITTLE RICHARD (12/58): *Keep a-Knockin'; By the Light of the Silvery Moon; Lucille; Hey-Hey-Hey-Hey; Ooh! My Soul; All around the World; Good Golly, Miss Molly; Baby Face; Boo-Hoo-Hoo-Hoo; Girl Can't Help It; Send Me Some Lovin'; Heeby-Jeebies.* FABULOUS LITTLE RICHARD (5/59): *Shake a Hand; Chicken Little Baby; All Night Long; Most I Can Offer; Lonesome and Blue; Wonderin'; She Knows How to Rock; Kansas City; Directly from My Heart; I'm Just a Lonely Guy; Maybe I'm Right; Whole Lotta Shakin'.* COMING HOME (11/63): *Just a Closer Walk with Thee; Coming Home; Search Me, Lord; I Want Jesus to Walk with Me; Milky White Way; Need Him; Everytime I Feel the Spirit; Does Jesus Care; God Is Real; I'm Trampin'; Jesus Walked This Lonesome Valley; Precious Lord.* LITTLE RICHARD'S BIGGEST HITS

(12/63): *Rip It Up; Lucille; Jenny Jenny; All around the World; Good Golly, Miss Molly; Long Tall Sally; Slippin' and Slidin'; Send Me Some Lovin'; Boo-Hoo-Hoo-Hoo; True, Fine Mama; Keep a-Knockin'; Tutti-Frutti.* KING OF THE GOSPEL SINGERS (10/64): *Joy, Joy, Joy; Do You Care; Captain Calls for You; Do, Lord, Remember Me; Ride On, King Jesus; Peace in the Valley; He's Not Just a Soldier; My Desire; He's My Star; It Takes Everything to Serve the Lord.* EXPLOSIVE LITTLE RICHARD (1/67): *I Don't Want to Discuss It; Land of 1,000 Dances; Commandments of Love; Money; Poor Dog; I Need Love; Never Gonna Let You Go; Don't Deceive Me (Please Don't Go); Function at the Junction; Well.* LITTLE RICHARD'S GREATEST HITS (6/67): *Lucille; Girl Can't Help It; Tutti-Frutti; Send Me Some Lovin'; Long Tall Sally; Get Down with It; True, Fine Mama; Jenny Jenny; Good Golly, Miss Molly; Whole Lotta Shakin' Goin' On; Anyway You Want Me; You Gotta Feel It.* THE RILL THING (8/70): *Freedom Blues; Greenwood, Mississippi; Two-Time Loser; Dew Drop Inn; Somebody Saw You; Spreadin' Natta What's the Matter; The Rill Thing; Lovesick Blues; I Saw Her Standing There.* KING OF ROCK AND ROLL (10/71): *King of Rock and Roll; Brown Sugar; In the Name; Dancing in the Streets; Midnight Special; The Way You Do the Things You Do; Green Power; I'm So Lonesome I Could Cry; Settin' the Woods on Fire; Born on the Bayou.* SECOND COMING (10/72): *Mockingbird Sally; Second Lie; Thomasine; Rockin' Boogie; Prophet of Peace; Nuki Suki; The Saints; Sanctified, Satisfied Toe Tapper; It Ain' What You Do, It's the Way That You Do It.*

Singles/*Tutti-Frutti/I'm Just a Lonely Guy* (11/55); *Long Tall Sally/Slippin' and Slidin'* (2/56); *Rip It Up/Ready Teddy* (5/56); *The Girl Can't Help It/All around the World* (12/56); *Lucille/Send Me Some Lovin'* (2/56); *Jenny Jenny/Miss Ann* (5/57); *Keep a-Knockin'/Can't Believe You Want to Leave Me* (8/57) *Good Golly, Miss Molly/Hey, Hey, Hey, Hey* (1/58); *Ohh! My Soul/True, Fine Mama* (4/58); *Baby Face/I'll Never Let You Go* (8/58); *Kansas City/Lonesome and Blue* (4/59); *Bama Lama Bama Loo/Annie Is Back* (6/64); *I Don't Know What You've Got but It's Got Me* (10/65); *Freedom Blues/Dew Drop Inn* (4/70); *Greenwood, Mississippi/I Saw Her Standing There* (8/70); *Shake a Hand/Somebody Saw You* (4/71); *Green Power/Dancing in the Street* (10/71); *Mockingbird Sally/Nuki Suki* (11/72).

NILS LOFGREN/Chicago-raised Nils Lofgren first attained rock status with his teenage Washington, D.C., group, Grin. Following Grin's demise, Lofgren embarked on a solo career which led to the release of his first album in 1975 entitled, for logic's sake, *NILS LOFGREN*. Nils' energetic approach to rock plus his adolescent vocals and distinctive, fluid guitar style have won him a large audience in the States and the basis for a cult following in England.

Albums/NILS LOFGREN (2/75): *Be Good Tonight; Back It Up; One More Saturday Night; If I Say It, It's So; I Don't Want to Know; Keith, Don't Go; Can't Buy a Break; Duty; The Sun Hasn't Set on This Boy Yet; Rock and Roll Crook; Two by Two; Goin' Back*. CRY TOUGH (3/76): *Cry Tough; It's Not a Crime; Incidentally . . . It's Over; For Your Love; Share a Little; Mud in Your Eye; Can't Get Closer; You Lit a Fire; Jailbait*. I CAME TO DANCE (2/77): *I Came to Dance; Rock Me at Home; Home Is Where the Hurt Is; Code of the Road; Happy Ending Kids; Goin' South; To Be a Dreamer; Jealous Gun; Happy*. NIGHT AFTER NIGHT (10/77): *Take You to the Movies; Back It Up; Keith, Don't Go; Like Rain; Cry Tough; It's Not a Crime; Goin' Back; You're the Weight; Beggars Day; Moon Tears; Code of the Road; Rock and Roll Crook; Goin' South; Incidentally . . . It's Over; I Came to Dance*.

Singles/*You're the Weight* (2/74); *Back It Up* (4/75); *Cry Tough* (4/76); *It's Not a Crime* (6/76); *I Came to Dance* (4/77).

LOGGINS AND MESSINA/Kenny Loggins is a Washington-born songwriter whose *House at Pooh Corner* became a moderate hit for the Nitty Gritty Dirt Band back in '71. Signed by Columbia Records, he was given Jim Messina as a producer for his first solo outing. Jim, a California musician, had achieved fame a few years earlier by vaulting from the position of recording engineer to the status of member/producer of Buffalo Springfield (he replaced Bruce Palmer). After Springfield packed it in, Jim teamed with Ritchie Furay and formed Poco. Messina eventually departed that band to embark on a career as a record producer. Loggins' album would be his first project.

Before too long, he found himself an integral part of Kenny's musical world, and the first long-player featured Messina *SITTIN' IN*. The twosome saw the light, joined forces and started producing lightweight, melodic fare that immediately caught on at progressive rock stations and college campuses throughout the nation. Their albums started going gold, topped by a smash single in 1972. *Your Mama Don't Dance.* As is often the case, recognition brought about some unhealthy situations as the band tried a bit too hard to emulate *Your Mama* in an attempt at another hit single. The pressure was on. Some of the music grew self-conscious. Albums of oldies took the place of new collections of tunes. The Loggins and Messina stage show remained virtually unchanged for two years. Stagnation began to set in.

Rather than cave in under the commercial aspects of the rock biz, the twosome rallied with *NATIVE SONS* before deciding to call it quits as *BEST OF FRIENDS.* Today, Kenny is actively pursuing a solo career, going on the road as an opening act for such top-flight bands as Fleetwood Mac. Jim is taking his sweet time getting his act together, but then again, he was pretty meticulous back in his Poco days as well.

Albums/SITTIN' IN (12/71): *Nobody but You; Back to Georgia; House at Pooh Corner; Danny's Song; Vahevela; Listen to a Country Song; Rock and Roll Mood; Same Old Wine.* LOGGINS AND MESSINA (10/72): *Good Friends; Whiskey; Your Mama Don't Dance; Long Tail Cat; Golden Ribbons; Think of You; Just Before the News; Till the Ends Meet; Holiday Hotel; Angry Eyes; Lady of My Heart.* FULL SAIL (10/73): *Lahaina; Travelin' Blues; My Music; A Love Song; You Need a Man; Coming to You; Watching the River Run; Pathway to Glory; Didn't I Know You When; Sailin' the Wind.* ON STAGE (4/74): *House at Pooh Corner; Danny's Song; You Could Break My Heart; Lady of My Heart; Long Tail Cat; Listen to a Country Song; Holiday Hotel; Just Before the News; Angry Eyes; Golden Ribbons; Another Road; Vahevela; Back to Georgia; trilogy; Lovin Me, To Make a Woman Feel Wanted, Peace of Mind; Your Mama Don't Dance; Nobody but You.* MOTHER LOAD (10/74): *Growin'; Be Free; Changes; Brighter Days; Time to Space; Lately My Love; Get a Hold; Keep Me in Mind; Fever Dream.* SO FINE (8/75): *Oh, Lonesome Me; My Baby Left Me; Wake Up Little Susie; I'm Movin' On; Hello Mary Lou; Hey Good Lookin'; Splish Splash; A Lover's Question; You Never Can Tell; I Like It Like That; So Fine; Honky Tonk Part II.* NATIVE SON (1/76) *Sweet Marie; Pretty Princess; My Lady, My Love; When I Was a Child; Wasting Our Time; Peace-*

maker; It's Alright; Fox Fire; Boogie Man. BEST OF FRIENDS
(10/76): *Angry Eyes; Be Free; Vahevela; Peace of Mind; My Mu-
sic; Thinking of You; House at Pooh Corner; Watching the River
Run; Danny's Song; Your Mama Don't Dance.* FINALE (10/77):
*Travelin' Blues; medley: Danny's Song, A Love Song, House at
Pooh Corner, Thinking of You; Pretty Princess; Keep Me in Mind.*
Singles/*Vahevela*/*Same Old Wine* (1/72); *Nobody but
You*/*Danny's Song* (5/72); *Peace of Mind*/*House at Pooh Corner*
(8/72); *Just Before the News* (10/72); *Your Mama Don't
Dance*/*Golden Ribbons* (10/72); *Thinking of You*/*Till the Ends
Meet* (2/73); *Danny's Song*/*Nobody but You* (3/73); *My Music*/*A
Love Song* (10/73); *My Music*/*Thinking of You* (4/74); *Your
Mama Don't Dance*/*Thinking of You* (9/74); *Changes*/*Get a Hold*
12/74); *Growin'*/*Keep Me in Mind* (3/75); *I Like It Like
That*/*Angry Eyes* (7/75); *A Lover's Question*/*Oh, Lonesome Me*
(10/75); *Watching the River Run*/*Travelin' Blues* (2/76);
Peacemaker/*When I Was a Child* (3/76); *Pretty Princess*/*Native
Son* (3/76); *Angry Eyes*/*Watching the River Run* (11/76).

LOVE/*Arthur Lee (guitar, vocals, piano, accordion, drums, harp,
organ), John Echols (lead guitar), Bryan Maclean (guitar vocals),
Ken Forssi (bass), Mike Stuart (percussion). Additional members:
Alban "Snoopy" Pfisterer (drums), Tjay Cantrelli (brass), Frank
Fayad (bass), George Sranovitch (drums), Jay Donellan (guitar),
Robert Rozelle (bass), Joe Blocker (drums), Melvan Whittington
(guitar), Sherwood Akuna (bass), John Sterling (guitar).*
One of the earliest of the Los Angeles rock groups, Love emerged
late in 1965 before anyone could foretell that there would be a San
Francisco music scene, let alone a successful one. Until that time,
L.A. had produced only the Byrds, Sonny and Cher, and the
Raiders—which explains in part why a serious group like Love
was an instant underground success. Their first album had a hard
Beatles-Byrds sound—a marriage of English and L.A. rock. Their
second album used a bit of orchestration, and their third had everything (considered a contemporary classic). Memphis-born lead
singer Arthur Lee (also known as Arthurly) was an oddity for his
time, a black singer in a predominantly white band playing a predominantly white sound. (Oddly enough, Lee wrote most of
Love's material). Marveled Lillian Roxon at the time: "It was
one of the first integrated groups. Arthur Lee produced one of the
most amusing paradoxes in rock—a Negro, he came on like Mick

Jagger, a white singer who built his whole style around accurate imitations of Negroes."

Love never made it as a supergroup, yet it was one of the first bands to attract an underground following (especially in England). They were innovative and experimental. They were one of the first bands to cover an entire side of a record (18:57 minutes) with one cut. The only thing they never did was make the best-seller lists—a fact which, obviously, flustered Lee. He constantly changed membership within the ranks. Eventually he changed labels as well, moving from initial home Elektra to newfound lair Blue Thumb. By 1971, the band was ready to call it quits. Lee merged one year later with a fairly boring album of his own, *VINDICATOR*. Three years later, he brought together an all-new Love for RSO records and released the promising *REEL TO REEL* LP. Unfortunately, the world of the seventies was not really ready to accept Love of the sixties. Nor was the psychedelic spirit of Lee ready to grasp the hard realities of the desensitized seventies. After *REEL TO REEL,* Love collapsed anew, leaving musical innovator Lee on his own to ponder his musical future.

Albums/LOVE (3/66): *My Little Red Book; Can't Explain; A Message to Pretty; My Flash to You; Softly to Me; No Matter What You Do; Emotions; You'll Be Following; Fazing; Hey Joe; Signed D.C.; And More; Colored Balls Falling; Mushroom Clouds.* DA CAPO (1/67): *Stephanie Knows Who; Orange Skies; Que Vida; Seven and Seven Is; The Castles; She Comes in Colors; Revelation.* FOREVER CHANGES (11/67): *Alone Again Or; A House Is Not a Motel; Andmoreagain; The Daily Planet; Old Man; The Red Telephone; Maybe the People Would Be the Times or Between Clark and Hillsdale; Live and Let Live; The Good Humor Man He Sees Everything Like This; Bummer in the Summer; You Set the Scene.* LOVE FOUR SAIL (7/69): *August; Your Friend and Mine; Neil's Song; I'm with You; Good Times; Singing Cowboy; Dream; Robert Montgomery; Nothing; Talking in My Sleep; Always See Your Face.* OUT HERE (12/69): *I'll Pray for You; Abalony; Signed D.C.; Listen to My Song; I'm Down; Stand Out; Discharged; Doggone; I Still Wonder; Love Is More Than Words or Better Late Than Never; Nice to Be; Car Lights On in the Day Time Blues; Run to the Top; Willow Willow; Instra-Mental; You Are Something; Gather 'Round.* LOVE REVISITED (7/70): *My Little Red Book; Softly to Me; Hey Joe; Signed D.C.; Seven and*

Seven Is; Orange Skies; Your Mind and We Belong Together; She Comes in Colors; Alone Again Or; Andmoreagain; Your Friend and Mine—Neil's Song; Good Times; You Set the Scene. FALSE START (11/70). REEL TO REEL (1974): *Be Thankful for What You Got; Good Old-Fashion Dream; Everybody's Gotta Live; Which Witch Is Which; With a Little Energy; You Said You Would; Time Is Like a River; Stop the Music; Singing Cowboy; Who Are You?; Busted Feet.*

Singles/*Alone Again Or*/*A House Is Not a Motel* (S66); *My Little Red Book*/*A Message to Pretty* (3/66); *Seven and Seven Is*/*Number Fourteen* (7/66); *Orange Skies*/*She Comes in Colors* (11/66); *Alone Again Or* (8/70).

THE LOVIN' SPOONFUL/*Steve Boone (bass), John Sebastian (harmonica, autoharp, lead vocals), Jerry Yester (guitar), Zal Yanovsky (guitar), Joe Butler (drums).*
For a lot of people in America, the Lovin' Spoonful was Liverpool-in-Manhattan. Our own little moptops, born and bred right here in the streets we walked each day, hanging around outside the coffeeshops, playing in the basket houses, making a nuisance of themselves in Izzy Young's Folklore Centre. Scores of kids must have gone the Lovin' Spoonful route at the same time as the Spoonful, but John Sebastian, son of a musician, had talent. And when all his folksy friends started making it before he did, he played harp on their albums.

Sebastian's involvement with the sixties' folk scene began at the start of the decade when, with Zal Yanovsky, he took part in the short-lived Mugwumps, a band that also featured future Mamas and Papas Denny Doherty and Cass Elliott. When the Mugwumps dissolved, Sebastian moved around, playing the traveling troubadour role. Finally returning to New York, he attempted to get things going, in a musical sense, brandishing a fairly strange mixture of folk, pop, and country. Nobody really wanted to hear it except future Spoonful producer Eric Jacobson, who had played banjo in a country band.

With Eric helping from the sidelines, the original Spoonful (Sebastian, Zal, Boone, and Butler) was formed in 1965. At the beginning, with all their talent, the Spoonful wasn't that good. The story goes—and it's such a legend now that everyone has forgotten what's true—that they were at the Night Owl and terrible, and that Joe Marra, the owner, told them to go away and practice. Zally and Joe had a room at the Albert Hotel then, mainly to store equipment. When they rehearsed there, there were complaints. So Miss Feldman, the assistant manager, suggested the basement. And that was it. The group made it.

Within a year, they were signed to Kama Sutra records and the good-time music of Sebastian and friends was heard coast to coast. *Daydream, Summer in the City, Do You Believe in Magic, Darlin', Be Home Soon,* and *Nashville Cats* demonstrated the full range of the Spoonful's all-inclusive style. Offstage and on, the Spoonful were bona fide characters. John sported sideburns and steel-rimmed glasses when both were new. Zally wore a cowboy hat all the time and occasionally great bearlike furs. None of the four ever dressed mod-English as other American groups did but, from the start, they wore the striped shirts and vests that were the uniform of every Village kid. American teens couldn't believe their luck. They finally had their own group.

The Spoonful toured and recorded rigorously. And, after two years of phenomenal success, the strain began to show. In 1967 there was a drug bust in San Francisco. Occurring before drug busts were common news in the music world, the charges against Zally and Steve proved fairly traumatic. The twosome identified their dealer and the source was jailed. They weren't. In San Francisco, in 1967, their name was mud. Their albums were used as doormats. Groupies were urged not to ball them. Jeez.

Zally left the band, disheartened, to pursue a disastrous solo career. Jerry Yester, former producer with the Association, joined the faltering entourage for one album. In 1968, the Spoonful disbanded, with Sebastian pursuing a helter-skelter career of his own. In 1969, Butler made a go of it using the Spoonful name for an album which can best be described as rancid. The group split a second time. They had done what they had set out to do. They had produced a lot of happy, infectious music. And on the way, they helped change the whole musical scene of the mid-sixties.

During an era when to be successful was to be British, the Spoonful proved that it was still possible to be inventive, accessible, and American (or stranger yet, from New Yawk).

Albums/DO YOU BELIEVE IN MAGIC (12/65): *Do You Believe in Magic; Blues in the Bottle; Sportin' Life; My Gal; You Baby; Fishin' Blues; Did You Ever Have to Make Up Your Mind;*

Wild about My Lovin'; Other Side of This Side of Life; Younger Girl; On the Road Again; Night Owl Blues. DAY DREAM (5/66): *Day Dream; There She Is; It's Not Time Now; Warm Baby; Day Blues; Let the Boy Rock and Roll; Jug Band Music; Didn't Want to Have to Do It; You Didn't Have to Be So Nice; Big Noise from Speonk; Butchie's Tune; Bald-Headed Lena.* WHAT'S UP, TIGER LILY? (7/66): *Responke; Grey Prison Blues; Introduction to Flick; Pow; Pow Revisited; Unconscious Minuet; Fishing Blues; Cool Millions; Phil's Love Theme; Speaking of Spoken; Looking to Spy; Theme from* What's Up, Tiger Lily. HUMS OF THE LOV-IN' SPOONFUL (1/67): *Summer in the City; Rain on the Roof; Full Measure; Lovin' You; Bes' Friends; Voo-Doo in My Basement; Darlin' Companion; Henry Thomas; Coconut Grove; Nashville Cats; Four Eyes.* YOU'RE A BIG BOY NOW (1/67): *Darlin', Be Home Soon; You're a Big Boy Now; Lonely; Wash Her Away; Kite Chase; Try and Be Happy; Peep Show Percussion; Letter to Barbara; Girl; Beautiful Girl; Dixieland Big Boy; Miss Thing's Thang; March.* BEST OF THE LOVIN' SPOONFUL (3/67): *You Didn't Have to Be So Nice; Did You Ever Have to Make Up Your Mind; Butchie's Tune; Jug Band Music; Night Owl Blues; Younger Girl; Day Dream; Do You Believe in Magic; Didn't Want to Have to Do It; Wild about My Lovin'; Blues in the Bottle; Summer in the City.* EVERYTHING IS PLAYING (11/67): *Six O'Clock; She Is Still a Mystery; Younger Generation; Old Folks; Only Pretty, What a Pity; Try a Little Bit; Close Your Eyes; Priscilla Millionaira; Boredom; Forever.* BEST OF VOL. II (3/68): *Lonely; She Is Still a Mystery; Six O'Clock; Darlin', Be Home Soon; Lovin' You; Boredom; Full Measure; Nashville Cats; Rain on the Roof; Old Folks; Darlin' Companion; Younger Generation.* REVELATION: REVOLUTION '69 (11/68): *Amazing Air; Never Going Back; The Prophet; Only Yesterday; War Games; Till I Run with You; Jug of Wine; Revelation; Revolution '69; Me about You; Words.* THE BEST . . . THE LOVIN' SPOONFUL (1976): *Do You Believe in Magic?; Summer in the City; Daydream; Younger Girl; Rain on the Roof; Did You Ever Have to Make Up Your Mind?; Nashville Cats; You Didn't Have to Be So Nice; Didn't Want to Have to Do It; Six O'Clock; Younger Generation; She Is Still a Mystery; Lovin' You; Jug Band Music; Never Going Back; Warm Baby; Till I Run with You; Darlin' Be Home Soon.*

Singles/*Do You Believe in Magic/On the Road Again* (7/65); *You Didn't Have to Be So Nice/My Gal* (10/75); *Day Dream/Night Owl Blues* (1/66); *Did You Ever Have to Make Up Your Mind?/Didn't Want to Have to Do It* (4/66); *Summer in the City/Butchie's Tune* (6/66); *Rain on the Roof/Pow* (9/66); *Nashville Cats/Full Measure* (10/66); *Darlin', Be Home Soon/Darlin' Companion* (1/67); *Lonely (Amy's Theme)/You're a Big Boy Now* (5/67); *She Is Still a Mystery/Only Pretty, What a Pity* (9/67); *Close Your Eyes/Money* (12/67); *Forever/Never Going Back* (6/68); *Me about You* (1/69).

ANDY FAIRWEATHER LOW/A zany Welsh artist with a voice that sounds like a lunch break at a gravel pit, Andy Fairweather Low has yet to really make it as a solo performer. The former lead singer with the legendary U.K. group the Amen Corner, Andy had a head-on collision with fame and fortune while still in his teens. When hits like *Bend Me, Shape Me* stopped coming, the group dissolved in 1970. Andy hit the comeback trail in 1974 with his debut LP *SPIDER JIVING*. The title should give you a hint as to where this artist is coming from. His slap-happy approach to rock has led to a Low cult following on both sides of the Atlantic.

Albums/SPIDER JIVING (9/74): *Spider Jiving; Drowning on Dry Land; Keep On Rocking; Same Old Story; I Ain't No Mountain; Every Day I Die; Standing on the Water; Mellow Down; The Light Is Within; Reggae Tune; Dancing in the Dark.* LA BOOGA ROOGA (9/75): *My Bucket's Got a Hole in It; Jump Up and Turn Around; Half Way to Everything; La Booga Rooga; Champagne Melody; If That's What It Takes; 8 Ton Crazy; Grease It Up; Wide-Eyed and Legless; Inner City Highwayman.* BE BOP 'N' HOLLA (1/77): *Shimmie-Do-Wah-Sae; Ain't No Fun Anymore; Da Doo Rendezvous; Hot Poop; Travelin' Light; Rocky Raccoon; Lighten Up; I Can't Take Much More; Rhythm 'n' Jazz; Checking Out the Checker; Be Bop 'n' Holla.*

Singles/*Spider Jiving* (1/75); *La Booga Rooga* (10/75); *Wide-Eyed and Legless* (1/76); *Wide-Eyed and Legless* (6/76).

LYNYRD SKYNYRD/*Ronnie Van Zant (vocals), Allen Collins (guitar), Gary Rossington (guitar), Billy Powell (keyboard), Leon Wilkeson (bass), Artimus Pyle (drums), Steve Gaines (guitar).*
They were rough and tough and plenty mean. They were one of

America's all time greatest, raunchiest, hardest-hitting rock bands. The razor-edged sounds of low-down Lynyrd Skynyrd started back in the early seventies in Jacksonville, Florida. Named for a high school gym teacher who just didn't understand the boys', uh, eccentricities, the band formed, woodsheded, and began playing around the South—tearing down bars and clubs (sometimes musically, sometimes literally) wherever they went. In 1973, while doing a gig in Atlanta, they were spotted by rocker Al Kooper, who was then starting his own label to be distributed by MCA. Al signed them pronto. He subsequently produced the band's premier long-player . . . much to everyone's dismay. He wasn't crazy about their attitude (too cocky). They weren't crazy about his producing (too boring). Nonetheless, the album made a bit of noise on the FM-radio level and Skynyrd's sparse, bare-boned rock style began to attract regional attention. Their big break came when, shortly after the release of *PRONOUNCED LEH'-NERD SKIN-NERD,* the mob of rock neophytes captured the opening spot on a coast-to-coast Who tour. They more than held their own.

Who fans, needless to say, know good hard rock when they hear it; thus, Lynyrd Skynyrd started hitting home on every possible level. Their second album went gold. Their next album, *NUTHIN' FANCY,* also went gold, spawning the hit single *Saturday Night Special.* During that time, the band initiated their famous "Torture Tour" behavior pattern wherein, in order to ensure the success of both album and single releases, they took to the road until they collapsed. While such tours are effective in terms of popularity and breaking attendance records, they tend to make some individuals mentally nauseous. That first tour cost Skynyrd Bob Burns and, eventually, guitarist Ed King. The band, however, continued slogging it out onstage, journeying to England for a '75 tour that paved the way for the headlining jaunt of '76.

The key to Skynyrd's success, aside from their crisp, clean brand of rock, was their no-nonsense visual approach to music. They traveled. They played. Period. No frills. They played well and often. They were hard-core rock and rollers and nobody, anywhere, could ever ask for more than that. Skynyrd's desire to give their fans their all ultimately resulted in tragedy.

On October 20, 1977, less than a week after the release of their exceptional *STREET SURVIVORS* LP, Skynyrd began a lengthy concert tour. The private plane rented by the band took off from Greenville, South Carolina, en route to Baton Rouge, Louisiana. In Gillsburg, Mississippi, the plane went down in a thickly wooded area, about two hundred yards from an open field where the pilot had apparently hoped to land. Dead were Ronnie Van Zant, Steve Gaines, background singer Cassie Gaines, and Dean Kilpatrick, a member of their road crew.

The crash robbed the world of several extraordinary human beings, phenomenal talents and one of the most inventive rock bands of the seventies. The surviving members of Skynyrd have vowed to continue playing, perhaps under a different name.

Albums/PRONOUNCED LEH'-NERD SKIN-NERD (8/73): *I Ain't the One; Tuesday's Gone; Gimme Three Steps; Simple Man; Things Goin' On; Mississippi Kid; Poison Whiskey; Free Bird.* SECOND HELPING (4/74): *Sweet Home Alabama; I Need You; Don't Ask Me No Questions; Workin' for MCA; The Ballad of Curtis Loew; Swamp Music; The Needle and the Spoon; Call Me the Breeze.* NUTHIN' FANCY (3/75): *On the Hunt; Cheatin' Woman; I'm a Country Boy; Saturday Night Special; Whiskey Rock-a-Rollers; Am I Losin'; Railroad Song; Made in the Shade.* GIMME BACK MY BULLETS (2/76): *Give Me Back My Bullets; Every Mother's Son; Trust; I Got the Same Old Blues; Double Trouble; Roll Gypsy Roll; Searching; Cry for the Bad Man; All I Can Do Is Write about It.* ONE MORE FROM THE ROAD (9/76): *Workin' for MCA; I Ain't the One; Searching; Tuesday's Gone; Saturday Night Special; Travellin' Man; Whiskey Rock-a-Roller; Sweet Home Alabama; Call Me the Breeze; T for Texas; The Needle and the Spoon; Crossroads; Free Bird; Give Me Three Steps.* STREET SURVIVORS (10/77): *What's Your Name; That Smell; One More Time; I Know a Little; You Got That Right; I Never Dreamed; Honky Tonk Night-Time Man; Ain't No Good Life.*

Singles/*Gimme Three Steps/Mr. Banker* (11/73); *Take Your Time/Don't Ask Me No Questions* (4/74); *Take Your Time/Sweet Home Alabama* (6/74); *Down South Jukin/Free Bird* (11/74); *Saturday Night Special/Made in the Shade* (5/75); *Double Trouble/Roll Gypsy Roll* (2/76); *Gimme Back My Bullets/All I Can Do Is Write About It* (5/76); *Free Bird/Searching* (11/76); *Gimme Three Steps/Travellin' Man* (2/77).

THE MAHAVISHNU ORCHESTRA (JOHN McLAUGHLIN)/
Started in 1972 as an informal gathering of sidemen on guitarist
John McLaughlin's *INNER MOUNTING FLAME* LP, the
Mahavishnu Orchestra became the first jazz-rock group to attain
national prominence in both the jazz and rock schools of fandom.
Composed of violinist Jerry Goodman, drummer Billy Cobham,
Jan Hammer on keyboards, and Rick Laird on bass, the original
Mahavishnu unit brought high-powered delight to music lovers
everywhere, dishing out innovative arrangements and spellbind-
ing instrumentation. As leader John began to delve deeper and
deeper into his Eastern philosophical womb, however, the band
began to waver in its musical direction. In 1974, the original
Mahavishnu Orchestra was dissolved and a new, larger organization took its place, featuring Jean Luc Ponty on violin, Michael
Walden on drums, Gayle Moran on keyboards and vocals, Bob
Knapp on reeds, Steve Frankovitch on reeds, Ralph Armstrong
on bass, and a four-piece string section composed of Marsha
Westbrook, Phil Hershi, Carol Shive, and Stephen Kinder. In
spite of its musical aspirations, the new improved Mahavishnu
proved an emotionally lackluster experience and, after two
albums, they too took a transcendental walk. After mulling over
his musical status for a few months, leader McLaughlin began
approaching jazz-fusion music once more on *INNER WORLDS,*
with some success. Briefly taking leave of the up-tempo treadmill,
he then delved into traditional Indian music with the group
Shakti. At present, the shape of the next installment of the
Mahavishnu Orchestra remains a question that only McLaughlin
can answer.

Albums/INNER MOUNTAIN FLAME (11/71): *Meeting of the
Spirits; Dawn; The Noonward Race; A Lotus on Irish Streams;
Vital Transformation; The Dance of Maya; You Know You Know;
Awakening.* BIRDS OF FIRE (1/73): *Birds of Fire; Miles Beyond;
Celestial Terrestrial Commuter; Sapphire Bullets of Pure Love;
Thousand Island Park; Hope; One Word; Sanctuary; Open Coun-
try Joy; Resolution.* BETWEEN NOTHINGNESS AND
ETERNITY (11/73): *Trilogy: The Sunlit Path, La Mere De La
Mer, Tomorrow's Story Not the Same; Sister Andrea; Dream.*
APOCALYPSE (5/74): *Power of Love; Vision Is a Naked Sword;
Smile of the Beyond; Wings of Karma; Hymn to Him.* VISIONS OF
THE EMERALD BEYOND (2/75): *Eternity's Breath (Parts One*

and Two); Lila's Dance; Can't Stand Your Funk; Pastoral; Faith;
Cosmic Strut; If I Could See; Be Happy; Earth Ship; Pegasus;
Opus 1; On the Way Home to Earth. INNER WORLDS (12/75):
All in the Family; Miles Out; In My Life; Gita; Morning Calls; The
Way of the Pilgrim; River of My Heart; Planetary Citizen; Lotus
Feet; Inner Worlds, Parts One and Two.

Singles/*Open Country Joy/Celestial Terrestrial Commuter* (4/73);
Sister Andrea (1/74); *Can't Stand Your Funk/Eternity's Breath*
(4/75).

THE MAMAS AND THE PAPAS/*Denny Doherty (vocals), Cass*
Elliott (vocals), John Phillips (vocals, guitar), Michelle Phillips (vocals).
The Mamas and the Papas were the royal family of American
rock during the mid-sixties. Not because their music kept evolving, leaping from one artistic plateau to another. It didn't. But,
along with the Spoonful, they were one of the biggest American
bands to emerge during the so-called British invasion. Formed by
John in 1965, the band was an extension of the New York folk
circuit.

Cass and Denny were veterans of the Mugwumps and John was
a resident New York folkie. As the Mamas and the Papas told it,
the four cemented band ties in the Virgin Islands, where there was
not too much more to do than sing, but still the blend was not
quite perfect until a piece of piping fell on Cass and changed her
voice. Whatever, Rock folks were like that back then.

The foursome set up camp in Los Angeles and John arranged
to have the band signed to ABC-Dunhill. Almost instantly, the
band was a popular live and recording act with both a unique
sound and a unique look. Tunes like *Monday, Monday, California*
Dreamin', and *Dedicated to the One I Love* took America by surprise. The satiny vocals and the ethereal arrangements covertly
knocked AM radio on its ear. Plus, the motley quartet foretold a
new era in the American youth culture. The word "hippie" was
not yet in common use, but the concept existed. Groups in beards
and boots and funny hats and strange clothes were still new at the
end of 1966 and not yet a cliché.

The way the Mamas and the Papas appeared, once the music
business got over the shock of it all, was a novelty and very pro-
motable. The band proved both successful and exciting. And
what was really exciting was that they managed to establish the
fact that there *was* an American youth scene independent of the

current British trends. As contrived—perhaps even prefabricated —as their getup may have been, the Mamas and the Papas were one of the first harbingers of the counter-culture wave. In 1967, John extended his role as rock entrepreneur to include financing rock events. The event was The Monterey Festival. The event spawned the film *Monterey Pop,* launched Jimi Hendrix, Janis Joplin, and the Who on phenomenal careers, and spotlighted the Mamas and the Papas (naturally).

Unfortunately, the festival also spotlighted the band's inherent shallowness during a time of musical experimentation. During the recording of their fourth album, they suddenly discovered that they could not function as a working unit any longer. A halt to production was called and the foursome split up in search of mental breathing space. John and Michelle's marriage was coming apart at the seams and Cass wanted a solo career. In 1968, the band called it quits, leaving the heavenly California sound behind them.

Cass went on to a semi-shmaltzy solo career, strung with occasional hits and general pathos. Michelle went on to devote her time to both singing and acting, with mixed results. John became a producer, a movie producer, and a solo artist with fair to middlin' results.

Albums/IF YOU CAN BELIEVE YOUR EYES AND EARS (1/66): *Monday, Monday; Straight Shooter; Got a Feelin'; I Call Your Name; Do You Wanna Dance; Go Where You Wanna Go; California Dreamin'; Spanish Harlem; Somebody Groovy; Hey Girl; You Baby; In Crowd.* THE MAMAS AND THE PAPAS (9/66): *No Salt on Her Tail; Trip, Stumble and Fall; Dancing Bear; Words of Love; My Heart Stood Still; Dancing in the Street; I Saw Her Again; Strange Young Girls; I Can't Wait; Even If I Could; That Kind of Girl; Once Was a Time I Thought.* DELIVER (1/67): *Dedicated to the One I Love; My Girl; Creeque Alley; Sing for Your Supper; Twist and Shout; Free Advice; Look through My Window; Boys and Girls Together; String Man; Frustration; Did You Ever Want to Cry; John's Music Box.* FAREWELL TO THE FIRST GOLDEN ERA (10/67): *Dedicated to the One I Love; Go Where You Wanna Go; Words of Love; Look through My Window; Dancing in the Street; Monday, Monday; Creeque Alley; Got a Feelin'; Twelve-Thirty; I Call Your Name; I Saw Her Again Last Night; California Dreamin'.* THE PAPAS AND THE MAMAS

PRESENT THE MAMAS AND THE PAPAS (4/68): *The Right Somebody to Love; Safe in My Garden; Meditation Mama; For the Love of Ivy; Dream a Little Dream of Me; Mansions; Gemini Child; Nothing's Too Good for My Little Girl; Too Late; Twelve-Thirty; Rooms; Midnight Voyage.* MAMAS AND PAPAS GOLDEN ERA, VOL. 2 (10/68): *My Girl; Sing for Your Supper; No Salt on Her Tail; Twist and Shout; Glad to Be Unhappy; Nothing's Too Good for My Little Girl; For the Love of Ivy; You Baby; String Man; Even If I Could; Spanish Harlem; Dream a Little Dream of Me.* 16 OF THEIR GREATEST HITS (8/69): *Monday, Monday, Creeque Alley; Dedicated to the One I Love; Twist and Shout; Dream a Little Dream of Me; For the Love of Ivy; I Saw Her Again Last Night; California Dreamin'; Go Where You Wanna Go; Words of Love; Twelve-Thirty; other titles.* PEOPLE LIKE US (10/71).

Singles/*California Dreamin'/Somebody Groovy* (11/65); *Monday, Monday/Got a Feelin'* (3/66); *I Saw Her Again/Even If I Could* (6/66); *Look through My Window/Once Was a Time I Thought* (9/66); *Words of Love/Dancing in the Street* (11/66); *Dedicated to the One I Love/Free Advice* (2/67): *Creeque Alley/Did You Ever Want to Cry* (4/67); *Twelve-Thirty/Straight Shooter* (8/67); *Glad to Be Unhappy/Hey Girl* (10/67); *Dancing Bear/John's Music Box* (11/67); *Safe in My Garden/Too Late* (5/68); *Dream/For the Love of Ivy* (8/68); Do You Wanna Dance (10/68); *Step Out* (12/71).

BARRY MANILOW/Brooklyn-born singer-songwriter-pianist Barry Manilow first came to the public's attention as Bette Midler's musical director and pianist. The twosome crossed paths in New York's (then) trendy Continental Baths in 1972, when stand-in pianist Manilow was asked to accompany the fledgling star. The multifaceted Manilow soon became an integral part of Bette's live and recorded music, arranging and co-producing her first two albums and playing and conducting her concert tours. During this time he also came into his own as a television and radio jingle writer and singer.

In 1973, he began to gain confidence in himself as a solo performer, touring with Bette as her official opening act. By 1974 he was ready for stardom, which surfaced in the guise of the smash single *Mandy*. The hits have not stopped coming since, with Manilow becoming one of the nation's largest-selling recording stars.

With the advent of Manilow's superstardom, he and Midler parted ways . . . for good.

Albums/BARRY MANILOW (1973): *Sing It; Sweetwater Jones; Cloudburst; One of These Days; Oh My Lady; I Am Your Child; Could It Be Magic; Seven More Years; Flashy Lady; Friends; Sweet Life.* BARRY MANILOW II (1974): *I Want to Be Somebody's Baby; Early Morning Strangers; Mandy; The Two of Us; Something's Comin' Up; It's a Miracle; Avenue C; My Baby Loves Me; Sandra; Home Again.* TRYIN' TO GET THE FEELING (1975): *New York City Rhythm; Tryin' to Get the Feeling Again; Why Don't We Live Together; Bandstand Boogie; You're Leaving Too Soon; She's a Star; I Write the Songs; As Sure As I'm Standin' Here; A Nice Boy Like Me; Lay Me Down; Beautiful Music.* THIS ONE'S FOR YOU (1976): *This One's for You; Daybreak; You Oughta Be Home with Me; Jump Shout Boogie; Weekend in New England; Riders to the Stars; Let Me Go; Looks Like We Made It; Say the Words; All the Time; Why Don't We See the Show Again.* LIVE: *Rider to the Stars; Why Don't We Live Together; Looks Like We Made It; New York City Rhythm; A Very Strange Medley; Jump Shout Boogie Medley; Jumpin' at the Woodside; Avenue C; Cloudburst; Bandstand Boogie; Beautiful Music; Daybreak; Lay Me Down; Weekend in New England; I Write the Songs; Beautiful Music II; Beautiful Music III; Could It Be Magic; Studio Musicians; Weekend in New England.*

Singles/*Mandy* (10/74); *It's a Miracle* (2/75); *Could It Be Magic* (5/75); *I Write the Songs* (10/75); *Looks Like We Made It* (1976).

MANFRED MANN/*Manfred Mann (organ, piano), Mike Hugg (drums), Tom McGuinness (bass), Michael D'Abo (vocals), Klaus Voorman (bass), Paul Jones (vocals), Mike Vickers (reeds, flute, guitar).*

In October 1964, not long after *I Want to Hold Your Hand* and *Can't Buy Me Love,* Manfred Mann became the third English group to have a number-one record in America (the Animals being the second with *House of the Rising Sun).* The song was *Do Wah Diddy Diddy,* the first in a string of chart successes. The band started out in 1964 as an R&B outfit before evolving into a pop-rock band. Original members Paul Jones and Tom McGuinness grew tired of the pop grind and left within two years of their initial success to pursue solo projects.

About this time, the band's career took a fairly bizarre turn. In England, the group kept on charting high with their releases. *Ha! Ha! Said the Clown, My Name is Jack, The Semi-Detached Suburban Mr. James,* and *Pretty Flamingo.* In the States, however, they virtually couldn't get arrested, let along crack the top twenty. Finally, in 1968, they scored big with a cover version of Bob Dylan's *The Mighty Quinn.* By this point, alas, the band was really tired of chasing after hit singles. They were musicians first and foremost and felt the constant pandering to popdom demeaning.

In 1969 the band broke up. D'Abo followed a rocky road as a singer-songwriter before taking part in Smith-D'Abo some six years later (and an equally rocky proposition that turned out to be). Voorman became a consummate sideman and Mann and Hugg formed Manfred Man Chapter Three, an experimental band which lasted two years. Shortly thereafter, Mann came back with Manfred Mann's Earth Band.

Albums/MANFRED MANN ALBUM (10/64): *Do Wah Diddy Diddy; Sock O Woe; Don't Ask Me What I Say; What You Gonna Do; Got My Mojo Working; I'm Your Hoochie Coochie Man; Smokestack Lightning; It's Gonna Work Out Fine; Down the Road Apiece; Untie Me; Bring It to Jerome; Without You.* FIVE FACES OF MANFRED MANN (2/65): *Sha La La; Come Tomorrow; She; Can't Believe It; John Hardy; Did You Have to Do That; Watermelon Man; I'm Your Kingpin; Hubble Bubble; You've Got to Take It; Dashing Away with the Smoothness of Iron.* MY LITTLE RED BOOK OF WINNERS (8/65): *My Little Red Book; Oh No, Not My Baby; What Am I to Do; One in the Middle; You Gave Me Somebody to Love; You're for Me; Poison Ivy; Without You; Brother Jack; Love Like Yours; I Can't Believe What You Say; With God on Your Side.* MANN MADE (2/66): *Since I Don't Have You; You're for Me; The Way You Do the Things You Do; Look Away; Bare Hugg; Abominable Snowman; Watch Your Step; Stormy Monday Blues; I Really Do Believe; Hi Lili, Hi Lo; You Don't Know Me; LSD; I'll Make It Up to You.* PRETTY FLAMINGO (10/66): *Pretty Flamingo; Let's Go Get Stoned; Tired of Trying; Bored with Living, Scared of Dying; I Put a Spell on You; It's Getting Late; You're Standing By; You Have to Do That.* GREATEST HITS (11/66): *Do Wah Diddy Diddy; Sha La La; Pretty Flamingo; Oh No, Not My Baby; You Don't Know; I Got You, Babe; My Little Red Book; Hi Lili, Hi Lo; Let's*

Go Get Stoned; Got My Mojo Workin'; Come Tomorrow; Satisfaction. UP THE JUNCTION (3/67): *Up the Junction; Sing Songs of Love; Walking Round; Love Theme from* Up the Junction; *Just More Me; Sheila's Dance; Belgravia; Wailing Horn; I Need Your Love.* MIGHTY QUINN (3/68): *Mighty Quinn; Ha! Ha! Said the Clown; Every Day Another Hair Turns Grey; It's So Easy Falling; Big Betty; Cubist Town; Country Dancing; Semi-Detached Suburban Mr. James; Vicar's Daughter; Each and Every Day; No Better, No Worse.*

Singles/*Do Wah Diddy Diddy*/*What You Gonna Do* (8/64); *Sha La La* (10/64); *Come Tomorrow*/*What Did I Do Wrong* (1/65); *Hi Lili, Hi Lo*/*She Needs Company* (1/66); *My Little Red Book*/*I Can't Believe What You Say* (4/66); *Pretty Flamingo* (6/66); *Just Like a Woman*/*I Wanna Be Rich* (7/66); *John Hardy*/*Sha La La* (10/66); *Semi-Detached Suburban Mr. James*/*Each and Every Day* (10/66); *Ha! Ha! Said the Clown*/*Feeling So Good* (3/67); *Mighty Quinn*/*By Request—Edwin Garvey* (1/68); *My Name is Jack*/*There Is a Man* (6/68); *Fox on the Run*/*Too Many People*/*A "B" Side* (4/69).

BOB MARLEY AND THE WAILERS/When reggae was touted as being the next big craze in rock a few years back, Bob Marley and his Jamaican band, the Wailers, were pegged as superstars. Unfortunately, reggae never did explode in the United States and Marley and his little group never did attain stardom. As a cult band, however, they have amassed a solid, if small, following and have brought the infectious Jamaican sound to many a stateside concert hall.

Marley, a Jamaica-born singer-songwriter-guitarist, first formed the Wailers back in 1964, the lineup being Marley, Peter Tosh, Junior Braithwaite, Beverley Kelso, and Bunny Livingston. The group began to hit the local charts in a big way and, by 1966, were established Jamaican stars. But '66 found original members Kelso and Braithwaite leaving the happening band. Marley and his crew continued to record, their string of regional hits being interrupted only by short jail terms for Marley and Livingston.

Upon their release, the music of the Wailers began to undergo serious change. A revolutionary, antihero tinge began to permeate a lot of their material, which made them cult-heroes on their own turf. Marley began to spread the influence of reggae worldwide via his association with Johnny Nash, a Texas-born R&B singer who had enjoyed success at home from the mid-fifties to the mid-sixties before bottoming out with a thud. Introducing Nash to reggae both established Marley as a songwriter first class (he penned the hits *Stir It Up* and *Guava Jelly*) and gave Nash's career a much needed shot in the arm with both a new style and a new sound . . . reggae.

The Barrett brothers, Carlton (drums) and Aston (bass), were added to the Wailers to insure a more contemporary sound and, soon, the band was signed to a worldwide label for the first time . . . Island. The Island Wailers albums became the "in" thing with critics on both sides of the Atlantic. And as the word of mouth spread on the alleged reggae revolution, so did the word on Marley. Triumphant tours of America and the United Kingdom greatly enhanced their reputations. Barbra Streisand recorded *Guava Jelly* (no comment) and Eric Clapton topped the charts with Bob's *I Shot the Sheriff.*

In 1975, Peter Tosh left to pursue solo antics and was quickly snatched by Columbia, Records, who have released two moderately successful Tosh long-players thus far. Marley regrouped a year later adding Seeco Patterson (percussion), China Smith (guitar), and Tyrone Downie (keyboards). Despite the global press and worldwide critical acclaim, neither reggae nor Marley has appealed to a mass audience. What the future holds for reggae is questionable. For Marley, however, only good music and a mushrooming following can lie ahead.

Albums/CATCH A FIRE (1972): *Concrete Jungle; Slave Driver; 400 Years; Baby, We've Got a Date (Rock It, Baby); Stir It Up; Kinky Reggae; No More Trouble; Midnight Ravers.* BURNIN' (1973): *Get Up, Stand Up; Hallelujah Tune; Put It On; Burnin' and Lootin'; I Shot the Sheriff; Small Axe; Pass It On; One Foundation; Rasta Man Chant; Duppy Conqueror.* NATTY DREAD (2/75): *Lively Up Yourself; No Woman, No Cry; Them Belly Full (But We Hungry); Rebel Music (3 O'Clock Roadblock); So Jah Seh; Natty Dread; Bend Down Low; Talkin' Blues; Revolution.* RASTAMAN VIBRATION (4/76): *Positive Vibration; Roots, Rock, Reggae; Cry to Me; Johnny Was; Want More; Crazy Baldhead; Who the Cap Fit; Night Shift; War; Rat Race.* LIVE (9/76): *No Woman, No Cry; I Shot the Sheriff; Get Up, Stand Up; Trenchtown Rock; Burnin' and Lootin'; Them Belly Full (But We*

Hungry); Lively Up Yourself. EXODUS (5/77): *Natural Mystic; So Much Things to Say; Guiltiness; The Heathen; Exodus; Jamming; Waiting in Vain; Turn Your Lights Down Low; Three Little Birds; One Love/People Get Ready.*

JOHN MAYALL/*Group members from 1963 to present: John Mayall (vocals, harmonica, piano, harpsichord, organ, harmonium, guitars), John McVie (bass), Bernie Watson (guitar), Roger Dean (guitar), Hughie Flint (drums), Eric Clapton (guitar), Jack Bruce (bass), Aynsley Dunbar (drums), Peter Green (guitar); Andy Fraser (bass), Chris Mercer (tenor and baritone saxes), Rip Kant (baritone sax), Dick Heckstall-Smith (tenor and soprano saxes), Jon Hixeman (drums, percussion), Keif Hartley (drums, percussion), Henry Lowther (cornet, violin), Mick Taylor (guitar), Tony Reeves (bass), Steve Thompson (bass), Colin Allen (drums), John Almond (reeds, flute), Jon Mark (acoustic guitar), Sugarcane Harris (violin), Larry Taylor (bass), Harvey Mandel (guitar), Ron Selico (drums), Blue Mitchell (trumpet), Clifford Solomon (sax), Freddy Robinson (sax), Dee McKinnie (vocals), Victor Gaskin (bass).*
There is probably no more prestigious position in the world of rock than the one John Mayall has taken—the position of doing things for art instead of money. In an industry in which the fast buck is, to say the least, much respected, and the position of a record on the charts is taken into consideration far too often by people who should know better, John Mayall is an almost holy figure, the patron saint of blues. Devoted to music and seemingly indifferent to financial pressures, he has never had a legitimate "hit," although he has helped launch the careers of a number of rock stars.

He fell in love with the blues in 1946, at the age of thirteen, when everyone else was in love with traditional jazz. While still a teen, he formed his own blues group, the Powerhouse Four. In 1962, he formed the Bluesbreakers in London (with McVie and Watson) and went professional in 1963 (dropping Watson, adding Dean and Flint). From the beginning, Mayall attracted a loyal following on both sides of the Atlantic. His fans appreciated both his sense of artistic serenity and his uncanny ability to attract only the finest musicians to his band. Looking back over Mayall's one and a half decades in rock, his list of group members reads like a Who's Who of British rockdom.

In 1965, Eric Clapton joined the band, followed less than a year later by Jack Bruce. The nucleus of Cream was formed within the Bluesbreakers. After a stint with Mayall Peter Green left to form the original Fleetwood Mac, a band conceptually very close to Mayall territory. An eighteen-year-old Mick Taylor entered Mayall's entourage in 1968. Two and a half years later he was playing axe for the Rolling Stones. The list of bands to emerge from John's group is practically endless. Coliseum. Mark-Almond. The Keef Hartley Band.

During the seventies, Mayall has expanded his musical frame of reference to include both acoustically oriented instrumentation and hectic jazz. He left his longtime U.S. label, Decca, in 1975 to join the roster at ABC. Over thirty years have elapsed since the blues bug first bit John Mayall. The infectious instrumentation is still going strong.

Albums/BLUES BREAKERS (1/67): *All Your Love; Hideaway; Little Girl; What'd I Say; Another Man; Double-Crossing Time; Key to Love; Parchman Farm; Have You Heard; Ramblin' on My Mind; Steppin' Out; It Ain't Right.* A HARD ROAD (7/67): *Hard Road; It's Over; You Don't Love Me; Stumble; Another Kind of Love; Hit the Highway; Leaping Christine; Dust My Blues; There's Always Work; Same Way; Someday, After a While; Supernatural; Top of the Hill; Living Alone.* CRUSADE (1/68): *Oh, Pretty Woman; Stand Back, Baby; My Time after a While; Snowy Wood; Man of Stone; Tears in My Eyes; Driving Sideways; Death of J.B. Lenoir; I Can't Quit You, Baby; Me and My Woman; Streamline; Checking On My Baby.* THE BLUES ALONE (5/68): *Brand New Start; Please Don't Tell; Down the Line; Sonny Boy Blow; Marsha's Mood; No More Tears; Catch That Train; Cancelling Out; Harp Man; Brown Sugar; Broken Wings; Don't Kick Me.* BARE WIRES (9/68): *Where Did I Belong; I Started Walking; Fire; Open Up a New Door; I Know Now; Look in the Mirror; I'm a Stranger; No Reply; Hartley Quits; Killing Time; She's Too Young; Sandy.* RAW BLUES (11/68): *Pretty Girls Everywhere; Burn Out Your Blind Eyes; Calcutta Blues; Long Night; Country Boy; Lonely Years; Evil Woman Blues; My Home in the Desert; Milkman Strut; 24 Hours; Bernard Jenkins; You Gonna Need My Help.* BLUES FROM LAUREL CANYON (1/69): *Vacation; Walking on Sunset; Laurel Canyon Home; 2401; Ready to Ride; Medicine Man; Somebody Acting Like a Child; The Bear; Miss*

James; First Time Alone; Long Gone Midnight; Fly Tomorrow.
LOOKING BACK (7/69): *Mr. James; Blue City Shakedown;
Stormy Monday; So Many Roads; Looking Back; Sitting in the
Rain; It Hurts Me, Too; Double Trouble; Suspicions (Part 2); Jenny; Picture on the Wall.* TURNING POINT (8/69). THE
DIARY OF A BAND (1/70): *Blood on the Night; Edmonton; I
Can't Quit You, Baby; Keef Hartley interview; Anzio Ann; Keef
Hartley interview and John Mayall; Snowy Wood; John Mayall
interview; God Save the Queen; The Lesson; My Own Fault.* LIVE
IN EUROPE (4/71): *The Train; Crying Shame; Local Boy Makes
Good; Help Me; Blues in B; Soul of a Short, Fat Man.* EMPTY
ROOMS (2/70): *Don't Waste My Time; Plan Your Revolution;
Don't Pick a Flower; Something New; People Cling Together;
Waiting for the Right Time; Thinking of My Woman; Counting the
Days; When I Go; Many Miles Apart; To a Princess; Lying in My
Bed.* USA UNION (9/70): *Nature's Disappearing; You Must Be
Crazy; Night Flyer; Off the Road; Possessive Emotions; Where Did
My Legs Go; Took the Car; Crying; My Pretty Girl; Deep Blue
Sea.* BACK TO THE ROOTS (3/71): *Prisons on the Road; My
Children; Accidental Suicide; Groupie Girl; Blue Fox; Home
Again; Television Eye; Marriage Madness; Looking at Tomorrow;
Dream with Me; Full Speed Ahead; Mr. Censor Man; Force of
Nature; Boogie Albert; Goodbye December; Unanswered Questions; Devil's Tricks; Travelling.* THRU THE YEARS (10/71):
*Crocodile Walk; My Baby's Sweeter; Crawlin' Up a Hill; Mama,
Talk to Your Daughter; Alabama Blues; Out of Reach; Greenie;
Curly; Missin' You; Please Don't Hide; Your Funeral; Suspicious
(Part 1); Knockers Step Forward; Hide and Seek; Key to Love; I'm
a Stranger; Sonny Boy Blow; Have You Heard; No Reply; Stand
Back, Baby; The Bear; Don't Kick Me; The Super Natural; Me
and My Woman.* MEMORIES (10/71). JAZZ BLUES FUSION
(5/72): *Country Road; Mess Around; Good Time Boogie; Change
Your Ways; Dry Throat; Exercise in C Major for Harmonica, Bass
and Shufflers; Got to Be This Way.* MOVING ON (9/72): *Worried Mind; Keep Our Country Green; Christmas '71; Things Go
Wrong; Do It; Moving On; Red Sky; Reasons; High Pressure Living.* DOWN THE LINE (1/73): *Oh, Pretty Woman; Broken
Wings; I Started Walking; Stormy Monday Blues; Hideaway; Man
of Stone; Fire; First Time Alone; Fly Tomorrow; Crawling Up a
Hill; I Wanna Teach You Everything; When I'm Gone; I Need Your*

Love; Hoot Owl; R and B Time; Crocodile Walk; What's the Matter with You; Doreen; Runaway; Heartache; Chicago Line. THE BEST OF JOHN MAYALL (1973): *Moving On; Things Go Wrong; Keep Our Country Green; Do It; Red Sky; Mess Around/Change Your Ways; Play the Harp; The Laws Must Change; Room to Move; Prisons on the Road; Boogie Albert; Full Speed Ahead; Deep Blue Sea; Good Looking Stranger; California Campground.* TEN YEARS ARE GONE (1973): *Ten Years Are Gone; Driving till the Break of Day; Drifting; Better Pass You By; California Campground; Undecided; Good Looking Stranger; I Still Care; Don't Hang Me Up; Sitting Here Thinking; Harmonica Free Form; Burning Sun; Dark of the Night.* THE LATEST EDITION (1974): *Gasoline Blues; Perfect Peace; Going to Take My Time; Deep Down Feelings; Troubled Times; The Pusher Man; Love Song; Little Kitten; A Crazy Game.* NEW YEAR, NEW BAND, NEW COMPANY (2/75): *Sitting on the Outside; Can't Get Home; Step in the Sun; To Match the Wind; Sweet Scorpio; Driving On; Taxman Blues; So Much to Do; My Train Time; Respectfully yours.* NOTICE TO APPEAR (1/76). A BANQUET OF BLUES (7/76): *Sunshine; You Can't Put Me Down; I Got Somebody; Turn Me Loose; Seven Days Too Long; Table Top Girl; Lady; Fantasyland.* PRIMAL SOLOS (1/77): *Maudie; It Hurts to Be in Love; Have You Ever Loved a Woman; Bye Bye Bird; I'm Your Hoochie Coochie Man; Look at the Girl; Wish You Were Mine; Start Walkin'.* LOTS OF PEOPLE (2/77). A HARD CORE PACKAGE (8/77): *Rock and Roll Hobo; Do I Please You; Disconnected Line; An Old Sweet Picture; The Last Time; Make Up Your Mind; Arizona Bound; Now and Then; Goodnight Dreams; Give Me a Chance.*

Singles/*Parchman Farm/Key to Love* (10/66); *All Your Love/Hideaway* (3/67); *Suspicions; Oh, Pretty Woman* (11/67); *Jenny/Picture on the Wall* (5/68); *Broken Wings/Sonny Boy Blow* (6/68); *Walking on Sunset/Living Alone* (10/68); *Don't Waste My Time* (9/69); *Step in theSun/Al Goldstein Blues* (4/75).

PAUL McCARTNEY/WINGS: *original members: Paul and Linda McCartney (bass, keyboards, vocals), Denny Laine (guitar), Denny Seiwell (drums). Present members: Paul and Linda McCartney, Laine, Joe English (drums). Former members: Henry McCullough (guitar), Geoff Britain (drums), Jimmy McCullough (guitar).*

Paul McCartney was the first Beatle openly to sever ties with the working band and, as such, incurred some harsh criticism from Beatle-4-Ever fans. Around the time of the Beatles' *LET IT BE* release, Paul brought forth *McCARTNEY,* a solo effort recorded with his wife, Linda, and featuring Paul on every instrument. The reviewers were not kind to this long-player (although it did produce *Maybe I'm Amazed),* nor were they particularly fond of the follow-up *RAM.* In spite of the public opinion, McCartney managed to survive the storm. (In the midst of it all, he hit the pop polls between the bullets with *Uncle Albert-Admiral Halsey).*

McCartney was aware that many of his fans felt that his albums were merely vehicles to allow him to work with his wife. Criticism aimed Linda's way sparked the creation of a legitimate band, Wings. Joining the McCartneys in the first ensemble were former Moody Blueser Denny Laine, Denny Seiwell, and, later, ex–Grease Band axe-wielder Henry McCullough. The first days of Wings were anything but triumphant. Their first single, *Give Ireland Back to the Irish,* was regarded as a token effort and their second, *Mary Had a Little Lamb,* was regarded as inane. A U.S. tour in '72 brought the critics out in droves, and the charges of Linda's getting a free musical ride once again found their way into print.

Undaunted, McCartney and his crew continued onward. Seiwell left the fold, to be replaced by Britain and later English. McCullough departed for a kamikaze solo career and ex–Thunderclap Newman guitarist Jimmy McCullough took his place. (Jimmy left abruptly in 1977 after an apparent row with Paul.) In spite of the criticism, McCartney led Wings on a tuneful trip through the top ten with release after release. The songs were kinetic and commercial and, while no one could call them inventive, they proved infectious to the growing number of Wings fans. *Jet, Band on the Run, Junior's Farm, Listen to What the Man Said, Silly Love Songs,* and *Let 'Em In* all proved solid hits for the Wings unit. Five years after their hasty beginnings, Wings has proved more than just a vehicle for Paul and Linda McCartney; the group has evolved into one of the most successful of modern-day pop ensembles.

Albums/McCARTNEY (with Linda McCartney; 4/70): *The Lovely Linda; That Would Be Something; Valentine Day; Every Night; Hot As Sun/Glasses; Junk; Man We Was Lonely; Oo-You; Momma Miss America; Teddy Boy; Singalong Junk; Maybe I'm*

Amazed; Kreen-Akrore. RAM (with Linda McCartney; 5/71): *Too Many People; 3 Legs; Ram On; Dear Boy; Uncle Albert-Admiral Halsey; Smile Away; Heart of the Country; Monkberry Moon Delight; Eat at Home; Long-Haired Lady; Ram On; Back Seat of My Car.* WILD LIFE (first Wings' album; 12/71): *Mumbo; Bip Bop; Love Is Strange; Wild Life; Some People Never Know; I Am Your Singer; Tomorrow; Dear Friend.* RED ROSE SPEEDWAY (4/73): *Big Bard Bed; My Love; Get on the Right Thing; One More Kiss; Litle Lamb Dragonfly; Single Pigeon; When the Night; Loup (1st Indian on the Moon); medley: Hold Me Tight, Lazy Dynamite, Hands of Love, Power Cut.* BAND ON THE RUN (11/73): *Jet; Band on the Run; Bluebird; Mrs. Vanderbilt; Let Me Roll It; Mamunia; No Words; Helen Wheels; Picasso's Last Words (Drink to Me); Nineteen Hundred and Eighty-five.* VENUS AND MARS (5/75): *Venus and Mars; Rock Show; Love in Song; You Gave Me the Answer; Magneto and Titanium Man; Letting Go; Venus and Mars (reprise); Spirits of Ancient Egypt; Medicine Jar; Call Me Back Again; Listen to What the Man Said; Treat Her Gently; Lonely Old People; Crossroads Theme.* WINGS AT THE SPEED OF SOUND (3/76): *Let Em In; The Note You Never Wrote; She's My Baby; Beware My Love; Wino Juno; Silly Love Songs; Cook of the House; Time to Hide; Must Do Something About It; San Ferry Anne; Warm and Beautiful.* WINGS OVER AMERICA (12/76): *Venus and Mars—Rock Show—Jet; Let Me Roll It; Spirits of Ancient Egypt; Medicine Jar; Maybe I'm Amazed; Call Me Back Again; Lady Madonna; The Long and Winding Road; Live and Let Die; Picasso's Last Words (Drink to Me); Richard Cory; Bluebird; Blackbird; I've Just Seen a Face; Yesterday; You Gave Me the Answer; Magneto and Titanium Man; Go Now; My Love; Listen to What the Man Said; Let 'Em In; Time to Hide; Silly Love Song; Beware My Love; Letting Go; Band on the Run; Hi, Hi, Hi; Soily.* LONDON TOWN (3/78): *Children, Children; Deliver Your Children; Don't Let It Bring You Down; London Town; Cafe on the Left Bank; I'm Carrying; Backwards Traveler/Cuff Link; I've Had Enough; With a Little Luck; Famous Groupies; Name & Address; Morse Moose and the Grey Goose; Girlfriend.*

Singles/*Another Day/Oh Woman, Oh Why* (2/71); *Uncle Albert-Admiral Halsey/Too Many People* (8/71); *Give Ireland Back to the Irish* (3/72); *Mary Had a Little Lamb/Little Woman Love* (6/72); *Hi, Hi, Hi/C Moon* (12/72); *My Love/The Mess* (4/73); *Live and*

Let Die/I Lie Around (6/73); *Helen Wheels/Country Dreamer* (11/73); *Jet/Let Me Roll It* (1/74); *Jet/Mamunia* (1/74); *Band on the Run/Nineteen Hundred and Eighty-five* (4/74); *Walking in the Park With Eloise/Bridge over the River Suite* (by Wings as the Country Hams; 11/74); *Junior's Farm/Salley G* (11/74); *Listen to What the Man Said/Love in Song* (5/75); *Letting Go/You Gave Me the Answer* (9/75); *Venus and Mars Rock Show/Magneto and Titanium Man* (11/75); *Silly Love Songs/Cook of the House* (4/76); *Let 'Em In/Beware My Love* (6/76); *Maybe I'm Amazed/Soily* (2/77); *Girls' School/Mull of Kintyre* (12/77).

ROGER McGUINN/After the collapse of the Byrds in 1973, founder–member–vocal trademark Roger McGuinn embarked on a solo career which, to this date, has been fairly erratic. On his own, Roger has been torn between assembling bands and writing tunes that are fairly Byrdslike in nature, and embarking on something totally new. This decision has been an almost impossible one to make (after all, Roger *was* the voice of the Byrds), so Roger has constantly hovered between the two extremes. As a result, he has yet to make it big on his own, although all his albums have been above par and his concert dates well received. His last attempt at getting a working band together, an aggregation dubbed Thunderbyrd, proved moderately successful, demonstrating the fact that there was life in that ol' Byrd yet. What the future holds for Roger, no one knows. But for his legions of devoted followers, which now spans some three generations, this grand old man of rock and roll can do no wrong.

Albums/ROGER McGUINN (6/73): *I'm So Restless; Heave Away; Lost My Drivin' Wheel; Draggin'; Time Cube; Bag Full of Money; Hanoi Hannah; Stone; My New Woman; My Linda; The Water Is Wide.* PEACE ON YOU (8/74): *Peace on You; Without You; Going to the Country; One More Time; Same Old Sound; Do What You Want To; Together; Better Change; Gate of Horn; The Lady.* ROGER McGUINN AND BAND (6/75): *Somebody Loves You; Knockin on Heaven's Door; Bull Dog; Painted Lady; Lover of the Bayou; Lisa; Circle Song; So Long; Easy Does It; Born to Rock and Roll.* CARDIFF ROSE (4/76): *Take Me Away; Jolly Roger; Rock and Roll Time; Partners in Crime; Up to Me; Round Table; Pretty Polly; Dreamland.* THUNDERBYRD (2/77): *All Night Long; It's Gone; Dixie Highway; American Girl; We Can Do It All Over Again; Why Baby Why; I'm Not Lonely*

Anymore; Golden Loom; Russian Hill.

Singles/*Draggin'/Time Cube* (9/73); *Gate of Horn/Same Old Sound* (8/74); *Peace on You/Without You* (10/74); *Take Me Away/Friend* (7/76); *American Girl/I'm Not Lonely Anymore* (5/77).

DON McLEAN/Born in New Rochelle, New York, *American Pie's* pop, Don McLean was an avid musicphile since childhood, seriously studying just about every type of melody he came in contact with. Starting off as a traveling folkie, he eventually caught the eye of folk legend Pete Seeger, who gave McClean a spot on his sloop, "Clearwater." The boat sailed up and down the Hudson River in New York, tunefully stressing the dangers of pollution to the river communities. McLean put his experiences into a book, *Songs and Sketches of the First Clearwater Crew,* and by the time the book was out, so was Don's first album. It sold moderately well (singer-songwriters often have a hard time getting their careers in gear), but in 1971 his career went through the roof with the release of *American Pie,* an eight-minute capsuled history of rock. Sadly, the song overwhelmed Don's subsequent compositions and his career has hovered in limbo since that time.

Albums/AMERICAN PIE (10/71): *American Pie; Till Tomorrow; Vincent; Crossroads; Winterwood; Empty Chairs; Everybody Loves Me, Baby; Sister Fatima.* TAPESTRY (1/72): *Castles in the Air; General Store; Magdelane Lane; Tapestry; Respectable; Orphans of Wealth; Three Flights Up; And I Love You So; Bad Girl; Circus Song; No Reason for Your Dreams.* DON McLEAN (11/72): *Narcississima; Dreidel; Bronco Bill's Lament; The Birthday Song; The Pride Parade; The More You Pay; Oh My, What a Shame; If We Try; On the Madzon; Falling through Time.* PLAYIN' FAVORITES (10/73): *Sitting on Top of the World; Living with the Blues; Mountains o Mourne; Mule Skinner Blues; Fool's Paradise; Love O Love; Bill Cheatham; Old Joe Clark; Everyday; Ancient History; Over the Mountains; Lovesick Blues; Happy Trails.* HOMELESS BROTHER (10/74): *Winter Has Me in Its Grip; La La Love You; Homeless Brother; Sunshine Life for Me; The Legend of Andrew McCrew; Wonderful Baby; You Have Lived; Great Big Man; Tangled (Like a Spider in Her Hair); Crying in the Chapel; Did You Know.* SOLO (9/76): *Magdelene Lane; Masters of War; Wonderful Baby; Where Were You Baby; Empty Chairs; Goerdie's Lost His Penker; Babylon; And I Love*

You So; Mactavish Is Dead; Cripple Creek; Muleskinner Blues; Great Big Man; Bronco Bill's Lament; Happy Trails; Circus Song; American Pie; Over the Waterfall; Homeless Brother; Arkansas Traveler; Three Flights Up; Castles in the Air; Lovesick Blues; Winter Has Me in Its Grip; The Legend of Andrew McCrew; Dreidel; Vincent; Till Tomorrow. PRIME TIME (12/77): *The Statue; Jump; Redwing; The Pattern Is Broken; Color TV Blues; When Love Begins; When a Good Thing Goes Bad; South of the Border; Down the Road/Sally Ann; Building My Body.*

Singles/*American Pie* (10/71); *American Pie (1 & 2)* (12/71); *Vincent/Castles in the Air* (2/72); *Dreidel/Bronco Bill's Lament* (12/72); *If We Try/The More You Pay the More It's Worth* (3/73); *Fool's Paradise/Happy Trails* (1/74); *Vincent/Dreidel* (8/74); *American Pie* (8/74); *La La Love You/Homeless Brother* (11/74); *Wonderful Baby/Birthday Song* (3/75).

LEE MICHAELS/For one brief moment, delightfully mad Lee Michaels had the musical world at his fingertips. The rollicking keyboard whiz soared to the top of the singles charts in 1972 with the carousel-sounding summer single *Do You Know What I Mean?* The underground following he had been building for four years exploded and an album, *LEE MICHAELS 5th,* shot up the LP charts. Within twenty-four months, however, Lee had disappeared with a shrug and a grin.

The laconic Lee first came to the attention of rock tastemakers in the mid-sixties when the L.A.-born musician toiled in such bands as the Sentinels and the Joel Scott Hill group. Beginning his own keyboard-powered band in 1967, he carved a niche in the West Coast music scene big enough to attract A&M Records, who signed him the following year. By 1969, however, Lee jettisoned the band and began recording and appearing in concert armed only with a mountain of keyboards and faithful drumming companion Frosty (Bartholomew Smith Frost). The multi-talented Lee offered an organ-laden brand of rock and roll that sounded like a roller-skating rink with a backbeat. It was funky, low, and fun and his following grew with the release of each underpublicized LP. By the time *LEE MICHAELS 5TH* was released, the world was ready for the easygoing, hum-along sound.

Shortly thereafter, a rift developed between Michaels and his label and Michaels and his drummer, Frosty. Frosty left to join the Columbia Records roster in a truly horrendous band, Sweathog (Frosty would later rejoin Lee when Lee was a Columbia artist). Michaels was being wooed by Columbia Records' president Clive Davis and the offer appealed to Lee for a number of reasons. A hastily constructed *SPACE AND FIRST TAKES* (with drummer Keith Knudsen) answered his label's pleas for another "hit single" with an album full of uncommercial jam sessions, and a double album, *LIVE,* fulfilled his contractual obligations to A&M.

Michaels' short stay at Columbia brought forth a large amount of advance money, two unsuccessful albums, much executive teeth-gnashing and a relaxed Lee Michaels walking into the sunset with Hawaiian home and California ranch waiting in the wings. Who says there are no rock success stories that end happily?

Albums/CARNIVAL OF LIFE (4/68): *Hello; Another One; Streetcar; Love; Why; Carnival of Life; Tomorrow; Sounding the Sleeping; My Friends.* RECITAL (10/68): *If I Lose You; Time Is Over; No Part of It; Fell in Love Today; Blind; Grocery Soldier; What Can He Do; Basic Knowledge; Gonna Leave; War; Spare Change.* LEE MICHAELS (7/69): *Tell Me How Do You Feel; (Don't Want No) Woman; My Friends; Frosty's; Think I'll Go Back; Stormy Monday; Who Could Want More; Want My Baby; Heighdy Hi.* BARREL (7/70): *Mad Dog; What Now, America; Uummmm My Lady; Thumbs; When Johnny Comes Marching Home; Murder in My Heart (for the Judge); Day of Change; Think I'll Cry; Games; Didn't Know What I Had; As Long As I Can.* 5TH (5/71): *Keep the Circle Turning; You Are What You Do; Willie and the Hand Jive; Didn't Have to Happen; Rock Me, Baby; Do You Know What I Mean; Ya Ya; Can I Get a Witness; Oak Fire; I Don't Want Her.* SPACE AND FIRST TAKES (2/72): *Own Special Way (As Long As); First Names; Hold On to Freedom; Space and First Takes.* LIVE (1972). NICE DAY FOR SOMETHING (4/73): *Your Breath Is Bleeding; Same Old Song; So Hard; High Wind; Olson Arrives at Two Fifty-Five; The Other Day (The Other Way); Rock and Roll Community; Bell; Went Saw Mama; Nothing Matters (It Doesn't Matter).* TAILFACE (2/74): *Met a Toucan; Politician; Slow Dancin' Rotunda; Roochie Toochie Loochie; Drink the Water; Lovely Lisa; Garbage Gourmet.*

Singles/*Hello/Love* (1968); *Sounding the Sleeping/Tomorrow* (1968); *If I Lose You/My Friends (1968); Goodbye, Goodbye/The War* (3/69); *Do You Know What I Mean* (6/71); *Can I Get a Witness* (10/71); *Same Old Song/Rock and Roll Community* (5/73).

BETTE MIDLER/The Divine Miss M, as she is known in Manhattan circles, first achieved fame as a solo artist in the early seventies via her cabaret appearances in New York's Continental Baths, an infamous gay gathering place. Prior to that, Midler was a featured player in Broadway's *Fiddler on the Roof,* starting out as a member of the chorus in 1966 and winding up in a featured role (as Tzeitel) before departing in 1969. After earning a solid grassroots following in New York, Bette signed a recording contract with Atlantic Records, which culminated with the release of her first album in 1973, *THE DIVINE MISS M.*

The album garnered her a Grammy in the Newcomer of the Year department and, for a while, it looked like Bette's show-biz dreams were to be fulfilled at last. Born in New Jersey, Bette was raised in Hawaii where she entertained notions of becoming an actress. A part as an extra in the film *Hawaii* earned her enough money to make the holy crusade to New York's Great White Way. Arriving in Manhattan in the mid-sixties, she took a series of odd jobs before landing the aforementioned chorus role in *Fiddler.*

After the release of her first LP, Bette's career took a gradual downswing. Her second album did not garner as much attention as her first and subsequent releases appealed only to her multitude of devoted fans. Bette's larger-than-life cabaret style had ridden the crest of a nostalgia wave that swept the country and as that fad faded, Bette found herself and her songs standing alone in the pop world.

Always the trouper, Bette rallied in 1977 with a network television special and an "in-concert" performance broadcast across the country on the cable-TV networks. With or without the nostalgia boom behind her, Midler proved that she was an artist to contend with.

Albums/THE DIVINE MISS M (1/72): *Do You Want to Dance; Chapel of Love; Superstar; Daytime Hustler; Am I Blue; Friends; Hello In There; Leader of the Pack; Delta Dawn; Boogie-Woogie Bugle Boy; Friends.* BETTE MIDLER (11/73): *Skylark; Drinkin' Again; Breaking Up Somebody's Home; Surabaya Johnny; I Shall*

Be Released; Optimistic Voice/Lullaby of Broadway; In the Mood; Uptown/Da Do Run Run; Twisted; Higher and Higher. SONGS FOR THE NEW DEPRESSION (1/76): *Strangers in the Night; I Don't Want the Night to End; Mr. Rockefeller; Old Cape Cod; Buckets of Rain; Shiver Me Timbers/Samedi et Vendredi; No Jestering; Tragedy; Marahuana; Let Me Just Follow Behind.* LIVE AT LAST (5/77): *Backstage; Friends/Oh My Way; Bang, You're Dead; Birds; Comic Relief; In the Mood; Hurry On Down; Shiver Me Timbers; The Vicki Eydie Show: Around the World/ Istanbul/Fiesta in Rio/South Seas Scene/Hawaiian War Chant/Lullabye of Broadway; Intermission; You're Moving Out Today; Delta Dawn; Long John Blues; Those Wonderful Sophie Tucker Jokes; The Story of Nanette: Nanette/Alabama Song/Drinking Again/Mr. Rockefeller; The Story of Nanette II: Ready to Begin Again/Do You Wanna Dance; Fried Eggs; Hello in There; finale: Up the Ladder to the Roof/Boogie-Woogie Bugle Boy.* BROKEN BLOSSOM (12/77): *Make Yourself Comfortable; Say Goodbye to Hollywood; I Never Talk to Strangers; A Dream Is a Wish Your Heart Makes; Paradise; You Don't Know Me; other titles.*

Singles/*Do You Want to Dance/Superstar* (1/72); *Boogie-Woogie Bugle Boy/Delta Dawn* (4/73); *Friends/Chapel of Love* (9/73); *Good As It Can Be/Drinking Again* (1/74); *Do You Want to Dance/Boogie-Woogie Bugle Boy* (1/74); *I'm in the Mood/Friends* (11/74); *Strangers in the Night/Samedi et Vendredi* (2/76); *Old Cape Cod/Tragedy* (4/76); *Strangers in the Night/Old Cape Cod* (11/76); *You're Movin' Out Today/Let Me Just Follow Behind* (1/77).

FRANKIE MILLER/Blue-eyed-soul belter Frankie Miller sounds a bit like Otis Redding but looks awfully like a fellow born in Glasgow, Scotland—the reason being that he was. Frankie was "discovered" in the early seventies by Robin Trower and Clive Bunker, two mainstay British musicians who had just departed their successful groups, Procol Harum and Jethro Tull, and were looking for upcoming talent for a projected new band . . . the ultimate in hard rock. They stumbled into a London pub in '71 and the roaring Scot on the stage impressed them enough to enlist his aid, along with bassist Jimmy Dewar (late of Stone the Crows), to form Jude. The group never actually got to the recording stage. Trower and Dewar left to form Trower's own group. Bunker disappeared and Miller was left on his lonesome, armed only with a gravel-tinged voice and a handful of rave reviews.

Miller began to record solo albums, none of them selling exceedingly well but all of them earning critical bouquets. At this point, that is still the case. Frankie now has a touring band, Full House, and is starting to pick up quite a grass-roots following on both sides of the Atlantic. Rest assured, however, that when this bellowing bloozer's career explodes . . . there will be enough shrapnel around to fill a few dozen long-players.

Albums/ONCE IN A BLUE MOON (U.S. release 3/77): *You Don't Need to Laugh (To Be Happy); I Can't Change It; Candlelight Sonata in F Major; Ann Eliza Jane; It's All Over; In No Resistance; After All (I Live My Life); Just Like Tom Thumb's Blues; Mailbox; I'm Ready.* HIGHLIFE (7/74): *High Life; Play Something Sweet (Brickyard Blues); Trouble; A Fool; Little Angel; With You in Mind; The Devil Gun; I'll Take a Melody; Shoo Rah; Just a Song; I'm Falling in Love Again.* THE ROCK (9/75): *A Fool in Love; The Heartbreak; The Rock; I Know Why the Sun Don't Shine; Hard on the Levee; Ain't Got No Money; All My Love to You; I'm Old Enough; Bridgeton; Drunken Nights in the City.* FULL HOUSE (4/77): *Be Good to Yourself; The Doodle Song; Jealous Guy; Searching; Love Letters; Take Good Care of Yourself; Down the Honkytonk; This Love of Mine; Let the Candlelight Shine; I'll Never Live in Vain.*

Singles/*A Fool in Love/I Know Why the Sun Don't Shine* (9/75); *Be Good to Yourself* (7/77).

STEVE MILLER/Singer-songwriter-guitarist can do no wrong these days. He just sits down on his farm, woodsheds with his band, and shows up a few months later with a hit album and a hit single. An overnight sensation. Like most overnight sensations, Miller has been hacking around the rock scene for years—for over a decade actually—turning out much-neglected albums that are considered classics by most devout rockologists.

Miller started playing guitar in a teen band while still living in Texas. His first group, the Marksmen, was started in his preteen days and featured another Dallas hopeful, Boz Scaggs. The two later journeyed to faroff University of Wisconsin, where they spearheaded yet another band, the Ardells. After school, Miller headed for Chicago where, immersed in the blues, he formed a blues band with Barry Goldberg. Nothing much happened and Miller made a hasty exit to San Francisco where the music scene was just beginning to explode. He formed a band and, together with Mother Earth and Quicksilver Messenger Service, contributed a song or two to the soundtrack of the long-forgotten (and rightfully so) film, *Revolution*. He and his band then backed Chuck Berry at the Fillmore, winding up on a "live" Berry LP.

Eventually, Miller signed with Capitol and, once again, he entered the studio with his band (which, by this time, once more had Scaggs in the lineup). Two albums, *CHILDREN OF THE FUTURE* and *BRAVE NEW WORLD,* were instant underground hits. Miller and Scaggs worked well together and both albums were amazingly ambitious for their time, with near-perfect production and fantastic execution. Nonetheless, Boz (who, while Steve was bloozing it in Chicago, had carved a niche for himself in Scandinavia as a folk singer) didn't find the psychedelic route to his liking and embarked on a solo route that would eventually lead him to supper-club soul. With various members entering and exiting, the Steve Miller Band toiled unrecognized for years. In 1972 Miller was afflicted with hepatitis and over a year and a half elapsed without any recording done. But when Miller came back, he came back with guns blazing.

Brandishing an off-the-cuff delivery, 1973's Miller hit hard with *THE JOKER* . . . an unprecedented success at every possible level. The style was easygoing but strong, the lyrics bemused and detached. It was infectious. Miller had it made. The laconic Steve, however, promptly followed this success up with another year-and-a-half retreat from the public eye, emerging in 1976 with *FLY LIKE AN EAGLE*. Instant fame again. A year later came *A BOOK OF DREAMS* and the world was his. From psychedelia to uptempo shrugs, Steve Miller has always come up with the best he had to offer. And that "best" is always the finest rock around.

Albums/CHILDREN OF THE FUTURE (4/68): *Children of the Future; Pushed Me to It; You've Got the Power; In My First Mind; Key to the Highway; Beauty of Time Is That It's Snowing; Baby's Callin' Me Home; Steppin' Stone; Roll with It; Junior Saw It Happen; Fanny Mae.* SAILOR (10/68); *Song for Our Ancestors; Dear Mary; My Friend; Living in the USA; Quicksilver Girl; Lucky*

Man; Gangster of Love; You're So Fine; Overdrive; Dime a Dance Romance. BRAVE NEW WORLD (6/69): *Brave New World; Celebration Song; Can't You Hear Your Daddy's Heartbeat; Got Love 'Cause You Need It; Kow Kow Calqulator; Seasons; Space Cowboy; Let's Midnight Dream; My Dark Hour.* YOUR SAVING GRACE (11/69): *Little Girl; Just a Passing Fancy in a Midnite Dream; Don't Let Nobody Turn You Around; Baby's House; Motherless Children; The Last Wombat in Mecca; Feel So Glad; Your Saving Grace.* NUMBER 5 (7/70): *Good Morning; I Love You; Going to the Country; Hot Chili; Tokin's; Going to Mexico; Midnight Tango; Industrial Military Complex Hex; Jackson-Kent Blues; Never Kill Another Man.* ROCK LOVE (9/71): *The Gangster Is Back; Blues With Out Blame; Love Shock; Let Me Serve You; Rock Love; Harbor Lights; Deliverance.* RECALL THE BEGINNING . . . A JOURNEY FROM EDEN (3/72): *Welcome; Enter Maurice; High on You, Mama; Heal Your Heart; The Sun Is Going Down; Somebody Somewhere Help Me; Love's Riddle; Fandango; Nothing Lasts; Journey from Eden.* ANTHOLOGY (10/72): *I Love You; Going to the Country; Baby's House; Kow Kow Calqulator; Don't Let Nobody Turn You Around; Little Girl; Celebration Song; My Dark Hour; Your Saving Grace; Going to Mexico; Space Cowboy; Living in the USA; Journey from Eden; Seasons; Motherless Children; Never Kill Another Man.* THE JOKER (9/73): *Sugar Babe; Mary Lou; Shu Ba Da Du; Your Cash Ain't Nothing but Trash; The Joker; Lovin' Cup; Come On in My Kitchen; Evil; Something to Believe In.* FLY LIKE AN EAGLE (5/76): *Space Intro; Fly Like an Eagle; Wild Mountain Honey; Serenade; Dance, Dance, Dance; Mercury Blues; Take the Money and Run; Rock'n Me; You Send Me; Blue Odyssey; Sweet Maree; The Window.* BOOK OF DREAMS (5/77): *Threshold, Jet Airliner; Winter Time; Swingtown; True Fine Love; Wish Upon a Star; Jungle Love; Electro Lux Imbroglio; Sacrifice; The Stake; My Own Space; Babes in the Wood.*

Singles/*Sittin' in Circles/Roll with It* (4/68); *Living in the USA/Quicksilver Girl* (9/68); *My Dark Hour/Song for Our Ancestors* (6/69); *Don't Let Nobody Turn You Around /Little Girl* (10/69); *Going to the Country/Never Kill Another Man* (7/70); *Steve Miller's Midnight Tango/Going to Mexico* (10/70); *Rock Love/Let Me Serve You* (11/71); *Fandango/Love's Riddle* (5/72); *The Joker/Something to Believe In* (9/73); *Your Cash Ain't Noth-*

ing but Trash/Evil (2/74); *Living in the USA/Kow Kow Calqulator* (5/74); *Take the Money and Run/Sweet Maree* (4/76); *Rock'n Me/Shu Ba Da Du* (9/76); *Fly Like an Eagle/Loving Cup* (12/76); *Jet Airliner/Babe in the Wood* (4/77); *Jungle Love* (7/77); *Swingtown* (10/77).

JONI MITCHELL/Tall, pale, slim, frail . . . the very model of a woman folk singer, Joni Mitchell emerged as a "personality" in 1968, with an album and some tasteful personal appearances. But to the music world she was already a name to be reckoned with as a songwriter. Prior to her emergence as a performer, Joni had gained acclaim as the composer of such songs as *The Circle Game* (immortalized by Tom Rush), *Both Sides Now* (introduced by Judy Collins), and *Eastern Rain* (furnished by Fairport Convention).

Her career started while she was still a teenager. Born in Alberta, Canada, Joni discovered folk music while attending the *Alberta College of Art* in Calgary. Toying with a ukelele before learning guitar from a play-it-yourself set of Pete Seeger records, she became a singer in local student bars. The Maripose Folk Festival in 1964 found the young singer leaving all thoughts of education behind, opting instead for a career as a folk singer in the Toronto area. An early marriage and a move to Detroit led to both success and failure—the marriage dissolved but her career blossomed. Her gigs in Detroit led to jobs in Manhattan, where her songs were quickly snatched by New York–based record companies and artists in search of new material.

In 1967, she was signed to Reprise Records and quietly began a recording career that would covertly overwhelm the industry. As her fame spread, so did the scope of her music. Initially a straight "folk" singer, Joni gradually began to incorporate strains of rock and jazz into her melodies. Her tune *Woodstock* was enshrined forever by the adenoids of Crosby, Stills, Nash and Young and, soon, Joni herself was on the charts with the uptempo *Big Yellow Taxi.*

During the seventies, her lyricism expanded to include intensely introspective moments, balanced nicely by her newfound tendency to use Los Angeles session musicians—most notably Tom Scott and the L.A. Express—on her album for a richer sound. In 1972 she moved to Asylum Records, where she still resides.

Albums/JONI MITCHELL (4/68): *I Had a King; Michael from Mountains; Night in the City; Marcie; Nathan La Franeer; Sisotowbell Lane; The Dawntreader; The Pirate of Penance; Song to a Seagull; Cactus Tree.* CLOUDS (4/69): *The Angel; Chelsea Morning; I Don't Know Where I Stand; That Song about the Midway; Roses Blue; The Gallery; I Think I Understand; Songs to Aging Children Come; The Fiddle and the Drum; Both Sides Now.* LADIES OF THE CANYON (4/70): *Morning Morgantown; He Played Real Good for Free; Conversation; Ladies of the Canyon; Willie; The Arrangement; The Priest; Blue Boy; Big Yellow Taxi; Woodstock; The Circle Game; Rainy Night House.* BLUE (6/71): *Carey; Little Green; My Old Man; All I Want; California; This Flight Tonight; A Case of You; The Last Time I Saw Richard; River.* FOR THE ROSES (11/72): *Banquet; Cold Blue Steel and Sweet Fire; Barangrill; Lesson in Survival; See You Sometime; Let the Wind Carry Me; For the Roses; Electricity; You Turn Me On, I'm a Radio; Blonde in the Bleachers.* COURT AND SPARK (1/74): *Court and Spark; Help Me; Free Man in Paris; People's Train; Raised on Robbery; Trouble Child; Twisted.* MILES OF AISLES (11/74): *Big Yellow Taxi; For Free; You Turn Me On, I'm a Radio; other titles.* THE HISSING OF SUMMER LAWNS (11/75): *In France They Kiss on Main Street; The Jungle Line; Edith and the Kingpin; Don't Interrupt the Sorrow; Shades of Scarlett Conquering; The Hissing of Summer Lawns; The Boho Dance; Harry's House Centerpiece; Sweetbird; Shadows and Light.* HEJIRA (11/76): *Coyote; Amelia; Furry Sings the Blues; A Strange Boy; Hejira; Song for Sharon; Black Crow; Blue Motel Room; Refuge of the Roads.* DON JUAN'S RECKLESS DAUGHTER (12/77): *Overture—Cotton Avenue; Talk to Me; Jericho; Paprika Plains; Otis and Marlena; The Tenth World; Dreamland; Don Juan's Reckless Daughter; Off Night Backstreet; The Silky Veils of Ardor.*

Singles/*I Had a King/Night in the City* (1/68); *Big Yellow Taxi/Woodstock* (4/70); *Carey/This Flight Tonight* (7/71); *Big Yellow Taxi/Carey* (4/72); *Chelsea Morning/Both Sides Now* (10/72); *You Turn Me On, I'm a Radio/Urge for Going* (10/72); *Raised on Robbery/Court and Spark* (11/73); *Help Me/Just Like This Train* (2/74); *Free Man in Paris/People's Parties* (6/74); *Jericho/Carey* (3/75); *In France They Kiss on Main Street/The Boho Dance* (1/76); *Coyote/Blue Motel Room* (1/77).

MOBY GRAPE/*Skip Spence (guitar, vocals), Jerry Miller (lead guitar, vocals), Bob Mosley (bass, vocals), Peter Lewis (guitar, vocals), Don Stevenson (drums, vocals).*
Moby Grape was one of the finest bands ever to emerge from the sixties. All five members wrote excellently, played phenomenally, and sang exceedingly well. They were capable of rock, jazz, country, and balladeering. They were, in essence, the perfect rock band. They also died a horrible death at the hands of record-company mavens. Formed near Marin County in 1967, Grape consisted of a group of musicians who were totally unknown, with the exception of Spence, who had served as drummer with the original Jefferson Airplane.

The band had everything. Miller's guitar work was without peer. Lewis had the voice of an angel. Mosley thundered both on bass and on vocals. Spence was a walking time bomb of musical energy and Stevenson could do drums rolls that sounded like a cattle stampede. Signed to Columbia Records that same year, they were the victims of one of the most dunderheaded hypes ever conceived in musicdom. Upon the release of their first album, the truly classic *MOBY GRAPE,* the band was marketed in a kamikaze fashion. *All ten* songs on the album were released on five singles (both A and B sides) on the same day. All the singles had the same cover which was, incidentally, the cover used on the album. In other words, in one day a record buyer was able to witness the arrival of a new band with six sleeves containing, essentially, rehashed material.

The hype boomeranged and Grape was forced to live it down for over a year. Seeking a fresh start, they released the inventive double album *WOW/GRAPE JAME,* one long-player being a studio album, the other being a collection of largely instrumental jams with the likes of Al Kooper and Mike Bloomfield. The record did not sell very well and Spence, one of the group's more erratic members, left to record *OAR,* a solo album recorded on a four-track machine with Spence singing, arranging, playing, composing, and producing everything. It stiffed.

Meanwhile, the remaining Grapers recorded a truly amazing record, *'69.* As wondrously successful as Grape's first effort, the album was cut down in a series of quick corporate decisions by the band's record company and left to fend for itself, untouted, at record stores. (Within a year of its release, the record company would panic, yank off one title from the long-player, stick on the cut *Omaha* from Grape's first LP, and retitle the '69 package *OMAHA* . . . selling it at discount prices.)

Discouraged, the band continued on. Mosley split and joined the Marines on a whim. After a few physical altercations with fellow defenders of the realm, he was discharged a year or two later. The remaining members of the band cut the low-keyed, countrified *TRULY FINE CITIZEN* with session bassist Bob Moore. It died a horrible death. The group broke up, re-uniting in 1972 on another label for the genuinely bizarre *20 GRANITE CREEK*. Sounding as if it were recorded 20,000 leagues under the sea, the album offered solid material with gross production. A subsequent tour proved disastrous. Mosley left to record his own album on Warner, a joyful excursion into high-handed noise that was as subtle as a sledgehammer.

In 1973, an attempt to repackage the "best of " Moby Grape with a few unreleased live cuts by Columbia never got off the ground because of management difficulties between the band and their first manager Matthew Katz, who owned the group's name. Miller, Lewis, and Mosley reformed the band in 1973, temporarily calling themselves Maby Grope until finally deciding upon Fine Wine. Fine Wine cut one unreleased album in 1974. The band was allegedly signed to a subsidiary label of Bell Records, a label that soon caved in before re-emerging as Arista. Somewhere along the line, Fine Wine disappeared. Lewis departed the scene in '74 as well, leaving Miller and Mosley to make a go of it. Miller, Mosley, and Lewis still appear in various West Coast clubs. Spence, rumored to be one of the legendary acid casualties of the psychedelia days, has suffered from bad health on occasion. His biggest musical feat in his post-Grape days was to help bring the Doobie Brothers demo tape to the proper sources. When last heard from, Stevenson had quit drumming in favor of bartending.

Albums/MOBY GRAPE (5/67): *Hey, Grandma; Mr. Blues; Fall on You; 8:05; Come in the Morning; Omaha; Naked, If I Want to: Someday; Ain't No Use; Sitting by the Window; Changes; Lazy Me; Indifference.* WOW/GRAPE JAM (4/68): *Murder in My Heart for the Judge; Bitter Wind; Can't Be So Bad; Motorcycle Irene; Three-Four; Place and the Time; Rose-Colored Eyes; Funky-Tunk; Miller's Blues; He; Just Like Gene Autry, Foxtrot;*

Naked, If I Want To; Never; Boysenberry Jam; Black Currant Jam; Marmalade; The Lake. 69 (1/69): *Ooh Mama Ooh; Ain't That a Shame; I Am Not Willing; It's a Beautiful Day Today; Hoochie; Trucking Man; If You Can't Learn from My Mistakes; Captain Nemo; What's to Choose; Going Nowhere; Seeing.* TRULY FINE CITIZEN (8/69): *Changes, Circles Spinning; Looper; Truly Fine Citizen; Beautiful Is Beautiful; Love Song; Right Before My Eyes; Open Up Your Heart; Treat Me Bad; Tongue-Tied; Long Son, Part Two.* OMAHA (12/70): Same selections as on 69, with *Omaha* added in lieu of *Ooh Mama Ooh.* GREAT GRAPE (12/71): *Omaha; Murder in My Heart for the Judge; Bitter Wind; It's a Beautiful Day Today; Changes; Motorcycle Irene; Trucking Man; Someday; 8:05; Ooh Mama Ooh; Naked, If I Want to.* 20 GRANITE CREEK (8/71): *Gypsy Wedding; I'm the Kind of Man That Baby You Can Trust; About Time; Goin' Down to Texas; Road to the Sun; Apocalypse; Chinese Song; Roundhouse Blues; Ode to the Man at the End of the Bar; Wild Oats Moan; Horse Out in the Rain.*

Singles/*Omaha*/*Someday* (5/67): *Fall on You/Changes* (5/67); *Sitting by the Window/Indifference* (5/67); *8:05/Mr. Blues* (5/67); *Hey Grandma/Come in the Morning* (5/67); *Omaha/Hey Grandma* (6/68); *Bitter Wind/Can't Be So Bad* (6/68); *If You Can't Learn from My Mistakes/Trucking Man* (2/69); *Ooh Mama Ooh/It's a Beautiful Day Today* (5/69); *Gypsy Wedding/Apocalypse* (9/71); *Goin' On Down to Texas/About Time* (11/71).

THE MONKEES/*Mike "Wool Hat" Nesmith (guitar, vocals), Davy Jones (vocals), Mickey Dolenz (drums, vocals), Peter Tork (bass, vocals).*
The Monkees were a swell band when everyone in the world loved swell bands. They smiled. They ran around corridors like Charlie Chaplin on speed. They fell in love with beautiful girls. They sang. They danced. They didn't have pimples. They were ideal.

They were also the biggest thing to hit nationwide TV in the mid-sixties. The Monkees were a prefabricated group put together by NBC and Don Kirshner in an attempt to recreate the excitement of the silver-screen endeavors of the Beatles on the small boob tube. It worked, to say the least. An ad in *Variety* brought forth hundreds of aspiring actors, musicians, singers, and lunatics to try out for the roles of four loveable moptops. The chosen few were Dolenz (an actor and sort of singer who had starred, years earlier, in the adventure show "Circus Boy" . . . later he would frizz his hair and try for James Brown's jungle), Nesmith (a musician), Tork (ditto), and Jones (a child actor who played the Artful Dodger in the British stage production of *Oliver*). Among those passed up was Steven Stills, who had lousy teeth.

Kirshner guided the boys into the magical land of hitdom. And, as likeable as the fellows were personally, a lot of "serious" rock fans (the folks with the long hair and the Owsley acid in their hip pockets) began to raise a ruckus when it was disclosed that the Monkees didn't even play their instruments on their debut LP. But the hits kept comin'. *I'm a Believer. Last Train to Clarksville. Daydream Believer.* Eventually the Monkees themselves grew tired of their status as king teenyboppers and insidiously set about making themselves "respectable."

Nesmith began singing and writing exceptional songs. Tork played down his role of dummy. Jones grew more post-adolescent and Dolenz nearly hurt himself with his James Brown shuffling on stage. A tour with Jimi Hendrix as an opening act caused quite a commotion (in more ways than one, with Hendrix being yanked off the tour after a few dates). Frank Zappa and Tim Buckley guested on the Monkees' second, schizoid TV season. Jack Nicholson guided the boys into the surrealistic turkey *Head,* a feature-length film that effectively lampooned the Monkees' plastic career and also destroyed it in the process.

Tork quit, disgusted with playing the Ringo of the band, and became a minstrel in California before opting for teaching. Nesmith began a phenomenally unsuccessful solo career on RCA that resulted in a horde of exceptional LPs, brimming with genius, and a complete lack of promotion on the part of the record company. He now cuts and distributes his own records. Dolenz resorted to doing TV commercials before reuniting with Jones in 1975 to bring about sort of a Monkee renaissance. The twosome joined with old Monkee songwriters Tommy Boyce and Bobby Hart and recorded an album for Capitol . . . one of the biggest bombs since Hiroshima. The latter foursome currently draw tremendous crowds at supper clubs and state fairs as Monkee retreads.

Ah well, it *was* great fun while it lasted.

Albums/THE MONKEES (10/66): *Theme from the Monkees; Saturday's Child; I Wanna Be Free; Tomorrow's Gonna Be Another Day; Poppa Jean's Blues; Take a Giant Step; Last Train to Clarksville; This Just Doesn't Seem to Be My Day; Let's Dance On; I'll Be True to You; Sweet Young Thing; Gonna Buy Me a Dog.* MORE OF THE MONKEES (1/67). *I'm a Believer; Steppin' Stone; She; When Loves Come Knockin' (At Your Door); Mary, Mary; Hold On, Girl; Your Auntie Grizelda; Look Out (Here Comes Tomorrow); The Kind of Girl I Could Love; Day We Fall in Love; Laugh; Sometime in the Morning.* HEAD-QUARTERS (6/67): *You Told Me; I'll Spend My Life with You; Forget That Girl; Band 6; You Just May Be the One; Shades of Gray; I Can't Get Her off of My Mind; For Pete's Sake; Sunny Girlfriend; Zilch; No Time; Early Morning Blues and Greens; Randy Scouse, Git; Mr. Webster.* PISCES, AQUARIUS, CAPRICORN AND JONES, LTD. (11 /67): *Words; Salesman; She Hangs Out; Door into Summer; Love Is Only Sleeping; Cuddly Toy; Hard to Believe; What Am I Doing Hangin' 'round; Daily Nightly; Don't Call on Me; Star Collector; Medley; Pleasant Valley Sunday; Peter Percival Patterson's Pet Pig Porky.* THE BIRDS, THE BEES, AND THE MONKEES (5/68): *Dream World; Valleri; Aunti's Municipal Court; We Were Made for Each Other; PO Box 9847; The Poster; I'll Be Back Up on My Feet; Writing Wrongs; Daydream Believer; Tapioca Tundra; Zir and Zam; Magnolia Simms.* HEAD (12/68): *Opening Ceremony; Porpoise Song; Ditty Diego—War Chant; Circle Sky; Supplicio; Can You Dig It; Neck Gravy; Superstitious; As We Go Along; Dandruff; Daddy's Song; Pull; Long Title; Do I Have To All Over Again; Swami—Plus Strings.* INSTANT REPLAY (3/69); *Through the Looking Glass; Don't Listen to Linda; I Won't Be the Same Without Her; Me without You; Just a Game; Don't Wait for Me; You and I; While I Cry; Tear Drop City; Girl I Left Behind Me; Man Without a Dream; Shorty Blackwell.* GREATEST HITS (6/69): *Last Train to Clarksville; I'm a Believer; Steppin' Stone; I Wanna Be Free; Valleri; other titles.* THE MONKEES PRESENT (10/69): *Good Clean Fun; Someday Man; other titles.*

Singles/*Last Train to Clarksville/Take a Giant Step* (8/66); *I'm a Believer/Steppin' Stone* (11/66); *A Little Bit Me, a Little Bit You/Girl I Knew Somewhere* (3/67); *Pleasant Valley Sunday/Words* (7/67); *Day Dream Believer/Going Down* (10/67);

Valleri/Tàpioca Tundra (5/68); *D. W. Washburn/It's Nice to Be With You* (5/68); *The Porpoise Song/As We Go Along* (10/68); *Tear Drop City* (1/69); *Listen to the Band/Someday Man* (5/69); *Good Clean Fun* (8/69); *Oh My My* (5/70).

THE MOODY BLUES/*Michael Pinder (keyboards, vocals), Justin Hayward (guitar, vocals), Graeme Edge (drums), John Lodge (bass, vocals), Ray Thomas (flute, vocals), Denny Laine (guitar, vocals), Clint Warwick (bass, vocals).*
The Moody Blues are one of the few groups to survive the British invasion of the early sixties and actually prosper, over a decade later, in the pop-oriented seventies. Begun in 1964, the original lineup consisted of Pinder, Edge, Thomas, Laine, and Warwick. The band scored heavily in 1965 with their beautiful rendition of *Go Now,* but that hit single proved an exception rather than the rule and the Moodies plunged quickly to the lower depths of the popularity charts. Warwick and Laine took a stroll and the remaining members brought in Lodge and Hayward.

Two years after their first popularity, the new Moodies emerged victorious with a lush, orchestrated sound on *DAYS OF FUTURE PAST,* a concept album recorded with the London Symphony Orchestra. Both a new audience and a new sound were discovered and, for the Moody Blues, *DAYS* marked a point of no return. Onward and upward they soared with a melodic (albeit slightly overbloated) sound. Before too long, the Moodies became the Holy Roman Empire of rock, weaving together majestic sounds and slightly pretentious lyricism. That combination, however, proved to be a long-lasting hit formula.

Nights in White Satin, a single culled from the 1967 LP, became a hit again in 1972, proving the power of the omniscient mellow rockers. The band began to grow tired of their format and fragmented in 1973–74. All five members went on to moderately successful solo projects before announcing a reunion in 1977.

Albums/MOODY BLUES NO. 1 (7/65): *I Go Crazy; And My Baby's Gone; Go Now; It Ain't Necessarily So; It's Easy, Child; Can't Nobody Love You; I Had a Dream; Let Me Go; I Don't Want to Go on Without You; From the Bottom of My Heart; True Story; Bye Bye Burd.* DAYS OF FUTURE PASSED (3/68): *Nights in White Satin; Dawn is a Feeling; Another Morning; Peak Hours; Forever Afternoon (Tuesday); Sun Set; Twilight Time.* IN

SEARCH OF THE LOST CHORD (9/68): *Departure; Ride My See-Saw; House of Four Doors; Dr. Livingstone, I Presume; Legend of a Mind; Voices in the Sky; Best Way to Travel; Visions of Paradise; Actor; Word; Om.* ON THE THRESHOLD OF A DREAM (4/69): *In the Beginning; Lovely to See You; Dear Diary; Send Me No Wine; To Share our Love; So Deep Within You; Never Comes the Day; Lazy Day; Are You Sitting Comfortably; The Dream; Have You Heart (Parts I and II); The Voyage.* TO OUR CHILDREN'S CHILDREN (12/69): *Higher and Higher; Eyes of a Child; Floating; Eyes of a Child II; I Never Thought I'd Live to Be a Hundred; Beyond; Out and In; Gypsy; Eternity Road; Candle of Life; Sun Is Still Shining; I Never Thought I'd Live to be a Million; Watching and Waiting.* A QUESTION OF BALANCE (7/70): *Questions; How Is It (We Are Here); And the Tide Rushes In; Don't You Feel Small; Tortoise and the Hare; It's Up to You; Minstrel's Song; Dawning is the Day; Melancholy Man; The Balance.* EVERY GOOD BOY DESERVES A FAVOR (7/71): *Procession; The Story in Your Eyes; Our Guessing Game; Emily's Song; After You Came; One More Time to Live; Nice to Be Here; You Can Never Go Home; My Song.* THE SEVENTH SOJOURN (9/72): *Lost in a Lost World; New Horizons; For My Lady; Isn't Life Strange; You and Me; The Land of Make-Believe; When You're a Free Man; I'm Just a Singer (In a Rock and Roll Band).* THIS IS THE MOODY BLUES (10/74): *Question; The Actor; The Word; Eyes of a Child; Dear Diary; Legend of a Mind; In the Beginning; Lovely to See You; Never Comes the Day; Isn't Life Strange; The Dream; Have You Heart (Parts I and II); The Voyage; Ride My See-Saw; Tuesday Afternoon; And the Tide Rushes In; New Horizons; Simple Game; Watching and Waiting; I'm Just a Singer (In a Rock and Roll Band); For My Lady; The Story in Your Eyes; Melancholy Man; Nights in White Satin; Late Lament.* CAUGHT LIVE +5 (5/77): *Gypsy; The Sunset; Dr. Livingstone, I Presume; Never Comes the Day; Peak Hour; Tuesday Afternoon; Are You Sitting Comfortably?; The Dream; Have You Heart (Parts I and II); The Voyage; Nights in White Satin; Legend of a Mind; Ride My SeeSaw; Gimme a Little Somethin'; Please Think About It; Long Summer Days; King and Queen; What Am I Doing Here?*

Singles/*Go Now/It's Easy Child* (1/65); *From the Bottom of My Heart* (5/65); *Stop!* (3/66); *This Is My House/Boulevard de la Madeline* (7/66); *I Really Haven't Got the Time/Fly Me High*

(6/67); *Nights in White Satin/Cities* (5/68); *Tuesday Afternoon/Another Morning* (7/68); *Voices in the Sky/Ride My See-Saw* (9/68); *Never Comes the Day* (6/69); *Questions/Candles of Life* (4/70); *The Story in Your Eyes/Melancholy Man* (7/71); *Isn't Life Strange/After You Came* (5/72); *Nights in White Satin* (7/72); *I'm Just a Singer (in a Rock and Roll Band)/For My Lady* (1/73).

MOR/MOR stands for middle-of-the-road music. In record-business language, this represents any type of song that is not quite youth-oriented but not exactly senior-citizen fodder. A perfect example of MOR today would be anything recorded by Barbra Streisand, Helen Reddy, or the Carpenters. The perfect example of what MOR is not today is anything recorded by Ted Nugent, the Sex Pistols, or Aerosmith.

VAN MORRISON/Van Morrison is one of the last sources of true magic left in the rock world. Enigmatic, erratic, and brilliant, Van is one of the prime movers in present-day music and one of the most invisible. He emerges every two years or so with an album or a tour that quickly reestablishes his reputation as a living musical sparkplug and then he trots off into seclusion again.

The Belfast singer-songwriter's career began professionally at the age of fifteen when he left school to form an R&B group, the Monarchs. After three years of gigs with that band, he formed the infamous British blues outfit Them. Them enjoyed most of their success in the U.K., offering such singles as *Gloria* (later a hit in America by the Shadows of Night) and *Here Comes the Night.* However, during Them's stormy existence, Morrison was constantly at odds with music-biz types who sought to enhance the band's "sound" with session musicians on wax and to reshape the band's image into rough, tough rockers via a few well-aimed press releases.

In 1967, Van quit the band in disgust and Them went on without him for a short eighteen months. Morrison, undaunted, opted for a solo career. Bert Berns, the songwriter responsible for *Here Comes the Night,* invited Morrison to join his New York–based Bang Records label. Morrison did so, cutting the single *Brown-Eyed Girl.* For the first time ever, Morrison had a smash U.S. single, with the record effectively slicing into the top-ten charts. Within months, however, Morrison was again on his own.

As Van's embryonic career grew, business troubles mounted. A hassle with Bang Records led to a few hard feelings, with Bang releasing an unauthorized Morrison album. Berns died later that year of a heart attack. Morrison was without a label.

Joe Smith, the president of Warner Records, quickly ushered the feisty talent into the Warner Brothers corner and, with the release of the album *ASTRAL WEEKS* a star and a driving force in popular music was born. In one long-player, Morrison effectively and uniquely fused together atavistic elements of jazz, rock, folk, and R&B. His loose, free-wheeling vocals were something totally new in the era of the dawning of "production" and his lyrics were both imaginative and intelligent. His total sound pricked the imagination of his listener on a multitude of levels. Morrison's music not only caused toes to tap but brows to furrow.

The album was a critical success but did not set the world on fire saleswise. To Warner's extreme credit, they supported Morrison through both his high and low points. With each subsequent album, Morrison's popularity grew. What started off as a college-oriented, underground following mushroomed throughout the early seventies. A hit single, *Domino,* gave Morrison wide exposure. *ST. DOMINIC'S PREVIEW* and *HARD NOSE THE HIGHWAY* led to amazing tours, with Morrison backed by a mini-orchestra of well-honed R&B and jazz players.

At this point in his career, Van Morrison does more than just compose and perform music. He creates events. His fans span two decades of musical appreciation and his scattergun approach to rock knows no bounds.

Albums/BLOWIN' YOUR MIND (9/67): *Brown-Eyed Girl; He Ain't Give You None; T.B. Sheets; Spanish Rose; Goodbye Baby (Baby Goodbye); Ro Ro Rosey; Who Drove the Red Sports Car; Midnight Special.* ASTRAL WEEKS (11/68): *Astral Weeks; Beside You; Sweet Thing; Cypress Avenue; Young Lovers Do; Madame George; Ballerina; Slim Slow Slider.* THE BEST OF VAN MORRISON (1968): *Spanish Rose; It's All Right; Send Your Mind; The Smile You Smile; The Back Room; Brown-Eyed Girl; Goodbye Baby (Baby Goodbye); Ro Ro Rosey; He Ain't Give You None; Joe Harper Saturday Morning.* MOONDANCE (2/70): *And It Stoned Me; Moondance; Crazy Love; Caravan; Into the Mystic; Come Running; These Dreams of You; Brand New*

Day; Everyone; Glad Tidings. HIS BAND AND THE STREET CHOIR (10/70): *Domino; Crazy Face; Give Me a Kiss; I've Been Working; Call Me Up in Dreamland; I'll Be Your Lover, Too; Blue Money; Virgo Clowns; Sweet Jannine; Gypsy Queen; If I Ever Needed Someone; Street Choir.* TUPELO HONEY (11/71): *Wild Night; (Straight to Your Heart) Lie A Cannonball; Old Old Woodstock; Starting a New Life; You're My Woman; Tupelo Honey; I Wanna Roo You (Scottish derivative); When That Evening Sun Goes Down; Moonshine Whiskey.* SAINT DOMINIC'S PREVIEW (7/72): *Jackie Wilson Said (I'm in Heaven When You Smile); Gypsy; I Will Be There; Listen to the Lion; Saint Dominic's Preview; Redwood Trees; Almost Independence Day.* HARD NOSE THE HIGHWAY (7/73): *Snow in San Anselmo; Warm Love; Hard Nose the Highway; Wild Children; The Great Deception; Green; Autumn Song; Purple Heather.* IT'S TOO LATE TO STOP NOW (2/74): *Ain't Nothing You Can Do; Warm Love; Into the Mystic; These Dreams of You; I Believe to My Soul; Bring It On Home to Me; Saint Dominic's Preview; Take Your Hand Out of My Pocket; Listen to the Lion; Here Comes the Night; Gloria; Caravan; Cypress Avenue; I've Been Working; Help Me; Wild Children; Domino; I Just Wanna Make Love to You.* VEEDON FLEECE (11/74): *Fair Play; Linden Arden Stole the Highlights; Who Was That Masked Man; Streets of Arklow; You Don't Pull No Punches but You Don't Push the River; Bulbs; Cul-de-sac; Comfort You; Come Here, My Love; Country Fair.* PERIOD OF TRANSITION (4/77): *You Gotta Make It through the World; It Fills You Up; The Eternal Kansas City; Joyous Sound; Flamingos Fly; Heavy Connection; Cold Wind in August.*

Singles/*Brown-Eyed Girl/Goodbye Baby (Baby Goodbye)* (6/67); *Ro Ro Rosey/Chick-a-Boom* (1967); *Crazy Love/Come Running* (4/70); *Domino/Sweet Jannine* (10/70); *Blue Money/Sweet Thing* (1/71); *Call Me Up in Dreamland/Sweet Choir* (4/71); *Wild Night/When That Evening Sun Goes Down* (9/71); *Tupelo Honey/Starting a New Life* (12/71); *Crazy Love/Moondance* (12/71); *Like a Cannonball/Old Old Woodstock* (3/72); *Jackie Wilson Said/You've Got the Power* (7/72); *Redwood Tree/Saint Dominic's Preview* (11/72); *Gypsy/Saint Dominic's Preview* (11/72); *Warm Love/I Will Be There* (3/73); *Ain't Nothing You Can Do/Wild Children* (3/74); *Bulbs/Cul-de-sac* (8/74); *Joyous Sound* (6/77).

MOTT THE HOOPLE/*Ian Hunter (guitar, vocals), Pete Watts (bass), Dale "Buffin" Griffen (drums, vocals), Morgan Fisher (keyboards), Nigel Benjamin (vocals), Ray Major (guitar), Verden Allen (keyboards), Mick Ralphs (guitar); Ariel Bender (guitar).*
One of the major injustices in the past ten years of rock history is that Mott the Hoople never attained stardom. God knows they deserved it, and they certainly tried hard for it. Formed in the mid-sixties by Allen and Ralphs, the original Hoople crew consisted of Allen, Ralphs, Griffen, Watts, and vocalist Stan Tippens, who would shortly become their road manager before progressing to manager. Stan's on-again off-again vocal condition led the Hoople to audition new lead singers. At this point, long-time folkie Ian Hunter showed up, a Dylanesque composer-guitarist who could honestly be described as a "croaker" as opposed to a singer. Hunter's raspy ramblings, however, struck a responsive chord within the group. He joined in '69, signaling the beginning of one of the most turbulent band careers in rock.

Producer Guy Stevens ushered the band into the studio and cut a series of quickly recorded, though classic, albums. *MOTT THE HOOPLE, MAD SHADOWS, WILDLIFE,* and *BRAIN CAPERS* quickly established the band as a schizoid, critically acclaimed troupe. However, on the sales level, Mott was the pits. This lack of sales, plus the constant vying between styles (Hunter's writing was a good 180 degrees away from Ralph's style) within the band, led to problems. In 1972, the group fragmented, but was brought back together by David Bowie, who produced the classic *ALL THE YOUNG DUDES* LP. The boys now had a new producer and a new label (Columbia replacing Atlantic).

A new Mott was sculpted from the glitter and glam prevailing in the early seventies. Hunter became the leader. Verden Allen left shortly thereafter. Bowie departed as a producer and Ralphs left the fold to form Bad Company in the middle of recording *MOTT.* Although Mott was certainly proving more successful on Columbia than they were in the old days, they were anything but superstars. Single after single stiffed in the States and Mott was growing frustrated.

Despite their rather tentative position in the rock pop polls, the band planned a coast-to-coast blowout of a tour for '73. Enlisting the aid of former Spooky Tooth guitarist Luthor Grosvenor (who, dressed in his Dale Arden stage costumes, called himself Ariel Bender), Mott the Hoople (regular blokes who liked a good drink every now and then) donned their best glitter costumes and, armed with oversized puppets, robots, flash powder, and dancing dolls, embarked on a killer tour. Although augmented by the excellent keyboard work of Morgan Fisher, the Mott the Hoople killer tour found Mott portraying the killee.

The outrageous stage antics detracted from the musical clout somewhat and negated any possible monetary profit. Several of the band members were clearly uncomfortable in their platform heels and Ariel Bender just didn't fit in on guitar. Soon Ariel was in the void and Mick Ronson was indoctrinated into the Mott realm of lunacy. The arrival of another dominant personality was too much for the group to bear. Although the band consistently performed exceedingly well on record during this somewhat erratic period, their personal lives were in turmoil.

Hunter left the band, entering a hospital after a stateside bout with total exhaustion. Ronson departed for an ill-fated solo career, and the remaining members of the band regrouped with newcomers Majors and Benjamin as simply Mott. The group got off to a shaky start but quickly picked up steam with albums *SHOUTING AND POINTING* and *DRIVE ON*. Hunter embarked on a critically acclaimed but commercially disastrous solo career. He was dropped by his label in 1977, as was Mott, who also severed ties with lead singer Benjamin.

Albums/MOTT THE HOOPLE (4/70): *You Really Got Me; At the Crossroads; Laugh at Me; Backsliding Fearlessly; Rock and Roll Queen; Rabbit Foot and Toby Time; Wrath and Wroll; Half Moon Bay.* MAD SHADOWS (9/70): *Thunderbuck Ram; No Wheels to Ride; You Are One of Us; Walkin' with a Mountain; I Can Feel; Threads of Iron; When My Mind's Gone.* WILD LIFE (3/71): *Whiskey Woman; Angel of Eighth Avenue; Wrong Side of the River; Waterlow; Lay Down; It Must Be Love; Original Mixed Up Kid; Home Is Where I Want to Be; Keep a'-Knockin'.* BRAIN CAPERS (1/72): *Death May Be Your Santa Claus; Your Own Backyard; Darkness Darkness; The Journey; Sweet Angeline; Second Love; The Moon Upstairs; The Wheel of the Quivering Meat Conception.* ALL THE YOUNG DUDES (10/72): *Sweet Jane; Mamma's Little Jewel; Sucker; All the Young Dudes; Jerkin' Crocus; One of the Boys; Soft Ground; Ready for Love; After*

Lights; Sea Diver. MOTT (7/73): *All the Way from Memphis; Whizz Kid; Hymn for the Dudes; Honaloochie Boogie; Violence; Drivin' Sister; Ballad of Mott the Hoople; I'm a Cadillac; El Camino Dolo Roso; I Wish I Was Your Mother.* THE HOOPLE (3/74): *Golden Age of Rock 'n' Roll; Marionette; Alice; Crash Street Kids; Born Late; Trudi's Song; Pearl 'n' Roy (England); Through the Looking Glass; Roll Away the Stone.* ROCK AND ROLL QUEEN (1974): *Rock and Roll Queen; The Wheel of the Quivering Meat Conception; You Really Got Me; Thunderbuck Ram; Walkin' with a Mountain; Death May Be Your Santa Claus; Midnight Lady; Keep a-Knockin'.* LIVE (11/74): *All the Way from Memphis; Sucker; Rest in Peace; All the Young Dudes; Walking with a Mountain; Sweet Angeline; Rose; Jerkin' Crocus; One of the Boys; Rock and Roll Queen; Get Back; Whole Lotta Shakin'; Violence.* DRIVE ON (9/75): *By Tonight; Monte Carlo; She Does It; I'll Tell You Something; Stiff Upper Lip; Love Now; Apologies; The Great White Wail; Here We Are; It Takes One to Know One; I Can Show You How It Is.* SHOUTING AND POINTING (6/76): *Shouting and Pointing; Collision Course; Storm; Career (No Such Thing As Rock 'n' Roll); Hold On; You're Crazy; See You Again; Too Short Arms (I Don't Care); Broadside; Outcasts; Good Times.* GREATEST HITS (10/76): *All the Way from Memphis; Honaloochie Boogie; Hymn for the Dudes; Born Late '58; All the Young Dudes; Roll Away the Stone; Ballad of Mott the Hoople; Golden Age of Rock and Roll; Foxy Foxy; Saturday Gigs.*

Singles/*All the Young Dudes/One of the Boys* (8/72); *One of the Boys/Sucker* (12/72); *Sweet Jane/Jerkin' Crocus* (1/73); *Honaloochie Boogie/Rose* (6/73); *All the Way from Memphis/The Ballad of Mott the Hoople* (9/73); *Roll Away the Stone/Through the Looking Glass* (6/74); *The Golden Age of Rock and Roll/Rest in Peace* (9/74); *All the Young Dudes/Rose* (2/75).

MOUNTAIN/*Leslie West (guitar, vocals), Felix Pappalardi (bass), Corky Laing (Drums), Steve Knight (keyboards), David Perry (rhythm guitar).*
One of the nicest, silliest, and loudest surprises of the late sixties, Mountain was the musical equivalent of a tag-team match between Godzilla and King Kong. Based upon guitarist West's soaring, searing lead licks and agonizing vocals, Mountain became the darling of the raunch-rock crowd and retained its supergroup status until fading from view in 1974.

Mountain came about when Felix Pappalardi, producer of Cream, the Youngbloods, and the Lovin' Spoonful, met up with New Yawk band the Vagrants' immense guitarist West. After both Cream and the Vagrants bit the dust, Felix produced a West solo album, *LESLIE WEST—MOUNTAIN*. So impressed was the visionary producer that he quickly formed a band around Leslie's unique talents. A friend of Pappalardi's, Steve Knight, was enlisted for keyboard work (destined to become the band's invisible member, Knight was doomed to sit in the shadows during concerts), and drummer Norm Smart was called in from the Boston band scene. Smart proved anything but and new drummer Corky Laing was marched in.

This lineup produced some of the finest Mountain songs *(For Yasgur's Farm, Mississippi Queen, Nantucket Sleighride)* and was still going strong when problems arose within the ranks. Pappalardi grew tired of being a performer and left the group in '72. Knight split as well, although it is rumored that no one noticed for six weeks afterward. West and Laing teamed with ex-Cream bassist Jack Bruce before embarking on the short-lived West, Bruce and Laing group ... which, after Bruce's departure, evolved into the even shorter-lived Leslie West's Wild West Show which, in 1974, evolved into a retreaded Mountain, with Pappalardi and David Perry joining the ranks for a few months.

By 1975, Mountain was a dead issue and Leslie West was beginning a stillborn solo career on RCA. Today, the sounds of West are no longer being captured on wax.

Albums/LESLIE WEST—MOUNTAIN (7/69): *Blood of the Sun; Long Red; Better Watch Out; Blind Man; Baby, I'm Down; Dreams of Milk and Honey; Story-Teller Man; This Wheel's on Fire; Look to the Wind; Southbound Train; Because You Are My Friend.* MOUNTAIN CLIMBING! (2/70): *Mississippi Queen; Theme for an Imaginary Western; Never in My Life; Silver Paper; For Yasgur's Farm; To My Friend; The Laird; Sittin' on a Rainbow; Boys in the Band.* NANTUCKET SLEIGHRIDE (1/71). FLOWERS OF EVIL (11/71). THE ROAD GOES EVER ON (4/72). BEST OF MOUNTAIN (2/73): *Never in My Life; Taunta; Nantucket Sleighride; Roll Over, Beethoven; For Yasgur's Farm; The Animal Trainer and the Toad; Mississippi Queen; King's Chorale; Boys in the Band; Don't Look Around; Crossroader; Theme for an Imaginary Western.* TWIN PEAKS

(2/74): *Never In My Life; Theme for an Imaginary Western; Blood of the Sun; Guitar Solo; Crossroader; Mississippi Queen; Silver Paper; Roll Over, Beethoven; Nantucket Sleighride I and II.* AVALANCHE (7/74): *Whole Lotta Shakin' Goin' On; Back Where I Belong; Swamp Boy; Satisfaction; Thumbsucker; You Better Believe It; I Love to See You Fly; Sister Justice; Last of the Sunshine Days.*
Singles/*Mississippi Queen* (3/70); *The Animal Trainer and the Toad* (2/71).

THE MOVE/*Roy Wood (guitar, vocals), Bev Beven (drums), Ace Kefford (bass), Trevor Burton (guitar, vocals), Carl Wayne (vocals).* The Move was one of the most unsuccessful successful bands ever not to make it in the United States. Formed in 1965 from the cream of the crop of Birmingham, England, musicians, the Move followed the leadership of musical wizard Roy Wood who guided them on a pop path fraught with Beatle-isms. His direction led them straight onto the British charts with such singles as *Night of Fear, Fire Brigade, Flowers in the Rain,* and *I Can Hear the Grass Grow.*

The image of being a "pop" band, however, didn't sit well with the members and they did their best to live it down. Instead of wrecking their instruments, as did the Who, they smashed television sets, pianos, cars. Once they destroyed an effigy of British Prime Minister Wilson, which contributed usefully to a publicity campaign designed to make them come across as junior thugs. That little incident also contributed to near-bankruptcy as a rather irate Wilson sued the band for damages.

As the years rolled by and the band learned to live with the fact that in spite of being a successful singles band in England, they were utter failures stateside; their spirit faltered. In the early seventies, the group attained a now-you-see-it, now-you-don't status as Beven, Wood, and the late Movecomer Jeff Lynne planned various musical projects which eventually mutated into the Electric Light Orchestra and Wizzard. The Move finally disbanded in 1972.

Albums/THE MOVE (released in England in 1968): *Yellow Rainbow; Kilroy Was Here; Here We Go 'round the Lemon Tree; Weekend; Walk upon the Water; Flowers in the Rain; Hey Grandma; Useless Information; Zing Went the Strings of My Heart; The*

Girl Outside; Fire Brigade; Mist on a Monday Morning; Cherry Blossom Clinic. SHAZAM (4/70): *Hello Susie; Beautiful Daughter; Cherry Blossom; Clinic Revisited; Fields of People; Don't Make My Baby Blue; The Last Thing on My Mind.* LOOKING ON (1971). MESSAGE FROM THE COUNTRY (1971): *Message from the Country; The Minister; The Words of Aaron; No Time; Ella James; Until Your Mama's Gone; It Wasn't My Idea to Dance; Tonight; Ben Crawley Steel Co.; Don't Mess Me Up; My Marge.* SPLIT ENDZ (1/73): *Do Ya; Message from the Country; Chinatown; The Minister; The Words of Aaron; Down on the Bay; California Man; No Time; Ella James; It Wasn't My Idea to Dance; Until Your Mama's Gone; Tonight.* THE BEST OF THE MOVE (4/74): *Yellow Rainbow; Kilroy Was Here; Here We Go 'round the Lemon Tree; Weekend; Walk upon the Water; Flowers in the Rain; Hey Grandma; Useless Information; Zing Went the Strings of My Heart; The Girl Outside; Fire Brigade; Mist on a Monday Morning; Cherry Blossom Clinic; Night of Fear; Disturbance; I Can Hear the Grass Grow; Wave Your Flag and Stop the Train; Something; Omnibus; Wild Tiger Woman; Blackberry Way; Curly; This Time Tomorrow; Lightning Never Strikes Twice; Brontosaurus.*

Singles/*Night of Fear/The Disturbance* (1/67); *I Can Hear the Grass Grow/Wave the Flag and Stop the Train* (4/67); *Here We Go 'round the Lemon Tree/Flowers in the rain* (2/68); *Fire Brigade/Walk upon the Water* (2/68); *Something/Yellow Rainbow* (7/68); *Blackberry Way* (1/69); *Curly* (9/69); *Chinatown/Down on the Bay* (12/71); *California Man/Do Ya* (6/72); *Tonight/My Marge* (2/73).

GRAHAM NASH/British singer-songwriter Graham Nash was still a teenager when he formed the original Hollies with fellow schoolmate Allan Clarke. Nash was responsible for most of the band's hits from 1963 to 1968. After a five-year stay, Nash departed the group, hooking up with Byrd-on-the-wing David Crosby and disenchanted Buffalo Springfielder Steve Stills. The trio of Crosby, Stills and Nash and, later, the quartet of Crosby, Stills, Nash and Young brought the album-oriented credibility that Nash had longed for while still with the Hollies.

As CSN&Y faltered during the early sixties, Nash embarked on what was destined to be a fairly routine solo career. He has, since his debut in 1971, gone on to greater fame as part of the duo Crosby and Nash and part of the re-formed Crosby, Stills and Nash.

Albums/SONGS FOR BEGINNERS (5/71): *Military Madness; Be Yourself; Wounded Bird; I Used to Be a King; Simple Man; Man in the Mirror; Sleep Song; There's Only One; Chicago; We Can Change the World.* WILD TALES (1/74): *Wild Tales; Hey You (Looking at the Moon); Prison Song; You'll Never Be the Same; And So It Goes; Grave Concern; Oh! Camil (The Winter Soldier); I Miss You; On the Line; Another Sleep Song.*

Singles/*Chicago/Simple Man* (6/71); *Military Madness/Sleep Song* (8/71); *Prison Song/Hey You* (2/74).

NAZARETH/*Dan McCafferty (vocals), Darryl Sweet (drums), Pete Agnew (bass), Manny Charlton (guitar).*
Hard-rocking Nazareth is best known for their cannon-volley rhythms and the truly lycanthropic wailing of lead vocalist Dan McCafferty. After a few years of hovering in limbo, the band broke big in the States with their 1975 single, *Love Hurts.* Prior to that, the Scotland-bred band had their share of ups and downs. Coming together in the late sixties, the band first attained crotch-rocking success in their homeland before they moved to London. Signed almost immediately, their first two albums, *NAZARETH* and *EXERCISE,* proved to be very *Un*Nazareth sounding, replete with lilting melodies, lush production, and not much rock and roll. A change in labels (from Warner to A&M) and a change in producers (Deep Purple's Roger Glover entered the picture about this time) brought Naz their first real bone-crusher, *RAZAMANAZ.*

A series of hard-rocking albums followed. Stateside, their fame lagged behind the recognition found in the United Kingdom. One big problem was that the band just never seemed to get a decent U.S. tour. (United States Record Company Axiom: If yer gonna get the album played, ya gotta get the band a tour. Not to be confused with the handy United States Record Company Anti-Axiom: We couldn't get yez a tour, 'cause we couldn't get the album played. You figure it out.)

Lack of tour dates kept the band fairly hidden from the limelight but, by 1975, all the right elements fell into place and the group hit the charts in a big way. They have yet to repeat their top-tenning antics but their albums are well received by their new-found fans. Of late, McCafferty has embarked on a solo career in between Naz activities. A solo album, released in 1975, proved a dud.

Albums/NAZARETH (4/72): *Dear John; Witchdoctor Woman; Empty Arms, Empty Heart; Real Light Lady; Fat Man; Country Girl; The King Is Dead; Morning Dew.* EXERCISES (8/72): *I Will Not Be Led; Cat's Eye . . . Apple Pie; In My Time; Woke Up This Morning; Called Her Name; Fool about You; Love, Now You're Gone; Madelaine; Sad Song; 1692 (Glen Coe Massacre).* RAZAMANAZ (7/73): *Razamanaz; Alcatraz; Vigilante Man; Woke Up This Morning; Night Women; Bad, Bad Boy; Sold My Soul; Too Bad, Too Sad; Broken-Down Angel.* LOUD 'N' PROUD (1/74): *Go Down Fighting; Not Faking It; Turn On Your Receiver; Teenage Nervous Breakdown; Freewheeler; This Flight Tonight; Child in the Sun; The Ballad of Hollis Brown.* RAMPANT (6/74): *Silver Dollar Forger (Parts 1 and 2); Glad When You're Gone; Loved and Lost; Shanghai'd in Shanghai; Jet Lag; Light My Way; Sunshine; Shapes of Things/Space Safari.* HAIR OF THE DOG (3/75): *Hair of the Dog; Miss Misery; Love Hurts; Changin' Times; Beggars Day; Rose in the Heather; Whiskey-Drinkin' Woman; Please Don't Judas Me.* CLOSE ENOUGH FOR ROCK 'N' ROLL (4/76): *Telegram; On Your Way, So You Want to Be a Rock 'n' Roll Star; Sound Check; Here We Are Again; Vicki; Homesick Again; Vancover Shakedown; Born under the Wrong Sign; Loretta; Carry Out Feelings; Lift the Lid; You're the Violin.* PLAY 'N' THE GAME (11/76): *Somebody to Roll; Down Home Girl; Flying; Waiting for the Man; Born to Love; I Want To (Do Everything for You); I Don't Want to Go On without You; Wild Honey; L.A. Girls.*

Singles/*Broken-Down Angel* (7/73); *Razamanaz* (8/73); *This Flight Tonight* (3/74); *This Flight Tonight* (7/74); *Love Hurts* (5/75); *Carry Out Feelings* (5/76); Loretta (8/76); *This Flight Tonight* (4/77).

NAZZ/*Todd Rundgren (guitar), Carson van Osten (bass), Robert Antoni (keyboards, vocals), Thom Mooney.*

Philadelphia-spawned Nazz is best known for being Todd Rundgren's first professional group. The band wallowed in a sound decidedly British and a lot of their early fans thought that these fab four truly hailed from the original fab four's birthplace. The Nazz quartet disbanded in 1969, a little over a year after their initial appearance.

Albums/THE NAZZ (8/68): *Open My Eyes; Back of Your Mind; See What You Can Be; Hello, It's Me; Wildwood Blues; If That's the Way You Feel; When I Get My Plane; Lemming Song; Crowded; She's Goin' Down.* NAZZ NAZZ (4/69): *Forget All about It; Not Wrong Long; Rain Rider; Gonna Cry Today; Meridian Leward; Under the Ice; Hang On, Paul; Kiddie Boy; Featherbedding Lover; Letters Don't Count; A Beautiful Song.* NAZZ III (11/70): *Some People; Only One Winner; Kicks; It's Not That Easy; Old Time Lovemaking; Magic Me; Loosen Up; Take the Hand; How Can You Call That Beautiful?; Plenty of Lovin'; Christopher Columbus; You Are My Window.*

Singles/*Hello, It's Me/Everybody's Talkin'* (8/68); *Under the Ice/Not Wrong Long* (5/69); *Hello, It's Me* (1/70).

NEW RIDERS OF THE PURPLE SAGE/*Buddy Cage (pedal steel), John Dawson (guitar and vocals), Spencer Dryden (drums), Stephen Love (bass and vocals), David Nelson (lead guitar and vocals), Previous members: Skip Battin (bass), Dave Torbert (bass), Jerry Garcia (pedal steel), Mickey Hart (drums), Phil Lesh (bass).* Formed in 1970 as an offshoot of the Grateful Dead, the New Riders of the Purple Sage espoused an off-the-cuff style of country-rock rambling that appealed to Dead fans. The first line-up included Dead alumni Jerry Garcia, Mickey Hart, and Phil Lesh. This trio, along with Nelson and Dawson, toured in conjunction with the Dead and were given quite a push as a result. Signed by CBS, the New Riders (NRPS to their fans) quickly achieved notoriety with their premier disc, *NEW RIDERS OF THE PURPLE SAGE.* Their twangy, unabashed cowboy antics leveled audiences from coast to coast.

The LP was more of a critical success than a commercial one, however, and when the time rolled around for another long-playing helping of countrified rhythm, the three members of the Dead found that working a double musical shift was impairing their creativity. NRPS quickly enlisted the talents of Torbert, Dryden, and Cage. This format lasted until 1974, when conflicts within the group led to Torbert's departure and Battin's arrival.

Battin, a former Byrd, lasted a year and a half, to be replaced by Stephen Love.

NRPS has always been a concert-goers' band. Their laid-back musical attitude has always kept them off the top numbers of the charts. Recently (1976) the band jumped labels and dropped their management affiliation in an effort to give the band a new, positive direction. They are not managed by member Dryden (a former Jefferson Airplane mainstay). At this point, Dryden is good-naturedly wondering which side of the stage is harder to survive on.

Albums/NEW RIDERS OF THE PURPLE SAGE (8/71): *I Don't Know; Whatcha Gonna Do; Portland Woman; Henry; Dirty Business; Glendale Train; Garden of Eden; All I Ever Wanted; Last Lonely Eagle; Louisiana Lady.* POWERGLIDE (4/72): *Dim Lights, Thick Smoke (and Loud, Loud Music); Rainbow; California Day; Sweet Lovin' One; I Don't Need No Doctors; Contract; Runnin' Back to You; Hello Mary Lou; Duncan and Brady; Willie and the Hand Jive.* GYPSY COWBOY (11/72): *Gypsy Cowboy; Groupie; Whiskey; Sutter's Mill; Death and Destruction; Linda; On My Way Back Home; Superman; She's No Angel; Long Black Veil; Sailin'.* THE ADVENTURES OF PANAMA RED (9/73): *Panama Red; It's Alright with Me; Lonesome L.A. Cowboy; Important Exportin' Man; One Too Many Stories; Kick in the Head; You Should Have Seen Me Runnin'; Teardrops in My Eyes; L.A. Lady; Thank the Day; Cement, Clay and Glass.* HOME, HOME ON THE ROAD (3/74): *Hi, Hello, How Are You; Groupie; She's No Angel; Kick in the Head; Truck Drivin' Man; Hello Mary Lou; Sutter's Mill; Dead Flowers; Henry; School Days; Sunday Suzie.* BRUJO (10/74): *Old Man Noll; Ashes of Love; You Angel You; Instant Armadillo Blues; Workingman's Woman; On the Amazon; Big Wheels; Singing Cowboy; Crooked Judge; Parson Brown; Neon Rose.* OH, WHAT A MIGHTY TIME (10/75): *Mighty Time; I Heard You Been Layin' My Old Lady; Strangers on a Train; Up Against the Wall, Redneck; Take a Letter, Maria; Little Old Lady; On Top old Old Smoke; La Bamba; Going 'Round the Horn; Over and Over; Farewell Angeline.* NEW RIDERS (5/76): *Fifteen Days under the Hood; Don't Put Her Down; Dead Flowers; She's Looking Better Every Beer; other titles.* THE BEST OF NRPS (10/76): *I Don't Know You; Glendale Train; Hello Mary Lou; Louisiana Lady; Kick in the Head; Panama Red; Last Lonely*

Eagle; Henry; I Don't Need No Doctor. WHO ARE THOSE
GUYS (1/77): *I Can Heal You; High Rollers; Peggy Sue; Just
Another Night in Reno; It Never Hurts to Be Nice to Somebody;
Love Has Strange Ways; Hold On, It's Coming; By and By When
I Need You; Home Grown; Red Hot Women and Ice Cold Beer.*

Singles/*I Don't Need No Doctor* (5/72); *Panama Red* (10/73);
Hello Mary Lou (1974); *Fifteen Days under the Hood/Don't Put
Her Down* (5/76); *Dead Flowers/She's Looking Better Every Beer*
(7/76); *Love Has Strange Ways/Red Hot Woman and Ice Cold
Beer* (2/77); *Just Another Night in Reno/Home Grown* (5/77).

THE NEW YORK DOLLS/*David Johannson (vocals), Jerry
Nolan (drums), Arthur Kane (bass), Silvain Silvain (guitar), Johnny
Thunder (guitar).*
The grandfathers of punk rock, the New York Dolls first thundered onto the New York club scene in 1973 (the Dark Ages),
flashing glitter, self-righteous swagger, and bone-shattering
rhythms. Sort of a lobotomized version of the vintage Rolling
Stones, the Dolls caused a considerable amount of controversy
immediately. Was it art? Was it rock? Was it alive? Recording
executive–visonary–writer Paul Nelson secured a recording contract and the brief career of the Dolls was launched with great
notoriety.
   Their first album, produced by Todd Rundgren, was raw and
then some. Johannson's vocals bordered on parody and the low-
lifed compositions both enraged and enraptured music lovers
worldwide. The LP only served to increase the arguing over the
band. Were they serious? If they were, should they be shot? Was
this the shape of things to come? Snickering and riffing their
hearts out, the Dolls began moving out of the small clubs and into
the large concert halls. A few problems with management and
changes within their record label hierarchy slowed the Dolls down
a bit at a crucial point. Their second album, produced by legendary Vanilla Fudge–dirge devotee Shadow Morton, brought the
band into the world of Mondo Stiffo and, by 1975, the Dolls were
no more.
   Pity. With the advent of punk rock and such stellar acts as the
Ramones, the Damned, the Clash, and the Stranglers, the Dolls
would have seemed positively *sophisticated* by now. Sort of the
Boston Pops of punk.

Albums/THE NEW YORK DOLLS (7/73): *Personality Crisis; Looking for a Kiss; Vietnamese Baby; Lonely Planet Boy; Frankenstein; Trash; Bad Girl; Subway Train; Pills; Private World; Jet Boy.* TOO MUCH TOO SOON (4/74): *Babylon; Stranded in the Jungle; Who Are the Mystery Girls; (There's Gonna Be a) Showdown; It's Too Lade; Puss 'n' Boots; Chatterbox; Bad Detective; Don't Start Me Talkin'; Human Being.*

Singles/*Personality Crisis/Trash* (8/73); *Stranded in the Jungle/Who Are the Mystery Girls* (4/74).

RANDY NEWMAN/Los Angeles mainstay Randy Newman will probably never top the charts. But then again, it's doubtful that he'll ever need to during the course of his career. Newman is one of the world's foremost songwriters (and alleged singers) and, although his albums sell moderately well, his songs have been heard more often than not being performed by other singers. Judy Collins' version of *I Think It's Going to Rain Today* first brought Newman to the attention of the record moguls in 1966. Since that time, Newman's compositions have been injected into every musical mode possible, from pop to blues to R&B. Joe Cocker covered *Guilty* and *I Think It's Going to Rain Today,* Ringo Star warbled *Have You Seen My Baby,* Three Dog Night broke into the top ten with *Mama Told Me Not to Come,* and Harry Nilsson cut an entire LP entitled *NILSSON SINGS NEWMAN.*

Newman is best known for his honest, irreverent, ironic lyrics, which hover somewhere between slapstick and tragedy. In late 1977, his tune *Short People* became an FM-radio anthem.

Albums/RANDY NEWMAN (6/68): *Love Story; Bet No One Ever Hurt This Bad; Living without You; So Long, Dad; I Think He's Hiding; Linda; Laughing Boy; Cowboy; Davy the Fat Boy; Beehive State; I Think It's Going to Rain Today.* 12 SONGS (2/70): *Have You Seen My Baby; Let's Burn Down the Cornfield; Mama Told Me Not to Come; Lucinda; Underneath the Harlem Moon; Lover's Prayer; Yellow Man; Old Kentucky Home; Rosemary; If You Need Oil; Uncle Bob's Midnight Blues.* LIVE (8/71): *Mama Told Me Not to Come; So Long, Dad; Living without You; Last Night I Had a Dream; I Think It's Going to Rain Today; Lover's Prayer; Maybe I'm Doing It Wrong; Cowboy; Yellow Man; Old Kentucky Home; Davy the Fat Boy; Lonely at the Top.* SAIL AWAY (5/72): *Lonely at the Top; He Gives Us All His*

Love; Old Man; Simon Smith and the Amazing Dancing Bear; Last Night I Had a Dream; Burn On; Political Science; Memo to My Son; God's Song; You Can Leave Your Hat On; Dayton, Ohio, 1903. GOOD OLD BOYS (9/74): *Rednecks; Birmingham; Guilty; Naked Man; Marie; Mr. President (Have Pity on the Working Man); Louisiana, 1927; Every Man a King; Kingfish; A Wedding in Cherokee County; Back On My Feet Again; Rollin'.* LITTLE CRIMINALS (11/77): *Baltimore; I'll Be Home; In Germany before the War; Jolly Coppers on Parade; Kathleen (Catholicism Made Easier); Little Criminals; Old Man on the Farm; Rider in the Rain; Short People; Sigmund Freud's Impersonation of Albert Einstein in America; Texas Girl at the Funeral of Her Father; You Can't Fool the Fat Man.*

Singles/*I Think It's Going to Rain Today/Beehive State* (5/68); *Hold On/Lover's Prayer* (2/70); *Political Science/Sail Away* (6/72); *You Can Leave Your Hat On/Memo to My Son* (11/72); *Naked Man/Guilty* (1/75); *Louisiana, 1927/Marie* (2/77); *Short People* (10/77).

OLIVIA NEWTON-JOHN/For some totally aberrant reason, perky Briton Olivia Newton-John is best known in America as a Grammy award–winning *country* singer. Uh-huh. Believe it or not, the doe-eyed lass the musical diabetics fear has garnered three Grammies and various awards from *Billboard, Cashbox, Record World,* The Country Music Association, The Academy of Country Music, AGVA and ASCAP. All that and barely out of her twenties!

Born in Cambridge, England, and raised in Melbourne, Australia, Olivia decided upon music as a career while still a teen. Deciding to forsake college in favor of singing, she won a talent contest at the age of sixteen and then traipsed off to England where she performed for two years as half of a singing duo with Australian friend Pat Carrol. When Pat's visa expired, she was packed off homeward. Olivia, however, stuck around and her first solo single, Dylan's *If Not for You,* assured her chart success. The singles kept a'coming in the United Kingdom, as did appearances on various BBC shows. The attractive, wholesome woman captured the hearts of millions and Olivia soon found herself billed as a star on the horizon. In 1973, her career exploded worldwide with *Let Me Be There* and it has continued to soar with such hits as *I Honestly Love You, Have You Ever Been Mellow,* and *Please, Mr., Please.* Her first feature film, *Grease,* has been completed and Olivia now seems bent on a multi-faceted show-biz lifestyle.

Albums/OLIVIA NEWTON-JOHN (9/71): *If Not for You; The Biggest Clown; Banks of the Ohio; It's So Hard to Say Goodbye; What Is Life; I'm a Small and Lonely Light; My Old Man's Got a Gun; Just a Little Too Much; Sail into Tomorrow; Take Me Home, Country Roads.* LET ME BE THERE (11/73): *Let Me Be There; Me and Bobby McGee; Banks of the Ohio; Love Song; If I Could Read Your Mind; Help Me Make It through the Night; Angel of the Morning; other titles.* IF YOU LOVE ME, LET ME KNOW (5/74): *If You Love Me (Let Me Know); Mary Skeffington; Country Girl; I Honestly Love You; Free the People; The River's Too Wide; Home Ain't Home Anymore; God Only Knows; Changes; You Ain't Got the Right.* HAVE YOU EVER BEEN MELLOW (2/75): *Have You Ever Been Mellow; Loving Arms; Lifestream; Goodbye Again; Water under the Bridge; I Never Did Sing You a Love Long; It's So Easy; The Air That I Breathe; Follow Me; And in the Morning.* CLEARLY LOVE (9/75): *Something Better to Do; Lovers; Slow Down Jackson; He's My Rock; Sail into Tomorrow; Crying, Laughing, Loving, Lying; Clear Love; Let It Shine; Summertime Blues; Just a Lot of Folk (The Marshmallow Song); He Ain't Heavy, He's My Brother.* COME ON OVER (3/76): *Jolene; Pony Ride; Come On Over; It'll Be Me; Greensleeves; Blue Eyes Crying in the Rain; Don't Throw It All Away; Who Are You Now?; Smile for Me; Small Talk and Pride; Wrap Me in Your Arms; The Long and Winding Road.* DON'T STOP BELIEVIN' (10/76): *Don't Stop Believin'; A Thousand Conversations; Compassionate Man; New Born Babe; Hey Mr. Dreammaker; Every Face Tells a Story; Sam; Love, You Hold the Key; I'll Bet You a Kangaroo; The Last Time You Loved.* MAKING A GOOD THING BETTER (6/77): *Making a Good Thing Better; Slow Dancing; Ring of Fire; Coolin' Down; Don't Cry for Me, Argentina; Sad Songs; You Won't See Me Cry; So Easy to Begin; I Think I'll Say Goodbye; Don't Ask a Friend; If Love Is Real.* GREATEST HITS (10/77): *Sam; Changes; If Not for You; Let Me Be There; Come On Over; If You Love Me; I Honestly Love You; Something Better to Do; Have You Ever Been Mellow; Please, Mr., Please; Don't Stop Believin'; Let It Shine.*

Singles/*If Not for You/The Biggest Clown* (4/71); *Banks of the Ohio/It's So Hard to Say Goodbye* (9/71); *What Is Life/I'm a Small and Lonely Light* (1/72); *My Old Man's Got a Gun/Just a Little Too Much* (9/72); *Take Me Home, Country Roads/Sail into Tomorrow* (4/73); *Let Me Be There/Maybe Then I'll Think of You* (7/73); *If You Love Me, Let Me Know/Brotherly Love* (3/74); *I Honestly Love You/Home Ain't Home Anymore* (7/74); *Have You Ever Been Mellow/Water under the Bridge* (1/75); *Please, Mr., Please/And in the Morning* (5/75); *Let Me Be There/I Honestly Love You* (9/75); *Something Better to Do/He's My Rock* (9/75); *Let It Shine/He Ain't Heavy, He's My Brother* (11/75); *Come On Over/Small Talk and Pride* (2/76); *Don't Stop Believin'/Greensleeves* (7/76); *Every Face Tells a Story/Let You Hold the Key* (10/76); *Sam/I'll Bet You a Kangaroo* (1/77); *Making a Good Thing Better/I Think I'll Say Goodbye* (5/77).

NILSSON/Harry Nilsson is an eccentric's eccentric. In the mid-sixties, he lurched into the spotlight in a fairly unorthodox manner with a handful of equally unorthodox songs. After writing *Cuddly Toy,* a good-timey (if somewhat gamey) toe-tapper for the Monkees, the Brooklynite demoed the song for RCA and was signed. He became a cause célèbre, of sorts.

He first attracted Beatle attention (and therefore world attention) with *You Can't Do That,* a clever collage of at least twelve Beatle songs. Derek Taylor, the Beatles' legendary press officer, heard about it and played it for John Lennon. Lennon, on his May, 1968, U.S. visit, talked of nothing else to anyone who would listen. (Lennon would later become a great drinking buddy of Harry's and a frequent musical collaborator.) Nilsson's first album, *PANDEMONIUM SHADOW SHOW,* which came out in 1967, made quite a splash.

After a brilliant start, the career of Nilsson faltered somewhat, with Harry recording a few albums that he obviously enjoyed but which were not geared toward the interest of the fans at large. He wormed his way into the good graces of the rock world with his epic fantasy, *THE POINT,* and furthered his career with the Richard Perry–produced *NILSSON SCHMILSSON,* an album that not only gave Harry a bona fide hit, *Without You* (his first big one since the Fred Neill penned *Everybody's Talking),* but established an identifiable sound for Harry as well. Of course, with fame waiting around the corner, he promptly chose to embark on a scattergun approach to music that would completely polarize his camp of fans. With half of his following considering him a genius and the other half opting for the label "self-indulgent," Nilsson slugged his way through a host of long-players which featured either renditions of golden oldies (from the twenties on) or fairly sophomoric satirical ditties that showed Harry to be above the whole sordid rock business.

Genius or fraud, Nilsson stands as being one of the most individualistic talents ever to stumble onto the charts. When he's not putting people on, or crooning tunes that would make Vaughn Monroe wince, or boring himself silly, Harry is capable of delivering emotionally jarring compositions with style and prowess.

Albums/PANDEMONIUM SHADOW SHOW (12/67): *Ten Little Indians; 1941; Cuddly Toy; She Sang Hymns out of Tune; You Can't Do That; Sleep Late; My Lady Friend; She's Leaving Home; There Will Never Be; Without Her; Freckles; It's Been So Long; River Deep Mountain High.* AERIAL BALLET (8/68): *Good Old Dark; Don't Leave Me; Together; Mr. Richland's Favorite Song; Little Cowboy; Everybody's Talkin'; I Said Goodbye to Me; Mr. Tinker; One; Wilting of the Willow; Bath.* HARRY (7/69): *Puppy Song; Nobody Cares about the Railroads Anymore; Open Your Window; Mother Nature's Son; Fairfax Rag; City Life; Mournin' Glory Story; Marchin' Down Broadway; I Guess the Lord Must Be in New York City; Rainmaker; Mr. Bojangles; Simon Smith and the Amazing Dancing Bear.* NILSSON SINGS NEWMAN (1970): *Vine St.; Love Story; Yellow Man; Caroline; Cowboy; The Beehive State; Living without You; Dayton, Ohio, 1903; So Long Dad.* THE POINT (1971): *Everything's Got 'Em; Me and My Arrow; Poli High; Think about Your Troubles; Are You Sleeping; Life Line; other titles.* NILSSON SCHMILSSON (11/71): *Gotta Get Up; Driving Alone; Moonbeam Song; Down; Early in the Morning; Without You; Coconut; Let the Good Times Roll; Jump into the Fire; I'll Never Leave You.* SON OF SCHMILSSON (6/72): *Take 54; Remember Christmas; Joy; Turn On Your Radio; You're Breakin' My Heart; Spaceman; I'd Rather Be Dead; The Most Beautiful Word in the World; The Lottery Song; At My Front Door.* A LITTLE TOUCH OF SCHMILSSON IN THE NIGHT (7/73): *Lazy Moon; For Me and My Girl; It Had to Be You;*

Always; Making Whoopie; You Made Me Love You; Lullaby in Ragtime; Nevertheless; This Is All I Ask; As Time Goes By; What'll I Do. SON OF DRACULA (4/74): *Is It He Who Will Be King; Daybreak; At My Front Door; Count Down Meets Merlin and Amber; Moonbeam; Remember; Perhaps This Is All a Dream; The End; Without Vulnerability; Merlin and the Operation; Intro; other titles.* PUSSY CATS (8/74): *Many Rivers to Cross; Subterranean Homesick Blues; Don't Forget Me; All My Life; Old Forgotten Soldier; Loop De Loop; Black Sails; Rock around the Clock; Mucho Mungo; Save the Last Dance for Me.* DUET ON MON DEAU (3/75): *Jesus Christ Your Tall; It's a Jungle Out There; Down by the Sea; Kojak Columbo; Easier for Me; Turn Out the Lights; Salmon Falls; Puget Sound; Good for God; Home; What's Your Sign.* SANDMAN (9/75): *I'll Take a Tango; Something True; Pretty Soon There'll Be Nothing Left for Everybody; The Ivy-Covered Walls; Here's Why I Did Not Go; The Work today; How to Write a Song; The Flying Saucer Song; Will She Miss Me.* THAT'S THE WAY IT IS (6/76): *Just One Look; Baby, I'm Yours; Sail Away; She Sits Down on Me; That I All; Zombie Jamboree; Daylight Has Caught Me; I Need You; A Thousand Miles Away; Moonlight Bandito.* KNNILLSSONN (6/76): *All I Think About Is You; I Never Thought I'd Get This Lonely; Who Done It?; Lean on Me; Goin' Down; Old Bones; Sweet Surrender; Blanket for a Sail; Laughin' Man; Perfect Day.*

Singles/*One*/*Sister Marie* (2/68); *Everybody's Talking/Don't Leave Me* (5/68); *Rainmaker/I Will Take You There* (11/68); *Everybody's Talking/Rainmaker* (5/69); *Maybe/Everybody's Talking* (7/69); *Maybe/The Clock* (10/69); *I'll Be Home/Waiting* (2/70); *Yellow Man/Caroline* (3/70); *Down in the Valley/Buy Me Aba* (6/70); *Everybody's Talking* (10/70); *Without You* (8/71); *Without You/Gotta Get Up* (11/71); *Jump into the Fire/Moonbeam Song* (2/72); *Coconut/Down* (5/72); *Spaceman/Turn On Your Radio* (9/72); *Remember/The Lottery Song* (11/72); *Jump into the Fire/Coconut* (3/73); *As Time Goes By/Lullaby in Ragtime* (7/73); *Day Break/Down* (3/74); *Many Rivers to Cross/Don't Forget Me* (7/74); *Subterranean Homesick Blues/Mucho Mungo* (9/74); *Don't Forget Me/Loop De Loop* (12/74); *Save the Last Dance for Me/All My Life* (1/75); *Kojak Columbo/Turn Out the Light* (6/75); *Sail Away/Moonshine Bandito* (4/76); *Just One Look—Baby I'm Yours; That Is All* (8/76).

TED NUGENT/When Ted Nugent first came to the public's attention, he was a psychedelic guitarist extraordinaire with the
Amboys Dukes, a Detroit-spawned band that attacked the world
with *Journey to the Center of Your Mind.* When the Dukes finally
staggered into oblivion in the early sixties, Nugent emerged as a
superstar himself. Clad in a loincloth and often sporting a bow
and arrow, Nugent stormed his way through the Midwest, staging
guitar duels to the death, glass-breaking guitar solos, and claims
of eating raw meat in public.

Although the self-imposed publicity helped keep Ted in the
public eye, his albums on Warners didn't exactly sell like hotcakes. At this point, the wild man of Detroit joined the Epic
Records' roster and a Ted Nugent explosion occurred. Leber-
Krebbs, the management genius behind Aerosmith, stepped in
and Ted hit the concert trail in earnest, sometimes playing six
nights a week.

His music is frantic and wild and slightly unhinged. For Ted
Nugent, crazed guitar-playing is more than a way of life . . . it is
a lethal weapon. Thus far he has killed three gold albums' worth
of eardrums.

Albums/AMBOY DUKES (12/67): *Let's Go Get Stoned; I Feel
Free; Baby, Please Don't Go; Young Love; Psalms of Aftermath;
Colors; Down on Philips Escalator; Lovely Lady; Night Time; It's
Not True; Gimme Love.* JOURNEY TO THE CENTER OF
YOUR MIND (4/68): *Mississippi Murder; Surrender to Your
King; Flight of the Bird; Scottish Tea; Journey to the Center of
Your Mind; Dr. Slingshot; Ivory Castles; Why Is a Carrot More
Orange Than an Orange; Missionary Mary; Death Is Life; St.
Philip's Friend; I'll Prove I'm Right.* MARRIAGE ON THE
ROCKS/ROCK BOTTOM (2/70; re-released 12/77): *Marriage:
Parts 1–3, Man, Woman, Music; Breast-Fed Gator; Get Yer Guns;
Non-Conformist Wildebeest Man; Today's Lesson; Children of the
Woods; Brain Games of Yesteryear; The Inexhaustible Quest for
the Cosmic Cabbage, Parts 1 and 2.* SURVIVAL OF THE FIT-
TEST LIVE (2/71; re-released 12/77): *Survival of the Fittest; Rat-
tle My Snake; Mr. Jones' Hanging Party; Papa's Will; Slidin' On;
Prodigal Man.* CALL OF THE WILD (2/74): *Sweet Revenge;
Pony Express; Ain't It the Truth; Renegade; Rot Gut; Cannon
Balls; Below the Belt.* TOOTH, FANG AND CLAW (9/74): *Hi-
bernation; Sasha; Lady Luck; Living in the Woods; Free Fight; No*

Holds Barred; The Great White Buffalo; Maybelline. TED
NUGENT (9/75): *Stranglehold; Stormtroopin'; Hey Baby; Just
What the Doctor Ordered; Snakeskin Cowboys; Motor City
Madhouse; Where You Been All My Life; You Make Me Feel
Right at Home; Queen of the Forest.* FREE FOR ALL (9/76):
*Free for All; Dog Eat Dog; Writing on the Wall; Turn It Up; Street
Rats; Together; Light My Way; Hammerdown; I Love You So I
Told You a Lie.* CAT SCRATCH FEVER (5/77): *Cat Scratch
Fever; Wang Dang . . . Sweet Poontang; Death by Misadventure;
Live It Up; Home Bound; Workin' Hard, Playin' Hard; Sweet
Salty; A Thousand Knives; Fist Fightin' Son of a Gun.*

Singles/*Baby, Please Don't Go*/*Psalm of Aftermath* (1967); *Journey to the Center of Your Mind*/*Mississippi Murder* (4/68); *Scottish Teach*/*You Talk Sunshine, I Breathe Fire* (1968); *Sweet
Revenge*/*Ain't It the Truth* (4/74); *Where Have You Been All My
Life*/*Motor City Madhouse* (11/75); *Hey Baby*/*Stormtroopin'*
(1/76); *Dog Eat Dog*/*Light My Way* (10/76); *Free for All*/*Street
Rats* (3/77).

LAURA NYRO/The reclusive Laura Nyro has been a revered
cult figure since her appearance in the late sixties. The young New
Yorker combined a mixture of jazz, gospel, and folk to create a
rather unique brand of balladeering during the time of flower
power and transcendental meditation for a buck and a half. It was
her individualism at the height of hippie-mania that caused Laura
to become one of rock's more elusive figures. Her songwriting
ability could not be contested, even during her early years. While
still in her twenties she penned hits for BS&T (*And When I Die*),
Streisand (*Stoney End*), and the Fifth Dimension (*Stoned Soul
Picnic, Wedding Bell Blues*). Her awkward, rather different concept of performing, however, completely alienated her from the
youth culture crowd. At the Monterey Pop Festival of 1967, she
was practically heckled off the stage during an attempt to create
a sort of white gospel feel (accompanied by three black gospel
singers). Turning inward, she began producing albums on a spo-
radic basis, making personal appearances even more sporadically.
For the most part, she has averaged an album every year or so,
with the exception of a period during the early seventies when
four years elapsed between the release of *GONNA TAKE A MIR-
ACLE* and *SMILE*. To this date, Laura Nyro has yet to conform

to rock industry standards of stardom (two albums a year, tour your butt off, say hello to the djs and smile at the guy from *Rolling Stone*), and she remains one of modern music's most faceless stars.

Albums/MORE THAN A NEW DISCOVERY (2/67): *Wedding Bell Blues; Goodbye Joe; Billy's Blues; And When I Die; Stoney End; Lazy Susan; Hands Off the Man (Flim Flam Man); Buy and Sell; He's a Runner; Blowin' Away; I Never Meant to Hurt You; California Shoe Shine Boys.* ELI AND THE THIRTEENTH CONFESSION (4/68): *Sweet Blindness; Luckie; Lu; Poverty Train; Lonely Woman; Eli's Coming; Timer; Stoned Soul Picnic; Emmie; Woman's Blues; Once It Was Alright Now (Farmer Joe); December's Boudoir; The Confession.* NEW YORK TENDABERRY (2/69): *Gibson Street; New York Tendaberry; Time and Love; The Man Who Sends Me Home; Sweet Lovin' Baby; Captain Saint Lucifer; You Don't Love Me When I Cry; Tom Cat Goodbye; Mercy on Broadway; Save the Country.* CHRISTMAS AND THE BEADS OF SWEAT (11/70): *Brown Earth; When I Was a Freeport and You Were the Main Drag; Blackpatch; Been on a Train; Up on the Roof; Upstairs by a Chinese Lamp; Map to the Treasure; Beads of Sweat; Christmas in My Soul.* GONNA TAKE A MIRACLE (11/71): *I Met Him on a Sunday; The Bells; Monkey Time; Dancing in the Street; Desire; You've Really Got a Hold on Me; Spanish Harlem; Jimmy Mack; The Wind; Nowhere to Run; Gonna Take a Miracle.* FIRST SONGS (re-issue of MORE THAN A NEW DISCOVERY; 1/73) SMILE (12/75): *Sexy Mama; Children of the Junks; Money; I Am the Blues; Stormy Love; The Cat Song; Midnight Blue; Smile.* SEASON OF LIGHTS (10/76): *Money; Sweet Lovin' Baby; And When I Die; The Morning News; Emmie; The Confession; Timer; Midnite Blue; Smile; Sweet Blindness; The Cat Song; Upstairs by a Chinese Lamp; I Am the Blues; Captain Saint Lucifer; When I Was a Freeport and You Were the Main Drag; Mars.* SEASON OF LIGHTS (9/77): *The Confession; And When I Die; Upstairs by a Chinese Lamp; Sweet Blindness; Captain Saint Lucifer; Money; The Cat Song; Freeport; Timer; Emmie.*

Singles/*And When I Die/Flim Flam Man* (4/67); *Eli's Coming/Sweet Blindness* (4/68); *Save the Country/Timer* (6/68); *Sweet Blindness/Stoned Soul Picnic* (10/68); *Farmer Joe/Lu*

(3/69); *And When I Die/I Never Meant to Hurt You* (3/69); *Eli's Coming/Save the Country* (6/69); *Time and Love/The Man Who Sends Me Home* (10/69); *New York Tendaberry/Save the Country* (1/70); *Up on the Roof/Captain Saint Lucifer* (8/70); *When I Was a Freeport/Been on a Train* (1/71); *It's Gonna Take a Miracle* (1/72); *Wedding Bell Blues/Flim Flam Man* (2/73).

OHIO PLAYERS/*Sugar Bonner (guitar, vocals), Merve Pierce (trumpet, flugelhorn), Billy Beck (keyboards, vocals), Pee Wee Middlebrooks (trumpet, trombone, sax), Diamond Williams (drums), Satch Stachell (sac, flute).*
With sultry, semi-clad ladies gracing their covers and fun ad infinitum in the grooves, the Ohio Players have finally made it big after some ten years of plugging away. Originating around the Dayton, Ohio, area, the group went through several stages before emerging as the Players in the late sixties. An album on Capitol in 1968 nearly won them an instant-oblivion award although, a few albums later on, Westbound began to plug the band as something hot to watch. Moving to Mercury in 1973, the band finally began to generate a lot of heat, via both their intense instrumentation and their hubba-hubba album covers. They are best known for their funky, droning sound and, at this point, have several gold alumbs (*SKIN TIGHT, FIRE, HONEY, CONTRADICTION*) and a few hit singles in their portfolio to prove just *how* well known they are.

Albums/PAIN (2/72). PAIN + PLEASURE = ECSTASY (1973). THE OHIO PLAYERS: *Here Today and Gone Tomorrow; Mother-in-law; Stop Lying to Yourself; Over the Rainbow; Find Someone to Love; Cold Cold World; Summertime; Bad Bargain; The Man That I Am; Lonely Street; Street Party.* SKIN TIGHT (4/74): *Skin Tight; Jive Turkey; It's Your Night/Words of Love; Is Anybody Gonna Be Saved; Heaven Must Be Like This; Streakin' Cheek to Cheek.* FIRE (10/74): *Fire; Together; Runnin' from the Devil; I Want to Be Free; Smoke; It's All Over; What the Hell; Together (reprise).* HONEY (7/75): *Honey; Fopp; Let's Love; Ain't Givin' Up No Ground; Sweet Sticky Thing; Love Roller Coaster; Alone.* CONTRADICTION (5/76): *Contradiction; Precious Love; Little Lady Maria; Far East Mississippi; Who'd She Coo?; My Life; Tell the Truth; My Ladies Run Me Crazy; Bi-Centennial.* OHIO PLAYERS GOLD (10/76): *Jive Turkey; Skin*

Tight; Fopp; Sweet Sticky Thing; Who'd She Coo?; I Want to Be Free; Love Rollercoaster; Far East Mississippi; Feel the Beat; Only a Child Can Love. ANGEL (3/77): *Merry Go Round; Angel; Don't Fight My Love; Glad to Know You're Mine; Can You Still Love Me; Faither; O-H-I-O; Body Vibes.* OHIO PLAYERS (4/77): *Fire; Players Balling; Singing in the Morning; Funky Worm; Walt's First Trip; I Wanna Hear from You; Laid It; Pleasure; Walked Away from You.* MR. MEAN (9/77): *Mr. Mean; Fight Me, Chase Me; The Controller's Mind; The Big Score; Magic Trick; Good Luck Charm; Speak Easy.*

Singles/*Pain* (11/71); *Funky Worm* (1/73); *Ecstasy* (7/73); *Jive Turkey/Streakin' Cheek to Cheek* (4/74); *Skin Tight/Heaven Must Be Like This* (7/74); *Fire/Together* (11/74); *Skin Tight/Jive Turkey* (1/75); *I Want to Be Free/Smoke* (3/75); *Ain't Givin' Up No Ground/Love Roller Coaster* (10/75); *Fire/Sweet Sticky Thing* (12/75); *Happy Holidays (Parts I and II)* (12/75); *Fopp* (2/76); *Bi-Centennial/Who'd She Coo?* (6/76); *Far East Mississippi/Only a Child Can Love* (10/76); *Contradiction/Feel the Beat* (12/76); *Body Vibes/Don't Fight My Love* (4/77); *O-H-I-O/Can You Still Love Me* (6/77).

ROBERT PALMER/Robert Palmer is known in some circles as the leading purveyor of blue-eyed soul. But the funky R&B belter actually started out his career as a mainstream rock and roller. Born in England but raised in Malta, Palmer joined the Alan Bown set while still a teenager. He left that band to join the short-lived jazz-rock band, Dada, a troupe that eventually evolved into the more rock-oriented Vinegar Joe. As a member of Vinegar Joe, Palmer found himself sharing vocal duties with Elkie Brooks and Pete Gage as well as playing rhythm guitar. The band fell apart in 1973, with both Brooks and Palmer entertaining plans for solo careers.

Palmer pursued his in earnest, demoing some R&B numbers he had penned and taking them to Island Records. His first solo album, *SNEAKIN' SALLY THROUGH THE ALLEY*, was released less than twelve months later. With three albums under his belt and a growing reputation as a primo R&B interpreter to his credit, Palmer has no direction to head but up.

Albums/SNEAKIN' SALLY THROUGH THE ALLEY (9/74): *Sailing Shoes; Hey, Julia; Sneakin' Sally through the Alley; Get*

Outside; Blackmail; How Much Fun; From a Whisper to a Scream; Through It All There's You. PRESSURE DROP (10/75): *Give Me an Inch; Work to Make It Work; Back in My Arms; River Boat; Pressure Drop; Here with You Tonight; Fine Time; Which of Us Is the Fool; Trouble.* SOME PEOPLE CAN DO WHAT THEY LIKE (9/76): *One Last Look; Keep in Touch; Man Smart, Woman Smarter; Spanish Moon; Have Mercy; Gotta Get a Grip on You; What Can You Bring Me; Off the Bone; Hard Head; Some People Can Do What They Want.*

GRAHAM PARKER/If ever a performer deserved the reputation of being "the next BIG thing" on the global rock front, it's feisty Graham Parker. Armed only with a buzz-saw vocal style and an explosively simplistic band, the Rumour, Parker fought his way into the limelight during a musical period frought with Ben Hurrish stage shows and the sounds of mega-bucks long-players. His musical message was short, sweet and to the point. Listen. Dance if you want to, sweat if you'd like.

Parker actually made the quantum jump from ordinary fellow to recording artist within the span of twelve months. A filling station attendant in Surrey, England, Parker put together a home-made demo tape of some of his songs and sent it to the Hope and Anchor Pub. This was during the Pub rock boom in the United Kingdom during the mid-seventies, and several musicians were itinerant hanger-outters at the pub in question. One of the primo names there was Brinsley Schwarz, one of Great Britain's finest (and most underrated) guitarists. He invited Parker over, after hearing the tape, and offered to back him up on a *real* demo session.

Brinsley called together Bob Andrews on keyboards, Martin Belmont on guitar, Andrew Bodnar on bass, and Stephan Goulding on drums. They combined forces for the demo and Graham Parker and the Rumour came into being. A copy of the demo found its way to Radio London where an A&R man from Phonogram/Mercury happened to be listening. The band was signed and Parker and the Rumour's first two albums, *HOWLIN' WIND* and *HEAT TREATMENT*, received a lot of airplay on both sides of the Atlantic.

At this point, Parker and crew have established a firm cult following with their bloozey approach to rock. If they choose to continue funkin' it up, their following is sure to grow.

Albums/HOWLIN' WIND (5/76): *White Honey; Nothin' Gonna Pull Us Apart; Silly Thing; Gypsy Blood; Between You and Me; Back to Schooldays; Soul Shoes; Lady Doctor; You've Got to Be Kidding; Howlin' Wind; Not If It Pleases Me; Don't Ask Me No Questions.* HEAT TREATMENT (10/76); *Heat Treatment; That's What They All Say; Turned Up Too Late; Black Honey; Hotel Chambermaid; Pourin' It All Out; Back Door Love; Something You're Going Through; Help Me Shake It; Fool's Gold.*

Singles/*You've Got to Be Kidding/Soul Shoes* (7/76); *Heat Treatment/Back Door Love* (11/76); Extended Player: *Hold Back the Night/(Let Me Get) Sweet on Your/White Honey (live)/Soul Shoes (live)* (3/77).

VAN DYKE PARKS/The enigmatic Van Dyke Parks first achieved notoriety in the late sixties as an accomplished producer, songwriter, and extremely eclectic recording artist. As a producer-collaborator he has worked with Brian Wilson, Harpers Bizarre, Arlo Guthrie, and Randy Newman. As an artist, he has worked mostly with himself and for himself. His first LP, *SONG CYCLE*, became *the* Art Rock album to talk about during the '67–'68 musical rush. Alas, the intricate musical workings on the album never caught on with the masses. Subsequent albums, few and far between, have suffered similar fates. Today Parks is still regarded as someone to talk about and a truly gifted producer.

Albums/SONG CYCLE (11/67): *Vine Street; Palm Desert; Widow's Walk; Laurel Canyon Boulevard; The All Golden Van Dyke Parks; Public Domain; Donovan's Colours; The Attic; By the People; Pot Pourri.* DISCOVER AMERICA (5/72): *Jack Palance; Bing Crosby; Streetband Music; FDR in Trinidad; Sweet Sweet; The 4 Mills Brothers; Be Careful; John Jones; Occapella; Sailin' Shoes; Riverboat; Ode to Tobago; Your Own Comes First; Stars and Stripes Forever; G-Man Hoover.* CLANG OF THE YANKEE REAPER (10/75): *City on the Hill; You're a Real Sweetheart; Another Dream; Soul Train; Iron Man; Love Is the Answer; Clang of the Yankee Reaper; other titles.*

Singles/*Ode to Tobago/Occapella* (6/72); *The Eagle and Me/On the Rolling Sea When Jesus Speaks to Me* (7/70).

PARLIAMENT-FUNKADELIC/*George Clinton (vocals), Bernie Worrell (keyboards), Bootsy Collins (bass), Cordell Mosson (bass),*

Michael Hampton (guitar), Glenn Goins (guitar), Gary Shider (guitar), Jerome Brailey (drums and percussion), vocals: Debbie Wright, Jeanette Washington, Lynn Mabry, Dawn Silva; horns: Fred Wesley, Maceo Parker, Rick Gardner, Richard Griffith, Clay Lawrey, Darryl Dixon, Valerie Drayton, Danny Cortez.
George Clinton, the man behind the P-Funk sound, claims that he has achieved success because he and bassist Bootsy Collins were buzzed by an honest-to-Ohm flying saucer. As a result, the world of Parliament-Funkadelic was soon enmeshed in out-of-this-world trappings based on Clinton's concept of the Mothership Connection. The band now appears onstage backed by a flying saucer, led by Dr. Funkenstein (Clinton), and surrounded by his clones (the musicians). The antics are spaced-out and funky as the band tears into such songs as *Mothership, Starchild,* and *Bop Gun.*

Clinton and Parliament first gained fame in 1968 with the hit *Testify.* Shortly thereafter, however, their label went under and with it their name (label-owned). Clinton took his entourage, reshaped them, rechristened them Funkadelic, and launched his men into an R&B–rock career of surreal proportions. A few years later when George regained the use of the name Parliament, he dubbed his Funkadelic troupe Parliament while still retaining the original Funkadelic term. In other words, George got two bands out of one group of musicians. He then signed the identical group to different labels using the two different names.

Both Parliament and Funkadelic still record simultaneously and the P-Funk experience is spreading, now including Bootsy's Rubber Band and the brassy Horny Horns (on a third label). Clinton's musical answer to *The War of the Worlds* is a high-stepping, low-riffing invasion from innerspace . . . and if anyone doesn't dig it, well, Dr. Funkenstein will set you straight.

Albums/FUNKADELIC (2/70): *Mommy, What's a Funkadelic; Music for My Mother; I Got a Thing, You Got a Thing, Everybody's Got a Thing; Good Old Music; Qualify and Satisfy; What Is Soul.* FREE YOUR MIND AND YOUR ASS WILL FOLLOW (9/70): *Free Your Mind and Your Ass Will Follow; Friday Night, August 14th; Funky Dollar Bill; I Wanna Know If It's Good to You; Some More; Eulogy and Light.* MAGGOT BRAIN (7/71): *Maggot Brain; Can You Get to That; Hit It and Quit It; You and Your Folks, Me and My Folks; Super Stupid; Back in Our*

Minds; Wars of Armageddon. AMERICA EATS ITS YOUNG (5/72): *A Joyful Process; We Hurt Too; Loose Booty; Philmore; You Hit the Nail on the Head; If You Don't Like the Effects, Don't Produce the Cause; Everybody Is Going to Make It This Time; Pussy; America Eats Its Young; Biological Speculation; That Was My Girl; Balance; Miss Lucifer's Love; Wake Up.* COSMIC SLOP (1973): *Nappy Dugout; You Can't Miss What You Can't Measure; March to the Witch's Castle; Let's Make It Last; Cosmic Slop; No Compute; Broken Heart; Trash a Go Go; Can't Stand the Strain.* STANDING ON THE VERGE OF GETTING IT ON (1974): *Red Hot Mama; Alice in My Fantasies; I'll Stay; Sexy Ways; Standing on the Verge of Getting It On; Jimmy's Got a Little Bit of Bitch in Him; Good Thoughts, Bad Thoughts.* LET'S TAKE IT TO THE STAGE (1975): *Good to Your Earhole; Better by the Pound; Be My Beach; No Head, No Backstage Pass; Let's Take It to the Stage; Get Off Your Ass and Jam; I Owe You Something Good; Stuffs and Things; The Song Is Familiar.* FUNKADELIC'S GREATEST HITS (1975): *I Got a Thing, You Got a Thing, Everybody's Got a Thing; I Wanna Know If It's Good for You; Standing on the Verge of Getting It On; Hit It and Quit It; Cosmic Slop; Can You Get to That; Loose Booty; Funky Dollar Bill; A Joyful Process; I'll Bet You.* TALES OF KID FUNKADELIC (1976): *Butt to Butt Resuscitation; Let's Take It to the People; Undisco Kid; Take Your Dead Ass Home; I'm Never Gonna Tell It; Tales of Kidd Funkadelic; How Do Yeaw View You.* HARDCORE JOLLIES (11/76): *Comin' 'round the Mountain; Smokey; If You Got Funk, You Got Style; Hardcore Jollies; Soul Mate; Cosmic Slop; You Scared the Lovin' outta Me; Adolescent Funk.* FUNKADELICS (5/77): *Cosmic Slop; Sexy Ways; Stupid Stud; No Compute; Can't Stand the Strain; Wake Up; Philmore; Funky Dollar Bill; Can You Get to That; I'll Bet You.*

Funkadelic Singles/*I'll Bet You* (9/69); *I Got a Thing, You Got a Thing, Everybody's Got a Thing* (2/70); *I Wanna Know If It's Good for You* (7/70); *You and Your Folks, Me and My Folks* (3/71); *Can You Get to That* (8/71); *Better by the Pound* (10/75).

Parliament Albums/OSMIUM (1970). UP FOR THE DOWN STROKE (7/74): *Testify; The Goose; I Can Move You (If You Let Me); I Just Get Back; From the Fantasy; A Head of Our Time in the Four Lands of Ellet; All Your Goodies Are Gone; Whatever Makes Baby Feel Good; Presence of a Brain.* CHOCOLATE

CITY (3/75): *Ride On; Together; Side Effects; What Comes Funky; Let Me Be; If It Don't Fit (Don't Force It); I Misjudged You; Big Footin'.* MOTHERSHIP CONNECTION (12/75): *P-Funk (Wants to Get Funked Up); Mothership Connection (Star Child); Unfunky UFO; Supergroovalisticprosifunstatication; Handcuffs; Give Up the Funk (Tear the Roof Off the Sucker); Night of the Thumpasorus Peoples.* THE CLONES OF DR. FUNKENSTEIN (9/76): *Prelude; Gamin' on Ya; Dr. Funkenstein; Children of Production; Gettin' to Know You; Do That Stuff; Everything Is on the One; I've Been Watchin' You (Move Your Sexy Body); Funkin' for Fun.* LIVE (4/77): *This Is the Way We Funk with You; Dr. Funkenstein; The Undisco Kid; The Girl Is Bad; Children of Production; Star Child; Swing Down, Sweet Chariot; P-Funk; Let's Take It to the Stage; Take Your Dead Ass Home; Do That Stuff; The Landing (of the Holy Mothership); Gamin' on Ya; Tear the Roof Off the Sucker medley: Give Up the Funk, Get Off Your Ass and Jam, Fantasy Is Reality, Night of the Thumpasorus Peoples.* FUNKENTELECKY VS. THE PLACEBO SYNDROME (10/77): *Bop Gun; Flash Light; Funkentelecky; Placebo Syndrome; Sir Nose D'Voidofunk (Pay Attention—B3M); Wizard of Finance.*

Parliament Singles/*(I Wanna) Testify* (6/67); *All Your Goodies Are Gone* (9/67); *Up for the Down Stroke* (9/74); *Testify* (11/74); *Chocolate City* (5/75); *Ride On* (7/75); *P-Funk* (1/76); *Tear the Roof Off the Sucker* (3/76); *Star Child (Mothership Connection)* (8/76); *Do That Stuff* (10/76); *Dr. Funkenstein* (1/77); *Fantasy Is a Reality* (7/77).

PEARLS BEFORE SWINE/*Tom Rapp (guitar, vocals), Jim Bohannon (keyboards), Roger Crissinger (keyboards), Wayne Harley (guitars), Lane Lederer (bass, guitar).*
Pearls Before Swine was one of those delightfully anemic groups that could have only happened during the slightly out-of-whack sixties. When everyone else was chasing their tails after acid rock, laconic and lisping Tom Rapp fashioned a band of local yokels that played acid folk. The results were endearing, engaging, and horrifying. Hearing Rapp wheeze his way through a song required a lot of energy on the part of the listener (you wound up cheering him onward by the final verse). Yet the Swine's delicate instrumentation did make for some engrossing moments.

The band was signed, in the mid-sixties, by underground label

ESP, a move that insured a band of a large amount of publicity and a good deal of poverty. (ESP's distribution could not exactly be called . . . huge.) In 1969, the band was signed by Warner-Reprise, an aboveground outfit that was rapidly becoming *the* most musically aware label in rock. (They still are, by the way.) Unfortunately, Pearls Before Swine did not fare all that well at their new musical headquarters. Sessionmen and actual arrangements marred the raw energy of the troupe. Within three years, Rapp was cutting solo albums, before fading into the woodwork.

To this day, the lisping, nasal strains of Pearls Before Swine are considered legend within the framework of the sixties' experimentation period. Most modern musicologists consider it "noise."

Albums/ONE NATION UNDERGROUND (10/67): *Another Time; Playmate; Ballad to an Amber Lady; (Oh Dear) Miss Morse; Drop Out; Morning Song; Regions of May; Uncle John; I Shall Not Care; The Surrealist Waltz.* BALAKLAVA (11/68): *Trumpeter Landfrey; Translucent Carriages; Images of April; There Was a Man; I Saw the World; Guardian Angels; Suzanne; Lepers and Roses; Florence Nightingale; Ring Thing.* THESE THINGS TOO (8/69): *Footnote; Sail Away; Look into Her Eyes; I Shall Be Released; Man in the Tree; Frog in the Window; If You Don't Want To; Green and Blue; When I Was a Child; These Things Too; Wizard of Is; Mon Amour.* THE USE OF ASHES (4/70): *The Jeweler; From the Movie; Rocket Man; God Save the Child; Song about a Rose; Tell Me Why; Margery; The Old Man; Regal; When the War Began.* THE CITY OF GOLD (4/71): *Sonnet #65; Once Upon a Time; Raindrops; Nancy; City of Gold; Seasons in the Sun; My Father; The Men; Casablanca; Wedding; Did You Dream Of.* BEAUTIFUL LIES YOU COULD LIVE IN (11/71): *Snow Queen; A Life; Butterflies; Simple Things; Everybody's Got Pain; Bird on a Wire; Island Lady; Come to Me; Freedom; She's Gone; Epitaph.*

Singles/*These Things Too/If You Don't Want To* (11/69); *Rocket Man/God Save the Child* (4/70); *Jeweler/Rocket Man* (9/70).

PENTANGLE/*Terry Cox (drums), Bert Jansch (guitar), Jacqui McShee (vocals), John Renbourn (vocals, guitar), Danny Thompson (bass).*
The delicate folk sounds of Pentangle first came to light in 1967 when two mainstay British folkies, Jansch (who inspired Donovan's career) and Renbourn, came together with a group in

mind. Soon the rest of the entourage fell into place and the pastoral-oriented Pentangle was formed. The group, very popular in England, just never caught on exceptionally well in the States. Overwhelmed by the rock market and the hard-rocking realm of hit singles, the band fragmented in 1973.

Albums/THE PENTANGLE (10/68): *Let No Man Steal Your Thyme; Bells; Hear My Call; Pentangling; Mirage; Way Behind the Sun; Bruton Town; Waltz.* SWEET CHILD (1/69): *Market Song; No More My Lord; Turn Your Money Green; Haitian Fight Song; A Woman Like You; Goodbye Pork Pie Hat; In Your Mind; I've Got a Feeling; The Trees They Do Grow High; Moon Dog; Hole in My Coat.* BASKET OF LIGHT (10/69): *Light Flight; Once I Had a Sweetheart; Springtime Promises; Train Song; Lyke-Wake Dirge; The Cuckoo; Hunting Song; Sally Go 'round the Roses; House Carpenter.* CRUEL SISTER (1/71): *A Maid That's Deep in Love; When I Was in My Prime; Lord Franklin; Cruel Sister; Jack Orioen.* REFLECTION (10/71): *Wedding Dress; Omie Wise; Will the Circle Be Unbroken; When I Get Home; Rain and Snow; Helping Hand; So Clear; Reflection.* SOLOMON'S SEAL (9/72): *Sally Free to Easy; The Cherry Tree Carol; The Snows; High Germany; People on the Highway; Willy of Winsbury; No Love Is Sorrow; Jump Baby Jump; Lady of Carslisle.*

PINK FLOYD/*Rick Wright (organ, piano, keyboards), Nick Mason (drums), Roger Waters (bass, piano), David Gilmore (lead guitar, replacing Syd Barret).*
Pink Floyd caused much excitement in England early in 1967 by being the first English rock band to come onstage armed with a light show. They were also one of the first English groups to play San Francisco–style psychedelic rock. Since then, trying to understand the music of Pink Floyd has become a sort of underground hobby in England. As with most experimental groups, it was difficult to decide what was sheer lack of control and what was courageous dabbling in the music of the future. The Floyd first started back in '65–'66 as a fairly un-psychedelic entourage. Mason, Wright, and Waters had met in college and had tried to make it, band-wise, under such names as Sigma 6, the T-Set, and the Screaming Abdabs. For some odd reason, neither the names nor the bands caught on. A friend of Waters', Syd Barret, eventually got into the musical hodgepodge as the band continued to re-

group and re-christen itself. Barret dubbed the entourage the Pink
Floyd Sound, inspired by a blues record he owned by Pink Anderson and Floyd Council. In 1967, the band was signed and,
before long, they were off and running with a hit British single,
See Emily Play. Gradually, under Barret's watchful eye, the band
became less structured, more free-formed. Success on the other
side of the Atlantic waited for nearly every musical move they
made.

Changes within the band, however, proved earth-shattering as
Barret became involved with the seedier side of psychedelia. With
his behavior becoming more and more erratic, the band allowed
Syd's long-time crony Dave Gilmour to join to pick up the slack
in the lead guitar area, playing in conjunction with Syd. Eventually, Syd departed (embarking on a brief career of his own) and
the newly formed foursome explored the realm of spacey music
with a renewed sense of interest. Their aura of Twilight Zone–ish
kineticism finally paid off around the world with their monumental album, *DARK SIDE OF THE MOON*. The album caught
on like wildfire. It went gold. Then it went platinum, selling more
than two million copies. Newly indoctrinated fans began buying
Floyd albums from the past and, before you could say Um-
magumma, their records were all over the charts. From this point
onward, they were internationally acclaimed superstars and
would never have to doubt their musical security. A subsequent
shift of record labels in the states saw the boys from Britain marketed in a big way, on the same level as, let's say, your Star Trek
line of toys. Their music has overcome the crassness surrounding
each release, though, and Floyd has remained high on the rungs
of rockdom's finest.

Albums/PINK FLOYD (3/68): *Gnome; See Emily Play; Chapter
24; Pow R Toch; Interstellar Overdrive; Take Up Thy Stethoscope
and Walk; Lucifer Sam; Matilda Mother; Scarecrow.*
SAUCERFUL OF SECRETS (9/68): *Let There Be More Light;
Remember a Day; Set the Controls for the Heart of the Sun; Cor-
poral Clegg; Saucerful of Secrets; See Saw; Jugband Blues.* UM-
MAGUMMA (11/69): *Astronomy Domine; Careful with That
Axe, Eugene; Set the Controls for the Heart of the Sun; Saucerful
of Secrets; Something Else; Syncopated Pandemonium; Storm Signal; Celestial Voices.* ATOM HEART MOTHER (9/70): *Atom
Heart Mother Suite (Father's Shout, Breast Milky, Mother Fore,*

Funky Dung, Mind Your Throats Please, Remergence); If; Summer 68; Fat Old Sun; Alan's Psychedelic Breakfast. RELICS (5/71): *Arnold Layne; Interstellar Overdrive; See Emily Play; Remember a Day; Paint Box; Julia Dream; Careful with That Axe, Eugene; Cirrus Minor; The Nile Song; Biding My Time; Bike.* MEDDLE (10/71): *One of These Days; A Pillow of Winds; Fearless; San Tropez; Seamus; Echoes.* OBSCURED BY CLOUDS (6/72): *Obscured by Clouds; When You're In; Burning Bridges; The Gold It's in the . . .; Wots . . . Uh the Deal; Mudmen; Childhood's End; Free Four; Stay; Absolutely Curtains.* DARK SIDE OF THE MOON (2/73): *Speak to Me; Breathe; On the Run; Time; The Great Gig in the Sky; Money; Us and Them; Any Color You Like; Brain Damage; Eclipse.* MORE (soundtrack; 7/73): *Cirrus Minor; The Nile Song; Crying Song, Up the Khyber; Green Is the Colour; Cymbaline; Party Sequence; Main Theme; Ibizar Bar; More Blues; Quicksilver; A Spanish Piece; Dramatic Theme.* A NICE PAIR (double album package composed of PINK FLOYD: THE PIPER AT THE GATES OF DAWN and SAUCERFUL OF SECRETS, their first two albums; re-released 11/73), SYD BARRETT: THE MADCAP LAUGHS AND BARRETT (American release of two previously unavailable solo albums; 7/74): *Terrapin; No Good Trying; Love You; No Man's Land; Dark Globe; Here I Go; If It's in You; Octopus; Golden Hair; Long Gone; She Took a Long Cold Look; Feel; Late Night; Baby Lemonade; Love Song; Dominoes; It Is Obvious; Rats; Maisle; Gigolo Aunt; Waving My Arms in the Air/I Never Lied to You; Wined and Dined; Wolfpack/Effervescing Elephant.* WISH YOU WERE HERE (9/75): *Shine on Your Crazy Diamond (Parts One through Nine); Have a Cigar; Wish You Were Here; Welcome to the Machine.* ANIMALS (2/77): *Pigs on the Wings (Parts One and Two); Dogs; Pigs (Three Different Ones); Sheep.*

Singles/*Arnold Layne/Candy and a Currant Bun; See Emily Play/ScareCrow* (1968); *Flaming/The Gnome* (1968); *One of These Days/Fearless* (11/71); *Free Four/Stay* (7/72); *Money/Any Colour You Like* (4/73); *Us and Them/Time* (2/74); *Have a Cigar/Welcome to the Machine* (10/75).

POCO/*Tim Schmit (bass, vocals), George Grantham (drums, vocals), Rusty Young (pedal steel, guitar), Paul Cotton (guitar, vocals). Previous members: Richie Furay (guitar, vocals), Jim*

Messina (guitar, vocals), Randy Mesiner (bass, vocals).
When Buffalo Springfield went under for the final time in 1967, members Furay and Messina decided to strike out on their own in an overtly countrified rock band. The result was called Pogo. This was later changed to Poco because of copyright problems involving the name, which was shared by a popular possum of comic-strip fame. Enlisted in the band were Young, Grantham, and Mesiner. From the outset, Poco was a top-notch band, dearly beloved by their fans, who just could not sell a ton of records. This perplexed both the band members and their label. Debuting in 1968 with a positively brilliant album, Poco embarked on a helter-skelter career littered with artistic high spots and commercial pits.

Throughout their career, the band has added and dropped members regularly. Mesiner left after the debut LP to join, first, the Stone Canyon Band and, then, the Eagles. Messina quit in '70 to form Loggins and Messina, making room for Paul Cotton to join the band. Finally, in 1973, after six years without a bona fide hit, Furay left to start the short-lived Souther-Hillman-Furay debacle. In 1975, Poco parted ways with their longtime Epic Records stomping grounds and put down roots at ABC.

They are still recording very fine albums, earning garlands of sincere critical praise, and not selling a hell of a lot of records.

Albums/PICKIN' UP THE PIECES (5/69): *What a Day; Grand Junction; Pickin' Up the Pieces; Oh Yeah; Short Changed; Make Me Smile; Consequently, So Long; Calico Lady; First Love; Tomorrow; Just in Case It Happens, Yes Indeed; Nobody's Fool.* POCO (5/70): *Hurry Up; You Better Think Twice; Honky Tonk Downstairs; Keep On Believin'; Anyway Bye Bye; Nobody's Fool; El Tonto de Nadie Regresa; Don't Let It Pass By.* DELIVERIN' (11/70): *C'mon; Hear That Music; A Man Like Me; Grand Junction; I Guess You Made It; other titles.* FROM THE INSIDE (9/71): *Hoe Down; Bad Weather; What Am I Gonna Do; You Are the One; Railroad Days; From the Inside; Do You Feel It Too; Ol' Forgiver; What If I Should Say I Love You; Just for Me and You.* A GOOD FEELIN' TO KNOW (10/72): *And Settlin' Down; Ride the Country; I Can See Everything; Go and Say Goodbye; Keeper of the Fire; Early Times; A Good Feelin' to Know; Restrain; Sweet Lovin'.* CRAZY EYES (8/73): *Blue Water; Fool's Gold; Here We Go Again; Brass Buttons; A Right Along; Crazy Eyes; Magnolia; Let's Dance Tonight.* SEVEN (7/74): *Skatin'; Drivin' Wheel;*

You've Got Your Reasons; Just Call My Name; Faith in the Families; Krikkit's Song (Passing Through); Rocky Mountain Breakdown; Angel. HEAD OVER HEELS (6/75): *Keep on Tryin'; Lovin' Arms; Let Me Turn Back to You; Makin' Love; Down in the Quarter; Sittin' on a Fence; Georgia Bind My Ties; Us; Flyin' Solo; Dallas; I'll Be Back Again.* THE VERY BEST OF POCO (7/75): *You Better Think Twice; Just for Me and You; Bad Weather; Fool's Gold; A Good Feelin' to Know; Another Time Around; Faith in the Families; medley: Just In Case It Happens, Yes Indeed; Grand Junction; Consequently So Long; Railroad Days; Sweet Lovin'; Rocky Mountain Breakdown; Here We Go Again; C'mon; A Right Along; A Man Like Me; And Settlin' Down; Skatin'; Pickin' Up the Pieces.* LIVE (2/76): *Bad Weather; Ride the Country; medley: Blue Water, Fool's Gold, Rocky Mountain Breakdown; Angel; High and Dry; A Good Feelin' to Know; Restrain.* ROSE OF CIMARRON (4/76). INDIAN SUMMER (4/77); *Twenty Years; Me and You; Downfall; Win or Lose; Living in the Band; Stay (Night Until Noon); Find Out in Time; The Dance; When the Dance Is Over; Never Gonna Stop; Reprise: When the Dance Is Over.*

Singles/*Pickin' Up the Pieces/First Love* (7/69); *My Kind of Love/Hard Luck* (11/69); *You'd Better Think Twice/Anyway Bye Bye* (7/70); *Pickin' Up the Pieces/My Kind of Love* (7/70); *C'mon/I Guess You Made It* (2/71); *Just for Me and You/Ol' Forgiver* (10/71); *Railroad Days/You Are the One* (11/71); *Good Feeling to Know/Early Times* (6/72); *Go and Say Goodbye /I Can See Everything* (2/73); *Here We Go Again/Fool's Gold* (10/73); *Magnolia/Blue Water* (3/74); *A Good Feeling/Here We Go Again* (4/74); *Faith in the Families/Rocky Mountain Breakdown* (6/74); *High and Dry/Bitter Blue* (1/75); *Keep On Tryin'* (8/75).

ELVIS PRESLEY/Elvis Presley was all things to all people. Starting out as a sneering rock-and-roller, he took thousands of teenage girls into new worlds of ecstasy, twisting his lips and fluttering his bedroom eyes ever-so-slightly. Simultaneously, his supercool demeanor and self-mocking sense of humor catapulted countless teenage boys into a state of rebel-without-a-causedom. When his own brand of rock began to falter, Elvis moved into high gear as a hip-swiveling movie star. When that faded, balladeering was at hand. He led his loyal legions of followers from rock to country to gospel to soul to Vegas. He was an original. Something special. Sitting on a stool with an acoustic guitar, he could still out-rock most fully equipped bands. He carried rock and roll into middle-aged territory before his death . . . and his fans loved him all the more for it.

In a sense, Elvis Presley *was* rock and roll. The Mississippi-born star took rock by the hand and dragged it to the top of the heap in the early fifties . . . despite the agonized cries of the respectable press, the pop music mavens, and the parental world at large. Presley's first record was actually a demo made for his mother's birthday. Cut in 1953, *My Happiness* made its way to Sam Phillips, the president of Memphis' Sun Records. Within a year, Phillips had Presley in the studio for real, cutting songs like *That's Alright, Mama.* It was a local hit and C&W fans appreciated the unique mixture of raunch and corn that Presley exuded.

Col. Tom Parker, a local manager, appreciated it as well. Signing the young artist to his company, Parker hyped and touted the talent until RCA was willing to make a bid. Although a pleasant, shy, and incredibly gentlemanly boy, Presley projected a fairly sultry image and record execs were sure that he would catch on big. He did. His first RCA recording, *Heartbreak Hotel,* released in 1956, skyrocketed to the top of the charts. When Presley appeared "live" to perform the song, his naturalistic gyrations caused even more of an uproar than his rebellious form of rock and roll. Elvis the Pelvis was soon a cause célèbre in the music industry—indeed, in all the world. *Hound Dog, Blue Suede Shoes,* and *Don't Be Cruel,* along with appearances on the popular *Ed Sullivan Show* and movies like *Love Me Tender* and *Loving You,* firmly established him as the king of rock and roll.

By 1957, Presley was both a recording and a movie star. His career nearly halted, however, in 1958, when he was drafted into the army. Fortunately, forethought on the part of the Colonel nipped that problem in the bud. With a wealth of material already recorded, Presley was assured new and timely releases every so often even during his army days. By the time he emerged from the military, Presley was an even greater star than he had been when drafted.

The post-army Elvis was a mellower type, though. Songs like *His Latest Flame* and *Are You Lonesome Tonight?* were remarkably more mature than previous rave-ups. Although Elvis still remained intensely popular, he began to lose ground in the early sixties. The Beatles, the Stones and the entire new wave of U.K.-oriented rock was bringing about rapid change in the music world. Presley retreated to films, cranking out dozens of colorful, feather-headed musicals (with essentially the same plot: Elvis meets girl, girl meets Elvis, Elvis likes girl, lots of dancing, hubba-hubba-ing, lots of dancing girls, a fight, they kiss, credits). While the movies didn't bowl over the critics, they certainly appealed to the masses. Every one was a money-maker and Presley continued his successful career.

Although the younger crowd trotted after the inhabitants of the British invasion, Elvis' fans grew up with him, sticking with him through thick and thin. In 1968, Elvis staged a semi-comeback via a tremendously successful television special. A flurry of pop hits followed. Presley started to play Las Vegas regularly, attracting rockophiles by the thousands. By the early seventies, he was an established Vegas star and a top TV draw. His appeal on the teen-rock scene was virtually nil, yet Presley's records continued to sell. When he wasn't on the pop charts, he was on country. When not on country, on gospel. His old albums sold like crazy during gift-giving seasons, and the soundtrack album to his 1973 *ELVIS: ALOHA FROM HAWAII VIA SATELLITE* went to the number-one position on the album charts.

That same year saw Presley enduring what was probably, next to the death of his mother, the most traumatic event of his life. He separated from his wife of six years, Priscilla, and his child, Lisa Marie. Although he continued touring, recording, and selling records, Presley grew more and more reclusive. His later years found him fighting a weight problem and some intimates hinted at a possible fixation with various prescription sleeping pills and stimulants.

He died on August 16, 1977, at the age of forty-two, of a nor-mally minor heart malfunction. Immediately, a book written by two of his former employees portraying him as a lost, erratic, drug-taking individual became a best-seller. Loyal fans, however, refused to believe such woeful tales. His funeral at Memphis was an Olympian affair and every one of his albums sold out of every record store in the nation. The RCA factories worked overtime to get more out to their customers quickly. The world realized that an era had passed. A god had departed. The King of Rock and Roll had relinquished his throne.

Presley's contribution to the rock world cannot be overemphasized. He nearly single-handedly championed the cause. He was more popular than Bill Haley and sturdier than Pat Boone. He spawned countless clone sex symbols in the fifties, from Fabian to Frankie Avalon, but never once worried about competition. He was part of the music machine yet seemed above it all. His charm was as lethal as his backbeat and he was one of the best door-to-door salesmen rock ever had, taking its high voltage world into millions of homes throughout the world. He was, is, and will be forevermore . . . a legend.

Albums/ELVIS PRESLEY (2/56): *Blue Suede Shoes; I'm Counting on You; I Got a Woman; One-Sided Love Affair; I Love You Because; Just Because; Tutti Frutti; Tryin' to Get to You; I'm Gonna Sit Right Down and Cry (over You); I'll Never Let You Go (Little Darlin'); Blue Moon; Money Honey.* ELVIS (10/56): *Rip It Up; Love Me; When My Blue Moon Turns to Gold Again; Long Tall Sally; First in Line; Paralyzed; So Glad You're Mine; Old Shep; Ready Teddy; Anyplace Is Paradise; How's the World Treating You; How Do You Think I Feel.* LOVING YOU (6/57): *Got a Whole Lot of Livin' to Do; Blueberry Hill; Mean Woman Blues; Teddy Bear; Loving You; Lonesome Cowboy; Hot Dog; Party; True Love; Don't Leave Me Now; Have I Told You Lately That I Love You?; I Need You So.* PEACE IN THE VALLEY (extended-player; 4/57): *Peace in the Valley; It Is No Secret; I Believe; Take My Hand; Precious Lord.* ELVIS' CHRISTMAS ALBUM (10/57): *Santa Claus Is Back in Town; White Christmas; Here Comes Santa Claus; I'll Be Home for Christmas; Blue Christmas; Santa, Bring My Baby Back; Oh Little Town of Bethlehem; Silent Night; Peace in the Valley; I Believe; Take My Hand; Precious Lord; It Is No Secret (What God Can Do).* LOVE ME TENDER (extended-player; 7/57): *Love Me Tender; Let Me; Poor Boy; We're Gonna Move.* JUST FOR YOU (extended-player; 8/57): *I Need You So; Have I Told You Lately That I Love You; Blueberry Hill; It Is So Strange.* ELVIS' GOLDEN RECORDS (3/58): *Hound Dog; Heartbreak Hotel; Jailhouse Rock; Love Me; Don't Be Cruel; Love Me Tender; Treat Me Nice; Anyway You Want Me; I Want You, I Need You, I Love You; Loving You; All Shook*

Up; Too Much; That's When Your Heartaches Begin; Teddy Bear.
KING CREOLE (8/58): *Troubled; Crawfish; King Creole; As Long As I Have You; Hard-Headed Woman; Dixieland Rock; Don't Ask Me Why; Lover Doll; Young Dreams; Steadfast, Loyal and True; New Orleans.* FOR LP FANS ONLY (2/59): *That's All Right; Lawdy, Miss Clawdy; Mystery Train; Playing for Keeps; Poor Boy; My Baby Left Me; I Was the One; Shake, Rattle and Roll; I'm Left, You're Right; She's Gone; You're a Heartbreaker.*
A DATE WITH ELVIS (8/59): *Blue Moon of Kentucky; Young and Beautiful; Baby, I Don't Care; Milkcow Blues Boogie; Baby, Let's Play House; Good Rockin' Tonight; Is It So Strange; We're Gonna Move; I Want to Be Free; I Forgot to Remember to Forget.*
50,000,000 ELVIS FANS CAN'T BE WRONG—ELVIS' GOLD RECORDS, VOLUME 2 (1/60): *;One Night; I Need Your Love Tonight; I Beg of You; A Fool Such As I; Won't You Wear My Ring around Your Neck; My Wish Came True; I Got Stung; A Big Hunk o' Love; Doncha Think It's Time.* ELVIS IS BACK! (4/60): *Make Me Know It; Fever; The Girl of My Best Friend; I Will Be Home Again; Dirty, Dirty Feeling; Thrill of Your Life; Soldier Boy; Such a Night; It Feels So Right; Girl Next Door Went a-Walking; Like a Baby; Reconsider, Baby.* G.I. BLUES (9/60): *Tonight Is So Right for Love; What's She Really Like; Frankfort Special; Wooden Heart; G.I. Blues; Pocketful of Rainbows; Shoppin' Around; Big Boots; Didja Ever; Blue Suede Shoes; Doin' the Best I Can.* ELVIS' CHRISTMAS ALBUM (12/60). HIS HAND IN MINE (12/60): *His Hand in Mine; I'm Gonna Walk Dem Golden Stairs; In My Father's House (Are Many Mansions); Milky White Way; Known Only to Him; I Believe in the Man in the Sky; Joshua Fit the Battle; He Knows Just What I Need; Swing Down, Sweet Chariot; Mansion over the Hilltop; If We Never Meet Again; Working on the Building.* SOMETHING FOR EVERYBODY (6/61): *Put the Blame on Me; Judy; There's Always Me; Give Me the Right; It's a Sin; Sentimental Me; Starting Today; Gently; I'm Coming Home; In Your Arms; I Want You with Me; I Slipped, I Stumbled, I Fell.* BLUE HAWAII (9/61): *Almost Always True; No More; Can't Help Falling in Love; Rock-a-Hula Baby; Moonlight Swim; Ito Eats; Slicin' Sand; Hawaiian Sunsets; Island of Love; Blue Hawaii; Aloha-Oe; Ku-U-I-Po (Hawaiian Sweetheart); Beach Boy Blues; Hawaiian Wedding Song.* POT LUCK (6/72): *I'm Yours; Kiss Me Quick; Just for Old Times' Sake; Gonna Get*

Me Back Home Somehow; Steppin' Out of Line; Something Blue; Suspicion; I Feel That I've Known You Forever; Night Rider; Fountain of Love; That's Someone You Never Forget. GIRLS! GIRLS! GIRLS! (11/62): *Girls! Girls! Girls!; I Don't Wanna Be Tied; Where Do You Come From; I Don't Want To; A Boy Like Me, a Girl Like You; Earth Boy; Return to Sender; Because of Love; Thanks to the Rolling Sea; Song of the Shrimp; The Walls Have Ears; We're Coming In Loaded; We'll Be Together.* IT HAPPENED AT THE WORLD'S FAIR (3/63): *Beyond the Bend; Relax; Take Me to the Fair; They Remind Me Too Much of You; One Broken Heart for Sale; I'm Falling in Love Tonight; Cotton Candy Land; A World of Our Own; How Would You Like to Be; Happy Ending.* ELVIS' GOLDEN RECORDS, VOLUME 3 (8/63): *It's Now or Never; Stuck on You; Fame and Fortune; I Gotta Know; Surrender; Are You Lonesome Tonight?; Good Luck Charm; Anything That's Part of You; She's Not You; I Feel So Bad; His Latest Flame; Little Sister.* FUN IN ACAPULCO (11/63): *Fun in Acapulco; El Toro; Marguerita; The Bullfighter Was a Lady; I Think I'm Gonna Like It Here; Bossa Nova, Baby; Guadalajara; Vino, Dinero y Amor; You Can't Say No in Acapulco; Love Me Tonight; Slowly but Surely; There's No Room to Rhumba in a Sports Car; Mexico.* KISSIN' COUSINS (3/64): *Kissin' Cousins; Barefoot Ballad; Catchin' On Fast; Once Is Enough; One Boy, Two Little Girls; Smokey Mountain Boy; Tender Feeling; There's Gold in the Mountains; Anyone Could Fall in Love with You; Kissin' Cousins (#2); Echoes of Love; It's a Long, Lonely Highway.* ROUSTABOUT (10/64): *Roustabout; Little Egypt; Poison Ivy League; Hard Knocks; It's a Wonderful World; Big Love, Big Heartache; One-Track Heart; It's Carnival Time; Carny on My Heels.* GIRL HAPPY (3/65): *Girl Happy; Spring Fever; Fort Lauderdale Chamber of Commerce; Startin' Tonight; Cross My Heart and Hope to Die; The Meanest Girl in Town; Puppet on a String; I've Got to Find My Baby; You'll Be Gone; Wolf Call; Do Not Disturb; Do the Clam.* ELVIS FOR EVERYONE (7/65): *Your Cheatin' Heart; Summer Kisses, Winter Tears; Finders Keepers, Losers Weepers; Memphis, Tennessee; For the Millionth and Last Time; Santa Lucia; I Met Her Today; In My Way; Forget Me Never; Sound Advice; When It Rains, It Really Pours; Tomorrow Night.* HARUM SCARUM (11/65): *Harem Holiday; Gold Coins; Hey Little Girl; My Desert Serenade;*

Kismet; Go East, Young Man; So Close Yet So Far; Mirage;
Shake That Tambourine; Animal Instinct; Wisdom of the Ages.
FRANKIE AND JOHNNY (5/66): *Frankie and Johnny; Come*
Along; Petunia, the Gardener's Daughter; Chesay; What Every
Woman Lives For; Look Out, Broadway; Beginner's Luck; Down
by the Riverside; And When the Saints Go Marching In; Shout It
Out; Hard Luck; Please Don't Stop Loving Me; Everybody Come
Aboard. PARADISE, HAWAIIAN STYLE (6/66): *Paradise,*
Hawaiian Style; This Is My Heaven; Scratch My Back; House of
Sand; A Dog's Life; Datin'; Queenie Wahine's Papaya; Drums of
the Island; Stop Where You Are; Sand Castles. SPINOUT
(10/66): *Spinout; Stop, Look and Listen; Adam and Evil; All That*
I Am; Never Say Yes; Am I Ready; Beach Shack; Smorgasbord;
I'll Be Back; Tomorrow Is a Long Time; Down in the Alley; I'll
Remember You. HOW GREAT THOU ART (2/67): *How Great*
Thou Art; In the Garden; Stand By Me; Farther Along; Without
Him; So High; Where Could I Go But to the Lord; By and By; If
the Lord Wasn't Walking by My Side; Run On; Where No One
Stands Alone; Crying in the Chapel; Somebody Bigger Than You
and I. DOUBLE TROUBLE (5/67): *Double Trouble; Long-*
Legged Girl; Baby, If You'll Give Me All Your Love; Could I Fall
in Love; City by Night; Old MacDonald; It Won't Be Long; I Love
Only One Girl; There Is So Much World to See; Never Ending;
Blue River; What Now, What Next, Where To. CLAMBAKE
(10/67): *Big Boss Man; You Don't Know Me; Houses That Have*
Everything; Guitar Man; Who Needs Money; Clambake; Con-
fidence; Hey, Hey, Hey; Girl I Never Loved; How Can You Lose
What You Never Had; Singing Tree; Just Call Me Lonesome.
ELVIS' GOLDEN RECORDS, VOLUME 4(2/68): *Love Let-*
ters; Witchcraft; It Hurts Me; Ask Me; What'd I Say; Please
Don't Drag That String Around; Indescribably Blue; You're the
Devil in Disguise; Lonely Man; Mess of Blues; Ain't That Loving
You Baby; Just Tell Her Jim Said Hello. SPEEDWAY (8/68):
Speedway; Your Time Hasn't Come Yet; Who Are You; He's Your
Uncle, Not Your Dad; Let Yourself Go; Five Sleepyheads; Western
Union; Mine; Going Home; Suppose. ELVIS (11/68): *Trouble;*
Guitar Man; Lawdy, Miss Clawdy; Baby, What You Want Me to
Do; Heartbreak Hotel; Hound Dog; All Shook Up; Can't Help
Falling in Love; Jailhouse Rock; Love Me Tender; Where Can I Go
but to the Lord; Over My Head; Saved; Blue Christmas; One

Night; Memories; Nothingville; Big Boss Man; Little Egypt; If I Can Dream; dialogue from Elvis' TV special. ELVIS SINGS FLAMING STAR (3/69): *Night Life; Do the Vega; Tiger Man; Flaming Star; other titles.* FROM ELVIS IN MEMPHIS (5/69): *Wearin' That Loved-On Look; Only the Strong Survive; I'll Hold You in My Heart (Till I Can Hold You in My Arms); Long Black Limousine; It Keeps Right on a-Hurtin'; I'm Moving On; Power of My Love; Gentle on My Mind; After Loving You; True Love Travels on a Gravel Road; Any Day Now; In the Ghetto.* FROM MEMPHIS TO VEGAS/FROM VEGAS TO MEMPHIS (10/69): *Blue Suede Shoes; Hound Dog; medley; Mystery Train; Tiger Man; Johnny B. Goode; All Shook Up; Are You Lonesome Tonight?; I Can't Stop Loving You; Words; In the Ghetto; Suspicious Minds; Can't Help Falling in Love; My Babe; Inherit the Wind; Stranger in My Own Home Town; A Little Bit of Green; And the Grass Won't Pay No Mind; Do You Know Who I Am; From a Jack to a King; You Think of Me; The Fair's Moving On; This Is the Story; Without Love (There Is Nothing).* LET'S BE FRIENDS (4/70). ON STAGE—FEBRUARY 1970 (5/70): *See See Rider; Release Me; Sweet Caroline; Runaway; The Wonder of You; Yesterday; Proud Mary; Walk a Mile in My Shoes; Let It Be Me.* ELVIS' WORLDWIDE 50 GOLD AWARD HITS, VOLUME 1 (7/70): *Heartbreak Hotel; I Was the One; I Want You, I Need You, I Love You; Don't Be Cruel; Hound Dog; Love Me Tender; Anyway You Want Me; Jailhouse Rock; Treat Me Nice; I Got Stung; I Feel So Bad; Little Sister; Ain't That Loving You, Baby; Wooden Heart; If I Can Dream; In the Ghetto; Suspicious Minds; Don't Cry, Daddy; Kentucky Rain; Too Much Playing for Keeps; I'm All Shook Up; That's When Your Heartaches Begin; Teddy Bear; I Beg of You; Loving You; Won't You Wear My Ring around Your Neck; Hard-Headed Woman; A Fool Such As I; A Big Hunk o' Love; Are You Lonesome Tonight?; I Gotta Know; Surrender; Can't Help Falling in Love; Rock-a-Hula Baby; Anything That's Part of You; Good Luck Charm; She's Not You; Return to Sender; Where Do You Come From; You're the Devil in Disguise; Bossa Nova Baby; Kissin' Cousins; Viva Las Vegas; Crying in the Chapel; One Broken Heart for Sale; excerpts from Elvis Sails.* ALMOST IN LOVE (10/70). BACK IN MEMPHIS (10/70): *Inherit the Wind; This Is the Story; Stranger in My Own Town; A Little Bit of Green; And the Grass Won't Pay No Mind;*

From a Jack to a King; The Fair's Moving On; You'll Think of Me;
Without Love (There Is Nothing). IN PERSON AT THE IN-
TERNATIONAL HOTEL (10/70): *Blue Suede Shoes; Tiger*
Man; Words; Suspicious Minds; My Babe; Hound Dog; Are You
Lonesome Tonight?; In the Ghetto; I Can't Stop Loving You; All
Shook Up; Johnny B. Goode; Can't Help Falling in Love; Mystery
Train. ELVIS—THAT'S THE WAY IT IS (11/70): *Twenty Days*
and Twenty Nights; How the Web Was Woven; You Don't Have to
Say You Love Me; Just Pretend; Stranger in the Crowd; The First
Step Is Love; Mary in the Morning; I Just Can't Help Believin';
Patch It Up; You've Lost That Lovin' Feelin'; I've Lost You; Bridge
over Troubled Water. ELVIS COUNTRY (12/70): *Snowbird; Lit-*
tle Cabin on the Hill; Whole Lotta Shakin' Goin' On; It's Your
Baby, You Rock It; The Fool; Faded Love; I Washed My Hands in
Muddy Waters; Tomorrow Never Comes; I Really Don't Want to
Know; There Goes My Everything; Funny How Time Slips Away;
Make the World Go Away. LOVE LETTERS FROM ELVIS
(6/71): *Love Letters; When I'm Over You; If I Were You; Got My*
Mojo Working; Only Believe; This Is Our Dance; I'll Never Know;
This Is Our Dance; Life; It Ain't No Big Thing; Cincy, Cindy.
ELVIS—THE OTHER SIDES—WORLDWIDE GOLD
AWARD HITS, VOLUME 2 (7/71). ELVIS SINGS THE
WONDERFUL WORLD OF CHRISTMAS (9/71): *O Come,*
All Ye Faithful; Silver Bells; Winter Wonderland; The First Noel;
other titles. I GOT LUCK (10/71). ELVIS NOW (2/72): *Help Me*
Make It through the Night; Miracle of the Rosary; Hey Jude; Put
Your Hand in the Hand of the Man Who Stilled the Water; United;
It's Time for You to Go; Sylvia; Fools Rush In; We Can Make the
Morning; Early Morning Rain; I Was Born About 10,000 Years
Ago. HE TOUCHED ME (4/72): *He Touched Me; I've Got Con-*
fidence; Amazing Grace; Seeing Is Believing; He Is My Everything;
Bosom of Abraham; Lead Me, Guide Me; I, John; An Evening
Prayer; There Is No God but God; A Thing Called Love. ELVIS AS
RECORDED LIVE AT MADISON SQUARE GARDEN
(6/72): *You Don't Have to Say You Love Me; The Impossible*
Dream; Suspicious Minds; For the Good Times; Can't Help Fallin'
in Love; I Can't Stop Loving You; American Trilogy; Hound Dog;
Funny How Time Slips Away; That's All Right; Proud Mary; Love
Me Tender; Heartbreak Hotel; Don't Be Cruel; Teddy Bear; All
Shook Up; You've Lost That Lovin' Feeling; Polk Salad Annie;

Never Been to Spain. ELVIS SINGS HITS FROM HIS MOVIES (7/72): *Kissin' Cousins; Spinout; Viva Las Vegas; other titles.* BURNING LOVE AND HITS FROM HIS MOVIES (10/72). ELVIS (7/73): *A Fool Such As I; Where Do I Go from Here; Love Me, Love the Life I Lead; It's Still Here; It's Impossible; For Lovin' Me; Padre; I'll Take You Home Again, Kathleen; I Will Be True; Don't Think Twice, It's All Right.* RAISED ON ROCK (10/73): *For Old Times' Sake; Raised on Rock; Are You Sincere; Find Out What's Happening; I Miss You; Girl of Mine; If You Don't Come Back; Just a Little Bit; Sweet Angeline; Three Corn Patches.* ELVIS—A LEGENDARY PERFORMER, VOL. 2 (11/73): *Love Me Tender; Peace in the Valley; Heartbreak Hotel; A Fool Such As I; Tonight's All Right for Love; Are You Lonesome Tonight?; Can't Help Falling in Love; That's All Right; I Love You Because; Love Me; Don't Be Cruel; Trying to Get to You.* GOOD TIMES (4/74): *Take Good Care of Her; Loving Arms; I Got a Feeling in My Body; If That Isn't Love; I've Got a Thing about You, Baby; My Boy; Spanish Eyes; Talk about the Good Times; Goodtime Charlie's Got the blues.* LIVE ON STAGE IN MEMPHIS (9/74): *Blueberry Hill; Help Me; An American Trilogy; Let Me Be There; My Baby Left Me; Lawdy, Miss Clawdy; I Got a Woman; Can't Help Falling in Love; See See Rider; I Got a Woman; Love Me Tender; Trying to Get to You; medley; Why Me, Lord.* PROMISED LAND (1/75): *Promised Land; There's a Honky Tonk Angel; It's Midnight; You Asked Me To; Think about You; If You Talk in Your Sleep; Your Love's Been a Long Time Coming; Mr. Songman; Love Song of the Year.* TODAY (5/75): *Trouble; And I Love You So; Woman without Love; Shake a Hand; Pieces of My Life; I Can Help; Bringing It Back; Green Green Grass of Home; Fairy Tale.* THE SUN SESSIONS (3/76): *That's All Right; Blue Moon of Kentucky; I Don't Care if the Sun Don't Shine; Blue Moon; Just Because; Mystery Train;;I Forgot to Remember to Forget; Little Darlin'; I Love You Because; Trying to Get to You; Baby, Let's Play House; I'm Left, You're Right, She's Gone; Milkcow Blues Boogie; Good Rockin' Tonight; Baby, Let's Play House.* GREATEST HITS (6/77): *In the Ghetto; A Big Hunk o' Love; Suspicious Minds; Burnin' Love; The Wonder of You; Steamroller Blues; other titles.* MOODY BLUES (6/77): *Unchained Melody; Moody Blue; Way Down; Pledging My Love; It's Easy for You; Little Darlin'; If You Love Me; other titles.*

Singles/*That's All Right*/*Blue Moon of Kentucky* (8/54); *Good Rockin' Tonight*/*I Don't Care If the Sun Don't Shine* (1954); *Milkcow Blues Boogie*/*You're a Heartbreaker* (1955); *Baby, Let's Play House*/*I'm Left, You're Right, She's Gone* (1955); *Mystery Train*/*I Forgot to Remember to Forget* (1955); *Heartbreak Hotel*/*I Was the One* (1/56); *Blue Suede Shoes* (1956); *I Want You, I Need You, I Love You*/*My Baby Left Me* (4/56); *Don't Be Cruel*/*Hound Dog* (7/56); *Blue Moon* (8/56); *Love Me Tender*/*Anyway You Want Me* (9/56); *Love Me*/*When My Blue Moon Turns to Gold Again*/*Paralyzed* (10/56); *Old Shep* (11/56); *Too Much Playing for Keeps* (12/56); *Poor Boy* (12/56); *All Shook Up*/*That's When Your Heartaches Begin* (3/57); *Peace in the Valley* (3/57); *Teddy Bear*/*Loving You* (5/57); *Jailhouse Rock*/*Treat Me Nice* (9/57); *Don't*/*I Beg of You* (12/57); *Won't You Wear My Ring around Your Neck*/*Doncha Think It's Time* (3/58); *Hard-Headed Woman*/*Don't Ask Me Why* (5/58); *One Night*/*I Got Stung* (10/58); *A Fool Such As I*/*I Need Your Love Tonight* (2/59); *A Big Hunk o' Love*/*My Wish Came True* (6/59); *Stuck on You*/*Fame and Fortune* (3/60); *It's Now or Never*/*A Mess of Blues* (6/60); *Are You Lonesome Tonight?*/*I Gotta Know* (10/60); *Surrender*/*Lonely Man* (1/61); *Flaming Star* (3/61); *I Feel So Bad*/*Wild in the Country* (4/61); *His Latest Flame*/*Little Sister* (8/61); *Can't Help Falling in Love*/*Rock-a-Hula Baby* (11/61); *Good Luck Charm*/*Anything That's Part of You* (2/62); *Follow That Dream* (4/62); *She's Not You*/*Just Tell Her Jim Said Hello* (7/62); *King of the Whole Wide World* (8/62); *Return to Sender*/*Where Do You Come From* (9/62); *One Broken Heart for Sale*/*They Remind Me Too Much of You* (1/63); *You're the Devil in Disguise* (5/63); *Bossa Nova Baby*/*Witchcraft* (9/63); *Kissin' Cousins*/*It Hurts Me* (1/64); *What'd I Say*/*Viva Las Vegas* (4/64); *Such a Night* (6/64); *Ask Me*/*Ain't That Loving You, Baby* (9/64); *Do the Clam* (1/65); *Crying in the Chapel* (3/65); *Easy Question*/*It Feels So Right* (5/65); *I'm Yours* (7/65); *Puppet on a String* (11/65); *Tell Me Why*/*Blue River* (12/65); *Frankie and Johnny*/*Please Don't Stop Loving Me* (2/66); *Love Letters* (6/66); *Spinout*/*All That I Am* (9/66); *Indescribably Blue* (12/66); *Long-Legged Girl*/*That's Someone You'll Never Forget* (4/67); *There's Always Me*/*Judy* (7/67); *Big Boss Man*/*You Don't Know Me* (9/67); *Guitar Man* (12/67); *U.S. Male*/*Stay Away* (2/68); *Let Yourself Go*/*Your Time Hasn't Come Yet, Baby* (5/68); *A Little Less*

Conversation/Almost in Love (8/68); *If I Can Dream/Memories* (10/68); *Memories* (2/69); *How Great Thou Art* (3/69); *In the Ghetto* (4/69); *His Hand in Mind* (4/69); *Clean Up Your Own Backyard* (6/69); *Suspicious Minds/You'll Think of Me* (8/69); *Don't Cry Daddy/Rubbernecking* (11/69); *Kentucky Rain/My Little Friend* (1/70); *I've Lost You/The Next Step Is Love* (7/70); *Patch It Up/You Don't Have to Say You Love Me* (10/70); *I Really Don't Want to Know* (12/70); *Let Yourself Go/Your Time Hasn't Come Yet, Baby* (12/70); *If I Can Dream/Edge of Reality* (12/70); *Charro/Memories* (12/70); *His Hand in Mine/How Great Thou Art* (12/70); *In the Ghetto/Any Day Now* (12/70); *Suspicious Minds/You'll Think of Me* (12/70); *Don't Cry Daddy/Rubbernecking* (12/70); *Where Did They Go, Lord/Rags to Riches* (2/71); *Only Believe/Life* (4/71); *Kentucky Rain/My Little Friend* (6/71); *I'm Leavin'/Heart of Rome* (6/71); *It's Only Love/The Sound of Your Crying* (9/71); *Merry Christmas Baby/O Come, All Ye Faithful* (11/71); *He Touched Me/Bosom of Abraham* (2/72); *American Trilogy/The First Time Ever I Saw Your Face* (4/72); *An American Trilogy/Until It's Time for You to Go* (10/72); *Steamroller Blues/Fool* (3/73); *Raised on Rock/For Old Times Sake* (9/73); *Take Good Care of Her/I've Got a Thing about You, Baby* (1/74); *If You Talk in Your Sleep/Help Me* (5/74); *It's Midnight/Promised Land* (10/74); *Trouble/Mr. Songman* (3/75); *Bringing It Back/Pieces of My Life* (9/75); *For the Heart/Hurt* (3/76); *Moody Blue/She Thinks I Still Care* (12/76); *Way Down/Pledging My Love; My Way/America* (11/77).

BILLY PRESTON/The Beatles' favorite keyboard ace, Billy Preston, actually started his funkafide career conducting a church choir. The Houston-born, Los Angeles–raised musician enjoyed a career in local gospel aggregations and church groups before moving into professional circles, adopting a sideman stance for such varied performers as Mahalia Jackson and Little Richard.

An ill-fated recording career in the early sixties led him to a semi-regular spot on the classic ABC-TVer *Shindig* and yet another fling at recording, this time in an almost straight gospel vein. Beatle George Harrison heard one of Billy's long-players and quickly ensnared him for a few Beatle sessions. After playing on *Get Back,* Billy was subsequently invited to participate in all the tracks on the Beatles' farewell *LET IT BE* album. As a result,

Preston also was featured in the film of the same name.

George then ushered the keyboard ace into the stable of the fledgling Apple Records, George supervised most of the recording of Billy's first two long-players, *THAT'S THE WAY GOD PLANNED IT* and *ENCOURAGING WORDS*. Determined to raise the Preston star above the horizon, Harrison gave the young musician a spotlight on the historic Bangla Desh Concert stage. As a result, Billy became a sought-after commodity. Signing a contract with A&M Records, Billy launched his newfound career with a string of hit singles including *I Wrote a Simple Song, Nothing from Nothing, Will It Go Round In Circles,* and *Outa Space.*

Of late, his career has slowed down a bit, surrounded by the omnipresent whining of disco droning.

Albums/THAT'S THE WAY GOD PLANNED IT (10/69): *That's the Way God Planned It; Do What You Want; She Belongs to Me; It Doesn't Matter; What about You; This Is It; Morning Star; I Want to Thank You; Let Us All Get Together; Everything's All Right.* ENCOURAGING WORDS (11/70); *Encouraging Words; Right Now; Little Girl; Use What You Got; My Sweet Lord; Let the Music Play; I've Got a Feeling; Sing One for the Lord; When You Are Mine; The Same Thing Again; I Don't Want You to Pretend; You've Been Acting Strange; All Things Must Pass.* I WROTE A SIMPLE SONG (11/71): *Should've Known Better; I Wrote a Simple Song; John Henry; Without a Song; The Bus; Outa-Space; The Looner Tune; You Done Got Older; Swing Down Chariot; God Is Great.* MUSIC IS MY LIFE (11/72): *We're Gonna Make It; One Time or Another; Blackbird; I Wonder Why; Goin' Around in Circles; Ain't That Nothin'; God Loves You; Make the Devil Mad (Turn to Jesus); Heart Full of Sorrow; Music's My Life.* EVERYBODY LIKES SOME KIND OF MUSIC (10/73): *Everybody Likes Some Kind of Music; You're So Unique; How Long Has the Train Been Gone; My Soul Is a Witness; You've Got Me for Company; Listen to the Wind; Space Race; Do You Love Me?; I'm So Tired; It's Alright Ma (I'm Only Bleeding); Minuet for Me.* THE KIDS & ME (8/74): *Tell Me You Need My Loving; Nothing from Nothing; Struttin'; Sister Sugar; You Are So Beautiful; Sad Sad Song; St. Elmo; Sometimes I Love You; John the Baptist; Little Black Boys and Girls; Creature Feature.* IT'S MY PLEASURE (6/75): *Fancy Lady; Found the Love; That's Life; Do It While You Can; It's My Pleasure; Song of Joy; I Can't Stand It;*

All of My Life. BILLY PRESTON (10/76): *Do What You Want; Girl; Bells; I've Got the Spirit; When You Are Mine; Bad Case of Ego; Take Time to Figure It Out; Let the Music Play; Simplify Your Life; Let's Make Love; Ecstasy.* A WHOLE NEW THING (11/77): *Whole New Thing; Disco Dancing; Complicated Sayings; Attitudes; I'm Really Gonna Miss You; Wide Stride; You Got Me Buzzin'; Sweet Marie; Happy; Touch Me, Love; You Don't Have to Go.*

Singles/*That's the Way God Planned It*/*What about You* (7/69); *Everything's All Right*/*I Want to Thank You* (10/69); *All That I've Got*/*As I Get Older* (2/70); *My Sweet Lord* (1/71); *Outa-Space*/*I Wrote a Simple Song* (12/71); *The Bus* (3/72); *Slaughter* (8/72); *Will It Go 'Round in Circles*/*Blackbird* (1/73); *Space Race* (8/73); *You're So Unique* (12/73); *Nothing from Nothing* (6/74); *Struttin'* (11/74); *Fancy Lady* (9/75); *Do It While You Can* (11/75); *I've Got the Spirit* (1/77); *Girl* (4/77).

PROCOL HARUM/*Keith Reid (lyrics), Gary Brooker (piano, vocals), Chris Copping (organ), Mick Grabham (guitar), Alan Cartwright (bass), B. J. Wilson (drums). Previous members: Matthew Fisher (organ), Robin Trower (guitar), Ray Rowyer (guitar), Dave Knights (bass), David Ball (guitar), Bob Harrison (drums).*
Since their early success with *Whiter Shade of Pale,* Procol Harum has gone on to become the Notre Dame Cathedral of rock and roll. Wielding lofty melodies and ofttimes surreal lyrical images, the band has lived up to their name: Latin for "beyond these things." From the onset, Procol Harum has offered the public at large something more than was expected.

The historic band had its origins in a humble but spunky (and totally forgettable) R&B band, the Paramounts, an early sixties British group that included Brooker, Copping, Wilson, and Trower in its membership. Dissatisfied with aping the popular soul tunes of the day, Brooker split and, together with lyricist Reid, decided to form a more meaningful rock band. After holding auditions, the first Procol lineup included Brooker, Reid (a non-performer but always present in spirit), Rowyer, Fisher, Harrison, and Knights.

The single *Whiter Shade of Pale* was an immediate success, jumping to the top five in both the United Kingdom and the United States. The song was built around a Bach cantata. Keith Reid's lyrics were a mixture of vestal virgins, flying ceilings, and fan-

Rita Coolidge

David Bowie

Jefferson Starship

Boz Scaggs

The Mothers of Invention

Earth, Wind & Fire

Billy Preston

Loggins & Messina

Olivia Newton-John

Roger Daltrey of The Who

Courtesy MCA Records

Steve Miller

Courtesy Capitol Records

The Band

Leon and Mary Russell

Jackson Browne

Paul Simon

dangos. Brooker decided to put it all to music above and around the Bach cantata *Sleepers Awake,* and the record sold two and a half million copies within a month of release. Never was a group less ready for success, however. Procol's personnel was changed almost immediately. Rowyer and Harrison were out. Trower and Wilson entered the scene.

Their outward appearance of uncertainty eventually cost the band a sense of momentum. A follow-up single never materialized and albums such as *SHINE ON BRIGHTLY, A SALTY DOG,* and *HOME* appealed only to die-hard fans. Procol quickly became an "underground" group, appealing to the FM-radio crowd. The lack of overt success caused stress within the group. After *A SALTY DOG,* Fisher and Knights departed, the pair being replaced by Copping. Trower was the next to leave, after the underrated *BROKEN BARRICADES.* Ball and Cartwright joined and Procol found themselves at the nadir of their career.

A live album with the Edmonton Symphony proved a flake hit and suddenly, Procol found themselves. Stunned, they discovered that they could do no wrong. A coast-to-coast tour proved phenomenal. A single, *Conquistador,* entered the top twenty. A re-release of *Whiter Shade of Pale* made the British top ten. Their follow-up album, *GRAND HOTEL* (featuring Grabham replacing Ball), pointed toward sure success. However, the album did not fare that well in numbers sold and, since that time, the band has returned to their FM-radio status.

Some ten years after their initial excursion into rockdom, Procol Harum remains a distinctive musical entourage, capable of regular flashes of brilliance—brilliance that simply captivates their devoted legions of fans.

Albums/*A WHITER SHADE OF PALE (8/67): Whiter Shade of Pale; She Wandered through the Garden Fence; Something Followed Me; Mabel; Cerdes (Outside the Gates of); Salad Days; Conquistador; Kaleidoscope; Repent Walpurgis; A Christmas Camel.* SHINE ON BRIGHTLY (9/68): *Quite Righly So; Shine On Brightly; Skip Softly (My Moonbeams); Wish Me Well; Ramblin' On; Magdalene (My Regal Zonophone); In Held 'Twas in I.* A SALTY DOG (4/69): *A Salty Dog; The Milk of Human Kindness; Too Much between Us; The Devil Came from Kansas; Boredom; Juicy John Pink; Wreck of the Hesperus; All This and More; Crucification Lane; Pilgrims Progress.* HOME (6/70): *Whisky Train; The Dead Man's Dream; Still There'll Be More; Nothing*

That I Didn't Know; About to Die; Barnyard Story; Piggy Pig Pig; Whaling Stories; Your Own Choice. BROKEN BARRICADES (4/71): *Simple Sister; Broken Barricades; Memorial Drive; Luskus Delph; Power Failure; Playmate of the Month; Poor Mohammed; Song for a Dreamer.* LIVE WITH THE EDMONTON SYMPHONY ORCHESTRA (4/72): *Conquistador; Whaling Stories; A Salty Dog; All This and More; In Held 'Twas in I: Glimpses of Nirvana/'Twas Teatime at the Circus/In the Autumn of My Madness/Look to Your Soul/Grand Finale.* A WHITER SHADE OF PALE (re-issue; 11/72). GRAND HOTEL (3/73): *Grand Hotel; Toujours l'Amour; A Rum Tale; T.V. Caesar; A Souvenir of London; Bringing Home the Bacon; For Licourice John; Fires (Which Burnt Brightly); Robert's Box.* THE BEST OF PROCOL HARUM (9/73): *A Whiter Shade of Pale; Lime Street Blues; Homburg; In the Wee Small Hours of Sixpence; Shine On Brightly; Quite Rightly So; A Salty Dog; Whisky Train; Simple Sister; Conquistador; Long Gone Geek.* EXOTIC BIRDS AND FRUIT (3/74): *Nothing but the Truth; Beyond the Pale; As Strong As Samson; The Idol; The Thin End of the Wedge; Monsieur R. Monde; Fresh Fruit; Butterfly Boys; New Lamps for Old.* PROCOL'S NINTH (8/75): *Pandora's Box; Fools Gold; Taking the Time; The Unquiet Zone; Final Thrust; I Keep Forgetting; Without a Doubt; The Piper's Tune; Typewriter Torment; Eight Days a Week.* SOMETHING MAGIC (3/77): *Something Magic; Skating on Thin Ice; Wizard Man; The Mark of the Claw; Strangers in Space; The Worm and the Tree: Introduction/Menace/Occupation/Enervation/Expectancy/Battle/Regeneration/Epilogue.*

Singles/*A Whiter Shade of Pale/Lime Street Blues* (5/67); *Homburg* (9/67); *A Salty Dog* (5/69); *Boredom* (8/69); *Whisky Train* (8/70); *Simple Sister* (8/71); *Conquistador* (5/72); *A Whiter Shade of Pale* (10/72); *Grand Hotel/Fires* (5/73); *In the Wee Small Hours of Sixpence* (6/73); *Bringing Home the Bacon/Toujours l'Amour* (7/73); *Nothing but the Truth/Drunk Again* (5/74); *Pandora's Box* (9/75).

PRODUCERS/Record production, which once was a mere technician's job, somewhere in the late sixties became an art form. Records came out, like the Beach Boys' *Good Vibrations* in 1966, with arrangements that were difficult if not impossible to duplicate in live performances. Groups like the Beatles and the Rolling Stones discovered what veteran producers like Phil (the Righteous Brothers, the Ronettes) Spector knew all along: the man who works the controls, who sits behind the console, can literally *dictate* how a group will sound. In essence, a producer is the man who pieces together all the raw ingredients in order to form a finished LP. He will suggest to the arranger that there should be a little more volume in one spot, a little less in another, and what sort of volume it should be. He can make things faster, slower, closer, more distant. In a way, he is the conductor of the symphony of studio sound. Some of the best producers are former engineers and musicians. Some of the worst are rock fans and recording executives.

GARY PUCKETT AND THE UNION GAP/*Gary Puckett (vocals), Dwight Bement (tenor sax), Karry Chater (bass), Paul Wheatbread (drums), Gary Withem (piano).*
The Union Gap, formed in California in 1967, had three million-selling records in a row during the late nineteen sixties. Unfortunately, they were all the same song sung sideways. It only goes to show how much the public liked it the first time. The main attraction of the band was sturdy Gary Puckett's booming crooning. The band's Civil War uniforms didn't hurt, either. Gradually, as Puckett emerged as the true star, the band began to fade into the distance. As the seventies approached and music attained a small sense of kineticism, Puckett faded into the woodwork as well.

Albums/THE UNION GAP (1/68): *Woman, Woman; M'Lady; By the Time I Get to Phoenix; Raindrops; I Want a New Day; Believe Me; You Better Sit Down, Kids; My Son; Kentucky Woman; To Love Somebody; Don't Make Promises.* GARY PUCKETT AND THE UNION GAP (5/68): *Young Girl; Lady Madonna; Kiss Me Goodbye; Pleasure of You; Dreams of the Everyday Housewife; I'm Losing You; Honey (I Miss You); Mighty Quinn; Wait till the Sun Shines on You; Since You've Been Gone; Say You Don't Need Me.* INCREDIBLE (10/68): *Over You; Now and Then; I'm Just a Man; Can You Tell; Common Cold; If the Day Would Come; Lady Willpower; Reverend Posey; Give In; Take Your Pleasure; I've Done All I Can.* THE NEW GARY PUCKETT AND THE UNION GAP ALBUM (11/69): *This*

Girl Is a Woman Now; Let's Give Adam and Eve Another Chance; Don't Give in to Him; other titles. GREATEST HITS (6/70): *Woman, Woman; Young Girl; Over You; Lady Willpower; This Girl Is a Woman Now; other titles.*

Singles/*Woman, Woman/Don't Make Promises* (9/67); *Young Girl/I'm Losing You* (2/68); *Lady Willpower/Daylight Stranger* (5/68); *If the Day Would Come/Over You* (10/68); *Don't Give in to Him* (2/69); *This Girl Is a Woman Now* (7/69); *Let's Give Adam and Eve Another Chance* (2/70).

PUNK ROCK/A decidedly British phenomenon, Punk Rock is the anarchistic first cousin to the atonal sounds of America's ol' Velvet Underground and Iggy and the Stooges (although "in-the-know" rock critics often refer to the Who's *My Generation* as the quintessential rebellion tune that started it all). Rising during 1974 and 1975, the punk school was an overtly defiant gesture aimed at the stagnant music scene. The music scene, seeing bucks to be made, quickly embraced the "New Wave" to its bosom, signing up the new anti-heroes and making them "legit," as it were. The nasty Stranglers became the "new Doors." The Jam was dubbed "the New Who." The Vibrators were "just like the old Stones." The only band not classifiable was the first big punk outfit, the Sex Pistols. Possibly due to this iconoclastic stand, the band wasn't signed for a year and a half by a major label.

In the States, punk was co-opted from the beginning. Having none of the anger of the British prototype but just as much punkola posturing, punk got off to a well-publicized if miniscule start via the New York club CBGB's. Bands like the Ramones and the Miamis had a go at it with minimal success. Thus far, punk rock has proved to be a non-event stateside, although rock writers find it fascinating copy. The torn T-shirts, pins through the earlobe, and all-important sneers make for nice photos as well.

QUEEN/*Roger Taylor (drums), Freddie Mercury (vocals), John Deacon (bass), Brian May (guitars).*
Queen is to heavy metal what the Vatican is to the local wooden church. Olympian in sound, majestic in scope and quite pretentious in nature, Queen first howled their way to fame in 1973 with the release of their first album entitled, logically enough, *QUEEN.* The long-player was derivative, to be sure, borrowing

heavily from the Led Zepplin school of musical though, but it was also a brilliant exercise in style and execution. Since their debut, Queen have gone on to bigger and better things but their sound, first developed in 1972, has remained virtually unscathed. Freddie Mercury's vocals are truly ethereal. May's guitar still sounds like the dogfight scenes in *Star Wars,* and Deacon and Taylor on bass and drums constantly conjur up visions of the *Titanic* bubbling to its fate. Their lyrics have always vacillated between sheer fantasy and earthy reality and their audience, both the teenies and the older fans, obviously enjoy both realms.

Albums/QUEEN (9/73): *Keep Yourself Alive; Doing All Right; Great King Rat; My Fairy King; Liar; The Night Comes Down; Modern Times Rock n Roll; Son and Daughter; Jesus; The Seven Seas of Rhye.* QUEEN II (4/74): *Procession; Father to Son; White Queen (As It Began); Some Day One Day; The Loser in the End; The Ogre Battle; The Fairy Feller's Master Stroke; Nevermore; The March of the Black Queen; Funny How Love Is; The Seven Seas of Rhye.* SHEER HEART ATTACK (11/74): *Brighton Rock; Tenement Funster; Killer Queen; Flick of the Wrist; Lily of the Valley; Now I'm Here; In the Lap of the Gods; Stone Cold Crazy; Dear Friends; Misfire; Bring Back That Leroy Brown; She Makes Me (Stormtrooper in Stilettoes); In the Lap of the Gods (revisited).* A NIGHT AT THE OPERA (12/75): *Death on Two Legs; Lazing on a Sunday Afternoon; I'm in Love with My Car; You're My Best Friend; Sweet Lady; Seaside Rendezvous; The Prophet's Song; Love of My Life; Good Company; Bohemian Rhapsody; God Save the Queen.* A DAY AT THE RACES (12/76): *Tie Your Mother Down; You Take My Breath Away; The Millionaire Waltz; You and I; Somebody to Love; White Man; Good Old-Fashioned Lover Boy; Drowse; Teo Torriatte (Let Us Cling Together).* NEWS OF THE WORLD (11/77): *We Will Rock You; We Are the Champions; Sheer Heart Attack; All Dead All Dead; Spread Your Wings; Fight from the Inside; Get Down, Make Love; Sleeping on the Sidewalk; Who Needs You; It's Late; My Melancholy Blues.*

Singles/*Keep Yourself Alive/Son and Daughter* (10/73); *Liar/Doing All Right* (2/74); *Seven Seas of Rhye/See What a Fool I've Been* (6/74); *Keep Yourself Alive/Lily of the Valley* (7/75); *Bohemian Rhapsody/I'm in Love with My Car* (12/75); *You're My*

Best Friend/39 (5/76); *Somebody to Love/White Man* (11/76); *Tie Your Mother Down/Drowse* (2/77); *Long Away/You and I* (6/77); *We Are the Champions/We Will Rock You* (10/77).

QUICKSILVER MESSENGER SERVICE/*Original Members: John Cipollina (guitar), Gary Duncan (guitar), David Freiberg (bass), Greg Elmore (drums).*
One of the very first bands to take part in the San Francisco rock scene of the sixties, Quicksilver can trace its roots back to 1965. They played mostly for the citizens of Haight-Ashbury at free concerts and for the patrons of the Fillmore and the Avalon at the height of the flower period in 1966 and 1967. They did not record until quite late in their careers, turning down offers until they considered themselves entirely together and ready for the studio. Their first album disappointed some of their fans in that it was a "studio" album in the traditional sense, with much of the band's in-concert power pasteurized (albeit magnificently). They more than made up for this lack of edge on their second album, *HAP-PY TRAILS,* one of the finest live albums ever recorded. Lead guitarist Cipollina's glittering, quivering guitar lines stole the show, making the hard-hitting band sound like the equivalent of a sea resort "happy feet" machine.

All systems were go when former member Dino Valenti was released from prison (drug bust) in 1969. He rejoined the band in 1970, assuming the role of guitarist/vocalist—neither job being handled with an inordinate amount of expertise. By their fourth long-player, Quicksilver had all but lost their "sound." Cippollina left and the original sense of direction was destroyed. The "new" band floundered along quite unspectacularly, having a single or two on the charts but doing nothing much by way of creativity. In 1975, the original foursome plus Valenti got together to produce *SOLID SILVER,* a travesty of a musical reunion.

Quicksilver is a good example of perfection gone astray. The original concept was fine, meticulous in its planning and expert at its performing. Once a hint of success found its way into the psychedelic stew, however, the rock gourmet's dream turned into beef jerky.

Albums /QUICKSILVER MESSENGER SERVICE (5/68): *Pride of Man; Light Your Windows; Dino's Song; Gold and Silver; It's Been Too Long; The Fool.* HAPPY TRAILS (3/69): *Who Do*

*You Love Suite; Who Do You Love; When You Love; Where You
Love; How You Love; Which Do You Love; Who Do You Love
(Part Two); Mona; Maiden of the Cancer Moon; Calvary; Happy
Trails.* SHADY GROVE (12/69): *Shady Grove; Flute Song; Three
or Four Feet from Home; Too Far; Holy Moly; Joseph's Coat;
Flashing Lonesome; Words Can't Say; Edward, the Mad Shirt
Grinder.* JUST FOR LOVE (8/70): *Wolf Run (Parts 1 and 2); Just
for Love (Parts 1 and 2); Cobra; The Hat; Freeway Flyer; Gone
Again; Fresh Air.* WHAT ABOUT ME (12/70): *What About Me;
Local Color; Baby Baby; Won't Kill Me; Long-Haired Lady; Sub-
way; Spindrifter; Good Old Rock and Roll; All in My Mind; Call
on Me.* QUICKSILVER (11/71): *Hope; I Found Love; Song for
Frisco; Play My Guitar; Rebel; Fire Brothers; Out of My Mind;
Don't Cry My Lady Love; The Truth.* COMIN' THRU (4/72):
*Doin' Time in the USA; Chicken; Changes; California State Cor-
rectional Facility Blues; Forty Days; Mojo; Don't Lose It.* AN-
THOLOGY (3/73): *Pride of Man; Dino's Song; The Fool; What
About Me; Don't Cry My Lady; Hope; Fire Brothers; I Found
Love; Bears; Mona; Edward, the Mad Shirt Grinder; Three or Four
Feet from Home; Fresh Air; Just for Love; Spindrifter; Local Col-
or.* SOLID SILVER (10/75): *Gypsy Lights; Heebie Jeebies; Cow-
boy on the Run; I Heard You Singing; Worryin' Shoes; The Letter;
They Don't Know; Flame; Witch's Moon; Bittersweet Love.*

Singles/*Pride of Man/Dino's Song* (5/68); *Stand by Me/Bears*
(11/68); *Who Do You Love/Which Do You Love* (7/69); *Holy
Moly/Words Can't Say* (11/69); *Shady Grove/Three or Four Feet
from Home* (4/70); *Fresh Air/Freeway Flyer* (9/70); *What about
Me/Good Old Rock and Roll* (2/71); *I Found Love/Hope* (11/71);
Doin' Time in the USA/Changes (5/72); *Fresh Air/Freeway Flyer*
(8/72); *Gypsy Light/Witch's Moon* (1/76).

R&B/Logical abbreviation for rhythm and blues, whence
blossomed the term "soul."

THE RASCALS/*Eddie Brigati (vocals), Felix Cavaliere (organ),
Gene Cornish (guitar), Dino Danelli (drums).*
If you were a kid in New Jersey you might have heard about the
Young Rascals very early in February, 1965, when they played
the Choo Choo Club in Garfield, New Jersey. Even then, as a new
group, they weren't amateurs. Dino had done a lot of work since
the age of fifteen with jazz people and later with a band backing

Sandy Cott in Las Vegas. Felix had also backed Miss Scott and had been one of Joey Dee's Starlighters after the Twist had died. And Gene and Eddie were also Starlighters toward the end of the Dee phenomenon. So even in 1965, they were something to listen to. If you weren't around New Jersey but had social aspirations you might have known of them that summer when they played the Barge, the first of the big discos at the Hamptons on Long Island. It was in *the* place to go that summer and it was also considered very chic in those circles to have a Rascal or two in tow. ("So cute, my dear," said the jet-set ladies, not realizing they had just gotten their first taste of being a groupie.)

If you were around early in 1966 and you hadn't seen the Young Rascals in the smaller New York Clubs, well, you had to have seen them in any one of the score of concerts (including James Brown's Madison Square Garden debut) where they would come on to do a very soulful, frantic, and raunchy version of *Good Lovin'* (with all four of them ridiculously clad in Little Lord Fauntleroy outfits). That song was probably the most-played single on disco jukeboxes, especially at the black discos like the Dom in New York's East Village, where they tended to play only black music but invariably included the Rascals, who were white.

The group went to England for a while, where their black sound (these guys were the kings of blue-eyed soul) predictably flipped out black-oriented prestige groups like the Stones and the Animals. Back in America, they were soon playing to the sort of packed house you thought only the Beatles got. The Rascal's primo years were 1965 to 1968, both in terms of success and artistry. The advance of orthodox psychedelia caught the band off-guard, however. Suddenly, being soulful was decidedly out.

The foursome quickly donned Nehru shirts and love beads, which totally blew the minds of their loyal fans and led to snickering within the ranks of flower power. The Rascals valiantly attempted to straddle the two musical worlds, falling unsuccessfully in the middle. By 1971, Brigati and Cornish called it quits. The two remaining Rascals regrouped and attempted to evolve into a "meaningful," album-oriented band. The experiment, while noble, was a dud and by 1972, the Rascals were no more.

Cornish and Danelli resurfaced about that time in a band called Bulldog, which had two albums to its credit and a few mid-chart singles before collapsing. Cavaliere embarked on a solo career that can only be termed non-existent.

Albums/YOUNG RASCALS (3/66): *Good Lovin'; Slow Down; Baby, Let's Wait; Just a Little; I Believe; Do You Feel It; Like a Rolling Stone; Mustang Sally; I Ain't Gonna Eat Out My Heart Anymore; In the Midnight Hour.* COLLECTIONS (11/66): *What Is the Reason; Since I Fell for You; I've Been Lonely Too Long; No Love to Give; Love Lights; Mickey's Monkey; Come On Up; Too Many Fish in the Sea; More; 1956; Love Is a Beautiful Thing; Land of 1,000 Dances.* GROOVIN' (7/67): *Girl Like You; Groovin'; I'm So Happy Now; Find Somebody; How Can I Be Sure; If You Knew; I Don't Love You Anymore; You Better Run; Place in the Sun; It's Love; Sueno.* ONCE UPON A DREAM (1/68): *Easy Rollin'; Rainy Day; Please Love Me; It's Wonderful; I'm Gonna Leave You; My Hawaii; My World; Silly Girl; Singin' the Blues Too Long; Sattva; Once upon a Dream.* TIME PEACE (GREATEST HITS) (6/68): *How Can I Be Sure; Groovin'; I've Been Lonely Too Long; In the Midnight Hour; I Ain't Gonna Eat Out My Heart Anymore; Good Lovin'; You Better Run; Come On Up; Mustang Sally; Love Is a Beautiful Thing; Girl Like You; It's Wonderful; Easy Rollin'; Beautiful Morning.* FREEDOM SUITE (3/69): *America the Beautiful; Me and My Friends; Any Dance'll Do; Look Around; Ray of Hope; Island of Love; Of Course; Love Was So Easy to Give; People Got to Be Free; Baby, I'm Blue; Heaven; Adrian's Birthday; Cute; Boom.* SEE (12/69): *See; I'd Like to Take You Home; Remember Me; I'm Blue; Stop and Think; Temptations 'bout to Get Me; Nubia; Carry Me Back; Away Away; Real Thing; Death's Reply; Hold On.* SEARCH AND NEARNESS (11/70): *Right On; I Believe; Thank You, Baby; You Don't Know; Nama; Almost Home; The Letter; Ready for Love; Fortunes; Glory Glory.* PEACEFUL WORLD (5/71): *Sky Trane; In and Out of Love; Bit of Heaven; Love Me; Mother Nature Land; Icey Water; Happy Son; Love Letter; Little Dove; Visit to Mother Nature Land; Getting Nearer; Peaceful World.* THE ISLAND OF REAL (3/72): *Lucky Day; Saga of New York; Be on the Real Side; Jungle Walk; Brother Tree; Island of Real; Hummin' Song; Echoes; Buttercup; Time Will Tell; Lament.*

Singles/*I Ain't Gonna Eat Out My Heart Anymore*/*Slow Down* (11/65); *Good Lovin'*/*Mustang Sally* (2/66); *Love Is a Beautiful Thing*/*You Better Run* (5/66); *Come On Up*/*What Is the Reason*

(8/66); *I've Been Lonely Too Long/If You Knew* (1/67); *Groovin'/Sueno* (4/67); *A Girl Like You/It's Love* (6/67); *Groovin' (Italian)/Groovin' (Spanish)* (6/67); *How Can I Be Sure/I'm So Happy Now* (8/67); *It's Wonderful/Of Course* (11/67); *Beautiful Morning/Rainy Day* (3/68); *People Got to Be Free/My World* (8/68); *Ray of Hope/Any Dance'll Do* (12/68); *Away Away/See* (5/69); *Love Me/Happy Song* (5/71); *Lucky Day/Love Letter* (10/71); *Brother Tree/Saga of New York* (2/72); *Hummin' Song/Echoes* (5/72); *Jungle Walk/Saga of New York* (6/72).

THE RASPBERRIES/*Original members: Eric Carmen (vocals, rhythm guitar, keyboards), Wally Bryson (guitar, vocals), David Smalley (brass, vocals), Jim Bonfanti (drums, vocals); Scott McCarl replaced Smalley and Michael McBride replaced Bonfanti.* The Raspberries died an untimely and unnecessary death in the music business, a demise their talent did not deserve. It was all a matter of image, you see. It just wasn't *right* for any band to be so overtly UNhip. None of the guys looked like Easy Rider out-takes when they started back in the early seventies. They also committed the sin of writing crisp, clean singles that didn't deal with the doings of tragic anti-heroes. Hailing from the Cleveland area, the foursome (high-school chums) demoed a few tunes that came to the attention of producer Jimmy (Teeth) Ienner. Jimmy brought them to Capital Records and produced their first (and subsequent) album(s). *THE RASPBERRIES* was released in 1972 with some suggestion of hype. The band's sound was pseudo-British, the execution flawless and their success almost immediate.

The boys in the band, fairly sophisticated in their idea of what success would bring, decided to play the image "goof" schtick to the hilt. They sounded so mid-sixties, they decided to dress it as well. It was all sort of humorous, you see.

Of course, no one thought it was funny. The critics hated what was going on and so, in turn, did the FM-oriented public. The Raspberries were taken aback. A few near-miss singles found them regarded with scorn at AM outlets as well. The word suddenly came down from above. The Raspberries were yesterday's news. This annoyed the foursome somewhat in that they were still turning out quality albums and singles. By the time the excellent *SIDE 3* was released, they were veritable rock lepers. Tensions increased within the band, leading to fragmentation. The

Raspberries regrouped and released their most ambitious album, *STARTING OVER*. The single *Overnight Sensation* should have been one but wasn't, and their supporting tour ended in defeat. The group collapsed. Carmen went solo and the rest of the foursome went their separate ways.

And as the legend (short though it was) of the Raspberries faded away, a few of their detractors started to say; "Hey, they were pretty good after all."

There are thousands of stories like this in the Naked City.

Albums/THE RASPBERRIES (4/72): *Go All the Way; Come Around and See Me; I Saw the Light; Rock and Roll Mama; Waiting; Don't Want to Say Goodbye; With You in My Life; Get It Moving; I Can Remember.* FRESH (11/72): *I Wanna Be with You; Goin' Nowhere Tonight; Let's Pretend; I Reach for the Light; Every Way I Can; If You Change Your Mind; Drivin' Around; It Seemed So Easy; Might As Well; Nobody Knows.* SIDE 3 (8/73): *Tonight; Last Dance; Making It Easy; On the Beach; Hard to Get Over a Heartbreak; I'm a Rocker; Should I Wait; Ecstasy; Money Down.* STARTING OVER (9/74): *Overnight Sensation; Play On; Party's Over; I Don't Know What I Want; Rose-Coloured Glasses; All through the Night; Cruisin' Music; I Can Hardly Believe You're Mine; Cry; Hands on You; Starting Over.* RASPBERRIES' BEST (5/76): *Go All the Way; Tonight; Ecstasy; I Wanna Be with You; I Can Remember; Overnight Sensation; Let's Pretend; Drivin' Around; Starting Over; Don't Want to Say Goodbye.*

Singles/*Don't Want to Say Goodbye* (2/72); *Go All the Way/With You in My Life* (5/72); *I Wanna Be with You/Goin' Nowhere Tonight* (10/72); *Let's Pretend/Every Way I Can* (2/73); *Tonight/Hard to Get Over a Heartbreak* (8/73); *I'm a Rocker/Money Down* (10/73); *Drivin' Around/Might As Well* (5/74); *Overnight Sensation/Hands on You* (8/74); *Party's Over/Cruisin' Music* (12/74).

HELEN REDDY/She is woman, folks, and also a multifaceted gold record winner. Born in Australia, songstress Helen entered the entertainment whirl while still a toddler, guided by members of her show-biz family. When barely out of her teens, she had her own television show. Realizing that her homeland could offer just so much in terms of artistic fulfillment, Helen journeyed to the States in search of stardom in the mid-sixties. It was long in coming. In 1967, she met and married agent Jeff Wald in New York City. Wald then attempted to pull Helen's singing career into shape. At that time, however, the music industry in general was more interested in strobe lighting than song-singing, so Helen found herself on the low end of the totem pole for a while. After struggling for a few years and, ultimately, leaving New York in favor of Los Angeles, Jeff snared a recording contract for his talented wife with Capitol records. Her first single, *I Don't Know How to Love Him* (the over-exposed tune from *Jesus Christ, Superstar*), caused a bit of a buzz on the airwaves but it was Helen's self-penned *I Am Woman* that shot her up the charts like a Nike Zeus missile. One album. One hit. One red-hot career started. Helen's subsequent albums and singles have met with similar success. With eight gold albums, four gold singles, three platinum LPs, one Grammy and three "Top Vocalist" awards from *Billboard, Cashbox,* and *Record World,* it is safe to assume that Helen Reddy will be around for a long time to come.

Albums/I DON'T KNOW HOW TO LOVE HIM (5/71): *Crazy Love; I Don't Know How to Love Him; How Can I Be Sure; Our House; I Am Woman; L.A. Breakdown; A Song for You; Don't Make Promises; I Believe in Music; Best Friend.* HELEN REDDY (11/71): *New Year's Resolution; How; I Think It's Going to Rain Today; Come On, John; No Sad Song; Summer of '71; I Don't Remember My Childhood; Tulsa Turnaround; Time; More Than You Could Take.* I AM WOMAN (11/72): *Where Is My Friend; And I Love You So; I Didn't Mean to Love You; Peaceful; Hit the Road, Jack; Where Is the Love; I Am Woman; What Would They Say; This Masquerade; The Last Blues Song.* LONG HARD CLIMB (8/73): *Leave Me Alone (Ruby Red Dress); Lovin' You; A Bit OK; Don't You Mess with a Woman; Delta Dawn; The West Wind Circus; If We Could Still Be Friends; Long Hard Climb; Until It's Time for You to Go; The Old-Fashioned Way.* LOVE SONG FOR JEFFREY (3/74): *That Old American Dream; You're My Home; Songs; I Got a Name; Keep On Singing; You and Me Against the World; Ah, My Sister; Pretty, Pretty; Love Song for Jeffrey; Stella by Starlight.* FREE AND EASY (10/74): *Angie Baby; Raised on Rock; I've Been Wanting You So Long; You Have Lived; I'll Be Your Audience; Emotion; Free and Easy; Loneliness; Think I'll Write a Song; Show Biz.* NO WAY TO TREAT A LADY (6/75): *Ain't No Way to Treat a Lady; Bluebird; Don't*

Let It Mess Your Mind; Somewhere in the Night; You Don't Need a Reason; Ten to Eight; Birthday Song; You Know Me; Nothing Good Comes Easy; Long Time Looking. GREATEST HITS (11/75): *I Am Woman; I Don't Know How to Love Him; Leave Me Alone (Ruby Red Dress); Delta Dawn; You and Me Against the World; Angie Baby; Emotion; Keep On Singing; Peaceful; Ain't No Way to Treat a Lady.* MUSIC, MUSIC (7/76): *Music, Music; Gladiola; Mama; Hold Me in Your Dreams; Get Off Me, Baby; I Can't Hear You No More; Ladychain; Music Is My Life; Nice to Be Around; You Make It So Easy; Lullaby.* EAR CANDY (4/77).

Singles/*I Don't Know How to Love Him* (1/71); *Crazy Love* (7/71); *No Sad Song* (11/71); *I Am Woman* (5/72); *Peaceful* (1/73); *Delta Dawn* (6/73); *Leave Me Alone (Ruby Red Dress)* (10/73); *Keep On Singing* (2/74); *You and Me against the World* (5/74); *Angie Baby* (10/74); *Emotion* (1/75); *Bluebird* (6/75); *Ain't No Way to Treat a Lady* (8/75); *Somewhere in the Night* (11/75); *I Can't Hear You No More* (7/76); *Gladiola* (10/76); *You're My World* (4/77).

LOU REED/The most successful survivor of the legendary (and ill-fated) Velvet Underground, Lou Reed's helter-skelter career has had more than its share of ups and downs. Starting his solo career in 1971, the New York–born guitarist has offered himself to the public, at one time or another, as everything from the high Priest of Hedonism to a caricature of androgyny. After leaving the Velvets in 1970, Reed spent a year in hibernation, finally being urged into present-day rock music by rock critic and producer Richard Robinson.

Richard was ditched after producing Reed's premier LP, *LOU REED,* and replaced by the very au-courrant antics of David Bowie. With *TRANSFORMER,* Reed's career as a slick decadent, a product of the glitter times, was launched. It was Brecht with a backbeat and a hit single, *Walk on the Wild Side,* rocketed monotoned Reed to the top ten. Almost immediately, however, the glam facade began to wear thin.

Subsequent albums proved mixed commercial affairs, with the music offered often being echoes of previous numbers. *BERLIN,* a concept piece, was generally dismissed as being a tad pretentious, although *ROCK 'N' ROLL ANIMAL* saved the day with some tremendous "in-concert" performances by sessionmen Dick

Wagner and Steve Hunter (later of the Alice Cooper touring band). Lou's career continued on a downward trend until the release of the infamous *METAL MACHINE MUSIC,* which officially buried it. The album was a double LP in electronic tonalities which strangely resembled tap hum. No lyrics. No melodies. And, according to most fans, "no nothing."

Although Reed attempted to justify the album as being a "Lou Reed presents" sort of affair and not a "Lou Reed record," the damage was done. RCA killed the record. The critics killed Reed. And so it goes. Reed jumped labels in 1976, switching to Arista Records and returning to the deadpanned, monotoned, sleepy-eyed, redundant sound he'd pioneered five years earlier.

Albums/LOU REED (5/72): *I Can't Stand It; Going Down; Walk and Talk It; Lisa Says; Berlin; I Love You; Wild Child; Love Makes You Feel; Ride into the Sun; Ocean.* TRANSFORMER (11/72): *Vicious; Andy's Chest; Perfect Day; Hangin' 'Round; Walk on the Wild Side; Make Up; Satellite of Love; Wagon Wheel; N.Y. Telephone Conversation; I'm So Free; Goodnight, Ladies.* BERLIN (10/73): *Berlin; Lady Day; Men of Good Fortune; Caroline Says; How Do You Think It Feels; Oh Jim; Caroline Says II; The Kids; The Red; Sad Songs.* ROCK AND ROLL ANIMAL (2/74): *Sweet Jane; Intro; Heroin; White Light/White Heat; Lady Day; Rock and Roll.* SALLY CAN'T DANCE (8/74): *Ride, Sally, Ride; Animal Language; Baby Face; N.Y. Stars; Kill Your Sons; Ennui; Sally Can't Dance; Billy.* LOU REED LIVE (3/75): *Satellite of Love; Oh Him; Sad Song; Vicious; Walk on the Wild Side; I'm Waiting for My Man.* METAL MACHINE MUSIC (1975). *CONEY ISLAND BABY (1/76):* Crazy Feeling; Charlie's Girl; She's My Best Friend; Kicks; Coney Island Baby; A Gift; Oooh Boy; Nobody's Business.* WALK ON THE WILD SIDE, THE BEST OF LOU REED (12/76): *Satellite of Love; Sweet Jane; Sally Can't Dance; Nowhere At All; Coney Island Baby; Walk on the Wild Side; N.Y. Telephone Conversation; I Love You; Wild Child; How Do You Think It Feels.*

Singles/*I Can't Stand It/Going Down* (5/72); *Walk on the Wild Side/Perfectly* (1/73); *Satellite of Love/Walk on the Wild Side* (5/73); *Vicious/Goodnight, Ladies* (7/73); *How Do You Think It Feels/Lady Day* (11/73); *Sweet Jane/Lady Day* (2/74); *Sally Can't Dance/Ennui* (10/74); *Charlie's Girl/Nowhere At All* (2/76); *Crazy Feeling/Nowhere At All* (4/76).

PAUL REVERE AND THE RAIDERS/*Mark Lindsay (lead vocals), Paul Revere (keyboards), Freddie Weller, Michael Smith (lead guitar), Joe Correro, Jim Valley, Drake Levin (drums), Charlie Coe, Phil Volk (bass).*
For years Paul Revere and the Raiders were on television every single day, camping it up in their revolutionary uniforms of jackets and tights. Any other group would have died of overexposure, but the Raiders became an integral part of the young girlhood of every American teeny of that period. They were the first rock group with Columbia Records to have a million dollar gold album *(JUST LIKE US* in 1966) and, inevitably, there was much looking down of noses by rivals as Revere and his boys stuck to the well-rehearsed formulas (choreographed down to the last shuffle kick) that the audiences adored.

They started out as a hard-rock group, the Downbeats, in Portland, Oregon in 1962, complete with piped collarless suits and swept-back pompadours. They became famous for the dances they ran in that area and released a single version of *Louie, Louie* which would have made it big had not another local band, the Kingsmen, stolen the tunder with their version. The single did get the band a recording contract, however, and their upward climb began.

Dick Clark's *Where The Action Is* TV show made them instant stars in April of 1965 and they enjoyed five good years of hitdom. Once the seventies appeared, Paul Revere and the Raiders' recording career eased off. Lindsay went solo for a while with a small amount of success. Finally, the band disappeared from recordom altogether. They occasionally perform, in one form or another, at state fairs and such.

Albums/HERE THEY COME (8/65): *You Can't Sit Down; Money; Louie, Louie; Do You Love Me; Big Boy Pete; Oh Poo Pah Doo; Sometimes; Gone; Time A Kiss to Remember You.* JUST LIKE US (3/66): *Steppin' Out; Doggone; Out of Sight; Baby, Please Don't Go; I Know; Night Train; Just Like Me; Catch the Wind; Satisfaction; I'm Crying; New Orleans; Action.* IN THE BEGINNING (4/66): *Shake, Rattle and Roll; Don't Be Cruel; Linda Lu; So Fine; Blues Stay Away; Work with Me Annie; Mojo Workout; Rinky Dink; Key Baby; Hard Tonk; Crisco; Irresistible You.* MIDNIGHT RIDE (7/66): *Kicks; There's a Useless Man; I'm Not Your Stepping Stone; There She Goes; All I Really Need*

*Is You; Get It On; Louie, Go Home; Take a Look at Yourself;
Melody for an Unknown Girl.* SPIRIT OF '67 (1/67): *Good Thing;
All About Her; Louise; In My Community; Why Why Why (Is It
So Hard); Oh to Be a Man; Hungry; Undecided Man; 1001 Arabi-
an Nights; Our Candidate; Great Airplane Strike.* GREATEST
HITS (6/67): *Ups And Downs; Steppin' Out; Just Like Me; Louie,
Louie; Louie, Go Home; Kicks; Hungry; Great Airplane Strike;
Good Things; Legend Of Paul Revere; Melody for an Unknown
Girl.* REVOLUTION (10/67): *Him or Me-What's It Gonna Be; I
Had a Dream; Reno; Upon Your Leaving; Mo'reen; I Hear a
Voice; Wanting You; Gone-Movin' On; Tighter; Make It With Me;
Ain't Nobody Who Can Do It Like Leslie Can.* GOING TO
MEMPHIS (4/68): *Boogaloo Down Broadway; Every Man Needs
a Woman; My Way; One Night Stand; Love You Sou; Soul Man;
I Don't Want Nobody; Cry on My Shoulder; I'm a Loser Too;
Peace of Mind; No Sad Songs; Goin' to Memphis.* SOMETHING
HAPPENED (9/68): *Happening Intro; Too Much Talk; Don't
Take It So Hard; Good Times; Happens Every Day; Communica-
tions; Burn Like a Candle; Free; Get Out of My Mind; Happening
'68; Love Makes the World Go Around; Observation from Flight
285.* CHRISTMAS PRESENT . . . & PAST (11/67): *Wear a
Smile for Christmas; Jingle Bells; Brotherly Love; Rain, Sleet,
Snow; Peace; Valley Forge; Dear Mr. Claus; Macy's Window;
Christmas Spirit; Heavy Christmas Message.* HARD 'N' HEAVY
(WITH MARSHMELLOW) (3/69): *Mr. Sun, Mr. Moon; Money
Can't Buy Me; Time after Time; Ride on My Shoulder; Without
You; Trishalana; Out on That Road; Hard and Heavy/5 String
Soul Bango; Where You Goin' Girl; Cinderella Sunshine; Call On
Me.* ALIAS PINK PUZZ (7/69): *Let Me; Thank You; Frankfort
Side Street; Louisiana Redbone; Here Comes the Pain; The Ori-
ginal Handy Man; I Need You; Down in Amsterdam; I Don't
Know; Freeborn Man.* COLLAGE (2/70): *Save the Country;
Think Twice; Interlude; Dr. Fine; Just Seventeen; Boys in the
Band; Tighter; Gone Movin' On; Wednesday's Child; We Gotta All
Get Together; Sorceress with Blue Eyes.* PAUL REVERE AND
THE RAIDERS FEATURING MARK LINDSAY (9/70): *Cin-
derella Sunshine; Ride On My Shoulder; Don't Take It So Hard;
Happens Every Day; The Original Handy Man; Observation from
Flight 285; I· Hear a Voice; Brotherly Love; Do Unto Others.*
GREATEST HITS II (12/70): *Let Me; Don't Take It So Hard; I*

Had a Dream; Too Much Talk; Just Seventeen; Mr. Moon; Do Unto Others; We Gotta All Get Together. ALL TIME GREATEST HITS (5/72): *Louie, Louie; Steppin Out; Just Like Me; Kicks; Hungry; Great Airplane Strike; Good Thing; Ups and Downs; Him Or Me-What's It Gonna Be; Legend of Paul Revere; I Had a Dream; Too Much Talk; Do Unto Others; Peace of Mind; Don't Take It So Hard; Cinderella Sunshine; Mr. Sun, Mr. Moon; Let Me; We Gotta All Get Together; Just Seventeen.*

Singles/*Like Long Hair* (3/61); *Louie, Louie* (1963); *Steppin Out* (8/65); *Just Like Me* (11/65); *Kicks* (3/66); *Hungry* (6/66); *The Great Airplane Strike/Hungry* (9/66); *Good Thing* (11/66); *Ups and Downs* (2/67); *Him or Me-What's It Gonna Be/Steppin' Out* (4/67); *I Had A Dream/Upon Your Leaving* (8/67); *Peace Of Mind/Do Unto Others* (11/67); *Too Much Talk/Happening '68* (2/68); *Don't Take It So Hard/Observation from Flight 285* (6/68); *Cinderella Sunshine/It's Happening* (10/68); *Mr. Sun, Mr. Moon* (2/69); *Let Me; I Don't Know* (5/69); *We Gotta All Get Together* (9/69); *Just Seventeen/Sorceress with Blue Eyes* (1/70); *Gone Movin On/Interlude* (4/70); *Indian Reservation/Terry's Tune* (2/71); *Birds of a Feather/The Turkey* (8/71); *Country Wine/It's So Hard Getting Up Today* (12/71); *Indian Reservation/Birds of a Feather* (2/72); *Powder Blue Mercedes Queen/Golden Girls Sometimes* (4/72); *Song Seller/A Simple Song* (9/72); *Love Music/Goodbye Number 9* (12/72); *All Over You/Seaboard Line Boogie* (7/73).

THE RIGHTEOUS BROTHERS/*Bobby Hatfield (vocals), Billy Medley (vocals). Additional member: Jimmy Walker (vocals).*
Bill Medley and Bobby Hatfield were among the first to produce what was later to be dismissed contemptuously as "blue-eyed soul." But the Righteous Brothers' brand of R&B was truly universal, as popular on lily-white pop stations (currently known as "vanilla markets" in the trade) as they were on black "soul" formats. They began singing together in 1962 and, less than a year later, found themselves on the charts with a Latin-raver, *Little Latin Lupe Lu.* Fame courted them in earnest when Phil Spector took over producing chores in 1964, unleashing the monster *You've Lost That Lovin' Feeling.*

From that point onward, with and without Spector behind the board, the Righteous Brothers specialized in a lush, orchestrated brand of soul that sounded as if it might have been recorded in St.

Patrick's Cathedral at the tail end of a High Mass. *Unchained Melody, Go Ahead and Cry,* and *You're My Soul and My Inspiration* kept the boys in the limelight and led to numerous television appearances. In 1968, however, the deep-throated Medley decided he could do just as well on his own.

He left to pursue a solo career that proved fantastically catatonic and Hatfield adopted another brother, Jimmy Walker, to continue the Righteous way of life. The new siblings proved anemic and the act faded into oblivion. Medley and Hatfield rejoined in 1974 and released the top-twenty necrophelia a go-go hit, *Rock 'n' Roll Heaven* (a nifty song which mentioned everyone's favorite dead rock stars).

This night of the living dead fluke proved a herring and after two LPs, the Righteous duo drifted out of the spotlight once again.

Albums/RIGHT NOW (12/63): *Let the Good Times Roll; My Baby; Bye Bye Love; B-Flat Blues; Little Latin Lupe Lu; My Prayer; In That Great Gettin' Up Mornin'; Georgia on My Mind; Koko Joe; I'm So Lonely; Love or Magic; Fee-Fi-Fidily-I-Oh.* SOME BLUE-EYED SOUL (1964): *Baby, What You Want Me to Do; I Just Want to Make Love to You; Bring Your Love to Me; My Tears Will Go Away; Fanny Mae; Something's Got a Hold on Me; This Little Girl of Mine; Try to Find Another Man; Night Owl; For Your Love.* YOU'VE LOST THAT LOVIN' FEELIN' (12/64): *You've Lost That Lovin' Feelin'; Ol' Man River; Summertime; What'd I Say; Angels Listened In; Ko Ko Mo; Look at Me; Over and Over; Sick and Tired; Soul City; There's a Woman.* JUST ONCE IN MY LIFE (4/65): *Just Once in My Life; Big Boy Pete; See That Girl; Unchained Melody; You Are My Sunshine; Sticks and Stones; Great Pretender; Oo-Oo-Pah-Doo; You'll Never Walk Alone; Guess Who; The Blues.* THIS IS NEW (5/65): *Justine; Burn On Love; I Still Love You; Gotta Tell You How I Feel; I Need a Girl; You Can Have Her; Cryin' Blues; At My Front Door; If You're Lying You'll Be Crying; There She Goes.* BACK TO BACK (11/65): *Ebb Tide; God Bless the Child; Hung on You; Hot Tamales; Hallelujah I Love Her So; She's Mine, All Mine; For Sentimental Reasons; White Cliffs of Dover; Loving You; Without a Doubt; Late, Late Night.* SOUL AND INSPIRATION (3/66): *You're My Soul and My Heart's Inspiration; He Will Break Your Heart; Stand By; In the Midnight Hour; He; I'm Leaving It Up to*

You; Turn On Your Love Light; Hey Girl; Mine All Mine; Change Is Gonna Come; Bring It On Home to Me; Rat Race. THE BEST OF THE RIGHTEOUS BROTHERS (4/66): *Georgia on My Mind; Little Latin Lupe Lu; For Your Love; Try to Find Another Man; You Can Have Her; Justine; I Just Want to Make Love to You; Fanny Mae; Something's Got a Hold on Me; My Prayer; Let the Good Times Roll; Bye Bye Love; At My Front Door; This Little Girl of Mine.* GO AHEAD AND CRY (8/66): *Go Ahead and Cry; Save the Last Dance for Me; Something You've Got; I've Got the Beat; I Believe; Let It Be Me; What Now My Love; Big Time Ben; Island in the Sun; Stagger Lee; Things Didn't Go Your Way; Drown in My Own Tears.* SAYIN' SOMETHIN' (3/67): *Along Came Jones; On This Side of Goodbye; Don't Fight It; Yes Indeed; Harlem Shuffle; Soulville; Hold On, I'm Comin'; Man without a Dream; Will You Love Me Tomorrow; Jimmy's Blues.* GREATEST HITS (8/67): *Great Pretender; Unchained Melody; You've Lost That Lovin' Feelin'; Ebb Tide; Hung On You; Georgia on My Mind; You'll Never Walk Alone; Just Once in My Life; See That Girl; Guess Who; White Cliffs of Dover; For Sentimental Reasons.* SOULED OUT (9/67): *Been So Nice; Stranded in the Middle of No Place; If Loving You Is Wrong; Here I Am; It's Up to You; So Many Lonely Nights Ahead; I Don't Believe in Losing; You Bent My Mind; Someone Like You; Without You I'd Be Lost; Love Keeps Callin' My Name.* STANDARDS (3/68): *That Lucky Old Sun; That's All; My Darling Clementine; All the Way; Country Boy; If I Ruled the World; Without a Song; Since I Fell for You; Come Rain or Come Shine; Secret Love; Somewhere.* ONE FOR THE ROAD (11/68): *Let the Good Times Roll; You're My Soul and Inspiration; Little Latin Lupe Lu; My Babe; You'll Never Walk Alone; That Lucky Old Sun; Oldies but Goodies medley and Gospel medley.* GREATEST HITS VOL. II (3/69). GIVE IT TO THE PEOPLE (6/74): *Dream On; Give It to the People; Rock and Roll Heaven; other titles.* THE SONG OF MRS. RIGHTEOUS (1975).

Singles/*Little Latin Lupe Lu* (4/63); *My Babe* (8/63); *You've Lost That Lovin' Feelin'* (11/64); *Bring Your Love to Me* (12/64); *Just Once in My Life* (3/65); *You Can Have Her* (4/65); *Justine* (6/65); *Unchained Melody/Hung On You* (6/65); *Ebb Tide* (11/65); *Georgia on My Mind* (1/66); *You're My Soul and Inspiration* (2/66); *He/He Will Break Your Heart* (5/66); *Go Ahead and Cry* (7/66);

On This Side of Goodbye (11/66); *Melancholy Music Man* (3/67); *Stranded in the Middle of No Place* (8/67); *Rock and Roll Heaven* (4/74); *Give It to the People* (8/74); *Dream On* (10/74).

ROCK REVIVAL/During the late sixties, the children of psychedelia suddenly rediscovered the rock and roll antics of the fifties. These were called "roots." Rock revival shows, spotlighting the "rootsy" sounds of Chuck Berry, Dion, Little Richard, and Fats Domino (as well as dozens of peer performers) made their way across the country, drawing both the old fans of the fifties (now grown up with rock and rollettes of their own at home) and young nostalgia buffs who enjoyed seeing where the Rolling Stones came from.

THE ROLLING STONES/*Original members: Mick Jagger (lead vocals, harmonica), Keith Richard (lead guitar, vocals), Brian Jones (rhythm guitar, harmonica, sitar), Charlie Watts (drums), Bill Wyman (bass guitar). Additional members: Mick Taylor (lead guitar), Ron Wood (lead guitar).*
Mixing menace with mascara, the Rolling Stones have taken their hard-hitting brand of R&B rock from the squalid clubs of London to the biggest concert stages in the world over a period of a decade and a half. Today, they are arguably the biggest rock attraction in existence. Their beginnings were a bit less spectacular, to say the least. The embryonic group, Brian Jones and Mick Jagger and the Rolling Stones, made their debut in June of 1962 at the Marquee club in London. Jagger, a blues fanatic, was on leave from Alexis Korner's Blues Inc., friend Richard was a musical associate from their the Blue Boys outfit, and Jones was a frustrated musician who played in various blues bands. Taking their name from a Muddy Waters song, the threesome got together with drummer Tony Chapman and pianist Ian Stewart. By year's end, the lineup consisted of Jagger, Jones, Richard, Stewart, ex-Blues Inc. drummer Charlie Watts, and new bassist Bill Wyman.

A few demo sessions and a long-lasting job at the Crawdaddy Club led to their meeting manager/producer Andrew Oldham in 1963. Oldham quickly played up the group's scruffy image (which led to Ian Stewart's gradual disappearance from the troupe) and secured a recording contract for the band with Decca Records in the United Kingdom, London Records in the States. By 1964 the group had proved their worth, causing a sensation on both sides of the Atlantic.

In an era of nicely trimmed Beatle bangs, carefully brushed mouthfuls of Herman's Hermit teeth, and zany cornpone antics of the likes of Freddie and the Dreamers, the Stones became *the* most identifiable British band. Jagger's sneer and R&B drawl, Jones' nasty-little-boy looks and the band's no-holds-barred, down-to-the-bone blues approach took them to the top of the charts within weeks of their debut album's (and single's) release.

As the band became more experienced, their sound became less derivative. Chuck Berry riffing and blues progressions made way for such classic tunes as *Satisfaction, Get Off My Cloud, As Tears Go By,* and *Paint It Black.* What the Beatles were to melody, the Stones were to backbeat. Next to the Fab Four, in fact, the Stones were the biggest rock attraction in the world. The band's fame grew, attracting new legions of followers and business advisors. Andrew Oldham faded into the woodwork, being replaced in a roundabout way by business manager Allen Klein. Taking over from the Stones' guiding light. Klein sought to guide the bad boys of rock and roll to new heights. Those heights, however, nearly became unattainable for a number of reasons.

In the midst of psychedelia and Sgt. Pepperdom, the Stones clung tenaciously to their hard-as-nails sound. A provocative single, *Let's Spend the Night Together,* was censored on *The Ed Sullivan Show.* (The Stones' choice: change it to read *Let's Spend Some Time Together* or drop the song. They dropped the song.) That same year found Jagger, Richard, and Jones involved in drug arrests. Meanwhile, back on the charts, the Beatles were dominating the globe with their lush Pepperisms. The Stones responded with the spaced-out *THEIR SATANIC MAJESTIES REQUEST* effort, a nicely done LP but a shock to many of their punkier fans.

Jones, an on-again, off-again drug user in earnest, began to experience the first signs of physical decay, further complicating the band's lifestyle. In December of 1967, he was admitted to a hospital. In May of 1968, he was arrested for drugs. During that hectic period, the Stones, as a working unit, managed to pull off quite a musical coup, releasing their finest LP in over a year, *BEGGAR'S BANQUET.* The most cohesive album in their history, *BANQUET* afforded the shot in the arm the band needed on the charts and led to the filming of the never-released TV special *Rock and Roll Circus*. Shortly thereafter, the erratic Jones left the band to be replaced four days later, on June 13, 1969, by former John Mayall guitarist Mick Taylor. On July 5, Jones was found dead in the swimming pool of his home. At the age of twenty-five, the rock and roller was allegedly the victim of too many downers plus a nearby pool. The official coroner's report listed his death as a result of "misadventure."

Two days later, at Hyde Park, Taylor made his debut at a free festival, which lapsed into a tribute to Jones. During the remainder of 1969, the Stones reached new heights with their *Honky Tonk Women* single. The band members began to tour at length (the most notorious concert being the one at Altamount, California, wherein Hells Angels hired as security guards overreached their bounds and murdered a concertgoer in front of the stage as the Stones performed—this event would later be documented in the film *Gimme Shelter*), and Jagger started an on-again off-again acting career via Ned Kelly and Performance.

In 1971, the Stones formed their own Rolling Stones Records label and launched their new, galvanized career with the single *Brown Sugar* and the album *STICKY FINGERS*. The band continued on an upward trend until December, 1974, when Taylor exited the band to be replaced by Ron Wood. Taylor's exit marked a declining period of Stones activity. In 1976, the *BLACK AND BLUE* album proved anticlimactic to say the very least and a subsequent live album in 1977 proved equally ordinary.

Although some of the fire has faded, the Stones still manage to crank out some of the bluesiest pieces of high-energy rock and roll ever to cross a turntable. Jagger's pout is still pagical, albeit slightly overdone (those jumpsuits could be retired as well), and Keith Richard is still one of the most distinctive guitarists to enter the rock limelight. A little bit older, a little more refined, the Rolling Stones are still the masters of R&B rock. For all their fans, the sound of the Stones is timeless.

Albums/THE ROLLING STONES (5/64): *Not Fade Away; Route 66; I Just Want to Make Love to You; Honest I Do; Now I've Got a Witness; Little by Little; I'm King Bee; Carol; Tell Me; Can I Get a Witness; You Can Make It If You Try; Walking the Dog.* 12 X 5 (12/64): *Around and Around; Confessin' the Blues; 2120 South Michigan Avenue; Empty Heart; Time Is on My Side;*

Good Times, Bad Times; It's All Over Now; Under the Boardwalk; Brown Up Wrong; Congratulations; If You Need Me; Susie Q. THE ROLLING STONES NOW (2/65): *Heart of Stone; Everybody Needs Somebody to Love; Little Red Rooster; Oh Baby We Got Such a Good Thing Goin'; Down the Road a Piece; Off the Hook; Pain in My Heart; Surprise, Surprise; Mona (I Need You Baby).* OUT OF OUR HEADS (7/65): *Mercy Mercy; Hitch Hike; Last Time; That's How Strong My Love Is; Good Times; I'm All Right; (I Can't Get No) Satisfaction; Cry to Me; Under Assistant West Coast Promotion Man; Play with Fire; Spider and the Fly; One More Try.* DECEMBER'S CHILDREN (11/65): *Get Off My Cloud; Blue Turns to Grey; She Said Yeah; Talkin' about You; You Better Move On; Look What You've Done; The Singer Not the Song; Route 66; I'm Free; As Tears Go By; Gotta Get Away; I'm Moving On.* BIG HITS (HIGH TIDE AND GREEN GRASS) (3/66): *19th Nervous Breakdown; (I Can't Get No) Satisfaction; Last Time; As Tears Go By; Time Is on My Side; It's All Over Now; Tell Me; Heart of Stone; Get Off My Cloud; Not Fade Away; Good Times, Bad Times; Play with Fire.* AFTERMATH (6/66): *Paint It Black; Stupid Girl; Lady Jane; Think; Under My Thumb; Doncha Bother Me; Flight; High and Dry; It's Not Easy; I Am Waiting; Going.* GOT "LIVE" IF YOU WANT IT (11/66): *Have You Seen Your Mother, Baby, Standing in the Shadow; Under My Thumb; Get Off My Cloud; Lady Jane; I've Been Loving You Too Long; Fortune Teller; Last Time; 19th Nervous Breakdown; Time Is on My Side; I'm Alright; (I Can't Get No) Satisfaction; Not Fade Away.* BETWEEN THE BUTTONS (1/67): Ruby Tuesday; Let's Spend the Night Together; Yesterday's Papers; Connection; All Sold Out; She Smiled Sweetly; Cool and Collected; My Obsession; Who's Been Sleeping Here; Complicated; Miss Amanda Jones; Something Happened to Me Yesterday. FLOWERS (6/67): *Ruby Tuesday; Have You Seen Your Mother, Baby, Standing in the Shadow; Let's Spend the Night Together; Lady Jane; Out of Time; My Girl; Back Street Girl; Please Go Home; Mother's Little Helper; Take It or Leave It; Ride On Baby; Sittin' on a Fence.* THEIR SATANIC MAJESTIES REQUEST (11/67): *Sing This All Together; Citadel; In Another Land; 2000 Man; Sing This All Together (See What Happens); She's a Rainbow; The Lantern; Gomper; 2000 Light Years from Home; On with the Show.* BEGGARS BANQUET (11/68): *Sympathy for the Dev-*

il; No Expectations; Dear Doctor; Parachute Woman; Jig-Saw Puzzle; Street Fighting Man; Prodigal Son; Stray Cat Blues; Factory Girl; Salt of the Earth. THROUGH THE PAST DARKLY (BIG HITS VOL. 2) (8/69): *Honky Tonk Woman; Ruby Tuesday; Jumpin' Jack Flash; Paint It Black; Street Fighting Man; Have You Seen Your Mother, Baby, Standing in the Shadow; Let's Spend the Night Together; 2000 Light Years from Home; Mother's Little Helper; She's a Rainbow; Dandelion.* LET IT BLEED (11/69): *Gimme Shelter; Love in Vain; Country Honk; Live with Me; Let It Bleed; Midnight Rambler; You Got the Silver; Monkey Man; You Can't Always Get What You Want.* GET YER YA-YA'S OUT (9/70): *Jumpin' Jack Flash; Carol; Stray Cat Blues; Love in Vain; Midnight Rambler; Sympathy for the Devil; Live with Me; Little Queenie; Honky Tonk Woman; Street Fighting Man.* STICKY FINGERS (4/71): *Brown Sugar; Sway; Wild Horses; Can't You Hear Me Knocking; You Gotta Move; Bitch; I Got the Blues; Sister Morphine; Dead Flowers; Moonlight Mile.* HOT ROCKS 1964– 1971 (12/71): *Brown Sugar; Wild Horses; Gimme Shelter; Honky Tonk Woman; Satisfaction; Paint It Black; Jumping Jack Flash; Street Fighting Man; Midnight Rambler (live); You Can't Always Get What You Want; Let's Spend the Night Together; Mother's Little Helper; 19th Nervous Breakdown; Ruby Tuesday; Get Off My Cloud; Play with Fire; Time Is on My Side; Heart of Stone; Under My Thumb; Sympathy for the Devil; As Tears Go By.* EX- ILE ON MAIN STREET (5/72): *Happy; Turd on the Run; Ventilator Blues; Just Wanna See His Face; Let It Loose; All Down the Line; Stop Breaking Down; Shine a Light; Soul Survivor; Rocks Off; Rip This Joint; Hip Shake; Casino Boogie; Tumbling Dice; Sweet Virginia; Torn & Frayed; Black Angel; Loving Cup.* MORE HOT ROCKS (BIG HITS AND FAZED COOKIES) (11/72): *Tell Me; Not Fade Away; The Last Time; Good Times, Bad Times; I'm Free; It's All Over Now; Out of Time; Lady Jane; Sittin' on a Fence; Have You Seen Your Mother, Baby, Standing in the Shadow; Dandelion; We Love You; She's a Rainbow; 2000 Light Years from Home; Child of the Moon; No Expectations; Let It Bleed; What to Do; Money; Come On; Poison Ivy; I Can't Be Satisfied; Long Long While; Bye Bye Johnnie; Fortune Teller.* GOAT'S HEAD SOUP (9/73): *Dancing with Mr. D; 100 Years Ago; Coming Down Again; Doo Doo Doo Doo Doo (Heartbreaker); Angie; Silver Train; Hide Your Love; Winter; Can You Hear the Music;*

Star Star. IT'S ONLY ROCK AND ROLL (10/74): *If You Can't Rock Me; Ain't Too Proud to Beg; It's Only Rock 'n' Roll (But I Like It); Till the Next Goodbye; Time Waits for No One; Luxury; Dance Little Sister; If You Really Want to Be My Friend; Short and Crulies; Fingerprint File*. METAMORPHOSIS (6/75): *Out of Time; Don't Lie to Me; Each and Every Day of the Year; Heart of Stone; I'd Much Rather Be with the Boys; Sleepy City; Try a Little Harder; I Don't Know Why; If You Let Me; Jiving Sister Fanny; Downtown Suzie; Family; Memo from Turner; I'm Going Down*. MADE IN THE SHADE (6/75): *Brown Sugar; Tumbling Dice; Happy; Dance Little Sister; Wild Horses; Bitch; It's Only Rock 'n' Roll; Angie; Doo Doo Doo Doo Doo (Heartbreaker); Rip This Joint*. BLACK AND BLUE (4/76): *Hey Negrita; Melody; Fool to Cry; Crazy Mama; Hot Stuff; Hand of Fate; Cherry Oh Baby; Memory Motel*. LOVE YOU LIVE (10/77): *Intro; Honky Tonk Woman; If You Can't Rock Me; Get Off of My Cloud; Happy; Hot Stuff; Star Star; Tumbling Dice; Fingerprint File; You Gotta Move; You Can't Always Get What You Want; Cracklin' Up; Little Red Rooster; Around and Around; It's Only Rock 'n' Roll; Brown Sugar; Jumping Jack Flash; Sympathy for the Devil; Mannish Boy*.

Singles/*I Wanna Be Your Man/Stoned* (2/64); *Not Fade Away/I Wanna Be Your Man* (3/64); *Tell Me/I Just Want to Make Love to You* (6/64); *It's All Over Now/Good Times, Bad Times* (7/64); *Time Is on My Side/Congratulations* (9/64); *Heart of Stone/What a Shame* (12/64); *The Last Time/Play with Fire* (3/65); *Satisfaction/Under Assistant West Coast Promotion Man* (5/65); *Get Off of My Cloud/I'm Free* (9/65); *As Tears Go By/Gotta Get Away* (12/65); *19th Nervous Breakdown/Sad Day* (2/66); *Paint It Black/Stupid Girl* (4/66); *Mother's Little Helper/Lady Jane* (6/66); *Have You Seen Your Mother, Baby, Standing in the Shadow/Who's Driving My Plane* (9/66); *Let's Spend the Night Together/Ruby Tuesday* (12/66); *We Love You/Dandelion* (8/67); *In Another Land/The Lantern* (11/67); *She's a Rainbow/2000 Light Years from Home* (12/67); *Jumpin' Jack Flash/Child of the Moon* (5/68); *Street Fighting Man/No Expectations* (8/68); *Honky Tonk Women/You Can't Always Get What You Want* (7/69); *Brown Sugar/Bitch* (4/71); *Wild Horses/Sway* (6/71); *Tumbling Dice/Sweet Black Angel* (4/72); *Happy/All Down the Line* (6/72); *Angie/Silver Train* (8/73); *Doo Doo Doo Doo Doo*

(Heartbreaker)/Dancing with Mr. D (12/73); *It's Only Rock 'n' Roll/Through the Lonely Nice* (7/74); *Ain't Too Proud to Beg/Dance Little Sister* (10/74); *Fool to Cry/Hot Stuff* (4/76).

MICK RONSON/Mick Ronson's career is one of those unique chains of events that could be labeled "a star is *not* brown." The superb guitar playing of this top session guitarist first attracted critical acclaim via his licks with David Bowie. A mini-sensation in his own right, Ronson attempted to launch his own career in a big way in 1974 under the aegis of Bowie's manager, Tony DeFries. Unfortunately, Mick's promotional and publicity campaign took on Quo Vadis proportions. With the world waiting for the album of albums, Ronson delivered the thoroughly average *SLAUGHTER ON TENTH AVENUE,* proving him an exceptional player but a pretty average songwriter and singer.

From that point onward, his career slid downhill. Burdened by the weight of the pre-LP hype, he retreated from the limelight, only to re-emerge a short time later as a member of Mott the Hoople. Although the association with Mott was short-lived, it was the beginning of an on-again, off-again musical romance with Mott's (then) leader, Ian Hunter. This association has led to the establishment, on various occasions, of a Hunter-Ronson touring band. Ronson released another solo LP, *PLAY, DON'T WORRY,* which also proved anticlimactic.

He has since re-established himself as a primo sessionman (touring with Dylan's Rolling Thunder Revue in 1975) and still entertains hopes of diving back into the rock scene with a monster band of his own design.

Albums/SLAUGHTER ON 10TH AVENUE (3/74): *Love Me Tender; Growing Up and I'm Fine; Only after Dark; Music Is Lethal; I'm the One; Pleasure Man; Hey Ma, Get Pa; Slaughter on 10th Avenue.* PLAY, DON'T WORRY (1/75): *Billy Porter; Angel #2; This Is for You; White Light/White Heat; Play, Don't Worry; Hazy Days; Girl Can't Help It; The Empty Bed; Woman.*

Singles/*Love Me Tender/Only after Dark* (2/74); *Slaughter on 10th Avenue/Growing Up and I'm Fine* (4/74); *Slaughter on 10th Avenue/Leave My Heart Alone* (5/74); *Billy Porter/Happy Days* (3/75).

LINDA RONSTADT/When Linda Ronstadt first took to the stage as a solo performer in the early seventies, she scored an easy two-digit win on a male-oriented hubba hubba scale of one to ten. Clad in tight jeans and flouncy blouses, Linda not only captured the hearts of her primarily male audience, but did wonders for their general anatomy as well. Born in Tucson, Arizona, Linda picked up the basics of music at home from her guitar-playing dad. At the end of her freshman year at the University of Arizona, Linda took off for the West Coast where, together with friends Kenny Edwards and Bob Kimmel, she formed the Stone Poneys —an acoustic trio known more for their spirit than their style. Nevertheless, the group was signed to Capitol and three erratic albums were the result. Their second contained the Mike Nesmith –penned *Different Drum,* which catapulted both the Poneys and Linda to fame.

In 1969, Linda left the band in pursuit of a career of her own —a career that was not easy to come by. Coming up with a disappointing premiere long-player, Linda's limited success in the early portion of her solo flight came from her live engagements. In 1971, she shifted into second gear and formed a new band which featured soon-to-be-Eagles Glenn Frey, Don Henley, and Randy Meisner. Her third album featured her short-lived group (the Eagles hatched six months later) and proved a turning point in her professional life. Before long, she had two record companies, Capitol and Asylum, bidding for her talent. For a while, she seesawed between the two companies with, happily enough, fantastic result. In 1974, her final Capitol album, *HEART LIKE A WHEEL,* yielded three gold singles. Her first Asylum album, *DON'T CRY NOW,* shot up the charts for a gold album award. Since that time, Linda has been a regular commuter on both the top-ten album and singles listings. And although, of late, she has muted her stage antics a bit . . . she still packs those doe-eyed boys into those concert halls.

Linda Ronstadt and the Stone Poneys Albums/THE STONE PONEYS (3/67): *Sweet Summer Blue and Gold; If I Were You; Just a Little Bit of Rain; Bicycle Song; All the Beautiful Things; Orion; Wild about My Lovin'; Back Home; Meredith (on My Mind); Train and the River; 2:10 Train.* EVERGREEN, VOLUME TWO (6/67): *December Dream; Song about the Rain; I'd*

Like to Know; Autumn Afternoon; Different Drum; Evergreen (2 Parts); Back on the Street Again; Toys in Time; New Hard Times. LINDA RONSTADT: STONE PONEYS AND FRIENDS (4/68): *Up to My Neck in High Muddy Water: other titles.* STONE PONEYS AND FRIENDS, VOLUME III (4/68): *Fragments; Golden Song, Merry-Go-Round, Love Is a Child; By the Fruits of Their Labor; Hobo; Star and a Stone; Let's Get Together; Up to My Neck in High Muddy Water; Aren't You the One; Wings; Stoney End; Some of Shelly's Blues.*

Linda Ronstadt Albums/HAND SOWN ... HOME GROWN (3/69): *Baby, You've Been On My Mind; Silver Threads and Golden Needles; Bet No One Ever Hurt This Bad; A Number and a Name; The Only Mama That'll Walk the Line; The Long Way Around; Break My Mind; I'll Be Your Baby Tonight; It's About Time; We Need a Lot More of Jesus (and a Lot Less Rock & Roll); The Dolphins.* SILK PURSE (3/70): *Lovesick Blues; Are My Thoughts with You?; Will You Love Me Tomorrow?; Louise; Nobodys; Long, Long Time; Mental Revenge; I'm Leavin' It All Up to You; He Dark the Sun; Life Is Like a Mountain Railway.* LINDA RONSTADT (1/72): *Rock Me on the Water; Crazy Arms; I Won't Be Hanging 'Round; I Still Miss Someone; In My Reply; I Fall to Pieces; Ramblin' 'Round; Birds; I Ain't Always Been Faithful; Rescue Me.* DON'T CRY NOW (9/73): *I Can Almost See It; Love Has No Pride; Silver Threads and Golden Needles; Desperado; Sail Away; Colorado; Don't Cry Now; The Fast One; Everybody Loves a Winner; I Believe in You.* DIFFERENT DRUM (1/74): *Different Drum; Rock Me on the Water; I'll Be Your Baby Tonight; Hobo; Stoney End; Long, Long Time; Up to My Neck in High Muddy Water; Some of Shelly's Blues; In My Reply; Will You Love Me Tomorrow?* HEART LIKE A WHEEL (11/74): *You're No Good; It Doesn't Matter Anymore; Faithless Love; The Dark End of the Street; Heart Is Like a Wheel; When Will I Be Loved?; Willing; I Can't Help It (If I'm Still in Love with You); Keep Me from Blowing Away; You Can Close Your Eyes.* PRISONER IN DISGUISE (9/75): *Love Is a Rose; Hey Mister, That's Me Up on the Jukebox; Roll 'Em Easy; Tracks of My Tears; Prisoner in Disguise; Sweetest Gift; Many Rivers to Cross; Heat Wave; You Tell Me That I'm Falling Down; I Will Always Love You; Silver Blue.* HASTEN DOWN THE WIND (8/76): *River of Babylon; Give One Heart; Try Me Again; Crazy; Down So*

Low; Lose Again; If He's Ever Near; That'll Be the Day; The Tattler; Lo Siento Mi Vida; Hasten Down the Wind. LINDA RONSTADT'S GREATEST HITS (12/76): *You're No Good; Silver Threads and Golden Needles; Desperado; Love Is a Rose; That'll Be the Day; Different Drum; When Will I Be Loved?; Love Has No Pride; Heat Wave; It Doesn't Matter Any More; Tracks of My Tears; Long, Long Time.* RETROSPECTIVE (4/77): *When Will I Be Loved?; Silver Threads and Golden Needles; Hobo; I Fall to Pieces; Birds; I Can't Help It (If I'm Still in Love with You); Different Drum; Some of Shelly's Blues; I'll Be Your Baby Tonight; Louise; Long, Long Time; Faithless Love; Rock Me on the Water; Rescue Me; Lovesick Blues; Just a Little Bit of Rain; The Long Way Around; You're No Good; Ramblin' Around; Crazy Arms; It Doesn't Matter Anymore; Will You Love Me Tomorrow?* SIMPLE DREAMS (8/77): *It's So Easy; Carmelita; Simple Man; Sorrow Lives Here; I Never Will Marry; Blue Bayou; Poor Poor Pitiful Me; Maybe I'm Right; Tumbling Dice; Old Paint.*

Singles/*The Long Way Around/The Dolphins* (3/69); *Will You Love Me Tomorrow?/Lovesick Blues* (3/70); *Long, Long Time/Nobodys* (6/70); *She's a Very Lovely Woman/The Long Way Around* (1/71); *I Fall to Pieces/Can It Be True?* (10/71); *Rock Me on the Water/Crazy Arms* (2/72); *Love Has No Pride/I Can Almost See It* (10/73); *Silver Threads and Golden Needles/Don't Cry Now* (1/74); *Colorado/Desperado* (6/74); *You're No Good/I Can't Help It* (11/74); *When Will I Be Loved?/Crazy Arms* (3/75); *When Will I Be Loved?/It Doesn't Matter Anymore* (3/75); *Love Is a Rose/Silver Blue* (8/75); *Heat Wave/Love Is a Rose* (9/75); *Tracks of My Tears/The Sweetest Gift* (12/75); *That Will Be the Day/Try Me Again* (8/76); *Someone to Lay Down Beside Me/Crazy* (11/76); *Lose Again/Lo Siento Mi Vida* (5/77); *Blue Bayou* (9/77); *It's So Easy* (10/77).

ROXY MUSIC/*Bryan Ferry (vocals, keyboards), Andrew Mackay (oboe, saxophone), Eno (synthesizer, tapes), Paul Thompson (drums), Phil Manzanera (guitar), John Porter (bass). Additional members: Edwin Jobson (strings, synthesizer, keyboards), John Gustafson (bass), Rik Kenton (bass).*

The exceedingly "visual" musical style of Roxy Music's demented world is the result of a meeting between art student Bryan Ferry and bassist Graham Stimpson in 1970. Ferry was trying to get a band together that would be eclectic but sound. The following year, Brian Eno, Andy Mackay, Dexter Lloyd, and Davey O'List were added to the ever-changing lineup of the soon-to-be Roxy. Soon O'List, Stimpson, and Lloyd were out, replaced by Thompson, Manzanera, and Kenton.

By 1972, Roxy was captured on wax and the world was greeted by a surreal little entourage that skipped merrily from rock to jazz fusion to satirical Broadway-show crooning. Initial critical reaction was positive to the nth power, and the band's literate style met with a fair amount of public acceptance in the United Kingdom. In the United States, however, Roxy was a bona fide dud. Both their first LP and their second, *FOR YOUR PLEASURE* (with new bassist Porter), were bona fide duds. Warner Brothers cut them out of their active list shortly thereafter.

It was clear that Roxy Music's career was not ascending the popularity charts as quickly as it should. A schism within the band was forming. Ferry, the ever-suave crooner-writer, was pushing the band into a more verbal, intellectually wry area, while Eno pulled the troupe toward an instrumentally challenging rockscape. The argument was settled with Eno's leaving the troupe in 1973.

Eddie Jobson and John Gustafson were enlisted for *STRANDED* and Roxy's career began to soar. Ferry's catchy, melodic ironies took hold on both sides of the Atlantic and Roxy's live show earned them a pocketful of newfound fans. During the fruitful 1973–75 Roxy period of music (topped with the hit single *Love Is the Drug*), several members of the band opted for simultaneous solo careers. Ferry, Mackay, and Manzanera all released long-players of their own, although none fared well saleswise.

As Roxy's future grew rosier, yet another difference of opinion grew, this time between Ferry and Mackay over differences of opinion similar to those once voiced by Ferry and Eno. The tiff resulted in a split of the band in 1976. While the band has never officially called it quits, their only recordings during the past two years have been "in concert" LPs and "best of" collections.

Albums/ROXY MUSIC (10/72): *Re-make/Re-model; Ladytron; If There Is Something; Virginia Plain; 2 H.B.; The Bob; Chance Meeting; Would You Believe; Sea Breezes; Bitters End.* FOR YOUR PLEASURE (5/73): *Do the Strand; Beauty Queen; Strict-*

ly Confidential; In Every Dream Home a Heartache; The Bogus Man; Grey Lagoons; For Your Pleasure. STRANDED (4/74): *Street Life; Just Like You; Amazona; Psalm; Serenade; A Song for Europe; Mother of Pearl; Sunset.* COUNTRY LIFE (12/74): *The Thrill of It All; Three and Nine; All I Want Is You; Out of the Blue; If It Takes All Night; Bitter-Sweet; Triptych; Casanova; A Really Good Time; Prairie Rose.* SIREN (11/75): *Love Is the Drug; End of the Line; Sentimental Fool; Whirlwind; She Sells; Could It Happen to Me?; Both Ends Burning; Nightingale; Just Another High.* VIVA! ROXY MUSIC (7/76): *Out of the Blue; Pyjamarama; The Bogus Band; Chance Meeting; Both Ends Burning; If There Is Something; In Every Dream Home a Heartache; Do the Strand.*

Singles/*Virginia Plain*/*The Numberer* (10/72); *Do the Strand*/*Editions of You* (6/73); *The Thrill of It All*/*Your Application's Failed* (2/75); *Love Is the Drug*/*Both Ends Burning* (11/75).

THE RUNAWAYS/*Original Members: Sandy West (drums and vocals), Cherie Currie (vocals and piano), Jackie Fox (bass and vocals), Joan Jett (guitar and vocals), Lita Ford (lead guitar).*

A profound mixture of hype and mascara, the Runaways were the first batch of girl rock and rollers really to capture the attention of the world at large. (Earlier, Fanny nearly made it, Isis didn't even come close, and Birtha bombed big). The band came together in '75 in L.A. (of course) under the watchful eye of veteran rock hypester/houdini Kim Fowley. Fowley, who has garnered himself a reputation (and rightfully so) of being *truly* crazed, fashioned a group containing young girls, all sixteen and seventeen. The girls, on command, played raunchy, overtly sexual music. In short, it was jailbait with a back-beat. The little boys (and the big boys, for that matter) went wild as the leather-encased, open-shirted batch of girls-next-door hit the road. Seeing the Runaways on stage, wielding their instruments like St. Valentine's Day assassins, was truly stirring, in a variety of ways. From the start, the music industry knew that if these kids made it, they'd make it big, with such show-stopping numbers as *Born to Be Bad, I Love Playin' with Fire, Cherry Bomb,* and *You Drive Me Wild.*

But, by the time their second album, *QUEENS OF NOISE,* was released, the girls were badmouthing Kim and Kim was responding in kind, each accused the other of having a profound

lack of talent. However, a short separation proved that each
needed the other and, as the group began to change members,
Kim returned to the fold.

Albums/THE RUNWAYS (5/76): *Cherry Bomb; You Drive Me
Wild; Is It Day or Is It Night; Thunder; Rock and Roll; Lovers;
American Nights; Black Mail; Secrets; Dead End Justice.*
QUEENS OF NOISE (1/77): *Queens of Noise; Take It or Leave
It; Midnight Music; Born to Be Bad; Neon Angels on the Road to
Ruin; I Love Playin' with Fire; California Paradise; Hollywood;
Hearbeat; Johnny Guitar.* WAITIN' FOR THE NIGHT (10/77):
*Little Sister; Wasted; Gotta Get Out Tonight; Wait for Me; Fan-
tasies; School Days; Trash Can Murders; Don't Go Away; Waitin'
for the Night; You're Too Possessive.*

Singles/*Cherry Bomb/American Nights* (6/76); *Heartbeat/Neon
Angels on the Road to Ruin* (1/77).

TODD RUNDGREN/Todd Rundgren, the multifaceted boy
wonder of rock and roll, emerged victoriously clad in mod apparel from the wilds of Pennsylvania in 1968, leading the pseudo-
British band the Nazz. The veddy English sound of the band
lasted until 1969, when the band toppled under the weight of public apathy. Rundgren immediately threw himself into a career
both as a solo artist (first album bearing his nickname, *RUNT*)
and as a session man-engineer-producer. The highpoint of his career as a solo artist came in 1972 with the release of his epic
SOMETHING/ANYTHING album, a masterfully conceived
two-record set featuring Todd on everything but the kitchen sink,
and launching the hit single *Hello It's Me*. His career as a performer has remained fairly consistent as he performs with his various bands, including the current Utopia enclave.

As a producer-engineer, he has worked with everyone from
Grand Funk Railroad and Paul Butterfield to Meat Loaf.

Albums/RUNT (9/71): *Broke Down and Busted; Believe in Me;
We Got to Get You a Woman; Who's That Man; Once Burned; I'm
in the Clique; There Are No Worlds; Birthday Carol; medley;
Devil's Bite.* SOMETHING/ANYTHING (2/72): *Black Maria;
One More Day; Little Red Lights; Couldn't I Just Tell You; Torch
Song; Piss Aaron; Hello, It's Me; You Left Me Sore; Slut; Some
Folks Is Even Whiter Than Me; Dust in the Wind; Money; I Saw
the Light; Wolfman Jack; Cold Morning Light; Breathless; Saving*

Grace; The Night the Carousel Burned Down; Marlene; I Went to the Mirror; Song of the Viking; Sweeter Memories; Cold; It Wouldn't Have Made Any Difference. A WIZARD, A TRUE STAR (3/73): *Does Anybody Love You; Just One Victory; medley; Hungry for Love; Is It My Name; Flamingo; Zen Archer; Never Never Land; A Wizard, a True Star; Dogfight Giggle; other titles.* TODD (12/73): *Sons of 1984; Don't You Ever Learn; The Spark of Life; Izzat Love; Useless Begging; Sidewalk Cafe; The Last Ride; Drunken Blue Rooster; No. 1 Lowest Common Denominator; Heavy Metal Kids; In and Out of the Chakras We Go; Lord Chancellor's Nightmare Song; A Dream Goes On Forever; I Think You Know; How About a Little Fanfare?; An Elpee's Worth of Toons.* INITIATION (5/75): *Real Man; Prana; The Internal Fire, Parts I, II & III; Born to Synthesize; Death of Rock and Roll; Fair Warning; Initiation; Eastern Intrigue.* FAITHFUL (6/76): *When I Pray; Cliche; Boogie; Rain; Good; The Verb "to Love"; If Six Was Nine; Strawberry Fields Forever; Love of the Common Man; Happening Ten Years Time Ago; Most Likely You'll Go Your Way, I'll Go Mine.*

Utopia Albums: UTOPIA (10/74). ANOTHER LIVE . . . UTOPIA (10/75). RA (1976). OOPS! WRONG PLANET (9/77).

Singles/*I Saw the Light/We Got to Get You a Woman* (10/70); *Be Nice to Me* (3/71); *A Long Time, a Long Way to Go* (8/71); *I Saw the Light/Marlene* (1/72); *Couldn't I Just Tell You/Wolfman Jack* (6/72); *Hello, It's Me/Cold Morning Light* (8/72); *I Saw the Light/We Got to Get You a Woman* (9/72); *Sometimes I Don't Know What to Feel/Does Anybody Love You* (4/73); *A Dream Goes On Forever/Heavy Metal Kids* (2/74); *Real Man* (3/75).

RUSH/*Neil Peart (drums), Geddy Lee (bass and vocals), Alex Lifeson (guitars).*
Rush is a band practically unknown in tastemaker circles but beloved by hundreds of thousands of science-fiction–rock fans in Canada and the United States. The band has successfully bridged the gap between fantasy proper and fantasy rock, emulating the works of Ayn Rand and, generally, slanting their power-trio antics toward ideas of the future. The band had its origins in a North Toronto basement when, awash with world-wide hard-rockitis (Cream, Hendrix, Zep), Alex, Geddy, and original drummer John Rutsey formed the first Rush . . . a bar band that paid

its dues playing in bars, hockey arenas, and high schools. Their first album, *Rush,* was financed independently after every major record label north of the border turned the band down.

An American booking agency, ATI, got wind of the talented trio and arranged a few bookings for them in 1974. Mercury Records saw what was happening and signed the band. By the time an American tour and a label deal were firm, however, Rutsey left and Peart joined immediately. Subsequent albums such as *FLY BY NIGHT, CARESS OF STEEL, ALL THE WORLD'S A STAGE,* and *2112* have pointed to a definite evolution in the Rush sound—one that has pleased their fans. Songs like *Cygnus X-1* (the first part of a proposed science-fiction epic concerning the effects of a black hole in space) and *Anthem* (inspired by Rand's work) have firmly established them as futuristic rockers first class.

Albums/RUSH (8/74): *Finding My Way; Need Some Love; Take a Friend; Here Again; What You're Doing; In the Mood; Before and After; Working Man.* FLY BY NIGHT (2/75): *Anthem; Best I Can; Beneath, Between and Behind; By-Tor and the Snow Dog; Fly by Night; Making Memories; Rivendell; In the End.* CARESS OF STEEL (9/75): *Bastille Day; I Think I'm Going Bald; Lakeside Park; Into Darkness (The Necromancer 1); Under the Shadow (The Necromancer 2); Return to the Prince (The Necromancer 3); In the Valley (The Fountain of Lamneth 1); Didacts and Narpets (The Fountain of Lamneth 2); No One at the Bridge (The Fountain of Lamneth 3); Panacea (The Fountain of Lamneth 4); Bacchus Plateau (The Fountain of Lamneth 5); The Fountain (The Fountain of Lamneth 6).* 2112 (3/76): *Overture: The Temples of Syrinx; Discovery; Presentation; Oracle; The Dream; Soliloquy; Grand Finale; A Passage to Bangkok; The Twilight Zone; Lessons; Tears; Something for Nothing.* ALL THE WORLD'S A STAGE (5/76): *Something for Nothing; Bastille Day; Anthem; Fly By Night/In the Mood; Lakeside Park; What You're Doing; Working Man/Finding My Way; 2112; Overture/The Temples of Syrinx/Presentation/Soliloquy/Grand Finale; By-Tor and the Snow Dog; In the End.* A FAREWELL TO KINGS (9/77): *A Farewell to Kings; Xanadu; Closer to the Heart; Cinderella Man; Madrigal; Cygnus X-1.*

Singles/*Need Some Love/Finding My Way* (9/74); *What You're Doing/In the Mood* (11/74); *Anthem/Fly by Night* (4/75); *Bastille*

Day/Lakeside Park (10/75); *The Twilight Zone/Lessons* (5/76);
Fly by Night—In the Mood/Something for Nothing (11/76); *Making Memories/The Temples of Syrinx* (4/77).

LEON RUSSELL/Oklahoma-born pounder Leon Russell first entered the music scene as a teenage trumpet player, replete with fake ID allowing him to play in liquor-serving clubs in the Tulsa area. He played briefly with Ronnie Hawkins and the Hawks (the Hawks eventually mutated into the Band) before moving out to Los Angeles, where his trumpet-playing and piano-tinkling skills (he had studied classical piano as a tyke) led him to a horde of session jobs. Before long, he was playing guitar as well, playing on most of Phil Spector's L.A. sessions, a few Byrds' tunes, and a Herb Albert album.

In the late sixties, he joined forces with fellow struggling musician Marc Benno and, in 1968, emerged as half of the Asylum Choir, a very Beatle-esque pairing of little or no interest to the public at large. As the Asylum Choir festered, Leon split to join the road show known as Delaney and Bonnie and Friends. His reputation as an instrumentalist was secure and his songwriting abilities were proven when Joe Cocker, at the behest of Russell friend Denny Cordell, cut *Delta Lady*. For Leon Russell, Cocker proved to be a gigantic green light, careerwise.

Playing on and co-producing most of Cocker's sessions from then on, Russell and Cordell grew so friendly that they formed their own label, Shelter, which launched Leon as a solo performer. His first album, *LEON RUSSELL,* was respectable but not commercially spectacular. This situation was soon remedied by Russell's involvement with 1970's Joe Cocker—Mad Dogs and Englishmen tour. Russell virtually ran the epic show. Somewhere along the way, Cocker was lost in the shuffle, with Russell emerging as a superstar on the horizon.

Soon, Leon's raspy voice could be heard from coast to coast via hit albums of his own *(CARNEY, LIVE, LEON RUSSELL AND THE SHELTER PEOPLE)* and on the epic Concert for Bangla Desh LP. In 1973–74, Russell's career began to take a downward slide. His interest in country-western resulted in the disastrous *HANK WILSON'S BACK* (cute cover, though) and his subsequent albums proved commercial goose eggs. In 1976, amidst a flurry of bad feelings, Leon departed Shelter and, together with his new bride, Mary, joined the Warner Brothers roster as part of the duo Leon and Mary Russell.

Albums/LEON RUSSELL (3/70): *A Song for You; Dixie Lullaby; I Put a Spell on You; Shoot Out on the Plantation; Hummingbird; Delta Lady; Old Masters; Prince of Peace; Give Peace a Chance; Pisces Apple Lady; Hurtsome Body; Roll Away the Stone.* LEON RUSSELL AND THE SHELTER PEOPLE (4/71): *Stranger in a Strange Land; Of Thee I Sing; It's a Hard Rain's Gonna Fall; Crystal Closet Queen; Home Sweet Oklahoma; Alcatraz; The Ballad of Mad Dogs and Englishmen; It Takes a Lot to Laugh, It Takes a Train to Cry; She Smiles Like a River; Sweet Emily; Beware of Darkness.* CARNEY (6/72): *Tight Rope; Out in the Woods; Me and Baby Jane; Manhattan Island Serenade; Cajun Love Song; Roller Derby; Carney; Acid Annapolis; If the Shoe Fits; My Cricket; This Masquerade; Magic Mirror.* LIVE (1973): *Delta Lady; Hummingbird; Give Peace a Chance; Mighty Quinn medley; Out in the Woods; Jumpin' Jack Flash; other titles.* HANK WILSON'S BACK (10/73): *Jumbalaya; I'm So Lonesome I Could Cry; The Battle of New Orleans; Goodnight Irene; other titles.* STOP ALL THAT JAZZ (1974): *Mona Lisa Please; Time for Love; Ballad of Hollis Brown; If I Were a Carpenter; Spanish Harlem; other titles.* WILL O' THE WISP (1975): *Will o' the Wisp; Little Hideaway; Make You Feel Good; Can't Get Over Losing You; My Father's Shoes; Stay Away from Sad Songs; Back to the Island; Down on Deep River; Bluebird; Laying Right Here in Heaven; Lady Blue.* WEDDING ALBUM (with Mary Russell; 3/76): *Rainbow in Your Eyes; Like a Dream Come True; Love's Supposed to Be That Way; Satisfy You; You Are on My Mind; Lavender Blue; Quiet Nights; Windsong; Daylight.* MAKE LOVE TO THE MUSIC (6/77): *Easy Love; Joyful Noise; Now Now Boogie; Say You Will; Make Love to the Music; Love Crazy; Love Is in Your Eyes; Hold On to This Feeling; Island in the Sun.*

Singles/*Tight Rope* (7/72); *Queen of the Roller Derby* (8/73); *If I Were a Carpenter* (3/74); *Lady Blue* (7/75); *Rainbow in Your Eyes/Love's Supposed to Be That Way* (4/76); *Satisfy You/Windsong* (9/76); *Love Crazy/Say You Will* (3/77).

MITCH RYDER AND THE DETROIT WHEELS/A brief flash in the late sixties, Mitch Ryder and The Detroit Wheels gave the somnambulistic psychedelic era a double shot of hard-nosed

R&B rock where it needed it most . . . right in the speakers. They went by the name Billy Lee and the Rivieras in Detroit until producer Bob Crewe wisely renamed them. Ryder was one of those white, blue-eyed soul singers who were doing every trick from the fifties R&B handbook. Onstage, he performed a series of choreographed grand mal seizures while the band bumped and ground in the background.

The Detroit Wheels fell apart after a few hits and Mitch found himself a solo performer. Although still a delightfully manic madman onstage, Ryder found himself outclassed by the musical expansiveness of the late sixties and early seventies. After a few unsuccessful releases, it became clear that record companies were just no longer interested in high-voltage sweat music. Mitch faded into the Michigan music scene, doing club work.

In 1977, he resurfaced, talking about a comeback and telling some grisly tales of his past fame and fortune (or conspicuous lack of same).

Albums/JENNY TAKE A RIDE (2/66): *Jenny Take a Ride; Come See about Me; I'll Go Crazy; Please, Please, Please; Shake a Tail Feather; Let Your Lovelight Shine; I Hope; Just a Little Bit; Sticks and Stones; Bring It On Home to Me; Baby Jane (Mo-Mo Jane).* BREAKOUT (7/66): *Little Latin Lupe Lu; Breakout; In the Midnight Hour; Walkin the Dog; I Had It Made; Oo Papa Do; I Like It Like That; You Got Your Kicks; Shakin' with Linda; Stubborn Kind of Fellow; Any Day Now; I Need Help.* SOCK IT TO ME (3/67): *Sock It to Me, Baby; I Can't Hide It; Takin' All I Can Get; Slow Fizz; Walk on By; I Never Had It Better; Shakedown; Face in the Crowd; I'd Rather Go to Jail; Wild Child.* ALL MITCH RYDER'S HITS (9/67): *Joy; Takin' All I Can Get; Sock It to Me, Baby; Devil with the Blue Dress On/Good Golly Miss Molly; Breakout; Jenny Take a Ride; Little Latin Lupe Lu; Too Many Fish in the Sea/Three Little Fishes; In the Midnight Hour.* WHAT NOW MY LOVE (11/67): *What Now My Love; Let It Be Me; I Make a Fool of Myself; Born to Lose; If You Go Away; Whole Lotta Shakin' Goin' On; Sally Go 'Round the Roses; Brown-Eyed Handsome Man; I Need Lovin' You; That's It, I Quit (I'm Movin' On).*

Singles/*Jenny Take a Ride/Baby Jane* (11/65); *Little Latin Lupe Lu/I Hope* (2/66); *Break Out/I Need Help* (5/66); *Takin' All I Can Get/You Got Your Kicks* (7/66); *Devil with a Blue Dress On*

—Good Golly Miss Molly/I Had It Made (9/66); *Sock It to Me, Baby/I Never Had It Better* (1/67); *Too Many Fish in the Sea— Three Little Fishes/One Grain of Sand* (4/67); *Joy/I'd Rather Go to Jail* (6/67); *What Now My Love/Blessing In Disguise* (8/67); *You Are My Sunshine/Wild Child* (9/67); *Personality & Chantilly Lace/I Make a Fool of Myself* (1/68); *Baby, I Need Your Loving/Ring Your Bell* (12/68).

SANTANA/*Carlos Santana (lead guitar, vocals), Greg Walker (vocals), Ndugu Leon Chancler (drums), Amando Paraza (percussion), Francisco Aquabella (percussion), David Brown (bass), Tom Coster (keyboards).*
Carlos Santana's droning, Latin style of guitar work first caught the country by surprise on the album *THE LIVE ADVENTURES OF MIKE BLOOMFIELD AND AL KOOPER.* Shortly thereafter, Carlos, together with Mike Shrieve, Gregg Rolie, David Brown, Mike Carrabello, and Jose Areas recorded the first Santana group album . . . the first overtly commercial blending of rock and Latin influences. The album was a tremendous underground success and, before long, the band hit the AM airwaves with *Black Magic Woman* and *Evil Ways.*
    Born in Mexico, Carlos' musical career started at a young age. His father was a mariachi musician and the Santana household was filled with percussive melodies. Santana's later move to San Francisco occurred during the height of that area's musical expansiveness and it was only natural that Carlos found himself a key ingredient in that scene. Once success had come Santana's way, his formula for hit music began to evolve . . . and this evolution did not always involve the original members of the Santana troupe. As a result, musicians came and went as the Santana sound grew more and more diffused. Carlos' affiliation with John McLaughlin led him to embrace John's Eastern philosophical influences. He soon shelved the Santana band in favor of a new lifestyle, a new melodic slant, and a new name, Divadip. A "new" Carlos Santana (and a new Santana band) emerged with *CARAVANSARI*, a spacey, jazz-latino effort that shook up some of Carlos' early fans and concerned record company executives alike. The group's popularity began to slide as their commercial activity slackened. *LOVE, DEVOTION AND SURRENDER* and *ILLUMINATIONS* established Carlos as an ambitious guitarist

but did not make a dent with the rock crowd. The thirteen-year-old fans did not particularly care that Carlos had seen the light. They came to concerts to get off and not hear about the connection between their lives and the infinite void. (Most of the audience carried their own personal voids in their stash pockets, anyway.) Of late, the band has seen yet another light and, led by a new and improved Carlos, they have attempted a return to the commercial sound of old with mixed success (although record-label veeps can sleep a bit more soundly at night). Carlos is presently managed by rock heavyweight Bill Graham.

Albums/SANTANA (8/69): *Waiting; Evil Ways; Shades of Tune; Savior; Jingo; Persuasion; You Just Don't Care; Soul Sacrifice.* ABRAXAS (9/70): *Singing Winds; Crying Beasts; Black Magic Woman; Gypsy Queen; Oye Como Va; Incident at Neshabur; Se a Cabo; Mother's Daughter; Sama Pa Ti; Hope You're Feeling Better; El Nicoya.* SANTANA (9/71): *Batuka; No One to Depend On; Taboo; Toussaint L'Overture; Everybody's Everything; Guajira; Jungle Strut; Everything's Coming Our Way; Par los Rumberos.* CARAVANSERAI (10/72): *Eternal Caravan; Reincarnation; Waves Within; Look Up; Just in Time to See the Sun; All the Love in the Universe; Future Primative; Stone Flower; Every Step of the Way; La Fuente del Ritmi.* WELCOME (11/73): *Going Home; Love, Devotion and Surrender; Samba de Sausalito; When I Look into Your Eyes; Yours Is the Light; Mother Africa; Lights of Life; Flame-Sky; Welcome.* GREATEST HITS (7/74): *Evil; Jingo; Hope You're Feeling Better; Samba Pa Ti; Persuasions; Black Magic Woman; Everything's Coming Our Way; Oye Coma Va; Si a Cabo; Everybody's Everything.* BORBOLETTA (10/74): *Spring Manifestation; Canto de los Flores; Life in Anew; Give and Take; One with the Sun; Aspirations; Practice What You Preach; Mirage; Here and Now; Flore de Canela; Promise of a Fisherman; Borboletta.* AMIGOS (3/76): *Dance Sister Dance; Take Me with You; Let Me; Gitana; Tell Me Are You Tired; Europa; Let It Shine.* FESTIVAL (1/77): *Carnival; Let the Children Play; Jugando; Give Me Love; Verao Vermelho; Let the Music Set You Free; Revelations; Reach Up; The River; Try a Little Harder; Maria Caracoles.* MOONFLOWER (10/77): *Dawn; Go Within; Carnival; Let the Children Play; Jugando; I'll Be Waiting; Zulu; Bahia; Black Magic Woman; Gypsy Queen; Dance Sister Dance; Europa; She's Not There; Flor d'Luna; Heads, Hands and Feet; El*

Morocco; Transcendence; Savor; Toussaint l'Overture; Soul Sacrifice.

Singles/*Jingo/Persuasion* (10/69); *Evil Ways/Waiting* (12/69); *Jingo/Evil Ways* (9/70); *Black Magic Woman/Hope You're Feeling Better* (10/70); *Oye Coma Va/Samba Pa Ti* (2/71); *Black Magic Woman/Oye Coma Va* (7/71); *Everybody's Everything/Guajira* (9/71); *No One to Depend On/Taboo* (1/72); *All the Love in the Universe* (12/72); *Just in Time to See the Sun* (2/73); *Just in Time to See the Sun/All the Love in the Universe* (2/73); *Everybodys Everything/No One to Depend On* (5/73); *When I Look into Your Eyes/Samba De Sausalito* (1/74); *Samba Pa Ti/Incident at Neshabur* (6/74); *Mirage/Flor de Canela* (11/74); *Give and Take/Life Is Anew* (1/75); *Let It Shine/Tell Me Are You Tired* (4/76); *Dance Sister Dance/Let Me* (6/76); *Europa/Take Me with You* (9/76); *Let the Children Play/Carnival* (2/77); *Give Me Love/Revelations* (4/77).

SAVOY BROWN/*Kim Simmonds (guitar), Tom Farnell (drums), Ian Ellis (bass, vocals), Paul Raymond (guitar, keyboards, vocals). Other members: Chris Youlden (vocals), Bob Hall (piano), Dave Peverett (guitar), Rivers Jobe (bass), Roger Earle (drums), Martin Stone (guitar), Ray Chappel (bass), Bryce Portius (vocals), Tony Stevens (bass), Dave Walker (vocals), Dave Bidwell (drums), Andy Sylvester (bass), Paul Raymond (keyboards), Andy Pyle (bass), Stan Webb (guitar), Eric Dillon (drums), James Leverton (bass), Miller Anderson (drums), Ray Chappel (bass), Leo Mannings (drums).*

The blues-belting sounds of Savoy Brown first originated in 1966 under the title of the Savoy Brown Blues Band. Always a favorite in America, the band has largely been the brainchild of guitarist Kim Simmonds, who has regrouped the boogie-oriented band constantly as his musical perspective has changed. In '66, Savoy was Simmonds, Stone, Chappell, Hall, Portius, and Mannings. By '68, Portius was gone and Youlden was in. In '70, Youlden was a lost cause and Peverett, Earn, and Stevens (who would later form the trio-nucleus of Foghat) were in. The 1971 edition of the band was Bidwell, Sylvester, Raymond, and Walker; in another change, in '73, Pyle was drafted to replace Sylvester. In 74, Savoy Brown was redubbed the Boogie Brothers (Simmonds, Anderson, Webb, Dillon, Leverton) in a fairly brainless attempt to crack the

American market anew. Savoy was reborn in '75 with Farnell, Ellis, and Raymond joining Simmonds for another stab at blues-rock.

Throughout its frantic career, Savoy Brown has always represented the quintessential sound of pile-driving rock and roll. In his own schizoid way, Simmonds has proven himself a hard-rocking genius.

Albums/GETTING TO THE POINT (8/68): *Flood in Houston; Stay with Me, Baby; Honey Bee; The Incredible Gnome Meets Jaxman; Gimme a Penny; Mr. Downchild; Getting to the Point; Big City Lights; You Need Love.* A STEP FURTHER (1/69): *Made Up My Mind; Waiting in the Bamboo Grove; Life's One-Act Play; I'm Tired; Where Am I; Savoy Brown Boogie; Feel So Good, Whole Lotta Shakin' Goin' On, Little Queenie, Purple Hazel, Hernando's Hideaway.* BLUE MATTER (2/69): *Train to Nowhere; Tolling Bells; She's Got a Ring in His Nose and a Ring on His Hand; Vicksberg Blues; Don't Turn Me from Your Door; May Be Wrong; Louisiana Blues; It Hurts Me Too.* RAW SIENNA (3/70); *A Hard Way to Go; That Same Feelin'; Master Hare; Needle and Spoon; A Little More Wine; I'm Crying; Stay While the Night Is Young; Is That So; When I Was a Young Boy.* LOOKING IN (4/71): *Gypsy; Poor Girl; Money Can't Save Your Soul; Sunday Night; Looking In; Take It Easy; Sitting an' Thinking; Leavin' Again; Romanoff.* STREET CORNER TALKING (8/71): *Tell Mama; I Can't Get Next to You; Let It Rock; Time Does Tell; Street Corner Talking; All I Can Do; Wang Dang Doodle.* HELLBOUND TRAIN (2/72): *Doin' Fine; Lost and Lonely Child; I'll Make Everything Alright; Troubled by These Days and Times; If I Could See an End; It'll Make You Happy; Hellbound Train.* LION'S SHARE (9/72); *Shot in the Head; Second Try; The Saddest Feeling; I Can't Find You; Howling for My Darling; So Tired; Denim Demon; Love Me Please; Hate to See You Go.* JACK THE TOAD (5/73): *Coming Down Your Way; Ride on, Babe; Hold Your Fire; If I Want To; Endless Sleep; Casting My Spell; Just Cos' You Got the Blues Don't Mean You Gotta Sing; Some People; Jack the Toad.* BOOGIE BROTHERS (3/74); *Highway Blues; Me and the Preacher; My Love's Lying Down; You Don't Love Me; Always the Same; Everybody Loves a Drinking Man; Rock 'n' Roll Star; Boogie Brothers; Threegy Blues.* WIRE FIRE (10/75): *Put Your Hands Together; Stranger Blues;*

Here Comes the Music; Ooh, What a Feeling; Hero to Zero; Deep Water; Can't Get On; Born into Pain. SKIN 'N' BONE (3/76): *Get On Up and Do It; Part Time Lady; This Day Is Gonna Be Our Last; She's the One; Skin 'n' Bone; Walkin' and Talkin'.* THE BEST OF SAVOY BROWN (1/77): *Train to Nowhere; Louisiana Blues; I'm Tired; Needle and Spoon; A Hard Way to Go; Tell Mama; Hellbound Train; Wang Dang Doodle.*

Singles/*Shake 'Em On Down (Parts I and II)* (10/68); *Grits Ain't Groceries/She's Got a Ring in His Nose and a Ring on His Hand* (3/69); *Train to Nowhere/Made Up My Mind* (7/69); *I'm Tired/Stay with Me, Baby* (10/69); *A Hard Way to Go/The Incredible Gnome Meets Jaxman* (3/70); *Sitting and Thinking/That Same Feelin'* (3/71); *Everybody Loves a Drinking Man/Ride On, Babe* (5/74); *Coming Down Your Way/I Can't Find You* (7/74).

LEO SAYER/Leo Sayer started his musical career as a sad-faced harlequin and wound up rising to stardom as a squeaky-voiced, high-stepping disco king. In 1972, the British singer-songwriter teamed with songwriter-musician David Courtney and began to write tunes in earnest. This pairing led to a commitment from manager Adam Faith, no slough in the singing category himself. Before too long, the songwriting pair were earning themselves quite a reputation through the efforts of Who vocalist Roger Daltry, who championed their cause via his first solo album, *DALTRY,* (produced by Faith and Courtney).

Soon Sayer emerged as a delicate, sad-faced singer on *SILVERBIRD,* one of his finest albums to date. A single by Leo, *The Show Must Go On,* was covered by Three Dog Night and became a hit (one of that group's last). Leo enjoyed success of his own with *Long Tall Glasses* from his gold album *JUST A BOY* but, within a year, record moguls feared that the waiflike qualities of Sayer might be overshadowed by the slick, glitzy pop sound of '75–'76. Producer Richard Perry was called in. Sayer and Courtney parted ways. A new, slicker, more commercial disco-oriented Leo emerged, replete with top-tenning tunes and falsetto crooning. While today Leo Sayer is certainly a hit "commodity" in terms of record sales, quite a bit of the *SILVERBIRD* magic has been sacrificed in the process of starmaking.

Albums/SILVERBIRD (12/73): *Innocent Bystander; Goodnight, Old Friend; Drop Back; Silverbird; The Show Must Go On; The*

Dancer; Tomorrow; Don't Say It's Over; Slow Motion; Oh Wot a Life; Why Is Everybody Going Home. JUST A BOY (1/75): *Telepath; Train; The Bells of St. Mary's; One Man Band; In My Life; When I Came Home This Morning; Long Tall Glasses; Another Time; Solo; Giving It All Away.* ANOTHER YEAR (9/75): *Bedsitterland; The Last Gig of Johnny B. Goode; On the Old Dirt Road; I Will Not Stop Fighting; Moonlighting; Streets of Your Town; Only Dreaming; The Kid's Grown Up; Another Year.* ENDLESS FLIGHT (10/76): *Hold On to My Love; You Make Me Feel Like Dancing; Reflections; When I Need You; No Business Like Love Business; I Hear the Laughter; Magdalena; How Much Love; I Think We Fell in Love Too Fast; Endless Flight.* THUNDER IN MY HEART (9/77): *Thunder in My Heart; Easy to Love; Leave Well Enough Alone; I Want You Back; It's Over; Fool for Your Love; World Keeps On Turning; There Isn't Anything; Everything I've Got; We Can Start All Over Again.*

Singles/*The Show Must Go On*/*Innocent Bystander* (1/74); *Long Tall Glasses*/*In My Life* (10/74); *Telepath*/*The Bells of St. Mary's* (5/75); *Moonlighting*/*The Streets of Your Town* (10/75); *You Make Me Feel Like Dancing*/*Magdelena* (9/76); *When I Need You*/*I Think We Fell in Love Too Fast* (2/77); *Thunder in My Heart* (9/77); *Easy to Love* (11/77).

BOZ SCAGGS/Before opting for blue-eyed soul, William Royce Scaggs was an Ohio-born, Texas-bred rock and roll lover. Starting out as a teenage singer in classmate Steve Miller's high school combo, the Marksmen, he was introduced to guitar by the future Joker. In college at Madison, Wisconsin, the Miller-Scaggs combination proved lethal in a band called the Ardells. After their college years, the twosome parted ways and Scaggs eventually found his way to England, where he attempted to launch a career as an R&B musician in a country already brimming with R&B and blues bands.

Eventually Scaggs began traveling across the Continent in the mid-sixties as a folksinger, cutting one album in Sweden. Returning to America in 1967, he joined the original Steve Miller Band in San Francisco. The premier psychedelic guitar band, Scaggs and Miller led the entourage into new and uncharted realms via *CHILDREN OF THE FUTURE* and *SAILOR*. Then Scaggs left the band to pursue a solo career.

He drifted from style to style and label to label, finally touching base at Columbia Records with a slick R&B style totally removed from both his Miller work and his fantastic (although hesitant) early efforts on his own *(BOZ SCAGGS, MOMENTS)*. Boz usually performs with a big band these days, complete with shoo-wopping female chorus and three-piece suit.

Albums/BOZ SCAGGS (8/69): *I'm Easy; I'll Be Long Gone; Another Day (Another Letter); Now You're Gone; Finding Her; Look What I Got; Waiting for a Train; Loan Me a Dime; Sweet Release.* MOMENTS (2/71): *We Were Always Sweethearts; Downright Woman; Painted Bells; Alone Alone; Near You; I Will Forever Sing the Blues; Moments; Hollywood Blues; We Been Away; Can I Make It Last.* BOZ SCAGGS AND BAND (11/71): *Monkey Time; Runnin' Blue; Up to You; Love Away; Flames of Love; Here to Stay; Nothing Will Take Your Place; Why Why; You're So Good.* SLOW DANCER (2/74): *You Make It So Hard; Slow Dancer; Angel; Lady; There Is Someone Else; Hercules; Pain of Love; Let It Happen; Sail on, White Moon; I Got Your Number; Take It for Granted.* SILK DEGREES (1/76): *What Can I Say; Georgia; Jump Street; What Do You Want the Girl to Do; Harbor Lights; Lowdown; It's Over; Love Me Tomorrow; Lido Shuffle; We're All Alone.* DOWN TWO THEN LEFT (12/77): *Still Falling for You; Hard Times; A Clue; Whatcha Gonna Tell Your Man; We're Waiting; Hollywood; Then She Walked Away; Gimme the Goods; 1993; Tomorrow Never Came; Tomorrow Never Came (reprise).*

Singles/*I'll Be Long Gone/I'm Easy* (10/69); *We Were Always Sweethearts/Painted Bells (3/71); Near You/Downright Woman* (7/71); *Runnin' Blue/Here to Stay* (1/72); *Dinah Flo* (8/72); *You Make It Hard/There Is Someone Else* (3/74); *Slow Dancer/Pain of Love* (9/74); *It's Over/Harbor Lights* (3/76); *Lowdown/Harbor Lights* (6/76); *What Can I Say/We're All Alone* (11/76); *Lido Shuffle/We're All Alone* (2/77); *Hard Times* (11/77).

SEALS AND CROFTS/The mild-mannered sounds of Seals and Crofts, present tense, is a far cry from their low-down and nasty days as members of the rock group the Champs, who vaulted into the top ten with the mindless hit single *Tequila* in 1958. After the Champs folded nearly ten years later, Seals and Crofts found god via the Baha'i faith and a solo career of their own, brotherhood-oriented design. Officially pairing in 1970, they became a popular college-campus attraction with their mandolin-backed tales of good vibes, organic living, and nice-niceness.

After two moderately successful albums, they moved to Warner Brothers records, where the Texas-born duo have garnered gold and platinum record awards via such hit singles as *Summer Breeze* and *Diamond Girl.* Jim Seals and Dash Crofts deal in music that is practically void of any controversial themes (although they did raise a rukus with their anti-abortion *UNBORN CHILD* LP, an album that some felt should have been aborted itself and is as palatable as can be. They are very nice.

So is Jello.

Albums/YEAR OF SUNDAY (11/71): *When I Meet Them; 'Cause You Love; Paper Airplanes; Year of Sunday; Antoinette; High on a Mountain; Irish Linen; Sudan Village; Ancient of the Old; Springfield Mill.* SUMMER BREEZE (7/72): *Hummingbird; Summer Breeze, East of Ginger Trees; Say; Funny Little Man; Fiddle in the Sky; Boy Down the Road; Yellow Dirt; Advance Guards; The Euphrates.* DIAMOND GIRL (3/73): *Diamond Girl; Wisdom; Dust on My Saddle; Jessica; It's Gonna Come Down; Standin' on a Mountain Top; Nine Houses; Intone My Servant; We May Never Pass This Way Again; Ruby Jean and Billie Lee.* UN-BORN CHILD (2/74): *Windflowers; Unborn Child; Desert People; Dance by the Light of the Moon; The Story of Her Love; Rachel; Ledges; Big Mac; Follow Me; King of Nothing; 29 Years from Texas.* SEALS AND CROFTS I and II (7/74): *Ridin' Thumb; Robin; Purple Hard; Cotton Mouth; Leave; Granny, Will Your Dog Bite; Today; Gabriel, Go On Home; Tin Town; Hollow Reed; Hand-Me-Down Shoes.* I'LL PLAY FOR YOU (12/74): *I'll Play for You; Truth Is But a Woman; Castles in Sand; Golden Rainbow; other titles.* GREATEST HITS (10/75): *Hummingbird; Diamond Girl; Unborn Child; Summer Breeze; We May Never Pass This Way Again; other titles.* GET CLOSER (3/76): *Baby Blue; Don't Fail; Million-Dollar Horse; Passing Thing; Red Long Ago; Goodbye, Old Buddie; Sweet Green Fields.* SUDAN VIL-LAGE (11/76): *Sudan Village; Advance Guards; Cause You Love; Baby, I'll Give It to You; Thunderfoot; East of Ginger Trees; Put Your Love in My Hands; Ark Traveler; Eighth of January.* ONE ON ONE (soundtrack); (9/77): *My Fair Share; This Day Belongs to Me; Janet's Theme; Picnic; Flyin'; Reflections; Love Conquers*

All; It'll Be All Right; Hustle; Time Out; The Party; The Basketball Game; This Day Belongs to Me (reprise).

Singles/*Summer Breeze/East of Ginger Trees* (6/72); *Diamond Girl/Wisdom* (3/73); *We May Never Pass This Way Again/Jessica* (8/73); *Unborn Child/Ledges* (1/74); *King of Nothing/Follow Me* (4/74); *I'll Play for You/Truth Is But a Woman* (1/75); *Castles in the Sand/Golden Rainbow* (7/75); *Get Closer/Don't Fail* (2/76); *Advance Guards/Baby I'll Give It All to You* (9/76); *Good Bye Old Buddie/Baby Blue* (1/77).

JOHN SEBASTIAN/New York–born folkie John Sebastian got his first taste of fame in 1965 when he formed the Lovin' Spoonful. Three years and several gold records later, Sebastian parted ways with the band and, moving to Los Angeles, he embarked on a solo career that was so low-keyed it was almost considered catatonic. In 1969, he appeared at the Woodstock festival and won over the hearts (but definitely not the minds) of the blissed-out crowd. A recording deal with Warner-Reprise resulted and led to a career that has appealed mostly to a diehard bunch of tie-dyers.

His biggest success came in 1976 when he reached number-one status with a recording of his theme song for the popular TV show, *Welcome Back, Kotter,* entitled (logically enough) *Welcome Back.*

Albums/JOHN B. SEBASTIAN (2/70): *Red Eye Express; She's a Lady; What She Thinks About; Magical Connection; You're a Big Boy Now; Rainbows All Over Your Blues; How Have You Been; Fa-Fana-Fa; I Had a Dream; The Room Nobody Lives In.* CHEAPO CHEAPO PRODUCTIONS PRESENT THE REAL LIVE JOHN SEBASTIAN (4/71): *Rooty Toot; Nashville Cats; Blue Suede Shoes; My Gal; Younger Generation; Amy's Theme; Goodnight Irene; Did You Ever Have to Make Up Your Mind; Younger Girl, other titles.* FOUR OF US (8/71): *Well, Well, Well; Black Snake Blues; I Don't Want Nobody Else; Apple Hill; We'll See; Sweet Muse; The Four of Us; Black Sailin' Kid.* TARZANA KID (9/74): *Harpoon, Sportin' Life; Singing the Blues; Wild Flower; Sitting in Limbo; Friends Again; Dixie Chicken; Stories We Could Tell; Face of Appalachia; Wild about My Lovin'.* WELCOME BACK (4/76): *Hideaway; She's Funny; You Go Your Way* *and I'll Go Mine; One Step Forward, Two Steps Back; Didn't Wanna Have to Do It; Let This Be Our Time to Get Along; A Song a Day in Nashville; I Needed Her Most When I Told Her to Go; Welcome Back; Warm Baby.*

Singles/*Magical Connection/Fa-Fana-Fa* (4/70); *What She Thinks About/Red Eye Express* (5/70); *I Don't Want Nobody Else/Sweet Muse* (7/71); *Well, Well, Well/We'll See* (10/71); *Give Us a Break/Music for People Who Don't Speak English* (2/72); *Welcome Back/Warm Baby* (2/76); *Hideaway/One Step Forward, Two Steps Back* (5/76).

THE SEEDS/*Sky Saxon (lead vocals), Daryl Hooper (piano, organ), Jan Savage (guitar), Rick Andridge (drums).*

One hit a career does not make. You and I may know that, but the Seeds didn't. The Seeds were a Los Angeles group that, in the wake of the 1967 flower power movement, followed up with flower music . . . sort of. *Pushin' Too Hard* was their hit. Countless other songs were their misses. When flower power faded, so did the Seeds. Sky Saxon attempted to refurbish their career by jumping on de blooze bandwagon, changing their name to the Sky Saxon Blues Band. Millions of fans replied with a terse "tee hee," and the Seeds went down the tubes.

Albums/THE SEEDS (6/66): *Can't Seem to Make You Mine; No Escape; Lose Your Mind; Evil Voodoo; Girl, I Want You; Pushin' Too Hard; Try to Understand; Nobody Spoil My Fun; It's a Hard Life; You Can't Be Trusted; Excuses, Excuses; Fallin' in Love.* WEB OF SOUND (10/66): *The Farmers; Tripmaker; Pictures and Designs; I Tell Myself; Faded Pictures; Rollin' Machine; Just Let Go; Up in Her Room.* FUTURE (8/67): *Thousand Shadows; March of the Flower Children; Travel with Your Mind; Painted Doll; Flower Lady and Her Assistant; Six Dreams; Out of the Question; Where Is the Entrance; Way to Play; Now a Man; Two Fingers Pointing on You; Fallin'.* SKY SAXON BLUES BAND: FULL SPOON OF SEEDY BLUES (1967): *Pretty Girl; Moth and the Flame; I'll Help You; Cry World; Plain Spoken; Gardner; One More Time Blues; Creepin' About; Buzzin' Around.* MERLIN'S MUSIC BOX (12/67): *Mr. Farmer; No Escape; Satisfy You; Up in Her Room; Night Time Girl; Gypsy Plays His*

Drums; Can't Seem to Make You Mine; Mumble Bumble; Nine Million Daily Making Love; Forest outside Your Door; Pushin' Too Hard.

Singles/*Pushin' Too Hard*/*Try to Understand* (11/66); *Mr. Farmer*/*No Escape* (2/67); *Can't Seem to Make You Mine*/*Daisey Mae* (4/67); *A Thousand Shadows*/*March of the Flower Children* (6/67); *Six Dreams*/*Wind Blows Your Hair* (1967).

BOB SEGER/Until recently, the king of raunch and roll, Detroit's own Bob Seger, was one of the best-kept secrets in rock and roll. A long-time staple of Motor City's mad diet of hard-rock delights, long-haired, raspy-voiced Seger just didn't get the breaks needed to punch his way into the nation's top-seller charts. He began his professional career in 1966 and released an initial single, *Heavy Music.* The tune proved a hit despite the collapse of Seger's record company, Cameo Parkway.

Unable to come up with a second "hit," Seger was considered a one-shot artist in some circles. He made a series of albums for Capitol Records which got nowhere fast and, by 1969, Seger was discouraged enough to put his guitar in mothballs for a college education (nice way of avoiding the draft, too). Out of school in '71, growling Bob jumped head first back into hard rock with a new band (aided by a host of Detroit pals including Teegarden and Van Winkle) and a new label (Warner-Reprise).

Two more LPs on Warners and Seger was again left out in the cold. Although critically acclaimed, his rough and tumble style just didn't catch on anywhere in the country but the MidWest. Seger was in the unique position of being a headlining attraction in Detroit and a complete unknown in other parts of the nation. He switched to Capitol Records and cut the universally praised *BEAUTIFUL LOSER* album in 1975. For once, Seger was in the right place at the right time. Although still a powerhouse of grit, *BEAUTIFUL LOSER* proved that Seger could be introspective and melodic as well.

The album went gold and its live followup, the double LP *LIVE BULLET,* went top five. Subsequent releases have consistently hit the top twenty in both the album and the single charts. At this point in his career, gravel-throated Seger doesn't seem to have to worry about a thing. He's still the toast of Detroit but, nowadays, he's a headliner wherever he goes. After a dozen or so years in the music business, Bob Seger has become an overnight sensation.

Albums/RAMBLIN' GAMBLIN' MAN (12/68): *Ramblin' Gamblin' Man; Tales of Lucy Blue; Ivory; Gone; Down Home; Train Man; White Wall; Black-Eyed Girl; 2+2=?; Doctor Fine; The Last Song (Love Needs to be Loved).* NOAH (9/69). MONGREL (8/70): *Song to Rufus; Evil Edna; Highway Child; Big River; Mongrel; Lucifer; Teachin' Blues; Leanin' on My Dream; Mongrel Too; River Deep—Mountain High.* BRAND NEW MORNING (10/71). SMOKIN' O.P.'s (9/72): *Bo Diddley; Love the One You're With; If I Were a Carpenter; Hummin' Bird; Let It Rock; Turn On your Love Light; Jesse James; Someday; Heavy Music.* BACK IN '72; (1/73): *Midnight Rider; So I Wrote You a Song; Stealer; Rosalie; Turn the Page; Back in '72; Neon Sky; I've Been Workin'; I've Got Time.* BOB SEGER 7 (3/74): *Get Out of Denver; Long Song Comin'; Need Ya; School Teacher; Cross of Gold; UMC; All Your Love; 20 Years from Now; Seen a Lot of Floors.* BEAUTIFUL LOSER (3/75): *Beautiful Loser; Black Night; Katmandu; Jody Girl; Travelin' Man; Momma; Nutbush City Limits; Sailing Nights; Fine Memory.* LIVE BULLET (4/76): *Nutbush City Limits; Travelin' Man; Beautiful Loser; Jody Girl; Lookin' Back; Get Out of Denver; Let It Rock; I've Been Working; Turn the Page; UMC; Bo Diddley; Ramblin' Gamblin' Man; Heavy Music: Katmandu.* NIGHT MOVES (10/76): *Rock and Roll Never Forgets; Night Moves; The Fire Down Below; Sunburst; Sunspot Baby; Mainstreet; Come to Poppa; Ship of Fools; Mary Lou.* STRANGER IN TOWN (5/78). *Hollywood Nights; Still the Same; Old Time Rock and Roll; Till It Shines; Feel Like a Number; Ain't Got No Money; We've Got Tonite; Brave Strangers; The Famous Final Scene.*

Singles/*Heavy Music* (1966); *2+2=?/Death Row* (2/68); *Ramblin' Gamblin' Man/Tales of Lucy Blue* (10/68); *Ivory/The Last Song* (4/69); *Noah/Lennie Johnson* (7/69); *Innervenus Eyes/Lonely Man* (10/69); *Lucifer/Big River* (2/70); *Lookin' Back/Highway Child (9/71);* *Turn On Your Love Light/Who Do You Love* (9/72); *Rosalie/Neon Sky* (2/73); *Need Ya/Seen a Lot of Floors* (8/73); *Get Out of Denver/Long Song Comin'* (5/74); *UMC/This Old House* (10/74); *Beautiful Loser/Fine Memory* (4/75); *Nutbush City Limits/Travelin' Man* (11/75); *Nutbush City Limits/Lookin' Back* (5/76); *Beautiful Loser/Travelin' Man* (7/76); *Night Moves/Ship of Fools* (11/76); *Main Street/Jody Girl* (4/77); *Rock and Roll Never Forgets/The Fire Down Below* (6/77).

THE SEX PISTOLS/*Johnny Rotten (lead vocals, spitting), Steve Jones (guitar), Sid Vicious (bass), Paul Cook (drums), Glen Matlock (bassist in exile).*
The most infamous of all punk rock bands, the Sex Pistols came about in Britain in 1975 via a traumatic series of anarchistic concert gigs and general mayhem. Known for their totally iconoclastic musical stance, the Sex Pistols started the Punk Rock wave almost single-handedly, throwing out any and all rules required by the music business. Audiences were spat upon, record executives razzed, and national figures debased via some tremendously uncommercial singles. As a result of all of the aforementioned traits, the Sex Pistols nearly got left behind once the Punk Rock "explosion" occurred in the United Kingdom. While peer groups such as the Stranglers, the Clash, the Damned, and the Jam quickly signed up with other labels and were promptly labeled as the "new" Doors, the "new" Who, etc., the Sex Pistols remained unclassifiable and untouched. A contract with EMI Records in late 1976 led to their being bounced in early 1977 with only one single, *God Save the Queen,* to their credit. A second recording contract in the spring of 1977 with A&M led to their being dropped less than two weeks later. Nasty chaps, these Sex Pistols. Finally, Warner Brothers intervened. By the end of 1977, the Sex Pistols' debut album was unleashed on both sides of the Atlantic. Their career in the U.K. was furthered by the release, although neither the album nor their truncated first American tour in January of 1978 made much noise stateside.
Album/NEVER MIND THE BOLLOCKS HERE'S THE SEX PISTOLS (12/77): *Liar; God Save the Queen; No Feelings; Pretty Vacant; New York; Seventeen; Anarchy in the U.K.; Bodies; EMI; Sub-Mission; Problems; Holidays in the Sun.*

SF-ROCK/Science fiction (SF) rock is a nickname for a fairly covert musical movement started in the early seventies by such artists as David Bowie and Yes. By transposing concepts of science fiction literature into the field of rock and roll, a new and exciting form of lyrical and melodic expression was offered by a few futuristic artists. *THE RISE AND FALL OF ZIGGY STARDUST AND THE SPIDERS FROM MARS* and *SPACE ODYSSEY* stand out as early examples of this flexible format.
The field has progressed since then, most notably by groups

like Rush (*2112*), Alan Parsons (*I ROBOT*), Wings (*VENUS AND MARS*), Meco (*STAR WARS, THE TIME MACHINE*), Kiss, Angel, Parliament-Funkadelic, and Spirit. The lyrical clout usually rests in the individual group's concept of the future (from a Brave New World to A Grave New World) and the musical spaciness is, for the most part, conjured up by electronic instruments.

SHAKTI/During a hiatus in his recording with the on-again, off-again Mahavishnu Orchestra, John McLaughlin brought forth the short-lived Shakti, a group which relied heavily on traditional Indian music. The band's album releases were slow in coming, although their concerts have been well received. At present, their future is in limbo as McLaughlin plans further Mahavishnu projects.

Albums/SHAKTI (4/76): *Joy (Parts One through Four); Lotus Feet; What Need Have I for This—What Need Have I for That—I am Dancing at the Feet of My lord—All Is Bliss—All Is Bliss (Parts One through Five).* JOHN MCLAUGHLIN AND SHAKTI (9/76): *La Danse de Bonhur; Lady L; India; Krite; Isis; Two Sisters.*

CARLY SIMON/Carly Simon's music personifies the word "slick." Everything about her career, from album-cover design to lush string arrangements, has been carefully planned . . . designed to achieve the optimum effect. And, judging from the mountains of gold records the songstress has amassed since 1971, her formula for success has been 100 percent effective.

Born in New York, Carly grew up in an affluent publishing family. She attended Sarah Lawrence College where she first began to perform before audiences as one-half of the Simon Sisters (the other half being Lucy Simon). After graduation, she traveled to France where she met Bob Dylan's manager, Albert Grossman. Albert, being a visionary, sought to mold Carly's career into that of a female Dylan. In 1966, Grossman ensnared long-time Dylan associate Bob Johnston to produce Carly's first album. The result was a lot of hard feelings all around, a split between Carly and Albert and, eventually, her signing with Elektra Records in 1969.

Carly's first album, *CARLY SIMON,* firmly established her as the Queen of Fluff, offering layers of breathy lyrics and soft melodies. Lyrically, Carly was given an able assist by good friend Jacob Brackman, a columnist for *Esquire*. The pair has penned some of Carly's more memorable tunes. In 1973, Carly married James Taylor, which cut down on her already sparse touring appearances. Today, she is a dutiful mother, a full-fledged recording star, and a devoted wife. And if she doesn't want to give all that up to play before twenty thousand screaming fans in a stuffy concert hall . . . well, who's going to argue logic?

Albums/CARLY SIMON (2/71): *That's the Way I Always Heard It Should Be; Alone; One More Time; The Best Thing; Just a Sinner; Dan, My Fling; Another Door; Reunions; Rolling Down the Hills; The Love's Still Growing.* ANTICIPATION (11/71): *Anticipation; Legend in Your Own Time; Our First Day Together; The Girl You Think You See; Summer's Coming Around Again; Share the End; The Garden; Three Days; Julie through the Glass; I've Got to Have You.* NO SECRETS (11/72): *Right Thing to Do; The Carter Family; You're So Vain; His Friends Are More Than Fond of Robin; We Have No Secrets; Embrace Me, You Child; Waited So Long; It Was So Easy; Night Owl; When You Close Your Eyes.* HOTCAKES (1/74): *Safe and Sound; Mind on My Man; Think I'm Gonna Have a Baby; Misfit; Forever; My Love; Mockingbird; Grownup; Haven't Got Time for the Pain; Hotcakes; Just Not True; Older Sister.* PLAYING POSSUM (4/75): *After the Storm; Love Out on the Street; Look Me in the Eyes; More and More; Slave; Attitude Dancing; Sons of Summer; Waterfall; Are You Ticklish; Playing Possum.* THE BEST OF CARLY SIMON (11/75): *That's the Way I've Always Heard It Should Be; The Right Thing to Do; Mockingbird; Legend in Your Own Time; Haven't Got Time for the Pain; You're So Vain; No Secrets; Night Owl; Anticipation; Attitude Dancing.* ANOTHER PASSENGER (6/76): *Half a Chance/It Keeps You Running; Fairweather Father; Cow Town; He Likes to Roll; In Times When My Head; One Love Stand; Riverboat Gambler; Darkness 'til Dawn; Libby; Be with Me; Dishonest Modesty.*

Singles/*That's the Way I've Always Heard It Should Be/Alone* (3/71); *Anticipation/The Garden* (11/71); *Legend in Your Own Time/Julie through the Glass* (2/72); *The Girl You Think You See/Share the End* (6/72); *You're So Vain/His Friends Are More Than Fond of Robin* (6/72); *The Right Thing to Do/We Have No Secrets* (3/73); *Mockingbird* (with James Taylor)/*Grownup*

(1/74); *Haven't Got Time for the Pain/Mind on My Man* (4/74); *Attitude Dancing/Are You Ticklish* (4/75); *Waterfall/After the Storm* (6/75); *More and More/Love Out in the Street* (9/75); *It Keeps You Runnin'/Be with Me* (5/76); *Half a Chance/Libby (8/76).*

PAUL SIMON/A native of Newark, New Jersey, Paul Simon is a living legend in the music world. As half of Simon and Garfunkel, he literally revolutionized the commercial folk idiom, taking balladeering from a straight, acoustic realm to a lavish, complexly arranged, harmonious one. After splitting with Garfunkel in 1970, Simon began a solo career that seemed to be in almost open rebellion against the lush sounds of the MOR (middle-of-the-road) oriented duo. His songs became personal statements and, at times, statements filled with wry, brazen humor. As a solo artist, Simon displays remarkable versatility; relying on sparse, to-the-point arrangements, he successfully jumps from emotionally jarring ballads to uptempo tunes and pseudo-gospel numbers. He is both introspective and outgoing. He is, perhaps, America's consummate pop artist.

Albums/MOTHER AND CHILD REUNION (1/72): *Mother and Child Reunion; Duncan; Everything Put Together Falls Apart; Run That Body Down; Armistice Day; Me and Julio Down by the Schoolyard; Hobo's Blues; Papa Hobo; Paranoia Blues; Congratulations.* THERE GOES RHYMIN' SIMON (5/73): *Kodachrome; Tenderness; Take Me to the Mardi Gras; Something So Right; One Man's Ceiling Is Another Man's Floor; American Tune; Was a Sunny Day; Learn How to Fall; St. Judy's Comet; Loves Me Like a Rock.* PAUL SIMON IN CONCERT (3/74): *Me and Julio Down by the Schoolyard; Homeward Bound; American Tune; El Condor Pasa (If I could); Duncan; The Boxer; Mother and Child Reunion; The Sounds of Silence; Jesus Is the Answer; Bridge over Troubled Water; Loves Me Like a Rock; American Tune.* STILL CRAZY AFTER ALL THESE YEARS (3/76): *Still Crazy after All These Years; My Little Town; I Do It for Your Love; 50 Ways to Leave Your Lover; Night Games; Gone At Last; Some Folks' Lives Roll Easy; Have a Good Time; You're Kind; Silent Eyes.* PAUL SIMON'S GREATEST HITS, ETC. (11/77): *Slip Slidin' Away; Stranded in a Limousine; Still Crazy after all These Years; Kodachrome; Duncan; 50 Ways to Leave Your Lover;*

Me and Julio Down by the Schoolyard; I Do It for Your Love; Have a Good Time; Something So Right; American Tune; Mother and Child Reunion; Loves Me Like a Rock; Take Me to the Mardi Gras.

Singles/*Mother and Child Reunion/Paranoia Blues* (1/72); *Me and Julio Down by the Schoolyard/Congratulations* (3/72); *Duncan/Run That Body Down* (6/72); *Loves Me Like a Rock/Learn How to Fall* (7/73); *American Tune/One Man's Ceiling Is Another Man's Floor (11/73); Loves Me Like a Rock/Kodachrome* (4/74); *Gone At Last/Take Me to the Mardi Gras* (8/74); *50 Ways to Leave Your Lover/Some Folks' Lives Roll Easy* (12/75); *Still Crazy after All These Years/I Do It for Your Love* (4/76); *Gone At Last/My Little Town* (11/76); *50 Ways to Leave Your Lover/Still Crazy after All These Years* (11/76); *Slip Slidin' Away* (10/77).

SIMON AND GARFUNKEL/Everybody loves a Cinderella story and Simon and Garfunkel are it. In 1957, when everything in rock is Elvis, these two precocious sixteen-year-old schoolboys in Queens, New York, come up with a hit, *Hey Schoolgirl.* They have flattop haircuts and call themselves Tom and Jerry. They get to play on Dick Clark's *American Bandstand* show. But they turn out to be more or less a one-hit wonder, and within a year they're has-beens. They adjust as well as can be expected. Years later, it's the sixties folk boom and Bob Dylan has just made *Blowin' in the Wind* and *The Times They Are a Changin'.* The two boys, now calling themselves Simon and Garfunkel, make a folk album with Dylan songs and some Simon songs on it. They call it *WEDNESDAY MORNING, 3 A.M.* Well, no one's heard of Simon and Garfunkel and late in 1964 everyone and his brother is recording Dylan, so nothing happens with the album. Simon splits for England, where American folk singers at least have novelty value. But meanwhile, The Cinderella story unfolds.

A disc jockey has fallen in love with one cut on *WEDNESDAY MORNING* and keeps playing it. Tom Wilson, a producer at Columbia who's nobody's fool, has watched the folk-rock explosion of 1965 and sees his chance. He gets the gentle folkie single *Sounds of Silence* and adds the standard rock backing of drums, bass and electric guitar. And before you can say S&G, it's a hit record, a number-one hit record. What happens is that the folkies buy it because it's one of their own, and the rockers latch onto it because they think it's some new kind of rock, which it is. Now that the market has been opened up for that fetching little combination, there's no stopping Simon and Garfunkel.

The duo reunite and Simon begins writing some of the most memorable songs of the sixties. His lyrics are clever, literate, and melancholy, reflecting the exasperating loneliness of universal adolescence. Their records begin to sell . . . and sell . . . and sell. The two boys who bombed in 1964 sell records by the millions a few years later, picking up as much as fifty thousand dollars for a single concert date. They are asked to do the sound track for the Mike Nichols film, *The Graduate*. It both establishes a new direction in film scoring and spawns a legitimate hit single, *Mrs. Robinson*. The success of the team spreads. Every American college student identifies with them. Then, with the advent of the youth movement of the late sixties, the criticism begins to filter in. They're too bland. Too sophomoric. Too commercial. Too safe. Simon and Garfunkel are accused of being the musical equal of farina, not possessing the magical charisma of Dylan or the Beatles.

Their critics forget that the team opened the door to a whole new strain of melodic sound, soft rock. The Simon and Garfunkel sound begins to loosen up, become more lavish as the criticism mounts. The low-keyed furor begins to irk Simon. He feels confined, frustrated. Art, too, senses an unrest. Yet they continue, coming up with the massive hit, *Bridge over Troubled Water,* the ultimate Simon and Garfunkel song. But by this time, two separate paths are visible where before there was one. Garfunkel is enamoured with the wide-screen world. Simon prefers music. When Art accepts a role in Nichols' *Catch 22,* Paul sees the handwriting on the wall. The two call it quits while still superstars. Art moves on to a multifaceted career, taking a lead role in *Carnal Knowledge* before moving into a solo musical career. Paul waits a year or so before launching his gold-record-laden solo antics. They part as friends. They part as innovators. They part as two of the most important musical figures to arise during the sixties.

Albums/WEDNESDAY MORNING, 3 A.M. (10/64): *You Can Tell the World; Last Night I Had the Strangest Dream; Bleecker Street; Sparrow; Benedictus; Sounds of Silence; He Was My Brother; Peggy-O; Go Tell It on the Mountain; Sun Is Burning;*

The Times Are a Changin'; Wednesday Morning, 3 A.M.
SOUNDS OF SILENCE (2/66): *Sounds of Silence; Leaves They
Are Green; Blessed; Kathy's Song; Somewhere They Can't Find
Me; Angie; Richard Cory; Most Peculiar Man; April Come She
Will; I Am a Rock; We've Got a Groovy Thing Goin'.* PARSLEY,
SAGE, ROSEMARY AND THYME (9/66): *Scarborough
Fair/Canticle; Homeward Bound; Patterns; For Emily, Whenever
I May Find Her; Big Bright Green Pleasure Machine; Poem on the
Underground Wall; Cloudy; Dangling Conversation; Simple Desul-
tory Philippie (Or How I Was Robert McNarmar'd into Sub-
mission); 59th Street Bridge Song; Flowers Never Bend with the
Rainfall; 7 O'Clock News/Silent Night.* THE GRADUATE
(3/68): *Sounds of Silence; Singleman Party Foxtrot; Mrs. Rob-
inson; Sunporch Cha-Cha-Cha; On the Strip; Scarborough Fair;
April Come She Will; The Folks; Great Effect; Big Bright Green
Pleasure Machine; Whew.* BOOKENDS (4/68): *Bookends Theme;
Save the Life of the Child; America; Overs; Voice of Old People;
Old Friends; Fakin' It; Punky's Dilemma; Hazy Shade of Winter;
At the Zoo; Mrs. Robinson.* BRIDGE OVER TROUBLED WA-
TER (1/70): *Bridge over Troubled Water; El Condor Pasa (If I
Could); Cecilia; Keep the Customer Satisfied; So Long, Frank
Lloyd Wright; The Boxer; Baby Driver; The Only Living Boy in
New York; Why Don't You Write Me; Bye Bye Love; Song for the
Asking.* SIMON AND GARFUNKEL'S GREATEST HITS
(6/72): *Mrs. Robinson; For Emily, Whenever I May Find Her; The
Boxer; 59th St. Bridge Song; Sounds of Silence; I am a Rock;
Scarborough Fair/Canticle; Homeward Bound; Bridge over Trou-
bled Water; America; Kathy's Song; El Condor Pasa (If I Could).*

Singles/*We've Got a Groovy Thing Goin'/Sounds of Silence (9/65);
Homeward Bound/Leaves That Are Green* (1/66); *That's My
Story/Tijuana Blues* (3/66); *Dangling Conversation/Big Bright
Green Pleasure Machine* (7/66); *Sounds of Silence/Homeward
Bound* (9/66); *A Hazy Shade of Winter/For Emily, Whenever I
May Find Her* (10/66); *At the Zoo/59th St. Bridge Song* (2/67);
Fakin' It/You Don't Know Where Your Interest Lies (7/67);
Scarborough Fair/April Come She Will (2/68); *Mrs.
Robinson/Old Friends/Bookends* (3/68); *Baby Driver/The Boxer*
(4/68); *Cecilia/The Only Living Boy in New York* (3/70); *El Con-
dor Pasa (If I Could)/Why Don't You Write Me* (8/70); *Bridge*

over Troubled Water/Cecilia (9/70); *For Emily, Whenever I May Find Her/America* (8/72).

SLY AND THE FAMILY STONE/*Sly Stone (organ, vocals), Rose Stone (electric piano, vocals), Freddie Stone (guitar, vocals), Larry Graham, Jr. (bass, vocals), Greg Errico (drums), Jerry Martini (saxophone, flute, accordion, piano), Cynthia Robinson (trumpet, vocals).*
The psychedelic-soulful sound of Sly and the Family Stone first came about in 1967, formed by former record producer, session-man, and disc jockey Sylvester Stewart (Sly Stone). Their first LP, released a year later, launched the horn-infested funk in a big way via the top-tenning single, *Dance to the Music.* For the next three years, Sly and the Family Stone proved popular to both black and white audiences and boasted such gold albums as *LIFE, DANCE TO THE MUSIC, STAND!* and *THERE'S A RIOT GOING ON.* The singles kept on coming as well, with titles such as *Everyday People, Thank You (Falettinme Be Mice Elf Agin),* and *I Want to Take You Higher* regularly making the top ten.

Led by supercharged, afro-encased Sly, the Family Stone garnered a fantastic following as the sixties melded into the seventies. Sly himself, however, became a somewhat enigmatic and fairly annoying figure. Rumors of drug use plagued the band and Sly's in-concert appearance, laconic to the point of catatonia, often proved a turnoff to his audiences. The troupe redeemed itself in the eyes of their fans with *THERE'S A RIOT GOING ON* in 1971 but, from that point onward, the golden era of the Family Stone was finished.

Personnel changes within the band weakened the overall sound and Sly began garnering a negative reputation concerning his consistent lateness for the concert dates. On occasion the band would go on one, two, or three hours late, enraging audiences to the point of no return. Married in 1974, Sly Stone has attempted a comeback of sorts during the past few years, penning and performing high-energy numbers that harken back to the *Dance to the Music* days of his original group. Thus far, success has eluded him the second time around.

Albums/WHOLE NEW THING (10/67): *Underdog; If This Room Could Talk; Run, Run, Run; Turn Me Loose; Let Me Hear*

It from You; Advice; I Cannot Make It; Trip to Your Heart; I Hate to Love Her; Bad Risk; Dog; That Kind of Person. DANCE TO THE MUSIC (3/68): *Dance to the Music; Higher; I Ain't Got Nobody (for Real); Ride the Rhythm; Color Me True; Are You Ready; Don't Burn, Baby; I'll Never Fall in Love Again; medley; Music Is Alive, Dance In, Music Lover.* LIFE (7/68): *Dynamite; Chicken; Plastic Jim; Fun; Into My Own Thing; Harmony; Life; Love City; I'm an Animal; M'Lady; Jane Is a Groupee.* STAND (4/69): *Stand! I Want to Take You Higher; Don't Call Me Nigger, Whitey; Somebody's Watching You; Sing a Simple Song; Everyday People; Sex Machine; You Can Make It If You Try.* GREATEST HITS (10/70): *I Want to Take You Higher; Everybody Is a Star; Stand!; Life; Fun; You Can Make It If You Try; Dance to the Music; Everyday People; Hot Fun in the Summertime; M'Lady; Sing a Simple Song; Thank You (Falettinme Be Mice Elf Again).* THERE'S A RIOT GOING ON (10/71): *Family Affair; Poet; Time; other titles.* FRESH (6/73): *In Time; If You Want Me to Stay; Let Me Have It All; Frisky; Thankful 'n' Thoughtful; Skin I'm In; I Don't Know (Satisfaction); Keep On Dancin'; Que Sera, Sera; If It Were Left Up to Me; Babies Makin' Babies.* SMALL TALK (6/74): *Small Talk; Say You Will; Mother Beautiful; Time for Livin'; Can't Strain My Brain; Loose Booty; Holdin' On; Wishful Thinking; Better Thee Than Me; Livin' While I'm Livin'; This Is Love.* HIGH ENERGY (3/75): *Underdog; If This Room Could Talk; Run, Run, Run; Turn Me Loose; Let Me Hear It from You; Advice; I Cannot Make It; Trip to Your Heart; I Hate to Love Her; Bad Risk; That Kind of Person; Dog; Dynamite; Chicken; Plastic Jim; Fun; Into My Own Thing; Harmony; Life; Love City; I'm an Animal; M'Lady; Jane Is a Groupee.* HIGH ON YOU (10/75): *I Get High on You; Crossword Puzzle; That's Lovin' You; Who Do You Love; Green-Eyed Monster Girl; Organize; Le Lo Li; My World; So Good to Me; Greed.* HEARD YA MISSED ME, WELL I'M BACK (11/76): *Heard Ya Missed Me, Well I'm Back; What Was I Thinkin; in My Head; Sexy Situation; Blessing in Disguise; Everything in You; Mother Is a Hippie; Let's Be Together; The Thing; Family Again.*

Singles/*Dance to the Music/Let Me Hear It from You* (11/67); *Life/M'Lady* (6/68); *Everyday People/Sing a Simple Song* (11/68); *Stand!/I Want to Take You Higher* (5/69); *Thank You (Falettinme Be Mice Elf Again)* (12/69); *I Want to Take You*

Higher (4/70); *Stand!* (9/70); *Everyday People* (9/70); *Smilin'* (3/72); *Family Affair* (4/73); *Frisky* (10/73); *If You Want Me to Stay* (4/74); *Time for Livin'* (6/74); *Loose Booty* (9/74); *Hot Fun in the Summer Time* (6/75); *I Get High on You* (8/75); *Le Lo Li* (11/75); *Crossword Puzzle* (2/76); *Family Again* (1/77).

THE SMALL FACES/*Steve Marriot (vocals, guitar), Ronnie Lane (bass), Kenn Jones (drums), Ian McLagan (organ).*
During a time of increased complication and layers of sound, the Small Faces offered a simplistic approach to rock that was almost innocent in its sound. As a result, they garnered a cult following in England but not much else. Stateside, they fared less spectacularly, appealing to the very few FM-radio buffs in the mid-sixties. In 1969, they parted ways, forming Humble Pie and the Faces.

Albums/THERE ARE BUT FOUR SMALL FACES (2/68): *Itchycoo Park; Talk to You; Up the Wooden Hills; My Way of Giving; I'm Only Dreaming; I Feel Much Better; Tin Soldier; Get Yourself Together; Show Me the Way; Here Comes the Nice; Green Circles; Have You Ever Seen Me.* ODGEN'S NUT GONE (9/68): *Ogden's Nut Gone Flake; Afterglow; Long Agos and Worlds Apart; Rene; Song of a Baker; Lazy Sunday; Happiness Stand; Rollin' Over; The Hungry Intruder; The Journey; Mad John; Happydaystoytown.* EARLY FACES (7/72).

Singles/*Hey Girl/Almost Grown* (5/66); *Itchycoo Park/I'm Only Dreaming* (9/67); *Tin Soldier/I Feel Much Better* (2/68); *Lazy Sun/Rollin' Over* (4/68).

PATTI SMITH/Watching Patti Smith perform onstage is like watching a head-on collision between Dondi and Machine Gun Kelly. On wax, she often sounds like a seance held at the Fillmore East during a typical late sixties blowout. She is alternately praised and damned for her literate (albeit bizarre) lyricism, erratic vocal delivery, and suicidal guitar style. Many of her fans claim that Patti Smith is, in part, responsible for the evolution of punk rock. Many of her detractors claim the same thing.

The singer-songwriter-guitarist-poet-punk was born in Chicago but raised in New Jersey. A poet-in-residence in New York since the late sixties, Patti first began appearing onstage in a musical setting during 1973–74 when, backed by rock writer Lenny Kaye on guitar, she alternately read, sang, and chanted her poetry in various New York clubs. In 1974, Patti and her newly formed band (led by Kaye) cut their first homemade single, *Piss Factory.* A number of local gigs followed which, ultimately, frightened most of the record companies in the New York metropolitan area into a state of near-stupor.

Clive Davis of Arista, however, was willing to take a chance on the New Wave's patron saint, so Patti and entourage were signed. An initial release in 1975, *HORSES,* made it to the lower half of the top LP charts and established Patti as an artist to be reckoned with. A second album, *RADIO ETHEOPIA,* released a year later, was less enthusiastically greeted.

Patti Smith, poet–rock star–artist, lists Bob Dylan, Jimi Hendrix, William Burroughs, and Arthur Rimbaud as her main influences.

Albums/HORSES (1975): *Gloria; Redondo Beach; Birdland; Free Money; Kimberly; Break It Up; Land; Elegie.* RADIO ETHEOPIA (10/76): *Ask the Angels; Ain't It Strange; Poppies; Pissing in a River; Pumping (My Heart); Distant Fingers; Radio Ethiopia; Abyssinia.*

Singles/*Piss Factory* (1974); *Gloria/My Generation* (1975); *Ask the Angels* (U.K. only, 1976).

SONNY/Detroit-born Salvatore (Sonny) Bono was beginning to make a name for himself as a songwriter *(Needles and Pins)* when his career exploded as half of a duo formed with his second wife, Cher. In 1968 he embarked on a terminal solo career which was aborted after one album. While Sonny's buzz-saw vocals, it seemed, were fine when confined to 50 percent of a record, 100 percent proved too much for most fans. After the Sonny and Cher duo finally called it quits (following a divorce and the end of a long-running television show) in 1976, Sonny embarked on a career as an actor.

Album/INNER VIEWS (8/68): *I Just Sit There; I Told My Girl to Go Away; I Would Marry You Today; My Best Friend's Girl Is Out of Sight; Pammie's on a Bummer.*

Singles/*Laugh at Me/Tony* (7/65); *The Revolution Kind/Georgia and John Quetzal* (10/65); *I Would Marry You Today/Circus* (1/68); *My Best Friend's Girl Is Out of Sight* (1968); *I Would Marry You Today/You're a Friend of Mine* (5/69).

SONNY AND CHER/The most famous couple in rock and roll history, Sonny and Cher started off as counter-culture heroes and wound up homogenized household words. Salvatore Bono, Detroit-born truck driver-laborer-struggling songwriter met aspiring actress Cherilyn Sakisian in 1963. By the time they met and married, Sonny was becoming known in the record industry, partly as a fledgling wordsmith but mostly as an assistant to Phil Spector. After unsuccessfully hyping Spector on Cher's vocal abilities, Sonny and Cher recorded an album under the name of Caesar and Cleopatra. The record was a monumental dud.

Changing their career names to Sonny and Cher, the twosome moved to Atco records where they inundated the pop world with a batch of catchy rock tunes. Borrowing heavily from the Spector school of producing and, lyrically, from whatever musical trend was happening, commercial-eared Sonny fashioned a bona fide hit sound that started with *I Got You, Babe* and continued into Cher's career as a solo artist.

I Got You, Babe brought the duo instant success and made their marriage a national institution. The perfect counter-culture couple: Cher with her willowy, *Vogue*-cover looks; Sonny with his pageboy haircut, fuzzy vests, and buzz-saw vocalizing. They were opposites in every way and, as such, they inspired a whole new generation of young and in-love and still-living-at-home fans.

Toward the end of the sixties, Cher embarked on a successful solo career with Sonny acting as her mentor, offering both tunes *(The Beat Goes On, Bang, Bang)* and producing skills. This solo outlet proved short-lived, however, and by 1970 the team was nearly broke. A self-financed feature length film, *Chastity,* stiffed. Sonny's attempt at solo work was mercifully short and, for Cher, the hits just stopped coming.

The seventies found them doing shtick in Las Vegas eateries. It was at this time that television knocked on their door. A Sonny and Cher mini-series led to a phenomenally successful series and the once-scruffy pair of young lovers made the transition to boob-tubedom, becoming everyone's ideal image of aging hipsters. Cher developed a remarkaby deadpan comic delivery and Sonny became the lovable fall guy, the braggart. Cher's recording career took a dramatic upswing on a new label (MCA) and with a new producer (Snuff Garrett).

However, all the Sonny and Cher bliss began to come crashing down to ankle-area in 1974 when Mr. and Mrs. Rock and Roll decided to divorce. The initial proceedings were exceedingly sticky. Their show was cancelled and they embarked on separate television careers. Sonny died a horrible death on ABC while Cher flourished on CBS. A run-in with the network censors over, of all things, whether Cher's navel should be shown on network television became a cause célèbre at CBS. An on-again, off-again marriage to on-again, off-again rock star Greg Allman damaged Cher's musical career in terms of fandom; soon, Sonny and Cher were back together again on TV in an effort to patch up their sagging professional lives. The show's run was short-lived and Cher returned to solo recording while Sonny set off on an acting career.

Albums/LOOK AT US (8/65): *I Got You, Babe; Unchained Melody; Then He Kissed Me; Sing C'est la Vie; It's Gonna Rain; 500 Miles; Just You; Letter; Let It Be Me; You Don't Love Me; You Really Got a Hold on Me; Why Don't They Let Us Fall in Love.* WONDROUS WORLD OF SONNY AND CHER (1/66): *Summertime; Tell Him; I'm Leaving It All Up to You; But You're Mine; Bring It On Home to Me; Set Me Free; What Now My Love; Leave Me Be; I Look for You; Laugh at Me; Turn Around; So Fine.* IN CASE YOU'RE IN LOVE (2/67): *Beat Goes On; Groovy Kind of Love; Podunk; You Baby; Monday; Love Don't Come; Little Man; We'll Sing in the Sunshine; Living for You; Misty Roses; Stand by Me; Cheryl's Going Home.* GOOD TIMES (4/67): *I Got You, Babe; It's the Little Things; I'm Gonna Love You; Good Times; Trust Me; Just a Name; Don't Talk to Strangers.* BEST OF (7/67): *Beat Goes On; What Now My Love; I Got You, Babe; Little Man; Just You; Sing C'est la Vie; Laugh at Me; Living for You.* LIVE (1972). ALL I EVER NEED IS YOU (1972). THE TWO OF US (8/72): *I Got You, Babe; Unchained Melody; Then He kissed Me; Sing C'est la Vie; It's Gonna Rain; Baby Don't Go; Just You; The Letter; Let It Be Me; You Really Don't Love Me; You've Really Got a Hold on Me; Why Don't They Let Us Fall in Love; The Beat Goes On; Groovy Kind of Love; You Baby; Monday; Love Don't Come; Podunk; Little Man; We'll Sing in the Sunshine; Misty Roses; Stand by Me; Living for You; Cheryl's Goin' Home.* MAMA WAS A ROCK AND ROLL SINGER, PAPA USED TO WRITE ALL HER SONGS (1973). THE BEAT GOES ON (11/75): *The Beat Goes On; I Got*

You, Babe; What Now My Love; Just You; Laugh at Me; Baby Don't Go; Little Man; Tonight I'll Be Staying Here with You; I Walk on Gilded Splinters; Sing C'est.la Vie; It's the Little Things; Do Right Woman, Do Right Man.

Singles/*Sing C'est la Vie/Just You* (3/65); *I Got You Babe/It's Gonna Rain* (5/65); *The Letter/Spring Fever* (10/65); *But You're Mine/Hello (11/65); What Now My Love/I Look for You* (1/66); *Leave Me Be/Have I Stayed Too Long* (5/66); *Little Man/Monday* (9/66); *The Beat Goes On/Love Don't Come* (12/66); *Podunk/Beautiful Story* (4/67); *It's the Little Things/Plastic Man* (5/67); *Don't Talk to Strangers/It's the Little Things* (7/67); *You and Me/Good Combination* (1/68); *You Gotta Have a Thing of Your Own/I Got You, Babe* (7/68); *You're a Friend of Mine/I Would Marry You Today* (5/69); *Get It Together/Hold You Tighter* (5/70); *All I Ever Need Is You* (9/71); *A Cowboy's Work Is Never Done* (1/72); *When You Say Love* (6/72); *Just You/I Got You Babe* (10/72); *What Now My Love/The Beat Goes On* (10/72).

THE SONS OF CHAMPLIN/*Bill Champlin (vocals, keyboards), Geoff Palmer (keyboards, vocals, reeds), Mike Andreas (woodwinds), Phil Wood (brass, keyboards), Terry Haggerty (guitar), Dave Schallock (bass, vocals), Jim Preston (drums), Mark Isham (brass, keyboards).*
A survivor of the San Francisco blitz of the mid-sixties, the Sons of Champlin have, in one form or another, been together since 1966 when Champlin, Palmer, and Haggerty got together with drummer Bill Bower, bassist Al Strong, reed player Tim Caine, and Jim Myers to record their first album. The album was never released, however, and it wasn't until the band signed with Capitol in 1969 that the keyboard-infested music of the Sons was heard across the nation. By that time membership began to fluctuate, with Myers being the first to leave. The Sons of Champlin then began to waver between calling themselves the Sons of Champlin and just the plain ol' the Sons. Professional schizophrenia is never a healthy sign in the life of a band, often causing personal craziness with the band members themselves. The Sons broke up in 1970. They then reformed at the end of 1970. In mid-1971, the band had an internal blowout with Strong and Bowen hitting the street. Ex-Big Brother Schallock joined, as

did drummer Bill Vitt. The Sons—Sons of Champlin question was solved when, during that same year, the name was changed to Yogi Phlegm. Oddly enough, that name just didn't catch on with the public at large. It didn't catch on with Bill Vitt, either, and he took a walk.

For anyone keeping score, that's three name changes, one breakup and six revolving-door members in five years. The band then changed their name back to the Sons or the Sons of Champlin and left Capitol in search of fame and fortune at Columbia Records. They found neither and, in 1975, signed with Ariola America . . . a label distributed by Capitol, whence they originally had come in 1969. (This rock life, it goes in circles, no?) Today, the Sons of whatever are making happy music in their usual off-the-cuff style. They are not stars in the traditional glitter –strobe–smoke bomb sense. Guitarist Terry has been known to sit on a stool for the entire set. Some of the band members never look at the audience during a concert. They don't really care about putting on a show. What they care about, and what they have always been known for, is making good music.

Albums/LOOSIN' UP NATURALLY (4/69): *Hello Sunlight; Freedom; Black and Blue Rainbow; 1982-A; other titles.* THE SONS (9/69): *Love of a Woman; Terry's Tune; Boomp Boomp Chop; Why Do People Run from the Rain; It's Time; Country Girl; You Can Fly.* FOLLOW YOUR HEART (4/71): *The Child Continued; Follow Your Heart; Children Know; Headway; A Sound Love; Before You Right Now; Greebish Delight; Well Done.* WELCOME TO THE DANCE (4/73): *Lightnin'; For Joy; Who; Heaven Only Knows; Right On; No Mo'; The Swim; Welcome to the Dance: a. Silence, b. Sound—Turn Around, c. Healthy Woman, d. Welcome to the Dance.* THE SONS OF CHAMPLIN (9/75): *Lookout; I'd Like to Get to Know You; Marp Interlude; Planet Ripper; All and Everything; Without Love; Rainbow's End; Geoff's Vibe; Queen of the Rain; Gold Mine.* CIRCLE FILLED WITH LOVE (5/76): *Hold On; Here Is Where Your Love Belongs; Follow Your Heart; Knickaknick; Imagination's Sake; Still in Love with You; Circle Filled with Love; For a While; Slippery When It's Wet; Helping Hand; To the Sea; You.* LOVING IS WHY (6/77): *Saved by the Grace of Your Love; Loving Is Why; Time Will Bring You Love; Doin' It for You; Where I Belong; Let That Be a Lesson;*

Love Can Take Me Now; Watcha Gonna Do; West End; Big Boss Man.

Singles/*Black and Blue Rainbow/1982-A* (3/69); *Freedom/Hello Sunlight* (6/69); *It's Time/Why Do People Run from the Rain* (10/69); *You Can Fly/Terry's Tune* (4/70); *Passing Through/The Swim* (4/73); *Welcome to the Dance/The Swim* (6/73); *Lookout/Queen of the Rain* (9/75); *Hold On/Still in Love with you* (6/76); *Imagination's Sake/You* (8/76); *Here Is Where Your Love Belongs/Follow Your Heart* (11/76); *Saved by the Grace of Your Love/West End* (6/77).

SOUTHER HILLMAN FURAY/*J. D. Souther (guitar, vocals), Chris Hillman (bass, guitar, vocals), Richie Furay (guitar, vocals), Al Perkins (pedal steel), Paul Harris (keyboards), Jim Gordon (drums).*
When the Souther Hillman Furay Band released their second album, *TROUBLE IN PARADISE,* they weren't kidding around. The super-trio's professional life was anything but tranquil at that point and the fur had been flying for quite a while. Formed in 1973 by leaving-Poco member Furay, ex-Byrd and -Burrito Hillman, and up-and-coming Eagles-songwriter Souther, the supergroup just never did happen, with all three driving wheels attempting to spin off in different directions simultaneously.

Furay allegedly suffered the most, having found religion the same time as stumbling over musical differences. The band faded from view after their second release with all three members pursuing rather mundane musical adventures.

Albums/THE SOUTHER-HILLMAN-FURAY BAND (6/74): *Fallin' in Love; Heavenly Fire; The Heartbreaker; Believe Me; Border Town; Safe at Home; Pretty Goodbyes; Rise and Fall; The Flight of the Dove; Deep, Dark and Dreamless.* TROUBLE IN PARADISE (5/75): *Trouble in Paradise; Move Me Real Slow; For Someone I Love; Mexico; Love and Satisfy; On the Line; Prisoner in Disguise; Follow Me Through; Somebody Must Be Wrong.*

Singles/*Fallin' in Love/Heavenly Fire* (7/74); *Mexico/Move Me Real Slow* (5/75); *Trouble in Paradise/On the Line* (7/75); *For Someone I Love/Move Me Real Slow* (9/75).

SPIRIT/*Original members: Randy California (vocals, guitar), Ed "Cass" Cassidy (drums), Mark Andes (bass, vocals), Jay Andes*

(bass, vocals), Jay Ferguson (vocals), John Locke (keyboards).
Spirit is a supergroup that just never caught on. In spite of fantastic albums, excellent live performances, and tremendous songwriting ability, the band always remained bogged down in the
"cult following" category. They had everything going for them
but no one in fandom was smart enough to notice.

The group can actually trace its roots back to the day when
barely teen-aged Randy was putting his first rock band together
on the West Coast. Drummer Ed (who had performed with Gerry
Mulligan, Thelonious Monk, and Cannonball Adderly) was dat-
ing Randy's mother. When she asked Ed to give thirteen-year-old
Randy some pointers in musicianship, he not only tutored the
sprout but joined the band as well. Eventually, Ed married
Randy's mother and the threesome packed up and moved to New
York, where California jammed a few times with up-and-coming
axe-wielder Jimi Hendrix (Hendrix's influences can especially be
heard on Randy's solo outing, *KAPTAIN KOPTER*). Moving
back to California in '65, the California-Cass team got together
with Ferguson, Locke, and Andes and a band called the Red
Roosters mutated into the original Spirit.

The group's sound was so clear and fresh as an ocean breeze,
arising during a time of intense psychedelia. Boasting controlled
playing, textured vocals, and jazz-tinged rock melodies, Spirit
brought forth a series of four superb albums in a row (three—
SPIRIT, THE FAMILY THAT PLAYS TOGETHER and *THE
TWELVE DREAMS OF DR. SARDONICUS*—are among the
finest albums to emerge during the last ten years). During the
torturous *SARDONICUS* sessions, however, the group began to
fragment, the years of toiling for little reward catching up with the
members. Andes and Ferguson moved on to Jo Jo Gunne (another cult band). Tragedy struck the remaining members when California was severely injured in a riding accident. While recuperat-
ing, Cassidy and Locke teamed with the Texas-born Staehely
twins to form yet another Spirit in a move that can best be termed
suicidal. The resulting album, *FEEDBACK*, is one of the best examples of recorded drek ever released.

California got back to his feet via 1973's *KAPTAIN KOPTER
AND THE TWIRLY BIRDS*, a long-player that was to rock what
Outer Limits was to prime-time television. He later revived Spirit
with Cass in 1973 as a tentative live experiment. Tours on both

sides of the Atlantic proved amazingly successful, so Spirit became a bona fide recording entity again, signing a long-term contract with Mercury Records. Cass and California have been the only steady members of the "new" Spirit and album quality has varied depending on what other Spirits were used on the sessions. Of the more recent efforts, *FARTHER ALONG* came closest to emulating the original excellence of the group. This album contained superb performances not only by Cass and California but also by original Spirit members John Locke and Mark Andes.

Albums/SPIRIT (1/68): *Fresh Garbage; Uncle Jack; Mechanical World; Taurus; Girl in Your Eye; Straight Arrow; Topanga Windows; Gramophone Man; Water Woman; The Great Canyon Fire in General; Elijah.* THE FAMILY THAT PLAYS TOGETHER (12/68): *I Got a Line on You; It Shall Be; Poor Richard; Silky Sam; The Drunkard; Darlin' If; All the Same; Jewish; Dream within a Dream; She Smiled; Aren't You Glad.* CLEAR (7/69): *Dark-Eyed Woman; Apple Orchard; Ground Hog; So Little Time to Fly; Cold Wind; Policeman's Ball; Ice; Give a Life, Take a Life; I'm Truckin'; Clear; Caught; New Dope in Town.* THE TWELVE DREAMS OF DR. SARDONICUS (11/70): *Animal Zoo; Morning Will Come; Mr. Skin; When I Touch You; Street Worm; Love Has Found a Way; Space Child; Prelude—Nothin' to Hide; Why Can't I Be Free; Life Has Just Begun; Nature's Way; Soldier.* FEEDBACK (6/72): *Chelsea Girls; Cadillac Cowboys; Puesta del Scam; Ripe and Ready; Darkness; Earth Shaker; Mellow Morning; Right On Time; Trancas Fog; Out; Witch.* THE FAMILY THAT PLAYS TOGETHER (re-released 6/72): THE BEST OF SPIRIT (6/73): *I Got a Line on You; Animal Zoo; Mr. Skin; 1984; Uncle Jack; Mechanical World; Nature's Way; Morning Will Come; Prelude—Nothin' to Hide; Dark-Eyed Woman; Fresh Garbage.* CLEAR (re-released 5/73). SPIRIT (re-released 5/73). SPIRIT OF '76 (5/75): *America the Beautiful/The Times, They Are a Changing; Victim of Society; Lady of the Lakes; Tampa Jam (I and II); Maunaloa; Sunrise; What Do I Have; Walking the Dog; Joker on the Run; When?; Like a Rolling Stone; Once Again; Feeling in Time; Happy; Jack Bond; My Road; Thank You, Lord; Uranita; Guide Me; Veruska; Hey, Joe; The Star-Spangled Banner; Jack Bond (Part II).* SON OF SPIRIT (10/75): *Holy Man; Looking into Darkness; Maybe You'll Find; Don't Go Away; Family; Magic Fairy Princess; Circle; The Other Song; Yesterday; It's*

Time Now. FARTHER ALONG (6/76): *Colossus; Mega Star; Phoebe; Don't Lock Up Your Door; Diamond Spirit; Nature's Way; Farther Along; Atomic Boogie; World Dog; Stoney Night; Pineapple.* FUTURE GAMES (1/77): *CB Talk; Stars Are Love; Kahauna Dream; Buried in My Brain; Bionic Unit; So Happy Now; All Along the Watchtower; Would You Believe; Jack Bond Speaks; Star Trek Dreaming; Interlude XM; China Doll; Hawaiian Times; Gorn Attack; Interlude 2001; Detroit City; Freakout Frog; Monkey See, Monkey Do; The Journey of Nomad; Ending; The Romulan Experience; Mt. Olympus.*

Singles/*Mechanical World/Uncle Jack* (4/68); *I Got a Line on You/She Smiled* (10/68); *I Got a Line on You/New Dope in Town* (8/69); *1984/Sweet Stella Baby* (12/69); *Animal Zoo/Red Light Roll On* (7/70); *Nature's Way/Soldier* (11/70); *Nature's Way/Mr. Skin* (1/71); *Soldier/Mr. Skin* (1/71); *Cadillac Cowboys/Darkness* (3/72); *I Got a Line on You/1984* (4/73); *Nature's Way/Mr. Skin* (6/73); *Lady of the Lakes/America, the Beautiful—The Times, They Are A-Changing* (6/75); *Holy Man/Looking into Darkness* (10/75); *Farther Along/Atomic Boogie* (7/76).

SPOOKY TOOTH/*Luther Grosvenor (guitar), Gary Wright (vocals, keyboards), Mike Harrison (vocals, keyboards), Greg Ridley (bass), Mike Kellie (drums). Additional members: Henry McCullough (guitar), Chris Stainton (keyboards), Mick Jones (guitar), Mike Patto (vocals), Chris Steward (bass), Alan Spenner (bass), Val Burke (bass), Bryson Graham (drums).*
One of the all-time kings of grunt-and-groan rock and roll, wailing, flailing Spooky Tooth was nearly nonexistent by the time they came to the attention of stateside audiences. Begun in 1968 by New Jerseyite Gary Wright (an American student in Europe) and veteran British musician Mike Harrison, the twosome guided the original Spooky Tooth through two initial LPs *(IT'S ALL ABOUT* and *SPOOKY TWO),* which effectively laid the groundwork for the band. The bass and drum combinations were lethal, sounding like an avalanche. Guitar soared into space while keyboards growled below and vocals screeched like aerial demons. Yet the band had problems getting off the ground.

In the States, their first album was not released until two years later under a different title *(TOBACCO ROAD).* Their second album was garnering them quite a following when Greg Ridley departed for Humble Pie fame and fortune. The band recorded an album with electronic music booster Pierre Henry. While not a Spooky Tooth album as such, it was labeled as one and a lot of crotch-rocking fans were stunned at the melodic, un-Spooky music thereon.

Still, the album was a U.S. chart-maker. By that time, Wright was getting restless; he parted ways with the maddening molar to begin his own disaster-prone outfit, Wonderwheel. Grosvenor faded into the woodwork to emerge a couple of years later in Mott the Hoople as the mascara-laden Ariel Bender. Uh-huh.

Founder Mike Harrison was in a quandary. In the United States, Spooky Tooth was gaining momentum and there wasn't an actual band. Grease Banders Stainton, McCullough, and Spenner were recruited to record the Tooth's "farewell" album, *LAST PUFF*. It was the band's biggest hit to date. Harrison was so encouraged that he embarked on a solo career himself. It was a dud.

With neither solo artist setting the world on fire, Harrison and Wright reunited in 1973 with a new, improved Spooky Tooth, featuring original teether Kellie and newcomers Mick Jones and Chris Stewart. This high-flying regrouping lasted two albums and by Tooth's final epic, *THE MIRROR*, the new lineup was Wright, Jones, Mike Patto, Bryson Graham, and Val Burke. The band folded, leaving behind a legacy of teeth-gnashing, fine rock and roll. Gary Wright saw the light and adopted a good-vibes stance, launching a cosmic career of his own with a large amount of success.

Albums/SPOOKY TWO (7/69): *Waiting for the Wind; Feelin' Bad; I've Got Enough Heartaches; Evil Woman; Lost in My Dream; That Was Only Yesterday; Better by You, Better Than Me; Hangman, Hang My Shell on a Tree.* CEREMONY (2/70): *Have Mercy; Jubilation; Confession; Prayer; Offering; Hosanna.* THE LAST PUFF (7/70): *I Am the Walrus; The Wrong Time; Something to Say; Nobody There At All; Down River; Son of Your Father; The Last Puff.* TOBACCO ROAD (5/71): *Society's Child; Love Really Changed Me; Here I Lived So Well; The Weight; Sunshine Help Me; It's All About a Roundabout; Tobacco Road; It Hurts You So; Forget It, I've Got It; Bubbles.* YOU BROKE MY HEART SO I BUSTED YOUR JAW (4/73): *Cotton-Growing Man; Old As I Was Born; This Time Around;*

Holy Water; Wildfire; Self-Seeking Man; Times Have Changed; Moriah. WITNESS (10/73): *Oceans of Power; Wings on My Heart; As Long As the World Keeps Turning; Don't Ever Stray Away; Dream Me a Mountain; Sunlight of My Mind; Pyramids.* THE MIRROR (1974): *Fantasy Satisfier; Two-Time Love; Kyle; Woman and Gold; Higher Circles; Hell or High Water; I'm Alive; The Mirror; The Hoofer.* THAT WAS ONLY YESTERDAY— GARY WRIGHT & SPOOKY TOOTH (3/76): *I Know; That Was Only Yesterday; The Wrong Time; Feelin' Bad; Two-Faced Man; Love to Survive; Wildfire; Nobody There At All; Sunshine Help Me; I Can't See the Reason; Waiting for the Wind; Cotton-Growing Man; Fascinating Things; Son of Your Father; Sing a Song; Something to say; Stand for Our Rights; Evil Woman; Holy Water.*

BRUCE SPRINGSTEEN/Poet? Street punk? Hype? Bruce Springsteen has been accused of being all three. In truth, the charismatic singer-songwriter-guitarist is a little bit of everything, encompassing the best elements of rock and roll from the fifties, sixties, and seventies. With street-urchin demeanor, mid-fifties guitar bravado ("Anybody who sees Elvis Presley and doesn't want to be like Elvis Presley has got to have something wrong with him"), and a raspy voice that alternately tears your heart out and hits you below the belt, the kinetic New Jerseyite has catapulted to fame with only three albums, no hit singles, and a cast of musical characters that makes the denizens of *West Side Story* look like the Little Rascals.

Born on September 23, 1949, and raised in Asbury Park, Bruce picked up the guitar during the sixties when playing in a rock band was *the* thing to do. With near-waist-length hair, he wailed his way through a host of admittedly terrible heavy-metal bands, including Steel Mill and Dr. Zoom and the Sonic Boom, (The latter featured any pal who happened to show up that day for a gig. "Sometimes someone would take a solo and we'd all fall down laughing," he recalls.) After serving a hefty apprenticeship in noise-making, Bruce decided to go it alone as a singer-songwriter. He found a manager who eventually brought him to the attention of John Hammond, Sr., the recording giant who discovered both Bessie Smith and Bob Dylan. Bruce sat down at the piano in Hammond's tiny office and warbled *It's So Hard to Be a Saint in the City.* Hammond knew star quality when he heard it and Bruce was signed shortly thereafter.

Springsteen's first two albums, *GREETINGS FROM ASBURY PARK, NEW JERSEY* and *THE WILD, THE INNOCENT AND THE E STREET SHUFFLE,* received critical acclaim, but it was not until the release of *BORN TO RUN* that Bruce began making it in a big way. Backed by an ace rock outfit, the E Street Band, Bruce took to the road nationally. Playing his hands off for two years running, he was awarded a gold album, cover shots on both *Time* and *Newsweek,* and the handle of being "the next big thing" in modern music. His tunes *(Blinded by the Light, Spirit in the Night, Thunder Road,* and *Growing Up)* have captured the hearts and imaginations of thousands of music lovers who recognize a little bit of their own lives in Bruce's lyrics. Springsteen's inspiration? "The stuff I write is what I live with," he says. "The stories are all around me. I just put 'em down."

Albums/GREETINGS FROM ASBURY PARK, NEW JERSEY (1/73): *Blinded by the Light; Growing Up; Mary Queen of Arkansas; Does This Bus Stop at 82nd Street?; Lost in the Flood; The Angel; For You; Spirit in the Night; It's Hard to Be a Saint in the City.* THE WILD, THE INNOCENT AND THE E STREET SHUFFLE (11/73): *The E Street Shuffle; 4th of July, Asbury Park (Sandy); Wild Billy's Circus Story; Incident on 57th Street; Rosalita (Come Out Tonight); New York City Serenade.* BORN TO RUN (8/75): *Thunder Road; Tenth Avenue Freeze-Out; Night; Backstreets; Born to Run; She's the One; Meeting across the River; Jungleland.*

Singles/*Blinded by the Light/Angel* (2/73); *Spirit in the Night/For You* (5/73); *Born to Run/Meeting across the River* (8/75); *Tenth Avenue Freeze-Out/She's the One* (12/75); *Born to Run/Spirit in the Night* (11/76).

RINGO STARR/After the Beatles broke up, most Beatlemaniacs were concerned over the wellbeing of loveable, and slightly dorky, drummer Ringo Starr. While it was true that Ringo was a delightful comic character in the Beatles films and fit in nicely with his cameo in the film *Candy,* no one was quite sure how he'd cut it musically all by his lonesome. Well, no one worried about Ringo for too long. Within two years after his debut as a solo performer, Starr had a top-tenning single on both sides of the Atlantic with *It Don't Come Easy.*

Shortly after the Beatles called it quits, he starred in the near-miss film, *The Magic Christian,* which afforded him a source of notoriety during a period when his first two long-players, *SENTIMENTAL JOURNEY* and *BEAUCOUPS OF BLUES* stiffed. The first, a collection of musty old songs, turned off dustfree teenage fans. The second, a potpourri of Nashville-recorded ditties, proved a pain in the grooves for city slickers.

In '73, Starr settled down to commerciality proper and, with the aid of producer Richard Perry, began releasing a glut of slickly done "singles" which quickly made their way into the top charts around the world. *Photograph, Oh My My,* & *You're Sixteen* were snatched from the resulting *RINGO* album (an LP which featured tunes penned by each of the three remaining Beatles).

By 1975, however, the hits slowed down and Ringo found himself in a state of creative flux. He formed his own record label, Ring' O Records, moved from Capitol in the States to Atlantic, and began seeking dynamite boss hits once again.

He is still loveable.

Albums/SENTIMENTAL JOURNEY (4/70): *Sentimental Journey; Night and Day; Whispering Grass (Don't Tell the Trees); Bye Bye Blackbird; I'm a Fool to Care; Star Dust; Blue, Turning Gray over You; Love Is a Many-Splendored Thing; Dream; You always Hurt the One You Love; Have I Told You Lately That I Love You?; Let the Rest of the World Go By.* BEAUCOUPS OF BLUES (9/70): *Beaucoups of Blues; Love Don't Last Long; Fastest Growing Heartache in the West; Without Her; Woman of the Night; I'd Be Talking All the Time; $15 Draw; Wine, Women and Loud Happy Songs; I Wouldn't Have You Any Other Way; Loser's Lounge; Waiting; Silent Homecome.* RINGO (10/73): *I'm the Greatest; Have You Seen My Baby; Photograph; Sunshine Life for Me (Sail Away, Raymond); You're Sixteen; Oh My My; Step Lightly; Six O'Clock; Devil Woman; You and Me (Babe).* GOODNIGHT VIENNA (11/74): *It's All Down to Goodnight Vienna; Oo-Wee; Husbands and Wives; Snookeroo; All by Myself; Call Me; No No Song/Skokiaan; Only You (and You Alone); Easy for Me; Goodnight Vienna (Reprise).* BLAST FROM YOUR PAST (12/75):

You're Sixteen; No No Song/Skokiaan; It Don't Come Easy; Photograph; Back Off Boogaloo; Only You (and You Alone); Beaucoups of Blues; Oh My My; Early 1970; I'm the Greatest. ROTO-GRAVURE (9/76): *A Dose of Rock 'n' Roll; Hey Baby; Pure Gold; Cryin'; You Don't Know Me At All; Cookin' (in the Kitchen of Love); I'll Still Love You; This Be Called a Song; Las Brisas; Lady Gaye; Spooky Weirdness.* RINGO IV (9/77): *Drowning in the Sea of Love; Tango All Night; Wings; Gave It All Up; Out on the Streets; Can She Do It Like She Dances; Sneaking Sally through the Alley; Gypsies in Flight; It's No Secret; Simple Love Song.*

Singles/*Beaucoups of Blues/Cooch Coochy* (10/70); *It Don't Come Easy/Early 1970* (4/71); *Back Off Boogaloo/Blindman* (4/72); *Photograph/Down and Out* (10/73); *You're Sixteen/Devil Woman* (12/73); *Oh My My/Step Lightly* (2/74); *Only You/Call Me* (11/74); *Snookeroo/No No Song* (1/75); *It's All Down to Goodnight Vienna/Oo-Wee* (6/75); *Hey Baby/Lady Gaye* (4/76); *Dose of Rock'n' Roll/Cryin'* (9/76).

STEELEYE SPAN/*Tim Hart (vocals, guitar), Maddy Prior (vocals), Bob Johnson (vocals, guitar), Peter Knight (vocals, mandolin, guitar), Nigel Pegrum (flute, drums), Rich Kemp (vocals, bass).*
In a rock world populated by Jekyll-and-Hyde working-class hero-superstars, it is reassuring to know that Steeleye Span is still Steeleye Span after nearly a decade in the music biz. One of the few remaining purveyors of British pastoral imagery, the lilting entourage had their beginning in 1969. Ashley Hutchings had just departed Fairport Convention when he met noted folkies Tim Hart and Maddy Prior and former electric folkies Gay and Terry Woods. The five joined forces and began recording *HARK, THE VILLAGE WAIT* (an album not made available in the United States until recently). By the end of the sessions, the Woods were out and Peter Knight and Martin McCarthy were in. Two more albums saw Hutchings and McCarthy departing and Bob Johnson and Rick Kemp enlisting. The band continued to release fantasy-laden albums, the first to be released stateside being *BELOW THE SALT*. With an American audience in mind, the group sought to expand their sound and drafted the services of drummer Nigel Pegrum for *PARCEL OF ROGUES*. Gradually, Steeleye began to develop a cult status on both sides of the At-

lantic. Thus far, the high point of their career has been their *ALL AROUND MY HAT* LP which offered them a hit single in England and a lot of airplay in the United States. Their sound is still traditional British folk but they have seen fit tastefully to expand its boundaries to include such diverse epics as *To Know Him Is to Love Him* and *New York Girls*. No matter what the song or its origin, Steeleye Span can be counted upon to perform it with grace and charm.

Albums/HARK, THE VILLAGE WAIT (9/76): *A Calling on Song; The Blacksmith; Fisherman's Wife; Blackleg Miner; Dark-Eyed Sailor; Copshawolme Fiar; All Things Are Quite Silent; The Hills of Greenmore; My Johnny Was a Shoemaker; Lowlands of Holland; Two Corbies; One Night As I Lay on My Bed.* PLEASE TO SEE THE KING (9/76): *The Blacksmith; Cold, Haily, Windy Night; jigs: Bryan O Lynn, The Hag with the Money; Prince Charlie Stuart; Boys of Bedlam; False Knight on the Road; The Lark in the Morning; The King; Lovely on the Water.* TEN MAN MOP OR MIR. RESERVOIR BUTLER RIDES AGAIN (9/76): *Gower Wassail; jigs: Paddy Clancey's Jig, Willie Clancy's Fancy; Four Nights Drunk; When I Was on Horseback; Marrowbones; Captain Couldston; reels: Dowd's Favorite, Ten-Pound Float, The Morning Dew; Skewball.* BELOW THE SALT (10/72): *Spotted Cow; Rosebud in June; jig: Sheep-Crook and Black Dog; Royal Forester; King Henry; Saucy Sailor; John Barleycorn.* PARCEL OF ROGUES (3/73): *One Misty Moisty Morning; Alison Gross; The Bold Poachers; The Ups and Downs; Robbery with Violins; The Wee Wee Man; The Weaver and the Factory Maid; Rogues in a Nation; Cam Ye O'er frae France; Hares on the Mountain.* NOW WE ARE SIX (3/74): *Seven Hundred Elves; Edwin; Drink Down the Moon; Now We Are Six; Thomas the Rhymer; The Mooncoin Jig; Long a-Growing; Two Magicians; Twinkle Twinkle Little Star; To Know Him Is to Love Him.* ALL AROUND MY HAT (10/75): *Black Jack Davy; Hard Times of Old England; Cadgwith Anthem; Sum Waves (Tunes); Gamble Gold/Robin Hood; All around My Hat; Dance with me; Bachelors Hall.* COMMONER'S CROWN (9/76): *Little Sir Hugh; Bach Goes to Limerick; Long Lankin; Dogs and Ferrets; Galtee Farmer; Demon Lover; Elf Call; Weary Cutters; New York Girls.* ROCKET COTTAGE (9/76): *London; The Bosnian Hornpipes; Orfeo/Nathan's Reel; The Twelve Witches; The Brown Girl; Fight-*

ing for Strangers; Sligo Maid; Sir James the Rose; The Drunkard.
THE STEELEYE SPAN STORY: ORIGINAL MASTERS
(6/77): *A Calling on Song; Thomas the Rhymer; Sir James the Rose; Black Jack Davy; The King; All around My Hat; Fighting for Strangers; Seven Hundred Elves; Little Sir Hugh; Demon Lover; Elf Call; Cam Ye O'er frae France; Bonnie Moorhen; Alison Gross; Dark-Eyed Sailor; Hard Times of Old England; Blackleg Miner; Skewball; Lovely on the Water; One Misty Moisty Morning; Gaudete; Saucy Sailor.*
Single/*Gaudete*/*Royal Forester* (10/72).

STEELY DAN/*Donald Fagan (keyboards, vocals), Walter Becker (bass and vocals), Denny Dias (guitar), Jim Hodder (drums), Dave Palmer (vocals), Jeff "Skunk" Baxter (guitar).*
Steely Dan is quite an atypical rock band. A super-literate on-again, off-again entourage named for a dildo appearing in William Burroughs' *Naked Lunch,* the band is a musical doctorate compiled by several graduates of the musical school of hard knocks. In this case, the campuses ranged from Ultimate Spinach to Jay and the Americans.

Steely Dan is the brainchild of Donald Fagan and Walter Becker (the only two "for sure" members of the group present). Becker and Fagan attended Bard college in upstate New York where they first began jamming and writing songs together. An early success, a movie soundtrack *(You Gotta Walk It Like You Talk It or You'll Lose That Beat)* did not exactly set the show-biz world on fire and subsequent jobs with Jay and the Americans as back-up musicians paid the rent but did little for peace of mind.

ABC producer Gary Katz saw the plight and the potential of the duo and helped them assemble the original Steely Dan, taking Becker and Fagan from their newfound posts as ABC West Coast songwriters. The twosome became the leaders of the "next big thing." Long-time friend Danny Dias was plucked from New York, as was Dave Palmer. From Boston came Hodder and Baxter (the latter a former member of Ultimate Spinach and sideman for Carly Simon).

The band scored big with their enigmatic lyrics and memorable melodies. Their debut LP, *CAN'T BUY A THRILL,* sent two singles—*Reelin in the Years* and *Do It Again*—reelin' up the charts. Steely Dan appeared to have made it. Hmmm. Their second album, *COUNTDOWN TO ECSTASY,* was critically acclaimed but contained no boffo singles. *PRETZEL LOGIC* delivered unto the AM-radio jocks *Rikki, Don't Lose That Number.* Shortly after its release, Steely Dan, as a working unit, collapsed.

Fagan and Becker hated to tour. For the rest of the band, however, touring was not only fun, it was their bread and butter. While Donald and Walter earned royalties on the songs that they penned, the band only made money from actually performing. Baxter joined the Dobies and the rest of the band scattered, with Fagan and Becker going on to form the nucleus of the present day Steely Dan: a band that is comprised of sidemen whenever an album is desired. The lyrics are still intense, the melodies still infectious, but for Steely Dan the days of live thrills are over.

Albums/CAN'T BUY A THRILL (10/72): *Do It Again; Dirty Work; Kings; Midnight Cruiser; Only a Fool Would Say That; Reeling In The Years; Fire in the Hole; Brooklyn; Change of the Guard; Turn That Heartbeat Over Again.* COUNTDOWN TO ECSTASY (8/73): *Bodhisattva; Razor Boy; The Boston Rag; Your Gold Teeth; Show Biz Kids; My Old School; Pearl of the Quarter; King of the World.* PRETZEL LOGIC (3/74): *Rikki Don't Lose That Number; Night by Night; Any Major Dude Will Tell You; Barrytown; Easy St. Louise Toodle-oo; Parker's Band; Through with Buzz; Pretzel Logic; With a Gun; Charlie Freak; Monkey in Your Soul.* KATY LIED (3/75): *Black Friday; Bad Sneakers; Rose Darling; Daddy Don't Live in That New York City No More; Doctor Wu; Everyone's Gone to the Movies; Your Gold Teeth II; Chain Lightning; Any World; Throw Back the Little Ones.* ROYAL SCAM (4/76): *Kid Charlemagne; Caves of Altamira; Don't Take Me Alive; Sign In, Stranger; The Fez; Green Earrings; Haitian Divorce; Everything You Did; The Royal Scam.* AJA (9/77): *Boddhisattva; Black Cow; Home At Last; I Got the News; Aja; Deacon Blues.*

Singles/*Dallas/Sail the Waterway* (3/72); *Do It Again/Fire in the Hole* (10/72); *Reeling In the Years/Only a Fool Would Say That* (2/73); *Razor Boy/Show Biz Kids* (6/73); *My Old School/Pearl of the Quarter* (9/73); *Riki, Don't Lose That Number/Any Major Dude Will Tell You* (4/74); *Through with Buzz/Pretzel Logic* (8/74); *Black Friday/Throw Back the Little Ones* (4/75); *Bad Sneakers/Chain Lightning* (7/75); *Green Earrings/Kid Charlemagne* (5/76); *Sign in, Stranger/The Fez* (8/76).

STEPPENWOLF/*John Kay (guitar, vocals), George Biando (bass, vocals), Jerry Edmonton (drums, vocals), Bobby Cochran (guitar), Wayne Cook (keyboards). Original members: Kay, Goldy McJohn (organ), Edmonton, Michael Monarch (guitar), John Russel Morgan (bass—replaced almost immediately by John Moreve).*
Led by croupy lead singer/swaggerer John Kay, Steppenwolf hit the rock and roll public betwixt the orbs back in the tail end of the sixties with their epic youth-culture-gone-bananas anthem, *Born to Be Wild.* After that the hits kept on coming with *Magic Carpet Ride, Monster,* and *Rock Me.*

Steppenwolf was the creation of East German–born Canadian Kay who formed a north-of-the-border blues band called Sparrow. As Sparrow made the rounds across the United States they gradually drifted from blues to gritty rock and changed their name to Steppenwolf at the behest of their first producer, Gabriel Mekler.

When the band hit, they hit big, with the aforementioned singles earning them a solid teen following and the long-winded *The Pusher* (a Hoyt Axton–penned tune) scoring them big points with the underground crowd. (You were cool if your nearby FM station even dared to play it.) The low-down and nasty group achieved even more fame via a double shot of Steppenwolf music in the counterculture-classic film *Easy Rider.* Success was theirs. Gold records. SRO concert dates. Even an occasional addition or deletion among the Hesse-inspired horde of musicians didn't break their stride. (Among the faces to come and go were John Morgan, bass, replaced by Nick St. Nicholas, replaced by George Biando, and Michael Monarch, guitar, replaced by Larry Byrom, replaced by Kent Henry, replaced by Bobby Cochran.)

When success got too much to handle, the band announced a split-up in 1972. Kay set off on a disastrous solo path. In 1974 the group was exhumed. Thus far, they have proven only moderately successful.

Albums/STEPPENWOLF (1/68): *Sookie, Sookie; Everybody's Next One; Berry Rides Again; Hootchie Kootchie Man; Born to Be Wild; Your Wall's Too High; Desperation; The Pusher; A Girl I Knew; Take What You Need; The Ostrich.* STEPPENWOLF THE SECOND (10/68): *Faster Than the Speed of Life; Tighten Up Your Wig; None of Your Doing; Spiritual Fantasy; Don't Step on the Grass Sam; 28; Magic Carpet Ride; Disappointment*

Number; Lost and Found by Trial and Error; Hodge Podge Strained through a Leslie; Resurrection; Reflections. STEPPENWOLF AT YOUR BIRTHDAY PARTY (3/69): *Don't Cry; Chicken Wolf; Lovely Meter; Round and Down; It's Never Too Late; Sleeping Dreaming; Jupiter Child; She'll Be Better; Cat Killer; Rock Me; God Fearing Man; Mango Juice; Happy Birthday.* EARLY STEPPENWOLF (8/69): *The Pusher; Tighten Up Your Wig; Power Play; Howlin' for My Darlin'; I'm Going Upstairs; Corina, Corina.* MONSTER (10/69): *Monster; Move Over; other titles.* LIVE STEPPENWOLF (2/70): *Hey Lawdy Mama; Magic Carpet Ride; Born to Be Wild; The Pusher; Monster; From Here to There Eventually.* STEPPENWOLF 7 (10/70): *Earschplittenloudenboomer; Foggy Mental Breakdown; 40 Days and 40 Nights; Snowblind Friend; Who Needs Ya; Ball Crusher; Hippo Stomp; Renegade; Fat Jack.* STEPPENWOLF GOLD (1/71): *Born to Be Wild; Rock Me; Screaming Night Hog; Magic Carpet Ride; Who Needs Ya; The Pusher; other titles.* FOR LADIES ONLY (8/71): *For Ladies Only; I'm Asking; Shackles and Chains; Tenderness; The Night Time's for You; Jaded Strumpet; Sparkle Eyes; Black Pit; Ride with Me; In Hopes of a Garden.* REST IN PEACE (5/72): *The Ostrich; Your Wall's Too High; Don't Step on the Grass, Sam; Desperation; Renegade; Foggy Mental Breakdown; Hippo Stomp; Take What You Need; Everybody's Next One; None of Your Doing.* STEPPENWOLF— 16 GREATEST HITS (1/73): *Born to Be Wild; It's Never Too Late; Rock Me; Hey Lawdy Mama; Move Over; Magic Carpet Ride; Who Needs Ya; The Pusher; Sookie, Sookie; Jupiter's Child; Screaming Night Hog; Monster; Ride with Me; Snowblind Friend; For Ladies Only; Tenderness (For Ladies Only).* SLOW FLUX (8/74): *Gang War Blues; Children of the Night; Justice Don't Be Slow; Get into the Wind; Jeraboah; Straight Shootin' Woman; Smokey Factory Blues; Morning Blues; A Fool's Fantasy; Fishin' in the Dark.* HOUR OF THE WOLF (8/75): *Caroline (Are You Ready for the Outlaw World); Annie, Annie Over; Two for the Love of One; Just for Tonight; Hard Rock Road; Someone Told a Lie; Another's Lifetime; Mr. Penny Pincher.* SKULLDUGGERY (3/76): *Skullduggery; Road Runner; Rock 'n' Roll Song; Train of Thought; Life Is a Gamble; Pass It On; Sleep; Lip Service.* REBORN TO BE WILD (10/76): *Straight Shootin' Woman; Hard Rock Road; Another's Lifetime; Mr. Penny Pincher; Smokey Fac-*

tory Blues; Caroline; Get into the Wind; Gang War Blues; Children of the Night; Skullduggery.

Singles/*Sookie, Sookie/Take What You Need* (2/68); *Born to Be Wild/Everybody's Next One* (6/68); *Girl I Knew/The Ostrich* (1968); *Magic Carpet Ride/Sookie, Sookie* (9/68); *Rock Me* (2/69); *It's Never Too Late/Happy Birthday* (5/69); *Move Over* (8/69); *Monster* (12/69); *Hey Lawdy Mama* (3/70); *Screaming Night Hog/Spiritual Fantasy* (7/70); *Who Needs Ya/Earschplittenloudenboomer* (10/70); *Snow Blind Friend/Hippo Stomp* (1/71); *Ride with Me* (6/71); *For Ladies Only/Sparkle Eyes* (10/71); *Straight Shootin' Woman/Justice Don't Be Slow* (8/74); *Get into the Wind/Morning Blue* (11/74); *Smokey Factory Blues/A Fool's Fantasy* (1/75); *Caroline/Angeldrawers* (5/75).

CAT STEVENS/In a little over a decade, Cat Stevens has gone from an overt pop personality crooning tunes like *I Love My Dog* to a satyrlike guru warbling *Peace Train.* The years in between have been riddled with success, emotional stress, and a good deal of mystery. A superstar who shuns the spotlight with a passion, Cat (or Steven Georgiou) took up folk music while in college. The son of Greek parents, London-born Cat was on the brink of giving up his educational experience in favor of an American lifestyle when he cut his first single, *I Love My Dog.* The song proved a British hit and Stevens was soon on his way to becoming a late sixties' pop idol with a followup single, *Matthew and Son.*

Cat's career came to a standstill in 1968 when, after contracting TB, he was forced to spend a year in a hospital on the mend. This year of professional inactivity led Stevens to concentrate on his songwriting skills. In 1970 he emerged with a minor classic of an album, *MONA BONE JAKON.* As evidenced on the album, a new Cat Stevens was entering the music business, a more introspective, lyrical performer. His newfound fame began to spread and, for the first time, American audiences began to take notice.

His next two albums, *TEA FOR THE TILLERMAN* and *TEASER AND THE FIRECAT,* proved amazingly successful, spawning hit singles *(Wild World, Morning Has Broken, Moonshadow)* and earning him the coveted status of Gold Record-dom. As his fame grew, Stevens' lifestyle became more and more reclusive. The tours became more infrequent and the albums were a year or more in coming. *Teaser and the Firecat* was produced as an animated short which spotlighted the single *Moonshadow.* Stevens' touring band fluctuated wildly and his music began to take on a more rambling character.

Of late, critics have begun to criticize Stevens' compositions as being mundane caricatures of earlier works. To his millions of fans, however, Cat Stevens is the premier singer-songwriter who can do no wrong.

Albums/MATTHEW AND SON (1967): *Matthew and Son; I Love My Dog; Here Comes My Baby; Bring Another Bottle; I've Found a Love; I See the Road; I'm Gonna Get a Gun; School is Out; Baby, Get Your Head Screwed On; Speak to the Flowers; Humming Bird; Lady.* NEW MASTERS (2/68): *Kitty; I'm So Sleepy; Northern Winds; The Laughing Apple; Smash Your Heart; Moonstone; First Cut Is the Deepest; I'm Gonna Be King; Ceylon City; Blackness of the Night; Shift That Log; I Love Them All.* MONA BONE JAKON (7/7): *Lady D'Arbanville Maybe You're Right; Pop Star; I Think I See the Light; Trouble; Mona Bone Jakon; I Wish, I Wish; Katmandu; Time; Fill My Eyes; Lilywhite.* TEA FOR THE TILLERMAN (11/70): *Where Do the Children Play; Hard-Headed Woman; Wild World; Sad Lisa; Miles from Nowhere; But I Must Die Tonight; Longer Boats; Into White; On the Road to Findout; Father and Son; Tea for the Tillerman.* MATTHEW AND SON/NEW MASTERS (3/71). TEASER AND THE FIRECAT (10/71): *The Wind; Rubylove; If I Laugh; Changes IV; How Can I Tell You; Tuesday's Dead; Morning Has Broken; Moonshadow; Bitterblue; Peace Train.* VERY EARLY AND YOUNG SONGS (11/71): *Here Comes My Wife; Lovely City; The Tramp; Come on and Dance; Image of Hell; Where Are You; It's a Super Duper Life; A Bad Night; Come On Baby; The View from the Top.* CATCH BULL AT FOUR (9/72): *Sitting; Boy with a Moon and a Star on His Head; Angelsea; Silent Sunlight; Can't Keep It In; 18th Avenue; Freezing Steel; O Caritas; Sweet Scarlet; Ruins.* FOREIGNER (7/73): *Foreigner Suite; The Hurt; How Many Times; Later; 100 I Dream.* BUDDHA AND THE CHOCOLATE BOX (3/74): *Music; Oh Very Young; Sun/C79; Ghost Town; Jesus; Ready; King of Trees; A Bad Penny; Home in the Sky.* GREATEST HITS (6/75): *Wild World; Oh Very Young; Can't Keep It In; Hard-Headed Woman; Moonshadow; Two Fine People; Peace Train; Ready; Father and Son;*

Sitting; Morning Has Broken; Another Saturday Night. NUM-
BERS (11/75): *Whistlestar; Novim' Nightmare; Majik of Majiks;
Drywood; Banapple Gas; Land o'Freelove and Goodbye; Zero;
Home; Monad's Anthem.* IZITSO (5/77): *Old Schoolyard; Life;
Killin' Time; Krypros; Bonfire; I Never Wanted to Be a Star;
Crazy; Sweet Jamaica; Was Dog a Doughnut?; Child for a Day.*

Singles/*I Love My Dog/Portobello Road* (1/67); *Matthew and
Son/Granny* (1/67); *I'm Gonna Get Me a Gun/School Is Out*
(4/67); *A Bad Night/The Laughing Apple* (8/67); *Lady
D'Arbanville* (8/70); *Wild World* (1/71); *Moon Shadow* (5/71);
Peace Train (9/71); *Morning Has Broken* (3/72); *The Hurt* (6/72);
Sitting (10/72); *Oh Very Young* (2/74); *Another Saturday Night*
(7/74); *Ready* (11/74); *Two Fine People* (9/75); *Banapple Gas*
(1/76); *Old School Yard* (6/77).

ROD STEWART/If young Rod Stewart had had his way, he
would have opted for a career as a soccer star instead of as a
gravel-voiced pop idol. The London-born Rod, after a stint at
manual labor (i.e., gravedigging) attempted to become a professional footballer while still a teen but was discouraged by the
menial tasks required of a "new kid." He left all thoughts of
sports behind and embarked on a nomadic existence across the
Continent before finally winding up in Spain. Broke and hungry,
he returned to England where he joined a Birmingham group,
Jimmy Powell and the Dimensions, as a harmonica-playing
singer. A series of gigs with various bands followed, including
Long John Baldry's Hootchie Coochie Men, Brian Auger's
Steampacket, and Mick Fleetwood and Peter Green's Shotgun
Express. Eventually he joined the Jeff Beck Group (c. 1968) where
he gained some degree of fame.

After two albums, Beck and Stewart reached an impasse as to
what direction the band should pursue. Stewart struck out on his
own path, simultaneously joining the revamped Faces (formerly
the Small Faces, until leader Steve Marriott jumped ship for
Humble Pie territory) as lead singer.

Rod's schizoid approach to his career eventually caught up
with his Faces stance. His solo albums achieved worldwide acclaim and, by 1971, he was a bona fide superstar on his own. His
Faces sessions, on the other hand, seemed listless by comparison
and the Faces "live" always proved a tentative proposition at

best. As the Faces suffered, Stewart soared with hit singles like *Maggie May* and *You Wear It Well.* At the height of his success, however, Rod became involved in a tug-of-war between his two labels, Mercury (solo) and Warners (Faces). The two labels fought over who "owned" Stewart and an album, *SMILER,* was delayed in being released for nearly a year.

In 1975, Stewart joined the Warner roster as a solo artist. Shortly thereafter, he severed ties with the Faces amidst a flurry of ill-chosen words and hard feelings on several members' parts. His albums on Warner have been slick, commercial affairs and, while they did well sales-wise, they also disappointed a lot of Stewart's older, raver-oriented fans. But no matter what direction his career takes at this point, the contribution made by Stewart to the school of rock and roll cannot be overlooked.

He was vocally subtle when the trend was to be garish. He was emotional when the rules called for supercool. He was gritty when the fad was smooth. His music was (and often still is) individualistic both in style and substance. There's no telling where his talent will lead him next.

Albums/THE ROD STEWART ALBUM (9/69): *Street Fighting Man; Man of Constant Sorrow; Blind Prayer; Handbags and Gladrags; An Old Raincoat Won't Ever Let You Down; I Wouldn't Ever Change a Thing; Cindy's Lament; Dirty Old Town.* GASOLINE ALLEY (5/70): *Gasoline Alley; It's All Over Now; Only a Hobo; My Way of Giving; Country Comfort; Cut Across Shorty; Lady Day; Jo's Lament; You're My Girl (I Don't Want to Discuss It).* EVERY PICTURE TELLS A STORY (5/71): *Reason to Believe; That's All Right; I'm Losing You; Tomorrow Is Such a Long Time; Seems Like a Long Time; Mandolin Wind; Every Picture Tells a Story; Maggie May.* NEVER A DULL MOMENT (8/72): *True Blue; Lost Paraguayos; Mama, You Been on My Mind; Italian Girls; Angel; Interludings; You Wear It Well; I'd Rather Go Blind; Twistin' The Night Away.* SING IT AGAIN ROD (6/73) *Reason To Believe; You Wear It Well; Mandolin Wind; Country Comfort; Maggie May; Handbags and Gladrags; Street Fighting Man; Twisting the Night Away; I'm Losing You; Lost Paraguayos; Pinball Wizard; Gasoline Alley.* SMILER (9/74): *Sweet Little Rock 'n' Roller; Lochinvar; Farewell; Sailor; Bring It On Home to Me/You Send Me; Let Me Be Your Car; A Natural Man; Dixie Toot; Hard Road; I've Grown Accustomed to Her Face; Girl from*

the North Country; Mine for Me. ATLANTIC CROSSING
(8/75): *Three Time Loser; Alright for an Hour; All in the Name of
Rock 'n' Roll; Drift Away; Stone Cold Sober; I Don't Want to Talk
About It; It's Not the Spotlight; Still Love You; This Old Heart of
Mine; Sailing.* THE BEST OF ROD STEWART (4/76): *Maggie
May; Cut Across Shorty; An Old Raincoat Won't Ever Let You
Down; I'm Losing You; Handbags and Gladrags; It's All Over
Now; Gasoline Alley; Street Fighting Man; Every Picture Tells a
Story; What's Made Milwaukee Famous (Has Made a Loser out of
Me); Oh! No, Not My baby; Jodie; You Wear It Well; Let Me Be
Your Car; Pinball Wizard; Sailor; Angel; Mine for Me.* A NIGHT
ON THE TOWN (7/76): *Tonight's the Night; The First Cut Is the
Deepest; Fool for You; The Killing of Georgie (Parts I and II); The
Balltrap; Pretty Flamingo; Big Bayou; The Wild Side of Life;
Trade Winds.* THE BEST OF ROD STEWART, VOL. II
(11/76): *Man of Constant Sorrow; Blind Prayer; Lady Day;
Tomorrow Is Such a Long Time; Country Comfort; Mandolin
Wind; That's All Right; My Way of Giving; I Don't Want to Dis-
cuss It; Find A Reason To Believe; Italian Girls; I'd Rather Go
Blind; Lost Paraguayos; True Blue; Sweet Little Rock 'n' Roller;
Hard Road; A Natural Man; Bring It On Home to Me/You Send
Me; Twistin' the Night Away.* FOOT LOOSE AND FANCY
FREE (11/77): *Hot Legs; You're Insane; You're in My Heart;
Born Loose; You Keep Me Hangin' On; (If Loving You Is Wrong)
I Don't Want to Be Right; You Got a Nerve; I Was Only Joking.*

Singles/*Street Fighting Man/An Old Raincoat Won't Ever Let
You Down* (12/69); *Handbags and Gladrags/Man of Constant Sorrow* (6/70); re-released 1/72); *Jo's Lament/It's All Over Now
(7/70); Gasoline Alley/Only a Hobo* (8/70); *Cut Across Shorty*
(11/70); *Dirty Old Town/My Way of Giving* (1/71); *Country Comfort* (3/71); *Reason to Believe/Maggie May* (6/71); *Mandolin
Wind/I'm Losing You* (10/71); *You Wear It Well/True Blue*
(8/72); *Angle/Lost Paraguayos* (10/72); *Twistin' the Night
Away/True Blue* (7/73); *Oh! No, Not My Baby/Jodie* (9/73);
Farewell/Mine for Me (10/74); *Sailor/Let Me Be Your Car*
(1/75); *Sailing/All in the Name of Rock 'n' Roll* (9/75); *This Old
Heart of Mine/Still Love You* (11/75); *Tonight's the Night/Fool
for You* (8/76); *Hard Road/A Natural Man* (11/76); *Sweet Little
Rock 'n' Roller* (11/76); *The First Cut Is the Deepest/The Balltrap*
(1/77).

STEPHEN STILLS/Stephen Stills has been a driving force in rock music for over a decade, although his career has received less fanfare than most. Born in Dallas, Stills first entered the music scene in New York during the halcyon days of the early sixties. The guitarist-singer-pianist-drummer quickly began playing in numerous house bands in Manhattan, including one called the Au Go Go Singers with one Richie Furay.

Stills eventually made his way from New York to the West Coast, where he answered the call of TV executives forming a ready-made rock troupe, the Monkees. Stills didn't pass the audition but, undaunted, went on to form Buffalo Springfield, one of the finest bands of that decade. Artistically triumphant, Springfield did little commercially, so, by 1968, Stills found himself without a band. Stills became a sideman and recorded several tracks with Joni Mitchell and Judy Collins. An album, *SUPER SESSION,* resulted from jams he held with Mike Bloomfield and Al Kooper.

Late in 1968, Stills helped put together Crosby, Stills and Nash (which later blossomed into Crosby, Stills, Nash and Young with the addition of ex-Springfield member Neil Young). At long last, Stills was enjoying commerciality. Success was quck in coming to CS&N. By 1970, however, the glamor was beginning to fade from the supergroup and in-house hassles led Stills to seek an outlet outside the band. His first solo album was the result.

When CSN&Y folded, Stills took to the solo route full-time. A second album was not as successful as its predecessor and Stills formed the shortlived Manassas. About this time the rumor machine of rock began operating overtime and Stills was portrayed as a low-keyed, hard-living superstar bent on self-destruction. Avoiding the rock limelight, Stills managed to keep the rumors to a minimum, as he continued churning out long-players. A marriage to Veronique Sanson was a joyous, albeit brief, turn of events in his life. A re-union with Crosby, Nash and Young in 1975 served as a springboard for a second stage of Stills' solo career. The same year, he moved to Columbia records, where he produced a debut album over a period of one and a half years.

Nineteen seventy-six and seventy-seven saw Stills reunited with Crosby and Nash on one album and with Neil Young on another. At this point, low-keyed musical maven Stills is still producing laid-back, melodious rock of the first magnitude for all his fans to relish. The problem is, his low-profile is making it easy for his legion of followers to dwindle.

Albums/STEPHEN STILLS (11/70): *Love the One You're With; Do for the Others; Church (Part of Someone); Old Times Good Times; Go Back Home; Sit Yourself Down; To a Flame; Black Queen; Cherokee; We Are Not Helpless.* STEPHEN STILLS 2 (6/71): *Change Partners; Nothin' to Do but Today; Fishes and Scorpions; Sugar Babe; Know You Got to Run; Open Secret; Relaxing Town; Singin' Call; Ecology Song; Word Game; Marianne; Bluebird Revisited.* MANASSAS (4/72): *Fallen Eagle; Jesus Gave Love Away for Free; Colorado; So Begins the Task; Hide It So Deep; Don't Look at My Shadow; It Doesn't Matter; Johnny's Garden; Bound to Fall; How Far; Move Around; The Love Gangster; Song of Love; Rock and Roll Crazies; Cuban Bluegrass; Jet Set (Sigh); Anyway; Both of Us (Bound to Lose); What to Do; Right Now; The Treasure; Blues Man.* DOWN THE ROAD (4/73): *Isn't It About Time; Lies; Pensamiento; So Many Times; Business on the Street; Do You Remember the Americans; Down the Road; City Junkies; Guaguanco de Vero; Rollin' My Stone.* STILLS (9/75): *Turn Back the Pages; My Favorite Changes; My Angel; In the Way; Love Story; To Mama from Christopher and the Old Man; First Things First; New Mama; As I Come of Age; Shuffle; Just As Bad; Cold Cold World; Myth of Sisyphus.* LIVE (12/75): *Change Partners; Crossroads; You Can't Catch Me; Everybody's Talkin' at Me; 4+20; World Game; Wooden Ships; Four Days Gone; Jet Set (Sigh); Rocky Mountain Way; Special Care.* ILLEGAL STILLS (4/76): *Buyin' Time; Midnight in Paris; Different Tongues; Soldier; The Loner; Stateline Blues; Closer to You; No Me Nieges; Ring of Love; Circlin'.* THE STILLS-YOUNG BAND: LONG MAY YOU RUN (10/76): *Long May You Run; Make Love to You; Midnight on the Bay; Black Coral Ocean Girl; Let It Shine; 12/8 Blues; Fontainebleau; Guardian Angel.* STILL STILLS (BEST OF) 12/76): *Love the One You're With; It Doesn't Matter; We Are Not Helpless; Marianne; Bound to Fall; Isn't It About Time; Change Partners; Go Back Home; Johnny's Garden; Rock and Roll Crazies; Cuban Bluegrass; Sit Yourself Down.*

Singles/*Love the One You're With/Change Partners* (10/70); *Sit Yourself Down/We Are Not Helpless* (2/71); *Change Partners/Relaxing Town* (5/71); *Marianne/Nothin' to Do but To-*

day (7/71); *It Doesn't Matter/Rock and Roll Crazies/Colorado* (4/72); *Isn't It About Time/So Many Times (3/73); Down the Road/Guaguanco de Vero* (6/73); *Turn Back the Pages* (10/75); *Buyin' Time/Soldier* (6/76).

THE STRANGLERS/*Hugh Cornwell (guitars and vocals), Jean Jacques Burnel (bass and vocals), Dave Greenfield (keyboards), Jet Black (drums and percussion).*
Probably the most musically cohesive punk rock band to emerge from Britain during the 1976–1977 Punk Rock bonanza, the Stranglers are a keyboard-oriented lot compared by many nostalgia buffs to the early Doors. Whether that comparison is valid or not, the Stranglers are one of the few bands involved in the New Wave to boast a distinctive, rumbling sound totally their own. Beginning in 1975, the group quickly attained a reputation for themselves, playing anywhere a band could possibly fit. In 1976, they played 184 separate dates. Their most prestigious jobs came in May of 1976 when they opened for Patti Smith on her tour of England. They were spotted by United Artists Records A&R man Andrew Lauder, who quickly signed them to the label. Lauder, one of the finest pairs of ears to grace the British music business, guided the foursome into the studio where, with Martin Rushent producing, they cut their first LP. A&M Records in the States signed the band in May of 1977. Although the Stranglers, like all of their punk peers, have yet to make a name for themselves in the United States, their organ-crazy sound shows the potential for a lot of development and expansion. Perhaps, when the fad is over, the Stranglers will be able to be heard for what they are: a truly hypnotic rock and roll outfit.
Albums/RATTUS NORVEGICUS (6/77): *Sometimes; Goodbye Toulouse; London Lady; Princess of the Streets; Hanging Around; Peaches; (Get a) Grip (on Yourself); Ugly; Down in the Sewer.* NO MORE HEROES (10/77): *I Feel Like a Wog; Bitching; Dead Ringer; Bring on the Nubiles; Something Better Change; Dagenham Dave; No More Heroes; Peasant in the Big Shitty; Burning Up Time; English Towns; School Mam.*
Singles/*Something Better Change/Straighten Out/(Get a) Grip (on Yourself)/Hanging Around* (extended player, 9/77).

THE STRAWBS/*Dave Cousins (vocals, guitar, banjo), Dave Lam-*

bert (guitar, vocals), Chas Cronk (bass), Rod Coombs (drums). Additional members: Blue Weaver (keyboards), Rick Wakeman (keyboards), John Ford (bass), Richard Hudson (drums), Tony Hooper (guitar, vocals), John Hawken (keyboards), Ron Chesterman (bass), Arthur Philips (mandolin).

The majestic sounds of the British band the Strawbs actually had their start in a bluegrass ensemble, the Strawberry Hill Boys, formed in 1967 by Leicester University student Cousins and friend-folkie Hooper. Eventually the band included Chesterman and Philips and the embryonic Strawbs (a shortening of the original name) was formed. The band joined forces with singer-songwriter Sandy Denny until her leap to fame via Fairport Convention. The Strawbs were then signed to A&M and, after two fairly ignored albums, regrouped. Cousins and Hooper were then joined by Hudson, Ford, and Wakeman.

Wakeman's interest in classical keyboard work led the band into a period of expansion, which resulted in the critically acclaimed *JUST A COLLECTION OF ANTIQUES AND CURIOS* long-player. In 1971, however, Wakeman (touted as a star on the horizon) left the band to join the fledgling Yes, being replaced by Blue Weaver. Despite Wakeman's departure, the Strawbs' momentum grew, climaxed by the magnificent *GRAVE NEW WORLD* release, which completely erased any and all traces of the band's earlier folkie days. While this album proved a tremendous success, it also served as a point of frustration for founding member Hooper, who left shortly thereafter.

Newcomer Dave Lambert entered the picture in time to witness an artistic difference between Cousins and songwriting duo Hudson-Ford. Following the *BURSTING AT THE SEAMS* album, Hudson, Ford, and Blue Weaver took leave of the band, allowing Cousins and Lambert to re-group with Hawken, Coombes, and Cronk. Two years later, in 1976, Hawken split, leaving the band to fend for themselves as a foursome. During the same year, they left A&M for the Polydor label. In both their high and low periods, the Strawbs have been a constant source of quality rock. With their musicians entering and exiting regularly, the Strawbs somehow retained an identifiable sound, led by the distinctive vocalizing of Dave Cousins.

Albums/JUST A COLLECTION OF ANTIQUES AND CURIOS (7/70): *Martin Luther King's Dream; Antique Suite (The*

Reaper, We Must Cross the River, Antiques and Curios, Hey, It's Been a Long Time); Temperament of Mind; Fingertips; Song of a Sad Little Girl; Where Is This Dream of Your Youth. FROM THE WITCHWOOD (7/71): *A Glimpse of Heaven; Witchwood; Thirty Days; Flight; The Hangman and Papist; Sheep; Canon Dale; The Shepherd's Song; In Amongst the Roses; I'll Carry On beside You.* GRAVE NEW WORLD (4/72): *Benedictus; Hey, Little Man . . . Thursday's Child; Queen of Dreams; Heavy Disguise; New World; Hey, Little Man . . . Wednesday's Child; The Flower and the Young Man; Tomorrow; On Growing Older, Ha Me, Ah My; Is It Today, Lord?; The Journey's End.* BURSTING AT THE SEAMS (3/73): *Flying; Lady Fuchsia; Stormy Down; Down by the Sea; The River; Part of the Union; Tears and Pavan; The Winter and the Summer; Lay Down; Thank You.* HERO AND HEROINE (1/74): *Autumn (Heroine's Theme, Deep Summer's Sleep, The Winter Long); Sad Young Man; Just Love; Shine On, Silver Sun; Hero and Heroine; Midnight Sun; Out in the Cold; Round and Round; Lay a Little Light on Me; Hero's Theme.* GHOSTS (2/75): *Ghosts (Sweet Dreams, Night Light, Guardian Angel); Lemon Pie; Starshine/Angel Wine; Where Do You Go (When You Need a Hole to Crawl In); The Life Auction (Impressions of Southhall from a Train, The Auction); Don't Try to Change Me; Remembering; You and I (When We Were Young); Grace Darling.* NOMADNESS (9/75): *To Be Free; Little Sleepy; The Golden Salamander; Absent Friend (How I Need You); Back on the Farm; So Shall Our Love Die?; Tokyo Rosie; A Mind of My Own; Hanging in the Gallery; The Promised Land.* DEEP CUTS (1976). BURNING FOR YOU (5/77): *Burning for Me; Cut Like a Diamond; I Feel Your Loving Coming On; Barcarole (For the Death of Venice); Alexander the Great; Keep On Trying; Back in the Old Routine; Heartbreaker; Carry Me Home; Goodbye (Is Not an Easy Word to Say).*

Singles/*The Man Who Called Himself Jesus* (10/68); *Heavy Disguise* (6/72); *Part of the Union* (2/73); *Lay Down* (6/73); *Or Am I Dreaming* (11/73); *Round and Round* (5/74); *Lemon Pie* (4/75).

DONNA SUMMER/The sultry sweetheart of the disco crowd, Donna Summer cooed her way to fame in 1975 with her epic dirge, *Love to Love You Baby.* As well as setting some sort of record for longevity, it helped to establish a disco tradition in terms of programming preferences for extra-long songs. Since her initial hit, she has gone onto still more gold-laden tunes as well as moving into the film-soundtrack area, singing the theme song from *The Deep.*

Albums/LOVE TO LOVE YOU BABY (8/75): *Love to Love You Baby; Full of Emptiness; Need-a-Man Blues; Whispering Waves; Pandora's Box; Full of Emptiness (reprise).* LOVE TRILOGY (3/76): *Try Me, I Know We Can Make It; Prelude to Love; Could It Be Magic; Wasted; Come with Me.* FOUR SEASONS OF LOVE (10/76): *Spring Affair; Summer Fever; Autumn Chances; Winter Melody; Spring Reprise.* I REMEMBER YESTERDAY (5/77): *I Remember Yesterday; Love's Unkind; Back in Love Again; I Remember Yesterday (reprise); Take Me; Black Lady; Can't We Just Sit Down and Talk It Over; I Feel Love.* THE DEEP SOUNDTRACK (6/77): *Deep Down Inside.* ONCE UPON A TIME (11/77): *Once Upon a Time; Faster and Faster to Nowhere; Fairy Tale High; Say Something Nice; Now I Need You; Working the Midnight Shift; Queen for a Day;If You Got It, Flaunt It; A Man Like You; Sweet Romance; Once Upon a Time; Dance into My Life; Rumour Has It; I Love You; Happily Ever After.*

Singles/*Love to Love You Baby (8/75); Could It Be Magic (3/76); Try Me, I Know We Can Make It* (5/76); *Spring Affair* (11/76); *Winter Melody* (1/77); *Can't We Just Sit Down and Talk It Over* (5/77).

SUPERTRAMP/*Roger Hodgson (vocals, keyboards, guitars), Richard Davies (vocals, keyboards), Dougie Thompson (bass), John Anthony Helliewell (wind instruments, vocals), Bob C. Benberg (drums, percussion).*
Supertramp waited half a decade in limbo before achieving status in 1974 with their *CRIME OF THE CENTURY* album. Originating in the late sixties, sponsored by a rich patron, the original lineup, consisting of Hodgson, Davies, Dave Winthrop (reeds), Richard Palmer (guitar), and Bob Miller (drums), didn't last very long. Miller was soon replaced by Kevin Currie. The band recorded two albums (only one, *INDELIBLY STAMPED,* was released stateside) and their career met with utter neglect on the part of the world at large. Joining forces with producer Ken Scott in 1974, they came up with *CRIME OF THE CENTURY* and *Bloody Well Right.* A tour of the States brought them some semblance of fame, and the future looks good for Supertramp to achieve superstatus.

Albums/INDELIBLY STAMPED (8/71): *Your Poppa Don't Mind; Travelled; Rosie Had Everything Planned; Remember; Forever; Potter; Coming Home to See You; Times Have Changed; Friend in Need; Aries.* CRIME OF THE CENTURY (9/74): *School; Bloody Well Right; Hide in Your Shell; Asylum; Dream; Rudy; If Everyone Was Listening; Crime of the Century.* CRISIS? WHAT CRISIS? (11/75): *Easy Does It; Sister Moonshine; Ain't Nobody but Me; A Soapbox Opera; Another Man's Woman; Lady; Poor Boy; Just a Normal Day; The Meaning; Two of Us.* EVEN IN THE QUIETEST MOMENTS (4/77): *Give a Little Bit; Lover Boy; Even in the Quietest Moments; Downstream; Babaji; From Now On; Fool's Overture.*

Singles/*Forever* (10/71); *Bloody Well Right* (1/75); *Lady* (2/76); *Ain't Nobody but Me* (4/76); *Give a Little Bit* (4/77).

SURFING MUSIC/Someone once defined surf music as wet rock and roll. Surf music was born in California with the Beach Boys in 1962. Everyone knows the story. The Wilson brothers and friends and relatives, not a group as yet, got together, wrote a song about surfing, sang it, recorded it, had a small local hit with it and went on to make three huge national hits on the same theme. Soon, the high-harmonied, melodic portraits of California, Hawaii, and the sounds of the sea went on to become a national rage with such other soggy peers as Jan and Dean, the Surfaris—even Chubby Checker got into the swim of things.

SWEET/*Brian Connolly (vocals), Andy Scott (guitar), Steve Priest (bass), Mick Tucker (drums).*
Begun in the late sixties by Brian Connolly and Mick Tucker, Sweet's early attempts at success proved sour as the band launched their career with a series of stifferoo singles. In 1970 they tied up with pop-rock Svengalis Nicky Chinn and Chapman, who agreed both to manage and produce the band. Chinn and Chapman, no slouches at writing, kept the band in the charts with a ton of catchy, bubblegum singles that kept Sweet in the spotlight but caused the group grief in terms of image. Only one of their United Kingdom tunes, *Little Willy,* caught on in the States. Briefly, the tune was irritating at best. In '74, Sweet parted ways with Chinn-Chapman in an all-out attempt to funk-up their career. Rockers they wanted to be. And, soon, rockers they were.

However, successful they weren't. As of now, Sweet is enjoying a sort of Jekyll-and-Hyde existence, alternately scoring big with Chinn-Chapman–sounding singles and floundering with more direct, heavier LPs. What's a band to do?

Albums/DESOLATION BOULEVARD (4/75): *Ballroom Blitz; Fox on the Run; The 6-Teens; A.C.D.C.; Sweet F.A.; No, You Don't; Solid Gold Brass; Set Me Free; I Wanna Be Committed; In to Night.* GIVE US A WINK (2/76): *Action; Yesterday's Rain; White Mice; Healer; The Lies in Your Eyes; Cockroach; Lady Starlight; Keep It In; 4th of July.* OFF THE RECORD (4/77): *Fever of Love; Lost Angels; Midnight to Daylight; Laura Lee; Windy City; Stairway to the Stars; Live for Today; Funk It Up; Hard Times; She Gimme Loving.*

Singles/*Co-Co* (9/71); *Little Willy* (1/73); *Blockbuster (5/73); Ballroom Blitz/Restless* (4/75); *Fox on the Run/Burn on the Flame* (10/75); *Action/Medusa* (2/76); *Fever of Love/Heartbreak Today* (5/77); *Stairway to the Stars/Funk It Up* (7/77).

JAMES TAYLOR/James Taylor's first sleepy-eyed hit single, *Fire and Rain,* concerned suicide, drug addiction, and confinement in a mental home. And that cheerful ditty served as a springboard for one of the most successful singer-songwriters to emerge during the seventies. The nasal warbler was born in Boston, Massachusetts, the son of a medical college dean and a soprano. Taylor as a youth was a moody lad, and his fits of depression led him to a short stay in a local mental hospital.

While still a teen he journeyed to New York, where he met up with boyhood chum Danny Kortchmar and joined Kootch's band, the Flying Machine. After a few aborted attempts at recording, the band broke up and, in 1967, Taylor set off for London. After playing gigs in town and demoing several of his self-penned tunes, Taylor made the rounds at some of London's record companies. He made a big impression on Apple Records' Peter Asher and was signed.

His first album on the Beatles' label, *JAMES TAYLOR,* was greeted with universal apathy. His career going nowhere fast, the songwriter lapsed into a period of drug abuse and, returning to the States, re-entered a rest home. Asher, however, goaded Taylor's talent into overcoming his depression. With Apple Records coming apart at the seams, Asher negotiated a contract for Taylor which resulted, after James' release from the hospital, in the *SWEET BABY JAMES* album. The LP spawned the single *Fire and Rain* and a star was born, phoenixlike, from the ashes of despair.

Taylor's on-again, off-again flirtation with drugs plagued the early stages of his career, although his albums never seemed to suffer for it. His long-players were always well received by his fans, and an occasional single on the charts added an extra boost to his career. In 1973, he married songwriter Carly Simon and the twosome settled down to well-publicized marital bliss. Later that year, Taylor made his movie debut, with Beach Boy Dennis Wilson, in the monumental disaster *Two Lane Blacktop,* a film only a whitewall tire could love. James' career as a singles artist picked up speed, however, at the same time his acting bug downshifted, via a song recorded with wife Carly, *Mockingbird,* a remake of the old rock and roll tune. The uptempo piece of catatonia broke into the top ten. This melodic feast was duplicated a year later with the similarly arranged *How Sweet It Is.*

In 1977, Taylor left his long-time musical home, Warner Brothers, for the money-laden banks of Columbia Records territory. Of late, Taylor's style has opened up a bit more, incorporating laconic strains of good old rock and roll with the waves of acoustic balladeering.

Albums/JAMES TAYLOR (2/69): *Don't Talk Now; Something's Wrong; Knocking 'round the Zoo; Sunshine Sunshine; Taking It In; Something in the Way She Moves; Carolina on My Mind; Night Owl; Rainy Day Man; Circle 'round the Sun; Blues Is Just a Bad Dream; Brighten Your Night with My Day.* SWEET BABY JAMES (3/70): *Sweet Baby James; Lo and Behold; Sunny Skies; Oh, Susanna; Fire and Rain; Blossom; Anywhere Like Heaven; Suite for 20 G; Steamroller; Oh, Baby, Don't You Loose Your Lip on Me.* MUD SLIDE SLIM AND THE BLUE HORIZON (4/71): *Love Has Brought You Around; You've Got a Friend; Soldiers; Riding on a Railroad; Mud Slide Slim and the Blue Horizon; Hey Mister; That's Me Up There on the Jukebox; You Can Close Your Eyes; Machine Gun Kelly; Let Me Ride; Long Ago and Far Away; Highway Song; Isn't It Nice to Be Home Again.* ONE MAN DOG (11/72): *One Man Parade; Chili Dog; Nobody but You; New Time; Hymn; Jig; Dance; Mescalito; Little David; Fanfare; Someone; Don't You Know; Back on the Street Again; Don't*

Spoonful; Losing the Dogs; Feelt I for Me; Love Until I Die; Don't Want You, Woman; Help Me. UNDEAD (7/68): *I May Be Wrong, but I Won't Be Wrong Always; Woodchopper's Ball; Spider in My Web; Summertime; Shantung Cabbage; I'm Going Home.* STONEDHENGE (11/68): *Going to Try; I Can't Live without Lydia; Woman Trouble; Skoobly-oobly-doobob; Hear Me Calling; A Sad Song; Three Blind Mice; Speed Kills; Faro; No Title.* SSSSH (7/69): *If You Should Love Me; Good Morning, Little Schoolgirl; I Woke Up This Morning; Stoned Woman; The Stomp; Bad Scene; I Don't That You Don't Know My Name; Two-Time Mama.* CRICKLEWOOD GREEN (3/70): *Sugar the Road; Working on the Road; 50,000 Miles beneath My Brain, Year 3,000 Blues; Me and My Baby; Love Like a Man; Circles; As the Sun Still Burns Away.* WATT (11/70): *I'm Coming On; My Baby Left Me; Think About the Time; I Say Yeah; The Band with No Name; Gonna Run; She Lies in the Morning; Sweet Little Sixteen.* A SPACE IN TIME (8/71): *One of These Days; Here They Come; I'd Love to Change the World; Over the Hill; Baby, Won't You Let Me Rock 'n' Roll You; Let the Sky Fall; Once There Was a Time; Hard Monkeys; I've Been There Too.* ALVIN LEE AND COMPANY (2/72): *The Sounds; Rock Your Mama; Hold Me Tight; Standing at the Crossroads; Portable People; Boogie On.* ROCK AND ROLL TO THE WORLD (9/72): *You Give Me Loving; Convention Prevention; Turned-Off TV Blues; Standing at the Station; Choo Choo Mama; You Can't Win Them All; Religion; Tomorrow I'll Be Out of Town; Rock and Roll Music to the World.* RECORDED LIVE (7/73): *One of These Days; You Give Me Loving; Good Morning, Little Schoolgirl; Hobbit; Help Me; Classical Thing; I Can't Keep from Crying Sometimes (I and II); Extension on One Chord; Silly Thing; I'm Going Home; Choo Choo Mama; Slow Blues in 'C.'* POSITIVE VIBRATIONS (4/74): *Nowhere to Run; Positive Vibrations; Stone Me; Without You; Going Back to Birmingham; It's Getting Harder; You're Driving Me Crazy; Look into My Life; Look Me Straight into the Eyes; I Wanted to Boogie.* GOIN' HOME (THEIR GREATEST HITS) (6/75): *Hear Me Calling; Going to Try; Love Like a Man; No Title; I Woke Up This Morning; Woodchopper's Ball; I'm Going Home.* CLASSIC PERFORMANCES OF TEN YEARS AFTER (10/76): *I'd Love to Change the World; Baby, Won't You Let Me Rock 'n' Roll You; Choo Choo Mama; I'm Going Home; It's Getting Harder; Positive*

Vibrations; Tomorrow I'll Be Out of Town; Good Morning, Little Schoolgirl; Rock and Roll Music to the World; One of These Days.
Singles/*Portable People/The Sounds* (7/68); *Hear Me Calling/I'm Going Home* (11/68); *Love Like a Man/If You Should Love Me* (3/70); *I'd Love to Change the World/Let the Sky Fall* (8/71); *Baby, Won't You Let Me Rock 'n' Roll You/Once There Was a Time* (12/71); *Choo Choo Mama/You Can't Win Them All* (11/72); *Tomorrow I'll Be Out of Town/Convention Prevention* (1/73); *I'm Going Home/You Give Me Loving* (8/73); *It's Getting Harder/I Wanted to Boogie* (5/74).

10 CC/*Original members: Kevin Godley (drums, vocals), Lol Creme (guitar, vocals), Eric Stewart (guitar, vocals), Graham Gouldman (bass, vocals).*
10 CC is rock and roll as interpreted by truly deranged minds. Led by Graham Gouldman and Eric Stewart (the chief song-writers), the foursome (now a twosome) started off with the absurd idea that rock could be funny as well as fun and wound up proving it via a slew of top-tenning album and singles. Songs like *Rubber Bullets* ("At the local dance at the local county jail"), *I'm Not in Love, Wall Street Shuffle,* and *The Things We Do for Love* have typed the band as schizoids-in-residence in the music biz. They have the ability to slide from straight to satire rock with grace, agility, and unabashed cheek.

Gouldman and Stewart first paired during the final days of the sixties' Mindbenders (originally Wayne Fontana and the Mindbenders until Wayne decided to go solo, beginning an innocuous career with singles like *Pamela, Pamela),* best known for their smash *Groovy Kind of Love* (which was *not* about corduroy). Eric was the lead singer at the time and the band was looking for a bassist/songwriter. Graham fit the bill, having written the Yardbirds' *For Your Love* and *Heart Full of Soul,* Herman's Hermits' *Listen People* and *No Milk Today,* and the Hollies' *Bus Stop* and *Look through Any Window.*

After the Mindbenders bent completely, Graham drifted into producing, where he met Godley and Creme. The threesome had an itch to record and, recruiting Stewart, formed the short-lived Hotlegs, and off-the-cuff entourage that had a million-selling send-up, *Neanderthal Man,* in 1970. After a short period of hibernation, Hotlegs mutated into what was to be known as 10 CC (a name hit upon by mad musical genius Jonathan King, who first brought the group to light in 1972). 10 CC's debut single was a fifties parody, *Donna*. It went top-five in England. *Rubber Bullets,* the follow-up tune, also smashed into the top-ten charts. Their first LP, in 1973, was an instant United Kingdom hit and, stateside, earned the band *Cashbox's* Best New Group award for that year.

The successes kept coming but the band's zaniness took a decidedly *unzany* turn. During the fall of '76, a rift appeared within the ranks and Creme and Godley decided to pursue projects of their own. Survivors Eric and Graham continued to run the show as a twosome and immediately scored with *The Things We Do for Love,* their biggest single to date.

And so, the two former Mindbenders march ever onward, hoping not only to bend, but twist, pummel and musically obliterate the minds of millions of fans via the deceptively normal sounds of 10 CC.

Albums/10 CC (10/73): *Johnny Don't Do It; Sand in My Face; Donna; The Dean and I; Headline Hustler; Speed Kills; Rubber Bullets; The Hospital Song; Ships Don't Disappear in the Nights (Do They); Fresh Air for My Mama.* SHEET MUSIC (6/74): *The Wall Street Shuffle; The Worst Band in the World; Hotel; Old Wild Men; Clockwork Creep; Silly Love; Somewhere in Hollywood; Baron Samedi; The Sacro-Iliac; Oh Effendi.* THE ORIGINAL SOUNDTRACK (3/75): *Une Nuit a Paris (One Night in Paris/Same Night in Paris/Later the Same Night in Paris); I'm Not in Love; Blackmail; The Second Sitting for the Last Supper; Brand New Day; Flying Junk Is a Minestrone; The Film of My Love.* 100 CC (8/75): *Old Wild Men; Wall Street Shuffle; Somewhere in Hollywood; Rubber Bullets; Waterfall; The Worst Band in the World; Donna; The Dean and I; Fresh Air for My Mama; Silly Love.* HOW DARE YOU! (1/76): *How Dare You; Lazy Ways; I Wanna Rule the World; I'm Mandy, Fly Me; Iceberg; Art for Art's Sake; Rock 'n' Roll Lullaby; Head Room; Don't Hang Up.* DECEPTIVE BENDS (4/77): *The Things We Do for Love; Marriage Bureau Rendezvous; People in Love; Modern Man Blues; Honeymoon with B Troop; I Bought a Flat Guitar Tuitor; You've Got a Cold; Reminisce and Speculation/Feel the Benefit (1); A Latin Break/Feel the Benefit (II); Feel the Benefit (III); Good Morning Judge.* LIVE AND LET LIVE (11/77): *The Second Sitting for the*

Last Supper; You've Got a Cold; Honeymoon with B Troop; Art for Art's Sake; People in Love; Wall Street Shuffle; Ships Don't Disappear in the Night (Do They?); I'm Mandy, Fly Me; Marriage Bureau Rendezvous; Good Morning Judge; The Things We Do for Love; Feel the Benefit; Waterfall; I'm Not in Love; Modern Man Blues.

Singles/*Donna/Hot Sun Rock* (12/72); *Rubber Bullets/Waterfall* (2/73); *Headline Hustler/Speed Kills* (2/74); *Wall Street Shuffle/Gismo My Way* (9/74); *I'm Not in Love/Channel Swimmer* (4/75); *Get In While You Can/Art for Art's Sake* (11/75); *I'm Mandy, Fly Me/How Dare You* (3/76); *Life Is a Minestrone/Lazy Ways* (5/76); *The Things We Do for Love/Hot to Trot* (12/76); *People In Love/Don't Squeeze Me Like Toothpaste* (4/77).

THEM/*Jim Armstrong (guitar, sitar, drums), David Harvey (drums), Alan Henderson (bass), Ray Elliot (organ), Ken McDowell (replacing Van Morrison; lead vocals).*
The original Them with Van Morrison started in Ireland in 1963, one of the few Irish groups to make an international name for itself. It was also one of the first rock groups to use an organ heavily, preceding the sound of later organ-based groups such as Traffic, the Band, and Steppenwolf. Until he left the group, Morrison, with his harsh voice and off phrasing, was the focus of the group. The band just never seemed to jell in terms of popularity, though. Morrison departed and McDowell was recruited for the band's final two albums. Them disbanded in late 1968.
Albums/THEM (6/65): *Here Comes the Night; Mystic Eyes; Don't Look Back; Little Girl; One Two Brown Eyes; Gloria; One More Time; If You and I Could Be As Two; I Like It Like That; I'm Gonna Dress in Black; Route 66; Go On Home, Baby.* THEM AGAIN (2/66): *Call My Name; Turn on Your Lovelight; Bad or Good; How Long, Baby; Don't You Know; My Lonely Sad Eyes; Bring 'Em on In; Something You Got; Out of Sight; I Can Only Give You Everything; It's All Over Now, Baby Blue; Could You, Would You.* NOW AND THEM (2/68): *I'm Your Witch Doctor; What's the Matter, Baby; Truth Machine; Square Room; You're Just What I Was Looking for Today; Dirty Old Man; Nobody Loves You When You're Down and Out; Walking in the Queen's Garden; I Happen to Love You; Come to Me.* TIME OUT! TIME IN FOR THEM (9/68): *Time Out for Time In; She Put a Hex on*

You; Bent Over You; Waltz of the Flies; Back Where I Started; We've All Agreed to Help; Market Place; Just One Conception; I Got a Woman; Lost. THEM (featuring Van Morrison; 6/72): *Could You, Would You; Something You Got; Turn on Your Love- light; I Can Only Give You Everything; My Lonely Sad Eyes; Out Of Sight; It's All Over Now, Baby Blue; Bad or Good; How Long, Baby; Bring 'Em on In; Gloria; Here Comes the Night; Mystic Eyes; Don't Look Back; Little Girl; One More Time; If Only You and I Could Be As Two; I Like It Like That; One Two Brown Eyes; Route 66.* BACKTRACKIN' (9/74): *Richard Cory; I Put a Spell on You; Just a Little Bit; I Gave My Love a Diamond; Half As Much; Baby, Please Don't Go; Hey, Girl; Don't Start Cryin' Now; All for Myself; Mighty Like a Rose.* THE STORY OF THEM (1/77): *The Story of Them; Time's Gettin' Tougher Than Tough; Stormy Monday Blues; Baby, What You Want Me to Do; Bright Lights, Big City; My Little Baby; I Got a Woman; Philosophy; Friday's Child.*

Singles/*Gloria* (5/65); *Here Comes the Night/All for Myself* (5/65); *Mystic Eyes/If You and I Could Be As Two* (10/65); *Gloria/Baby, Please Don't Go* (3/66); *Richard Cory/Don't You Know* (7/66); *I Can Only Give You Everything/Don't Start Crying Now* (8/66); *Gloria/Bring 'Em on In* (7/72); *The Story of Them/Time's Gettin' Tougher Than Tough* (1/77).

THIN LIZZY/*Phil Lynnot (vocals, bass), Scott Gorham (guitar), Brian Robertson (guitar), Brian Downey (drums). Original mem- ber: Eric Bell (guitar). Auxiliary member: Gary Moore (guitar on tour, '76–'77).*
A tiny bit of old Ireland and a large hunk of hard rock make up the essence of Thin Lizzy's clout. Led by street-talking poet Phil Lynnot, Lizzy is yet another example of an "overnight sensation" that took years to happen. During their meteoric rise to fame in 1976 with a hit single *(The Boys Are Back in Town)*, a hit album *(JAILBREAK)*, and an SRO tour, very few fans took the time to track down Lizzy's beginnings, which actually arose from tradi- tional Irish folk melodies. Lynnot and Downey first worked to- gether in their native Ireland in a group called the Black Eagles. During their endless club gigs they bumped into guitarist Eric Bell, then wasting away in an MOR (middle of the road)-oriented show band. The three pooled their musical resources and came up

with Thin Lizzy, a threesome that soon took the Irish pub-rock scene by storm.

Subsequently, after being voted Ireland's number-one band for two years running, Thin Lizzy moved to London. In early 1973, the band finally hit it big in Britain with their hit *Whiskey in the Jar,* a riffy re-working of a traditional Irish tune. The band found the song to be a dead-end careerwise, however, in that it was atypical of their rock-iron style. Their first album never saw the light of day in the States and, although they began to raise a critical ruckus with their second LP, *VAGABONDS OF THE WESTERN WORLD* (a minor masterpiece), they lost their American label.

Switching to Mercury in the States, the band had begun to make headway when guitarist Bell collapsed on stage during a performance on New Year's Eve, 1973. After endless auditioning, the band chose Robertson and Gorham to step in, thus establishing the familiar double-riff guitar style of Lizzy today. The new lineup brought forth a number of critically acclaimed LPs, but it wasn't until the release of '76's *JAILBREAK* that Lynnot's space-age fantasies took hold on the charts. And while the tastemakers debated on whether Lynnot sounded like Van Morrison or Bruce Springsteen, the band began to tour—drawing rave reviews wherever they went.

Although Thin Lizzy is a bona fide success on both sides of the Atlantic at this point, playing some of the finest rock around, bad luck has plagued them throughout their rise. In both 1976 and 1977, illness and injury hurt their live shows. Lynnot cancelled a tour in '76 because of illness and, later, a close friend of the band, Gary Moore, had to step into the live situation after guitarist Robertson injured his hand in a quick punch-up in a London pub. Since that time, Brian has become an on-again, off-again proposition for Lizzy, floating in and out of recording sessions and tour schedules.

Albums/THIN LIZZY (6/71): *The Friendly Ranger at Clontarf Castle; Honesty Is No Excuse; Diddy Levine; Ray-Gun; Look What the Wind Blew In; Eire; Return of the Farmer's Son; Clifton Grange Hotel; Saga of the Aging Orphan; Remembering.* VAGABONDS OF THE WESTERN WORLD (4/74): *Mama Nature Said; The Hero and the Madman; Slow Blues; The Rocker; Vagabond of the Western World; Little Girl in Bloom; Gonna*

Creep Up on You; A Song for While I'm Away. NIGHT LIFE (12/74): *She Knows; Night Life; It's Only Money; Still in Love with You; Frankie Carroll; Showdown; Banshee; Philomena; Sha-la-la; Dear Heart.* FIGHTING (7/75): *Rosalie; For Those Who Love to Live; Suicide; Wild One; Fighting My Way Back; King's Vengeance; Spirit Slips Away; Silver Dollar; Freedom Song; Ballad of a Hard Man.* JAILBREAK (3/76): *Jailbreak; Angel from the Coast; Running Back; Romeo and the Lonely Girl; Warriors; The Boys Are Back in Town; Fight or Fall; Cowboy Song; Emerald.* JOHNNY THE FOX (12/76): *Johnny; Rocky; Borderline; Don't Believe a Word; Fool's Gold; Johnny the Fox Meets Jimmy the Weed; Old Flame; Massacre; Sweet Marie; Boogie Woogie Dance.* ROCKER (1971–1974; released in the U.S. 1/77): *Black Boys on the Corner; Honesty Is No Excuse; Randolph's Tango; Little Girl in Bloom; Sitamoia; Little Darling; Remembering; Gonna Creep Up on You; Whiskey in the Jar; The Rocker.* BAD REPUTATION (9/77): *Soldier of Fortune; Bad Reputation; Opium Trail; Southbound; Dancing in the Moonlight; Killer without a Cause; That Woman's Gonna Break Your Heart; Dear Lord.*

Singles/*Whiskey in the Jar/Black Boys on the Corner* (1/73); *Randolph's Tango/Broken Dreams* (10/73); *Little Darling/The Rocker* (7/74); *Night Life/Showdown* (2/75); *Freedom Song/Wild One* (8/75); *Jailbreak/The Boys Are Back in Town* (4/76); *Half-Caste/Rocky* (11/76); *Old Flame/Johnny the Fox Meets Jimmy the Weed* (12/76); *Don't Believe a Word/Boogie Woogie Dance* (2/77); *Dancing in the Moonlight* (8/77).

THREE DOG NIGHT/*Cory Wells, Chuck Negron, and Danny Hutton (vocals), Floyd Sneed (drums), Joe Schermie (bass), Jim Greenspoon (keyboards), Mike Allsup (guitar).*
For a lot of kids growing up in the early seventies, Three Dog Night was the perfect rock band. They were safe. None of that nastiness found in that drug-laden psychedelia. None of that gritty sensuality found in (ugh) soul. They were pasteurized rockers and, as such, they achieved fame and fortune. They also got a fair share of "abuse" from the more "serious" rock aficionados. They racked up fourteen gold albums, ten gold singles, and sold nearly fifty million records. And, when their career began to sag, their

loyal fans left them decidedly in the lurch, moving on to the next act on the bill.

Danny Hutton was the driving force behind the band, getting together with Negron and Wells in the mid-sixties with the idea of forming a rock band with three lead vocalists. They got a band of sidemen together and began gigging on the West Coast. As their reputation as a live revue grew, so did record-company interest. ABC signed them and turned them over to Steppenwolf mentor Gabriel Mekler; from that union came the hit sounds of *One* and *Try a Little Tenderness*. With their style established and their career on the upswing, Three Dog Night embarked on a blitzkrieg attack on the singles and albums charts, brandishing fistsful of under-three-minute, designed-for-hitdom tunes.

To their credit, the denizens of hitboundland took other composers' tunes (Nyro, Axton, Newman) and worked them into a suitably infectious format. Gold records were the ultimate reward. By 1972, the band's career was slowing down. The singles weren't quick in coming and some fans felt disgruntled. A series of underwhelming albums commenced, with an occasional single finding its way onto the charts. Rumors of drug-involvement haunted the troupe, disillusioning some of the younger crowd. In '73, original band member Schermie abandoned ship, to be replaced by Jack Ryland. A second keyboard artist, Skip Konte, also joined at this time. Three Dog's career stumbled to a halt as quickly as it had begun. They have contributed virtually nothing to the musical scene during the past few years and have confined their in-concert activities to lounge-oriented venues and middle-of-the-road gatherings. Their fading into oblivion was truly an ironic ending for a band that offered so many different types of music to so many different fans for so many years.

Albums/THREE DOG NIGHT (1/69): *One; Try a Little Tenderness; Chest Fever; Nobody; Heaven Is in Your Mind; It's for You; One.* SUITABLE FOR FRAMING (8/69): *Eli's Coming; Easy to Be Hard; Celebrate; Feeling Alright; Lady Samantha; Circle for a Landing.* CAPTURED LIVE AT THE FORUM (10/69): *One; Eli's Coming; Try a Little Tenderness; Easy to Be Hard; Nobody; Feeling Alright.* IT AIN'T EASY (3/70): *Mama Told Me Not to Come; Cowboy; Woman; Out in The Country; Good Time Living; Your Song.* NATURALLY (12/70): *One Man Band; It Ain't Easy; I Can Hear You Calling; I'll Be Creeping; Fire*

*Eater; Can't Get Enough of It; Sunlight; Heavy Church; Liar; I've
Got Enough Heartache; Joy to the World.* GOLDEN BISQUITS
(2/71): *One; Eli's Coming; Easy to ·Be Hard; Mama Told Me Not
to Come; Try a Little Tenderness; Nobody; Woman; other titles.*
HARMONY (9/71): *Never Been to Spain; My Impersonal Life;
An Old-Fashioned Love Song; Never Dreamed You'd Leave Me in
Summer; Jam; You; Night in the City; Murder in My Heart for the
Judge; The Family of Man; Intro Poem; Mistakes and Illusions,
Peace of Mind.* SEVEN SEPARATE FOOLS (7/72): *Black and
White; My Old Kentucky Home; Prelude to Morning; Pieces of
April; Going in Circles; Chained; Tulsa Turnaround; In Bed; Free-
dom for the Stallion; The Writing on the Wall; Midnight Runaway.*
LIVE IN CONCERT AROUND THE WORLD (2/73). CYAN
(9/73): *Happy Song; Play Children Play; Storybook Feeling;
Ridin' Thumb; Shambala; Singer Man; Let Me Serenade You; Lay
Me Down Easy; Into My Life.* HARD LABOR (8/74): *Prelude;
Sure As I'm Sittin' Here; Anytime Babe; Put Out the Light; Sitting
in Limbo; I'd Be So Happy; Play Something Sweet; On the Way
Back Home; The Show Must Go On.* JOY TO THE WORLD:
THEIR GREATEST HITS (11/74). COMING DOWN YOUR
WAY (5/75): *'Til the World Ends; You Can Leave Your Hat On;
Good Old Feeling; Mind over Matter; Midnight Flyer; Kite Man;
Coming Down Your Way; When It's Over; Lean Back, Hold
Steady; Yo Te Quiero Hablar.* AMERICAN PASTIME (3/76):
*Everybody's a Masterpiece; Easy Evil; Billy the Kid; Mellow
Down; Yellow Beach Umbrella; Hang On; Southbound; Drive On,
Ride On; Dance the Night Away.*

Singles/*Try a Little Tenderness* (1/69); *One* (4/69); *Easy to Be
Hard* (8/69); *Eli's Coming* (10/69); *Celebrate* (2/70); *Mama Told
Me (Not to Come)* (5/70); *Out in the Country* (5/70); *One Man
Band/It Ain't Easy* (11/70); *I Can Hear You Calling/Joy to the
World* (2/71); *Liar/Can't Get Enough of It* (6/71); *An Old-Fash-
ioned Love Song* (10/71); *Never Been to Spain/Mistakes and Il-
lusions, Peace of Mind* (12/71); *The Family of Man* (2/72); *Black
and White/Freedom for the Stallion* (7/72); *Pieces of April/The
Writing's on the Wall* (10/72); *Shambala/Our B Side* (5/73); *Let
Me Serenade You/Storybook Feeling* (10/73); *The Show Must Go
On/On the Way Back Home* (3/74); *Sure As I'm Sittin'
Here/Anytime Babe* (6/74); *I'd Be Happy/Play Something Sweet*
(8/74); *'Til the World Ends/Yo Te Quiero Hablar* (6/75); *You Can*

Leave Your Hat On/Lean Back, Hold Steady (3/76); *Everybody's a Masterpiece/Drive On, Ride On* (5/76).

TINY TIM (HERBERT KHAURY)/Financially, 1969 was the year of Tiny Tim, with $50,000-a-week engagements at Las Vegas, a best-selling album, English concerts, adulation, world fame, the whole long glittering predictable star trip. The roly-poly, pancake-makeuped figure was the biggest thing to hit show biz since, well, talking dog acts. Tall, thin (like a pear is thin), hawk-nosed, long-haired, and owner of an overbite, Tiny Tim waddled into the hearts of millions when he appeared on the NBC-TV premier of *Laugh-In,* bravely wielding his ukelele and chirping, in the highest falsetto imaginable, *Tip-Toe thru the Tulips with Me.*

The record business took a shine to the lad, and soon Tiny Tim records were in every type of store imaginable, from supermarkets to Sam Goody's. Actually, Tim's overnight success was long in coming. He had knocked around the New York folk scene for nearly a decade, mincing onto the stage and performing both parts of Nelson Eddy–Jeanette MacDonald duets. While all of his audiences agreed that he was indeed a different type of performer, no one would actually say *why.* In the late sixties, Tiny became a legend. Everyone knew of his pumpkinseed habit, his romantic worship of the fair sex, his aversion to physical contact with that same sex, and his penchant for showering two or three times a day.

When Tiny Tim's career ended, it came with a bang. A trusting soul, he was rooked out of money by promoters and various shady characters. A made-in-heaven marriage to a young lass, Miss Vicki, ended in traumatic divorce after he refused to, uh, well. Alone, unpopular, and nearly broke, Tiny cheerfully took to playing the saloon route. Miss V. became a go-go dancer in sleezoid clubs. Talk about grim fairy tales.

Currently, the guitar-strumming vocalizer called Tiny Tim is planning a comeback—a comeback that has been in the works for five years.

Albums/GOD BLESS TINY TIM (5/68): *Welcome to My Dream; Tip-Toe thru the Tulips with Me; Livin' in the Sunlight, Lovin' in the Moonlight; On the Old Front Porch; Viper; Stay Down Here Where You Belong; Then I'd Be Satisfied with Life; Strawberry Tea; Other Side; Ever Since You Told Me That You*

Love Me; Daddy, Daddy, What Is Heaven Like; Coming Home Party; Fill Your Heart; I Got You, Babe; This Is All I Ask. TINY TIM'S 2ND ALBUM (11/68): *Come to the Ball; My Dreams Are Getting Better All the Time; We Love It; When I Walk with You; Community; She's Just Laughing at Me; Have You Seen My Little Sue; Christopher Brady's Old Lady; Great Balls of Fire; Neighborhood Children; Can't Help but Wonder Where I'm Bound; It's Alright Now; medley; I'm Glad I'm a Boy; My Hero; As Time Goes By.* FOR ALL MY LITTLE FRIENDS (8/60): *On the Good Ship Lollipop; Sunshine Cake; Mickey the Monkey; I'm a Lonesome Little Raindrop; Chickery Chick; Oliphant the Elephant; Two Times a Day; Hot and Cold Water; Sadie the Seal; The Viper; What the World Needs Now Is Love; other titles.*

Singles/*Tip-Toe thru the Tulips with Me/Fill Your Heart* (5/68); *Bring Back Those Rockabye Baby Days* (7/68); *Be My Love/Hello Hello* (9/68); *Great Balls of Fire* (1/69); *I'm a Lonesome Little Raindrop/What the World Needs Now Is Love* (10/69); *Why/The Spaceship Song* (12/70).

PETE TOWNSHEND/The dynamic lead guitar flailer of the Who, Pete Townshend embarked on a tentative career as a singer-songwriter in 1972, during one of the Who's more turbulent periods. His career lasted but one album before he decided to concentrate his efforts on the pursuit of Whodom.

Album/WHO CAME FIRST (10/72): *Pure and Easy; Evolution; Forever's No Time at All; Nothing Is Everything; Time Is Passing; Heartache; Sheraton Gibson; Content; Parvardigar.*

TRAFFIC/*Original band: Steve Winwood (keyboards, vocals), Chris Wood (reeds), Jim Capaldi (drums), Dave Mason (bass, guitar, sitar).*
The Traffic story starts with the Spencer Davis Group. Davis started a band in 1963 with three other musicians, two of whom were brothers already playing together. One of those brothers was a lad named Steve Winwood, aged fifteen. Like the Beatles, he came out of the skiffle craze of 1959 (he was only eleven when he was in a skiffle band). He had lived and breathed American blues from the start, learned from the record collections of friends. It was Steve's voice, his songs, his organ and piano work that made Spencer Davis' band soar. *I'm a Man* and *Gimme Some Loving,*

done under the Davis unbrella, were so black and strong it took
a lot of adjusting to get used to the fact that they were coming
from a seventeen-year-old English kid from Birmingham. In 1967,
Steve decided to leave Davis (life on the road was messing his
mind) and started his own group.

With a maturity and wisdom you don't find in most older musicians, Steve took himself and his new musician peers off to a quiet
country cottage in Berkshire to work and get themselves together
as people, as a band, as musicians. Photographers were barred.
Reporters were barred. Under-assistant promotion men were
barred. It was all peace and quiet there, with green grass, and
roaring logs on the fire at night—an idyllic setting that was immediately reflected on the very first Traffic singles, *Paper Sun* and
Hole in My Shoe.

For a long time, Traffic looked like it would be a great band,
a nicely balanced blend of four good musicians. Winwood's voice
was strong; Capaldi's drums were powerful; Chris Wood on flute,
Mason on sitar and Winwood on organ were gentle and peaceful.
Traffic was in the process of changing the whole mood of popular
music when Mason either left or was forced out of the group
(depending on whose story you believe). By the time the first
album was released stateside, Mason had been obliterated from
the cover and credit lines, although his songs, his playing, and his
influence were present on wax. Traffic held together as a working
trio for a bit; they were quietly on the upswing when
founder/member Steve decided to join the ultimate supergroup
Blind Faith (Eric Clapton, Ginger Baker, and Rick Gretch).

Fortunately for Traffic fans, Blind Faith required just that
from their listeners and the ill-quartet bit the dust quite unceremoniously. Soon, Traffic, minus Mason, was back together,
more or less, turning out interesting (although sometimes erratic)
long-players. As the band's career progressed, the musical
kineticism of its members regressed. They became well known for
semi-comatose concert sets with various members playing riffs
from off in the ozones, while others scowled in disgust or disin-
terest. (Interestingly enough, Traffic's albums always held together while most of their concert shows fell apart.) A major revamp
occurred in 1973 when session musicians Roger Hawkins, David
Hood, and Rebop Jwaku Baah were included in the Traffic lineup
to bolster the sagging sound. While this injection of new blood

did add life to the band, it merely slowed down the gradual disintegration as opposed to halting it. The group was streamlined in time for their final LP, with Rosko Gee joining the three original Traffic-ers Wood, Winwood, and Capaldi for *WHEN THE EAGLE FLIES*. Traffic simply went away after that, with Capaldi diving head-first into a solo career. In 1977, Winwood released his first full-fledged solo long-player, after several collaborative "jam" LPs.

Albums/MR. FANTASY (3/68): *Dear Mr. Fantasy; Paper Sun; Hole in My Shoe; Dealer; Coloured Rain; No Face, No Name and No Number; Heaven Is in Your Mind; House for Everyone; Berkshire Poppies; Giving to You; Smiling Phases; We're a Fade, You Missed This.* TRAFFIC (10/68): *You Can All Join In; Pearly Queen; Don't Be Sad; Who Knows What Tomorrow Will Bring; Feeling Alright; Vagabond Virgin; 40,000 Headmen; Cryin' to Be Heard; No Time to Live; Means to an End.* LAST EXIT (4/69): *Just for You; Shanghai Noodle Factory; Something's Got a Hold of My Toe; Withering Tree; Medicated Goo; Feelin' Good; Blind Man.* THE BEST OF TRAFFIC (12/69): *Dear Mr. Fantasy; Paper Sun; Feeling Alright; Paper Sun; other titles.* JOHN BARLEYCORN MUST DIE (6/70): *Glad; Freedom Rider; Empty Pages; Stranger to Himself; John Barleycorn; Every Mother's Son.* WELCOME TO THE CANTEEN (9/71): *Medicated Goo; Sad and Deep As You; 40,000 Headmen; Shouldn't Have Took More Than You Gave; Dear Mr. Fantasy; Gimme Some Lovin'.* THE LOW SPARK OF HIGH-HEELED BOYS (11/71): *Hidden Treasure; The Low Spark of High-Heeled Boys; Light Up or Leave Me Alone; Rock and Roll Stew; Many a Mile to Freedom; Rainmaker.* SHOOT OUT AT THE FANTASY FACTORY (1/73): *Shoot Out at the Fantasy Factory; Roll Right Stones; Evening Blue; Tragic Magic; (Sometimes I Feel So) Uninspired.* ON THE ROAD (10/73): *Low Spark of High-Heeled Boys; Shoot Out at the Fantasy Factory; (Sometimes I Feel So) Uninspired; Light Up or Leave Me Alone.* WHEN THE EAGLE FLIES (9/74): *Something New; Walking in the Wind; Dream Gerrard; Memories of a Rock 'n' Rolla; Graveyard People; When the Eagle Flies; Love.* HEAVY TRAFFIC (3/75): *Dear Mr. Fantasy; 40,000 Headmen; Smiling Phases; Shanghai Noodle Factory; Paper Sun; Feelin' Alright; Heaven Is in Your Mind; Medicated Goo; Coloured Rain; Empty Pages.* MORE HEAVY TRAFFIC (8/75): *Hole in My Shoe;*

Gimme Some Lovin'; John Barleycorn; You Can All Join In; Cryin' to Be Heard; Pearly Queen; No Face, No Name and No Number; Who Knows What Tomorrow May Bring; Means to An End; Vagabond Virgin.

Singles/*Paper Sun/Coloured Rain* (8/67); *Here We Go 'round the Mulberry Bush/Mr. Fantasy* (4/68); *Smiling Phases/Hole in My Shoe* (1968); *Feelin' Alright/Withering Tree* (10/68); *Empty Pages/Stranger to Himself* (8/70); *Gimme Some Lovin (Parts One and Two)* (10/71); *Rock and Roll Stew* (12/71); *Glad (Parts One and Two)* (9/72); *Paper Sun/Empty Pages* (1/73); *Walking in the Wind/Walking in the Wind—Instrumental Version* (8/74).

ROBIN TROWER/Guitarist Robin Trower is known, in some circles, as the high priest of the Church of Hendrix. Taking the dense, textured, layered sound of the late Jimi, Trower has expanded upon its inherent qualities and taken it into unexplored regions of musical time and space. The British musician, now well established as the king of intergalactic distortion, began in quite an earthbound band, the Parliaments, a funky R&B group which eventually mutated into Procol Harum. Trower served faithfully as Procol's lead guitarist during the band's early days. It was on Procol's *BROKEN BARRICADES* album, however, that Robin suddenly realized that the full extent of his guitar work would never be realized within the rather severe confines of Harum. His *Song for a Dreamer* (a tribute to Jimi Hendrix) was both a stand-out track on the album and a total departure from Procol's regimented imagery. "It made me see the limitless possibilities of the guitar as a music-making instrument, rather than just as a lick-turner-outer," Trower once remarked on the song. "Hendrix showed me how to make ethereal, beautiful music, beautiful rock, if you like."

Trower left Procol and after an aborted attempt at forming a group named Jude, formed instead the Robin Trower Group, featuring bassist James Dewar and drummer Reg Isadore. Their debut album, *TWICE REMOVED FROM YESTERDAY*, established Trower's new direction . . . the heavens. His space-laden sound has won him fans worldwide and has remained by and large unchanged since its inception (the lone change in Robin's thrust being a change in drumming, Bill Lordan replacing Isadore). Trower has become one of the most respected musical figures of the seventies, a virtually faceless superstar—identified only by his truly distinctive brand of music.

Albums/TWICE REMOVED FROM YESTERDAY (3/73): *I Can't Wait Much Longer; Daydream; Hannah; Man of the World; I Can't Stand It; Rock Me Baby; Twice Removed from Yesterday; Sinner's Song; Ballerina.* BRIDGE OF SIGHS (3/74): *Day of the Eagle; Bridge of Sighs; In This Place; The Fool and Me; Too Rolling Stoned; About to Begin; Lady Love; Little Bit of Sympathy.* FOR EARTH BELOW (2/75): *Shame the Devil; It's Only Money; Confession Midnight; Fine Day; Alethea; A Tale Untold; Gonna Be More Suspicious; For Earth Below.* ROBIN TROWER LIVE (4/76): *Too Rolling Stoned; Daydream; Rock Me Baby; Lady Love; I Can't Wait Much Longer; Alethea; Little Bit of Sympathy.* LONG MISTY DAYS (9/76): *Same Rain Falls; Long Misty Days; Hold Me; Caledonia; Pride; Sailing; S.M.O.; I Can't Live without You; Messin' the Blues.* CITY DREAMS (11/77): *Somebody Calling; Sweet Wine of Love; Bluebird; Falling Star; Farther Up the Road; Smile; Little Girl; Love's Gonna Bring You Round; In City Dreams.*

Singles/*Man of the World/Take a Fast Train* (3/73); *Too Rolling Stoned (Parts One and Two)* (4/76); *Caledonia/Messin' the Blues* (10/76).

THE TUBES/*Bill Spooner (guitar, vocals), Roger Steen (guitar, vocals), Fee Waybill (lead vocals), Re Styles (vocals), Prairie Prince (drums), Vince Welnick (keyboards), Rick Anderson (bass), Michael Cotton (synthesizers), Mingo Lewis (percussion).*

Begun in the early seventies by Bill Spooner and a group of former art-school cronies, the Tubes is the closest thing to *One Flew over the Cuckoo's Nest* as you will ever get in rock. With jaundiced eye and tongue planted firmly in cheek, the tubes introduced a satirical brand of rock and roll to a receptive San Francisco audience—a type of rock that lampooned everything from superstardom to super soul. The Tubes' answer to the ultimate gold-record king was nod-out hero Quay Lude, who wobbled onto the concert stage wearing platform heels that only King Kong could identify with (or climb, probably). Dr. Strangekiss was a crippled neo-Nazi who, on cue, could and often would transform himself into a Tom Jones sound-alike and gyrate to the tune of *It's Not Unusual.*

With visuals as out-of-whack as their musical lunacy, the Tubes began offering to the world at large (often when the world at large wasn't asking for it) such toetappers as *Don't Touch Me There, White Punks on Dope, Mondo Bondage, Slipped My Disco,* and *Young and Rich.* By the time their third album rolled around in 1977, however, it was clear that the rock public was not ready for what the Tubes had to offer. Enlisting the aid of Mingo Lewis, the Tubes calmed down somewhat and produced an extremely sane-sounding musical treat called *NOW.* The record, which featured such Tubes tunes as *Cathy's Clone* and *You're No Fun,* did not fare well and the band retrenched to rethink their rock strategy.

If the Tubes fail in their melodic mission it has nothing to do with their musical capabilities. It is very hard to parody a musical lifestyle that is, for the most part, a caricature to begin with.

Album/THE TUBES (6/75): *Up from the Deep; Haloes; Space Baby; Malaguena Salerosa; Mondo Bondage; What Do You Want from Life; Boy Crazy; White Punks on Dope.* YOUNG AND RICH (4/76): *Tubes World Tour; Brighter Day; Pimp; Stand Up and Shout; Don't Touch Me There; Slipped My Disco; Proud to be an American; Poland Whole/Madam I'm Adam; Young and Rich.* NOW (5/77): *Smoke (La Vie en Fumer); Hit Parade; Strung Out on Strings; Golden Boy; My Head Is My Only House Unless It Rains; God-Bird-Change; I'm Just a Mess; Cathy's Clone; This Town; Pound of Flesh; You're No Fun.*

Singles/*White Punks on Dope* (9/75); *What Do You Want from Life* (11/75); *Don't Touch Me There* (5/76).

JETHRO TULL/*Ian Anderson (vocals, flute, guitar), John Glascock (bass), Barrie Barlow (drums), Martin Barre (guitar), John Evan (keyboards). Previous members: Glenn Cornick (bass), Jeffrey Hammond-Hammond (bass), Mick Abrahams (guitar), Clive Bunker (drums).*

The image of long-haired Ian Anderson, with his eyes gleaming and with one leg perched, flamingo style, on the other while he blows breathlessly into his flute, is the essence of Jethro Tull. Led by the demonic flautist, Jethro Tull has become one of the most widely respected (and controversial) "progressive" English bands to survive the sixties.

Begun in 1967, Tull originated from the ashes of a band that just didn't cut it on the London scene, the John Evans Band. Out of its seven members, Anderson, Evan, Barlow, Cornick, and Hammond-Hammond would eventually find their way into Tull. In the beginning, however, it was Cornick and Anderson who joined forces with Bunker and Abrahams to form the first Jethro Tull, named for an eighteenth-century agriculturist, the inventor of the mechanical crop drill. Their brand of blues-jazz-rock quickly caught on in a musical marketplace brimming with the sounds of Ten Years After and Fleetwood Mac. A well-received guest spot at the National Jazz and Blues Festival of 1968 ensured their first LP, *THIS WAS,* a proper reception. Which it got.

The maniacal presence of Ian Anderson, with his tattered overcoat and Captain Hook demeanor, was welcome addition to a rock scene fraught with hot 'n' nasty guitarists. The band's cult status mushroomed, enduring an early personnel change when Abrahams left to be replaced by Barre. With Abrahams out of the outfit, Anderson began moving the band out of the blues area and into an unchartered realm of sophisticated wit, perverse pastoral imagery, and flute-led minstral magic.

The group's career soared to the top with the release of 1971's *AQUALUNG* (featuring new members Hammond-Hammond and Evan), a concept album detailing the adventures of a down-and-outer who looked suspiciously like Ian Anderson. The album went gold cracking the top ten. Jethro Tull became a headlining act and their stage show grew to titanic proportions. Soon, madman Ian would be surrounded by butlers, giant rabbits, and assorted props and extras on stage as Tull gradually moved into the realm of rock theatrics.

The band endured a bit of a critical backlash however, when a revamped Tull (Bunker out, Barlow in) offered *THICK AS A BRICK,* a concept album fan's concept album. Although it went gold and the fans loved it, there was rumblings in the rock press that Anderson was overdoing it. *A PASSION PLAY,* the crew's followup, was creamed in print and, in 1973, Ian Anderson told the press to take the reviews and do anything they wanted with them. Jethro Tull was finished. No more live tours. Goodbye. Farewell. Finis.

By the mid seventies, Tull was at it again with *WAR CHILD* and tours of both the United States and the United Kingdom in

1974 and 1975. A single, *Bungle in the Jungle,* brought them to the American top twenty once more and, of late, the band has concentrated on *non*-concept LPs.

No matter how schizoid their careers have been, the members of Jethro Tull have always presented to their fans remarkably well-played, well-constructed, and well-executed phantasmagoric views of the old vs. the new. With minstral-like qualities clashing head-on with present day lyrics and concepts, the music of Jethro Tull is a true standout in today's music world.

Albums/THIS WAS (1/69): *My Sunday Feeling; Some Day the Sun Won't Shine for You; Beggar's Farm; Move On Alone; Serenade to a Cuckoo; Dharma for One; It's Breaking Me Up; Cat's Squirrel; A Song for Jeffrey; Round.* STAND UP (7/69): *A New Day Yesterday; Jeffrey Goes to Leicester Square; Bouree; Back to the Family; Look into the Sun; Nothing Is Easy; Fat Man; We Used to Know; Reason for Waiting; For a Thousand Mothers.* BENEFIT (3/70): *Son; Nothing to Say; Inside; With You There to Help Me; For Michael Collins, Jeffrey and Me; To Cry You a Song; A Time for Everything; Teacher; Play in Time; Lossity: You're a Woman.* AQUALUNG (8/71): *Aqualung; Cross-Eyed Mary; Cheap Day Return; Mother Goose; Wond'ring Aloud; Up to Me; My God; Hymn; Slipstream; Locomotive Breath; Wind Up.* THICK AS A BRICK (4/72): *Side One; Side Two.* LIVING IN THE PAST (10/72): *Wond'ring Again; Hymn 43; Life Is a Long Song; Up the Pool; Dr. Bogenbroom; From Later, Nursie; Song for Jeffrey; Love Story; Christmas Song; Living in the Past; Driving Song; Bouree; Sweet Dream; Singing All Day; Teacher; Witch's Promise; Alive and Well and Living In; Just Trying to Be; By Kind Permission Of; Dharma for One.* A PASSION PLAY (7/73): *A Passion Play; The Story of the Hare Who Lost His Spectacles.* WAR CHILD (7/74): *War Child; Queen and Country; Ladies; Back-door Angels; SeaLion; Skating Away on the Thin Ice of the New Day; Bungle in the Jungle; Only Solitude; The Third Hoorah; Two Fingers.* M.U. THE BEST OF JETHRO TULL (3/75): *Teacher; Aqualung; Thick as a Brick Edit #1; Bungle in the Jungle; Locomotive Breath; Fat Man; Loving in the Past; A Passion Play Edit #8; Skating Away on the Thin Ice of the New Day; Rainbow Blues; Nothing Is Easy.* MINSTREL IN THE GALLERY (9/75): *Minstrel in the Gallery; Cold Wind to Valhalla; Black Satin Dancer; Requiem; One White Duck/0^{10} = Nothing at All;*

Baker Street Muse. TOO OLD TO ROCK AND ROLL, TOO YOUNG TO DIE (5/76); *Quizz Kid; Crazed Institution; Salamander; Taxi Grab; From a Dead Beat to an Old Greaser; Bad-Eyed and Loveless; Big Dipper; Too Old to Rock 'n' Roll: Too Young to Die; Pied Piper; The Chequered Flag (Dead or Alive).* JETHRO TULL (Christmas E.P.; 12/76): *Ring Out, Solstice Bells; March, the Mad Scientist; Pan Dance.* SONGS FROM THE WOOD (3/77): *Songs from the Wood; Jack-in-the-Green; Cup of Wonder; Hunting Girl; Ring Out, Solstice Bells; Velvet Green; The Whistler; Pibroch (Cap in Hand); Fire at Midnight.* REPEAT: THE BEST OF JETHRO TULL, VOL. II (10/77): *Minstrel in the Gallery; Cross-Eyed Mary; A New Day Yesterday; Bouree; Thick As a Brick Edit #4; Warchild; A Passion Play; To Cry You a Song; Too Old to Rock 'n' Roll: Too Young to Die; Glory Row.*

Singles/*The Witch's Promise/Teacher* (3/70); *Inside/A Time for Everybody* (6/70); *Hymn 24/Mother Goose* (6/71); *Hymn 43* (7/71); *Locomotive Breath/Wind Up* (11/71); *Living in the Past/Christmas Song* (9/72); *Passion Play Edit #8/Passion Play Edit #9* (4/73); *Passion Play Edit #10/Passion Play Edit #6* (8/73); *Living in the Past/Cross-Eyed Mary* (1/74); *Bungle in the Jungle/Backdoor Angels* (8/74); *Skating Away/Sea Lion* (12/74); *Minstrel in the Gallery/Summer Day Send* (8/75); *Locomotive Breath/Fat Man* (11/75); *Bungle in the Jungle/Minstrel in the Gallery* (11/75); *Too Old to Rock 'n' Roll: Too Young to Die/Bad-Eyed and Loveless* (6/76).

THE TURTLES/*Howard Kaylan (lead vocals), Mark Volman (vocals), John Barbata (drums), Jim Tucker (rhythm guitar), Jim Pons (bass, vocals), Al Nichol (lead guitar). Additional members: John Seiter (drums), Chuch Portz (bass), Don Murray (drums).*
The Turtles started in Los Angeles in 1965 just when the concept of melding folk with rock was developing in that city. The Byrds had just had a huge hit with *Mr. Tambourine Man*, the first rock version of a Dylan song. When the Turtles put out their version of Dylan's *It Ain't Me, Babe*, it couldn't have been more timely. They had a best-seller on their hands and instant stardom. After this initial hit, however, the original band (Kaylan, Volman, Murray, Portz, Nichol, Tucker) fell into a creative lull. Murray left and was replaced by Barbata.

By 1967, the band was rolling again with sunshiny singles that everyone seemed to love. *Happy Together, She'd Rather Be with Me, You Know What I Mean,* and *She's My Girl* kept the smiling band in the rock spotlight for quite a while. Strangely enough, however, the band was composed of real strange folks who didn't particularly relish the fact that they were catagorized as a hit-single band. Kaylan and Volman, possessors of truly wry senses of humor, began to sneak little pieces of musical satire onto the B sides of their singles. By the time their careers were just about over as the Turtles, the band released the incredible *BATTLE OF THE BANDS,* an album featuring the band under a number of different names performing in a number of different styles. It was a genius stroke of insanity. By the time the band broke up in 1970, Barbata, Portz, and Tucker had been replaced by Pons and Seiter and everyone was sick of the pop shtick.

Kaylan and Volman resurfaced as Flo and Eddie and, after serving time with the Mothers Of Invention, went off on their own. Barbata is currently with the Jefferson Starship.

Albums/IT AIN'T ME, BABY (9/65): *It Ain't Me, Babe; Like a Rolling Stone; It Was a Very Good Year; Wanderin' Kind; Eve of Destruction; Your Maw Said You Cried; Glitter and Gold; Let Me Be; Let the Cold Winds Blow; Walk in the Sun; Last Laugh; Love Minus Zero.* YOU BABY (3/66): *You Baby; Let Me Be; Down in Suburbia; Give Love a Trial; Flyin' High; I Know That You'll Be There; House of Pain; Just a Room; I Need Someone; Pallbearing, Ballbearing World; All My Problems; Almost There.* HAPPY TO-GETHER (3/67): *Happy Together; Makin' My Mind Up; Guide for the Married Man; Think I'll Run Away; Walking Song; Me About You; She'd Rather Be with Me; Too Young to Be One; Person without a Care; Like the Seasons; Rugs of Woods and Flowers.* TURTLES' GOLDEN HITS (10/67): *Happy Together; You Know What I Mean; You Baby; It Ain't Me, Babe; She'd Rather Be with Me; So Goes Love; Let Me Be; Grim Reaper of Love; Can I Get to Know You Better; Outside Chance; Is It Any Wonder.* THE TURTLES PRESENT THE BATTLE OF THE BANDS (12/68): *Battle of the Bands; The Last Thing I Remember; Elenore; Too Much Heartsick Feeling; Oh Daddy; Buzz Saw; Surfer Dan; I'm Chief Kamanananalea (We're the Royal Macadamia Nuts); You Showed Me; Food; Chicken Little Was Right; Earth Anthem (All).* TURTLE SOUP (10/69): *You Don't Have to Walk in the*

*Rain; Lady-O; Love in the City; Somewhere Friday Night; other
titles.* MORE GOLDEN HITS (3/70): *Elenore; You Showed Me;
Lady-O; Eve of Destruction; other titles.* HAPPY TOGETHER
AGAIN (1974): *It Ain't Me, Babe; You Know What I Mean; Love
in the City; Lady-O; You Baby; Grim Reaper of Love; Elenore; Let
Me Be; Outside Chance; Me About You; Guide for the Married
Man; The Story of Rock and Roll; You Don't Have to Walk in the
Rain; She'd Rather Be with Me; She's My Girl; Can I Get to Know
You Better; Somewhere Friday Night; Happy Together; Sound
Asleep; You Want to Be a Woman; You Showed Me; Battle of the
Bands; Gas Money; Like It or Not; Can I Go Now; Can't You Hear
the Cows; Teardrops; There You Sit Lonely; Santa and the Side-
walk Surfer.*

Singles/*It Ain't Me, Babe/Almost There* (5/65); *Let Me Be/Your
Maw Said You Cried* (9/65); *You Baby/Wanderin' Kind* (10/65);
Grim Reaper of Love/Come Back (3/66); *We'll Meet Again/An
Outside Chance* (4/66); *Making My Mind Up/Outside Chance*
(6/66); *Can I Get to Know You Better/Like the Seasons* (7/66);
Happy Together/Like the Seasons (11/66); *She'd Rather Be with
Me/Walking Song* (2/67); *Guide for the Married Man/Think I'll
Run Away* (2/67); *You Know What I Mean/Rugs of Woods and
Flowers* (5/67); *She's My Girl/Chicken Little Was Right* (9/67);
Sound Asleep/Umbassa and the Dragon (2/68); *The Story of Rock
and Roll/Can't You Hear the Cows* (5/68); *Elenore/Surfer Dan*
(9/68); *You Don't Have to Walk in the Rain* (5/69); *Love in the
City* (9/69); *Lady-O* (11/69); *Eve of Destruction* (5/70); *Me About
You* (9/70).

UFO/*Phil Mogg (vocals), Michael Schenker (guitar), Danny Pay-
ronel (keyboards), Pete Way (bass), Andy Parker (drums).*
Before releasing their first stateside album in 1974 (produced by
Ten Years After mainstay Leo Lyons), UFO had already made a
dent in the European market with two long-players, *FLYING* and
UFO. They have since gone on to moderate success in America
with a series of frantic concert dates and manic albums. Their
sound is slightly spacey but forceful and a good example of seventies' hard rock.

Albums/PHENOMENON (7/74): *Too Young to Know; Crystal
Light; Doctor Doctor; Space Child; Rock Bottom; Oh My; Time
on My Hands; Built for Comfort; Lipstick Traces; Queen of the*

Deep. FORCE IT (7/75): *Let It Roll; Shoot Shoot; High Flyer; Love Lost Love; Out in the Street; Mother Mary; Dance Your Life Away; This Kid's; Including between the Walls; Too Much of Nothing.* NO HEAVY PETTING (5/76): *Natural Thing; I'm a Loser; Can You Roller Her; Belladonna; Reasons Love; Highway Lady; On with the Action; A Fool in Love; Martian Landscape.* LIGHTS OUT (5/77): *Too Hot to Handle; Try Me; Lights Out; Just Another Suicide; Gettin' Ready; Alone Again or; Electric Phase; Love to Love.*

Singles/*Doctor Doctor*/*Lipstick Traces* (6/74); *Too Hot to Handle* (6/77).

THE VANILLA FUDGE/*Carmine Appice (drums), Tim Bogert (bass), Vinnie Martell (guitar), Mark Stein (organ).*

If you had been around at George Harrison's house in the summer of 1967, you would have heard an astonishing version of the Beatles' *Eleanor Rigby,* a version that sounded like Godzilla jamming with Mitch Ryder and a sedated Detroit Wheels. It gave one the feeling that the tempo had been slowed down by as much as four times—or if not the tempo, then your mind. That was the Vanilla Fudge. They were just another white Long Island R&B-rock group until they started interpreting contemporary rock songs so uniquely that even the Beatles were sitting up and taking notice. That summer George Harrison played their album to anyone who would listen.

Their first single, an incredibly slow-motioned version of the Supremes' fast-paced *You Keep Me Hanging On,* was a huge hit in England immediately after release. A year later it hit in the States. It was the Vanilla Fudge at their most musically effective, the song seemingly destined to go on forever. *Eleanor Rigby,* too, seemed to have been put on a rock and stretched out . . . tortured to the point where the tension was no longer bearable. As a matter of fact, the key to the initial success of the Fudge sound was the overt pain present in their dinosaur arrangements. Instrumental riffs were carried out to the point of extinction. Vocals quivered, cracked, and sputtered. Singers gasped in between ominous keyboard rumbling and tortured guitar solos. It was like listening to a stereophonic martyrdom. St. Stephen a go-go.

The Vanilla Fudge made the whole notion of interpretation interesting again. But their live performance left a bit to be desired. What came across as heartfelt pain on wax often looked like ad-

vanced catatonia onstage. The band's sound soon began to grow
a tad pretentious, with the Fudge moving from *Ticket to Ride* and
Bang Bang to *18th Century Variations on a Theme by Mozart,* and
The Windmills of Your Mind. By the time the Fudge decided to
call it quits, their only receptive fans wore hairshirts to concerts.

Appice and Bogert have stuck it out as a duo, for the most part,
first forming Cactus, then joining Jeff Beck and, of late, sitting in
with a British band, Boxer.

Albums/VANILLA FUDGE (7/67): *You Keep Me Hanging On;
Ticket to Ride; People Get Ready; She's Not There; Bang Bang;
Illusions of Childhood (3 parts); Take Me for a Little While;
Eleanor Rigby.* THE BEAT GOES ON (1/68): *Sketch; The Beat
Goes On; Fur Elise; Moonlight Sonata; 18th Century Variations on
a Theme by Mozart; Voices in Time; The Merchant; Game Is Over.*
RENAISSANCE (7/68): *She Cried . . . When I Was a Boy;
Thoughts; Paradise; That's What Makes a Man; Faceless People;
Spell Comes After; Season of the Witch.* NEAR THE BEGIN-
NING (2/69): *Shotgun; Some Velvet Morning; Where Is Happi-
ness; Break Song.* ROCK AND ROLL (7/69): *Need Love; Lord in
the Country; I Can't Make It Alone; Street Walking Woman;
Church Bells of St. Martins; The Windmills of Your Mind; If You
Gotta Make a Fool of Somebody.*

Singles/*You Keep Me Hanging On* (6/67); *Where Is My
Mind/The Look of Love* (1/68); *You Keep Me Hanging On* (6/68);
Take Me for a Little While/Thoughts (9/68); *Season of the Witch
(Parts 1 and 2)* (11/68); *Shotgun/Good Good Lovin'* (2/69); *Some
Velvet Morning/People* (4/69); *Need Love/I Can't Make It Alone*
(7/69); *Lord in the Country/The Windmills of Your Mind* (2/70);
You Keep Me Hanging On/Take Me for a Little While (10/72).

THE VELVET UNDERGROUND/*Lou Reed (guitar, vocals),
Sterling Morrison (bass, rhythm guitar), Maureen Tucker (drums),
Doug Yule (guitar, organ, vocals), Nico (vocals), John Cale (piano,
bass, electric viola). Additional member: Billy Yule (drums).*
The Velvet Underground's debut in 1967 marked the first appearance of overt anarchy in rock and roll. Backed by Andy Warhol (and the Exploding Plastic Inevitable environment show), the
Underground owed musical allegiance to no one. They were punk
in a time of flower power. Spiteful in a time of love. Kinky when

the rules called for gettin' back to nature through LSD. Though never commercially popular, their music sent ripples zinging through the rock world, ripples that are still felt in punk rock mimics. The band was conceived as a four-piece unit in 1966, consisting of Reed, Cale, Morrison, and Tucker. Reed was a songwriter-poet; Cale was a classically trained avant-grade musician; Moe Tucker drummed in a number of local groups; Morrison was a former trumpet player. After Reed had worked his way through such bands as the Warlocks and the Primitives, the Velvets came into being.

They were immensely unpopular with club owners from the start. Fortunately, Andy Warhol intervened and, adding the eternally tranquil Teutonic songstress Nico to the troupe, sponsored their first excursion into wax. Their first album, *THE VELVET UNDERGROUND AND NICO,* boasted a Warhol cover and a host of distinctive, provocative tunes that jarred the listener, both instrumentally and lyrically, with powerful tales of sado-masochism, narcissism, drug abuse, and despair. While the Velvets didn't have the mass appeal of the Monkees, they sent the New York scene reeling in awe.

Their fame, or infamy, was short-lived. In 1967 Nico left the band to pursue a fairly surreal career. Andy Warhol began to ease out of his musical project. A second album, *WHITE HEAT/WHITE LIGHT,* was all but ignored. Reed and Cale began to squabble and, by 1969, Cale was out and Doug Yule was in. From that point onward, the Underground began to lose momentum.

The band jumped labels in 1969, dropping Moe Tucker and picking up Billy Yule. In '70, Reed took a walk, leaving Yule to keep the band together until 1972, when the artifact collapsed in a heap of sour notes. Quite a few compilation albums were released following their demise and the rise of Lou Reed to superstar status in the early seventies. Nico's solo career has been fairly nonexistent. John Cale's solo career, while critically acclaimed, has not set the world on fire in terms of records sold. His work as a producer, however, is without peer, (witness Patti Smith's *Horses* LP). Sterling Morrison settled in Texas as a teacher.

Even in their most normal moments, the Velvet Underground's musicians provided the world with some of the most intelligent, visionary rock songs ever recorded. They were not exactly ahead of their time. They certainly weren't behind it. Their sound defied time . . . space . . . and any other boundaries you can imagine. Iconoclastically immortal, it can still be heard in the echoes of some of today's brasher, brazen bands.

Albums/THE VELVET UNDERGROUND AND NICO (3/67): *Sunday Morning; I'm Waiting for the Man; Femme Fatale; Venus in Furs; Run, Run, Run; All Tomorrow's Parties; Heroin; There She Goes Again; I'll Be Your Mirror; European Son to Delmore Schwartz; Black Angel's Death Song.* WHITE LIGHT/WHITE HEAT (1/68): *White Light/White Heat; The Gift; Lady Godiva's Operation; Here She Comes Now; I Heard Her Call My Name; Sister Ray.* THE VELVET UNDERGROUND (4/69): *Candy Says; What Goes On; Some Kinda Love; Pale Blue Eyes; Jesus; Beginning to See the Light; I'm Set Free; That's the Story of My Life; The Murder Mystery; After Hours.* LOADED (11/70): *Who Loves the Sun; Sweet Jane; Rock and Roll; Cool It Down; New Age; Head Held High; Lonesome Cowboy Bill; I Found a Reason; Train 'round the Bend; Oh! Sweet Nuthin'.* LIVE AT MAX'S KANSAS CITY (5/72): *I'm Waiting for the Man; Sweet Jane; Lonesome Cowboy Bill; Beginning to See the Light; I'll Be Your Mirror; Pale Blue Eyes; Sunday Morning; New Age; Femme Fatale; After Hours.* LOU REED AND THE VELVET UNDERGROUND (1973): *That's the Story of My Life; Sister Ray; Lady Godiva's Operation; Heroin; Sunday Morning; All Tomorrow's Parties; There She Goes Again; White Light/White Heat; Femme Fatale.* 1969 (1974): *Waiting for My Man; Lisa Says; What Goes On; Sweet Jane; We're Gonna Have a Real Good Time Together; Femme Fatale; New Age; Rock and Roll; Beginning to See the Light; Ocean; Pale Blue Eyes; Heroin; Some Kinda Love; Over You; Sweet Bonnie Brown/It's Just Too Much; White Light/White Heat; I'll Be Your Mirror.* ARCHETYPES (1974): *White Light/White Heat; The Gift; Lady Godiva's Operation; Here She Comes Now; Sister Ray; I Heard Her Call My Name.*

Singles/*Here She Comes Now/White Light/White Heat* (11/67); *Jesus/What Goes On* (5/69); *Who Loves the Sun/Oh! Sweet Nuthin'* (5/71).

RICK WAKEMAN/The helter-skelter career of keyboard master Rick Wakeman began in the late sixties when the teenage London resident came to the attention of the music industry via his extraordinary talents. He instantly became one of the hottest session men on the English music scene before embarking on a "professional" career as a founder-member of the Strawbs. Two albums later, Rick was ready to enlist with Yes, a band whose style he helped shape. Rick's first solo effort, *THE SIX WIVES OF HENRY VIII*, was released during his last months with Yes. It was obvious that Rick's keyboard-oriented, majestic direction was not compatible with the vocally oriented fantasy paths being blazed by Yes.

Rick embarked on a solo career which garnered him fame and accusations of pretentiousness and cost him nearly all his money. Albums such as *JOURNEY TO THE CENTRE OF THE EARTH* and *THE MYTHS AND LEGENDS OF KING ARTHUR AND THE KNIGHTS OF THE ROUND TABLE* rankled quite a few rock critics who promptly labeled Wakeman's artistry "pompous" and "overbloated." Undaunted, Rick sought to take his grandiose sounds on the concert trail in an equally grandiose manner. He organized a small orchestra in 1974 for the Verne-inspired opus. A heart attack followed. One year later, he organized nearly one hundred musicians and singers to back up *KING ARTHUR*. Near-bankruptcy was the net result.

Lowering his sights a bit, Wakeman subsequently toured with smaller units before rejoining Yes in the winter of '76–'77.

Albums/THE SIX WIVES OF HENRY VIII (2/73): *Catherine of Aragon; Anne of Cleves; Catherine Howard; Jane Seymour; Anne Boleyn; 'The Day Thou Gavest, Lord, Hath Ended'; Catherine Parr.* JOURNEY TO THE CENTRE OF THE EARTH (5/74): *The Journey; Recollection; The Battle; The Forest.* THE MYTHS AND LEGENDS OF KING ARTHUR AND THE KNIGHTS OF THE ROUND TABLE (3/75): *Arthur; Lady of the Lake; Guinevere; Sir Lancelot and the Black Knight; Merlin the Magician (Parts I–IV); Sir Galahad; The Last Battle.* LISZTOMANIA (10/75): *Rienzi/Chopsticks Fantasia; Love's Dream; Dante Period; Orpheus Song; Hell; Hibernation; Excelsior Song; Master Race; Rape, Pillage and Clap; Funeralles; Free Song; Peace At Last.* NO EARTHLY CONNECTION (4/76): *The Warning; The Maker; The Spaceman; The Realisation; The Reaper; The Prisoner; The Lost Cycle.* WHITE ROCK (1/77): *White Rock; Searching for Gold; The Loser; The Shoot; Lax'X; After the Ball; Montezuma's Revenge; Ice Run.* RICK WAKEMAN'S CRIMI-

NAL RECORD (11/77): *Statue of Justice; Crime of Passion; Chamber of Horrors; Birdman of Alcatraz; The Breathalyser; Judas Iscariot.*

Singles/*Annie* (5/73); *White Rock* (4/77).

JOE WALSH/New Yorker Joe Walsh is reknowned as a guitarist's guitarist. Moving from rock to jazz to progressive country, he has hopped, skipped, and jumped from the James Gang to a solo career to the Eagles within the span of a decade. A Kent state student in the late sixties, he formed the Measles before joining the James Gang as both lead singer and lead guitarist. After quitting the band in 1971, he embarked on a critically acclaimed solo career that firmly established him as a "cult" artist. In 1976 he became a new member of the amazingly successful Eagles.

Albums/BARNSTORM (8/72): *Here We Go; Midnight Visitor; One and One; Giant Behemoth; Mother Says; Birdcall Morning; Home; I'll Tell the World about You; Turn to Stone; Comin' Down.* THE SMOKER YOU DRINK, THE PLAYER YOU GET (5/73): *The Smoker You Drink, the Player You Get; Meadows; Walk Away; Rocky Mountain Way; Prayer; other titles.* SO WHAT (12/74): *Welcome to the Club; Falling Down; Pavane; Time Out; All Night Laundry Mat Blues; Turn to Stone; Help Me thru the Night; County Fair; Song for Emma.* YOU CAN'T ARGUE WITH A SICK MIND (3/76): *Walk Away; Meadows; Rocky Mountain Way; Time Out; Help Me thru the Night; Turn to Stone.*

Singles/*Mother Says/I'll Tell the World about You* (9/72); *Rocky Mountain Way/Day Dream Prayer* (1/74); *Turn to Stone/All Night Laundry Mat Blues* (1/75); *Time Out/Help Me thru the Night* (6/75); *Walk Away/Help Me thru the Night* (4/76).

WAR/*Harold Brown (drums, vocals), B. B. Dickerson (bass), Papa Dee Allen (percussion), Lonnie Jordan (keyboards, vocals), Lee Oskar (harmonica, vocals), Howard Scott (guitar, vocals).*
War was one of America's first low-down, funky black groups to hit white rock audiences where it counted, in between the ears. The band started off when young Harold Brown traded in his classical violin for a snare drum, a stand, and a pair of sticks. Before long he was driving the neighbors crazy, practicing in his

garage. He did manage to attract the attention of Charles Miller, a kid who lived down the block. Miller asked Brown to join a group he had. The other members of the group were Scott and Dickerson. Lonnie Jordan joined thereafter and the young band was dubbed the Night Shift.

The Night Shift began playing around L.A. where, eventually, they came to the attention of Eric Burdon, fresh out of the Animals and looking for a new career. In the era of Peace and Love, the Night Shift was re-christened War. Burdon joined forces with the band and, after adding friend Lee Oskar to the troupe, used War as his backup group. Two Eric Burdon and War albums, *ERIC BURDON DECLARES WAR* and *BLACK MAN'S BURDON,* were released in '70 and '71. Although War found themselves on record, they still weren't producing their own style of music. Burdon left the Warfare in '71 and by the end of that year, War was a solo act on United Artists records. A funky outfit, War is capable of venturing into almost any musical turf, from solid R&B to jazz-fusion skirmishes.

Albums/WAR (2/71): *War; Sun Oh Son; Lonely Feelin'; other titles.* ALL DAY MUSIC (11/71): *All Day Music; Get Down; That's What Love Will Do; There Must Be a Reason; Nappy Head; Slippin' into Darkness; Baby Brother.* THE WORLD IS A GHETTO (12/72): *The Cisco Kid; Where Was You At; City, Country, City; Four Cornered Room; The World Is a Ghetto; Beetles in the Bog.* DELIVER THE WORD (8/73): *H2 Overture; In Your Eyes; Gypsy Man; Me and Baby Brother; Deliver the Word; Southern Part of Texas; Blisters.* WAR LIVE (3/74): *Introduction/Sun Oh Sun; The Cisco Kid; Slippin' into Darkness; All Day Music; Ballero; Lonely Feelin' Intro; Get Down.* WHY CAN'T WE BE FRIENDS? (5/75): *Don't Let No One Get You Down; Heartbeat; Lotus Blossom; Leroy's Latin Lament; Lonnie Dreams; The Way We Feel; La Fiesta; Lament; Smile Happy; So; Low Rider; In Mazatlan; Why Can't We Be Friends?* GREATEST HITS (7/76): *All Day Music; Slippin' into Darkness; The World Is a Ghetto; The Cisco Kid; Gypsy Man; Me and Baby Brother; Southern Part of Texas; Low Rider; Summer.* PLATINUM JAZZ (6/77): *River Niger; H2 Overture; L.A. Sunshine; I Got You; Platinum Jazz; Slowly We Walk Together; War Is Coming, War Is Coming; Nappy Head; Smile Happy; City, Country, City; Deliver the World; Four Cornered Room.* GALAXY (11/77): *Galaxy;*

Baby Face; Sweet Fighting Lady; Hey Senorita; The Seven Tin Soldiers.

Singles/*Sun oh Son/Lonely Feelin'* (2/71); *War* (3/71); *Get Down/All Day Music* (7/71); *Slippin' into Darkness/Nappy Head* (11/71); *The World Is a Ghetto/Four Cornered Room* (10/72); *The Cisco Kid/Beetles in the Bog* (2/73); *Where Was You At/Country, City, Country* (1973); *Beetles in the Bog/Four Cornered Room* (5/73); *Gypsy Man/Deliver the Word* (6/73); *Me and Baby Brother/In Your Eyes* (5/73); *Gypsy Man/Deliver the Word* (6/73); *Me and Baby Brother/In Your Eyes* (10/73); *Ballero/Slippin' into Darkness* (5/74); *Why Can't We Be Friends?/In Mazatlan* (4/75); *Low Rider/So* (8/75); *Summer/All Day Music* (6/76); *L.A. Sunshine/Slowly We Walk Together* (6/77).

THE WHO/*Pete Townshend (guitar, John Entwistle (bass), Keith Moon (drums), Roger Daltry (vocals).*

If *One Flew Over the Cuckoo's Nest* is ever transformed into a rock musical, you can count on the Who to star. The Who have always been ... er ... odd. They have also always been innovative. Put the two traits together and you have musical fireworks. Along with the Rolling Stones, the Who are one of the last visible traces of the British invasion of the early sixties' rock scene. Born of a time of mod–rockers clashes, summer dances in Brighton, and the orthodox worship of the songs of Eddie Cochran, the Who, as a unit, was almost a contradiction in terms from the outset. From the beginning, they possessed the angry, scruffy flair of the British R&B bands, but physically they had more to do with the fashion-plated mod crowds. Onstage they were dangerous, with Moon smashing his drums, Daltry swinging his mike like an old-fashioned mace, and Townshend windmilling his guitar to death before finally smashing it during the finale. This was not exactly a publicity gimmick, either. The Who possessed energy that they just didn't know what to do with. Dangerous mods, these. What the Rolling Stones' hinted at onstage, the Who delivered.

The Who was originally called the Highnumbers, first surfacing in '63, a bit after the Yardbirds and the Stones. Chris Stamp and Kit Lambert were two lads in search of a group, their heads full of Brian Epstein fantasies, when they first espied the scruffy entourage. First they changed the name to the Who, then the already mod leanings of the foursome were amplified. Before long, the Who had a readymade mod audience for the taking. Townshend's Union Jack coat became *the* rage (one must remember that this was back in the dark ages, before national flags found their way onto everything from ashtrays to toilet paper), and handsome Roger's frills made the girls swoon. In short, the Who clicked. *My Generation,* the forerunner of punk rock, became the national anthem of the under-twenty-fives in England and shot up the charts to number one. Their career began to soar. A few problems still existed, however—problems that would prevent the Who from attaining true success for quite a while. For one thing, the Who's habit of destroying 90 percent of their equipment at the end of each concert date took its toll moneywise. The band was constantly in debt and the money they made from the British rock scene simply wasn't enough to stave it off.

The big bucks were to be found in the States. The States, of course, proved remarkably uninterested in the nasty Who, preferring the sound of Herman's Hermits and Gerry and the Pacemakers. The band was stymied. A 1967 American tour found them playing Murray the K's Easter Show in New York City. (Murray had this habit of assembling bands on a marathon concert show. You know, seven bands playing for twenty minutes each. If you were British, you fit on the British show, etc.) They played two numbers and no one in the audience knew who they were. Gradually things changed for the better.

FM radio began to happen in the mid- to late-sixties. Unlike today, it was not very easy to be musically knowledgeable in the dark daze of the early sixties. There was no FM radio, ergo, there were no cool, hip, heavy, poetic FM jocks to tell you what was meaningful and what wasn't. The only music to be heard was found on AM and most of that was shlock. By '67, however, FM was beginning to get a toehold in the country and the Who's *My Generation* and, later, *Happy Jack,* were exposed to an audience that *cared.* An apocalyptic appearance at the 1967 Monterey Pop Festival (preserved forever on film, no less) brought the Who instant acclaim, and the wryly humorous *Happy Jack* found its way to select AM outlets as well as FM.

The Who's popularity in the States began to spread. They became underground heroes. By 1968 they were bona fide cult stars.

THE WHO SELL OUT album, constructed in a rock-opera sort of way around a series of annoyingly real radio commercials, became *the* cause célèbre of '68. With tongue planted firmly in cheek, the Who assailed the very medium through which they brought their messages. Then, in mid-1969, the career of the Who exploded. No longer would they be in debt. No more would they worry about their career. Tommy. Tommy happened.

Tommy was a rock opera—the first, really. Tommy was also a character, a rock everyman. A deaf, dumb, and blind boy who goes from pinball wizardry to messiah tomfoolery to martyrdom. Townshend had created both the ultimate in rock achievements and a frankenstein monster. *Tommy* firmly established the Who as rock innovators first class. A tour of the Who performing the entire work was an SRO affair in both London and New York. A single, *Pinball Wizard,* became that year's anthem. But Tommy, the beguiling character, was not content to stop there. He became truly commercial!

A stage performance.

A special rock-star-studded album version.

A full-length motion picture.

A motion picture soundtrack.

TOMMY. TOMMY. TOMMY. Five years after the release of the original record, the public wanted *Tommy.* The Who's subsequent works were always compared to it (the *new* standard by which to judge all), and future ambitious projects inevitably suffered for it, such as the double album *QUADROPHENIA.* Townshend, the thinking man's musician, delved into eastern philosophy about the same time that *Tommy* became a megabucks property. Tempers flared within the Who. Members would say things to local rock reporters they would later regret. Various members began aborted solo careers. After ten years in the rock world, it looked as though the Who were about to pack it in. Happily, though, they have weathered the storm. The Who doesn't perform as often now as it did fifteen years ago and the albums don't come as frequently, but when the Who does create as a unit . . . the music is always worth the wait.

Albums/Albums by Who individuals: Entwistle: SMASH YOUR HEAD AGAINST THE WALL (9/71). WHISTLE RYMES (10/72). RIGOR MORTIS SETS IN (6/73). MAD DOG (2/75). Singles/*My Size/I Believe in Everything* (11/71); *I Wonder/Who*

Cares? (1/73); *Made in Japan/Roller Skate Kate* (5/73). Keith Moon: TWO SIDES OF MOON (3/75). Singles/*Don't Worry Baby/Teenage Idol* (9/74); *Crazy Like a Fox/In My Life* (6/75). Townshend: WHO CAME FIRST (10/72). Daltry: DALTRY (5/73). RIDE A ROCK HORSE (7/75). ONE OF THE BOYS (6/77). Singles/*Giving It All Away/Way of the World* (4/73); *Thinking/There Is Love* (7/73); *Come and Get Your Love/Heart's Right* (8/75); *Oceans Away/Feeling* (1/76).

Who Albums/MY GENERATION (4/66): *Out in the Street; The Good's Gone; La La La Lies; Much Too Much; My Generation; The Kids Are Alright; It's Not True; A Legal Matter; Instant Party; The Ox; I Don't Mind; Please, Please, Please.* HAPPY JACK (4/67): *Run, Run, Run; Boris the Spider; I Need You; Whiskey Man; Cobwebs and Strange; Happy Jack; Don't Look Away; See My Way; So Sad about Us; A Quick One While He's Away.* THE WHO SELL OUT (12/67): *Armenia City in the Sky; Heinz Baked Beans; Mary Ann with the Shaky Hands; Odorono; Tattoo; Our Love Was, Is; I Can See for Miles; I Can't Reach You; Spotted Henry; Relax; Silas Stingy; Sunrise; Rael.* MAGIC BUS (9/68): *Disguises; Run, Run, Run; Dr. Jekyll and Mr. Hyde; I Can't Reach You; Our Love Was, Is; Call Me Lightning; Someone's Coming; Doctor, Doctor; Bucket T.; Magic Bus.* TOMMY (5/69): *Overture; It's a Boy; You Didn't Hear It; Amazing Journey; Sparks; Eyesight to the Blind; Christmas; Cousin Kevin; The Acid Queen; Underture; Pinball Wizard; Do You Think It's Alright; Fiddle About; There's a Doctor I've Found; Go to the Mirror Boy; Tommy, Can You Hear Me; Smash the Mirror; Miracle Cure; Sensation; Sally Simpson; I'm Free; Tommy's Holiday Camp, Welcome; We're Not Gonna Take It; See Me, Feel Me; Finale from We're Not Gonna Take It.* LIVE AT LEEDS (5/70): *My Generation; Magic Bus; Young Man Blues; Summertime Blues; Shakin' All Over.* WHO'S NEXT (8/71): *Baba O'Riely; Bargain; Love Ain't for Keeping; My Wife; Song Is Over; Gettin' in Tune; Behind Blue Eyes; Won't Get Fooled Again.* MEATY, BEATY, BIG AND BOUNCEY (11/71): *I Can't Explain; The Kids Are Alright; Happy Jack; I Can See for Miles; Pictures of Lily; My Generation; The Seeker; Pinball Wizard; A Legal Matter; The Magic Bus; I'm a Boy; Substitute; Boris the Spider; Anyway, Anyhow, Anywhere.* QUADROPHENIA (10/73): *I Am the Sea; The Real Me; Quadrophenia; Cut My Hair; The Punk Meets the Godfather; I'm One;*

The Dirty Jobs; Helpless Dancer; Is It in My Head; I've Had Enough; Sea and Sand; Drowned; Bell Boy; Dr. Jimmy; The Rock; Love, Reign o'er Me. ODDS AND SODS (1/74): *Postcard; Now I'm a Farmer; Put the Money Down; Little Billy; Too Much of Anything; Glow Girl; Pure and Easy; Faith in Something Bigger; I'm the Face; Naked Eye; Long Live Rock.* MAGIC BUS/MY GENERATION (re-issues of earlier albums; 11/74), A QUICK ONE/THE WHO SELL OUT (re-issue of HAPPY JACK and THE WHO SELL OUT; 11/74). THE WHO BY NUMBERS (10/75): *Slip Kid; However Much I Booze; Squeeze Box; Dreaming from the Waist; Imagine a Man; Success Story; They Are All in Love; Blue, Red and Gray; How Many Friends; In a Hand or a Face.*

Singles/*I Can't Explain/Bald-Headed Woman* (12/64, 8/73); *Anyway, Anyhow, Anywhere/Anytime You Want Me* (6/65); *My Generation/Out in the Street* (11/65); *The Kids Are Alright/A Legal Matter* (7/66); *I'm a Boy/in the City* (12/66); *Happy Jack/Whiskey Man* (3/67); *Pictures of Lily/Doctor, Doctor* (7/67); *I Can See for Miles/Mary-Anne with the Shaky Hands* (10/67); *Call Me Lightning/Dr. Jekyll and Mr. Hyde* (3/68); *Magic Bus/Someone's Coming* (8/68); *Pinball Wizard/Dogs, Part Two* (3/69); *I'm Free/We're Not Gonna Take It* (6/69); *The Seeker/Here for More* (4/70); *Summertime Blues/Heaven and Hell* (6/70); *See Me, Feel Me/Tommy Overture* (9/70); *Won't Get Fooled Again/I Don't Even Know Myself* (7/71); *My Wife/Behind Blue Eyes* (10/71); *Join Together/Baby Don't You Do It* (6/72); *The Relay/Wasp Man* (11/72); *Love, Reign o'er Me/Water* (10/73); *The Real Me/I'm One* (1/74); *Postcard/Put the Money Down* (10/74); *Squeeze Box/Success Story* (11/75); *Slip Kid/Success Story* (8/76).

JESSE WINCHESTER/Hearing Jesse Winchester sing a song is a bit like listening to an out-of-town uncle give you a piece of sound advice. For the most part, Jesse's simplistic, down-home tunes are fraught with simultaneous strains of wry humor and twinges of everyday sadness. Coupled with Jesse's strong, clear vocals, this combination proves a potent one indeed. Jesse's first LP appeared during the dawn of the seventies. Since that time he has established himself as one of modern music's leading song poets. Not bad for a performer who was forbidden to play in the country of his birth, the United States, until 1977. Jesse Winchester—guitarist, singer, songwriter—was, in the eyes of Uncle Sam, nothing more than a draft dodger.

Born in Shreveport, Louisiana, Jesse picked up piano and guitar in his pre-teen years. In 1967, while a student in Munich, Germany, Jesse received his draft notice. Rather than return home, he opted for Canada. Settling down and raising a family, Jesse began to dabble in music professionally. In 1970, he met Robbie Robertson who got Jesse a recording deal with the doomed Ampex label. The first album, *JESSE WINCHESTER,* went practically unnoticed in the states but contained two classic tunes, *Brand New Tennessee Waltz* and *Yankee Lady.*

The two compositions from Jesse's premier disc were covered by numerous other artists, quickly establishing Jesse as a song-writer to be reckoned with. Unfortunately, Ampex Records was not exactly a cornerstone of either stability or longevity. Soon after the release of the LP, it disappeared from sight and Jesse found himself on Bearsville Records. His subsequent albums, from *THIRD DOWN, 110 TO GO* on, were quiet triumphs of taste, talent, and low-keyed brilliance. Before too long, the critics began to take notice of Jesse, and soon the public at large was following the saga of the exiled American who put his feelings into words so beautifully. In 1977, President Jimmy Carter al-lowed many draft evaders to return home. Winchester crossed the Canadian border for the first time in a decade and both his family and the press were there to greet him. A short tour of the United States followed.

True to form, however, Jesse returned to his newfound home, Canada, after a short visit and the mini-tour. When he needed solace, Canada had offered it. When his music needed nurturing, Canada had provided the backdrop. This year, and, it is hoped, for many years to come, Jesse Winchester will toil north of the border on some of the simplest, most evocative musical composi-tions ever to grace the world of modern music.

Albums/JESSE WINCHESTER (1971). THIRD DOWN, 110 TO GO (8/72): *Isn't That So?; Dangerous Fun; Full Moon; 'Nother Star; Do It; Lullaby for the First Born; Midnight Bus; Glory to the Day; Do La Lay; God's Own Jukebox; Silly Heart; All Your Stories.* LEARN TO LOVE IT (8/74): *Wake Me; Every Word You Say; How Far to the Horizon; L'Air de la Louisiane;*

Mississippi, You're on My Mind; Third-Rate Romance; Defying Gravity; Tell Me Why You Like Roosevelt; Pharaoh's Army; Laisse les Bons Temps Rouler; The End Is Not in Sight; I Can't Stand Up Alone. LET THE ROUGH SIDE DRAG (6/76): *Let the Rough Side Drag; Damned If You Do; Step by Step; Lay Down Your Burden; Everybody Knows but Me; Blow On, Chilly Wind; Working in the Vineyard; How About You; It Takes More Than a Hammer and Nails to Make a House a Home; The Only Show in Town; The Brand New Tennesse Waltz (reprise).* NOTHING BUT A BREEZE (3/77): *Nothing but a Breeze; My Songbird; Seems Like Only Yesterday; You Remember Me; Twigs and Seeds; Gilding the Lily; Bowling Green; Pourquoi M'Aimes-tu Pas?; It Takes a Young Girl; Rhumba Man.*

JOHNNY WINTER/Somewhere in the deep heart of America at this very moment is a man or woman, black, white, or brindle, who, if properly promoted, packaged, booked, and handled, could be bigger than Elvis and the Beatles put together. The question is where? Or, if you prefer, who? When the December 1968 edition of *Rolling Stone* mentioned almost in passing, in an article on the Texas scene, a totally unknown cross-eyed albino who played Delta Blues, New York club owner Steve Paul snapped like a divining rod that had at last stumbled onto water. He left on the first plane to Texas and didn't return until he'd tracked down the pale, thin cowboy with the white hair and the black voice.

Johnny Winter may not have been the *new* legendary unknown destined to reign as the greatest song hero since Bob Dylan, but he was an exciting discovery to make in early 1969 when everyone had seen everything except a cross-eyed albino who could sing. Columbia Records believed in him to the extent of a six-figure contract, and his lean white presence and silky hair brought an unexpected new twist to a musical scene already heavily dominated by a Black Is Beautiful philosophy.

America's first albino bluesman learned his sound from the black radio stations he listened to as a child. When he first became a professional entertainer in Texas (Johnny Winter and the Black Plague, he called his group—later renamed It and Them, featuring his brother Edgar), he played little blues, just hits of the time, R&B and soul. Nobody played blues for fun and profit in the rock and roll decade of 1956–66 but, when the blues revival of '66–'67 began, Steve Paul felt that Johnny's popularity as a blues guitarist par excellence was sure to cause some waves.

It did. Sort of. By mid-'69, Winter's vintage blues licks had clicked with most of the insiders and tastemakers. Then the mass media moved in and billed him, much to everyone's chagrin, as the most talented and irresistible freak since Tiny Tim. If the pitch didn't show where Johnny was musically, at least it sold records. Everyone agreed that, from that point onward, there was nowhere to go but up. Everyone was wrong.

Much to the music scene's amazement, the career of Johnny Winter never soared as high as was predicted. Caught in the traumatic transition between the spirit of musical adventure in the sixties and the commercial cretinism of the seventies, Johnny found himself an outsider . . . an artifact, dutifully playing gut-busting blues when the world at large was becoming more and more enamoured of the likes of Deep Purple and Black Sabbath. The blues revival was dead. Heavy metal was coming into its own. Gradually, Johnny drifted into Chuck Berry territory, forsaking roughneck blues for riff-rocking screamers. Still, he just never could achieve commerciality. A brief flirtation with drugs nearly ruined Johnny's life, not to mention career. Seeing the self-destructive path he was choosing, the plucky guitarist decided to call it quits until he could come to terms with himself as a human being as well as a musician. After a two-year hiatus to restructure both head and music, Johnny returned triumphant with a powerful album, *STILL ALIVE AND WELL.* No one really cares whether Johnny Winter ever becomes the "next big thing" anymore. No one really wants him to be. They're just happy to have him around, healthy and strong and churning out high-powered long-players and high-flying concert shows. Johnny Winter is a true blues artist; and artists really don't have to go out of their way to prove their worth to the world. As soon as they show up and perform . . . the world sits up and takes notice.

Albums/THE PROGRESSIVE BLUES EXPERIMENT (1968): *Rollin' and Tumblin'; Tribute to Muddy; I Got Love If You Want It; Bad Luck and Trouble; Help Me; Mean Town Blues; Broke Down Engine; Black Cat Moan; It's My Own Fault; Forty-Four.* JOHNNY WINTER (4/69): *I'm Yours and I'm Hers; Be Careful with a Fool; Dallas; Mean Mistreater; Leland, Mississippi; Good*

Morning Little School Girl; When You Got a Good Friend; I'll Drown in My Own Tears; Back Door Friend. SECOND WINTER (10/69): *Memory Pain; I'm Not Sure; The Good Love; Slippin' and Slidin'; Hustled Down in Texas; I Hate Everybody; Fast Life Rider; I Love Everybody; Miss Ann; Johnny B. Goode; Highway 61 Revisited.* JOHNNY WINTER AND (7/70): *Guess I'll Go Away; Ain't That a Kindness; No Time to Live; Rock and Roll Hoochie Koo; Am I Here?; Look Up; Prodigal Son; On the Limb; Let the Music Play; Nothin' Left; Funky Music.* JOHNNY WINTER LIVE (2/71): *Good Morning Little School Girl; It's My Own Fault; Jumpin' Jack Flash; medley: Great Balls of Fire; Long Tall Sally, Whole Lotta Shakin Goin' On, Mean Town Blues, Johnny B. Goode.* STILL ALIVE AND WELL (3/73): *Rock Me Baby; Can't You Feel It; Silver Train; Cheap Tequila; All Tore Down; Rock and Roll; Ain't Nothing to Me; Still Alive and Well; Let It Bleed; Too Much Seconal.* JOHN DAWSON WINTER III(1974): *Rock and Roll People; Golden Olden Days of Rock and Roll; Self-Destruction Blues; Raised on Rock; Stranger; Mind Over Matter; Roll with Me; Love Song to Me; Pick Up on My Mojo; Lay Down Your Sorrows; Sweet Papa John.* SAINTS AND SINNERS (2/74): *Stone County; Blinded by Love; Thirty Days; Stray Cat Blues; Bad Luck Situation; Rollin' 'cross the Country; Riot in Cell Block #9; Hurtin' So Bad; Boney Maronie; Feedback on Highway 101.* JOHNNY WINTER AND LIVE (re-issue of earlier album; 9/75). CAPTURED LIVE (2/76): *Bony Maronie; Roll with Me; Rock and Roll People; It's All Over Now; Highway 61 Revisited; Sweet Papa John.* NOTHIN' BUT THE BLUES (6/77): *Tired of Tryin'; TV Mama; Sweet Love and Evil Women; Drinkin' Blues; Mad Blues; It Was Rainin'; Bladie Mae; Walking through the Park.*

Singles/*I'm Yours and I'm Hers/I'll Drown in My Own Tears* (5/69); *Johnny B. Goode/I'm Not Sure* (11/69); *Rock and Roll Hoochie Koo/21st Century Man* (10/71); *Jumpin' Jack Flash/Good Morning Little School Girl* (4/71); *Silver Train/Rock and Roll* (5/73); *Can't You Feel It/Rock and Roll* (7/73); *Stone County/Bad Luck Situation* (1/74); *Bony Maronie/Hurtin' So Bad* (4/74); *Raised on Rock/Pick Up My Mojo* (12/74); *Golden Olden Days of Rock and Roll/Stranger* (3/75); *Let the Good Times Roll (with Edgar Winter)/Soul Man* (7/76).

STEVIE WONDER/No one can ever accuse Stevie Wonder of *not* living up to his name. Blind from birth, the composer-singer-pianist-harmonica player had his first top-ten record at the age of twelve *(Fingertips)*, his first hit album the same year *(THE 12-YEAR-OLD GENIUS)*, was compared to Ray Charles before he reached his teens, became a regular resident in the top five when not yet twenty years of age, and is currently one of the most influential and respected artists-producers-arrangers-composers alive. He will not be thirty until 1980.

Stevie was born Steveland Morris in Saginaw, Michigan. While still a tot, his family moved to Detroit where he was turned on to R&B via the local radio stations. Motor city, the home of the Motown label, gave Stevie ample opportunity to absorb different musical modes. His passion for music increased as he got older. In 1961, at the grand old age of eleven, he was brought to Motown by a young friend's big brother, Ronnie White of the Miracles. The company promptly dubbed him Little Stevie Wonder. Within one year, an entire nation knew of the boy's exceptional talents.

A series of Motown-sponsored tours increased the teen's popularity and as his fandom grew, so did his musical abilities. Songs like *Uptight, I Was Made to Love Her, For Once in My Life,* and *My Cherie Amour* proved his talent in the songwriting area and, by the end of the decade, he was an accomplished producer, arranger, and businessman as well.

At the age of twenty-one, he legally received all of his childhood earnings, which had been held by a state-appointed guardian. He promptly moved to a new home, got married, and emerged on a grandiose musical adventure that has yet to reach an end. Moving from the more traditional, pop-oriented sounds of the sixties, Wonder began experimenting with more subtle strains, incorporating shadows of jazz, traditional, rock, and R & B, with spectacular results.

MUSIC OF MY LIFE firmly established Wonder as a serious composer. Playing all instruments heard on the record, Stevie sought to open up his music as far as it would go, to break out of the style Motown had established for him over the years. He succeeded. He became a reborn cause célèbre. Touring with the Rolling Stones in 1972 brought his newfound sound to millions, live. In June of the following year, his *INNERVISIONS* continued the musical odyssey and his fandom increased even more, with the album going gold and then platinum within weeks.

A near-disaster nearly brought the journey to an end prematurely. On August 6 of that year, Wonder was involved in a head-on collision with a logging truck on a highway outside Durham, North Carolina. He fell into a coma. Miraculously, within seven months he was not only up and about but performing as well. *INNERVISIONS* led him to win five Grammy awards the following year. A subsequent album, *FULFILLINGNESS' FIRST FINALE,* shipped gold, held the number-one position for three weeks running, and won five more Grammys. His *SONGS IN THE KEY OF LIFE,* released in 1976, copped yet another five awards. And his career shows no signs of slowing down.

In February of 1977, Wonder spent two weeks in Nigeria exploring his musical heritage with local musicians at FESTAC '77, the second world Black and African cultural festival.

Albums/12-YEAR-OLD GENIUS (6/63): *Fingertips (two parts); Soul Bongo; Drown in My Own Tears; La La La La La; Masquerade Is Over (I'm Afraid); Hallelujah! I Love Her So; Don't You Know.* TRIBUTE TO UNCLE RAY: *Hallelujah! I Love Her So; Ain't That Love; Mary Ann; Don't You Know; Masquerade; My Baby's Gone; Frankie and Johnny; Drown in My Own Tears; Come Back, Baby; Sunset.* JAZZ SOUL: *Fingertips; Square; Soul Bongo; Manhattan at Six; Some Other Time; Wandering; Session 112; Bam; Paulsby.* WITH A SONG IN MY HEART: *Dream; With a Song in My Heart; Get Happy; Put on a Happy Face; When You Wish upon a Star; Smile; Make Someone Happy; Without a Song; On the Sunny Side of the Street; Give Your Heart a Chance.* AT THE BEACH: *Red Sails in the Sunset; Party at the Beach; Happy Street; Beachcomber; Castles in the Sand; Beyond the Sea; Sad Boy; Beachstomp; Hey, Harmonica Man.* UPTIGHT (5/66): *Uptight (Everything Is Alright); Nothing's Too Good for My Baby; Love a Go-Go; Ain't That Asking for Trouble; Blowin' in the Wind; Hold Me; Teach Me Tonight; I Want My Baby Back; Pretty Little Angel; Contract on Love; With a Child's Heart.* DOWN TO EARTH (12/66): *Place in the Sun; Bang Bang; Thank You, Love; Mr. Tambourine Man; Hey Love; Sixteen Tons; Down to Earth; Sylvia; Lonesome Road; My World Is Empty without You; Angel Baby; Be Cool, Be Calm and Keep Yourself Together.* I WAS

MADE TO LOVE HER (5/67): *I Was Made to Love Her; My Girl; I Got a Witness; Baby, Don't You Do It; Respect; I Pity the Fool; Send Me Some Lovin'; I'd Cry; Everybody Needs Somebody; Fool for You; Please, Please, Please; Every Time I See You I Go Wild.* SOMEDAY AT CHRISTMAS (12/67): *Someday at Christmas; What Christmas Means to Me; Silver Bells; Christmas Song; Little Drummer Boy; Ave Maria; other titles.* GREATEST HITS (3/68): *Uptight; I Was Made to Love Her; I'm Wondering; Hey Love; Place in the Sun; Blowin' in the Wind; Contract on Love; Workout, Stevie, Workout; Fingertips; Hey, Harmonica Man; Nothing's Too Good for My Baby; Castles in the Sand.* FOR ONCE IN MY LIFE (12/68): *For Once in My Life; Shoo-Be-Doo-Be-Doo-Da-Day; You Met Your Match; I Wanna Make Her Love Me; I'm More Than Happy (I'm Satisfied); I Don't Know Why; Sunny; I'd Be a Fool Right Now; Ain't No Lovin'; God Bless the Child; Do I Love Her; The House on the Hill.* MY CHERIE AMOUR (9/69): *My Cherie Amour; Hello, Young Lovers; At Last; Light My Fire; The Shadow of Your Smile; You and Me; Somebody Knows, Somebody Cares; Yester-me, Yester-you, Yesterday; Angie Girl; Give Your Love; I've Got You.* STEVIE WONDER LIVE (3/70): *Intro/Pretty World; Sunny; love theme from* Romeo and Juliet; *Shoo-Be-Doo-Be-Doo-Da-Day;Everybody's Talking; My Cherie Amour; Yester-me, Yester-you, Yesterday; I've Gotta Be Me/Once in a Lifetime; A Place in the Sun; Down to Earth; Blowin' in the Wind; By the Time I Get to Phoenix; Ca' Purange; Alfie; For Once in My Life/Thank You, Love.* SIGNED, SEALED & DELIVERED (7/70): *Never Had a Dream Come True; We Can Work It Out; Signed, Sealed, Delivered I'm Yours; Heaven Help Us All; You Can't Judge a Book by Its Cover; Don't Wonder Why; Anything You Want Me to Do; I Can't Let My Heaven Walk Away; Joy (Takes over Me); I Gotta Have a Song; Something to Say.* WHERE I'M COMING FROM (4/71): *Look Around; Do Yourself a Favor; Think of Me As Your Soldier; Something out of the Blue; If You Really Love Me; I Wanna Talk to You; Take Up a Course in Happiness; Never Dream You'd Leave in Summer; Sunshine in Their Eyes.* GREATEST HITS, VOL. 2 (10/71): *Shoo-Be-Doo-Be-Doo-Da-Day; Signed, Sealed, Delivered I'm Yours; If You Really Love Me; For Once in My Life; We Can Work It Out; You Met Your Match; Never Had a Dream Come True; Yester-me, Yester-you, Yesterday; My Cherie Amour; Never*

Dreamed You'd Leave in Summer; Travelin' Man; Heaven Help Us All. MUSIC OF MY MIND (3/72): *Love Having You Around; Superwoman; I Love Every Little Thing about You; Sweet Little Girl; Happier Than the Morning Sun; Girl Blue; Seems So Long; Keep On Running; Evil.* TALKING BOOK (10/72): *Sunshine of My Life; Maybe Your Baby; You and I; Tuesday Heartbreak; You've Got It Bad, Girl; Superstition; Big Brother; Blame It on the Sun; Lookin' for Another Pure Love; I Believe.* INNERVISIONS (9/73): *Too High; Visions; Living for the City; Golden Lady; Higher Ground; Jesus Children of America; All in Love Is Fair; Don't You Worry 'bout a Thing; He's a Missta Know-It-All.* FULFILLINGNESS' FIRST FINALE (1974): *Smile Please; Heaven Is 10 Zillion Light Years Away; Too Shy to Say; Boogie on, Reggae Woman; Creepin'; You Haven't Done Nothin'; It Ain't No Use; They Won't Go When I Go; Bird of Beauty; Please Don't Go.* SONGS IN THE KEY OF LIFE (10/76): *I Am Singing; Love's in Need of Love Today; Have a Talk with God; Village Ghetto Land; Sir Duke; I Wish; Knock Me Off My Feet; Pass-Time Paradise; Summer Soft; Ordinary Pain; Isn't She Lovely; Joy inside My Tears; Black Man; If It's Magic; As; Another Star; Saturn; Ebony Eyes; All-Day Sucker; Contusion; Another Star; Easy-Going Evening (My Mama's Call).* LOOKING BACK (12/77): *Hey, Harmonica Man; Uptight; Nothing's Too Good for My Baby; Place in the Sun; Blowin' in the Wind; I Was Made to Love Her; Signed, Sealed, Delivered I'm Yours; My Cherie Amour; For Once in My Life; Fingertips; I Call It Pretty Music; other titles.*

Singles/*Little Water Boy/La La La* (10/62); *Contract on Love/Sunset* (12/62); *Fingertips (Parts I and II)* (5/63); *I Call It Pretty Music (Parts I and II)* (8/63); *Workout, Stevie, Workout/Monkey Talk* (9/63); *Castles in the Sand/He's a Good Guy* (1/64); *Hey, Harmonica Man/This Little Girl* (5/64); *Sad Boy/Happy Street* (9/64); *Kiss Me, Baby/Tears in Vain* (3/65); *High Heel Sneakers/Funny* (8/65); *Uptight/Purple Raindrops* (11/65); *Nothing's Too Good for My Baby/With a Child's Heart* (3/66); *Blowin' in the Wind/Ain't That Asking for Trouble* (5/66); *I'm Wondering/Everytime I See You, I Go Wild* (9/66); *A Place in the Sun/Sylvia* (10/66); *Someday at Christmas/The Miracles of Christmas* (11/66); *Travelin' Man/Hey Love* (2/67); *I Was Made to Love Her/Hold Me* (5/67); *Shoo-Be-Doo-Be-Doo-Da-*

Day/Why Don't You Lead Me to Love (3/68); *You Met Your Match/My Girl* (6/68); *For Once in My Life/Angie Girl* (10/68); *My Cherie Amour/Don't Know Why I Love You* (2/69); *Yester-me, Yester-you, Yesterday/I'd Be a Fool Right Now* (9/69); *Never Had a Dream Come True/Somebody Knows, Somebody Cares* (1/70); *Signed, Sealed, Delivered/I'm More Than Happy, I'm Satisfied (5/70); Heaven Help Us All/I Gotta Have a Song* (9/70);*We Can Work It Out/Never Dreamed You'd Leave in Summer* (2/71); *If You Really Love Me/Think of Me As Your Soldier* (7/71); *Super Woman/I Love Every Little Thing* (4/72); *Keep On Running/Evil* (8/72); *Superstition/You've Got It Bad, Girl* (10/72); *You Are the Sunshine of My Life* (2/73); *Higher Ground* (7/73); *Living for the City* (10/73); *Don't You Worry 'bout a Thing* (3/74); *You Haven't Done Nothin'* (7/74); *Boogie on Reggae Woman* (10/74); *Isn't She Lovely* (1976); *Sir Duke* (1977); *Another Star* (1977); *As* (10/77).

GARY WRIGHT/Spooky Tooth's lead screamer has found peace of mind in the sanctuary of a synthesizer and gone off to the world of solo gold with apparent ease. New Jersey–born Gary Wright is currently knocking out crowds worldwide with his spacey keyboard antics and high-pitched vocals. In 1976, his *THE DREAM WEAVER* album (and single) put him in the top ten for months. Subsequent recordings haven't proved as popular, but have managed to keep the likeable songwriter in the top-fifty album charts for three months at a time, sparking solid tours across country.

Gary's earlier solo efforts weren't all that earth-shattering, though. Leaving Spooky Tooth first in 1970, he started the brief group Wonderwheel, a band more off the record than on. Two solo albums, *EXTRACTION* and *FOOTPRINT,* proved to be top secrets in terms of popularity and, in 1973, Wright rejoined the re-formed Spooky Tooth for another stab at fame. The wounds proved superficial, however, and by 1974, Wright was a solo entity. He began to noodle in earnest with the sounds of synthesized space and, donning a silver jumpsuit for stage appearances, he created the *DREAM WEAVER*. The hits haven't stopped coming since. Better living through science.

Albums/EXTRACTION (11/70): *Get on the Right Road; Get Hold of Yourself; Sing a Song; We Try Hard; The Wrong Time; Over You Now; Too Late to Cry; I've Got a Story.* FOOTPRINT

(10/71): *Give Me the Good Earth; Two-Faced Man; Love to Survive; Whether It's Right or Wrong; Stand for Our Rights; Fascinating Things; Forgotten; If You Treat Someone Right.* DREAM WEAVER (7/75): *Love Is Alive; Let It Out; Can't Find the Judge; Made to Love You; Power of Love; Dream Weaver; Blind Feeling; Much Higher; Feel for Me.* THAT WAS ONLY YESTERDAY (Gary Wright and Spooky Tooth; 3/76): *I Know; That Was Only Yesterday; The Wrong Time; I've Got Enough Heart; Two-Faced Man; Love to Survive; Wildfire; Nobody There At All; Sunshine Help Me; I Can't See the Reason; Waitin' for the Wind; Cotton-Growing Man; Fascinating Things; Son of Your Father; Sing a Song; Something to Say; Stand for Our Rights; Evil Woman; Holy Water.* THE LIGHT OF SMILES (3/77): *Water Sign; Time Machine; I Am the Sky; Who Am I; Silent Fury; Phantom Writer; The Light of Smiles; I'm Alright; Empty Inside; Are You Weepin'; Child of Light.* TOUCH AND GONE (9/77): *Touch and Gone; Stay Away; Lost in My Emotions; Starry-Eyed; Sky Eyes; Something Very Special; The Love It Takes; Night Ride; Can't Get above Losing You.*

Singles/*Feelin' Bad* (8/69); *That Was Only Yesterday* (11/69); *Get on the Right Road* (2/71); *Stand for Our Rights* (5/71); *Fascinating Things* (11/71); *Love Is Alive/Much Higher* (9/75); *Dream Weaver/Let It Out* (11/75); *Made to Love You/Power of Love* (8/76); *Phantom Writer/Child of Light* (1/77); *Water Sign/Empty Inside* (4/77).

THE YARDBIRDS/*Jimmy Page (guitar), Jeff Beck (guitar), Eric Clapton (guitar), John Paul Jones (bass, organ), Paul Samwell-Smith (bass, organ), Robert Plant (vocals), John Bonnham (drums), Jimmy McCarty (drums), Keith Relf (vocals), Chris Dreja (rhythm guitar).*

In late 1963 and early 1964, when the British "scene" was having its birth pangs, the Yardbirds followed the Rolling Stones into the Crawdaddy Club as house band. Like the early Stones, they used standard material—Bo Diddley, Muddy Waters, Sonny Boy Williamson—though always remaining more faithful to the original than the variation-prone Stones. This was important at a time when the concept of original material was not as overworked as it was to become in 1967–69. Also, man for man, the Yardbirds were better instrumentalists than the Stones. Formed in London in 1963, the original Yardbirds evolved from a group called the Metropolis Blues Quartet, which featured Dreja, Samwell-Smith, Relf, and McCarty. Clapton joined and the Yardbirds were formed. Their fame spread instantly; soon they were top contenders with the fledgling Stones for the "best blues band" around. Although the Yardbirds excelled musically, they were no match for Mick Jagger's pouting charisma.

By 1964, the Beatles had hit America, The Stones had hit America. EVERYone from England had hit America. Except the Yardbirds. They were somehow lost in the shuffle. A first album proved a technical dud and the Yardbirds had to rely on their in-concert jams (rave-ups) to sustain their popularity. Fortunately, guitarist Eric Clapton proved more than adept at keeping the Yardbirds popular.

Professional opinions were called in to help the sagging record life of the group. Graham Gouldman (later of 10 cc.) penned a hit single for the band, *For Your Love.* It gave the band status. It also gave them problems. Clapton, displeased with the non-blues direction the band was pursuing, left, eventually joining John Mayall. Fortunately, he was replaced by guitar wild-man Jeff Beck, who quickly led the band back up the charts with two more Gouldman hits, *Heart Full of Soul* and *Evil-Hearted You.* By 1966, the Yardbirds seemed a sure thing. Two more singles, *Shapes of Things* and *Over Under Sideways Down,* brought them near the top of the charts again. Trouble within the ranks, a classic pattern here, slowed down their rising star. Samwell-Smith quit. Dreja picked up the bass and Jimmy Page was enlisted as a rhythm guitarist. Illness forced Beck out of the picture for a while, allowing Page to step in as head axeman. When Beck returned to his legion, the group had two hot 'n' nasty lead men playing duel riffs.

By 1967, however, Beck was gone, out to start his own group. Donovan producer Mickie Most hit the band where it hurt most —on record—and produced the syrupy mess, *LITTLE GAMES.* By now, the Yardbirds were catatonic. They were not blues. They were not rock. They were not pop. They were finished.

They broke up in 1968, leaving Jimmy Page holding the name, the bag, and contracts to quite a few European dates. He quickly formed a group called the New Yardbirds, Robert Plant, John Bonham, and John Paul Jones, and embarked on a European tour.

By the time the foursome returned to England, they had a new name and a growing reputation. Led Zeppelin had been born.

Albums/FOR YOUR LOVE (6/65): *For Your Love; I'm Not Talking; I Ain't Got You; Got to Hurry; I Ain't Done Wrong; I Wish You Would; Certain Girl; Sweet Music; Good Morning, Little Schoolgirl; My Girl Sloopy.* HAVING A RAVE UP WITH THE YARDBIRDS (11/65): *I'm a Man; You're a Better Man Than I; Evil-Hearted Woman; Still I'm Sad; Heart Full of Soul; Train Kept a-Rollin'; Smokestack Lightning; Respectable; Here 'Tis.* YARDBIRDS WITH SONNY BOY WILLIAMSON (2/66; re-released 5/70 as ERIC CLAPTON AND THE YARD-BIRDS LIVE WITH SONNY BOY WILLIAMSON): *Bye Bye, Bird; Mister Downchild; 23 Hours Too Long; Out of Water Coast; Baby, Don't Worry; Pontiac Blues; Take It Easy, Baby; I Don't Care No More; Do the Weston.* OVER UNDER SIDEWAYS DOWN (7/66): *Lost Woman; Over Under Sideways Down; I Can't Make Your Way; Farewell; Hot House of Omargarashid; Jeff's Boogie; He's Always There; Turn into Earth; What Do You Want; Ever Since the World Began.* GREATEST HITS (3/67): *Shapes of Things; Still I'm Sad; New York City Blues; For Your Love; Over Under Sideways Down; I'm a Man; Happenings Ten Years Time Ago; Heart Full of Soul; Smokestack Lightning; I'm Not Talking.* LITTLE GAMES (7/67): *Little Games; Smile on Me; White Summer; Tinker, Tailor, Soldier, Sailor; Glimpses; No Excess Baggage; Drinking Muddy Water; Only the Black Rose; Stealing, Stealing; Little Soldier Boy.* THE YARDBIRDS, FEATURING PERFORMANCES BY JEFF BECK, ERIC CLAPTON AND JIMMY PAGE (9/70): *Shapes of Things; For Your Love; Over Under Sideways Down; Little Games; Smokestack Lightning; other titles.* YARDBIRDS FAVORITES (3/77): *Smokestack Lightning; Good Morning, Little Schoolgirl; New York City Blues; I'm a Man; Here 'Tis; Evil-Hearted You; Putty (in Your Hands); A Certain Girl; Got to Hurry; You're a Better Man Than I.* GREAT HITS (3/77): *For Your Love; Heart Full of Soul; Still I'm Sad; I'm Not Talking; Shapes of Things; Train Kept a-rollin'; I Wish You Would; I Ain't Done Wrong; I Ain't Got You; I'm a Man.*

Singles/*I Wish You Would/A Certain Girl* (8/64); *For Your Love* (4/65); *Heart Full of Soul* (6/65); *I'm a Man* (9/65); *Shapes of Things/I'm a Man* (2/66); *Over Under Sideways Down* (5/66);

Happenings Ten Years Time Ago/Nazz Are Blue (11/66); *Little Games/Puzzles* (3/67); *Over Under Sideways Down/Happenings Ten Years Time Ago* (5/67); *Ha Ha Said the Clown/Tinker, Tailor, Soldier, Sailor* (7/67); *Drinking Muddy Water/Ten Little Indians* (10/67); *Think about It/Goodnight Sweet Josephine* (3/68).

YES/*Jon Anderson (vocals); Chris Squire (bass, vocals), Peter Banks (guitar). Tony Kaye (keyboards), Bill Bruford (drums). Present members: Anderson, Squire, Patrick Moraz (keyboards), Alan White (drums), Steve Howe (guitar).*

The world of Yes is musically majestic and fantasy-laden. Ech of their present-day excursions into song stands as being sort of a rock leap into Tolkien territory with bizarre imagery peppering both the record itself and the album cover design. The intricate band was born in 1968 when singer Anderson and bassist Squire decided to form a band that would do "more" than just play good ol' rock and roll. The first Yes albums were somewhat hesitant affairs, with the band alternately offering original material and re-arranging semi-standard stuff to fit their eclectic style.

Finally, by their third release, *THE YES ALBUM,* the group had found a suitable phantasmagoric approach and their careers were launched. During the years, the faces of Yes have changed almost as much as their musical topography. Banks was the first to leave, starting the ill-fated Flash. Tony Kaye set off to pursue Badger, a promising band that released two albums in the States on two different labels and with two different sets of musicians. Howe replaced Banks, and Rick Wakeman joined to fill in the keyboard slot. Wakeman left in '73 to chase solo rainbows and Moraz was tapped. In '72, Bruford jumped into King Crimson's court and White's aid was enlisted. All of Yes' present members have released individual albums of their solo works.

Albums/YES (10/69). TIME AND A WORD (11/70): *No Opportunity Necessary, No Experience Needed; Then; Everydays; Sweet Dreams; The Prophet; Clear Days; Astral Traveler; Time and a Word.* THE YES ALBUM (3/71): *Yours Is No Disgrace; The Clap; Starship Trooper: Life Seeker, Disillusion, Wurm; I've Seen All Good People—Your Move, All Good People; A Venture; Perpetual Change.* FRAGILE (1/72): *Roundabout; Cans and Brahms; We Have Heaven; South Side of the Sky; Five Per Cent for Nothing; Long Distance Runaround; The Fish; Mood for a Day;*

Heart of the Sunrise. CLOSE TO THE EDGE (9/72): *Close to the the Edge; The Solid Time of Change, The Total Mass Retain, Get Up/Get Down, Seasons of Man; And You and I: Cord of Life, Eclipse, The Preacher, The Teacher, Apocalypse; Siberian Khatru.* YESSONGS (5/73): *Opening (excerpt from "Firebird Suite"); Siberian Khatru; Heart of the Sunrise; Perpetual Change; And You and I; Mood for a Day; Excerpts from "The Six Wives of Henry VIII" Roundabout; Your Move; All Good People; Long Distance Runaround; The Fish; Close to the Edge; Yours Is No Disgrace; Starship Trooper.* TALES FROM TOPOGRAPHIC OCEANS (1/74): *The Revealing Science of God; The Remembering; The Ancient; Ritual.* RELAYER (12/74): *The Gates of Delirium; Sound Chaser; To Be Over.* YESTERDAYS (2/75): *America; Looking Around; Time and a Word; Sweet Dreams; Then Survival; Astral Traveler; Dear Father.* GOING FOR THE ONE (6/77): *Wondrous Stories; Going for the One; Parallels; Awaken; Turn of the Century.*

Singles/*Yessongs*/*Every Little Thing* (1/70); *Your Move/Clap* (7/71); *Roundabout/Long Distance Runaround* (1/72); *America/Total Mass Retain* (7/72); *And You and I (Parts One and Two)* (10/72); *Roundabout/Long Distance Runaround* (1/74); *America/Your Move* (11/74); *Soon/Sound Chaser* (1/75).

JESSE COLIN YOUNG/Following the demise of the Youngbloods in 1971, ethereal-voiced lead singer Jesse Colin Young embarked on a solo career. Still going strong, the laconic singer-songwriter-guitarist is a major draw at college campuses, where his songs of pastoral plenty go over bigger than a mid-semester break.

Albums/THE SOUL OF A CITY BOY (recorded 1964, released 1967 & 1974): *Four in the Morning; You Gotta Fix It; Rye Whiskey; Whoa, Baby; Suzanne; Black-Eyed Susan; Same Old Man; Talk to Me; Drifter's Blues; Stranger Love; I Think I'll Take to Whiskey.* TOGETHER (1/72): *Good Times; Together; Peace Song; Sweet Little Sixteen; Child; Six Days on the Road; It's a Lovely Day; Creole Belle; Pastures of Plenty; 6,000 Miles; Born in Chicago.* SONG FOR JULIE (9/73): *Morning Sun; Song for Julie; Ridgetop; Evenin'; Miss Hesitation; T-Bone Shuffle; Lafayette Waltz; Jambalaya (on the Bayou); Country Home.* LIGHT SHINE (3/74): *California Suite; California Child; Grey Day;*

Light Shine; Pretty and the Fair; Barbados; Motorcycle Blues; The Cuckoo; Susan. SONGBIRD (2/75): *Songbird; Before You Came; Daniel; Josianne; Again; Slick City; 'Til You Come Back Home; Sugar Babe; Motorhome.* ON THE ROAD (4/76): *Corinna; Have You Seen My Baby; T-Bone Shuffle; Miss Hesitation; Sunlight; Walkin' Off the Blues; What's Goin' On; Peace Song; Mercy Mercy Me.* LOVE ON THE WING (3/77): *Higher and Higher; Love on the Wing; Workin'; Hey, Good Lookin'; Fool; Drift Away; Do It Slow; California Cowboy; Louisiana Highway; Your Lovin' Hobo.*

Singles/*Peace Song/Pretty and the Fair* (9/70); *Good Times/Peace Song* (4/72); *It's a Lovely Day/Sweet Little Child* (8/72); *Morning Sun/Evenin'* (10/73); Light Shine/The Cuckoo (4/74); *Susan/Barbados* (9/74); *Songbird/Till You Get Back Home* (5/75); *Motorhome/Sugar Babe* (7/75); *Love on the Wing/California Cowboy* (3/77); *Higher and Higher/Fool* (5/77).

NEIL YOUNG/Born in Toronto, nasal-voiced, sleepy-eyed Neil Young first achieved fame as the brooding second lead guitarist in the L.A.-based band, Buffalo Springfield. A shy, reclusive sort, Neil was initially too backward to sing his own lyrics in the band. Finally, his self-confidence was bolstered enough to participate and the thin, haunting vocal strains of Young became one of the band's most effective trademarks.

When the band split in 1968, Neil plunged into solo work with mixed results. An initial long-player, *NEIL YOUNG,* was practically ignored by the public at large, although it stands as being one of Young's most cohesive and brooding works to date. A second, more up-tempo LP, *EVERYBODY KNOWS THIS IS NOWHERE* (with Crazy Horse) firmly established Young as a rock star first class with the FM-radio hit, *Down by the River* (with that famous guitar solo that sounds a bit like a fully grown Yak choking on a soupbone). Bolstered by Crazy Horse (Billy Talbot on bass, Ralph Molina on drums, Danny Whitten on guitar), Young's future as a solo artist seemed assured.

Success on another front, however, put a crimp in Neil's solo style. His brief fling with Crosby, Stills and Nash produced one exceptional album, *DEJA VU,* and a bitter, intriguing single, *Ohio.* Simultaneously, Young was soaring to new heights with albums like *AFTER THE GOLDRUSH* (with young Nils Lofgrin onboard as a new Crazy Horser).

An unexpected string of Neil Young hits between 1970 and 1972 *(Cinnamon Girl, Only Love Can Break Your Heart, Heart of Gold,* and *Old Man)* put Young in·the uneasy position of a pop star. The moody musician reacted in a fairly iconoclastic manner, best represented by the collosal dud *JOURNEY THROUGH THE PAST,* an opulently banal retrospective album touted as a soundtrack to a film no one had ever seen. A follow-up album, *TIME FADES AWAY,* dealt with the overdose deaths of two of Young's friends. Not exactly commercial fodder.

For the past few years, the career of Neil Young, rock recluse, has faltered somewhat in terms of monetary success. His die-hard fans have stuck with him through all his musical idiosyncracies. Of late, he has taken an upswing of sorts. His *ZUMA* (1976) was fairly upbeat and his *STILLS-YOUNG BAND* contributions could not be termed downers by any means. In 1977, Warners issued a Neil Young retrospective package tracing the artist's career from his Buffalo Springfield days to the present. When seen in perspective, Neil Young's career is indeed unique to the mass-marketed seventies. A talent of enormous stature, capable of conjuring up powerfully introspective visions, Young has retained his individualistic stance and has slugged it out, careerwise, for the right to remain unique.

Albums/NEIL YOUNG (11/68): *The Emperor of Wyoming; The Loner; If I Could Have Her Tonight; I've Been Waiting for You; The Old Laughing Lady; String Quartet from Whiskey Boot Hill; Here We Are in the Years; What Did You Do to My Life; I've Loved Her So Long; The Last Trip to Tulsa.* EVERYBODY KNOWS THIS IS NOWHERE (5/69): *Cinnamon Girl; Everybody Knows This Is Nowhere; Round and Round; Down by the River; The Losing End; Running Dry (requiem for the Rockets): Cowgirl in the Sand.* AFTER THE GOLDRUSH (9/70): *Tell Me Why; After the Goldrush; Only Love Can Break Your Heart; Southern Man; Till the Morning Comes; Oh, Lonesome Me; Don't Let It Bring You Down; Birds; When You Dance I Can Really Love; I Believe in You; Cripple Creek Ferry.* HARVEST (2/71): *Heart of Gold; Harvest; Old Man; There's a World; Alabama; The Needle and the Damage Done; Words; Are You Ready for the*

Country; A Man Needs a Maid; Out on the Weekend. JOURNEY THROUGH THE PAST (soundtrack; 11/72): *For What It's Worth/Mr. Soul; Rock and Roll Woman; Find the Cost of Freedom; Ohio; Southern Man; Are You Ready for the Country; Let Me Call You Sweetheart; Alabama; Words; Relativity Invitation; Handel's* Messiah; *King of Kings; Soldier; Let's Go Away for a While.* TIME FADES AWAY (8/73): *Journey through the Past; L.A.; Time Fades Away; Love in Mind; Don't Be Denied; The Bridge; Yonder Stands the Sinner; Last Dance.* ON THE BEACH (7/74): *Walk On; See the Sky About to Rain; Revolution Blues; For the Turnstiles; Vampire Blues; On the Beach; Motion Pictures; Ambulance Blues.* TONIGHT'S THE NIGHT (6/75): *Tonight's the Night; Speakin' Out; World on a String; Come On, Baby/Let's Go Downtown; Mellow My Mind; Roll Another Number; New Mama; Lookout Joe; Tired Eyes; Albuquerque; Tonight's the Night.* ZUMA (11/75): *Don't Cry No Tears; Danger Bird; Pardon My Heart; Lookin' for a Love; Barstool Blues; Stupid Girl; Drive Back; Cortez the Killer; Through My Sails.* AMERICAN STARS 'n' BARS (5/77): *The Old Country Waltz; Saddle Up the Palomino; Hey Babe; Hold Back the Tears; Bite the Bullet; Star of Bethlehem; Will to Love; Like a Hurricane; Homegrown.* DECADE (10/77): *Down to the Wire; Burned; Mr. Soul; Broken Arrow; Expecting to Fly; Sugar Mountain; I Am a Child; The Loner; The Old Laughing Lady; Cinnamon Girl; Down by the River; Cowgirl in the Sand; I Believe in You; After the Goldrush; Southern Man; Helpless; Ohio; Soldier; Old Man; A Man Needs a Maid; Harvest; Heart of Gold; Star of Bethlehem; The Needle and the Damage Done; Tonight's the Night; Tired Eyes; Walk On; For the Turnstiles; Winterlong; Deep Forbidden Lake; Like a Hurricane; Love Is a Rose; Cortez the Killer; Campaigner; Long May You Run.*

Singles/*Oh, Lonesome Me/I've Been Waiting for You* (2/70); *Cinnamon Girl/Sugar Mountain* (4/70); *Only Love Can Break a Heart/Birds* (9/70); *When You Dance I Can Really Love/Sugar Mountain* (2/71); *When You Dance I Can Really Love* (2/71); *Heart of Gold/Sugar Mountain* (12/71); *War Song (with Graham Nash)/The Needle and the Damage Done* (6/72); *Time Slips Away/Last Trip to Tulsa* (11/73); *Walk On/For the Turnstiles* (5/74); *Looking for a Love/Sugar Mountain* (1/76); *Drive Back/Stupid Girl* (3/76).

THE YOUNGBLOODS/*Jesse Colin Young (guitar, bass, vocals), Jerry Corbitt (guitar, vocals), Joe Baur (drums), Banana (guitar, keyboards).*

Formed on the East Coast in the mid-sixties, the folkie-oriented Youngbloods really didn't take the music world by storm until they moved to the West Coast. Their first two albums, produced by Felix Pappalardi, set the stage for their popular West Coast *ELEPHANT MOUNTAIN* LP. Shortly thereafter, Corbitt left the band, leaving the Youngbloods to forge onward as a trio. In 1971, Michael Kane was brought in on bass but, by the end of the year, the group broke up to pursue solo projects. Banana(and the bunch)'s solo career proved a dud, as did Jerry Corbitt's and Joe Bauer's. Jesse Colin Young has enjoyed much success on a regional level as a wandering troubadour.

Albums/THE YOUNGBLOODS (1/67): *Grizzly Bear; All over the World; Statesboro Blues; Get Together; One-Note Man; Other Side of This Life; Tears Are Falling; Four in the Morning; Foolin' Around; Ain't That Lovin' You Baby; See See Rider.* EARTH MUSIC (10/67): *Euphoria; All My Dreams Blue; Monkey Business; Dreamer's Dream; Sugar Babe; Long and Tall; I Can Tell; Don't Play Games; Wine Song; Fool Me; Reason to Believe.* ELEPHANT MOUNTAIN (4/69): *Darkness, Darkness; Smug; On Sir Francis Drake; Sunlight; Beautiful; Turn It Over; Rain Song; Trillium; Quicksand; Black Mountain Breakdown; Sham; Ride the Wind.* BEST OF THE YOUNGBLOODS (8/70): *Get Together; Grizzly Bear; Beautiful; Sugar Babe; other titles.* ROCK FESTIVAL (9/70): *It's a Lovely Day; Prelude; Faster All the Time; Josiane; Sea Cow Boogie; Misty Roses; Fiddler a Dran; Ice Bag; Peepin' and Hidin'; Interlude; On Beautiful Lake Spenard.* RIDE THE WIND (2/71): *Dolphin; Beautiful; Get Together; Ride the Wind; Sunlight; Sugar Babe.* RIDE THE WIND (re-released on second label, 6/71). SUNLIGHT (7/71): *Sunlight; Reason to Believe; Foolin' Around; Statesboro Blues; On Sir Francis Drake; One-Note Man; Dreamer's Dream; Long and Tall; I Can Tell; Ain't That Lovin You, Baby.* GOOD AND DUSTY (11/71): *Stagger Lee; That's How Strong My Love Is; Willie and the Hand Jive; Good and Dusty; Let the Good Times Roll; Hippie from Olena#5; Pontiac Blues; Drifting and Drifting; Will the Circle Be Unbroken; Light Shine; I'm a Hog for You, Baby; The Moonshine Is the Sun-*

shine. HIGH ON A RIDGETOP (11/72): *Speedo; She Caught the Katy; I Shall Be Released; Dreamboat; She Came in through the Bathroom Window; Donna; La Bamba; Kind-Hearted Woman; Running Bear; Going by the River.*

Singles/*Grizzly Bear/Tears Are Falling* (1/67); *Merry-Go-Round/Foolin' Around* (3/67); *Euphoria/The Wine Song* (5/67); *Get Together/All My Dreams Blue* (7/67); *Fool Me/I Can Tell* (10/67); *Quicksand/Dreamer's Dream* (1/68); *Darkness Darkness* (3/69); *Get Together/Beautiful* (6/69); *Sunlight/Trillium* (10/69); *Darkness Darkness/On Sir Francis Drake* (9/70); *Hippie from Olena/Misty Roses* (11/70); *Sunlight/Reason to Believe* (4/71); *It's a Lovely Day/Ice Bag* (6/71); *Light Shine/Will the Circle Be Unbroken* (2/72); *Running Bear/Kind-Hearted Woman* (11/72); *Dreamboat/Kind-Hearted Woman* (1/73).

FRANK ZAPPA (THE MOTHERS OF INVENTION)/It's impossible to describe the world of Frank Zappa without using each of the following adjectives at least once: innovative, original, imaginative, crazed, aberrated, cacaphonous, brilliant, classical, jazzy, serious, absurd, eclectic, erratic, pop-oriented, misanthropic, progressive, bizarre, hypnotic, and larger-than-life. Now that the required descriptive phrases have been dispensed with, suffice it to say that Frank Zappa is *not* your ordinary rock musician—and his music is equally distinctive.

Zappa first came into prominence in the mid-sixties with an entourage of strange-looking musicians calling themselves the Mothers. For Zappa, it was the first step in a master plan designed to bring the musical world to either its senses or its knees. Baltimore-born, California-raised Francis Vincent Zappa launched his fairly schizoid musical career while still a teen. Nurtured on a diet of both R&B and experimental music (Edgar Varese being a strong influence), Frank dubbed his first high-school band the Blackouts. By the time he was in college, Zappa was gigging in cocktail lounges and writing the scores to low-budget "B" pictures.

As the money from his efforts entered his household, Frank made sure it exited said household very quickly, investing in musical equipment and a small three-track studio. Frank began experimenting in the studio with friends Don Van Vliet (soon to become notorious as Captain Beefheart) and future members of the first Mothers of Invention. The original group, the Mothers (formerly the Soul Giants), consisted of Frank, Ray Collins, Jimmy Carl Black, Roy Estrada and Dave Coranada. Coranada left, a victim of Frank's progressive instincts, and soon the West Coast was treated to the first only underground sensation of rock and roll.

From the outset, the Mothers was not your average rock band. Combining hunks of R&B, rock, jazz, and (my god!) classical music with fantastically satirical lyrics, the Mothers conjured up vivid musical pictures of the society in the sixties. Without blinking an eye, Frank and his crew could leap from *Trouble Every Day* (a mesmerizing account of the Watts race riots) to *Hungry Freaks, Daddy* (psychedelia goes gritty) and somehow pull the style change off with ease. The Mothers were part of a new wave of music. They heralded the shape of things to come. Verve producer Tom (the Velvet Underground, Bob Dylan) Wilson caught their act at the Whiskey A Go-Go in Los Angeles and got them signed to MGM. Their first album, *FREAK OUT,* was a live double album (unheard-of for a new band), which swayed precariously from satirical R&B send-ups *(Go Cry on Somebody Else's Shoulder)* to free-form rock mantras *(Help, I'm a Rock).* *FREAK OUT* may not have cracked the top ten, but in its own subtle way it completely revolutionized the rock industry and firmly established both Zappa and the Mothers (now called the Mothers of Invention) as *the* underground trendsetters in the nation.

From that point onward, there was no stopping Zappa and his band (whose membership changed with marked regularity . . . or perhaps, irregularity). *ABSOLUTELY FREE* was a concept LP to end all concept LPs. *WE'RE ONLY IN IT FOR THE MONEY* devastated not only *SGT. PEPPER* but also the "wear-some-flowers-in-your-hair-in-Scarsdale" trendiness superbly. *LUMPY GRAVY,* Zappa's first solo effort, combined classical nuances with autobiographical spoken word pieces and R&B blasts from the past. *RUBEN AND THE JETS* was pre-Fonzie nostalgia and *UNCLE MEAT* was jazz-tinged brilliance.

All during this recording period, Zappa was introducing the concept of stage theatrics to the rock realm as well. From the Mothers' first major gig in Greenwich Village's Garrick Theater in 1966 to their no-holds-barred funfests at the Fillmore, Zappa littered the stage with props, invited audience participation (and abuse), and had individual group members perform musically related skits. Every Mothers concert was as well-choreographed as it was played. By the end of the sixties, Zappa had garnered a cult following.

Still, the financial rigors of touring with a large band proved too much for Zappa to handle. Angered at the lack of mass acceptance of his progressive ideas, Frank disbanded the Mothers in 1969, concentrating on his two new Warner-distributed labels (Bizarre and Straight) and his producing activities (the GTOs, Captain Beefheart, Wild Man Fisher, Alice Cooper). A solo album, *HOT RATS*, earned him much respect in the rock realm (hmmmm, that freak can play pretty well). By 1970, Frank was ready to have another go with the Mothers via a feature-length film, *200 Motels*. Although the film stiffed, the soundtrack proved popular. Zappa returned to the road where, despite fire (all the Mothers' equipment was destroyed in Switzerland in a quick blaze), personality changes within the ranks (keeping up with the Mothers on a first-name basis is nearly impossible), verbal abuse (Frank has had several well-phrased jousts in print with both Captain Beefheart and Flo and Eddie) and injury (during a concert in London in 1971, Frank was hurled from the stage by a male fan enraged over his girlfriend's interest in the lion-maned star—Frank was bedridden for nearly a year), he has remained since—playing his best and drawing ever-increasing crowds (he even had a hit single a few years back). In a rock biz filled with imitation to the point of extinction, Zappa has remained a guiding light and a source of total joy for nearly two decades.

His hair is still good in the back too, *FREAK OUT* fans.

The Mothers-at-a-Glance Dept. Mothers #1: Zappa, Ray Collins, Jimmy Carl Black, Roy Estrada, Elliott Ingber, with additional help provided by Jim Fielder, Henry Vestine, Jim Guercio, Jeanne Vassoir and Van Dyke Parks. Mothers #2: Zappa, Collins, Black, Estrada, Don Preston, Bunk Garner, Jim "Motorhead" Sherwood, and Bill Mundi. Mothers #3: Zappa, Collins, Black, Estrada, Preston, Sherwood, Mundi and Ian Underwood. Mothers #4: Zappa, Collins, Black, Estrada, Preston, Gardner, Sherwood, Underwood, and Art Tripp, with additional help from Lowell George. Mothers #5: Zappa, Underwood, Aynsley Dunbar, George Duke, Mark Volman and Howard Kaylan (Flo and Eddie), Jeff Simmons, Don Preston, and Ruth Underwood.

Mothers #6: Zappa, Underwood, Volman, Kaylan, Dunbar, Preston, and Jim Pons. Mothers #7 (including Grand Wazoo): Dunbar, Preston, Duke, Erroneous, Janet Neville-Ferguson, Sal Marquez, Earl Dumler, Tony Ortega, Mike Altshul, Johnny Rotella, Joanne Caldwell McNabb, Fred Jackson, Malcolm McNabb, Bill Byers, Ken Shroyer, Ernie Tack, Bob Zimmitti, Alan Estes, Tony Duran, and Joel Peskin. Mothers #8: Preston, Bruce Fowler, Jim Gordon, Guerin, Dunbar, Jack Bruce, Erroneous, Harris, Jean-Luc Ponty, Collins, Kerry McNabb, Susie Glover, Debbie, Lynn, Ruben Ladron De Guevara, Frog Camarena, and Duran. Mother #9: Ruth Underwood, Tom Fowler, George Duke, Napoleon Brock, Chester Thompson, Bruce Fowler, Ralph Humphrey, Don Preston, Walt Fowler, and Jeff Simmons, Mothers #10: Zappa, Duke, Beefheart, Denny Walley, Terry Bazzio, Tom Fowler, Brock, Bruce Fowler.

Albums/FREAK OUT (8/66): *Hungry Freaks, Daddy; I Ain't Got No Heart; Who Are the Brain Police; Go Cry on Somebody Else's Shoulder; Motherly Love; How Could I Be Such a Fool; Wowie Zowie; You Didn't Try to Call Me; Any Way the Wind Blows; I'm Not Satisfied; You're Probably Wondering Why I'm Here; Trouble Comin' Every Day; Help, I'm a Rock; Return of the Son of Monster Magnet.* ABSOLUTELY FREE (5/67): *Plastic People; Duke of Prunes; Amnesia Vivace; Duke Regains His Chops; Call Any Vegetable; Soft-Sell Conclusion; Status Back Baby; Son of Suzy Creamcheese; Brown Shoes Don't Make It; America Drinks and Goes Home; Uncle Bernie; Invocation and Ritual Dance of the Young Pumpkin; America Drinks.* WE'RE ONLY IN IT FOR THE MONEY (1/68): *Are You Hung Up; Who Needs the Peace Corps; Concentration Moon; Mom and Dad; Bow Tie Daddy; Harry, You're a Beast; What's the Ugliest Part of Your Body; Absolutely Free; Flower-Punk; Nasal Retentive Calliope Music; Let's Make the Water Turn Black; Idiot Bastard Son; Lonely Little Girl; Take Your Clothes Off When You Dance; Mother People; Hot Poop; Chrome Plated Megaphone of Destiny.* LUMPY GRAVY (5/68): *Lumpy Gravy Parts I and II.* CRUISING WITH RUBEN AND THE JETS (11/68): *Cheap Thrills; Love of My Life; How Could I Be Such a Fool; Desri; I'm Not Satisfied; Jelly Roll Gum Drop; Anything; Later That Night; You Didn't Try to Call Me; Fountain of Love; No, No, No; Anyway the Wind*

Blows; Stuff Up the Cracks. MOTHERMANIA—THE BEST OF THE MOTHERS (3/69). UNCLE MEAT (4/69): *Uncle Meat; The Voice of Cheese; Nine Types of Industrial Pollution; Zolar Czakl; Dog Breath in the Year of the Plague; The Legend of the Golden Arches; The Dog Breath Variations; Sleeping in a Jar; The Uncle Meat Variations; Our Bizarre Relationship; Electric Aunt Jemina; Prelude to King Kong; God Bless America; A Pound for a Brown on the Buss; Ian Underwood Whips It Out; Mr. Green Genes; We Can Shoot You; The Air; If We'd All Been Living in California . . .; Project X; Cruising for Burgers; King Kong Itself; King Kong; King Kong (as Motorhead explains it); King Kong (the Gardner varieties); King Kong (as played by 3 deranged Good Humor trucks); King Kong (live on a flat bed diesel in the middle of a race track at a Miami Pop Festival . . . the Underwood ramifications).* HOT RATS (10/69): *Peaches en Regalia; Willie the Pimp; Son of Mr. Green Genes; Little Umbrellas; The Gumbo Variations; It Must Be a Camel.* BURNT WEENY SANDWICH (10/69): *WPLJ; Igo's Boogie, Phase 1; Overture to a Holiday in Berlin; Igor's Boogie, Phase 2; Theme from Burnt Weeny Sandwich; Aybe Sea; Little House I Used to Live In; Valerie; Holiday in Berlin, Full Blown.* WEASELS RIPPED MY FLESH (8/70): *Didja Get Any Onya; Directly from My Heart to You; Prelude to the Afternoon of a Sexually Aroused Gas Mask; Toads of the Short Forest; Get a Little; Eric Dolphy Memorial Barbecue; Dwarf Nebula Processional March & Dwarf Nebula; My Guitar Wants to Kill Your Mama; Oh No; The Orange County Lumber Truck; Weasels Ripped My Flesh.* CHUNGA'S REVENGE (10/70): *Transylvania Boogie; Road Ladies; Twenty Small Cigars; The Nancy and Mary Music; Tell Me You Love Me; Would You Go All the Way?; Chunga's Revenge; The Clap; Rudy Wants to Buy Yez a Drink; Sharleena.* FILLMORE EAST, JUNE 1971 (9/71): *Little House I Used to Live In; The Mud Shark; What Kind of Girl Do You Think We Are?; Latex Solar Beef; Bwana DIK; Will the Pimp (Parts 1 and 2); Do You Like My New Car?; Happy Together; Peaches en Regalia; Tears Began to Fall; Lonesome Electric Turkey.* 200 MOTELS (soundtrack; 9/71). JUST ANOTHER BAND FROM L.A. (4/72): *Bill the Mountain; Call Any Vegetable; Eddie, Are You Kidding?; Dog Breath; Magdalena.* WAKA/JAWAKA—HOT RATS (7/72): *Big Swifty; Your Mouth; It Just Might Be a One-Shot Deal; Waka/Jawaka.* GRAND WAZOO (11/72): *For*

Calvin; The Grand Wazoo; Cleetus Awreetus-Awrightus; Eat That Question; Blessed Relief. APOSTROPHE (3/74): *Don't Eat the Yellow Snow; Nanook Rubs It; St. Alfonzo's Pancake Breakfast; Cosmik Debris; Excentrifugal Forz; Apostrophe; Uncle Remus; Stink-Foot.* ROXY AND ELSEWHERE (9/74): *Preamble (four parts); Penguin in Bondage; Pygmy Twylyte; Dummy Up; Village of the Son; Echidna's Arf (of You); Don't You Ever Wash That Thing?; Cheepnis; Son of Orange County; More Trouble Every Day; Be-Bop Tango (of the Old Jazzmen's Church).* ONE SIZE FITS ALL (6/75): *Inca Roads; Can't Afford No Shoes; Sofa No. 1 & 2; Po-Jama People; Andy; San Ber-dino; Evelyn, a Modified Dog; Florentine Pogen.* BONGO FURY (10/75): *Debra Kadabra; Carolina Hard-Core Ecstasy; Poofter's Frothy Wyoming Plans Ahead; Sam with the Showing Scalp Flat Top; 200 Years Old; Cucamonga; Advance Romantic; Man with the Woman Head; Muffin Man.* ZOOT ALLURES (10/76): *Find Her Finer; Wonderful Wino; Friendly Little Finger; Disco Boy; Zoot Allures; Wind Up Workin' at a Gas Station; The Torture Never Stops; Ms. Penby.*

Singles/*Big Leg Emma/Why Don't You Do Me Right* (4/67); *Mother People/Lonely Little Girl* (11/67); *Anyway the Wind Blows/Jelly Roll Gum Drop* (12/68); *Peaches en Regalia/Little Umbrellas* (1/70); *Tell Me You Love Me/Would You Go All the Way?* (11/70); *Tears Began to Fall/Junior Mintz Boogie* (10/71); *Cleetus Awreetus-Awrightus/Eat That Question* (11/72); *I'm the Slime/Montana* (10/73); *Don't Eat the Yellow Snow/Cosmik Debris* (9/74); *Find Her Finer/Zoot Allures* (11/76).

THE ZOMBIES/*Rod Argent (piano, organ, harmonica, violin, clarinet, vocals), Hugh Grundy (drums), Paul Atkinson (guitar, violin, harmonica), Chris White (bass, guitar, vocals), Colin Blunstone (guitar, tambourine, lead vocals).*
When the Beatles gave America the English sound in 1964, they opened up a transatlantic door in music. One of the early English groups to pass through that door was the Zombies. Led by pianist-composer Rod Argent, they came up with a subtle style of minor-mood tunes that were unlike anything that had yet come in from England and certainly unlike anything that was happening in America—a major feat in itself, considering the band was made up of schoolmates from St. Albans who vaulted into fame via a

talent contest. While initial hits such as *She's Not There* and *Tell Her No* won the group a small but loyal following, their lack of stateside touring assured their following in the United States a diminutive stance for keeps.

The group dropped out of sight for a while, resurfacing with *ODYSSEY AND ORACLE,* an album that gave them their biggest hit in 1968, *Time of the Season.* Ironically, the band had disbanded shortly before the release of the album. Argent went on to form the group name. Blunstone resurfaced in the seventies as a solo performer and Paul Atkinson got into the business end of record-dom, serving as an A&R man for both CBS London and CBS in the States.

Albums/THE ZOMBIES (2/65): *She's Not There; Summertime; It's Alright with Me; You've Really Got a Hold on Me; I Don't Want to Know; Sometimes; I've Got My Mojo Working; Woman; Tell Her No; Work 'n' Play; Can't Nobody Love You; What More Can I Do.* ODYSSEY AND ORACLE (7/68): *Care of Cell 44; A Rose for Emily; Maybe after He's Gone; Beechwood Park; Brief Candles; Hung Up on a Dream; Changes; I Want Her, She Wants Me; This Will Be Our Year; Butcher's Tale (Western Front 1914); Friends of Mine; Time of the Season.* EARLY DAYS (5/69): *Whenever You're Ready; Don't Go Away; She's Not There; I Love You; Leave Me Be; Indication; She Does Everything for Me; You Make Me Feel Good; Tell Her No; I Want You Back Again; Kinda Girl; I Must Move.* TIME OF THE ZOMBIES (1974): *She's Not There; Tell Her No; Whenever You're Ready; Is This the Dream; Summertime; I Love You; You Make Me Feel Good; She's Coming Home; She Loves the Way They Love Her; Imagine the Swan; Smokey Day; If It Don't Work Out; I Know She Will; Don't Cry for Me; Walking in the Sun; I'll Call You Mine; plus the entire ODYSSEY AND ORACLE selection.*

Singles/*She's Not There/You Make Me Feel So Good* (9/64); *Tell Her No/Leave Me Be* (12/64); *She's Coming Home/I Must Move* (3/65); *Whenever You're Ready/I Love You* (8/65); *Remember/Just out of Reach* (9/65); *Is This the Dream/Don't Go Away* (2/66); *Indication/How Were We Before* (6/66); *Care of Cell 44/Maybe After He's Gone* (11/67); *Butcher's Tale (Western Front 1914)/This Will Be Our Year* (6/68); *Time of the Season/Friends of Mine* (11/68); *Conversation on Floral Street/Imagine the Swan* (5/69).

Z.Z. TOP/*Billy Gibbons (guitar, vocals), Frank Beard (drums), Dusty Hill (bass, vocals).*

Texas' own power trio, Z.Z. Top was formed in late 1970 by three local musicians who had paid their dues in both psychedelic and blues bands. The net result was raunch and roll boogie power plus, a brand of music that the critics either ignored or looked down upon for the first two or three LPs of Z.Z.'s career. The public, however, didn't need much prodding to get into Z.Z.'s music and before long the boys were whooping up the charts with both hit singles and gold albums.

Albums/FIRST ALBUM (1/71): *(Somebody Else Been) Shaking Your Tree; Brown Sugar; Quank; Goin' Down to Mexico; Old Man; Neighbor, Neighbor; Certified Blues; Bedroom Thing; Just Got Back from Baby's; Backdoor Live Affair.* RIO GRANDE MUD (3/72): *Francene; Just Got Paid; Mushmouth Shoutin'; Ko Ko Blue; Chevrolet; Apologies to Pearly; Bar-B-Q; Sure Got Cold after the Rain Fell; Whiskey 'n' Mama; Down Brownie.* TRES HOMBRES (7/73): *Waitin' for the Bus; Jesus Just Left Chicago; Beer Drinkers and Hell Raisers; Master of Sparks; Hod Blue and Righteous; Move Me On Down the Line; Precious and Grace; La Grange; Shiek; Have You Heard?* FANDANGO (4/75): *Tush; Thunderbird; Jailhouse Rock; Backdoor medley: Backdoor Love Affair/Mellow Down Easy/Backdoor Love Affair No. 2/Long Distance Boogie; Nasty Dogs and Funky Kings; Blue Jean Blues; Save Me (Save Me/Epilog/The Still); Heard It on the X; Mexican Blackbird; Balinese.* TEJAS (12/76): *It's Only Love; Arrested for Driving While Blind; El Diablo; Snappy Kakkie; Enjoy and Get It On; Ten-Dollar Man; Pan Am Highway; She's a Heartbreaker; Avalon's Highway; Asleep in the Desert.* BEST OF Z.Z. TOP (11/77): *Heard It on the X; Just Got Paid; Tush; Francine; Jesus Just Left Chicago; Backdoor Love Affair; Waitin' for the Bus; Blue Jean Blues; Beer Drinkers and Hell Raisers.*

Singles/*Francene* (English version)/*Francene* (Spanish) (4/72); *La Grange/Just Got Paid* (2/74); *Tush/Blue Jean Blues* (6/75); *Arrested for Driving While Blind/It's Only Love* (2/77); *Enjoy and Get It On/El Diablo* (5/77).

INDEX

559